Police Psychology and Its Growing Impact on Modern Law Enforcement

Cary L. Mitchell
Pepperdine University, USA

Edrick H. Dorian
Los Angeles Police Department, USA

A volume in the Advances in Psychology, Mental Health, and Behavioral Studies (APMHBS) Book Series

IGI GLOBAL
DISSEMINATOR OF KNOWLEDGE

www.igi-global.com

Published in the United States of America by
IGI Global
Information Science Reference (an imprint of IGI Global)
701 E. Chocolate Avenue
Hershey PA, USA 17033
Tel: 717-533-8845
Fax: 717-533-8661
E-mail: cust@igi-global.com
Web site: http://www.igi-global.com

Library of Congress Cataloging-in-Publication Data

Names: Mitchell, Cary L., 1955-, editor. | Dorian, Edrick H., 1973-, editor.
Title: Police psychology and its growing impact on modern law enforcement / Cary L. Mitchell and Edrick H. Dorian, editors.
Description: Hershey : Information Science Reference, 2017. | Includes bibliographical references and index.
Identifiers: LCCN 2016023702| ISBN 9781522508137 (hardcover) | ISBN 9781522508144 (ebook)
Subjects: LCSH: Police psychology. | Police--Job stress--United States. | Counseling.
Classification: LCC HV7936.P75 P6527 2017 | DDC 363.201/9--dc23 LC record available at https://lccn.loc.gov/2016023702

This book is published in the IGI Global book series Advances in Psychology, Mental Health, and Behavioral Studies (APMHBS) (ISSN: pending; eISSN: pending)

British Cataloguing in Publication Data
A Cataloguing in Publication record for this book is available from the British Library.

All work contributed to this book is new, previously-unpublished material. The views expressed in this book are those of the authors, but not necessarily of the publisher.

For electronic access to this publication, please contact: eresources@igi-global.com.

Advances in Psychology, Mental Health, and Behavioral Studies (APMHBS) Book Series

Bryan Christiansen
PryMarke, LLC, USA

ISSN: pending
EISSN: pending

Mission

The complexity of the human mind has puzzled researchers and physicians for centuries. While widely studied, the brain still remains largely misunderstood.

The **Advances in Psychology, Mental Health, and Behavioral Studies (APMHBS)** book series presents comprehensive research publications focusing on topics relating to the human psyche, cognition, psychiatric care, mental and developmental disorders, as well as human behavior and interaction. Featuring diverse and innovative research, publications within APMHBS are ideally designed for use by mental health professionals, academicians, researchers, and upper-level students.

Coverage

- Emotional Health
- Treatment & Care
- Substance Abuse
- Eating Disorders
- Human Interaction
- Trauma & Stress
- Psychiatry
- Mental Health & Disorders
- Socialization
- Personality Disorders

IGI Global is currently accepting manuscripts for publication within this series. To submit a proposal for a volume in this series, please contact our Acquisition Editors at Acquisitions@igi-global.com or visit: http://www.igi-global.com/publish/.

The Advances in Psychology, Mental Health, and Behavioral Studies (APMHBS) Book Series (ISSN pending) is published by IGI Global, 701 E. Chocolate Avenue, Hershey, PA 17033-1240, USA, www.igi-global.com. This series is composed of titles available for purchase individually; each title is edited to be contextually exclusive from any other title within the series. For pricing and ordering information please visit http://www.igi-global.com/book-series/advances-psychology-mental-health-behavioral/110200. Postmaster: Send all address changes to above address.

Titles in this Series

For a list of additional titles in this series, please visit: www.igi-global.com

Seduction in Popular Culture, Psychology, and Philosophy
Constantino Martins (Nova University of Lisbon, Portugal) and Manuel Damásio (Lusófona University, Portugal)
Information Science Reference • copyright 2017 • 332pp • H/C (ISBN: 9781522505259) • US $175.00 (our price)

Chronic Mental Illness and the Changing Scope of Intervention Strategies, Diagnosis, and Treatment
Barre Vijaya Prasad (Dharwad Institute of Mental Health and Neurosciences, India)
Medical Information Science Reference • copyright 2017 • 404pp • H/C (ISBN: 9781522505198) • US $220.00 (our price)

Identifying, Treating, and Preventing Childhood Trauma in Rural Communities
Marion Baker (Center of Hope Arizona, USA) Jacqueline Ford (Center of Hope Arizona, USA & Walden University, USA) Brittany Canfield (Center of Hope Arizona, USA & Fielding Graduate University, USA) and Traci Grabb (Arizona's Children Association, USA & Center of Hope Arizona, USA)
Information Science Reference • copyright 2016 • 306pp • H/C (ISBN: 9781522502289) • US $185.00 (our price)

Handbook of Research on Diagnosing, Treating, and Managing Intellectual Disabilities
Rejani Thudalikunnil Gopalan (Gujarat Forensic Sciences University, India)
Information Science Reference • copyright 2016 • 496pp • H/C (ISBN: 9781522500896) • US $210.00 (our price)

Neuroeconomics and the Decision-Making Process
Bryan Christiansen (PryMarke LLC, USA) and Ewa Lechman (Gdansk University of Technology, Poland)
Business Science Reference • copyright 2016 • 354pp • H/C (ISBN: 9781466699892) • US $195.00 (our price)

Integrating Technology in Positive Psychology Practice
Daniela Villani (Università Cattolica del Sacro Cuore, Italy) Pietro Cipresso (Università Cattolica del Sacro Cuore, Italy & I.R.C.C.S. Istituto Auxologico Italiano, Italy) Andrea Gaggioli (Università Cattolica del Sacro Cuore, Italy & I.R.C.C.S. Istituto Auxologico Italiano, Italy) and Giuseppe Riva (Università Cattolica del Sacro Cuore, Italy & I.R.C.C.S. Istituto Auxologico Italiano, Italy)
Information Science Reference • copyright 2016 • 447pp • H/C (ISBN: 9781466699861) • US $185.00 (our price)

Global Perspectives on Youth Gang Behavior, Violence, and Weapons Use
Simon Harding (Middlesex University, UK) and Marek Palasinski (Liverpool John Moores University, UK)
Information Science Reference • copyright 2016 • 425pp • H/C (ISBN: 9781466699380) • US $185.00 (our price)

IGI GLOBAL
DISSEMINATOR OF KNOWLEDGE
www.igi-global.com

701 E. Chocolate Ave., Hershey, PA 17033
Order online at www.igi-global.com or call 717-533-8845 x100
To place a standing order for titles released in this series, contact: cust@igi-global.com
Mon-Fri 8:00 am - 5:00 pm (est) or fax 24 hours a day 717-533-8661

To Sharon, for your incredible support and encouragement, and to Nicole, Sarah, and Erin.
--C.L.M.
To Arlet, Sophia, and Vaughn, my inspiration, always.
--E.H.D.

Table of Contents

Detailed Table of Contents

This chapter briefly identifies important societal events and governmental responses that set the stage for the emergence of the specialty of police psychology, provides the names and departments of early practitioners (1963-1990) of police psychology, and explains how the current definition of police psychology was developed, with its four domains and 55 proficiencies. The maturation of the specialty is outlined from its recognition as an American Psychological Association (APA) proficiency, to the creation of an American Board of Police & Public Safety Psychology (ABPPSP) specialty board, and most recently to its recognition as an APA specialty.

The psychological screening of law enforcement officer applicants represents a core practice area in police psychology. Significant advances have been made in recent years regarding the development of practice guidelines and standards. This chapter provides an overview of the essential components of this specialized form of high-stakes psychological assessment. Important legal principles are highlighted and key resources are identified. The core steps in a contemporary screening model are described and the psychological self-report measures most widely used in psychological screenings are profiled. Factors impacting the validity and usefulness of psychological test results are discussed. The critical need for preemployment psychological screenings of police officer candidates to be culturally sensitive is addressed, as are some of the criticisms that have been identified in the literature. The chapter stresses the need for preemployment assessments of police officer candidates to be evidence-based, ethically attuned, and consistent with recent advances in police psychology.

The MMPI-2 Restructured Form (MMPI-2-RF) is the current, most up-to-date version of the most widely used self-report measure of personality and psychopathology. Prior versions of the test were studied and used extensively in police candidate assessments. This chapter reviews the legal and empirical foundations for using the MMPI-2-RF in preemployment evaluations of police officer candidates and provides practical guidance for doing so. A detailed review of a series of recent studies on using the MMPI-2-RF in identification of high risk candidates is presented, followed by practical suggestions for integrating MMPI-2-RF findings with other sources of information when conducting preemployment evaluations of police candidates. The MMPI-2-RF Police Candidate Interpretive Report is highlighted.

The Five Factor Model (FFM) is widely accepted as a valid descriptor of normal personality and commonly used as a framework for prediction of job performance. As an inventory that operationalizes the FFM, the NEO PI-R is often utilized in personnel selection. The California Commission on Peace Officer Standards and Training has identified ten dimensions that increasingly serve as a template for the screening of police officer applicants. These screening dimensions are based on the FFM. The NEO PI-R thus appears well suited to serve as an inventory used for screening police officer applicants. A literature review is provided and strengths and weaknesses of the inventory discussed.

Courts throughout the United States have ruled that that the "awesome powers" entrusted to law enforcement officers, and the safety-sensitive nature of their positions, impose on their public employers a responsibility to ensure that they are fit to perform their duties. But, as with an officer's powers, the authority of a police employer to mandate a psychological fitness-for-duty evaluation (FFDE) is not without boundaries. This chapter addresses the legal authority of a police employer to require an FFDE, the limits to that authority, and the implications of these constraints both for police employers and the psychologists who conduct these evaluations on their behalf. Written by two prominent experts in police employment law and police psychology, this chapter concerns itself with both the law and professional standards of practice. Key topics include the legal threshold for requiring an FFDE, limitations to the content of an FFDE report, and evaluator qualifications.

Section 3
Clinical Intervention and Prevention

Police officers are exposed to many critical incidents throughout their careers. This chapter discusses critical incident exposure and psychological sequelae in police officers, police culture, obstacles to mental health care, currently utilized early interventions, existing research for these approaches, alternative evidence-based early interventions, emerging models, and directions for future research. Given the frequency and potential impact of critical incidents, early intervention for exposed police officers is of central importance. One of the most commonly utilized group early interventions, Critical Incident Stress Debriefing (CISD), has limited empirical support, such that some departments are being advised against its use. That said, there are important challenges in identifying better, evidence-based alternatives.

Mass Casualty Events (MCE) have an extraordinary impact on an entire community. The impact on victims' families, survivors, and community members is often the subject of significant attention; however, rarely does the impact on first responders (law enforcement officers, firefighters, dispatchers, crime scene investigators/photographers, etc.) garner the same coverage. Additionally, agencies can quickly become overwhelmed by the magnitude of the response causing them to overlook the psychological impact of these incidents on their personnel. Serving as specialists in police and public safety psychology, crisis intervention, and trauma recovery, the authors reflect on lessons learned from their response to multiple MCEs, including the 1999 Columbine High School shooting and the 2012 Aurora Century 16 Theater shooting, and offer recommendations to agencies regarding crisis response and trauma recovery.

Over two million United States military service members have served in the theaters of Iraq and Afghanistan since 2001. Many of these military service members are seeking employment in law enforcement upon discharge from active duty. The skills acquired from military service are complementary to many of the essential job functions of a law enforcement officer, thus a natural fit. In addition, military reserve police officers have seen activations for deployment to combat regions. These National Guard and Reserve service members make a rapid transition from military fatigues to a police uniform upon their return from deployment. After outlining the scope of the military deployment cycle, reintegration programs and

developing resources that support police officers' physical, mental, emotional, and social wellbeing. Police agencies are encouraged to draw from model programs and national guidelines to develop sustainable, cost-effective health and wellness programs. Such efforts are likely to fit local needs, foster positive community relations, and support police officer resiliency.

Peer supporters are a vital resource for members of the public safety community. Peers are often the first to notice when colleagues are exhibiting symptoms of psychological distress. Due to the cultural norms and the personality traits of those drawn to this career field, many public safety officers prefer to confide in peers rather than to obtain the assistance of mental health professionals. Further, peer supporters can give public safety officers the reassurance and support they need to enlist the services of mental health professionals. This chapter reviews the development and application of peer support teams, addresses issues in selecting peer support team members and developing a program, reviews team organization options and training needs, and addresses common challenges.

As early as the 1970s, some police agencies began to develop education and training initiatives as well as specialized response initiatives to assist police in responding to calls for service involving people with mental health problems. Various versions of Memphis's Crisis Intervention Team program as well as various co-response models have become increasingly common. However, the effectiveness of these often stand-alone programs remains unclear. What has become clear is that police agencies require a strategic approach to interactions between police and vulnerable populations including those with mental health problems. This chapter, which provides an overview of the evolution of these specialized police responses, proposes that there is a need for a more comprehensive third generation approach—a strategic approach—rather than solely a "program" approach. Identification is made of specific areas in which the unique skills of psychologists are important in furthering the success of the necessary strategic approach.

This chapter addresses the interaction of law enforcement officers and people who are psychologically impaired as a result of mental illness, emotional disturbance, or severe intoxication. The chapter consists of three major sections. Part One provides an overview of the larger legal and social factors that increasingly

Preface

In 1972, Martin Reiser, widely considered the father of police psychology, wrote in the preface of his pioneering book *The Police Department Psychologist*, that the book's main purpose was to "explicate some of the dimensions of this fascinating position for psychologists…with the expectation that in the future the psychologist will be less of a rare bird in the police profession" (p. vii). Over four decades later, we are very pleased to produce a volume entitled *Police Psychology and Its Growing Impact on Modern Law Enforcement*. As the title implies, the police psychologist is no longer a rare bird, but rather an integral, contributing figure in present-day police agencies, providing support in the areas of personnel assessment, individual and organizational intervention, consultation, and operational assistance.

So much has occurred in the development and expansion of police psychology in the five years since Jack Kitaeff's (2011) important volume *Handbook of Police Psychology* was published. For example, in that same year, the American Board of Professional Psychology (ABPP) recognized Police & Public Safety Psychology as its 14th specialty board (American Board of Professional Psychology, n.d.). This hard-won acknowledgement helped ensure that psychology's most rigorous professional practice standards would be applied to police psychology, to the benefit of law enforcement agencies and the communities they serve. In 2013, the American Psychological Association (APA) officially recognized Police & Public Safety Psychology as a specialty, having earlier accorded it proficiency status (American Psychological Association, n.d.). APA's recognition set the stage for police psychology to further mature and grow in regard to its breadth, empirical foundation, and impact. It is our hope that the present book represents a valuable contribution to that growth by providing leading police psychologists, many of whom are among the first generation of professionals to achieve ABPP board certification in Police & Public Safety Psychology, an opportunity to write about current practices and emerging trends in a number of the specialty's core areas.

Today, police psychologists face unprecedented opportunities and challenges. In 2015, the *President's Task Force on 21st Century Policing* emphasized the essential importance of trust "between law enforcement agencies and the people they protect and serve" (p. 1). Police psychologists are ideally situated to support law enforcement agencies in their efforts to strengthen and build trust with the communities they serve. Resources such as this book are intended to contribute to those efforts by shedding light on best practices, identifying recent and cutting-edge research and developments, and calling attention to important challenges and growth areas that remain.

This book is intended for practicing police psychologists, researchers, students of police psychology, and others with particular interest in the specialty, including law enforcement executives and personnel. The chapters address current practices and recent advances, informed by the research literature and the latest guidelines developed by leading police psychology professional organizations. Our contributing authors are a combination of seasoned police psychologists, academics, researchers, and other subject matter experts who are uniquely qualified to comment on the growing impact of police psychology on modern law enforcement.

We open with Trompetter's chapter, which offers a personal take on the history of police psychology and an overview of the major practice areas encompassed by the specialty. The book is then organized into five additional sections, beginning with "Assessment and Evaluation." Assessment has factored prominently in the development of police psychology and that importance is reflected in four chapters on the topic. Mitchell (co-editor) provides an introductory and overview chapter on the preemployment psychological evaluation of police officer applicants. Ben-Porath, Tarescavage, and Corey describe the use of the MMPI-2-RF in preemployment screenings, highlighting the impressive empirical support associated with the measure. Detrick and Chibnall share their insights on using the NEO PI-R, widely regarded as the instrument of choice in regard to the Five Factor Model of personality, in preemployment screenings. Finally, Mayer and Corey offer their perspectives on fitness for duty evaluations in a comprehensive chapter that provides an up-to-the-moment distillation of important considerations in this form of high-stakes assessment.

Section 3, "Clinical Interventions and Prevention," begins with a rigorous review chapter on interventions for critical incidents, authored by Brucia, Cordova, and Ruzek. Next, Garrido and Nicoletti address first responder recovery in the wake of mass casualty events, drawing from the literature and their firsthand experience as police psychologists. The timely matter of transition and reintegration of military personnel to law enforcement careers is examined by Curran, Holt, and Afanador. Clark and White review law enforcement officer suicide, with attention to empirical trends, management of risk, and prevention.

Section 4 explores themes of "Employee Wellness and Support" in law enforcement agencies. Axelrod describes the benefits that accrue to organizations from employee assistance programs and reviews models of service delivery. Kelly and Hoban consider health and wellness programs for law enforcement officers, and share their insights on the intersection of ethics and officer well-being.

In Section 5, two chapters examine aspects of "Operational Consultation." Cotton and Coleman survey the literature on police interactions with individuals who have mental health problems and based on their review, advocate for new, strategic approaches. Christopher and Tsushima look closely at social factors underlying police officer interactions with persons in crisis and provide recommendations based on their experience directing a program in an urban police department.

We conclude our book with a section on "Current Trends and Developments." Bradford, McElroy, and Rosenblatt address the impact of contemporary cultural phenomena, including generational shifts, social media, and legalization of marijuana, upon law enforcement agencies' hiring practices and identity development. McCutcheon examines distinctive ethical challenges and opportunities associated with police psychology, while calling for an emphasis on aspirational ethics.

Cary. L. Mitchell
Pepperdine University, USA

Edrick H. Dorian
Los Angeles Police Department, USA

REFERENCES

American Board of Professional Psychology (ABPP). (n.d.). *Police & public safety psychology*. Retrieved from http://www.abpp.org/i4a/pages/index.cfm?pageid=3606

American Psychological Association (APA). (n.d.). *Recognized specialties and proficiencies in professional psychology*. Retrieved from http://www.apa.org/ed/graduate/specialize/recognized.aspx

Kitaeff, J. (Ed.). (2011). *Handbook of police psychology*. New York, NY: Routledge.

President's Task Force on 21st Century Policing. (2015). *Final report of the president's task force on 21st century policing*. Washington, DC: Office of Community Oriented Policing.

Reiser, M. (1972). *The police department psychologist*. Springfield, IL: Thomas.

Acknowledgment

We would like to acknowledge that this volume would not be possible without the contributions of many talented people. First and foremost, we thank each one of the authors for their high-quality chapters and their participation as double-blind peer reviewers, providing valuable feedback to fellow authors and contributing significantly to strengthening the book. Without their time, expertise, and commitment this book would not have become a reality. In addition, we wish to recognize the pioneering police psychologists upon whose shoulders we stand. We hope with this book we humbly take up the torch they lit and carry it a little further. Finally, we must thank the men and women of law enforcement, from whom we have learned so much, and for whom we strive to learn much more. The police psychologist—no longer the rare bird—knows all too well the extraordinary challenges faced by today's police officers.

Cary. L. Mitchell
Pepperdine University, USA

Edrick H. Dorian
Los Angeles Police Department, USA

Section 1
Introduction

Chapter 1
A History of Police Psychology

Philip S. Trompetter
Stanislaus-Area Law Enforcement, USA

ABSTRACT

This chapter briefly identifies important societal events and governmental responses that set the stage for the emergence of the specialty of police psychology, provides the names and departments of early practitioners (1963-1990) of police psychology, and explains how the current definition of police psychology was developed, with its four domains and 55 proficiencies. The maturation of the specialty is outlined from its recognition as an American Psychological Association (APA) proficiency, to the creation of an American Board of Police & Public Safety Psychology (ABPPSP) specialty board, and most recently to its recognition as an APA specialty.

INTRODUCTION

There are few public interests more compelling than public safety. The ability of a police force to conduct its activities safely, effectively, efficiently, and in conformance with statutory and constitutional requirements depends in large part on the functional health of police professionals and the agencies in which they work. Police officers are the only occupational position in a civilian, democratic society with the statutory authority to use lethal force and to conduct criminal investigations. These responsibilities expose police officers to chronic and often traumatic stressors while, at the same time, requiring a high level of competence and resilience. Assisting in identifying police officer applicants capable of carrying out these duties, as well as identifying those who are wholly unsuitable, is one role performed by psychologists specializing in Police and Public Safety Psychology (Council of Organizations in Police Psychology [COPP] Petition, 2011).

The assessment of police officer candidates was not the only activity in which psychology and law enforcement interacted during the formative years. The specialty of Police and Public Safety Psychology commenced in the early 20th century but accelerated following the civil unrest in the United States in the 1960s and further advanced once the specialty was precisely defined in 2007 (Aumiller & Corey, 2007). This chapter captures the key moments of this evolution, noting along the way the significant entry of psychologists who provided a variety of services to law enforcement between 1963 and 1990,

DOI: 10.4018/978-1-5225-0813-7.ch001

from whose work today's police psychology was distilled. Many of these pioneering psychologists continue to practice today but they are recognized here more for the course they set for today's specialty practice than for their many contributions along the way. The chapter concludes with the definition of the functional domains, competencies, and proficiencies of police psychology.

IN THE BEGINNING

While police officer selection was psychology's first contribution to modern law enforcement, helping to maintain effective functioning of police professionals through clinical intervention, training, research, and organizational consulting emerged as other aspects of police and public safety psychology. These milieu-adapted practices of the specialty of police psychology have recent origins. In the early twentieth century, only a small number of mental health professionals were involved within the broader criminal justice system. These professionals engaged in activities such as criminal profiling, eyewitness memory and identification, hypnosis, and early attempts at selection to measure the aptitudes necessary to become a police officer, to name a few.

Involvement in police selection (i.e., assessment) was a turning point for the expansion of police psychology into not one but four domains: assessment, intervention, operational support, and organizational consultation. Scrivner and Kurke (1995), as well as Reese (1995), describe "three traditions of police psychology." The "first tradition" of police psychology was created by the applied research spurred by the 1968 Law Enforcement Assistance Administration and its predecessor, the Department of Justice's Office of Justice Programs, particularly two of its affiliate agencies, the National Institute of Justice and the Bureau of Justice Assistance. The roots of the first tradition originated from Lewis Terman's use in 1916 of the Stanford revision of the Binet-Simon Scale that became known as the Stanford-Binet IQ Test for measuring intelligence with children (Terman, 1917). Terman began using an abbreviated form of the Stanford-Binet to test San Jose (CA) Police Department officers in order to assess their intelligence as a step toward establishing job-related criteria for police selection. Terman published his results in 1917 and concluded that intelligence testing could be potentially valuable as a selection tool (Weiss & Inwald, 2010). Terman's work was soon followed by L. Louis Thurstone (Thurstone, 1922), who used the Army Alpha Intelligence Test to assess officers in the Detroit (MI) Police Department and found that patrolmen scored higher (mean IQ = 71.44) than their lieutenants (mean IQ = 57.80). Other departments followed suit including the Los Angeles (CA) Police Department in 1954 when they administered an MMPI, group Rorschach, projective drawing, and a clinical interview to police officer applicants (Weiss & Inwald, 2010). In 1975, Joe Fabricatore was hired by the Personnel Department of the City of Los Angeles as the first full time psychologist dedicated solely to designing and implementing an objective and legally defensible preemployment psychological evaluation program for law enforcement (personal communication, May 24, 2015).

Societal and cultural shifts in the 1960s provided increased demand for psychological assessment in police selection. During the late 1950s and into the early 1960s, the crime rate in the United States increased dramatically (Pinker, 2011). Coupled with the civil rights movement and protests against the war in Vietnam, President Lyndon B. Johnson formed the Commission on Law Enforcement and Administration of Justice in 1965. He charged the members of the commission to determine the causes of crime and to recommend what society could do to reduce it. *The Presidential Commission on Law Enforcement and the Administration of Justice* (President's Commission, 1967) report urged law enforcement agencies to implement sweeping reforms in personnel structure, officer selection and training, community relations, and overall management practices. The Commission's stress on selection and the importance of assessing emotional stability in police officer candidates was a milestone event for police psychology. Subsequently, in 1973 the National Advisory Commission on Criminal Justice Standards and Goals (National Advisory Commission, 1974) published its recommendations for improvements with specific recommendations for upgrading the quality of police personnel, which included the recommendation that police agencies employ a psychological evaluation in the hiring process.

While the National Advisory Commission on Criminal Justice Standards and Goals report emphasized only one particular aspect of police psychology (the psychological assessment of all law enforcement applicants), within the next ten years, other services followed (e.g., SWAT/crisis negotiation, field consultation, critical incident intervention, Employee Assistance Programs, etc.). Forty years after the National Advisory Commission on Criminal Justice Standards and Goals report, Corey and Borum (2013) noted that 38 states had established preemployment or pre-certification requirements for the emotional, mental, or psychological health, functioning, fitness, or suitability of peace officers, and most agencies in the remaining 12 states conducted such evaluations in compliance with standards of the Commission on Accreditation for Law Enforcement Agencies (CALEA). Many states have followed the lead of California's Commission on Peace Officers Standards and Training (POST) *Peace Officer Psychological Screening Manual* (1984) and its revision two decades later (2014). In their 2010 application for specialty status with the American Board of Professional Psychology (ABPP), the American Board of Police and Public Safety Psychology (ABPPSP) estimated that there were approximately 100,000 preemployment evaluations performed each year by as many as 4,000 psychologists (Initial Application for ABPP Affiliation of Police & Public Safety Psychology as a Specialty Board, 2010). Of these, approximately 542 psychologists self-identified as being involved in police and public safety psychology through membership in one or more of the national organizations.

The focus on federally-funded research and program development led to the "second tradition" in police psychology: the delivery of direct psychological services to police agencies (Reese, 1995; Scrivner & Kurke, 1995). In the wake of the 1967 Presidential Commission on Law Enforcement and the Administration of Justice recommendations, several psychologists were drawn to provide comprehensive psychological services to law enforcement, the earliest notably being Jim Shaw with the King County (WA) Sheriff's Department in 1963 (personal communication, September 15, 2015), and Martin Reiser with the Los Angeles Police Department in 1968 (personal communication with S. Saxe-Clifford, October 25, 2015). Jim Shaw was a new Ph.D. when he was hired part-time by the King County Sheriff in 1963 to conduct research in the custodial division. The Sheriff put Shaw through a basic police training academy and he became a deputy assigned full time as the department psychologist where he provided intervention, consultation, and assistance with applicant screening and selection (personal communication, May 9, 2015). In 1968, after working with autistic children at the San Fernando Valley (CA) Child Guidance Clinic, when the announcement of an opening at the Los Angeles Police Department (LAPD) caught his eye, Martin Reiser became what most consider to be the father of police psychology because of his pioneering work in the specialty (Kurke & Scrivner, 1995). He provided critical incident debriefings for officers who had been involved in shootings or other situations that were particularly gruesome or frightening. He trained 750 field sergeants to discern early warnings of damaging stress and reached out to undercover officers. He kept a tactical vest in his car for emergencies, responded to hostage standoffs, and advised negotiators. In high-profile cases such as the Hillside Strangler murders of the late 1970s, he developed psychological profiles that aided detectives. Reiser was a prominent advocate for the use of hypnosis to help victims and witnesses remember elusive details. He became board certified through ABPP in Clinical Psychology. He retired in the early 1990s and died at the age of 87 on April 11, 2015 (Chawkins, 2015). Another early practitioner was Guy Seymour, who started providing services to the Boston (MA) Police Department in 1969 (personal communication, September 22, 2015).

In the early 1970s, others joined the growth of the fledgling specialty by providing specialized consultative, operational, or intervention services to law enforcement agencies, in addition to assessment[1]. The names, law enforcement departments or regions served, and beginning year of service of many early police psychologists in the United States are provided below. In some cases, additional contributions are detailed:

- Mike Roberts, San Jose (CA) Police Department, 1971; Roberts was the third full-time police psychologist to be hired by a major agency;
- Irv Guller, New Jersey-area agencies, 1972;
- Susan Saxe-Clifford; Los Angeles (CA)-area agencies, 1976; initially hired as a predoctoral employee by LAPD in 1970 to work with Martin Reiser, Saxe-Clifford later provided services to the Los Angeles Sheriff's Department and other agencies;
- Harvey Schlossberg, New York (NY) Police Department, 1972; detective and psychologist, Schlossberg developed an influential framework for hostage negotiations in 1972-73 following the massacre of Israeli athletes at the 1972 Munich Summer Olympics; he is also regarded as the first police officer to earn a doctorate in psychology (Reese, 1995);
- Al Somodevilla, Dallas (TX) Police Department, 1983;
- Penny Dralle (and later Gabe Rodriguez), New Orleans (LA) Police Department, 1975;
- Jim Turner, United States Military Police units, 1976;
- Mark Axelberd, South Florida-area agencies, 1977;
- Phil Trompetter, Modesto (CA)-area agencies, 1977;
- Neil Hibler, Federal and National Security agencies, 1977;
- John Nicoletti, Denver (CO)-area agencies, 1977;
- David Smith, Washington State Patrol, 1977; Smith was a former Washington State police officer who earned a doctorate and became the first psychologist in his department;
- Stephen Seeman, Hampton (NH) Police Department, 1977;
- Thomas Hickey, Memphis (TN) Police Department, 1977;
- Gregory Riede, Houston (TX) Police Department, 1978;
- Robin Inwald, New York State Corrections, 1978; Inwald went on to distinguish herself as the developer and publisher of several psychological tests frequently used in police assessments;
- Ellen Scrivner, Fairfax (VA) Police Department, 1978;
- Rick Bradstreet, Austin (TX) Police Department, 1978;
- Gerry Serafino, Roswell (NM) Police Department, 1978;
- Roger Solomon, Colorado Springs (CO) Police Department, 1979;
- Bob Jones, Salem (OR) Police Department, 1979;
- Patrick Cook, Tallahassee (FL) Police Department, 1979.

The "third tradition" of police psychology arose in the late 1970s but blossomed in the 1980s with the largest influx of new specialists in the history of the specialty. Early names for this time period are presented below.

- Eloise Archibald, New York (NY) Police Department, 1980;
- Eric Gruver, Anaheim (CA) Police Department, 1980;
- Dave Corey, Northern California-area agencies, 1980; Corey later provided services to the Portland (OR) Police Bureau;
- Debbi Glaser, Los Angeles (CA) Police Department, 1980;
- Richard Blak, Fresno County (CA) Sheriff's Department, 1980;
- Tony Stone, Georgia agencies, 1980;
- James Greenstone, Dallas (TX) County Sheriff's Department, early 1980s;
- Pete DiVasto, New Mexico agencies, 1980;
- JoAnne Brewster, Staunton (VA) Police Department, 1981;
- Marilyn Wooley, Redding (CA)-area agencies, 1981;
- Gary Kaufmann, Michigan State Police, 1981;
- Eric Ostrov, Chicago (IL) Police Department, 1981;
- Joe Elam, Oklahoma Department of Public Safety, 1981; earlier, Elam was an officer with the Oklahoma Highway Patrol; Vesta Gettys preceded him at the Oklahoma Department of Public Safety;
- Larry Blum, Southern California-area agencies, 1981;
- Mike McMains, San Antonio (TX) Police Department, 1982;
- Rick Wihera, National agencies, 1982; Wihera worked for Colorado agencies starting in 1986;
- Ira Grossman, San Diego (CA)-area agencies, 1982;
- Doug Gentz, Tulsa (OK) Police and Fire Departments, 1982;
- Scott Allen, Miami Dade (FL) Police Department, 1983;
- Ginger Hayes, Fairfax (VA) Police Department, 1983;
- Gordon Wolf, Fresno (CA) Police Department, 1983;
- Michael Cuttler, Greensboro (NC)-area agencies, 1983;
- Ellen Kirschman, Palo Alto (CA) Police Department, 1983;
- Steve Curran, Maryland State Police, 1983;
- Robin Greene, Los Angeles (CA) Police Department, 1983;
- Jack Kitaeff, Arlington County (VA) Police Department, 1983;
- Herb Gupton, Federal agencies and U.S. Army, 1983; Gupton later provided services to the Honolulu (HI) Police Department;
- Gary Aumiller, Suffolk County (NY)-area agencies, 1984;
- Dan Goldfarb, Suffolk County (NY)-area agencies, 1985;
- George Hargrave, California Highway Patrol and California POST, 1984;
- Deirdre Hiatt, California Highway Patrol and California POST, 1984;
- Mark Zelig, Salt Lake City (UT)-area agencies, 1985;
- Linda Forsberg, Detroit (MI)-area agencies, 1985;
- Mike Mantell, San Diego (CA) Police Department, 1985;
- Darlene Hoyt, San Diego (CA) Police Department, 1986;
- Katherine Ellison, Montclair (NJ) Police Department, 1985;
- Jim Janik, Chicago (IL) Police Department, 1985;
- Nancy Bohl, San Bernardino County (CA) Sheriff's Department, 1985; though not a licensed psychologist, Bohl has been a pioneering contributor to police psychology;
- Charles Milofsky, Illinois agencies, 1985;

- Mike Campion, Decatur (IL) Police Department, 1985;
- Audrey Honig, Los Angeles (CA) Sheriff's Department, 1985;
- James Fico, Wisconsin agencies, 1986;
- Rob Tannenbaum, Philadelphia (PA)-area agencies, 1986;
- Paul Detrick, St. Louis (MO)-area agencies, 1986;
- Lorraine Greene, Nashville (TN) Police Department, 1987;
- Adrienne Bradford, Atlanta (GA) Police Department, 1987;
- Cristina Cullens, Los Angeles (CA) Sheriff's Department, 1986;
- John Warren III, Winston-Salem (NC) Police Department, 1987;
- Anne Kopp, Northern California-area agencies, 1987;
- Elizabeth White, San Diego (CA) Police Department, 1987; White later provided services to the Los Angeles (CA) Sheriff's Department;
- Gerard Sumprer, California Highway Patrol, 1988;
- Jon Moss, Richmond (VA) Police Department, 1989;
- Jack Leeb, Maryland agencies, 1988;
- Michael Comer, Kalamazoo (MI)-area agencies, 1989;
- Kris Mohandie, Los Angeles (CA) Police Department, 1989;
- Alexis Artwohl, Portland (OR)-area agencies, late 1980s.

The "third tradition" had its origins in federal law enforcement agencies, where psychologists were engaged in behavioral science research or policy matters related to their agencies' missions. Their activities included further development of selection testing and assessment; career development; program planning; and practical application of psychological knowledge to police operations such as hostage negotiations, criminal profiling, and methods to improve witness recall, to name but a few. While police selection had matured significantly by the 1980s with increasing acceptance of psychologists by law enforcement, agencies started asking for additional services including employee assistance for their officers, critical incident interventions following officer-involved shootings, field consultation for CNT callouts, and other forms of operational and organizational consultation.

Contemporaneous with the growth of the specialty practice was the beginning of specialty-specific professional groups and conferences for specialty-specific continuing education. Indeed, since graduate training in police psychology was not available for the early practitioners, the newly developed organizations and their conferences provided the bulk of their specialty training. In September 1984, the first and most important gathering of police psychologists ever assembled was hosted by the FBI's Jim Reese, with the assistance of Harvey Goldstein (Reese, 1995). Never before had there been such an organized and concerted effort to highlight the specialty and bring together most of the professionals who were currently providing psychological services to law enforcement agencies across the United States. Subsequently, there were another five gatherings (1985, 1993, 1995, 1998, 1999) organized by Reese, assisted by psychologists John Stratton, Gary Aumiller, Ellen Scrivner, Roger Solomon, and John Yuille. A pioneer criminal profiler with the FBI's Behavioral Science Unit, Jim Reese retired from the FBI in 1995 as Assistant Unit Chief. Each of the FBI symposia resulted in a publication of the submitted works that formed the first extensive foundation of evidence-based police psychology[2]. The United States Department of Justice, Federal Bureau of Investigation provided airfare, lodging, and food to all attendees in exchange for the attendees presenting an original, publishable paper related to the conference theme of a law enforcement issue (e.g., domestic violence, suicide, operations, family issues).

The expansion of police psychological activity in the 1980s coincided with the development of the three main police psychological professional associations still in existence. The Society for Police and Criminal Psychology (SPCP) formed in 1973 (Kitaeff, 2011) through a consortium of police psychologists and law enforcement professionals with the initial sponsorship of the Tucson (AZ) Police Department. Its first journal focusing on police psychology was published in 1985. In the early 1980s, a group of police psychologists in the Baltimore-District of Columbia area began to meet informally on a monthly basis. This group, known as the Law Enforcement Behavioral Sciences Association (LEBSA), recognized the national significance of their experiences, needs, and aspirations. One of its members, Harvey Goldstein, provided the leadership necessary to form a new section within APA Division 18, Psychologists in Public Service, and the Police & Public Safety Section was established in 1982 (Reese, 1995). Lastly, it was at the 1984 FBI gathering that several attendees discussed and later helped form the Police Psychological Services Section (PPSS) of the International Association of Chiefs of Police (IACP), whose first meeting occurred in 1985 (Kitaeff, 2011).

POLICE PSYCHOLOGY MATURES INTO AN APA SPECIALTY

While the three major professional groups held annual conferences, it was not until 2005 that several leading police psychologists and police psychological organizations embarked on a process to more precisely define police psychology as a specialty and seek specialty recognition with the APA. The three main national police psychology organizations – SPCP, IACP-PPSS, and APA Division 18 PPSS, collectively named the Council of Organizations in Police Psychology (COPP; Aumiller & Corey, 2007), for the first time precisely defined the activities of police psychology, successfully established Police and Public Safety Psychology as the fourteenth specialty board in the ABPP on October 21, 2011, and prepared and submitted an application[3] to APA that resulted in the official recognition of police psychology on July 31, 2013, as a *specialty* (it had been approved as a *proficiency* on August 13, 2008). This application, which was presented to APA in 2011, provided a comprehensive definition of police psychology:

Police [& Public Safety] Psychology is concerned with assisting law enforcement and other public safety personnel and agencies in carrying out their missions and societal functions with optimal effectiveness, safety, health, and conformity to laws and ethics. [It] consists of the application of the science and profession of psychology in four primary domains of practice: assessment, clinical intervention, operational support, and organizational consulting. Police [& Public Safety] Psychology requires, at a minimum, distinctive knowledge of the following: essential functions of police and public safety personnel, working conditions unique to their respective positions, common and novel stressors inherent in public safety work, normal and abnormal adaptation to occupational stress and trauma, research pertinent to resilience and recovery in public safety personnel, and the unique aspects of confidentiality and testimonial privilege when providing services to public safety personnel and/or agencies. Specialized knowledge beyond this foundation is needed for practice within each of the four domains. (COPP, 2011, p. 2)

The police psychology proficiencies can be clustered or organized into four distinct domains of practice: (1) assessment-related activities, (2) intervention services, (3) operational support, and (4) organizational/management consultation. An overview of each of the primary proficiencies of police psychology within each of the four domains is provided below (COPP, 2011, pp. 213-237):

I. Assessment Domain

Job Analysis

Job and task analysis methodology is the primary vehicle for identifying, describing, and quantifying the performance components of a position, including both essential and marginal functions. The results of job and task analysis form the empirical framework for design and validation of selection instruments and processes (preemployment and/or promotional) as well as training needs assessments, performance measurement instruments, career development plans, and other personnel related instruments. Job and task analysis methodology typically involves a survey of incumbents and superiors in order to identify tasks, responsibilities and other job requirements as well as the knowledge, skills and abilities (KSAs) necessary to perform these job components. Once these components are identified, their relative contribution to performance is calculated; usually in terms of importance, frequency, and criticality.

Preemployment, Post-Offer Psychological Evaluations of Job Candidates

Statutory requirements, regulations, and national accreditation have established preemployment, post-offer psychological evaluations of police officer candidates as a nearly universal standard. These evaluations help to ensure that candidates are free of job-relevant mental impairments; possess adequate stress resilience and emotional hardiness; are able to meet the behavioral, social, ethical, and cognitive demands of modern policing; or satisfy other criteria determined by law or agency requirements. Post-offer psychological evaluations involve, at a minimum, the administration of one or more objective, standardized written measures of abnormal psychological functioning, and a clinical interview, both of which must be administered by a qualified psychologist or psychiatrist. The IACP Police Psychological Services Section publishes and maintains guidelines for this area of practice ("Preemployment Psychological Evaluation Guidelines").

Psychological Fitness-for-Duty Evaluations of Incumbents

This highly specialized area of practice involves the psychological evaluation of an incumbent police officer's ability to safely and effectively carry out the essential functions of his or her position. Fitness-for-duty evaluations are indicated whenever there is objective evidence leading to a reasonable belief that the employee may be substantially psychologically impaired or pose a direct threat to him/herself. The IACP Police Psychological Services Section publishes and maintains guidelines for this area of practice ("Psychological Fitness-for-Duty Evaluation Guidelines").

Evaluations for FMLA Eligibility

Under circumstances defined by the federal Family and Medical Leave Act (FMLA) and its state progeny, employers may require employees to submit to an independent medical evaluation when applying for FMLA benefits. Psychologists conducting these evaluations should be familiar with the eligibility requirements in the employer's jurisdiction and be qualified to evaluate or diagnosis mental health functioning.

Evaluations for Reasonable Accommodation

Under circumstances defined by the federal Americans with Disabilities Act (ADA) and its state progeny, employers may require qualified employees with a disability to submit to an independent medical evaluation when requesting reasonable accommodation. Psychologists conducting these evaluations should be familiar with the federal and state ADA requirements and case law, be qualified to evaluate or diagnose mental health functioning, and have an adequate understanding of the requirements and working conditions of the employee's position.

Evaluations (Medical) for High-Risk, High-Demand Assignments

Some agencies require psychological evaluations for police special assignments (e.g., SWAT, hostage negotiator, canine officer, undercover officer, drug and vice officer, etc.) to ensure that they meet minimum requirements for emotional stability or other standards. When any of the inquiries or procedures used by the examining psychologist are "medical" in nature, as defined by state or federal law, psychologists conducting these evaluations should be familiar with federal and state ADA procedures, statutes and case law and be qualified to evaluate or diagnose mental health functioning. These evaluations are also referred to by the acronym PEPSA (psychological evaluations for police special assignments).

Direct Threat Assessments

This activity is a type of fitness-for-duty evaluation where the referral question centers on whether or not the employee poses a direct threat to himself or others, as opposed to general fitness to perform essential functions. The standards governing this inquiry are defined in statutory and case law related to the Americans with Disabilities Act, both federal and state. Therefore, psychologists conducting these evaluations should be familiar with federal and state ADA statutes and case law and be qualified to evaluate or diagnose mental health functioning. The IACP Police Psychological Services Section publishes and maintains guidelines for this area of practice ("Psychological Fitness-for-Duty Evaluation Guidelines").

Workplace Violence Assessments

Arguably a variation of direct threat assessments, the focus of workplace violence assessments generally goes beyond the question of whether or not the employee poses a direct threat, as defined by relevant statutes, and includes a focus on risk management strategies (e.g., how identified risk factors might be minimized, and protective factors might be optimized, in order to reduce the risk of violence). As with direct threat assessments, the standards governing this inquiry are defined in statutory and case law related to the Americans with Disabilities Act, both federal and state. Therefore, psychologists conducting these evaluations should be familiar with federal and state ADA statutes, pertinent case law and research, and be qualified to evaluate or diagnose mental health functioning. The IACP Police Psychological Services Section publishes and maintains guidelines for this area of practice ("Psychological Fitness-for-Duty Evaluation Guidelines").

Emergency Consultations Concerning the Seriously Mentally Ill

Police psychologists provide direct and indirect assessment of individuals identified by police officers as potentially suicidal, imminently dangerous to self or others, unable to provide for basic personal needs as a result of a mental disease or disorder, incapable of understanding risks to health and safety as the result of a mental disorder, using drugs or alcohol in a manner that might endanger the safety of the individual or others, or who are extremely combative in association with a mental disease or disorder. The police psychologist consults with police officers on de-escalation, crisis intervention, and referral to a medical treatment facility for voluntary or involuntary emergency psychiatric evaluation.

Supervision of Psychological Assistants, Interns, Residents, or Fellows

Police psychologists provide supervision of psychological assistants, residents, interns, and fellows in accordance with the "Guidelines and Principles for Accreditation of Programs in Professional Psychology" (American Psychological Association, 2005). These guidelines require that there be formally designated licensed psychologists (including at least one police psychologist) with exclusive responsibility for supervision who: (1) develop a police psychology training program including philosophy, objectives, and training plan; (2) secure program resources sufficient to accomplish the program's service delivery, training, and supervision goals; (3) maintain program dynamics to promulgate eligibility for a training program in police psychology, which prepares supervisees for professional practice in police psychology; (4) create, accurately describe, disclose, and document relevant information relating to the training model, program goals and objectives, selection procedures, requirements for training completion, training facilities/settings, service recipient populations, administrative policies and procedures, and other resources; (5) participate in a program of self-assessment and quality enhancement; and (6) ensure positive supervisor-supervisee relations.

Pre-Offer Suitability Screening of Job Applicants (Normal Traits and Competencies)

Some agencies use a bifurcated procedure to evaluate the psychological suitability of job candidates, with a non-medical assessment of normal traits, behaviors, and competencies taking place prior to the conditional offer of employment, and the medical assessment (i.e., tests and inquiries capable of revealing an underlying mental disability) occurring after the conditional offer of employment. Pre-offer suitability screening involves the administration and scoring of tests, personal history questionnaires, and/or other instruments predicting suitability to complete training and perform the duties of a law enforcement officer. These predictions are validated against content, construct and/or criterion measures that are directly and demonstrably linked to the critical performance attributes of the target position. These measures are not designed to identify, describe, or diagnose mental disability or illness, as these can only be assessed after the conditional offer of employment.

Promotional Assessments (Normal Traits and Competencies)

The focus of these evaluations is usually assessment of personal management style and general "fit" of the candidate with the job in question. They are administered to candidates for promotion to supervisory and/or executive ranks, and consist of tests of ability, personality, and interactive style combined with a structured comprehensive personal interview by a police psychologist. Since these assessments address general attributes (rather than specifically defined performance attributes such as job knowledge), they are usually conducted in conjunction with other agency promotional selection processes and serve as an adjunctive, rather than definitive, tool for making key personnel appointments. They also may serve to identify individual strengths, weaknesses, and/or areas for improvement. As such, results of this process may be incorporated into a career development program. These assessments often address performance attributes such as intellectual (problem solving) ability, emotional characteristics, skill in human relations, insight into human behavior, and ability to plan, organize and direct.

Assessment Center Development and Administration

Assessment centers are standardized job simulation exercises designed to allow candidates to demonstrate skills and abilities identified by job analysis as essential for success in a given position. These exercises are scored by multiple trained observers whose ratings and judgments are pooled through consensus or by a statistical integration process. The term "assessment center" is a catch-all term that can consist of some or all of a variety of exercises. Most assessment centers usually include some sort of in-basket exercise simulating the disposition of items found in the in-basket for the job that is being tested. Other typical exercises include oral presentations, counseling simulations, problem analysis exercises, interview simulations, role play exercises, written report/analysis exercises, and leaderless group exercises. Psychologists are often involved in developing the various simulation exercises contained in an assessment center, conducting the related validation research, and administering the overall assessment program.

Psychological Evaluations (Normal Traits and Competencies) for High-Risk, High-Demand Assignments

Psychologists frequently contribute to the assessment and selection of officers assigned to high-risk, high-demand positions (e.g., SWAT, undercover, narcotics and vice, etc.). These evaluations usually include administration of psychological assessment instruments as well as an interview conducted by a police psychologist. However, psychologists may also design and/or participate in other selection processes and activities such as oral board interviews, and simulations. Although the traits, competencies and constructs assessed by these instruments are rationally linked to performance, the focus of these evaluations is usually to "screen out" individuals with a high probability of performance difficulties rather than to predict individual competency relative to other team members. They also are not designed to assess medical conditions and/or to comment on overall fitness for duty.

Psychological Autopsies (Intended for Purposes Other Than Case Resolution)

A psychological autopsy is a postmortem, postdictive psychological investigative procedure by which a person's circumstances and psychological state of mind at the time leading up to his/her death is reconstructed, in order to help determine the manner of death, whether suicide, homicide, or accidental. Psychological autopsies are most useful when the evidence of the decedent's intention is equivocal, and they entail reviewing medical and police reports, photos, drawings, and records, interviewing witnesses and people who knew the victim, visiting the scene, and using knowledge of personality theory, suicidology, and psychology in general, to form an integrated picture of the subject's personality characteristics and state of mind, and the circumstances leading up to his/her death. Findings from psychological autopsies aid law enforcement agencies in designing programs to reduce the incidence of future suicides and to minimize liability by implementing behavioral or policy changes that mitigate factors that may have contributed to suicide.

Test Development

Development of psychologically-based tests or assessment instruments involves the conceptualization, design, construction and validation of psychometric assessment instruments, which typically are used for selection and/or assessment of individual strengths and weaknesses. Examples include content validated tests of specific knowledge skills and abilities used to measure job knowledge, management decision-making, facility at written expression, construct validated measures of specific interactive traits related to special assignments, and/or criterion validated measures of performance such as work samples. The test development process typically consists of critical incident review, item writing, initial linkage, pilot administration, item/cluster analysis (and/or other measures of internal consistency), and post hoc validation.

Assessment-Related Education and Training

Psychologists performing these activities develop and present training materials and programs to instruct agency personnel in the proper use and interpretation of assessment instruments as well as to assure the implementation of proper policies for dissemination and storage of assessment related information. They also perform personal and/or group consultation to aid in design/modification of preemployment and promotional selection policies that are consistent with professional standards (e.g., Standards for Educational and Psychological Testing AERA/APA; Principles for the Validation and Use of Personnel Selection Procedures, SIOP; CFR Title29 Part 1607).

Assessment-Related Research

These activities involve evaluating and documenting validity, reliability, and objectivity (disparate impact) of the assessment instruments and processes currently in use at an agency, as well as recommending, designing, and/or implementing modifications to maximize effectiveness, validity, and defensibility.

Assessment-Related Process Improvement

Psychologists conducting assessment related process improvement evaluate and document the overall results of agency assessment processes. For example, one focus of evaluation might be on efficiency (fiscal, manpower, time lines, etc.) as reflected in recruitment yield, training yield, quality of new hire performance, etc. Data to support these efforts may be derived from objective data and/or surveys of academy personnel, training officers, etc. Once the data are gathered and analyzed, the psychologist/consultant may make recommendations for improvement and/or participate in agency-based task forces, problem-solving committees, etc.

Assessment-Related Consultation

This activity involves personal and/or group consultation to aid in design/modification of preemployment and promotional selection policies that are consistent with professional standards (e.g., Standards for Educational and Psychological Testing AERA/APA; Principles for the Validation and Use of Personnel Selection Procedures, SIOP; CFR Title29 Part 1607).

II. Intervention Domain

Employee Assistance Counseling

Employee assistance counseling is a psychological service provided for law enforcement employees who may be experiencing personal, psychological, or behavioral problems that may adversely affect their job performance and productivity. The services provided vary from agency to agency. Although many programs were originally designed to provide counseling for substance abuse, particularly alcohol-related problems, many employee assistance counseling programs have expanded to address a wide variety of problems, including psychological and stress-related disorders, marital and family problems, financial difficulties, and problems adjusting to retirement. Some employee assistance counseling programs also offer services to the eligible dependents of law enforcement employees. Police psychologists provide early detection of employee problems, problem assessment, short-term counseling, referral to longer-term outside treatment resources, follow-up services, employee education, and training for management in how to make appropriate use of the counseling program, in an effort to foster growth, resiliency and effectiveness in the individual and in the work place. Employee assistance counseling may be provided as one component of a broader array of psychological services that may also include long-term treatment. Law enforcement employee assistance counseling is tailored to meet the needs of a unique culture and a specialized work force (e.g., a closed community in a quasi-military structure, functioning under the cumulative weight of several stressors, including shift-work and insomnia). The police psychologist must have a thorough understanding of the law enforcement culture and work environment in order to assess where his/her skills and resources might be of greatest assistance.

Individual Therapy or Counseling

Individual therapy and counseling are broad terms used to describe a variety of psychological services provided to individuals, typically in a one-on-one, face-to-face meeting with a police psychologist. In the law enforcement setting, this includes providing treatment or advice concerning a wide range of possible concerns related to the individual's goals, needs, values, attitudes, conflicts, personal and interpersonal styles, education and career choice, academic and work functions, and developmental and social challenges unique to law enforcement personnel. Individual therapy or counseling may focus on stressors and problems most relevant to law enforcement personnel and the unique nature of their jobs that adversely impact their families, marriages, health, finances, and work performance/productivity. Therapy and counseling can consist of psycho-education, behavioral training, cognitive training, and a variety of other techniques intended to assist law enforcement personnel in identifying maladaptive or problematic patterns of thought and behavior that result in emotional distress, social, and/or occupational problems. Normally, individual therapy and counseling are provided with legal and ethical guarantees of confidentiality on the part of the therapist or counselor, and information about the services can only be disclosed by the therapist or counselor with the written, informed consent of the individual client. In some jurisdictions, qualified psychologists may be authorized to prescribe psychotropic medication, as well.

Group, Couple, Family Therapy or Counseling

Group, couple, and family therapy or counseling are broad terms used to describe a variety of psychological services provided to more than one individual at a time. In the law enforcement setting, groups typically consist of law enforcement employees. Couple therapy or counseling focuses on the law enforcement employee and his/her spouse. Similarly, family therapy or counseling focuses on the law enforcement employee and his/her family members. These forms of psychological service address the same issues addressed in individual therapy and employ many of the same techniques. They additionally allow participants to practice more adaptive interpersonal interactions in a controlled environment, and give them greater access to the perspectives of others, enabling them to develop more adaptive interpersonal response patterns. These services are provided with legal and ethical guarantees of confidentiality on the part of the therapist or counselor. However, maintenance of confidentiality in a group, couple, or family therapy setting is inherently more difficult due to the number of participants who are not legally bound to maintain confidentiality of the material discussed. Police psychologists may also provide services to groups that consist of the spouses of police officers, or other family members of police officers, without the participation of the officers themselves. Police psychologists may provide information to spouses or family members about the unique working conditions of law enforcement, the types of stresses experienced by police officers, effective ways to support and interact with the family member who is a law enforcement officer, and other information intended to facilitate positive and satisfying interactions within the couple or the family.

Critical Incident Early Intervention

Police officers in the course of their job duties may be exposed to critical incidents, which are traumatic events that are outside the range of normal human experience. These types of events include, but are not limited to, witnessing or being involved in situations involving accidents, natural disasters, deaths, serious injuries, or extreme danger. These types of events would be expected to produce a significant physiological, emotional, psychological, or behavioral reaction in anyone, and they often temporarily overwhelm the normal coping abilities of the individual. Although it is assumed that temporary negative reactions to a critical incident would be expected from almost anyone exposed to a similar incident, if such experiences are not dealt with properly, the individual may subsequently develop Posttraumatic Stress Disorder (PTSD) or other disturbances of psychological and behavioral functioning. Critical incident early intervention - including debriefing, "psychological first aid", defusing, etc. - encompasses initial, immediate efforts to meet the needs of law enforcement officers impacted by a critical incident. Ideally, it takes place from one to a few days after the incident, or up to three to four weeks after a mass disaster. Depending on methods and goals, services can be provided individually, or in groups of individuals affected by the same incident, in sessions that typically last from one to three hours. Intervention typically consists of providing opportunities for the affected individual(s) to describe the event and their reactions to it, in a setting that provides emotional support and reassurance, and education about the wide range of expected and typical responses to such an event. The intervention is designed to: (1) address the need for acute symptom reduction while not interfering with natural recovery processes, (2) preclude the development of maladaptive responses or maladaptive problem-solving, (3) facilitate social support and effective communications, (4) restore individual(s) to a pre-crisis, independent level of functioning, (5) provide closure, if possible, and (6) refer for more advanced care as necessary.

Critical Incident Therapy or Counseling

Critical incident therapy or counseling refers to a broad range of psychological services provided to individuals impacted by a critical incident. These services are provided after the initial, immediate time period following the critical incident, when it has become clear that the individual's reaction to the incident has not resolved. Critical incident therapy or counseling is intended to treat continuing symptoms of a pathological stress reaction. Services may be provided to individuals, groups, couples, or families. The approach with the most empirical support is Cognitive Behavioral Therapy (CBT), but other approaches such as Emotion Focused Therapy (EFT) have also been shown to be effective. Counseling approaches generally are based on the military intervention principles of immediacy, proximity, and expectancy, the process of grieving, the understanding of normal developmental life crisis, and the nature of emotionally hazardous situations.

Counseling to Cope with Unique or Chronic Job Stressors (e.g., Deep Undercover, Homicide, Child Abuse, Sex Crimes, Etc.)

Police officers frequently confront extremely unpleasant situations and behavior in the performance of their job (e.g., accidents; homicides; violent crimes and crime scenes; domestic violence; child abuse; hostage situations; suicides, officer-involved shootings or line-of-duty deaths; and handling human remains after disasters or other deaths). Some assignments, such as investigation of homicides, child abuse, or sex crimes, regularly expose officers to such unpleasant events. Other specialized assignments, such as undercover assignments, create a unique variety of stressors, such as the constant vigilance required to maintain an alternate identity, fears of exposure, separations from family and friends, and even pressures to commit criminal acts. The cumulative effect of such regular stressors may cause temporary or chronic psychological distress and/or problems with functioning, similar to that experienced by officers who have been exposed to a particularly traumatic critical incident. Police psychologists can identify these types of reactions in officers, and use a variety of counseling or therapy techniques designed to assist officers in recognizing and understanding their reactions to these cumulative "everyday" police stressors, and ameliorating the negative psychological or behavioral effects that they may be experiencing.

Disability Recovery

Disabilities are not necessarily permanent and in fact have recovery rates that can be understood in terms of various demographic and psychosocial resource variables. In the event that a psychological disability prevents a police officer from properly performing his/her assigned duties, the police psychologist may assist the officer and the department by assessing and documenting the presence of the disability, which might otherwise be mistaken for a disciplinary problem or some other sort of difficulty. In the case of medical and/or psychological disabilities, the police psychologist can also provide assistance in obtaining certain disability benefits, such as modified occupational duties, reasonable accommodations, vocational rehabilitation, and psychological assessment and services. The police psychologist may also review applicable policies and procedures allowing the injured officer to work within his/her medical or psychological restrictions/capabilities in temporary or permanent work assignments.

Substance Abuse Treatment

Substance abuse treatment is an umbrella term used to refer to the processes of medical and/or psychotherapeutic treatment for dependency on psychoactive substances such as alcohol, prescription drugs, and illegal drugs of abuse, such as cocaine, heroin or methamphetamines. The goal of the police psychologist is to provide or facilitate the provision of intervention services to enable the police officer to cease substance abuse in order to avoid the psychological, legal, financial, social, and physical consequences that can result.

Mental Attitude Preparation

Police psychologists assist law enforcement officers with psychological preparation that helps them to gain self-confidence and an ability to coordinate cognitions, emotions, and behavior in an optimally adaptive manner. The police psychologist prepares the officer not just in terms of technical skill and knowledge, but also in terms of an optimally adaptive attitude that enables him/her to be flexible and innovative. The general goal is to train the officer in an attitude that leads him/her to view situations as challenges or opportunities rather than risks or potential failures. Mental attitude preparation may also involve more specific training to inculcate the proper orientation and attitude toward an assignment that may present unique difficulties. For example, without prior mental preparation, an officer might hesitate or even fail to shoot at a legitimate target that is not consistent with his or her stereotyped expectations.

Wellness Programs

Many agencies have created programs aimed at preventing or reducing the negative impact of stress on health. These wellness programs are health protection programs that promote physical and mental fitness and well-being, and environmental and occupational health. Many varieties of wellness programs exist, many of which focus primarily on physical fitness. Ideally, such programs should also include elements for enhancing stress management, social communication skills, psychological/mental health, nutrition and diet, cessation of maladaptive habits, and substance dependence treatment and education. The police psychologist's role in wellness training is to assist law enforcement officers toward improving their lifestyles through learning new, health-enhancing behaviors and coping mechanisms to more effectively deal with the inherent stressors of police work that adversely impact job performance. Through the improvement of physical and mental health behaviors, wellness programs are intended to reduce health care costs, improve job performance and morale, decrease absenteeism, increase productivity, generate higher health satisfaction, and facilitate achievement of the agency's operational missions.

Life Coaching

Life coaching is the practice of assisting law enforcement personnel to determine and achieve personal goals. A police psychologist, serving as a coach, will use a variety of methods tailored to the client's needs, to move him/her through the process of setting and reaching goals. Coaching is not targeted at psychological illness, and coaches are not functioning as therapists (although therapists may be coaches). Life coaching in law enforcement is typically used to address: (1) development of high-potential leaders and leadership effectiveness, (2) change in required competencies or job skills, (3) change in management and succession planning, (4) improvement of under-performing police supervisors or executives, (5) departmental and personnel needs to surpass perceived potential limits or performance stagnation, (6) problems involving cultural misalignments with law enforcement job requirements, and (7) breakdowns in communication.

Intervention-Related Education and Training

Intervention-related education and training conducted by police psychologists consists of attempts to prevent and/or ameliorate problematic behaviors in law enforcement officers by providing individual or group education and training about the causes and consequences of such behaviors, as well as techniques for changing behavior. Such training typically focuses on critical issues in law enforcement, such as understanding and controlling: (1) police use of deadly force; (2) deviant or corrupt police behavior; (3) police prejudice and discrimination; (4) the violence-prone police officer; or (5) substance abuse by police officers. Police psychologists might also provide information about stress management or other psychological health and wellness issues within an educational or work setting, rather than in a clinical setting.

Intervention-Related Research

Police psychologists provide many services and interventions designed to prevent occupational stress-related problems in law enforcement officers and to restore officers to optimal functioning when such problems exist. The practical imperative of ensuring the effective use of finite resources, together with an ethical imperative to demonstrate that such interventions are effective, require that the methodology of police psychologists be based on sound empirical evidence. Intervention-related research by police psychologists provides that empirical evidence, through the use of the scientific method to develop and test hypotheses concerning effective interventions for police officers and police organizations. Ideally, such research will focus on the effectiveness of interventions with the law enforcement population itself and will take into account the unique culture and working conditions of law enforcement, however, more general clinical research designed to answer questions about the effectiveness of various intervention methods can also sometimes be successfully generalized to law enforcement. Such research, for example, might explore the impact of a variety of occupational factors on physical and mental health and functioning of law enforcement officers, or might compare the efficacy of alternative intervention methods in the prevention or treatment of stress-related problems.

Intervention-Related Process Improvement

Psychologists engaged in intervention-related process improvement employ interdisciplinary and intergroup partnerships, which view ongoing learning as an essential process for attaining and maintaining optimal functioning of the individual and the organization. It can be understood as "learning by collaborative design." It generally entails (1) increasing awareness of various performance improvement options, (2) proposing an intervention or a series of interventions to eliminate a performance gap, (3) selecting interventions with a view toward their systemic impact, and (4) learning how to implement and refine interventions more effectively. Intervention related process improvement includes a program of process and peer review. The police psychologist reviews and evaluates service programs and client services to ensure adherence to accepted standards of practice and legal parameters and submits clinical work before peers for review.

Intervention-Related Consultation

Intervention-related consultation consists of systemic principles, approaches, and models of consultation designed to ameliorate technical, social, and emotional performance problems exhibited by members of an organization and to enhance organizational as well as individual competence. The principle objective of intervention-related consultation is to improve the accessibility, availability, effectiveness, and appropriateness of law enforcement services. Objectives include, but are not limited to: (1) identifying gaps in existing law enforcement mental health training and related services (e.g., ensure that officers are equipped with the right skills and competences used to manage encounters with the seriously mentally ill offender); (2) developing and evaluating multidisciplinary and culturally-sensitive law enforcement consultation services that specializes in mental health evaluation and treatment; (3) facilitating access to expertise in mental health by developing a network of police psychologists, clinicians, databases, and internet resources; and (4) offering ongoing professional training to promote the development of competency in law enforcement intervention among mental health practitioners, particularly those who offer frontline or primary care services.

III. Operational Domain

Criminal Intelligence

Criminal intelligence encompasses a broad range of activities and involves the application of psychological knowledge, principles, and methods to aid police in criminal investigations. Criminal intelligence is used by law enforcement organizations to prevent, detect and/or disrupt criminal or potential criminal activity. These activities can include gathering, organizing, integrating, or interpreting case information, and specialized operational support (e.g., direct and indirect assessment, criminal profiling, psychological autopsies, threat assessment, crisis/hostage negotiation, debriefing undercover operatives).

Criminal Profiling

Criminal profiling involves the identification of personality, behavioral, and demographic factors characteristic of the perpetrators of particular crimes or criminal patterns. Criminal profiles are used by police investigators to help narrow the scope of criminal suspects or to aid in generating investigative leads.

Psychological Autopsies (for Case Resolution)

In the Operational Domain, psychological autopsies are used to support death investigations and to facilitate case resolution. A psychological autopsy is a postmortem, postdictive psychological investigative procedure by which a person's circumstances and psychological state of mind at the time leading up to his/her death are reconstructed, in order to help determine the manner of death, whether suicide, homicide, or accidental. Psychological autopsies are most useful when the evidence of the decedent's intention is equivocal. They entail reviewing medical and police reports, photos, drawings, and records, interviewing witnesses and people who knew the victim, visiting the scene, and using knowledge of personality theory, suicidology, and psychology in general, to form an integrated picture of the subject's personality characteristics and state of mind, and the circumstances leading up to his/her death.

Crisis and Hostage Negotiation

Police psychologists routinely serve on an agency's Crisis Negotiation Unit (CNU) to support the achievement of a peaceful, nonlethal resolution of critical incidents, such as barricaded subjects, suicidal persons, and active threats of serious violence against persons or property. The psychologist has several functions as a CNU consultant, including the ongoing and continuous monitoring of negotiations, translating relevant information and behavior of the hostage taker, assessing violence risk, managing the stress level of the negotiator and liaisons, recommending strategies to the negotiator for managing the behavior and emotions of the hostage taker, and helping to assess the hostage taker's motivations.

Indirect Assessment

Indirect assessment encompasses a wide array of activities in which the psychologist relies on third-party information to form conclusions about the psychological traits, behavioral proclivities, functioning, and intentions of a particular person. It is used whenever the psychologist is asked to form opinions or make predictions about a person without the benefit of direct contact, and it is fundamental to many of the proficiencies described elsewhere under the Operational Domain (e.g., Psychological Autopsies, Criminal Profiling, etc.). The IACP Police Psychological Services Section has published guidelines for this area of practice (see "Guidelines for Consulting Police Psychologists").

Threat Assessments

Threat assessment is employed to identify, evaluate, obstruct, reduce, and manage threats of substantial criminal harm to public safety, the safety of third parties and/or to an entity's personnel or assets. When the source of the threat is an employee, the assessment occurs in the context of a "Workplace Violence Assessment" or "Fitness-for-Duty Evaluation" (see definitions for these proficiencies under the Assessment Domain). Threat assessment concerns itself with the factors that increase (risk factors) and decrease (protective factors) the likelihood of harm, as well as methods for minimizing or managing risk.

Operations-Related Education and Training

Police psychologists frequently are called upon to educate police personnel on a wide variety of psychological topics central to police operations, including criminal psychology, psychopathology (e.g., psychotic disorders, personality disorders, substance use disorders, etc.), and memory. Psychologists also assist in operational training, such as enhancing performance under peak stress conditions, crisis negotiation (e.g., active-listening skills, persuasion techniques, crisis intervention, assessment of personality types, threat assessment, aggression potential, and high-fidelity role playing), survival training, and suicide prevention.

Operations-Related Research

Police psychologists carry out research on a broad range of topics designed to support police operations, including factors associated with successful vs. unsuccessful operational outcomes; demographic and personality factors of criminal perpetrators; and risk vs. protective factors under various conditions of threat.

Operations-Related Process Improvement

As ancillary participants in police operations who are also skilled process observers, police psychologists are uniquely qualified to identify potential improvements to operational processes, both investigative and tactical.

Operations-Related Consultation

This activity involves individual and/or group consultation to support achievement of operational goals and objectives. The IACP Police Psychological Services Section has published guidelines for this area of practice (see "Guidelines for Consulting Police Psychologists").

IV. Consulting Domain

Development of Performance Appraisal Systems

This activity involves the design and development of organizational policies, processes and instruments for measurement and feedback of individual job performance. Typically, these appraisals are completed by supervisors and other relevant members of the chain of command. However, some performance appraisals may also include data from others (peers, subordinates, community member, etc.). The primary purpose of any performance appraisal system is to provide meaningful, actionable feedback to the incumbent for purpose of individual performance improvement and career development. However, in some settings, performance appraisal data may also be used as a component of promotional selection and or for selection to special assignments. Composite data from performance appraisals may also be used by management for training needs assessments and manpower/succession planning. When performance appraisals are utilized as a component of selection processes, content validity as well as precise attention to construction of measurement components, training of assessors, assessment policy, etc. is critical. The psychologist/consultant may design and deliver these processes/instruments in total or may participate as a professional advisor to an agency task force.

Organizational Development

Whereas individual employees are the focus of performance appraisal, organizational development programs focus on improving organizational performance. Most organizational development programs start with an organizational assessment yielding actionable data in regard to training needs, leadership climate, morale, values/culture, etc. Organizational development goals are then formulated and program components are designed and implemented in order to achieve these goals. Organizational development program components frequently include, but are not limited to, leadership development training, employee problem-solving groups, content-based training programs, specialized training programs (e.g., management decision making, ethics, communication, field training/performance coaching, relationship/diversity training, etc.), evaluation of policies and procedures, and strategic planning. Periodic program evaluation (and modification when appropriate) is a critical component of any organizational development program.

Executive Consultation

Psychologists engage in consultation with agency executives for a variety of purposes including, but not limited to, personnel-related issues (selection, individual performance issues, interpersonal problems, etc.), leadership-related issues (style, impact, relationships, team building), organizational issues (agency mission and strategy, values, culture) general performance issues (coaching) and/or personal issues. These consultations are typically focused, time limited, and confidential in nature.

Management Consultation

Psychologists engage in consultation with agency managers for a variety of purposes including, but not limited to, training needs assessment, recommendation or design of training programs and/or shift staffing policies, time management consultation, etc. Management consultation may also include the activities described under "executive consultation."

Supervisor Consultation

This activity centers on specific supervision-related issues such as counseling problem employees, managing relationships with subordinates and superiors, effective management of disciplinary incidents, time management, etc. These consultations may also include some of the activities described under "executive consultation."

Process Consultation

Process consultation involves a process by which the consultant engages in mutual inquiry designed to create a shared responsibility for diagnosing problems and generating solutions, but also to enable the consultant to pass on some of his or her own diagnostic and intervention skills. Process consultation is generally contrasted with "expert consultation" in which the consultant independently diagnoses and fixes problems. Nearly all management and organizational consulting involves a mix of expert and process models, with the consultant frequently shifting roles to meet the needs of the situation.

Mediation

Psychologists trained in mediation theory and techniques often facilitate the resolution of interpersonal conflict among individuals within an organization, between organizational units, and between the agency and members of the public. Mediation also is used effectively in resolving policy disputes, labor conflicts, and other grievances. Many states provide mediation with statutory protections, including protections against compulsory disclosure of mediation related communications, if the mediator and the mediation process meet certain statutory requirements (e.g., minimum training and experience, use of standard mediation agreement language, etc.).

Implementation of Multirater Feedback Systems

Multirater feedback, also known as multisource or 360-degree feedback, involves performance evaluation feedback gathered about a person from two or more rating sources, including self, supervisor, peers, direct reports, internal stakeholders, external stakeholders, and vendors or suppliers. Consulting psychologists often design and/or implement multirater feedback systems, and many also integrate them with personality assessment in order to assist the subject or "target" of the feedback in understanding how his or her behavior may contribute to strengths and developmental needs.

Consulting Psychology-Related Education and Training

Consulting psychologists provide education and training to assist agency personnel in optimizing their leadership, management, and supervisory effectiveness. The broad array of consulting psychology topics amenable to education and training efforts include organizational change, leadership transformation, ethical decision making, managing in a multicultural workforce, etc.

Consulting Psychology-Related Research

Consulting police psychologists engage in empirical research intended to aid executives and managers in better understanding, anticipating, and managing the complexities of organizational behavior, particularly in paramilitary settings.

With police psychology now formally defined, in 2007 the IACP-PPSS, APA Division 18 PPSS, and the SPCP collaborated in petitioning APA's Commission for the Recognition of Specialties and Proficiencies in Professional Psychology (CRSPPP) for recognition of Police Psychology as a proficiency in professional psychology (COPP, 2010). At that time, CRSPPP's definition of a proficiency was substantially broader than it is today, and it allowed for "near specialties" to be recognized as proficiencies on their way to full recognition as a specialty. The petition for professional recognition was unanimously approved by CRSPPP, the APA Board of Directors, and the Council of Representatives (COR) in August 2008. The American Board of Professional Psychology (ABPP) recognizes 15 specialties, one of which is Police & Public Safety Psychology, which became a specialty board in 2011. The third entity involved in recognizing specialties is the Council of Specialties in Professional Psychology (CoS). CoS is composed of organizations responsible for oversight of the specialties, and in January 2013, CoS recognized Police & Public Safety Psychology as a member specialty. Finally, on December 31, 2011, ABPPSP submitted a 688-page petition to APA for recognition of Police and Public Safety Psychology as a specialty (COPP, 2011). After a 90-day period of public comment and careful review, CRSPPP voted in May 2011 to defer action on the petition. The Commission sought clarification about the specialty's formal education and training (E&T) model—namely, the sequential, integrated program of study and training that enables psychologists to develop the necessary competence in the specialty—and requested that ABPPSP submit a revised petition that detailed their postdoctoral/post-licensure structure for obtaining specialty competence. The ABPPSP Board of Directors submitted its revised petition on December 31, 2011. During another period of public comment, the petition received support from a broad range of APA boards and committees, including the Board of Professional Affairs, which had opposed ABPPSP's initial petition. On May 10, 2013, CRSPPP voted to recommend recognition of Police & Public Safety Psychology as a specialty in professional psychology and this was ratified by the APA Board of Directors and by the APA Council of Representatives on July 31, 2013, during their annual conference in Honolulu. Police and Public Safety became the 13th specialty recognized by the American Psychological Association.

CONCLUSION

Police Psychology started taking shape with Jim Shaw and Martin Reiser in the 1960s and has grown steadily since then. In the past half century, police psychology has evolved and developed into an APA-recognized specialty with a specialty board under the American Board of Professional Psychology. Police Psychology is now recognized in statutes and case law as a well ingrained area of specialty knowledge. The American Academy of Police and Public Safety Psychology (the academy associated with ABPPSP) now promotes ABPP board certification in police and public safety psychology, provides continuing professional education, and helps develop graduate programs in the specialty. As a result, the specialty grows better equipped to offer law enforcement the psychological services that have become vital to the well-being of the men and women who provide protection and service to the public.

REFERENCES

Aumiller, G. S., & Corey, D. M. (2007). Defining the field of police psychology: Core domains & proficiencies. *Journal of Police and Criminal Psychology*, *23*(1), 23–48.

Ben-Porath, Y. S., Fico, J. N., Hibler, N. S., Inwald, R., Kruml, J., & Roberts, M. R. (2011, August). Assessing the psychological suitability of candidates for law enforcement positions. *The Police Chief*, 64–70.

Bohl, N. (1995). Professionally administered critical incident debriefing for police officers. In M. I. Kurke & E. M. Scrivner (Eds.), *Police psychology into the 21st century* (pp. 169–188). Hillsdale, NJ: Lawrence Erlbaum.

Butler, W. M., Leitenberg, H., & Fuselier, G. D. (1993). The use of mental health professional consultants to police hostage negotiation teams. *Behavioral Sciences & the Law*, *11*(2), 213–221. doi:10.1002/bsl.2370110210 PMID:10150230

Chawkins, S. (2015, April 16). Martin Reiser dies at 87: LAPD's first police psychologist. *The Los Angeles Times*. Retrieved from http://www.latimes.com/local/obituaries/la-me-martin-reiser-20150417-story.html

Corey, D. M., & Borum, R. (2013). Forensic assessment for high-risk occupations. In R. K. Otto & I. B. Weiner (Eds.), *Handbook of psychology* (Vol. 11, pp. 246–270). Hoboken, NJ: Wiley.

Council of Organizations in Police Psychology. (2010). *Initial application for ABPP affiliation of police & public safety psychology as a specialty board, submitted by the Council of Organizations in Police Psychology (COPP).* Unpublished manuscript.

Council of Organizations in Police Psychology. (2011). *Petition to the American Psychological Association Commission on Recognition of Specialties and Proficiencies in Professional Psychology (CRSPPP) for the recognition of police and public safety psychology as a specialty in professional psychology.* Unpublished manuscript.

Fuselier, G. D. (1988). Hostage negotiation consultant: Emerging role for the clinical psychologist. *Professional Psychology, Research and Practice, 19*(2), 175–179. doi:10.1037/0735-7028.19.2.175

Gelles, M. G. (1995). Psychological autopsy: An investigative aid. In M. I. Kurke & E. M. Scrivner (Eds.), *Police psychology into the 21st century* (pp. 337–356). Hillsdale, NJ: Lawrence Erlbaum.

Gupton, H. M., Axelrod, E., Cornell, L., Curran, S. F., Hood, C. J., Kelly, J., & Moss, J. (2011, August). Support and sustain: Psychological intervention for law enforcement personnel. *The Police Chief*, 92–97.

Hargrave, G. E., & Berner, J. G. (1984). *Peace officer psychological screening manual.* Sacramento, CA: California Commission on Peace Officers Standards and Training (POST).

Hatcher, C., Mohandie, K., Turner, J., & Gelles, M. G. (1998). The role of psychologists in crisis/hostage negotiation. *Behavioral Sciences & the Law, 16*(4), 455–472. doi:10.1002/(SICI)1099-0798(199823)16:4<455::AID-BSL321>3.0.CO;2-G PMID:9924767

Kirschman, E. F. (1995). Organization consultation to law enforcement: An essay from the field. In M. I. Kurke & E. M. Scrivner (Eds.), *Police psychology into the 21st century* (pp. 375–389). Hillsdale, NJ: Lawrence Erlbaum.

Kitaeff, J. (2011). History of police psychology. In J. Kitaeff (Ed.), *Handbook of police psychology* (pp. 1–59). New York, NY: Routledge.

Kurke, M. I. (1995). Organizational management of stress and human reliability. In M. I. Kurke & E. M. Scrivner (Eds.), *Police psychology into the 21st century* (pp. 391–415). Hillsdale, NJ: Lawrence Earlbaum.

Kurke, M. I., & Scrivner, E. M. (1995). *Police psychology into the 21st century*. Hillsdale, NJ: Lawrence Erlbaum.

Murray, H. A., & MacKinnon, D. W. (1946). Assessment of OSS personnel. *Journal of Consulting Psychology, 10*(2), 76–80. doi:10.1037/h0057480

Nicoletti, J., Allen, S., Baum, K., Deisinger, G., Garrido, S., Gelles, M., & Kirschman, E. et al. (2011, August). Police psychologist as consultant. *The Police Chief*, 54–62.

Ones, D. S., Viswesvaran, C., & Dilchert, S. (2004). Cognitive ability in selection decisions. In O. Wilhelm & R. W. Engle (Eds.), *Handbook of understanding and measuring intelligence* (pp. 431–468). Thousand Oaks, CA: Sage.

Ones, D. S., Viswesvaran, C., & Schmidt, F. L. (2003). Comprehensive meta-analysis of integrity test variables: Findings and implications for personal selection and theories of job performance. *The Journal of Applied Psychology*, *78*(4), 679–703. doi:10.1037/0021-9010.78.4.679

Pinker, S. (2011). *In the better angels of our nature: Why violence has declined*. New York, NY: Viking.

President's Commission on Law Enforcement and Administration of Justice. (1967). *The challenge of crime in a free society: A report by The President's Commission on Law Enforcement and Administration of Justice*. Washington, DC: U.S. Government Printing Office.

Reese, J. T. (1995). A history of police psychological services. In M. I. Kurke & E. M. Scrivner (Eds.), *Police psychology into the 21st century* (pp. 31–45). Hillsdale, NJ: Lawrence Erlbaum.

Reiser, M. (1982). *Police psychology: Collected papers*. Los Angeles, CA: Lehi Publication.

Scrivner, E. M., & Kurke, M. I. (1995). Police psychology at the dawn of the 21st century. In M. I. Kurke & E. M. Scrivner (Eds.), *Police psychology into the 21st century* (pp. 3–29). Hillsdale, NJ: Lawrence Erlbaum.

Sellbom, M., Fischler, G. L., & Ben-Porath, Y. S. (2007). Identifying MMPI-2 predictors of police officer integrity and misconduct. *Criminal Justice and Behavior*, *34*(8), 985–1004. doi:10.1177/0093854807301224

Spilberg, S. W., & Corey, D. M. (2014). *Peace officer psychological screening manual*. Sacramento, CA: California Commission on Peace Officers Standards and Training (POST), Standards, Evaluation, and Research Bureau.

Terman, L. M. (1917). A trial of mental and pedagogical tests in a civil service examination for policemen and firemen. *The Journal of Applied Psychology*, *1*(1), 17–29. doi:10.1037/h0073841

The National Advisory Commission on Criminal Justice Standards and Goals. (1974). *U.S. Dept. of Justice, Law Enforcement Assistance Administration*. Retrieved March 5, 2016, from https://www.ncjrs.gov/App/Publications/abstract.aspx?ID=10865

Thurstone, L. L. (1922). The intelligence of policemen. *Journal of Personnel Research*, *1*, 64–74.

Weiss, P. A., & Inwald, R. (2010). A brief history of personality assessment in police psychology. In P. A. Weiss (Ed.), *Personality assessment in police psychology: A 21st century perspective* (pp. 5–28). Springfield, IL: Charles C. Thomas.

ENDNOTES

1 These names and related facts were obtained initially from a review of the extant literature and supplemented by a solicitation to the discussion forum of the International Association of Chiefs of Police – Police Psychological Services Section (IACP-PPSS) and the curriculum vitae submitted to the American Board of Police and Public Safety Psychology (ABPPSP). The author obtained

additional and clarifying information via personal communications with each living psychologist in September 2015. Every effort was made to include all early police psychologists but important contributors have likely been inadvertently omitted.

2 The books are Psychological Services for Law Enforcement (Reese & Goldstein, 1986); Police Psychology: Operational Assistance (Reese and Horn, 1988); Critical Incidents in Policing (Reese, Horn, & Dunning, 1991); Law Enforcement Families: Issues and Answers (Reese & Scrivner, 1994); and Organizational Issues (Reese & Solomon, 1995). He also wrote History of Psychological Services in Law Enforcement Organizations in the United States, (Reese, 1987).

3 On September 7, 2007, the Joint Committee on Police Psychology Competencies (Dave Corey, Scott Allen, Gary Aumiller, JoAnne Brewster, Michael Cuttler, Herb Gupton and Audrey Honig), consisting of representatives from SPCP, APA Division 18 PPS Section, and IACP-PPSS, submitted a comprehensive review of the "domains and competencies" that comprise the diverse activities of the specialty. The committee proposed a definition of police psychology that identified 4 domains and 57 (reduced to 55 in 2016) professional proficiencies.

Section 2
Assessment and Evaluation

Chapter 2
Preemployment Psychological Screening of Police Officer Applicants:
Basic Considerations and Recent Advances

Cary L. Mitchell
Pepperdine University, USA

ABSTRACT

The psychological screening of law enforcement officer applicants represents a core practice area in police psychology. Significant advances have been made in recent years regarding the development of practice guidelines and standards. This chapter provides an overview of the essential components of this specialized form of high-stakes psychological assessment. Important legal principles are highlighted and key resources are identified. The core steps in a contemporary screening model are described and the psychological self-report measures most widely used in psychological screenings are profiled. Factors impacting the validity and usefulness of psychological test results are discussed. The critical need for preemployment psychological screenings of police officer candidates to be culturally sensitive is addressed, as are some of the criticisms that have been identified in the literature. The chapter stresses the need for preemployment assessments of police officer candidates to be evidence-based, ethically attuned, and consistent with recent advances in police psychology.

INTRODUCTION

The preemployment psychological evaluation of law enforcement officer applicants represents one of the earliest real-world applications of modern psychological assessment. For nearly one hundred years psychologists in the United States have utilized their competence in assessment to contribute to the selection of public safety officers. One of the first examples is that of Terman (1917), who early in the 20th century conducted preemployment psychological evaluations of police and fire department applicants to explore whether this contributed to the effectiveness of selection. By 1939 the cities of Wilmington, DE

DOI: 10.4018/978-1-5225-0813-7.ch002

and Toledo, OH were requiring preemployment mental and personality assessment of all law enforcement applicants (Gottesman, 1975). More recently a national survey of municipal police departments showed that over 90% required psychological assessment of all police officer recruits (Cochrane, Tett, & Vandecreek, 2003). Today, at least 38 states mandate that peace officer applicants be psychologically screened to determine whether they are free of mental or emotional conditions that might interfere with the safe and effective performance of peace officer duties (Corey & Borum, 2013). Moreover, nearly all police agencies serving communities of 25,000 or more in the U.S. require some form of preemployment psychological evaluation (Reaves, 2010), regardless of whether they are compelled to do so by their respective state laws. It has been estimated that 100,000 preemployment assessments of police officer applicants are conducted each year in the U.S., by up to 4,500 participating psychologists (Cuttler, 2011; Corey, Cuttler, & Moss, 2009). Clearly the preemployment screening of law enforcement applicants has emerged as a core practice area of police psychology (Ben-Porath et al., 2011). And, in contrast to the early years, psychologists practicing in this area now have the benefit of a great number of published resources including empirical research findings, recommendations for best practices, and professional guidelines.

The purpose of this chapter is to provide an overview of the psychological screening process for law enforcement applicants, with particular attention to recent advances in this distinctive professional practice area. Following some background considerations and identification of key resources, a number of relevant legal principles will be highlighted, including government mandated requirements and landmark cases. The nature of the preemployment psychological screening process for police officer applicants will be described, including consideration of how screenings contribute to but differ from competitive selection. The core features of a basic screening model will be reviewed, followed by consideration of psychological disqualification and appeals. Brief introductions to the major psychological instruments utilized in screenings will be provided, including recently developed and emerging measures. Two considerations that impact the use of psychological tests employed in screenings will be explored: socially desirable responding and range restriction. Recent developments in the identification of psychological qualification standards for peace officers will be considered. Finally, the need for psychological screenings to be culturally sensitive will be discussed, and some major concerns and critiques will be identified. Preemployment psychological screening is applicable to a range of law enforcement occupations including correctional officer and public safety dispatcher. However, the focus of this chapter will be on police officers.

BACKGROUND AND GUIDELINES

The history of preemployment screening of police officer applicants has been explored in depth elsewhere (e.g., Devan, 2003; Kitaeff, 2011; Spilberg & Corey, 2014; Weiss & Inwald, 2010). It is safe to say that while the practice of psychological screenings of law enforcement applicants may have started early in the 20th century, for decades there were few resources available to guide psychologists in this form of high-stakes assessment. In the second half of the 20th century, various federal entities issued reports that called for more attention to psychological factors in the recruitment of police officers. In 1967, the Presidential Commission on Law Enforcement and the Administration of Justice recommended psychological assessment of the emotional stability of all police officer candidates. In 1973, the National Advisory Commission on Criminal Justice Standards and Goals stated that all police agencies should engage psychologists or psychiatrists to conduct assessments of the psychological suitability of police applicants. Currently, police departments that seek national accreditation through the Commission on Accreditation for Law Enforcement Agencies (CALEA) must have formal preemployment psychological screening programs in place.

At the state level, there were likewise significant developments that provided direction and shaped practices in this important area of police psychology. California's Commission on Peace Officer Standards and Training (POST) published its first Psychological Screening Manual in 1984, for use by state and local law enforcement agencies (Hargrave & Berner, 1984). This document summarized relevant research, addressed critical issues such as adverse impact, and provided guidelines that were consistent with state and federal laws at that time. In 2014, California's POST published a greatly expanded Peace Officer Screening Manual (Spilberg & Corey, 2014). California's POST manual is a comprehensive and informative document that represents essential reading on the state of the art in preemployment psychological screening of peace officer applicants. The standards established by California's POST are more highly developed than in most states and are impacting screening practices in other jurisdictions (Tarescavage, Corey, Gupton, & Ben-Porath, 2015).

According to Borum, Super, and Rand (2003), the most widely used and influential guidelines were developed by the Police Psychological Services Section of the International Association of Chiefs of Police (IACP). First adopted in 1998, the Preemployment Psychological Evaluation Guidelines are updated every five years and are available at the IACP website (IACP, 2014). The IACP Guidelines reflect best practices and shape the implementation of psychological screening programs throughout the U.S. (Ben-Porath et al., 2011). These and other relevant resources help equip police psychologists for comprehensive, appropriate preemployment psychological screenings.

LEGAL CONSIDERATIONS

Numerous federal and state laws directly impact the performance of preemployment psychological screenings for law enforcement applicants. Practitioners must familiarize themselves with applicable laws to ensure the interests and rights of individuals, agencies, and communities are respected and protected. Psychologists engaged in this type of high stakes practice must also commit to staying informed throughout their careers about changes and new developments in the federal or state laws that impact screenings.

The relevant federal laws include the Civil Rights Act of 1991, which makes it unlawful to engage in employment discrimination due to disparate treatment or disparate impact (Spilberg & Corey, 2014). The concept of adverse impact is particularly relevant to psychological screenings because employment practices that result in any protected class having a selection rate that is less than four-fifths of the selection rate for the majority group is likely to be in violation of equal opportunity requirements. The Civil Rights Act also prohibits the use of differing cutoff scores on job-relevant tests based on applicants' race or gender (Borum, Super, & Rand, 2003; Padilla, 2001). Consequently, combined gender norms are utilized for psychological tests in preemployment psychological screenings for police applicants.

The Americans with Disabilities Act of 1990 (ADA) protects disabled persons from discrimination in the workplace and addresses issues such as reasonable accommodation. To be consistent with ADA, preemployment psychological screenings for law enforcement applicants must take place after conditional offers of hire, must be conducted by qualified professionals, must be required of all applicants for the positions, must focus on the applicant's ability to perform essential job functions, and must be confidential (Spilberg & Corey, 2014). Because of public safety and officer safety concerns, there may be few degrees of freedom available in regard to reasonable accommodation for police officer positions. However, screening psychologists should be in dialogue with hiring agencies about such matters to ensure that the rights of all applicants are protected.

The Genetic Information Nondiscrimination Act of 2008 (GINA) is the federal law that prohibits discrimination in health coverage and employment based on genetic information. To be consistent with GINA, preemployment psychological screenings must not include information about family genetic or health status, including family history of mental disorders or substance use disorders. Consideration of GINA and its implications is yet another way in which preemployment screenings differ from traditional clinical evaluations and therefore call for specialized training.

State laws also greatly impact the practice of psychological screenings. For example, in California, Government Code 1031(f) stipulates that before they can be appointed, peace officer applicants must be found to be free of any physical, emotional, or mental condition that would interfere with carrying out the duties of a peace officer. California's Fair Employment and Housing Act (FEHA) also has employment-related provisions that directly impact how screenings must be conducted. Psychologists who conduct preemployment screenings of law enforcement applicants must familiarize themselves with all relevant laws and regulations in the jurisdictions where they practice.

States may also vary in the extent to which their laws and regulations emphasize screening out applicants who do not meet minimum psychological qualification standards vs. "selecting in" applicants who demonstrate positive, job-relevant psychological attributes. According to Corey and Borum (2013), 45% of the 38 states with some form of preemployment psychological suitability requirements for peace officer applicants have regulations or laws that emphasize screening out applicants with mental or emotional conditions that would interfere with the performance of peace officer duties. Thirteen states (34%) have laws or regulations that focus on suitability or fitness, and three states (8%) have laws that combine emphases on screening out and selecting in. In addition, there are three states (8%) with generally stated "pass" criteria and two states (5%) that simply defer screening decisions to an examining physician (Corey & Borum). Once again the need for screening psychologists to be well versed on all relevant laws and regulations in the states where they practice cannot be overstated.

IMPORTANT CASES

Case law has certainly been important in shaping the practice of preemployment psychological screenings of police officer applicants. For example, courts have ruled that public safety officer agencies do have the right to require psychological evaluations of applicants (*Conte v. Horcher*, 1977; *McCabe v. Hoberman*, 1969; *McKenna v. Fargo*, 1978; *Miller v. City of Springfield*, 1998). The case of *Bonsignore v. City of New York* (1982) addressed the "vicarious liability" of employers and showed that law enforcement agencies may be held liable for the actions of their employees who were not adequately screened or evaluated (Flanagan, 1995). The timing of a preemployment psychological screening has also been the focus of court rulings. For example, *Leonel v. American Airlines* (2005) showed that medical and disability-related exams, including preemployment psychological screenings, must only take place after a conditional offer of hire has been extended to an applicant.

Confidentiality issues and the right of applicants to have access to the results of preemployment psychological evaluations have been the focus of multiple cases, with varying outcomes. Some courts have ruled that the essential features of a "doctor-patient" relationship, including patient access to records, extend also to the relationship between a psychologist conducting a preemployment screening and the police officer applicant/examinee (e.g., *Cleghorn v. Hess*, 1993). On the other hand, some courts have denied examinees access to their preemployment psychological screening records (*Roulette v. Department of Central Management Services*, 1987; *Schroeder v. Detroit*, 1997). Even in jurisdictions where the courts have denied access to records to examinees who are police officer applicants, Borum, Super, and Rand cautioned, "...an individual applicant may still be granted access under civil service rules or medical records statutes (*Cremer v. Macomb*, 1994)" (2003, p. 248).

It is generally accepted that psychologists are exempted from providing feedback to examinees in preemployment psychological screenings, however this must be explained when psychologists obtain informed consent (Corey & Borum, 2013). The agency for which an evaluation was conducted would have to consent for feedback to be provided to an applicant, and such feedback would need to be restricted to findings that were relevant to an applicant's suitability for a specific position within a particular law enforcement department (Borum, Super, & Rand, 2003). In addition to having familiarity with relevant case law, psychologists need training and supervised experience in order to learn to manage these complex considerations.

POLICE OFFICER SCREENING VS. SELECTION

Selection refers to the competitive process of identifying well-qualified applicants for peace officer positions. Law enforcement agencies typically utilize a variety of standardized procedures and criteria to identify the most qualified candidates. These include educational requirements, written examinations, individual or panel interviews, physical ability tests, comprehensive background investigations, and polygraph or computer voice stress analysis (CVSA) exams (Cochrane et al., 2003; Gamez & Collins, 2012).

The psychological screening process is qualitatively different than selection. Most typically, its core purpose is to determine whether a candidate meets minimum psychological qualification standards for peace officer employment as mandated by the statutes and regulations in force in the jurisdiction where the evaluation takes place. Candidates are screened out when there is a finding of mental or emotional conditions, including psychological disorders, personality traits, or problematic attitudes, that could interfere with the safe and effective performance of peace officer duties (Spilberg & Corey, 2014). Psychological screenings inevitably cover sensitive and personal information that would never be deemed relevant or appropriate to explore in a competitive selection process. As noted earlier, ADA stipulates that medical exams, including all psychological exams that assess for the presence of mental or emotional impairment, shall not take place until after a conditional offer of hire. Consequently, psychological screenings must take place after a legitimate conditional offer of hire has been extended and when it has already been determined that a candidate meets a hiring agency's criteria for peace officer employment (Detrick, Chibnall, & Rosso, 2001). This expectation extends to both the written and oral components of psychological exams, whenever such exams are conducted to assess for the presence of psychopathology, including substance abuse or dependence.

In addition to ruling out applicants with psychological characteristics that would significantly interfere with successful job performance (Lowmaster & Morey, 2012), screenings contribute to peace officer selection by helping ensure that individuals who are well adjusted and possess good coping skills are hired (Beutler, Nussbaum, & Meredith, 1988; Scogin, Schumacher, Gardner, & Chaplin, 1995). There is nothing to prevent a hiring agency from establishing psychological suitability criteria that go beyond a minimum level (Spilberg & Corey, 2014; IACP, 2014), particularly when justified for particular job classifications. In such cases, hiring agencies should work closely with screening psychologists to ensure that such additional criteria are job-relevant, well defined, and measurable at the preemployment screening level.

There is also nothing to prevent hiring agencies from assessing normal personality traits and characteristics early in the peace officer selection process, before a job offer has been extended. This is often referred to as the bifurcated model (Corey & Borum, 2013) and some have advocated for the advantages of this two-stage approach (e.g., Hitchcock, Weiss, Weiss, Rostow, & Davis, 2010). In the bifurcated model, normal-range psychological dimensions are assessed pre-offer and this information is used to help select individuals with desirable characteristics for peace officer employment (Spilberg & Corey, 2014). At the post-offer stage, the psychological screening takes place, and candidates not meeting minimum criteria for psychological suitability are disqualified. An important limitation of the bifurcated model is that pre-offer psychological evaluations must never stray into the assessment of psychopathology or impairment, including exploration of substance abuse. In other words, the pre-offer assessment cannot take on the character of a medical exam as defined by ADA.

BASIC SCREENING MODEL

The basic elements of the preemployment psychological screening process have been well described in a number of sources (e.g., Ben-Porath et al., 2011; Borum, Super, & Rand, 2003; Corey & Borum, 2013; Cuttler, 2011; IACP, 2014; Spilberg & Corey, 2014). Many of the core elements, principles, and considerations are summarized below.

1. Preemployment psychological screenings of police officer applicants are specialized assessments that take place after a conditional offer of hire.
2. The hiring agency is the evaluating psychologist's client, not the police officer applicant. However, the psychologist does have ethical obligations and professional role-related responsibilities that extend to the applicant (Corey & Borum, 2013).
3. Informed consent should be obtained from the applicant to ensure he or she understands the key features and limitations of this specialized evaluation.
4. At least two psychological tests that have been validated for preemployment screening of police officer applicants are typically used: one of normal personality and one that measures psychopathology and/or impairment.
5. A face-to-face interview with a qualified psychologist is an essential component of the preemployment screening. Psychologists must have specialized training to conduct preemployment psychological screenings; they also need in-depth understanding of the job functions performed in the law enforcement positions for which they are conducting screenings. Knowledge of law enforcement agency culture is also critically important, as is in-depth understanding of the training processes for new hires (e.g., police academy, field training program, length and scope of probationary supervision, etc.).
6. Prior to the screening interview, the psychologist should review the written psychological test results, any psychological history questionnaires that have been used, the results of the background

investigation (if available), the results of the polygraph or CVSA (if available), and psychological/psychiatric treatment and evaluation records for applicants who report prior histories of mental health treatment and/or psychiatric disability. Records pertaining to any history of job stress leaves should also be obtained and reviewed prior to the interview.

7. The psychological interview should systematically review all the relevant domains of history, behavior, and functioning, with particular emphasis upon job-relevant issues and concerns. The interview is an opportunity to contextualize and confirm the results of the psychological testing, as well as to follow up on important themes from the background investigation and other sources of information. The interview allows the examiner to address inconsistencies in the applicant's records or statements; it provides an opportunity to explore the applicant's motivation for and understanding of the nature of the peace officer position; and it allows the examiner to learn more about the applicant's psychological suitability, including strengths and coping resources.
8. Depending upon the jurisdiction and applicable laws and regulations, the examining psychologist renders a decision or recommendation regarding whether the applicant meets minimum psychological qualification standards for suitability. The recommendation or decision is based upon an integration of all the relevant evidence and information, including careful consideration of the essential job functions, the needs of the hiring agency, and all applicable laws and regulations. The outcome of the evaluation is communicated to the hiring agency in a written report that summarizes the essential and relevant findings, including any limitations or constraints regarding the decision or recommendation.
9. The hiring agency provides follow-up information to the examining psychologist about the job performance and job-relevant outcomes of candidates who were hired. Such feedback permits the examining psychologist to continually improve and refine the psychological screening process over time and better meet the needs of all the parties involved, including the hiring agency, the applicants, and the community. Follow-up also allows the hiring agency and psychologist to examine whether hiring decisions have any adverse impact upon particular classes of applicants (IACP, 2014).
10. The examining psychologist engages in ongoing educational and professional development activities, including consultation with colleagues, to ensure high levels of competence at preemployment psychological screening of police officer applicants.

While the core elements described above are generally applicable, actual practices may vary across states and jurisdictions. Ongoing communication and consultation with the hiring agency is critically important and allows the psychologist to refine, adapt, and improve the screening process. Hiring agencies may vary in their risk tolerance and in their capacity to support the development of police officer recruits. Dialogue with the hiring agency will help the psychologist better understand and respond to such parameters.

PSYCHOLOGICAL DISQUALIFICATION

Given that psychological screenings occur after a candidate has successfully cleared a background investigation and other aspects of a competitive selection process, it is not surprising that psychological disqualification rates tend to be relatively low. A general principle is that the more thorough and comprehensive the background investigation, the lower the psychological disqualification rate (Spilberg

& Corey, 2014). Psychological disqualification rates are rarely reported or discussed in the peer review literature on psychological screenings. In a review by Cochrane et al. (2003), psychological disqualification rates that ranged from 5% to 15% are reported. Considering the recent literature, psychological disqualification rates of 24% (Tarescavage et al., 2015d), 12% (Detrick & Chibnall, 2014), and 8% (Lowmaster & Morey, 2012) are among those that have been reported. Disqualification rates will likely vary across job classifications, departments, jurisdictions, and examining psychologists. The amount of feedback a disqualified applicant receives is also likely to vary a great deal and to reflect the policies and regulations observed by the hiring agency.

APPEALS AND SECOND OPINIONS

In the interest of fundamental fairness, comprehensive psychological screening programs should include some reasonable type of appeal process for those applicants who are disqualified (Hargrave & Kohls, 1984; Serafino, 2010). Many jurisdictions permit second opinion evaluations when an applicant disagrees with a psychological disqualification. In most cases, the applicant must locate a psychologist for the second opinion and pay for it with his or her own funds (Khadivi, 2010). The quality of second opinion evaluations is therefore understandably variable. The IACP guidelines (2014) stipulate that second opinion evaluations should be based on the same criteria used in the initial psychological evaluations. However, the psychological tests used in a second opinion screening sometimes differ from those used in the initial evaluation (Ben-Porath et al., 2011; Corey & Borum, 2013).

Arcaya (2011) addresses the complexities of psychological disqualifications in preemployment screenings. He asserts that in order to manage risk, some police psychologists may be inclined to err in the conservative direction and may recommend against some applicants who should be cleared. Arcaya calls for more probing of applicants' positive accomplishments to ensure that examining psychologists have the whole picture. Khadivi (2010) recommends obtaining consent from applicants to pursue collateral information during second opinion evaluations. He reasons that interviews of an applicant's employers, coaches, and/or teachers may shed important light on the screening dimensions of concern. However, he does not articulate how such collateral information would be superior to the collateral interviews conducted by the background investigator. Moreover the costs incurred by applicants for expansive second opinion evaluations need to be considered. Regardless, the point is well taken that second opinion evaluations should be carefully planned and executed to generate appropriate, evidence-based recommendations and to ensure the rights of all involved. Preemployment psychological screening should not be viewed as a panacea or a guarantee that peace officers will not develop any psychological problems over a long term of employment (Hargrave & Berner, 1984).

PSYCHOLOGICAL INSTRUMENTS

The IACP Preemployment Psychological Evaluation Guidelines (2014) call for the use of a written psychological test battery in preemployment screenings, with particular emphasis on objective, job-relevant psychological measures. The tests used to help make screening decisions need demonstrated reliability and validity, and there should be empirical evidence supporting their use in the preemployment screening of law enforcement applicants. As noted earlier, a standard or basic model that has wide applicability is the use of one self-report inventory of psychopathology and one of normal personality traits. According to Serafino (2010), most preemployment screenings feature this approach and this model is likely to be useful across jurisdictions, regardless of varying legal criteria. Semi-structured interviews, conducted by qualified psychologists, are typically an essential component of the preemployment psychological screening process and must take place after the written psychological tests have been administered and scored (Ben-Porath et al., 2011). Administration of a comprehensive psychological history questionnaire is also standard practice and usually takes place at the same time of the post-offer written psychological testing. Preemployment psychological screening decisions represent a complex, high-stakes assessment task that should be evidence-based. Screening decisions are not typically made on the basis of a single data source (Spilberg & Corey, 2014), but rather reflect the thoughtful integration of multiple data sources.

Desirable characteristics for written measures to be considered appropriate for use in preemployment screenings of police officers include that adequate levels of reliability and validity have been demonstrated; that the measure has been validated specifically for use in preemployment screenings of public safety officer applicants; that the measure includes one or more scales or indices of test-taking attitude; that combined gender norms are available; and that police officer applicant norms have been published or are readily available from the test publisher (Detrick & Chibnall, 2013; Spilberg & Corey, 2014). The psychological measures that are most widely used in preemployment screenings of police officer applicants are introduced and summarized below.

Minnesota Multiphasic Personality Inventory-2

The Minnesota Multiphasic Personality Inventory-2 (MMPI-2; Butcher, Dahlstrom, Graham, Tellegen, & Kaemmer, 1989) is among the most commonly used psychological measures in preemployment screenings of law enforcement applicants (Jacobs, Cushenberry, & Grabarek, 2011). It has been referred to as one of the "workhorses of police psychology" (Rostow & Davis, 2004) and is widely utilized not only in preemployment screenings but also in fitness for duty evaluations of incumbent officers. The MMPI-2 has 567 items and a True/False response format. It is designed primarily to measure mental, emotional, and behavioral problems and therefore represents a medical test for the purposes of preemployment psychological screenings of police officer applicants (P. Weiss & Weiss, 2010). According to Graham (2012), the MMPI-2 has demonstrated its usefulness and validity for the preemployment screening of public safety officer applicants. The test includes an array of validity and clinical scales that have often been examined for their relevance to preemployment screenings of law enforcement applicants and to various aspects of job performance in law enforcement (e.g., Aamodt, 2004; Bartol, 1991; Detrick et al., 2001; Hiatt & Hargrave, 1988; Laguna, Agliotta, & Mannon, 2015; Sellbom, Fischler, & Ben-Porath, 2007; Weiss, Vivian, Weiss, Davis, & Rostow, 2013).

MMPI-2-Restructured Form

The MMPI-2-Restructured Form (MMPI-2-RF; Ben-Porath & Tellegen, 2008) is a recently developed measure based on 338 items drawn from its parent inventory, the MMPI-2. The test items are reorganized into validity and clinical scales that reflect contemporary models of scale construction and psychopathology (Ben-Porath & Archer, 2014). As described in depth in another chapter in the present volume, a growing body of empirical literature supports the validity and usefulness of the MMPI-2-RF in the preemployment psychological screening of police officer applicants (e.g., Detrick & Chibnall, 2014;

Tarescavage, Brewster, Corey, & Ben-Porath, 2015; Tarescavage, Corey, & Ben-Porath, 2015; Tarescavage et al., 2015c; Tarescavage et al., 2015d). Research has demonstrated the equivalence of MMPI-2-RF profiles whether scored from the MMPI-2 item booklet or from the stand-alone administration of the 338 MMPI-2-RF items (Tarescavage et al., 2015b). Like the MMPI-2, the MMPI-2-RF is considered primarily a measure of psychopathology and therefore is appropriate for post-offer screenings.

Personality Assessment Inventory

The Personality Assessment Inventory (PAI; Morey, 1991) is a 344-item self-report measure of psychopathology that employs a four-point response scale (Totally False, Slightly True, Mainly True, and Very True). The PAI items are organized into 22 non-overlapping validity, clinical, treatment consideration, and interpersonal scales (Morey, 2014). Research, though limited, has supported the usefulness and validity of the PAI in the preemployment screening of law enforcement applicants (e.g., Lowmaster & Morey, 2012; Weiss, Hitchcock, Weiss, Rostow, & Davis, 2008; W. Weiss & Weiss, 2010).

Inwald Personality Inventory/Inwald Personality Inventory-2

The Inwald Personality Inventory (IPI; Inwald, 1982) is a 310-item self-report measure of psychopathology, problematic behaviors, and personality characteristics that was developed specifically for application to law enforcement and other high-risk occupations (Inwald, 2010). The IPI features a True/False response format; it includes one validity and 25 clinical scales. Multiple research studies have supported the test's usefulness for the screening of law enforcement applicants (e.g., Chibnall & Detrick, 2003; Cortina, Doherty, Schmitt, Kaufman, & Smith, 1992; Detrick & Chibnall, 2002; Inwald, 2010; Mufson & Mufson, 1998; Ones, Viswesvaran, & Schmidt, 1993; Scogin et al., 1995). The Inwald Personality Inventory-2 (IPI-2) is a briefer version of the test that includes 202 items drawn from the original IPI item pool (Institute for Personality and Ability Testing, 2011). Outdated items were removed and the 202 IPI-2 items have been reorganized into 16 discrete, non-overlapping content scales and one validity scale.

Matrix-Predictive Uniform Law Enforcement Selection Evaluation Inventory

The Matrix-Predictive Uniform Law Enforcement Selection Evaluation Inventory (M-PULSE; Davis & Rostow, 2008) is a 455-item self-report measure that was developed specifically for the assessment of law enforcement candidates. The inventory utilizes a four-point response scale (Strongly Agree, Agree, Disagree, and Strongly Disagree) and is organized into two validity scales; 18 liability scales that identify risk for officer misconduct; 16 empirical scales and subscales that measure attitudes, values, and beliefs considered to be relevant to work in law enforcement; and 10 "California POST Scales" that are considered relevant to job success in law enforcement. The M-PULSE is intended to identify risk for job problems among law enforcement applicants. According to Davis and Rostow, "The M-PULSE Inventory was specifically designed to have utility at both the pre-offer and post-conditional offer phases of the hiring or selection process" (2010, p. 145). However, the inclusion of scales that assess for risk related to chemical abuse/dependency and substance abuse raise some questions about whether M-PULSE could be construed as a medical exam (Spilberg & Corey, 2014). Though the M-PULSE has not often been the focus of peer reviewed publications, it was normed on a substantial number of law enforcement applicants, it has been favorably reviewed (e.g., Blackbourn, Thomas, & Fillingim, 2010; Dean, 2010), and it has generated multiple doctoral dissertations and conference presentations.

California Psychological Inventory

The California Psychological Inventory (CPI; Gough, 1975) is a 434-item self-report measure of normal personality traits and characteristics. The CPI utilizes a True/False response format and is organized into 20 individual scales, three vector or personality dimension scales developed from factor analysis, and validity scales (Groth-Marnat, 2009). The CPI is regarded as one of the most respected of the personality inventories and has a long history of application to police psychology (Kitaeff, 2011). Multiple empirical studies have supported its validity and usefulness in law enforcement applications (e.g., Hargrave & Hiatt, 1989; Hogan & Kurtines, 1975; Mills & Bohannon, 1980).

Sixteen Personality Factor Questionnaire

The 16 Personality Factor Questionnaire, Fifth Edition (16-PF; Russell & Karol, 1994) is a 187-item self-report measure of normal personality. The test utilizes a response format with three options: True, False, and Indeterminate (?). Like the CPI the 16-PF has a long history of application in law enforcement settings (Kitaeff, 2011). The inventory has three validity indices, 16 factor scales, and five global factor scales. The 16-PF's usefulness in preemployment psychological screening of peace officer applicants has been addressed in multiple studies and publications (e.g., Aamodt, 2004; Drew, Carless, & Thompson, 2008; Fabricatore, Azen, Schoentgen, & Snibbe, 1978; Lorr & Strack, 1994).

NEO Personality Inventory, Revised

The NEO Personality Inventory, Revised (NEO PI-R; Costa & McCrae, 1992) is a 240-item self-report measure of normal personality traits. It utilizes a five-point response scale (Strongly Disagree, Disagree, Neutral, Agree, Strongly Agree). The NEO PI-R is often described as a comprehensive measure of the Five Factor Model of personality (Costa & McCrae, 2014). The inventory includes five primary factor scales, plus six facet scales for each factor, resulting in a total of 35 personality scales or subscales. Its usefulness in preemployment psychological screenings is explored in depth in another chapter of the present volume. Given that validity scales have been developed from the item pool (Schinka, Kinder, & Kremer, 1997) and that police officer norms have been published (Detrick & Chibnall, 2013), the NEO PI-R would appear poised for greater use in preemployment screenings of police officer applicants in the future. Early research findings have supported its validity and usefulness for law enforcement applications (e.g., Black, 2000; Chibnall & Detrick, 2003; Detrick, Chibnall, & Luebbert 2004; Miller, Mire, & Kim, 2009; Detrick, Chibnall, & Call, 2010; Salters-Pedneault, Ruef, & Orr, 2010).

Factors Impacting Test Results: Socially Desirable Responding

Socially desirable responding refers to selecting test responses in order to create a more favorable impression for the examiner or others. This response tendency may reflect deliberate impression management (IM), or it may derive from an internalized, dispositional, and perhaps self-deceptive (SD) tendency to view the self in highly favorable terms (Bagby & Marshall, 2004; Paulus, 1991; Vispoel & Kim, 2014).

The context of preemployment psychological screenings has a profound impact upon how individuals approach both the written psychological tests and the face-to-face psychological interview. Given the high-stakes nature of such evaluations, it is to be expected that most applicants will engage in some degree of socially desirable responding, positive impression management, and/or underreporting of psychological problems (Detrick & Chibnall, 2014; Greene, 2011; Weiss, Weiss, Cain, & Manley, 2009). For example, research has shown that peace officer applicants often show average elevations of one standard deviation or more above the mean on MMPI-2 validity scales that measure defensiveness and socially desirable responding such as L and K (Detrick et al., 2001). In fact, the absence of socially desirable responding is unusual in preemployment screenings and might conceivably be cause for some concern (Ben-Porath et al., 2011). Nevertheless, underreporting of psychological problems has been identified as the most salient threat to the validity of psychological test results in preemployment screenings (Tarescavage et al., 2015b). Psychologists who conduct preemployment screenings of police officer applicants must therefore become adept at managing the challenges associated with socially desirable responding.

As has been described earlier in this chapter, applicants who reach the preemployment psychological screening stage have survived what is often a complex, rigorous selection process. Individuals who might have produced elevated scores on scales of psychopathology are less likely to have cleared the hurdles encountered in a hiring agency's selection process. Not surprisingly, the applicants who receive conditional offers of hire rarely show elevations on scales of psychopathology and have often been described as better adjusted than the general population (Hitchcock, Weiss, Weiss, Rostow, & Davis, 2010; Spilberg & Corey, 2014). In addition to whatever defensiveness they are inclined to show on the preemployment psychological testing, their positive adjustment itself may elevate their scores on scales of socially desirable responding (Tarescavage et al., 2015a). More research is needed on how to differentiate positive impression management from the realistic strengths or virtues that applicants possess.

An area that has received considerable attention in the general clinical psychology literature is the impact of coaching and tutorial information upon test takers' attempts to underreport psychological problems on self-report inventories (e.g., Hartmann & Hartmann, 2014). The police psychology literature would likely benefit from more attention to this concern.

Despite the challenges presented by socially desirable responding, the screening psychologist must conduct a thorough interview and psychological evaluation of each applicant. When high levels of socially desirable responding are evident in the written psychological test results, the evaluator must rely more heavily on extra-test sources to determine whether significant, job-relevant psychopathology is present and whether minimum psychological qualification standards have in fact been met.

Range Restriction

It has frequently been noted that because police officer applicants seen in preemployment screenings are often psychologically healthy, their mean scores on measures of psychopathology tend to be low and restricted in range (Chibnall & Detrick, 2003; Lowmaster & Morey, 2012; Sellbom et al., 2007). Studies have also indicated that police officer applicants are often more defensive than the general population, which adds to range restriction of their test scores (Tarescavage et al., 2015c). Despite these realities, significant associations between applicants' test scores and their job performance as police officers are often obtained and reported in the literature (Lowmaster & Morey, 2012). However, range restriction may obscure or limit the usefulness of self-report measures of personality and psychopathology that are utilized in screenings.

An important development in recent years has been the application of statistical corrections to address the problem of range restriction. This advancement has permitted researchers to better understand the validity of measures used in preemployment psychological screenings, including the MMPI-2, MMPI-2-RF, and PAI (Sellbom et al., 2007; Lowmaster & Morey, 2012; Tarescavage et al., 2015c). A parallel development has been the determination of relative risk ratios associated with psychological test scores obtained by applicants. This has enhanced the practical usefulness of psychological testing by indicating the increased risk of job problems associated with subclinical variations in test scores. For example, Sellbom et al. (2007) found that *T* scores as low as 55 on some MMPI-2 Clinical and Restructured Clinical scales were associated with elevated risk for job problems among police officer applicants. While *T* scores of 55 are one standard deviation below the usual cutoff for clinical significance on the MMPI-2, scores at this level (T=55) are quite rare among police officer applicants on many clinical scales. Psychologists who conduct preemployment screenings can make better use of psychological test results by understanding the empirical findings that are emerging from this line of recent research.

PSYCHOLOGICAL SCREENING DIMENSIONS

Psychologists conducting preemployment screenings must have a thorough understanding of the specific nature of the job classifications sought by law enforcement applicants. A clear sense of the psychological qualities or attributes associated with the successful performance of peace officer duties is also essential. According to Detrick and Chibnall (2013), the most sophisticated and ambitious effort yet to operationally define those psychological qualities was produced by the California Commission on Peace Officer Standards and Training (POST). Spilberg and Corey (2014) describe in careful detail the results of a comprehensive job analysis for the position of police officer that was undertaken by POST. That landmark effort yielded ten psychological screening dimensions and included identification of both productive and counterproductive behaviors associated with each dimension. POST's ten psychological screening dimensions are: Social Competence; Teamwork; Adaptability/Flexibility; Conscientiousness/Dependability; Impulse Control/Attention to Safety; Integrity/Ethics; Emotional Regulation/Stress Tolerance; Decision-Making/Judgment; Assertiveness/Persuasiveness; and Avoiding Substance Abuse and Other Risk-Taking Behaviors. The POST psychological screening dimensions represent an important advance in identifying evidence-based criteria to be considered in preemployment psychological screenings of peace officer applicants.

CULTURALLY SENSITIVE ASSESSMENT

A core requirement for the competent practice of preemployment psychological evaluation of law enforcement applicants is awareness of how cultural and linguistic factors may impact the psychological tests used in such assessments (Ben-Porath et al., 2011). For an evaluation process to have multicultural assessment validity, psychologists must take into account examinees' cultural and idiographic experiences, including factors related to cultural identity, acculturation, socioeconomic status, education, language, and other individual difference variables (Ridley, Tracy, Pruitt-Stephens, Wimsatt, & Beard, 2008). Psychologists conducting legal and employment-related evaluations must be attuned to cultural factors and must ensure that all findings and recommendations are culturally informed in ways that are consistent with sound practice (Johnson, 2011). Moreover, psychologists conducting preemployment psychological screenings need to attend to the ethical guidelines of the American Psychological Association (2010), particularly in regard to Principle D, Justice; Principle E, Respect for People's Rights and Dignity; and Section 9, Assessment.

In a classic paper on cultural factors in psychological assessment, Jones and Thorne (1987) stressed the potential of the clinical interview as an opportunity to clarify the meaning and validity of test results in intercultural assessment contexts. The face-to-face interview conducted as part of a preemployment psychological screening represents an ideal example of such an opportunity. Consider the hypothetical case described below.

Mr. R, a 29-year-old single male for whom English was a second language, was seen for a preemployment psychological screening after receiving a conditional offer of hire for a sworn peace officer position. At the item level, the MMPI-2 findings suggested the possible presence of unusual perceptual or sensory experiences of a kind rarely reported among nonclinical samples. At the scale level, all the relevant clinical and validity scales were essentially consistent with law enforcement norms. During the interview, the screening psychologist asked the applicant to comment on whether he had ever had any unusual perceptual experiences. The applicant described having seen what he considered to be "the face of God" on one occasion after having worked a long day in a security-related job. Follow-up questioning determined that this was an isolated incident that appeared unrelated to any factors such as substance use, medications, or mental or medical disorders. The experience did not cause undue distress nor was it associated with any impairment or disturbance in the applicant's daily functioning, including his relationships and the carrying out of his varied responsibilities. The applicant coped with the experience by discussing it with a trusted mentor and he came to view it as a positive incident that was generally consistent with spiritual experiences and practices within his faith community. He added that he drew some reassurance from the experience, particularly as he was going through the demanding peace officer application and qualification process in his state. In the absence of any other job-relevant concerns, and given the applicant's excellent track record at work, at the community college he formerly attended, in his social relationships, and in regard to his substance use history, psychological history, legal history, finances, and driving record, the psychologist found the applicant to meet minimum psychological qualification standards. Follow up showed that the applicant performed satisfactorily in his law enforcement academy, and he likewise met or exceeded standards in all phases of his post-academy field training.

The generalizability of the above vignette is unknown. However, the vignette helps demonstrate the importance of the interview. In this example, the semi-structured face-to-face interview allowed the psychologist to place the psychological test findings in context and integrate all of the relevant data while making an appropriate recommendation.

In addition to the power imbalance between examiner and applicant in preemployment screenings, there may be significant differences in socioeconomic status (SES) and related variables. Smith (2005) has written thoughtfully of the subtle and overt ways that classist attitudes of psychologists can undermine their efforts to provide psychological services to consumers who vary in SES. Screening psychologists potentially face similar challenges. Serafino (2010) provides a number of practical recommendations about how to respectfully and honestly engage with applicants. Respectful, professional, and constructive engagement with applicants is certainly consistent with the ethical principles that should guide all professional practice in psychology.

It has been noted that becoming culturally competent in psychological practice is a complex aspiration that involves self-awareness, cultural knowledge, specific skills, and key virtues such as courage, openness to other perspectives, and commitment to social justice (Fowers & Davidov, 2006). While addressing cultural factors in personality assessment Cheung observed, "...the discipline can no longer ignore the cultural contexts of our knowledge base" (2009, p. 54). Certainly more attention to cultural competence is needed in the police psychology literature, including the literature on preemployment psychological screening of police officer applicants.

CONCERNS

Khadivi (2010) posited that a major challenge in conducting preemployment screenings is that the criteria for psychological disqualification are unclear. Arcaya (2011) suggested that attribution error might lead screening psychologists to regard applicants' past instances of poor judgment as examples of stable personality characteristics rather than as problems that were transcended. Such critiques speak to concerns about the fairness and validity of decisions made by screening psychologists. Dantzker (2011) is among those who have called for greater consistency across psychologists and hiring departments in regard to how preemployment screenings are conducted. Dantzker recommends greater uniformity of practice, including one standard battery of psychological tests for screenings. However, the rationale for restricting screening psychologists and hiring agencies to a uniform battery of psychological tests when multiple psychological measures have been empirically validated for preemployment screenings is unclear. In a reply to Dantzker, Detrick (2012) noted that the IACP has generated useful, comprehensive guidelines and California's POST has produced job-relevant criteria of unprecedented scope with its ten psychological screening dimensions. Detrick also advocates for an evidence-based approach when it comes to the issue of which psychological tests to use.

Police psychology is a relatively new specialty area. Its growth and development should continue and will certainly be enhanced by well-conceived research and by the vision and commitment of the involved professional organizations and stakeholders.

CONCLUSION

Preemployment psychological screening of police officer applicants represents a core element of police psychology. This chapter provides an overview and addresses the need for preemployment psychological screenings to be characterized by sound practices that are empirically supported, ethically attuned, culturally informed, and endorsed by leading professional groups and stakeholders. Psychologists conducting preemployment screenings according to the rigorous standards that have emerged in recent years have the opportunity to make positive and substantive contributions to the communities where they practice and to the discipline of police psychology.

REFERENCES

Aamodt, M. G. (2004). *Research in law enforcement selection*. Boca Raton, FL: Brown Walker Press.

American Psychological Association. (2010). *Ethical principles of psychologists and code of conduct* (2002, Amended June 1, 2010). Washington, DC: Author. Retrieved from http://www.apa.org/ethics/code/index.aspx

Americans with Disabilities Act of 1990, Pub. L., No. 101-336, § 2, 104 Stat. 328 (1991).

Arcaya, J. M. (2011). Challenging the police de-selection process during the psychological interview: How gullibility spells hiring doom for the unwary. In J. Kitaeff (Ed.), *Handbook of police psychology* (pp. 227–236). New York, NY: Routledge.

Bagby, R. M., & Marshall, M. B. (2004). Assessing underreporting response bias on the MMPI-2. *Assessment, 11*(2), 115–126. doi:10.1177/1073191104265918 PMID:15171459

Bartol, C. R. (1991). Predictive validation of the MMPI for small-town police officers who fail. *Professional Psychology, Research and Practice, 22*(2), 127–132. doi:10.1037/0735-7028.22.2.127

Ben-Porath, Y. S., & Archer, R. P. (2014). The MMPI instruments. In R. P. Archer & S. R. Smith (Eds.), *Personality assessment* (2nd ed.; pp. 89–146). New York, NY: Routledge.

Ben-Porath, Y. S., Fico, J. M., Hibler, N. S., Inwald, R., Kruml, J., & Roberts, M. R. (2011, August). Assessing the psychological suitability of candidates for law enforcement positions. *The Police Chief*, 64–70.

Ben-Porath, Y. S., & Tellegen, A. (2008). *MMPI-2-RF (Minnesota Multiphasic Personality Inventory-2 Restructured Form): Manual for administration, scoring, and interpretation*. Minneapolis, MN: University of Minnesota Press.

Beutler, L. E., Nussbaum, P. D., & Meredith, K. E. (1988). Changing personality patterns of police officers. *Professional Psychology, Research and Practice, 19*(5), 503–507. doi:10.1037/0735-7028.19.5.503

Black, J. (2000). Personality testing and police selection: Utility of the "Big Five." *New Zealand Journal of Psychology, 29*, 2–9.

Blackbourn, J. M., Thomas, C., & Fillingim, J. G. (2010). Review of the Matrix-Predictive Uniform Law Enforcement Selection Evaluation Inventory. In R. A. Spies, J. F. Carlson, & K. F. Geisinger (Eds.), *The eighteenth mental measurements yearbook* (pp. 324–326). Lincoln, NE: Buros Institute of Mental Measurements.

Bonsignore v. City of New York, 683 F.2d 635 (1982).

Borum, R., Super, J., & Rand, M. (2003). Forensic assessment for high-risk occupations. In I. B. Weiner (Series Ed.) & A. M. Goldstein (Vol. Ed.), *Comprehensive handbook of psychology: Forensic psychology* (vol. 11, pp. 133-147). Hoboken, NJ: Wiley. doi:10.1002/0471264385.wei1108

Butcher, J. N., Dahlstrom, W. G., Graham, J. R., Tellegen, A., & Kaemmer, B. (1989). *Minnesota Multiphasic Personality Inventory-2 (MMPI-2): Manual for administration and scoring*. Minneapolis, MN: University of Minnesota Press.

Cheung, F. M. (2009). The cultural perspective in personality assessment. In J. N. Butcher (Ed.), *Oxford handbook of personality assessment* (pp. 44–56). New York, NY: Oxford University Press.

Chibnall, J. T., & Detrick, P. (2003). The NEO-PI-R, Inwald Personality Inventory, and MMPI-2 in the prediction of police academy performance: A case for incremental validity. *American Journal of Criminal Justice*, *27*(2), 233–248. doi:10.1007/BF02885696

Civil Rights Act of 1991, Pub. L 102-166. (1991).

Cleghorn v. Hess, 853 P.2d 1260 (Nev. 1993).

Cochrane, R. E., Tett, R. P., & Vandecreek, L. (2003). Psychological testing and the selection of police officers: A national survey. *Criminal Justice and Behavior*, *30*(5), 511–537. doi:10.1177/0093854803257241

Conte v. Horcher, 365 N.E.2d 567 (Ill.App. 1977).

Corey, D. M., & Borum, R. (2013). Forensic assessment for high-risk occupations. In R. K. Otto & I. B. Weiner (Eds.), *Handbook of psychology* (Vol. 11, pp. 246–270). Hoboken, NJ: Wiley.

Corey, D. M., Cuttler, M. J., & Moss, J. A. (2009, December). *Pre-application discussion with the ABPP Board of Trustees regarding a proposed Specialty Board in police an public safety psychology*. Presentation made to the Board of Trustees, American Board of Professional Psychology. Chapel Hill, NC.

Cortina, J. M., Doherty, M. I., Schmitt, N., Kaufman, G., & Smith, R. (1992). Big five personality factors in the IPI and MMPI. *Personnel Psychology*, *45*, 119–139. doi:10.1111/j.1744-6570.1992.tb00847.x

Costa, P. T. Jr, & McCrae, R. R. (1992). *Revised NEO Personality Inventory (NEO-PI-R) and NEO Five-Factor Inventory (NEO-FFI) professional manual*. Odessa, FL: Psychological Assessment Resources.

Costa, P. T. Jr, & McCrae, R. R. (2014). The NEO inventories. In R. P. Archer & S. R. Smith (Eds.), *Personality assessment* (2nd ed.; pp. 229–260). New York, NY: Routledge.

Cremer v. City of Macomb Board of Fire and Police Commissioners, 260 Ill.App.3d 765, 632 N.E.2d 1080, 198 Ill.Dec. 469 (1994).

Cuttler, M. J. (2011). Pre-employment screening of police officers: Integrating actuarial practice models with practice. In J. Kitaeff (Ed.), *Handbook of police psychology* (pp. 135–163). New York, NY: Routledge.

Dantzker, M. L. (2011). Psychological preemployment screening for police candidates: Seeking consistency if not standardization. *Professional Psychology, Research and Practice*, *42*(3), 276–283. doi:10.1037/a0023736

Davis, R. D., & Rostow, C. D. (2008). *Matrix-Predictive Uniform Law Enforcement Selection Evaluation (M-PULSE) Inventory: Technical Manual*. North Tonawanda, NY: Multi-Health Systems, Inc.

Dean, G. J. (2010). Review of the Matrix-Predictive Uniform Law Enforcement Selection Evaluation Inventory. In R. A. Spies, J. F. Carlson, & K. F. Geisinger (Eds.), *The eighteenth mental measurements yearbook* (pp. 326–327). Lincoln, NE: Buros Institute of Mental Measurements.

Detrick, P. (2012). Police officer preemployment evaluations: Seeking consistency if not standardization? *Professional Psychology, Research and Practice*, *43*(2), 162. doi:10.1037/a0026874

Detrick, P., & Chibnall, J. T. (2002). Prediction of police officer performance with the Inwald Personality Inventory. *Journal of Police and Criminal Psychology*, *17*(2), 9–17. doi:10.1007/BF02807111

Detrick, P., & Chibnall, J. T. (2013). Revised NEO Personality Inventory normative data for peace officer selection. *Psychological Services*, *13*, 1541–1559. PMID:23398091

Detrick, P., & Chibnall, J. T. (2014). Underreporting on the MMPI-2-RF in a high-demand police officer context: An illustration. *Psychological Assessment*, *26*(3), 1044–1049. doi:10.1037/pas0000013 PMID:24978133

Detrick, P., Chibnall, J. T., & Call, C. (2010). Demand effects on positive response distortion by police officer applicants on the Revised NEO Personality Inventory. *Journal of Personality Assessment*, *92*(5), 410–415. doi:10.1080/00223891.2010.497401 PMID:20706927

Detrick, P., Chibnall, J. T., & Luebbert, M. C. (2004). The Revised NEO Personality Inventory as predictor of police academy performance. *Criminal Justice and Behavior*, *31*(6), 676–694. doi:10.1177/0093854804268751

Detrick, P., Chibnall, J. T., & Rosso, M. (2001). Minnesota Multiphasic Personality Inventory-2 in police officer selection: Normative data and relation to the Inwald Personality Inventory. *Professional Psychology, Research and Practice*, *32*(5), 484–490. doi:10.1037/0735-7028.32.5.484

Devan, J. L. (2003). *A taxometric analysis of impression management and self-deception on the MMPI-2 among law enforcement applicants* (Doctoral dissertation). Retrieved from ProQuest Information and Learning Company. (UMI Number: 3112951)

Drew, J., Carless, S. A., & Thompson, B. M. (2008). Predicting turnover of police officers using the Sixteen Personality Factor Questionnaire. *Journal of Criminal Justice*, *36*(4), 326–331. doi:10.1016/j.jcrimjus.2008.06.003

Fabricatore, J., Azen, S., Schoentgen, S., & Snibbe, H. (1978). Predicting performance of police officers using the Sixteen Personality Factor Questionnaire. *American Journal of Community Psychology*, *6*(1), 63–70. doi:10.1007/BF00890100

Flanagan, C. L. (1995). Legal issues regarding police psychology. In M. I. Kurke & E. M. Scrivner (Eds.), *Police psychology into the 21st century* (pp. 93–107). New York, NY: Lawrence Erlbaum Associates.

Fowers, B. J., & Davidov, B. J. (2006). The virtue of multiculturalism: Personal transformation, character, and openness to the other. *The American Psychologist*, *61*(6), 581–594. doi:10.1037/0003-066X.61.6.581 PMID:16953746

Gamez, A. M., & Collins, G. C. (2012). Psychological evaluations of law enforcement applicants: The search for ethical officers. In B. D. Fitch (Ed.), *Law enforcement ethics: Classic and contemporary issues* (pp. 29–47). Thousand Oaks, CA: Sage Publications, Inc.

Genetic Information Nondiscrimination Act of 2008 (GINA). Pub. L. 110-233, 122 Stat. 881, 42 U.S.C. 2000 (2008).

Gottesman, J. (1975). *The utility of the MMPI in assessing the personality patterns of urban police applicants*. Hoboken, NJ: Stevens Institute of Technology.

Gough, H. G. (1975). *Manual for the California Psychological Inventory*. Palo Alto, CA: Consulting Psychologists Press, Inc.

Graham, J. R. (2012). *MMPI-2: Assessing personality and psychopathology* (5th ed.). New York, NY: Oxford University Press.

Greene, R. L. (2011). *The MMPI-2/MMPI-2-RF: An interpretive manual* (3rd ed.). Boston, MA: Allyn & Bacon.

Groth-Marnat, G. (2009). *Handbook of psychological assessment* (5th ed.). Hoboken, NJ: John Wiley & Sons.

Hargrave, G. E., & Berner, J. G. (1984). *POST psychological screening manual*. Sacramento, CA: California Commission on Peace Officer Standards and Training.

Hargrave, G. E., & Hiatt, D. (1989). Use of the California Psychological Inventory in law enforcement officer selection. *Journal of Personality Assessment*, *53*(2), 267–277. doi:10.1207/s15327752jpa5302_5

Hargrave, G. E., & Kohls, J. W. (1984, January). Psychological screening of police officers: A clinical-industrial psychological process. *The Police Chief*, 25–28.

Hartmann, E., & Hartmann, T. (2014). The impact of exposure to Internet-based information about the Rorschach and the MMPI-2 on psychiatric outpatients' ability to simulate mentally health test performance. *Journal of Personality Assessment*, *96*(4), 432–444. doi:10.1080/00223891.2014.882342 PMID:24528223

Hiatt, D., & Hargrave, G. E. (1988). Predicting job performance problems with psychological screening. *Journal of Police Science and Administration*, *16*, 122–125.

Hitchcock, J. H., Weiss, P. A., Weiss, W. U., Davis, R. D., & Rostow, C. D. (2010). The future of personality assessment research in police psychology: What's next and what do we need? In P. A. Weiss (Ed.), *Personality assessment in police psychology: A 21st century perspective* (pp. 279–296). Springfield, IL: Charles C. Thomas.

Hogan, R., & Kurtines, W. (1975). Personological correlates of police effectiveness. *The Journal of Psychology*, *91*(2), 289–295. doi:10.1080/00223980.1975.9923955

Institute for Personality and Ability Testing. (2011). *Inwald Personality Inventory-2 manual*. Champaign, IL: Author.

International Association of Chiefs of Police (IACP). (2014). *Preemployment psychological evaluation guidelines: Ratified by the Police Psychological Services Section*. Orlando, FL: Author.

Inwald, R. E. (1982). *Inwald Personality Inventory (IPI) technical manual*. New York, NY: Hilson Research.

Inwald, R. E. (2010). Use of the Inwald Personality Inventory, Hilson Tests, and Inwald Surveys for selection, "fitness-for-duty" assessment, and relationship counseling. In P. A. Weiss (Ed.), *Personality assessment in police psychology: A 21st century perspective* (pp. 91–131). Springfield, IL: Charles C. Thomas.

Jacobs, R., Cushenberry, L., & Grabarek, P. (2011). Assessments for selection and promotion of police officers. In J. Kitaeff (Ed.), *Handbook of police psychology* (pp. 193–210). New York, NY: Routledge.

Johnson, R. (2011). The integration section of forensic psychological evaluation reports in law enforcement: Culturally responsive ending words. In J. Kitaeff (Ed.), *Handbook of police psychology* (pp. 211–226). New York, NY: Routledge.

Jones, E. E., & Thorne, A. (1987). Rediscovery of the subject: Intercultural approaches to clinical assessment. *Journal of Consulting and Clinical Psychology, 55*(4), 488–495. doi:10.1037/0022-006X.55.4.488 PMID:3624605

Khadivi, A. (2010). Conditional second opinion psychological evaluation of law enforcement candidates. In P. A. Weiss (Ed.), *Personality assessment in police psychology: A 21st century perspective* (pp. 333–346). Springfield, IL: Charles C. Thomas.

Kitaeff, J. (2011). History of police psychology. In J. Kitaeff (Ed.), *Handbook of police psychology* (pp. 1–59). New York, NY: Routledge.

Laguna, L., Agliotta, J., & Mannon, S. (2015). Pre-employment screening of police officers: Limitations of the MMPI-2 K scale as a useful predictor of performance. *Journal of Police and Criminal Psychology, 30*(1), 1–5. doi:10.1007/s11896-013-9135-9

Leonel v. American Airlines, Inc., 400 F.3d 702 (9th Cir. 2005).

Lorr, M., & Strack, S. (1994). Personality profiles of police candidates. *Journal of Clinical Psychology, 50*(2), 200–207. doi:10.1002/1097-4679(199403)50:2<200::AID-JCLP2270500208>3.0.CO;2-1 PMID:8014241

Lowmaster, S. E., & Morey, L. D. (2012). Predicting law enforcement officer job performance with the Personality Assessment Inventory. *Journal of Personality Assessment, 94*(3), 254–261. doi:10.1080/00223891.2011.648295 PMID:22224672

McCabe v. Hoberman, 33 A.D.2d 547 (1st Dept. 1969).

McKenna v. Fargo, 451 F.Supp. 1355 (1978).

Miller, H. A., Mire, S., & Kim, B. (2009). Predictors of job satisfaction among police officers: Does personality matter? *Journal of Criminal Justice, 37*(5), 419–426. doi:10.1016/j.jcrimjus.2009.07.001

Miller v. City of Springfield, 146 F.3d 612 (1998).

Mills, C. J., & Bohannon, W. E. (1980). Personality characteristics of effective state police officers. *The Journal of Applied Psychology, 65*(6), 680–689. doi:10.1037/0021-9010.65.6.680

Morey, L. C. (1991). *Personality Assessment Inventory professional manual*. Odessa, FL: Psychological Assessment Resources.

Morey, L. C. (2014). The Personality Assessment Inventory. In R. P. Archer & S. R. Smith (Eds.), *Personality assessment* (2nd ed.; pp. 181–228). New York, NY: Routledge.

Mufson, D. W., & Mufson, M. (1998). Predicting police officer performance using the IPI: An illustration from Appalachia. *Professional Psychology, Research and Practice, 29*, 59–62. doi:10.1037/0735-7028.29.1.59

National Council on Crime and Delinquency. (1973). *Criminal justice standards and goals of the National Advisory Commission.* Digested from a National Strategy to Reduce Crime. Harrisburg, PA.

Ones, D. S., Viswesvaran, C., & Schmidt, F. L. (1993). Comprehensive meta-analysis of integrity test validation: Findings and implications for personnel selection and theories of job performance. *The Journal of Applied Psychology, 78*(4), 679–703. doi:10.1037/0021-9010.78.4.679

Padilla, A. M. (2001). Issues in culturally appropriate assessment. In L. A. Suzuki, J. G. Ponterotto, & P. J. Meller (Eds.), *Handbook of multicultural assessment* (2nd ed., pp. 5–27). San Francisco, CA: Josey-Bass.

Paulhus, D. L. (1991). Measurement and control of response bias. In J. P. Robinson, P. R. Shaver, & L. S. Wrightsman (Eds.), *Measures of personality and social psychological attitudes* (pp. 17–59). San Diego, CA: Academic Press. doi:10.1016/B978-0-12-590241-0.50006-X

President's Commission on Law Enforcement and Administration of Justice. (1967). *The challenge of crime in a free society: A report by The President's Commission on Law Enforcement and Administration of Justice.* Washington, DC: U.S. Government Printing Office.

Reaves, B. A. (2010). *Local police departments, 2007. Publication NCJ 231174.* U.S. Department of Justice, Office of Justice Programs, Bureau of Justice Statistics.

Ridley, C. R., Tracy, M. L., Pruitt-Stephens, L., Wimsatt, M. K., & Beard, J. Multicultural assessment validity: The preeminent ethical issue in psychological assessment. In L. A. Suzuki & J. G. Ponterotto (Eds.), *Handbook of multicultural assessment* (3rd ed.; pp. 22–33). San Francisco, CA: John Wiley & Sons.

Rostow, C. D., & Davis, R. D. (2004). *A handbook of fitness-for-duty evaluations for law enforcement.* Binghamton, NY: Haworth.

Roulette v. Department of Central Management Services, 490 N.E. 2d 60 (Ill.App. 1 Dist. 1986).

Russell, M., & Karol, D. (1994). *16 PF Fifth Edition: Administrator's manual.* Chicago, IL: Institute for Personality and Ability Assessment.

Salters-Pedneault, K., Ruef, A. M., & Orr, S. P. (2010). Personality and psychophysiological profiles of police officer and firefighter recruits. *Personality and Individual Differences, 49*(3), 210–215. doi:10.1016/j.paid.2010.03.037

Schinka, J. A., Kinder, B. N., & Kremer, T. (1997). Research validity scales for the NEO-PI-R: Development and initial validation. *Journal of Personality Assessment, 68*(1), 127–138. doi:10.1207/s15327752jpa6801_10 PMID:16370773

Schroeder v. Detroit, 221 Mich.App. 364, 561 N.W.2d 497 (1997).

Scogin, F., Schumacher, J., Gardner, J., & Chaplin, W. (1995). Predictive validity of psychological testing in law enforcement settings. *Professional Psychology, Research and Practice, 26*(1), 68–71. doi:10.1037/0735-7028.26.1.68

Sellbom, M., Fischler, G. I., & Ben-Porath, Y. S. (2007). Identifying MMPI-2 predictors of police officer integrity and misconduct. *Criminal Justice and Behavior, 34*(8), 985–1004. doi:10.1177/0093854807301224

Serafino, G. F. (2010). Fundamental issues in police psychological assessment. In P. A. Weiss (Ed.), *Personality assessment in police psychology: A 21st century perspective* (pp. 29–55). Springfield, IL: Charles C. Thomas.

Smith, L. (2005). Psychotherapy, classism, and the poor: Conspicuous by their absence. *The American Psychologist, 60*(7), 687–696. doi:10.1037/0003-066X.60.7.687 PMID:16221002

Spilberg, S. W., & Corey, D. M. (2014). *Peace officer psychological screening manual.* Sacramento, CA: California Commission on Peace Officer Standards and Training: Standards, Evaluation, and Research Bureau.

Tarescavage, A. M., Brewster, J., Corey, D. M., & Ben-Porath, Y. S. (2015a). Use of prehire Minnesota Multiphasic Personality Inventory-2-Restructured Form (MMPI-2-RF) police candidate scores to predict supervisor ratings of posthire performance. *Assessment, 22*(4), 411–428. doi:10.1177/1073191114548445 PMID:25169624

Tarescavage, A. M., Corey, D. M., Gupton, H. M., & Ben-Porath, Y. S. (2015c). Criterion validity and practical utility of the Minnesota Multiphasic Personality Inventory-2-Restructured Form (MMPI-2-RF) in assessments of police officer candidates. *Journal of Personality Assessment, 97*(4), 382–294. doi:10.1080/00223891.2014.995800 PMID:25588076

Tarescavage, A. M., Fischler, G. L., Cappo, B. M., Hill, D. O., Corey, D. M., & Ben-Porath, Y. S. (2015d). Minnesota Multiphasic Personality Inventory-2-Restructured Form (MMPI-2-RF) predictors of police officer problem behavior and collateral self-report test scores. *Psychological Assessment, 27*(1), 125–137. doi:10.1037/pas0000041 PMID:25383586

Tarescavage, C., Corey, D. M., & Ben-Porath, Y. S. (2015b). Minnesota Multiphasic Personality Inventory-2-Restructured Form (MMPI-2-RF) predictors of police problem behavior. *Assessment, 22*(1), 116–132. doi:10.1177/1073191114534885 PMID:24875465

Terman, L. M. (1917). A trial of mental and pedagogical tests in a civil service examination for policemen and firemen. *The Journal of Applied Psychology, 1*(1), 17–29. doi:10.1037/h0073841

Vispoel, W. P., & Kim, H. Y. (2014). Psychometric properties for the Balanced Inventory of Desirable Responding: Dichotomous versus polytomous conventional and IRT scoring. *Psychological Assessment, 26*(3), 878–891. doi:10.1037/a0036430 PMID:24708082

Weiss, P. A., Hitchcock, J. H., Weiss, W. U., Rostow, C., & Davis, R. (2008). The Personality Assessment Inventory Borderline, Drug, and Alcohol Scales as predictors of overall performance in police officers: A series of exploratory analyses. *Policing and Society, 18*(3), 301–310. doi:10.1080/10439460802091708

Weiss, P. A., & Inwald, R. (2010). A brief history of personality assessment in police psychology. In P. A. Weiss (Ed.), *Personality assessment in police psychology: A 21st century perspective* (pp. 5–28). Springfield, IL: Charles C. Thomas.

Weiss, P. A., Vivian, J. E., Weiss, W. U., Davis, R. D., & Rostow, C. D. (2013). The MMPI-2 L scale, reporting uncommon virtue, and predicting police performance. *Psychological Services, 10*(1), 123–130. doi:10.1037/a0029062 PMID:22774705

Weiss, P. A., & Weiss, W. U. (2010). Using the MMPI-2 in police psychological assessment. In P. A. Weiss (Ed.), *Personality assessment in police psychology: A 21st century perspective* (pp. 59–71). Springfield, IL: Charles C. Thomas.

Weiss, W. U., & Weiss, P. A. (2010). Use of the Personality Assessment Inventory in police and security personnel selection. In P. A. Weiss (Ed.), *Personality assessment in police psychology: A 21st century perspective* (pp. 72–90). Springfield, IL: Charles C. Thomas.

Weiss, W. U., Weiss, P. A., Cain, S., & Manley, B. (2009). Impression management in police officer candidacy on the MMPI-2. *Journal of Police and Criminal Psychology*, *24*(2), 120–125. doi:10.1007/s11896-009-9044-0

Chapter 3
Using the MMPI-2-RF in Preemployment Evaluations of Police Officer Candidates

Yossef S. Ben-Porath
Kent State University, USA

David M. Corey
Corey & Stewart, USA

Anthony M. Tarescavage
Kent State University, USA

ABSTRACT

The MMPI-2 Restructured Form (MMPI-2-RF) is the current, most up-to-date version of the most widely used self-report measure of personality and psychopathology. Prior versions of the test were studied and used extensively in police candidate assessments. This chapter reviews the legal and empirical foundations for using the MMPI-2-RF in preemployment evaluations of police officer candidates and provides practical guidance for doing so. A detailed review of a series of recent studies on using the MMPI-2-RF in identification of high risk candidates is presented, followed by practical suggestions for integrating MMPI-2-RF findings with other sources of information when conducting preemployment evaluations of police candidates. The MMPI-2-RF Police Candidate Interpretive Report is highlighted.

DISCLOSURES

Yossef S. Ben-Porath is a paid consultant to the MMPI Publisher, the University of Minnesota, and Distributor, Pearson. As co-author of the MMPI-2-RF he receives royalties on sales of the test. Along with David M. Corey he is co-author of the MMPI-2-RF Police Candidate Interpretive Report (PCIR) and receives royalties on its sales. He has also received research funding from the test publisher.

David M. Corey is a co-author of the MMPI-2-RF PCIR and receives royalties on sales of the report and has received research funding from the Publisher.

Anthony M Tarescavage has received research funding from the MMPI Publisher, the University of Minnesota.

DOI: 10.4018/978-1-5225-0813-7.ch003

INTRODUCTION

The MMPI-2 Restructured Form (MMPI-2-RF; Ben-Porath & Tellegen, 2008/2011; Tellegen & Ben-Porath, 2008/2011) is the current, most up-to-date version of the most widely used self-report measure of personality and psychopathology. Prior versions of the test[1] were studied and used extensively in police candidate assessments. Building on the initial work of Sellbom, Fischler, and Ben-Porath (2007), over the past several years a series of studies has provided a comprehensive empirical foundation for using the MMPI-2-RF in these evaluations (Detrick, Ben-Porath, & Sellbom, 2015; Detrick & Chibnall, 2014; Tarescavage, Brewster, Corey, & Ben-Porath, 2015; Tarescavage, Corey, & Ben-Porath 2015; Tarescavage, Corey, & Ben-Porath, 2016; Tarescavage, Corey, Gupton, & Ben-Porath, 2015; Tarescavage, Fischler, Cappo, Hill, Corey, & Ben-Porath, 2015). This research has also been incorporated in the Police Candidate Interpretive Report (PCIR; Corey & Ben-Porath, 2014), a computer-generated interpretive report designed to assist police candidate evaluators.

This chapter is intended to inform the reader about the legal and empirical foundations for using the MMPI-2-RF in preemployment evaluations of police officer candidates and provide practical guidance in this area. We begin with a review of the legal matters related to using clinical assessment measures such as the MMPI in preemployment evaluations of police candidates. The second section includes a historical review of the literature on use of the Original MMPI and MMPI-2 in police candidate assessments. The third section provides a detailed discussion of the MMPI-2-RF literature just described. The final section provides recommendations for integrating MMPI-2-RF findings in general, and PCIR results in particular, with other sources of information when evaluating police candidates.

LEGAL MATTERS

Psychologists who use the MMPI in the conduct of police officer candidate preemployment evaluations should be aware of the laws and regulations governing this practice, recognizing that whereas federal laws and regulations apply throughout the U.S., individual states may, and often do, have their own complementary requirements. The following discussion of these legal matters should be viewed as an orientation to the topic, not legal advice, which should be sought from one's own legal counsel. We focus here on two primary federal laws that impact use of the MMPI tests in assessments of police officer candidates throughout the U.S. -- the Americans with Disabilities Act (1990) and the Civil Rights Act (1964, 1991). A more detailed discussion of these and other federal and national laws and guidelines is presented by Spilberg and Corey (2014).

Americans with Disabilities Act (1990)

Prior to passage of the Americans with Disabilities Act of 1990 (ADA), federal and state laws were largely silent on the matter of using clinical assessment devices such as the MMPI in evaluations of police officer candidates. With enactment of the ADA, this legal landscape changed considerably. Title I of the ADA applies strict limits on (but does not prohibit) making disability-related medical inquiries of job candidates (ADA, 1990), including ones that *may*[2] reveal a mental disability. These restrictions also apply to professionals retained or employed by police agencies to conduct preemployment evaluations. Under the ADA, an examination is deemed medical if, among other factors, it seeks information about possible physical or mental impairments or health. Because the MMPI includes items that address these topics, the test is considered a medical examination subject to the restrictions imposed by the ADA (*Karraker v. Rent-A-Center, Inc.* [2005] 411 F.3d 831 [7th Cir. Ill.]).

The ADA does not prohibit police agencies from requiring that officer candidates' mental health be evaluated, but it does impose restrictions on the circumstances under which this can occur. The statute allows an agency to require that a candidate submit to a medical (including psychological) examination if (1) all non-medical information needed to make the hiring decision has already been obtained, (2) the candidate is subsequently given a conditional offer of employment, contingent upon the results of the examination, and (3) all candidates applying for the position are required to take the examination. Consequently, the preemployment psychological evaluation, including administration of the MMPI-2-RF, must occur "post-conditional offer"; that is, after a candidate has successfully passed the non-medical assessment phase and has been tendered a conditional offer of employment.

Civil Rights Act (1964, 1991)

The Civil Rights Act (CRA, 1964), and its subsequent update (CRA, 1991), prohibits discrimination in the workplace on the basis of race, color, religion, sex, or national origin. The CRA has two primary implications for using the MMPI-2-RF in preemployment evaluations of police candidates. The first involves the concept of d*isparate impact*, which is an employment practice that results in a disproportionate number of affected class members (e.g., women) being adversely impacted. The federal agency charged with enforcing the CRA, the Equal Employment Opportunity Commission (EEOC), has operationalized disparate impact as occurring if a protected class (in this example, women) is hired at less than fourth-fifths the rate of the majority group (men, who make up the vast majority of police officers). For example, if an agency hires 60 percent of male candidates but only 40 percent of females, the hiring rate for females (40 percent) divided by the hiring rate for males (60 percent) is 66.67 percent, falling below the 80 percent (four-fifths) requirement, thus demonstrating disparate (or adverse) impact.

Differential MMPI-2-RF findings occur when different rates of a protected class versus the majority score at or above designated cutoffs (at a rate exceeding the four-fifths standard). These differential MMPI-2-RF findings *alone* are unlikely to lead to a finding of disparate impact in hiring decisions stemming from use of the inventory because of two considerations. First, as discussed later, a candidate should not be routinely disqualified on the basis of any single test score or set of test scores alone. Second, an employer can justify hiring practices that do result in disparate impact if it can demonstrate that these practices (e.g., use of a given test) are job-related (i.e., valid predictors of job outcomes) and consistent with business necessity (i.e., the need to avoid negligent hiring of individuals who pose a risk to public safety). Because the literature reviewed later in this chapter demonstrates that MMPI-2-RF scores are associated with a broad range of adverse outcomes in law enforcement officers, they can be demonstrated to be job-related and consistent with business necessity; therefore, these scores can be relied upon in making hiring recommendations regardless of whether disparate impact occurs.

A specific provision, introduced in the 1991 CRA update, states, "It shall be an unlawful employment practice for a respondent, in connection with the selection or referral of applicants or candidates for employment or promotion, to adjust the scores of, use different cutoff scores for, or otherwise alter the results of, employment related tests on the basis of race, color, religion, sex, or national origin" (CRA, 1991, Sec. 106). This prohibition of considering race, color, religion, sex, or national origin in the conduct of preemployment evaluations makes it illegal to use demographically-based norms in these assessments. In the case of the MMPI, which traditionally always had separate norms for men and women, this necessitated the development of a third set of non-gendered norms for the MMPI-2 (Ben-Porath & Forbey, 2003). In addition to providing raw-to-T-score conversions for the MMPI-2, Ben-Porath and Forbey (2003) examined the impact of using non-gendered versus gender-based MMPI-2 norms and found it negligible. This led to the decision to develop only one set of norms (non-gendered) for the MMPI-2-RF. Moreover, as discussed later, the Police Officer Candidate MMPI-2-RF comparison group is made up of an equal number (1,037 each) of female and male candidates, to comply with the CRA prohibition against using an interpretation standard that is weighted differentially for a given demographic group. Given the fact that approximately 85% of police candidates across the United States are male (Langton, 2010), comparison groups that simply aggregate candidate scores are inherently weighted differentially by gender.

RESEARCH ON THE ORIGINAL MMPI AND MMPI-2 IN POLICE CANDIDATE EVALUATIONS

A substantial body of empirical research was available to guide use of the Original MMPI and later the MMPI-2 in preemployment police candidate evaluations. The following review is not intended to be exhaustive, but rather to provide examples of the main findings of this research and some issues raised that remain pertinent to contemporary use of the MMPI-2-RF.

The Original MMPI

Early empirical studies conducted with the Original MMPI found that several scales were effective in identifying police candidates at risk for post-hire counterproductive behaviors. Marsh (1962) reported the results of a 10-year longitudinal study conducted with the Los Angeles County Sheriff's Department. The subjects were 619 male deputy sheriffs hired between 1947 and 1950. Marsh reported that scores on MMPI Clinical Scales 9 (positively) and 2 (negatively) correlated with preventable auto accidents during an officer's first and second years on the force. Ten years later, Azen, Snibbe, and Montgomery (1973) conducted a follow-up study of 95 deputies from this cohort. These authors replicated and extended Marsh's findings, finding in particular that officers' pre-hire MMPI Scale 9 scores were associated with an increased risk for being involved in any type of traffic accident over the course of 20 years of service.

In one of the most comprehensive, early MMPI studies, Blum (1964) conducted a longitudinal study of 87 male police applicants who were subsequently hired by a major metropolitan police agency. Seven years after testing, each officer's personnel records were reviewed for evidence of negative outcomes (charges of misconduct, motor vehicle accidents, sick leave use, termination) and positive outcomes (career progression and commendations). Blum reported significant correlations (.20 or higher) between MMPI scale scores and various outcomes, with the validity scale F and Clinical Scale 8 having the highest number of significant correlations (three each) with negative outcomes. Blum concluded that "personality problems loom largest in determining the chances for later misconduct as a policeman; they also play a role in risk for accidents and illness. They seem to play no role in whether or not a man is commended" (p. 131).

Saxe and Reiser (1976) compared MMPI scores of three police candidates groups: 100 who were rejected, 100 who were hired but separated from service within three years, and 100 who were hired and served successfully for at least three years. They reported significant group differences between rejected and successful candidates, and between separated and successful officers, on most MMPI scales. However, they noted that most subjects scored within normal limits, even on scales that differentiated successful from unsuccessful candidates, which they viewed as limiting the ability of the test to identify potentially problematic ones when using clinically elevated scores on these scales. They recommended that the use of "successful officer norms" be explored, and they demonstrated that the separated officers scored approximately one-half of a standard deviation above the mean of successful officers on Clinical Scale 7. The absence of clinically significant elevations among police candidates has figured prominently in criticisms of the utility of the MMPI in screening law enforcement candidates. We return to this topic later in this section.

Beutler, Storm, Kirkish, Scogin, and Gaines (1985) examined the prediction of negative outcomes in officers sampled from a variety of departments, finding that scores on Clinical Scales 1, 2, 4, 6, and 7 were associated significantly with subsequent police supervisor ratings and various measures of post-hire counterproductive behavior. The most notable correlations were between: Clinical Scale 6 and technical proficiency; Clinical Scales 4 and 7 and at-fault motor vehicle accidents; Clinical Scale 1 and use-of-force reprimands; and Clinical Scale 2 and letters of complaint. Like Saxe and Reiser (1976), Beutler and colleagues commented on the absence of clinically significant elevations among officers who exhibited counterproductive behaviors, but they noted that this was the result of automatic disqualification of candidates who produced elevated scores on MMPI scales associated with emotional and thought dysfunction. The authors observed that they were able to detect substantial associations between MMPI scale scores and outcomes in spite of the absence of clinically elevated scores.

The MMPI-2

The release of the MMPI-2 (Butcher, Dahlstrom, Graham, Tellegen, & Kaemmer, 1989) raised some initial questions about the comparability of scores generated with the original and revised versions of the inventory, and whether Original MMPI findings such as the ones just reviewed could be assumed to carry over to the MMPI-2. Hargrave, Hiatt, Ogard, and Carr (1994) administered both versions of the test to a sample of incumbent police officers. When MMPI-2 raw scores were converted to Original MMPI T scores, Clinical Scale scores were essentially interchangeable across the two versions, indicating that minor rewording and loss of a small number of items had no appreciable effect on officers' Clinical Scale scores. When scored using the MMPI-2 norms, Clinical Scale scores were appreciably (at least 5 T score points) lower on Scales 2, 3, 4, 6, and 9 for both genders, and Scales 5 and 7 for men. This was consistent with findings for other samples, and the differences were addressed by lowering the cutoff for clinically significant elevation from 70 on the Original MMPI to 65 on the MMPI-2. The authors concluded that the two versions of the inventory would yield comparable results when used as a component of the preemployment assessment process, but noted the need for new MMPI-2 validation studies.

Boes, Chandler, and Timm (1997) studied Original MMPI and MMPI-2 scores of police officers who had been administered the test as part of their preemployment psychological evaluations. Their sample included 439 known-offender officers from 69 police departments and a sample of matched controls from the same departments. The authors reported finding few MMPI score differences between the groups, but they did report higher scores on Clinical Scale 4 and on the L scale when scores of integrity violators where compared with those of the non-violator control subjects. This dataset was revisited in a subsequent MMPI-2-RF study (Tarescavage, Ben-Porath, & Corey, 2016) discussed in the following section of this chapter.

Detrick, Chibnall, and Rosso (2001) provided descriptive data for, and reported correlations between, MMPI-2 scores and scores on the Inwald Personality Inventory (IPI; Inwald, 1992), an instrument designed specifically for assessment of police officer candidates, for a sample of 461 Midwestern law enforcement candidates who were administered these tests as part of a preemployment evaluation. This was one of the first MMPI-2 studies published following the CRA legislation discussed earlier, which prohibited use of gender-based norms in preemployment evaluations. The authors provided the first descriptive findings for police candidates using the MMPI-2 non-gendered norms. Consistent with prior studies with the Original MMPI, and accentuated by the overall lowering of T scores on the MMPI-2, mean Clinical Scale T scores were substantially lower than the general population mean (50T). The standard deviations associated with these lower means were also substantially smaller than the general population standard T score deviations (10T). Finally, Detrick and colleagues noted that whereas correlations between MMPI-2 Clinical Scale and IPI scale scores were generally moderate and in the expected direction, this was true only for non-K-corrected Clinical Scale scores. Applying the standard K correction to the five Clinical Scales with which it was used (1, 4, 7, 8, and 9) substantially attenuated their correlations with relevant IPI scales, in some cases reducing sizable correlations to zero. This study led MMPI-2 experts (e.g., Graham, 2012 and Greene, 2011) to recommend that non-K-corrected scores be relied upon when the test is used in preemployment evaluations. These data were also revisited in the context of the MMPI-2-RF in a study by Detrick, Ben-Porath, and Sellbom (2016), discussed later in this chapter.

Sellbom, Fischler, and Ben-Porath (2007): A Paradigm Shift

Sellbom, Fischler, and Ben-Porath (2007) conducted the most comprehensive, prospective police candidate study carried out with the MMPI-2. It was the first to include the Restructured Clinical (RC) Scales (Tellegen et al., 2003), which are also part of the MMPI-2-RF. The authors examined the ability of pre-hire MMPI-2 scores of 426 candidates to predict future misconduct of police officers who, at the time of the study, had been employed from seven to nine years. In addition to reporting associations between pre-hire MMPI-2 scores and a host of outcome variables, these authors sought to address two challenges raised by the findings of prior research. As noted earlier, descriptive statistics reported for both Original MMPI and MMPI-2 scores of police officer candidates indicated that, as a group, they score considerably lower than the general population and evidence substantially reduced scale score variability.

Sellbom and colleagues (2007) reasoned that the lower scores with reduced variability observed in police officer candidates were likely the product of preselection and selection effects. *Preselection* effects are ones that limit the range of scores of individuals referred by law enforcement agencies for a preemployment psychological evaluation. These include any self-selection that may occur among those who choose to seek employment in law enforcement as well as any exclusions that might apply (e.g., a significant criminal record). The impact of preselection factors likely increased substantially following enactment of the ADA (discussed earlier) and the requirement that candidates receive a conditional offer of employment prior to being referred for a preemployment psychological evaluation. Whereas prior to the ADA police agencies could refer potential candidates for a psychological evaluation before determining that they were prepared to hire them, post-ADA candidates, as discussed earlier, must be given a bona fide conditional offer of employment prior to being referred for an evaluation.

Selection factors stem from the use of MMPI scores as part of the pre-hire decision-making process, where it stands to reason that candidates whose MMPI scores raise suitability concerns are less likely to be hired. For example, in the study by Beutler and colleagues (1985) discussed earlier, candidates with clinically elevated scores on any of a number Clinical Scales were automatically disqualified and, therefore, unavailable for the follow-up part of the study.

Sellbom and colleagues (2007) estimated preselection effects in their sample by comparing the means and associated standard deviations of MMPI-2 T scores of the full sample of 426 candidates with the known means and standard deviations of the general population (T scores 50 and 10, respectively). Mean scores on the Clinical Scales (particularly the more informative non-K-corrected scores) and the RC Scales were generally 5-15 T score points lower than those of the general population, and standard deviations were generally 2 to 5 T score units lower (e.g., a 20-50 percent reduction in scale score variability). Selection effects were estimated by comparing mean scores and standard deviations of the 426 candidates with the 291 individuals among them who "passed" the psychological evaluation and were hired. Selection effects were considerably smaller than those produced by preselection, but they still resulted in further lowering of mean scores and their associated standard deviations.

These preselection (in particular) and selection effects have both significant research and practice implications. The reduced variability characteristic of pre-hire scale scores attenuates correlations between these scores and the criteria used in studying their validity as predictors of subsequent counterproductive behaviors. Correlations essentially reflect the extent to which variance in a predictor variable (MMPI score) is associated with variance in a criterion (counterproductive behavior). Reduced variance in the predictor variable (stemming from preselection and selection factors) artificially attenuates its correlations with outcome variables. Sellbom and colleagues (2007) applied a formula derived from the work of Hunter and Schmidt (1990) to estimate the true correlation between MMPI-2 scores and outcome variables in their study:

$$r_c = \frac{r_u \cdot (SD \div SD_r)}{\sqrt{(1 + r_u^2) + (r_u^2) \cdot (SD \div SD_r)^2}}$$

where r_c is the estimated correct correlation between the predictor and criterion variable, r_u is the uncorrected or observed correlation, SD_r is the restricted or observed standard deviation, and SD_u is the unrestricted standard deviation. To correct for preselection factors, Sellbom and colleagues (2007) set SD_r to equal 10 (the standard deviation of T scores in the general population) and inserted the r_u and SD_u values obtained in their analyses to calculate the corrected validity coefficient, r_c.

From a practice standpoint, the absence of clinically elevated scores stemming from preselection and selection factors creates a need to identify non-clinically elevated cutoffs associated with an estimated increased risk for a subsequent adverse outcome. To address this need, Sellbom and colleagues (2007) reported relative risk ratios associated with T score cutoffs of 60 and 55. Relative risk ratios quantify the increased risk for a given outcome associated with scoring at or above the designated cutoff versus scoring below the cutoff. For example, a relative risk ratio equal to 2.0 for a cutoff 55T on a given scale indicates that those who score at or above 55T on that scale are at twice the risk of the associated negative outcome as are those who score below 55T on that scale.

Applying the Hunter and Schmidt (1990) correction for range restriction just mentioned, Sellbom and colleagues (2007) reported for a sample of 291 male police officers uncorrected and range-restriction-corrected correlations between pre-hire scores on the MMPI-2 Clinical, RC, and Substance Abuse scales and post-hire internal affairs and civilian review authority complaints, termination of employment for cause, and supervisory ratings. Sellbom and colleagues (2007) found that the RC Scales, particularly RC3 (Cynicism), RC4 (Antisocial Behavior), RC6 (Ideas of Persecution), and RC8 (Aberrant Experiences), had the best predictive utility among the MMPI-2 scales they examined. For example, higher scores on RC6 were significantly associated with termination for cause, complaints from members of the public, use of excessive force, rude behavior, displaying a bad attitude toward members of the public, being uncooperative toward supervisors, being a defendant in civil litigation, deceptiveness, abuse of authority, failure to take responsibility for mistakes, using one's position for personal advantage, showing biased attitudes toward others, poor response to constructive feedback, and an indication that, given an opportunity to reconsider the initial hire decision, the officer's supervisor would not rehire him or her. The uncorrected correlations between pre-hire RC6 scores and the outcomes just listed ranged from .15 to .29. The range-restriction-corrected correlations were from .35 to .60.

Sellbom and colleagues' (2007) results indicate that even utilizing an interpretive cutoff of 60T yielded low elevation rates for the RC scales. For example, 1.7% and 0.4% of employed officers scored ≥ 60T on RC3 and RC4, respectively. Furthermore, Sellbom and colleagues (2007) noted that as a result of various preselection and selection factors, none of the officers included in their study scored above 60T on RC6. Thus, the correlates just mentioned reflect associations between non-clinically elevated RC6 scores and the outcome variables. This, in turn, indicates that substantial deviations from the mean RC6 score of police candidates are associated with substantially increased risk for negative outcomes at levels well below 65 (the T score cutoff used typically to interpret MMPI-2 scores in clinical settings). To quantify this risk, Sellbom and colleagues calculated relative risk ratios (RRRs) for statistically significant correlations. They reported, for example, that 26.3% of officers who, during the pre-hire evaluation, scored at or above 55T on RC6 were identified by their supervisors several years later as having engaged in rude behavior toward members of the public. Only 6.5% of those who scored below 55T on RC6 in the pre-hire testing were similarly identified, producing a RRR of roughly 4 (26.3/6.5), indicating that candidates who score at or above this cutoff on RC6 have a four-times greater risk for engaging in rude behavior toward civilians compared with those who score below 55 on this scale.

Sellbom, Fischler, and Ben-Porath's (2007) results demonstrated several important considerations pertaining to use of the MMPI in pre-hire assessments of police candidates. First, these authors found that, when corrected for range restriction, correlations between pre-hire scores and subsequent counterproductive behaviors were of a meaningful magnitude reflecting medium to large effect sizes. Second, Sellbom and colleagues demonstrated the need for and appropriateness of using lower (than the traditional 65T) cutoffs to properly interpret police candidates' MMPI-2 scale scores. Sellbom and colleagues' (2007) results also replicated those of Detrick and colleagues (2001) in finding generally stronger validity for non-K-corrected versus K-corrected Clinical Scale scores. Finally, their findings indicated that the RC Scales developed by Tellegen et al. (2003), described in the next section of this chapter, provided substantial improvements above the non-K-corrected Clinical Scale scores in prospective prediction of police candidates' problematic behavior.

Summary

In summary, 50 years of empirical research demonstrated the validity of Original MMPI and MMPI-2 scale scores as predictors of negative outcomes in police candidates, although studies using different outcome criteria did not necessarily produce consistent findings (i.e., different scales were found to work best across these studies). The substantial improvement resulting from restructuring the Clinical Scales reported by Sellbom and colleagues (2007) was a positive indicator of the prospects for using the MMPI-2-RF, which includes the RC Scales complemented by additional measures constructed with similar methods, in preemployment assessments of police candidates. Their findings also introduced important methodological considerations for future research in this area, including use of range restriction corrections and identification of sub-clinical cutoffs.

THE MMPI-2-RF

Before turning to a detailed review of the research available to guide use of the MMPI-2-RF in preemployment evaluations of police officers, we provide here a brief overview of the MMPI-2-RF. Sources containing more detailed information about the inventory are listed at the conclusion of this section.

Test Development and Composition

The Minnesota Multiphasic Personality Inventory-2 Restructured Form (MMPI-2-RF; Ben-Porath & Tellegen, 2008/2011; Tellegen & Ben-Porath, 2008/2011) consists of 338 items that are presently scored on 51 scales. As discussed by Ben-Porath (2012), the authors' goal for the MMPI-2-RF was to represent the clinically significant substance of the MMPI-2 item pool with a comprehensive set of psychometrically adequate measures. This objective reflected the authors' view that the MMPI item pool had a strong, long-standing record of providing test users relevant information about the clinical functioning (mainly dysfunctioning) of individuals who completed the inventory. This confidence in the item pool existed in spite of the fact that the primary sources of information on the Original MMPI and MMPI-2, the Clinical Scales of the inventory, had some long-recognized limitations.

The first phase of the restructuring effort focused on addressing the psychometric shortcomings of the Clinical Scales. This work, which culminated first in the addition of the resulting Restructured Clinical (RC) Scales to the MMPI-2, and in subsequent development of the MMPI-2-RF, began shortly after the MMPI-2 was released. It was initiated by Auke Tellegen, a member of the committee that developed the MMPI-2. The ten-year project that culminated in a restructuring of the Clinical Scales is recounted in detail by Tellegen, Ben-Porath, McNulty, Arbisi, and Kaemmer (2003). A brief description of the rationale for, and the methods used in this work, is provided next.

A primary limitation of the Clinical Scales involved their discriminant abilities. Because of unexpectedly high correlations between them (unexpected based on what is known about the rates of co-occurrence of the constructs they were intended to assess), amplified by considerable item overlap, the Clinical Scales had limited discriminant validities, particularly with respect to differentiation between emotional dysfunction and other types of psychopathology. This shortcoming was in part a product of how the empirical keying technique was applied when items were assigned to the Clinical Scales, based primarily on their ability to discriminate between patient groups and a common "normal" comparison sample. Because essentially the same normal reference group was used in their construction, each of the eight original Clinical Scales wound up including some items that characterized the designated patient group, in addition to others that reflected common (across disorders) differences between being a patient and not being one. A second critical limitation of the Clinical Scales was their heterogeneous makeup, which diminished their convergent validity. Finally, a near-total absence of theory to help guide their interpretation restricted the ability of MMPI users to rely on construct validity in Clinical Scale interpretation.

Tellegen's goal was to restructure the Clinical Scales in a manner that would directly address the limitations just noted and make available a parsimonious set of scales with improved discriminant and/or convergent validities, which can be linked to contemporary theories and models of personality and psychopathology. Scale development proceeded in four steps. The first involved devising a marker of the MMPI common factor, which as just discussed was overrepresented in the Clinical Scales as a result of how they were constructed. Tellegen et al. (2003) labeled this factor *Demoralization*, and conceptualized it within the framework of Watson and Tellegen's (1985) two-factor model of affect as the MMPI-2 equivalent of pleasant versus unpleasant or happy versus unhappy mood. Ben-Porath (2012) provides a detailed discussion of this construct as it applies to the MMPI-2-RF.

Step 2 was designed to identify the major distinctive core component of each Clinical Scale, and it was hypothesized that each would consist of something other than Demoralization. Factor analyses were conducted separately, with the items of each Clinical Scale combined with the Demoralization markers identified in Step 1. The first factor that emerged in each case included the Demoralization markers as well as specific (to a given scale) Clinical Scale items primarily correlated with this construct. The second (and in some cases third) factor included items representing a core component of the Clinical Scale that was distinct from Demoralization. In Step 3, these core markers were refined further to yield a maximally distinct set of *Seed* scales. This step included the removal of all item overlap and retention of core items that correlated maximally with a given Seed scale and minimally with remaining candidate Seed scales. Step 4 involved correlational analyses with the entire MMPI-2 item pool. An item was added to a Seed scale and included on the final Restructured Scale derived from it if: (1) that item correlated more highly with that Seed scale than it did with the others; (2) the correlation exceeded a certain specified value; and (3) it did not correlate beyond a specified level with any other Seed scale. The specific criteria varied across scales as specified by Tellegen et al. (2003).

The result of this four-step process was a set of nine non-overlapping scales representing Demoralization and a major distinctive core component of each of the eight original Clinical Scales. Restructured Scales were not developed for Clinical Scales 5 (Masculinity-Femininity) or 0 (Social Introversion) because the focus of the RC Scales was on assessment of psychopathology. Further development efforts, described later, included the distinctive core components of these two scales. The final set of nine RC Scales consisted of 192 MMPI-2 items. Research reported initially by Tellegen et al. (2003), and later in the peer-reviewed literature, demonstrated that the RC Scales had successfully met their developers' goals and showed substantial improvement in discriminant and convergent (and therefore also construct) validity, including, as discussed earlier, in the context of assessing law enforcement candidates (Sellbom, Fischler, & Ben-Porath, 2007).

At the conclusion of the monograph introducing the RC Scales, Tellegen et al. (2003) noted:

The introduction of the RC Scales may stimulate additional MMPI-2 scale development. It may prove worthwhile to search for and measure distinctive core features of important MMPI-2 scales other than the MMPl-2 Clinical Scales, some of which may also be confounded with a strong Demoralization component. Investigations along these lines may lead to additional measures that are incrementally informative beyond the RC Scales. Through such efforts it may be possible eventually to capture the full range of attributes represented by the large body of MMPI-2 constructs with a set of new scales more transparent and effective than those currently available. (pp. 85-86)

Efforts along these lines led to the development and publication of the MMPI-2-RF (Ben-Porath & Tellegen, 2008/2011; Tellegen & Ben-Porath, 2008/2011). The nine RC Scales, designed to assess major distinctive core components of the Original MMPI Clinical Scales, were carried over to the MMPI-2-RF in identical composition and augmented by 33 substantive measures and 9 validity indicators intended to canvass the full range of constructs that can be reliably and validly assessed with the MMPI-2 item pool. A central aspect of the development of the MMPI-2-RF was to link the test to contemporary concepts and models of personality and psychopathology. Ben-Porath (2012) provides a detailed description of the constructs assessed by the 42 MMPI-2-RF substantive scales and the literature supporting their construct validity.

Listed and described briefly in Table 1 (in the appendix), the MMPI-2-RF scales are divided into six sets. The *Validity Scales* include nine MMPI-2-RF measures designed to alert the interpreter to various threats to the validity of an individual test protocol. They include measures of inconsistent responding, overreporting, and underreporting. The remaining 42 substantive scales include three *Higher-Order Scales,* which indicate whether and to what extent a test-taker is likely experiencing problems in the domains of mood and affect, thought processes, and/or behavior; the nine *Restructured Clinical Scales* just discussed, which provide an indication of the individual's standing on the nine psychological constructs identified by Tellegen et al. (2003) as major distinctive core components of the original MMPI Clinical Scales; 23 *Specific Problems Scales,* the most narrowly focused MMPI-2-RF measures, which are subdivided into indicators of somatic and cognitive complaints, internalizing difficulties, externalizing behaviors, and interpersonal functioning; two *Interest Scales,* derived from the original MMPI Scale 5; and five *Personality Psychopathology Five (PSY-5) Scales,* which are revised versions of similarly labeled MMPI-2 scales, designed, as noted previously, to provide a dimensional perspective on features of personality disorder-related psychopathology.

Details about the MMPI-2-RF norms and the procedures used to derive standard scores for the 51 scales are provided by Ben-Porath and Tellegen (2008/2011). One feature of particular relevance to use of the instrument in preemployment evaluations of police officer candidates is the decision to only develop non-gendered norms for the instrument. As described earlier in the context of the Civil Rights Act of 1991, a set of non-gendered norms had previously been developed for the MMPI-2 by Ben-Porath and Forbey (2003), who found that these norms generate interpretably comparable T scores when contrasted with gender-specific MMPI-2 standard scores. Based on this observation, the MMPI-2-RF authors decided to adopt a single normative standard for the inventory, using the same non-gendered sample. A primary problem with gendered norms is that they can mask genuine gender differences by setting the mean T score for each gender to be the same (50). A comparison of non-gendered T scores across genders is the only way to meaningfully compare men and women's MMPI-2-RF standard scores and discern any differences.

Three source documents are available to facilitate use of the inventory. The *MMPI-2-RF Manual for Administration, Scoring and Interpretation* (Ben-Porath & Tellegen, 2008/2011) includes information about intended uses of the inventory, the normative sample and methods used to develop standard scores for the scales, and guidelines for standard administration, scoring, and interpretation of test results. Unlike the MMPI-2 manual, this document includes detailed interpretive guidelines that establish a common standard for interpreting test results in a clinical context. The *MMPI-2-RF Technical Manual* (Tellegen & Ben-Porath, 2008/2011) includes a description of the test development procedures and detailed information about the psychometric properties (reliability and validity) of scores on the 51 scales of the inventory. The third source document, the *MMPI-2-RF User's Guide for Reports* (Ben-Porath & Tellegen, 2011) provides information on two of the software-based reports available for the test, the *MMPI-2-RF Score Report,* which includes scale scores and item-level information, and the *MMPI-2-RF Interpretive Report for Clinical Settings*, which, in addition to all of the elements of the Score Report, provides a clinically-focused interpretation of the results. Because of its clinical focus, this report is not recommended for use in assessments of police candidates. Instead, a specialized report, the *MMPI-2-RF Police Candidate Interpretive Report* (PCIR; Corey & Ben-Porath, 2014) is available and described later in this chapter. Another resource available for MMPI-2-RF users is the book *Interpreting the MMPI-2-RF* (Ben-Porath, 2012), which provides a detailed review of the evolution of the MMPI instruments, a description of the construction of the instrument, a framework for interpreting Validity Scale scores, and, as just mentioned, a detailed discussion of the constructs assessed by the 42 substantive scales of the inventory.

The MMPI-2-RF Technical Manual (Tellegen & Ben-Porath, 2008/2011) and scoring software (Ben-Porath & Tellegen, 2011) include comparison group data designed to facilitate interpretation of test results by contrasting the test-taker's scores with those of a cohort of individuals tested in a similar setting and/or under similar circumstances. These include a Police Candidate comparison group made up of a sample of 2,074 individuals tested as part of a preemployment evaluation for law enforcement candidates throughout North America. Information about this sample is provided later in this chapter.

Research on the MMPI-2-RF in Police Candidate Evaluations

After the MMPI-2-RF was released in 2008, Weiss and Weiss (2010) identified it as having "considerable promise in the area of pre-employment screening" (p. 68). They listed as particular benefits the availability of law enforcement applicant norms in the *MMPI-2-RF Technical Manual* (Tellegen & Ben-Porath, 2008/2011), inclusion of the Restructured Clinical (RC) Scales with their evidence of predictive validity for police officer performance (Sellbom, Fischler, & Ben-Porath, 2007; discussed in detail earlier in this chapter), and the smaller number of items (338 versus 567 in the MMPI-2), which makes the test easier to administer with additional testing in a preemployment evaluation. These authors also commented on the need for research to support use of the MMPI-2-RF in preemployment assessments of police candidates.

Since Weiss and Weiss (2010) issued their call, a comprehensive body of empirical research has been published and is available to guide use of the MMPI-2-RF in assessment of police candidates. Some of this research was conducted with archival MMPI-2 datasets, from which the MMPI-2-RF scales were scored. Use of archival data for this purpose is possible because the 338 MMPI-2-RF items are embedded in the 567-item MMPI-2 booklet, and is supported by findings that MMPI-2-RF scores derived from the MMPI-2 and MMPI-2-RF booklets are essentially interchangeable (Tarescavage, Alosco, Ben-Porath, Wood, & Luna-Jones, 2014; Tellegen & Ben-Porath, 2008/2011; van der Heijden, Egger, & Derksen, 2010).

We begin our review of this literature by examining the results of an innovative study of the assessment of underreporting in police candidates, followed by six investigations that provide empirical correlates (including longitudinal outcomes) of MMPI-2-RF scores produced by men and women undergoing preemployment evaluations for law enforcement positions. Altogether, the studies described in this chapter include data obtained from 1,892 police candidates tested throughout the United States. The vast majority (93%) of these candidates were men, reflecting the relatively small proportion of female law enforcement officers (10%-20% nationally, depending upon agency size), which for several of these studies did not allow for meaningful analyses by gender. This underscores the need to follow up with additional studies with larger samples of female candidates.

Detrick and Chibnall (2014) examined the impact of the demand characteristics associated with preemployment evaluations of police officer candidates, which incentivize test takers to present in a favorable manner by underreporting problems, a ubiquitous challenge in this type of assessment. They also investigated the sensitivity of the MMPI-2-RF Validity Scales, Uncommon Virtues (L-r) and Adjustment Validity (K-r), to underreporting by police candidates. Employing a differential prevalence research design, the authors compared scores generated by a sample of 62 police candidates (54 men and 9 women) tested twice, first under high-demand conditions and a second time in a low-demand context. The *high-demand* condition involved completion of the MMPI-2-RF as part of their routine preemployment evaluation. For the *low-demand* condition the subjects of the study were administered the MMPI-2-RF a second time after completing a six-month academy. Participants were informed that the post-academy assessment results would be used strictly for research purposes and there would be no consequences to them resulting from this testing, nor would the results be shared with any police personnel.

Consistent with the authors' hypothesis that the low-demand condition would result in a greater willingness to acknowledge psychological problems, participants scored higher in the low-demand condition on several MMPI-2-RF substantive scales, with some of the highest effect sizes found on measures of externalizing dysfunction. Participants also had higher scores in the low-demand condition on measures of emotional dysfunction and the interpersonal scales. Also as expected, participants scored higher on L-r and K-r in the high-demand condition, demonstrating the sensitivity of these scales to underreporting. With an innovative set of regression analyses, Detrick and Chibnall (2014) found that elevations on L-r were associated with a proclivity to underreport behavioral dysfunction and cynicism whereas higher K-r scores were associated with underreporting of emotional dysfunction and cynicism.

Detrick, Ben-Porath, and Sellbom (2015) reported correlations between MMPI-2-RF substantive scale scores and results on the *Inwald Personality Inventory* (IPI; Inwald, Knatz, & Schusman, 1982), which, as discussed earlier, is a psychological test specifically designed and validated to screen police candidates. Their sample consisted of 277 male police officer candidates from four Midwestern police agencies varying in size. The authors tested a series of conceptually-based hypotheses about correlations between scores on these two measures, which were administered to the sample as part of a post-offer preemployment psychological evaluation. Findings were largely consistent with the authors' conceptually-formed hypotheses, supporting the construct validity of MMPI-2-RF scales in this police candidate sample.

Tarescavage, Brewster, Corey, and Ben-Porath (2015) examined associations between pre-hire MMPI-2-RF scores and post-hire performance ratings for a sample of 131 male police officers employed in the northeastern United States. After consulting with several police chiefs and supervisory personnel, the second author of the study created a supervisor survey of police officer performance. Supervisors completed the survey after they had observed officers' behavior for a time period ranging from one month to 2.5 years (M = 1.1, SD = 0.5 years). The authors selected 39 survey items that addressed constructs related to the California POST screening dimensions (Spilberg & Corey, 2014), as well as one global rating, as the criteria in their investigation.

Uncorrected and range-restriction-corrected correlations (see earlier discussion of Sellbom, Fischler, & Ben-Porath, 2007) between MMPI-2-RF scores and the selected criteria indicated that scales from the emotional dysfunction domain were substantially associated with emotional control and stress problems, routine task performance problems, decision-making and judgment problems, and problem-solving difficulties. Scores on MMPI-2-RF scales from the thought dysfunction domain were associated with marksmanship problems and difficulty predicting situational outcomes. Scores from measures included in the behavioral dysfunction domain were correlated with various outcomes related to acting out, such as integrity problems and alcohol and drug use. Scores on MMPI-2-RF measures of interpersonal functioning were associated with problems such as failing to utilize training under stressful conditions, difficulties with assertiveness and social skills, and shortcomings in oral communication skills. Overall, the corrected correlations were mainly of a medium effect size.

Tarescavage, Corey, and Ben-Porath (2015) investigated the predictive validity of the MMPI-2-RF in a sample of 136 male police officers hired by the Portland (Oregon) Police Bureau. Supervisor ratings of performance and problem behaviors were obtained during the officers' initial probationary period, when they were closely monitored by a field training officer. The officers were evaluated daily during the field training program, and these daily evaluations were subsequently used by training division personnel to complete the Selection Validation Survey (SVS), a measure developed to assess police officers' performance during their initial probationary period. Scores on scales in the emotional domain of the MMPI-2-RF were moderately correlated with various emotional control and stress problems, as well as with routine task performance problems, problems in the areas of conscientiousness and commitment, and with an overall negative performance evaluation. Scales in the thought dysfunction domain were not correlated substantially with most of the SVS criteria. By contrast, scores on the MMPI-2-RF behavioral dysfunction measures were correlated with problems such as failure to accept feedback and interpersonal difficulties. Scores on the BXD, RC9, and DISC-r scales were negatively correlated with failure to engage subjects, indicating that particularly low scores on these measures were associated with problematic performance. Scales in the somatic domain did not have many meaningful associations with SVS ratings. On the other hand, the MMPI-2-RF measures of interpersonal function were associated with assertiveness and control problems, interpersonal difficulties, and problems with teamwork.

Tarescavage, Corey, Gupton, and Ben-Porath (2015) examined the predictive validity of MMPI-2-RF scores of 145 male police officers employed by the Honolulu Police Department applying the methods just described in connection with the Portland, Oregon study (Tarescavage, Corey, & Ben-Porath, 2015). After correction for range restriction, scores on scales from all the domains assessed by the MMPI-2-RF were correlated with various negative outcomes with medium to large effect sizes. In the emotional domain, some of the strongest correlations were found for scores on RC2 and problems in the areas of emotional control and stress, routine task performance, decision-making and judgment, and social competence and teamwork. Higher scores on scales in the thought dysfunction domain were correlated with learning problems, navigation problems, radio operation difficulties, and problems with multitasking. As was the case in the study by Tarescavage, Corey, and Ben-Porath (2015), scores in the externalizing domain were negatively correlated with a number of variables (assertiveness, social competence and teamwork, and interpersonal problems), indicating that particularly low scores on these scales are associated with negative outcomes. Scales on the MMPI-2-RF measures of interpersonal functioning were also correlated with a number of negative outcomes.

Tarescavage, Corey, and Ben-Porath (2016) used an archival dataset collected by Boes, Chandler, and Timm (1997), who examined the ability of pre-hire MMPI scores to predict police officers' future serious integrity violations. These authors surveyed over 2,000 police departments throughout the United States, seeking to locate officers with one of ten pre-specified integrity violations that resulted in termination. They identified 439 officers with at least one of the ten designated violations and matched them with 439 officers of the same gender, age, and length of employment who did not have any of the designated violations. These officers were employed by 69 agencies in 29 states spread throughout the country, including departments in the northeast, south, midwest, southwest, and west (Boes et al., 1997).

To examine the predictive validity of MMPI-2-RF scores, Tarescavage, Corey, and Ben-Porath (2016) introduced and provided empirical support for a new prorating procedure for estimating MMPI-2-RF scores from original MMPI responses. They identified a subsample of 161 officers (out of 417 for whom MMPI data were available) who had not committed any of the integrity violations or other disciplinary infractions that were the focus of the original investigation and contrasted their scores with those of individuals who committed each violation and infraction. Several estimated MMPI-2-RF Substantive Scale scores were meaningfully correlated (with range-restricted corrected correlations typically of a small to medium effect size) with future integrity violations and disciplinary infractions. Estimated scale scores from the emotional, thought, and behavioral domains were positively associated with use of excessive force, supervisory problems, substandard work performance, conduct unbecoming, procedural violations, private use of equipment, failure to attend court, embezzlement/fraud, accidents, dropping cases inappropriately, and off-duty violations.

Tarescavage, Fischler, et al. (2015) reported descriptive findings and correlations between pre-hire MMPI-2-RF scores and selected scales from the *California Psychological Inventory* (CPI; Gough, 1956) and the IPI (described earlier) for a sample of 588 male and 124 female police candidates from two Midwestern states, as well as correlations with outcome data for 426 of the male candidates who were subsequently hired. A subset of the men in this sample was also included in the MMPI-2 study reported by Sellbom, Fischler, and Ben-Porath (2007), which was discussed earlier. Descriptive analyses indicated that the male and female candidates produced very similar means and standard deviations on the MMPI-2-RF scales, with the exception that hired men scored approximately five T-score points higher than hired women on the DISC-r scale.

Correlations between pre-hire MMPI-2-RF and CPI scores were reported for the female candidates. The CPI scales examined in this investigation included special measures developed by Roberts and Johnson (2001) for police candidate evaluations. Several substantial associations were found between females' MMPI-2-RF scores and the special CPI scale indexes. For example, RC7 scores were substantially correlated with a CPI composite predicting a history of job performance problems; RC1, RC7, MLS, and HPC scores were associated with an index predicting increased risk of being rated poorly by the evaluating psychologist; and RCd, RC3, RC6, and BRF scores were correlated with an indicator of increased risk for being fired for cause. Scores on several externalizing scales also were correlated with a wide range of CPI risk indicators. Of note is that the vast majority of women included in this study scored below 65T on most MMPI-2-RF scales, indicating that, as is the case with male candidates, subclinical deviations from the mean are associated with a wide range of risk factors in female candidates.

Male candidates produced similar (to the females) patterns of correlations with the CPI risk indicators. Correlations between MMPI-2-RF scales and scores on the IPI were generally consistent with those reported by Detrick, Ben-Porath, and Sellbom (2015) for a different sample (described earlier). In the subset of men for whom outcome data were available, higher scores on the substantive scales were associated substantially with a broad range of negative outcomes. For example, higher pre-hire MMPI-2-RF scores on the measures of emotional dysfunction were correlated with complaints from members of the public, use of excessive force and inappropriate language, and poor ethics. Scores on the thought dysfunction measures were associated with outcomes such as deceptive behavior, rude behavior, being uncooperative toward peers, missing court appearances, and being fired for cause. Behavioral dysfunction measures were correlated with sustained internal affairs complaints, missing court appearances, and poor response to feedback. Interpersonal functioning measures were correlated with outcomes such as inappropriate sexual attitudes, conduct unbecoming, and poor integrity ratings.

To summarize, meaningful associations between pre-hire MMPI-2-RF scores and a broad range of job-relevant counterproductive behaviors were replicated in a series of studies conducted with police candidates and officers throughout all regions of the U.S. In all these investigations, MMPI-2-RF descriptive statistics indicated that candidates produced mean substantive scale scores and associated standard deviations that were (a) very similar to those of the 2,074-member MMPI-2-RF Police Officer Candidate comparison group (Corey & Ben-Porath, 2014) and (b) for the most part appreciably lower (generally 10-15 T-score points) and more range-restricted (20%-50% smaller standard deviations) than comparable statistics for the MMPI-2-RF normative sample. In several of these investigations, the authors reported Relative Risk Ratio analyses similar to the ones discussed earlier in the context of the study by Sellbom, Fishler, and Ben-Porath (2007). These analyses demonstrated consistently that cutoffs in the range of T scores 50-60 (i.e., in the non-clinically-elevated range) are associated with appreciably increased risk for a broad range of concurrent and future counterproductive behaviors.

The MMPI-2-RF Police Candidate Interpretive Report (PCIR)

The literature just reviewed illustrates that non-clinically-elevated scores on pre-hire MMPI-2-RF substantive scales are associated with a variety of job-relevant counterproductive behaviors, and that scores on these scales need not reach the cutoff for clinical significance (65T) for a substantially increased risk for these negative outcomes to be indicated. Corey and Ben-Porath (2014) developed the MMPI-2-RF Police Candidate Interpretive Report (PCIR) to facilitate integration of information from this research and data from the Police Officer Candidate comparison group when using the test in a preemployment suitability evaluation. As with any computer-generated report, the PCIR is not intended to take the place of the examiner, who is tasked with considering the information it provides in the context of other relevant sources, including additional test findings, a clinical interview, psychosocial history, and other background information. Corey and Ben-Porath (2014) provide a detailed description of the various elements of the PCIR. We highlight here several innovative features of the report.

The *Protocol Validity* section of the PCIR provides information about three types of threats to the validity of the test results: content non-responsiveness (unscorable and/or inconsistent responses), overreporting, and underreporting. This section includes features designed to address the unique challenges associated with the detection and impact of underreporting in police candidate preemployment evaluations. Underreporting is the most common threat to protocol validity in these assessments. Corey and Ben-Porath (2014) report that for the 2,074 members of the Police Officer Candidate comparison group the mean scores on L-r and K-r are 59 (*SD* = 13) and 63 (*SD* = 8) respectively, approximately one standard deviation above the general population mean T score (50). As discussed earlier, police candidates are highly vetted before receiving a conditional offer of employment, and it is reasonable to expect that many, if not most, of these candidates are, as these scores suggest, more virtuous and better adjusted than the general population. This is also reflected in the data reported by Detrick and Chibnall (2014), where police candidates tested under low-demand conditions (see previous section for a more detailed description of this study), although scoring lower than when initially tested as part of their preemployment evaluation, still score considerably higher than members of the MMPI-2-RF normative sample on L-r and K-r. On the other hand, some candidates approach psychological testing with a level of defensiveness or even deception that renders their responses to substantive scales uninterpretable.

Special PCIR features are designed to assist examiners in making this distinction. In cases where L-r is substantially elevated, the report prints MMPI-2-RF items with *potentially verifiable historical content* to aid the examiner in detecting discrepancies from other self-report and/or background information. The report authors selected these items from the entire booklet if they were deemed to include potentially verifiable content (e.g., a history of "trouble with the law"). To maintain test security, the content of these items is not listed here. When evaluating what inferences to draw from elevated underreporting scores, a test-taker's responses to these items, when considered in the context of collateral information, can aid test users in differentiating naive responses (often occurring in individuals with a background stressing traditional values) from intentionally deceptive ones. It is important to note in this context that discrepancies between self-report and collateral sources have been found to be predictive of post-hire integrity violations (Sarchione, Cuttler, Muchinsky, & Nelson-Gray, 1998).

A section of the PCIR labeled *Comparison Group Findings* provides construct-based statements that describe implications of clinically elevated substantive scale scores, as well as statements about implications of uncommonly high (but not clinically elevated) scores for police officer candidates. Base-rate information (derived from the Police Officer Candidate comparison group) is provided for both clinically elevated and non-elevated scores that generate interpretive statements. The 2,074 members of this comparison group (1,037 men and 1,037 women), described in detail by Corey and Ben-Porath (2014), were assessed as a component of preemployment evaluations conducted throughout North America. Non-clinically-elevated findings that generate statements in this section are typically limited to scores that fall at least two standard deviations above the mean for the Police Officer Candidate comparison group. For example, the mean comparison group T score on the Self-Doubt (SFD) scale is 43, with a standard deviation of 4. Thus, a T score of 56 on this scale falls more than three standard deviations above the comparison group mean and would trigger the statement: "The test taker reports a comparatively high level of self-doubt for a police officer candidate. Only 2.8% of comparison group members convey this or a greater lack of confidence."

A PCIR section titled *Job-Relevant Correlates* consists of interpretive statements supported by the literature reviewed in the previous section of this chapter. This information is organized into ten job performance problem domains, which correspond closely to the California POST Psychological Screening Dimensions (Spilberg & Corey, 2014), variants of which are used by most states. These domains were derived from a comprehensive meta-analysis of more than 19,000 criterion-validity coefficients obtained in studies that examined associations between scores on personality measures and police officer job performance (Cullen & Ones, 2001). A list of the ten PCIR problem domains, and a description of the job-relevant difficulties associated with each domain, are presented in Table 2. The Job-Relevant Correlates statements included in the PCIR were derived from a comprehensive analysis of the concurrent and prospective MMPI-2-RF job-performance-related correlates reported in the literature just reviewed.

A particularly helpful feature of the PCIR is its *annotation*. Every statement in the report is annotated with information about which scale score(s) generated it and whether the statement is based on empirical correlates, scale item content, or is an inference of the report authors. For correlate-based statements, such as the ones in the section reporting Job-Relevant Correlates, annotation includes a list of references to studies (from among those reviewed in the previous section) that support it. This transparency makes it possible for PCIR users to cite literature in support of their MMPI-2-RF-based conclusions. If the PCIR is viewed on an internet-connected device, hyperlinks allow the user to view the abstract and options for downloading any article cited in the report.

Additional PCIR features include a *Synopsis* section highlighting the main findings, a *Clinical Findings* section that provides a psychopathology-focused interpretation of clinically-elevated MMPI-2-RF scores, an optional section that includes *Diagnostic Considerations*, and detailed *Item-Level Information*. This last section includes a list of *Unscorable Responses* – items left unanswered or answered both "true" and "false" and the scales on which they appear; *Critical Responses* – responses in the keyed direction to items that appear on seven MMPI-2-RF scales designated by the MMPI-2-RF authors as having critical content (Ben-Porath & Tellegen, 2011); *User-Designated Item-Level Information* – an optional section where users can choose any scale for which they would like to see item responses; and *Critical Follow-up Items* – any response in the keyed direction to a series of items designated by police officer screening experts as having critical content. The PCIR authors (Corey & Ben-Porath, 2014) recommend strongly that users who choose to follow-up with a test-taker concerning item-level responses do so by paraphrasing item content rather than reading specific item content verbatim. Spilberg and Corey (2014) point out that asking candidates to explain their responses to individual test items usually yields little helpful information since, once alerted to the examiner's concern, they typically reply that they misunderstood the item content or incorrectly recorded their answers. A more useful strategy may be to use the item content to construct probing interview questions designed to assess the underlying issue.

INTEGRATING MMPI-2-RF FINDINGS IN A POLICE PREEMPLOYMENT EVALUATION

A commonly used model for preemployment psychological evaluations of police officer candidates includes administrating two broadband personality measures, one assessing abnormal behavior and functioning, the other assessing normal personality, followed by a clinical interview and consideration of personal history information (Serafino, 2010; Spilberg & Corey, 2014). This model is adopted by a large proportion of state and federal regulations governing the selection and hiring of police officers (Corey & Borum, 2013). Spilberg and Corey (2014) recommend a six-step process for integrating information derived from multiple sources in a police candidate evaluation:

1. Evaluate test scores for evidence of response inconsistency, overreporting, and underreporting.
2. Identify and interpret relevant findings, using standard norms and peace officer norms.
3. Evaluate relevant personal history information from all sources to determine if any information meets agency standards for disqualification and how the information is convergent with, divergent from, or complements relevant test findings and interpretations.
4. Evaluate relevant clinical observations to determine how they are convergent with, divergent from, and/or complementary of relevant test findings and personal history information.

5. Determine whether the weight of the collective evidence (convergent, complementary, and divergent findings) supports or refutes the conclusion that the candidate meets the selection standards.
6. Obtain feedback from the hiring agency to determine the status of hired candidates and make adjustments to the prediction strategy as necessary.

PCIR data are pertinent to each of the six steps in this process. For Step 1, the MMPI-2-RF validity scales provide well-validated information about these three types of threats to the validity of a candidate's test scores (see Ben-Porath, 2012 for a detailed discussion of the threats and their assessment), and there is growing evidence that MMPI-2-RF Validity Scale findings generalize to other co-administered measures (Crighton, Tarescavage, Gervais, & Ben-Porath, 2015; Forbey & Lee, 2011; Forbey, Lee, Ben-Porath, Arbisi, & Gartland, 2013). Regarding Step 2, the report includes both the candidate's scores on the 51 MMPI-2-RF scales based on the general population test norms and, for each scale, the percent of the Police Officer Candidate comparison group members who score at or below the test-taker, a statistic analogous to a percentile value. For example, a T score of 56 on the Self-Doubt Scale, which is approximately one-half of a standard deviation above the general population mean score for that scale, corresponds to the 99.1st percentile among law enforcement candidates. Steps 3-5 involve consideration of the known validity of the various sources of information relied upon in a police candidate preemployment evaluation. In this context, Spilberg and Corey (2014) note that of the various sources of information considered in an evaluation, empirically-validated test correlates (of the kind included in the *Job-Relevant Correlates* section of the PCIR) are the ones most likely to have documented validity (in contrast, for example, to clinical interview findings), and should, therefore, be accorded the greatest weight when integrating information from multiple sources in in a police candidate evaluation. Step 6 is, essentially, the foundation of the PCIR, in that the collaborative validation work called for in this step led to the research guiding development of the report. Corey and Ben-Porath (2016) provide detailed guidelines and case illustrations of integrating MMPI-2-RF results with these other sources when conducting preemployment evaluations of police officer candidates. For a more detailed discussion of integrating the various types of information in a preemployment evaluation the reader is directed to Spilberg and Corey's (2014) discussion of this topic.

CONCLUSION

The MMPI has been among the most widely used measures in preemployment evaluations of police candidates for over six decades. Use of the most up-to-date version of the inventory, the MMPI-2-RF, builds on this decades-long experience coupled with a comprehensive, modern literature documenting associations between pre-hire scores and a broad range of job-relevant variables. The PCIR combines this empirical literature with base rate information on the MMPI-2-RF scores of the 2,074-member Police Officer Candidate comparison group and provides an empirically-grounded, annotated (i.e., transparent) interpretation of a candidate's test scores.

Although broad insofar as the type and geographic location of the agencies involved, and comprehensive in the scope of extra-test variables it incorporates, the literature supporting use of the MMPI-2-RF in police candidate assessments can benefit from being expanded in several ways. First, as discussed earlier, there is relatively limited published research on use of the test with female candidates. This reflects in part the relative distribution of male and female law enforcement officers; however, as the proportion of female police officers continues to grow the need for research documenting associations between pre-hire scores and job-relevant correlates in females will become more pressing. Based on extensive research with samples representing other populations, and reported in detail in the MMPI-2-RF Technical Manual (Tellegen & Ben-Porath, 2008/2011), there is good reason to expect that the findings with male samples will be replicated with female candidates. Collaborative efforts combining relatively small samples of female police officer candidates across agencies to achieve adequately-powered analyses are needed.

With regard to other demographic variables, the empirical studies cited earlier were conducted with demographically and geographically diverse samples, as is the composition of the Police Officer Candidate comparison group. Original MMPI literature reviewed by Campos (1989) indicated little to no evidence of potential adverse impact (as defined by the EEOC and discussed in the first part of this chapter). The one exception was the original L scale, on which Hispanic candidates scored higher than Caucasians. However, as discussed in the *Legal Matters* section of this chapter, a test score alone cannot have direct adverse impact, which is contingent on how the score is interpreted and used. Moreover, the cutoffs for interpreting L-r on the PCIR (Corey & Ben-Porath, 2014) are considerably higher than those recommended for use in general clinical assessments (Ben-Porath & Tellegen, 2008/2011), and examinations conducted by the report authors showed no evidence of adverse impact using EEOC definitions (discussed earlier).

Finally, as just discussed, the MMPI-2-RF is one component of the broader range of procedures used to assess police officer candidates. When integrated with the results of normal personality testing, a clinical interview, and psychosocial and background information derived from a variety of sources, MMPI-2-RF findings provide the examiner empirically-validated information about a candidate's psychological suitability for service as a police officer. Corey and Ben-Porath (2016) provide detailed guidelines for using the instrument in this manner in preemployment assessments of police officer candidates.

REFERENCES

Americans with Disabilities Act (ADA) of 1990, 42 U.S.C.A. 12101 *et seq.*

Azen, S. P., Snibbe, H. M., & Montgomery, H. R. (1973). A longitudinal predictive study of success and performance of law enforcement officers. *The Journal of Applied Psychology*, *57*(2), 190–192. doi:10.1037/h0037124

Ben-Porath, Y. S. (2012). *Interpreting the MMPI-2-RF*. Minneapolis, MN: University of Minnesota Press.

Ben-Porath, Y. S., & Forbey, J. D. (2003). *Non-gendered norms for the MMPI-2*. Minneapolis, MN: University of Minnesota Press.

Ben-Porath, Y. S., & Tellegen, A. (2008/2011a). *Minnesota Multiphasic Personality Inventory-2 Restructured Form: Manual for administration, scoring and interpretation*. Minneapolis, MN: University of Minnesota Press.

Ben-Porath, Y. S., & Tellegen, A. (2008/2011b). *Minnesota Multiphasic Personality Inventory-2 Restructured Form: User's guide for reports* (2nd ed.). Minneapolis, MN: University of Minnesota Press.

Beutler, L. E., Storm, A., Kirkish, P., Scogin, F., & Gaines, J. A. (1985). Parameters in the prediction of police officer performance. *Professional Psychology, Research and Practice*, *16*(2), 324–335. doi:10.1037/0735-7028.16.2.324

Blum, R. H. (1964). *Police selection*. Springfield, IL: Charles C. Thomas.

Boes, J. O., Chandler, C. J., & Timm, H. W. (1997). *Police integrity: Use of personality measures to identify corruption-prone officers* (pp. 97–003). Monterey, CA: Defense Personnel Security Research Center, Publication No. PERSTR.

Butcher, J. N., Dahlstrom, W. G., Graham, J. R., Tellegen, A., & Kaemmer, B. (1989). *Minnesota Multiphasic Personality Inventory: Manual for administration, scoring and interpretation* (2nd ed.). Minneapolis, MN: University of Minnesota Press.

Butcher, J. N., Graham, J. R., Ben-Porath, Y. S., Tellegen, A., Dahlstrom, W. G., & Kaemmer, B. (2001). *MMPI-2 (Minnesota Multiphasic Personality Inventory-2) manual for administration, scoring, and interpretation* (Rev. ed.). Minneapolis, MN: University of Minnesota Press.

California Commission on Peace Officer Standards and Training (POST) Regulation 1955. (n.d.). Retrieved from https://www.post.ca.gov/peace-officer-selection-requirements-regulations.aspx#c1955

Campos, L. E. (1989). Adverse impact, unfairness, and bias in the psychological screening of Hispanic peace officers. *Hispanic Journal of Behavioral Sciences*, *11*(2), 122–135. doi:10.1177/07399863890112002

Carpenter, B. N., & Raza, S. M. (1987). Personality characteristics of police applicants: Comparisons across subgroups and with other populations. *Journal of Police Science & Administration*, *15*(1), 10–17.

Castaneda, L. W., & Ridgeway, G. (2010). *Today's police and sheriff recruits: Insights from the newest members of America's law enforcement community*. Santa Monica, CA: The RAND Corporation.

Civil Rights Act of 1991, Pub. L. 102-166 (1991).

Cochrane, R. E., Tett, R. P., & Vandecreek, L. (2003). Psychological testing and the selection of police officers: A national survey. *Criminal Justice and Behavior*, *30*(5), 511–537. doi:10.1177/0093854803257241

Corey, D. M., & Ben-Porath, Y. S. (2014). *User's guide for the MMPI-2-RF Police Candidate Interpretive Report*. Minneapolis, MN: University of Minnesota Press.

Corey, D. M., & Ben-Porath, Y. S. (2017). *Assessing police and public safety personnel using the MMPI-2-RF: A practical guide*. Minneapolis, MN: University of Minnesota Press.

Corey, D. M., & Borum, R. (2013). Forensic assessment for high-risk occupations. In R. K. Otto & I. B. Weiner (Eds.), *Handbook of psychology: Vol. 11. Forensic psychology* (2nd ed.; pp. 246–270). Hoboken, NJ: John Wiley & Sons, Inc.

Corey, D. M., & Wolf, G. D. (1992). An integrated approach to reducing stress injuries. In J. C. Quick, L. R. Murphy, & J. J. Hurrell (Eds.), *Stress and well-being at work: Assessments and interventions for occupational health* (pp. 64–78). Washington, DC: American Psychological Association. doi:10.1037/10116-005

Crighton, A. H., Tarescavage, A. M., Gervais, R. O., & Ben-Porath, Y. S. (2015). The generalizability of over-reporting across a battery of self-report measures: An investigation with the Minnesota Multiphasic Personality Invemtory-2 Restructured Form (MMPI-2-RF) and the Personality Assessment Inventory (PAI) in a civil disability sample. *Assessment*. doi:10.1177/1073191115621791

Cullen, M. J., & Ones, D. S. (2001, April). *Dimensions used in police selection: A meta-analysis.* Paper presented at the 16th annual conference of the Society for Industrial and Organizational Psychology, San Diego, CA.

Detrick, P., Ben-Porath, Y. S., & Sellbom, M. (2016). Associations between MMPI-2-RF (Restructured Form) and Inwald Personality Inventory (IPI) scale scores in a law enforcement preemployment screening sample. *Journal of Police and Criminal Psychology, 31,* 81-95. doi:10.1007/s11896-015-9172-7

Detrick, P., & Chibnall, J. T. (2014). Underreporting on the MMPI-2-RF in a high-demand police officer selection context: An illustration. *Psychological Assessment, 26*(3), 1044–1049. doi:10.1037/pas0000013 PMID:24978133

Detrick, P., Chibnall, J. T., & Rosso, M. (2001). Minnesota Multiphasic Personality Inventory-2 in police officer selection: Normative data and relation to the Inwald Personality Inventory. *Professional Psychology, Research and Practice*, *32*(5), 484–490. doi:10.1037/0735-7028.32.5.484

Forbey, J. D., & Lee, T. T. C. (2011). An exploration of the impact of invalid MMPI-2 protocols on collateral self-report measure scores. *Journal of Personality Assessment*, *93*(6), 556–565. doi:10.1080/00223891.2011.608757 PMID:21999379

Forbey, J. D., Lee, T. T. C., Ben-Porath, Y. S., Arbisi, P. A., & Gartland, D. (2013). Associations between MMPI-2-RF Validity Scale scores and extra-test measures of personality and psychopathology. *Assessment, 20*(4), 448–461. doi:10.1177/1073191113478154 PMID:23443819

Graham, J. R. (2012). *MMPI-2: Assessing personality and psychopathology* (5th ed.). New York, NY: Oxford University Press.

Greene, R. L. (2011). *MMPI-2/MMPI-2-RF: An Interpretive Manual* (3rd ed.). New York, NY: Allyn & Bacon.

Hargrave, G. E., Hiatt, D., Ogard, E. M., & Karr, C. (1994). Comparison of the MMPI and the MMP-2 for a sample of peace officers. *Psychological Assessment*, *6*(1), 27–32. doi:10.1037/1040-3590.6.1.27

Hunter, J. E., & Schmidt, F. L. (1990). *Methods of meta-analysis: Correcting error and bias in research findings*. Newbury, CA: Sage Publications.

Inwald, R., Knatz, H., & Shusman, E. (1982). *Inwald Personality Inventory manual.* Kew Gardens, NY: Hilson Research.

Langton, L. (2010). *Census of law enforcement gang units: Gang units in large local law enforcement agencies: 2007*. U.S. Department of Justice, Office of Justice Programs.

Marsh, S. H. (1962). Validating the selection of deputy sheriffs. *Public Personnel Review*, *23*, 41–44.

Roberts, M. D., & Johnson, M. (2001). *CPI police and public safety selection report: Technical manual.* Los Gatos, CA: Law Enforcement Psychological Services, Inc.

Saxe, S. J., & Reiser, M. (1976). A comparison of three police applicant groups using the MMPI. *Journal of Police Science & Administration*, *4*(4), 419–425.

Sellbom, M., Fischler, G. L., & Ben-Porath, Y. S. (2007). Identifying MMPI-2 predictors of police officer integrity and misconduct. *Criminal Justice and Behavior*, *34*(8), 985–1004. doi:10.1177/0093854807301224

Serafino, G. F. (2010). Fundamental issues in police psychological assessment. In P. A. Weiss (Ed.), *Personality assessment in police psychology: A 21st century perspective* (pp. 29–55). Springfield, IL: Charles C. Thomas.

Spilberg, S. W., & Corey, D. M. (2014). *POST peace officer psychological screening manual.* Sacramento, CA: California Commission on Peace Officer Standards and Training.

Tarescavage, A. M., Alosco, M. L., Ben-Porath, Y. S., Wood, A., & Luna-Jones, L. (2015). Minnesota Multiphasic Personality Inventory-2-Restructured Form (MMPI-2-RF) scores generated from the MMPI-2 and MMPI-2-RF test booklets: Internal structure comparability in a sample of criminal defendants. *Assessment*, *22*(2), 188–197. doi:10.1177/1073191114537347 PMID:24934218

Tarescavage, A. M., Brewster, J., Corey, D. M., & Ben-Porath, Y. S. (2015). Use of pre-hire MMPI-2-RF police candidate scores to predict supervisor ratings of post-hire performance. *Assessment*, *22*, 411–428. doi:10.1177/1073191114548445 PMID:25169624

Tarescavage, A. M., Corey, D. M., & Ben-Porath, Y. S. (2015). Minnesota Multiphasic Personality Inventory Restructured form (MMPI-2-RF) predictors if police officer problem behavior. *Assessment*, *22*(1), 116–132. doi:10.1177/1073191114534885 PMID:24875465

Tarescavage, A. M., Corey, D. M., & Ben-Porath, Y. S. (2016). A prorating method for estimating MMPI-2-RF Scores from MMPI responses: Examination of score fidelity and illustration of empirical utility in the PERSEREC Police Integrity Study sample. *Assessment*, *23*(2), 173–190. doi:10.1177/1073191115575070 PMID:25848124

Tarescavage, A. M., Corey, D. M., Gupton, H. M., & Ben-Porath, Y. S. (2015). Criterion validity and clinical utility of the Minnesota Multiphasic Personality Inventory-2-Restructured Form (MMPI-2-RF) in assessments of police officer candidates. *Journal of Personality Assessment*, *97*(4), 382–394. doi:10.1080/00223891.2014.995800 PMID:25588076

Tarescavage, A. M., Fischler, G. L., Cappo, B., Hill, D. O., Corey, D. M., & Ben-Porath, Y. S. (2015). Minnesota Multiphasic Personality Inventory-2-Restructured Form (MMPI-2-RF) predictors of police officer problem behavior and collateral self-report test scores. *Psychological Assessment*, *27*(1), 125–137. doi:10.1037/pas0000041 PMID:25383586

Tellegen, A., Ben-Porath, Y. S., McNulty, J. L., Arbisi, P. A., Graham, J. R., & Kaemmer, B. (2003). *The MMPI-2 Restructured Clinical Scales: Development, validation, and interpretation.* Minneapolis, MN: University of Minnesota Press.

Watson, D., & Tellegen, A. (1985). Toward a consensual structure of mood. *Psychological Bulletin*, *98*(2), 219–235. doi:10.1037/0033-2909.98.2.219 PMID:3901060

Weiss, P. A., & Weiss, W. U. (2010). Using the MMPI-2 in police psychological assessment. In P. A. Weiss (Ed.), *Personality assessment in police psychology* (pp. 59–71). Springfield, IL: Charles C. Thomas.

ENDNOTES

1 A terminological note: Throughout this chapter we use the generic term MMPI to refer to all versions of the inventory. Specific versions are identified as the Original MMPI, MMPI-2, and MMPI-2-RF.

2 The word "may" is emphasized here to reflect the fact that a candidate need not have an *actual* disability to be protected by the ADA. ADA limitations on disability-related inquiries apply to all job applicants, regardless of disability status.

APPENDIX

Table 1: The MMPI-2-RF Scales

Validity Scales

Variable Response Inconsistency (VRIN-r) – Random responding
True Response Inconsistency (TRIN-r) – Fixed responding
Infrequent Responses (F-r) – Responses infrequent in the general population
Infrequent Psychopathology Responses (Fp-r) – Responses infrequent in psychiatric populations
Infrequent Somatic Responses (Fs) – Somatic complaints infrequent in medical patient populations
Symptom Validity (FBS-r) – Somatic and cognitive complaints associated at high levels with overreporting
Response Bias Scale (RBS) – Exaggerated memory complaints
Uncommon Virtues (L-r) – Rarely claimed moral attributes or activities
Adjustment Validity (K-r) – Avowals of good psychological adjustment associated at high levels with underreporting

Higher-Order (H-O) Scales

Emotional/Internalizing Dysfunction (EID) – Problems associated with mood and affect
Thought Dysfunction (THD) – Problems associated with disordered thinking
Behavioral/Externalizing Dysfunction (BXD) – Problems associated with under-controlled behavior

Restructured Clinical (RC) Scales

Demoralization (RCd) – General unhappiness and dissatisfaction
Somatic Complaints (RC1) – Diffuse physical health complaints
Low Positive Emotions (RC2) – Lack of positive emotional responsiveness
Cynicism (RC3) – Non-self-referential beliefs expressing distrust and a generally low opinion of others
Antisocial Behavior (RC4) – Rule breaking and irresponsible behavior
Ideas of Persecution (RC6) – Self-referential beliefs that others pose a threat
Dysfunctional Negative Emotions (RC7) – Maladaptive anxiety, anger, irritability
Aberrant Experiences – (RC8) Unusual perceptions or thoughts
Hypomanic Activation – (RC9) Over-activation, aggression, impulsivity, and grandiosity

Specific Problems (SP) Scales

Somatic Scales

Malaise (MLS) – Overall sense of physical debilitation, poor health
Gastrointestinal Complaints (GIC) – Nausea, recurring upset stomach, and poor appetite
Head Pain Complaints (HPC) – Head and neck pain
Neurological Complaints (NUC) – Dizziness, weakness, paralysis, loss of balance, etc.
Cognitive Complaints – (COG) Memory problems, difficulties concentrating

Internalizing Scales

Suicidal/Death Ideation (SUI) – Direct reports of suicidal ideation and recent suicide attempts
Helplessness/Hopelessness (HLP) – Belief that goals cannot be reached or problems solved
Self-Doubt – (SFD) Lack of confidence, feelings of uselessness
Inefficacy – (NFC) Belief that one is indecisive and inefficacious
Stress/Worry (STW) – Preoccupation with disappointments, difficulty with time pressure
Anxiety – (AXY) Pervasive anxiety, frights, frequent nightmares
Anger Proneness (ANP) – Becoming easily angered, impatient with others
Behavior-Restricting Fears (BRF) – Fears that significantly inhibit normal activities
Multiple Specific Fears – (MSF) Fears of blood, fire, thunder, etc.

Externalizing Scales

Juvenile Conduct Problems (JCP) – Difficulties at school and at home, stealing
Substance Abuse (SUB) – Current and past misuse of alcohol and drugs
Aggression (AGG) – Physically aggressive, violent behavior
Activation (ACT) – Heightened excitation and energy level

Interpersonal Scales

Family Problems (FML) – Conflictual family relationships
Interpersonal Passivity (IPP) – Being unassertive and submissive
Social Avoidance (SAV) – Avoiding or not enjoying social events
Shyness (SHY) – Bashful, prone to feel inhibited and anxious around others
Disaffiliativeness (DSF) – Disliking people and being around them

Interest Scales

Aesthetic-Literary Interests (AES) – Literature, music, the theater
Mechanical-Physical Interests (MEC) – Fixing and building things, the outdoors, sports

Personality Psychopathology Five (PSY-5) Scales

Aggressiveness-Revised (AGGR-r) – Instrumental, goal-directed aggression
Psychoticism-Revised (PSYC-r) – Disconnection from reality
Disconstraint-Revised (DISC-r) – Under-controlled behavior
Negative Emotionality/Neuroticism-Revised (NEGE-r) – Anxiety, insecurity, worry, and fear
Introversion/Low Positive Emotionality-Revised (INTR-r) – Social disengagement and anhedonia

Table 2: Problem Domains Used in the PCIR JOB-Relevant Correlates Section

Domain 1: Emotional Control and Stress Tolerance Problems

This domain involves deficits in the ability to maintain emotional and behavioral control under pressure and other adverse circumstances. Counterproductive behaviors related to this domain include overreaction to provocation or challenge, moodiness and irritability, inaction or excessive hesitancy in the face of emergency or other high-stress conditions, poor stress tolerance or resilience, and failing to properly employ tactics and knowledge under stress conditions. This domain is distinguished from Impulse Control Problems (Domain 10) by its focus on stress conditions, whereas Domain 10 is concerned with impulsive behavior under normal conditions.

Domain 2: Routine Task Performance Problems

This domain pertains to problems in the ability to apply job-relevant knowledge, skills, and abilities in the context of routine demands. Counterproductive behaviors related to this domain include performing with little or no confidence, avoiding challenges, difficulty performing routine tasks and job functions (including report writing and navigation).

Domain 3: Decision-Making and Judgment Problems

This domain pertains to problems in the ability to plan, prioritize, take decisive action, and make decisions under normal conditions. Counterproductive behaviors related to this domain include failing to make decisions or take action, not "thinking on one's feet," failing to make midcourse corrections when needed, and not seeing the "big picture."

Domain 4: Feedback Acceptance Problems

This domain involves deficits in the ability to consider one's own role in or contribution to problems and, in the face of constructive criticism, to integrate feedback into a plan for self-improvement. Counterproductive behaviors related to this domain include excessive defensiveness, blaming others, and dismissing or minimizing the credibility of negative feedback.

Domain 5: Assertiveness Problems

This domain involves limitations in the ability to interact confidently with others, act assertively, and, when necessary, exert dominance and control over others. Counterproductive behaviors related to this domain include failure to engage others, isolating oneself or avoiding interpersonal contact, being overly submissive or timid, lacking "command presence," and communicating unclearly.

Domain 6: Social Competence and Teamwork Problems

This domain pertains to problems in the ability to communicate with tact and sensitivity, work effectively with others, accept authority and direction, and function as an effective member of a team. Counterproductive behaviors related to this domain include generating interpersonal conflict and complaints, showing bias, behaving rudely, resisting authority, denigrating others, failing to cooperate, and alienating citizens and/or co-workers.

Domain 7: Integrity Problems

This domain involves failure to maintain high standards of morality and ethics in one's personal and professional conduct. This includes noncompliance with organizational and societal rules, and exploiting the privileges and access of one's position for personal and/or other illegitimate interests. Counterproductive behaviors related to this domain include corruption, exploitation, dishonesty and deception, misrepresentation, boundary violations, and illegal behavior.

Domain 8: Conscientiousness and Dependability Problems

This domain involves problems in the ability to diligently and reliably fulfill employment and other obligations. Counterproductive behaviors related to this domain include taking impermissible short-cuts, disorganization, safety violations and property damage due to neglect or inattention, missing deadlines, missing court and mandatory appearances, failing to complete assignments, and a lack of initiative and/or perseverance.

Domain 9: Substance Use Problems

This domain pertains to the problematic use of alcohol or drugs. Counterproductive behaviors related to this domain include fights or arguments, employment problems, arrests or other legal problems, and tardiness or absenteeism due to substance use.

Domain 10: Impulse Control Problems

This domain involves impulsive and/or unnecessarily risky behavior that threatens the safety or interests of oneself or others, or reacting to situations without the proper degree of emotional and behavioral restraint and control. Counterproductive behaviors related to this domain include driving beyond the limits of one's abilities, failing to take proper precautions during high-risk activities, and recklessness.

Chapter 4
A Five-Factor Model Inventory for Use in Screening Police Officer Applicants:
The Revised NEO Personality Inventory (NEO PI-R)

Paul Detrick
Florissant Psychological Services, USA

John T. Chibnall
Saint Louis University School of Medicine, USA

ABSTRACT

The Five Factor Model (FFM) is widely accepted as a valid descriptor of normal personality and commonly used as a framework for prediction of job performance. As an inventory that operationalizes the FFM, the NEO PI-R is often utilized in personnel selection. The California Commission on Peace Officer Standards and Training has identified ten dimensions that increasingly serve as a template for the screening of police officer applicants. These screening dimensions are based on the FFM. The NEO PI-R thus appears well suited to serve as an inventory used for screening police officer applicants. A literature review is provided and strengths and weaknesses of the inventory discussed.

INTRODUCTION

The federal government has long supported the use of psychological evaluations to screen police officer candidates (National Advisory Commission on Criminal Justice Standards and Goals, 1973) and police departments have been held responsible for selecting a capable and healthy workforce (*Bonsignore v. City of New York,* 1981; *Woods v. Town of Danville, WV*, 2010). The psychological screening of police officer applicants has thus become a widespread practice (Cochrane, Tett, & Vandecreek, 2003; Bureau of Justice Statistics, 2010). Guidelines for preemployment psychological evaluations have been promulgated

DOI: 10.4018/978-1-5225-0813-7.ch004

by the International Association of Chiefs of Police (2014) and recommend that a written test battery be relevant to the purpose of the evaluation and that test instruments possess documented empirical reliability and validity supporting their use for police officer selection (Guideline 7.1). The California Commission on Peace Officer Standards and Training (CA POST), in the largest applied research project of its kind to date, identified 10 dimensions associated with both effective and counterproductive police officer job performance and mapped these dimensions against the Five Factor Model (FFM) personality domains, facets, and compound personality traits using a taxonomy created by Hough and Ones (2002). CA POST mandates assessment of police officer applicants according to the following FFM oriented job-related dimensions: Social Competence, Teamwork, Adaptability and Flexibility, Conscientiousness and Dependability, Impulse Control, Integrity and Ethics, Emotional Regulation and Stress Tolerance, Decision Making and Judgment, Assertiveness and Persuasiveness, and Avoiding Substance Use and Other Risk-Taking Behavior (Spilberg & Corey, 2014). These screening dimensions represent validated, behaviorally-defined police officer work behaviors associated with FFM psychological factors and serve as a standard template for police officer applicant evaluation findings across departments and examiners. Consequently, FFM-based objective personality inventories appear especially suited for the screening of police officer applicants; the NEO Personality Inventory-Revised (NEO PI-R), in particular, has empirical evidence that supports its use for this purpose.

Five-Factor Model and Job Performance

The Five-Factor Model (FFM) is a hierarchical structure of personality traits representing five fundamental domains: Neuroticism, Conscientiousness, Extraversion, Agreeableness, and Openness. Although the FFM and "Big Five" have differing origins, these labels are commonly used interchangeably (De Fruyt, McCrae, Szirmak, & Nagy, 2004). There is general agreement that the FFM is a valid descriptor of normal personality (Mount & Barrick, 1998; Mount, Barrick, & Stewart, 1998). It also has been widely used as a framework for the prediction of job performance (Barrick & Mount, 2005; Hogan, 2005, Hough & Oswald, 2005; Mount, Barrick, & Stewart, 1998; Ones, Viswesvaran, & Dilchert, 2004).

FFM personality traits have demonstrated validity for a wide array of work performance measures (Barrick & Mount, 1991; Hurtz & Donovan, 2000; Mount & Barrick, 1995; Salgado, 1997; Tett, Jackson, & Rothstein, 1991). Neuroticism and Conscientiousness predict work motivation and performance across most job functions, while Extraversion, Openness, and Agreeableness are characterized as "niche" traits predictive of performance in specific occupations and according to particular job functions (Barrick & Mount, 2005). Contextual job performance, including citizenship behavior that supports, maintains, and enhances task performance, has also been associated with FFM traits (Chiaburu, Oh, Berry, Li, & Gardner; 2011).

FFM Meta-Analyses and Police Officer Job Performance

Several meta-analyses report associations between FFM assessments and police officer job performance. As one aspect of a pioneering meta-analysis of FFM measures as indicators of job performance on a wide array of jobs, Barrick and Mount (1991) found Conscientiousness to possess the strongest estimated true correlation ($\hat{\rho}$) with police officer job performance ($\hat{\rho}$ = .22). Weaker associations with job performance were found for Neuroticism ($\hat{\rho}$ = .10), Agreeableness ($\hat{\rho}$ = .10), and Extraversion ($\hat{\rho}$= .09). No association between job performance and Openness to Experience was noted. Job performance as a broad outcome measure reflected an assortment of more narrow measures including job proficiency (primarily reflecting performance ratings), personnel data (e.g. salary level, turnover, status change and tenure), and training proficiency ratings. The relatively small number of primary studies involving police officer job performance prevented analysis by the more narrow performance outcome criteria. Salgado (1997), based on four primary studies, found a similar pattern of results for European police officer job performance (estimated true validity at the construct level, ρ) regarding Conscientiousness, Neuroticism, Extraversion, and Agreeableness (ρ = .39, .22, .20, and .14, respectively); however, in contrast to the findings of Barrick and Mount (1991), Openness also correlated with job performance, especially that reflecting training proficiency (ρ = .18). Aamodt (2004) found Conscientiousness, Neuroticism, and Openness to be associated with police academy grades, performance ratings, and discipline problems. Conscientiousness had the strongest correlation with performance ratings (r = .12), Neuroticism (Emotional Stability) with discipline problems (r = -.09), and Openness with grades (r = .22).

Finally, as noted earlier, CA POST commissioned a comprehensive meta-analysis to assess the validity of personality traits as job performance predictors (Ones et al., 2004). Independently-developed POST Psychological Screening Dimensions served as the basis for hypotheses regarding personality constructs expected to be most relevant to aspects of police officer job performance and for identifying measures of those constructs. Meta-analyses were conducted for the Big Five traits, facets, or compound traits/facets. Findings indicated that all performance criteria were significantly related to multiple FFM personality variables: for Overall Job Performance there were 16 associations, 13 for Interpersonal Behavior, 11 for Training Performance, 10 for Task Performance, and 10 for Teamwork. Awards/Commendations and Substance Abuse were each significantly correlated with eight personality variables. Numerous significant associations were obtained for Agreeableness, Conscientiousness and its facets, Emotional Stability and its facets, and Extraversion and its facets. Little operational validity support was obtained for the facets of Openness to Experience, but results suggested potential relationships with training performance. Among the compound traits, the strongest pattern of results was found for compound variables that included elements of Conscientiousness and Emotional Stability. One compound trait, labeled as Self-Destructive Autonomy and consisting of facets of Emotional Stability, Extraversion, and Conscientiousness, was predictive of a wide range of performance criteria (Spilberg & Corey, 2014).

With regard to primary associations between FFM measures and Screening Dimensions: Emotional Stability was associated with Social Competence, Integrity/Ethics, Emotional Regulation/Stress Tolerance, and Self-Destructive Autonomy (-); Extraversion with Adaptability/Flexibility, Conscientiousness/Dependability, Assertiveness/Persuasiveness, Avoiding Substance Abuse/Risk Taking (Thrill Seeking), and Self-Destructive Autonomy; Openness to Experience with Social Competence, Adaptability/Flexibility, Decision Making/Judgment, and Avoiding Substance Abuse/Risk Taking (Thrill Seeking); Agreeableness with Social Competence, Teamwork, and Integrity/Ethics; and Conscientiousness with Social Competence, Adaptability/Flexibility (-), Conscientiousness/Dependability, Impulse Control, Integrity/Ethics, Emotional Regulation/Stress Tolerance, Avoiding Substance Abuse/Risk Taking (Thrill Seeking) (-), and Self-Destructive Autonomy (-) (Ones et al., 2004).

A FFM MEASURE: THE NEO PI-R

The NEO PI-R (Costa & McCrae, 1992) is a 240-item inventory designed to operationalize the FFM. Examinees respond to items on a (1)-strongly disagree to (5)-strongly agree Likert-type scale, with the order of the labels balanced across items to control for acquiescence and nay-saying effects. The NEO PI-R yields five broad domain scores that represent the basic personality dimensions of the FFM. These domains are: Neuroticism (N; the tendency to experience negative affect like anxiety, frustration, worry, low self-confidence, poor coping skills), Extraversion (E; tendency toward assertiveness, high activity, friendliness, warmth, energy, adventurousness, optimism), Openness (O; tendency to be open to new experiences, imaginative, intellectually curious, possess wide ranging interests, and be open to training opportunities), Agreeableness (A; tendency toward trust, cooperation, generosity, modesty, directness), and Conscientiousness (C; tendency toward dependability, ambition, organization, deliberation). Within each broad domain, there are six narrow facets (Costa & McCrae, 1995). For example, the Conscientious domain is composed of six facets: C1-Competence, C2-Order, C3-Dutifulness, C4-Achievement Striving, C5-Self-Discipline, and C6-Deliberation (Table 1).

Each facet is measured by eight items. Norms are established for men and women separately, and combined for use in personnel selection. Scores are reported as T scores (normative mean = 50, *SD* = 10). Definitions for the domains and associated facets are provided in the publication manuals (Costa & McCrae, 1992; McCrae & Costa, 2010). The NEO PI-R requires a 6th grade reading level and is appropriate for people age 17 and over. The NEO PI-R may be administered individually or in a group. Hand-scoring and scannable answer sheets are available. The NEO PI-R can also be scored and/or administered electronically using the NEO Software System™ (PAR; www.parinc.com).

Although the NEO PI-R items are non-invasive and possess face validity, as is true of objective personality inventories in general, the items are also transparent and thus vulnerable to response distortion or bias. Response bias may be positive or negative. Positive response bias (faking good, impression management, socially desirable responding) is most common in the personnel selection context (a circumstance in which applicants are motivated to present themselves in a positive light to obtain a desired job). The

Table 1. NEO PI-R domain and associated facet scales

Domains	Facets	
Neuroticism	*N1: Anxiety* *N2: Angry Hostility* *N3: Depression*	*N4: Self-Consciousness* *N5: Impulsiveness* *N6: Vulnerability*
Extraversion	*E1: Warmth* *E2: Gregariousness* *E3: Assertiveness*	*E4: Activity* *E5: Excitement Seeking* *E6: Positive Emotions*
Openness to Experience	*01: Fantasy* *02: Aesthetics* *03: Feelings*	*04: Actions* *05: Ideas* *06: Values*
Agreeableness	*A1: Trust* *A2: Straightforwardness* *A3: Altruism*	*A4: Compliance* *A5: Modesty* *A6: Tender-Mindedness*
Conscientiousness	*C1: Competence* *C2: Order* *C3: Dutifulness*	*C4: Achievement Striving* *C5: Self-Discipline* *C6: Deliberation*

impact of response bias continues to be debated (Dilchert, Ones, Viswesvaran, & Deller, 2006), with some studies showing no impact on criterion-related validity (e.g. Ones, Viswesvaran, & Reiss, 1996), while others (e.g. Griffith, Chmielowski, & Yoshito, 2007; Rosse et al., 1998; Schmit and Ryan, 1993) indicate an impact on applicant rankings and thus hiring decisions. This ongoing controversy may in part reflect differences in research designs and methodological problems inherent in each design (Griffith et al., 2007). The research designs most commonly employed in studies of response bias include: (1) studies in which simulated high demand conditions are created by instructing participants to "fake good"; (2) studies using measures of response bias (typically validity scales) as proxies for demand condition; and (3) studies comparing job applicants to incumbents. In a meta-analysis on positive response bias, it was found that individuals who were instructed to "fake good" (simulated high demand condition) were on average able to improve scores on personality inventories by approximately 0.5 standard deviation units (Viswesvaran & Ones, 1999). Simulated high demand instructional sets, however, appear to produce larger effect sizes than actual applicant high demand circumstances and thus may not accurately reflect "real" high demand conditions (Edens & Arthur, 2000). Using a validity scale as a proxy or indicator of "faking good" in a high demand condition may provide some information about the construct validity of these scales, but the information is limited with respect to how such bias impacts specific scales and consequently how it may affect predictions of subsequent job performance (Detrick, Chibnall, & Call, 2010). Comparing incumbent with applicant scores similarly has shown that applicants tend to score higher than incumbents, indicative of response bias, (e.g. Schmit & Ryan, 1993). These studies, however, are only capable of inferring that a difference is an effect of demand condition and consequently provide limited information regarding construct validity. A within-subjects design comparing individuals under different demand or motivational conditions is most appropriate for studying the construct validity of measures of response bias (Griffith et al., 2007).

The authors of the NEO PI-R maintain that empirical evidence does not support the use of validity scales (Costa & McCrae, 1992; McCrae & Costa, 2010). Instead, three simple items are included at the conclusion of the inventory asking examinees if they tried to respond to items in an honest and accurate manner, if they answered all items, and if responses were entered in the correct space. In response to criticism of the lack of formal validity scales (Ben-Porath & Waller, 1992), three NEO PI-R research validity scales were developed by Schinka, Kinder, and Kremer (1997): the Inconsistent Responding scale, to assess random responding; the Negative Presentation Management scale, to assess negative response distortion/overreporting or "faking bad"; and the Positive Presentation Management (PPM) scale, to assess positive response distortion/underreporting or "faking good." Demand-simulation and clinical studies have provided support for the validity of these scales in clinical applications (Ballinger, Caldwell-Andrews, & Baer, 2001; Caldwell-Andrews, Baer, & Berry, 2000; Morasco, Gfeller, & Elder, 2007; Morey et al., 2002; Sellbom & Bagby, 2008; Young & Schinka, 2001) and Reid-Seiser and Fritzsche (2001) offered qualified support for the validity of the PPM scale in personnel selection.

Detrick et al. (2010) utilized a within-subject design that "naturalistically" manipulated applicant motivation to engage in positive response bias. Police officer applicant NEO PI-R profiles obtained under the high demand condition of personnel selection were compared with profiles from the same individuals obtained approximately six months later under low demand conditions (i.e., after successful completion of the police academy and hiring). The Neuroticism domain and all of its facets were significantly lower under high demand in comparison to scores under low demand (Cohen's d ranged from -1.01 for the Neuroticism domain score to -.64 for the Impulsiveness facet). Extraversion domain scores were not significantly different as a function of demand condition; however, lower facet scores on Excitement-Seeking, *d* = -.53, and higher facet scores on Warmth, *d* = .72, Gregariousness, *d* = .45, Assertiveness, *d* = .44, and Positive Emotions, *d* = .28, were noted in the high as opposed to low demand condition. No difference on the Openness domain scale was noted; however, among Openness facets, lower scores on Fantasy, *d* = -.72, and Feelings, *d* = -.30, and higher scores on Actions, *d* = .35, and Ideas, *d* = .38, were observed under high demand. The Agreeableness domain score, *d* = .75, and facets of Trust, *d* = .77, Straightforwardness, *d* = .64, Altruism, *d* = .54, and Compliance, *d* = .85, were all higher under high demand. With respect to Conscientiousness, the domain score and all of the facets except Order were higher in the high demand condition than in the low demand condition (Cohen's *d* ranged from .72 to .43). Of the 35 comparisons (five domains and 30 facets), 27 were significant at $p \leq .001$. Overall, positive response bias was illustrated by lower scores on Neuroticism and accentuated scores on Agreeableness and Conscientiousness under high demand. PPM (the validity scale of greatest relevance in the personnel selection context) was elevated under the high as opposed to the low demand condition, thus providing some support for the construct validity of this scale. PPM was able to predict demand-induced variation in Neuroticism scores only, thus providing only modest support for the construct validity of PPM as a measure of positive response bias in the context of police officer selection. There is some evidence that response sets on validity scales may generalize across inventories (as well as other extra-test measures), therefore potentially allowing for additional response bias information through comparisons of validity scale scores from different inventories (Forbey et al., 2013). It is noteworthy, however, that very few within-subject studies on the validity scales of personality inventories exist; as a consequence, understanding of the construct validity of these scales in general is limited. Additional research in this area utilizing a within-subject design is much needed.

Psychometric Properties of the NEO PI-R

As detailed in the Professional Manual (Costa & McCrae, 1992), the NEO PI-R has substantial psychometric research to support its use as a comprehensive measure of normal adult personality, and has been used in hundreds of clinical and basic research studies. Costa and McCrae (1992) provide detailed information and references regarding the psychometric development of the NEO PI-R. Based on several large normative samples, internal consistency reliabilities range from 0.86 (Agreeableness) to 0.92 (Neuroticism) for the 48-item domain scores, and 0.56 (Tender-Mindedness) to 0.81 (Depression) for the 8-item individual facet scores. Similarly, retest reliabilities for the domain and facet scores range from 0.66 to 0.92 across various samples and time frames (ranging from weeks to years). The factor analytic structure of the NEO PI-R strongly supports a five-domain model with six facets per domain. Finally, a large number of studies has provided strong support for the content, criterion-related, and construct (convergence/discrimination) validity of the NEO PI-R domain and facet scores. Additional studies relating to the reliability and validity of the NEO PI-R are presented in the most recent *NEO Inventories Professional Manual* (McCrae & Costa, 2010). As a primary representative of the FFM, the NEO PI-R has been widely utilized in personality research across cultures, and its five-factor structure has been repeatedly replicated, including across gender and age groups. A comprehensive online bibliography pertaining to the NEO PI-R is available at www.parinc.com in the *NEO PI-R Supplemental Product Resources* section.

The normative sample on which the NEO PI-R self-report form is based includes 405 men and women from the Augmented Baltimore Study of Aging (ABLSA), 320 ABLSA participants who completed the NEO PI-R by computer administration between 1989 and 1991, and 1,539 participants in a national study of job performance. In addition, 500 men and 500 women were selected from these groups to match U.S. Census projections for 1995 (Costa & McCrae, 1992). NEO PI-R norms for police officer applicants are also available and indicate that applicants score at high levels on Conscientiousness and Extraversion and low levels on Neuroticism (Detrick & Chibnall, 2013).

Development of the NEO PI-R

The NEO PI-R was derived from the NEO Personality Inventory (NEO-PI), first published in 1985, and this in turn was an adaptation of an earlier three-factor inventory (Costa & McCrae, 1985). The initial three-factor inventory included the domain scales Neuroticism, Extraversion, and Openness; Agreeableness and Conscientiousness were added several years later. The NEO-PI was succeeded by the NEO PI-R in 1992 (Costa & McCrae, 1992). The NEO PI-R differed from the earlier version primarily in the inclusion of facet scales for the Agreeableness and Conscientiousness domains. Recently, 37 items on the NEO PI-R were revised or edited to lower the required reading level and make the instrument appropriate for adolescents as young as 12 years of age (McCrae & Costa, 2010). This most recent revision, the NEO PI-3, retains the reliability and validity of the NEO PI-R, but is more appropriate for younger examinees or adults with lower educational levels.

The NEO Inventories are unique in that they include both traditional self-report assessment (Form S), as well as observer assessment (Form R). While self-report data are commonly obtained in the personnel selection context, circumstances may arise where observer ratings are an important source of information. In some contexts, like personnel selection, observer ratings may be more valid than self-report, in part because they are less susceptible to positive response distortion under high demand conditions (Hogan, 1991; Mount, Barrick, & Strauss, 1994). Short forms of the NEO inventories are also available; they have weaker validity, however, and their use for personnel selection purposes is therefore not recommended. In addition, the short forms yield only domain scores.

Although the NEO PI-3 supersedes the NEO PI-R, the current *NEO Inventories Professional Manual* (McCrae & Costa, 2010) notes that "Researchers and clinicians who have extensive experience with the NEO PI-R may wish to continue using that version and the norms with which they are familiar. The NEO PI-R will continue to be made available in both print and computer versions" (p. 1). The authors also note that the NEO PI-3 and NEO PI-R domain and facet scales are highly correlated. Since there is no need in police officer personnel selection contexts for non-adult measures and the literature pertaining to the construct validity of the NEO inventories for use in peace officer selection is based on the NEO PI-R (no police officer norms for the NEO PI-3 are available to date), the NEO PI-R is featured in this chapter.

NEO PI-R Construct Validity for Police Officer Selection

In addition to being widely used in personnel selection, a number of studies have provided support for the construct validity of the NEO PI-R for police officer selection. Bishop et al. (2001) found relationships between coping styles and NEO PI-R personality measures for police officers in Singapore. Neuroticism predicted avoidant behavior; Conscientiousness predicted problem solving; and Extraversion, Agreeableness, and Openness predicted positive reinterpretation and growth when faced with stress.

Other studies have reported associations between NEO PI-R scales and police academy performance (Black, 2000; Detrick, Chibnall, & Luebbert, 2004). In a study of recruits in New Zealand, Black (2000) found that a measure of overall training performance (based on 17 practical and academic tests including firearms, self-defense, cognitive ability and driving) was most strongly correlated with Conscientiousness (r = .27) and its facets (Competence, r = .23; Order, r = .20; Dutifulness, r = .21; Achievement Striving, r = .22; Self-Discipline, r = .25; and Deliberation, r = .14). Significant associations were also reported for Neuroticism (r = -.16) and two of its facets (Impulsiveness, r = -.17, and Vulnerability, r = -.17). Extraversion was associated with a physical performance measure (r = .13), as were two of its facets (Assertiveness, r = .15; Activity, r = .23; and Excitement-Seeking, r = .18).

Detrick et al. (2004) found that, after controlling for demographics, higher Openness domain facet scores on Values ($\beta = .33, p \leq .05$) and lower scores on Extraversion domain facet Excitement-Seeking ($\beta = -.29, p \leq .001$) predicted academic performance. Firearms performance was predicted by lower scores on the Neuroticism domain facet Anxiety ($\beta = -.22, p \leq .05$). Physical performance was predicted by lower scores on the Conscientiousness domain facet Deliberation ($\beta = -.43, p \leq .001$), lower scores on the Openness domain facet Fantasy ($\beta = -.43, p \leq .001$), and higher scores on the Extraversion domain facet Activity ($\beta = .31, p \leq .05$). Lastly, absenteeism was predicted by lower scores on the Neuroticism domain facet Self-Consciousness ($\beta = -.30, p \leq .05$). This study, in contrast to the Black (2000) study, focused on facet measures because of their hypothesized stronger link with more specific performance outcome measures (Hurtz & Donovan, 2000).

In an incremental validity study, the Minnesota Multiphasic Personality Inventory-2, Inwald Personality Inventory, and NEO PI-R were each found to contribute significantly to the prediction of police academy performance (Chibnall & Detrick, 2003). The three inventories together predicted between 50% and 55% of the variance in performance (demographic variables accounted for 20%). The NEO PI-R, however, was unique in its ability to predict physical performance and demonstrated the highest level of incremental validity of the three inventories.

Hogan (1991) and others (Mount, Barrick, & Strauss, 1994) have suggested that observer ratings may be more valid than self-report in the context of personnel selection because of the likely reduction in impression management. Metchik (1999) and Scrivner (1995) have also argued for a "screening-in" as opposed to a "screening-out" process that identifies the personality characteristics of high performing entry-level police officers (as opposed to identifying personality risk factors for poor performance). Thus, in an "observer-rating" study identifying "positive, screening-in" personality characteristics, field training officers were asked to describe the characteristics of the "best" entry-level police officer that they had supervised, using the Observer Form of the NEO PI-R (Detrick & Chibnall, 2006). The resulting profile was notable for low scores on Neuroticism (M = 40.8, SD = 6.3) and its facets of Angry Hostility (M = 41.7, SD = 4.8), Depression (M = 43.7, SD = 7.3), and Vulnerability (M = 37.4, SD = 7.2); high scores on Extraversion (M = 56.3, SD = 5.8) and its facets of Assertiveness (M = 55.9, SD = 8.0) and Excitement-Seeking (M = 59.7, SD = 6.2); and high scores on Conscientiousness (M = 55.9, SD = 7.3) and its facets of Achievement Striving (M = 58.1, SD = 7.3) and Self-Discipline (M = 56.8, SD = 6.3).

Finally, entry-level police officer applicant norms for the NEO PI-R have recently become available (Detrick & Chibnall, 2013). The NEO PI-R profile of the successful police officer applicant is notable for low scores on Neuroticism (M = 37.0, SD = 6.8), especially the facets of Vulnerability (M = 37.9, SD = 7.6) and Impulsiveness (M = 37.8, SD = 8.5); high scores on Extraversion (M = 55.3, SD = 6.2), especially the facets of Gregariousness (M = 59.5, SD = 7.5), Assertiveness (M = 60.8, SD = 7.8), and Excitement-Seeking (M = 57.5, SD = 8.1); and high scores on Conscientiousness (M = 57.3, SD = 8.3), especially the facets of Competence (M = 59.5, SD = 8.7), Achievement-Striving (M = 60.5, SD = 7.9), Self-Discipline (M = 59.3, SD = 7.1), and Deliberation (M = 60.2, SD = 9.3). Of note, these successful police officer applicant self-report norms are consistent with the NEO PI-R Observer norms for "best" recruits (Detrick & Chibnall, 2006). This paper also reports normative data for the PPM scale, which had a mean of 27.2 (*SD* = 3.9) on a 0-40 raw score scale.

General Issues

The NEO PI-R, with its derivation in the FFM, is an attractive option for use as a measure of normal personality functioning in peace officer applicants. The constructs assessed by the NEO PI-R translate well to the Psychological Screening Dimensions that are the focus of the California Post Screening Manual. Despite widespread recognition that FFM measures, and the NEO PI-R in particular, are valid predictors of job performance, the NEO PI-R has had limited use in the selection of police officers. Until recently, the lack of police officer applicant norms and formal validity scales for the NEO PI-R were significant factors that hampered its use. With the availability of NEO PI-R police officer applicant norms (Detrick & Chibnall, 2013) and the PPM research validity scale as a measure of response bias, this inventory is more attractive. As noted previously, the PPM validity scale is a useful measure of impression management in police officer selection, although it appears to be most sensitive to changes on the Neuroticism domain, and less so with respect to Agreeableness and Conscientiousness. It is also worth noting that encouraging examinee cooperation with testing, obtaining observer ratings, and comparing test results with other collateral sources of data are important methods for detecting and understanding response distortion (McCrae & Costa, 2010). Although a measure of normal personality functioning, the NEO PI-R possesses a considerable body of literature relating to diagnostic/clinical applications (Costa & Widiger, 2002; Piedmont, 1998). Therefore, the NEO PI-R is likely to be considered a "medical" test as defined by the Americans with Disability Act of 2008 (ADA, 2009), and thus is most appropriately administered as a component of a preemployment psychological evaluation at the post-conditional offer stage. There are no empirical data to support the use of cut-off scores on the NEO PI-R for police officer selection. Gender differences on the NEO PI-R are generally small in comparison to individual variation within genders. Women tend to describe themselves as higher on Neuroticism, Agreeableness, Warmth, and Openness compared to men, while men score higher on Assertiveness and Ideas (Costa, Terracciano, & McCrae, 2001). The FFM and NEO Inventories in particular have become the focus of personality research worldwide and have been translated into more than 50 languages (McCrae & Costa, 2010). Compared to other personality inventories commonly used in personnel selection, the NEO Inventories, including the NEO PI-R, are of relatively recent development.

Primary Limitations to Use of the NEO PI-R

Although it is difficult to compare the construct validity of validity scales for various personality inventories commonly used in police officer selection because of a relative lack of within-subject studies, the PPM research validity scale on the NEO PI-R appears to be primarily associated with scores on Neuroticism, to the exclusion of Agreeableness and Extraversion scores, indicating only modest construct validity (Detrick et al, 2010). This validity scale could be strengthened by including items in these two domains. At present there are also no predictive validity studies relating to the NEO PI-R and police officer job performance. Finally, although the authors of the NEO PI-R encourage continued use of the NEO PI-R as needed, the NEO PI-3 is a more recent version and reportedly possesses improved psychometric properties. At this time, however, no police officer norms for the NEO PI-3 have been published.

CONCLUSION

Given the dominant status of the FFM as a descriptor of normal personality functioning, the common use of the FFM as a framework for the prediction of job performance (including the CA POST Screening Dimensions), the recognition that the NEO PI-R operationalizes the FFM, and the growing body of literature supporting the construct validity of the NEO PI-R for use in police officer selection, the NEO PI-R appears well-suited for use as an inventory for police officer selection.

ACKNOWLEDGMENT

Thanks to CA POST for granting permission for material to be included in this chapter from information on the NEO PI-R (Detrick, 2014) that was written by the first author and linked to the California Post Peace Officer Psychological Screening Manual (Spilberg & Corey, 2014).

REFERENCES

Aamodt, M. G. (2004). *Research in law enforcement selection*. Boca Raton, FL: Brown Walker.

Americans with Disability Act of 2008. Pub. L. 110-325 (2009).

Ballinger, J. F., Caldwell-Andrews, A., & Baer, R. A. (2001). Effects of positive impression management on the NEO Personality Inventory-Revised in a clinical population. *Psychological Assessment*, *13*(2), 254–260. doi:10.1037/1040-3590.13.2.254 PMID:11433800

Barrick, M. R., & Mount, M. K. (1991). The big five personality dimensions and job performance: A meta-analysis. *Personnel Psychology*, *44*(1), 1–26. doi:10.1111/j.1744-6570.1991.tb00688.x

Barrick, M. R., & Mount, M. K. (2005). Yes, personality matters: Moving on to more important matters. *Human Performance*, *18*(4), 359–372. doi:10.1207/s15327043hup1804_3

Ben-Porath, Y. S., & Waller, G. (1992). "Normal" personality inventories in clinical assessment: General requirements and the potential for using the NEO Personality Inventory. *Psychological Assessment*, *4*, 23–25. doi:10.1037/1040-3590.4.1.23

Bishop, G. D., Tong, E. M. W., Diong, W. M., Enkelmann, H. C., Why, Y. P., Khader, M., & Ang, J. C. H. (2001). The relationship between coping and personality among police officers in Singapore. *Journal of Research in Personality*, *35*(3), 353–374. doi:10.1006/jrpe.2001.2319

Black, J. (2000). Personality testing and police selection: Utility of the "Big Five." *New Zealand Journal of Psychology*, *29*, 2–9.

Bonsignore v. City of New York, 521 F.Supp. 394 (1981).

Bureau of Justice Statistics. (2010). *Local Police Departments, 2007*. Washington, DC: Author.

Caldwell-Andrews, A., Baer, R. A., & Berry, D. T. T. (2000). Effects of response set on NEO PI-R scores and their relations to external criteria. *Journal of Personality Assessment*, *74*(3), 472–488. doi:10.1207/S15327752JPA7403_10 PMID:10900573

Chiaburu, D. S., Oh, I.-S., Berry, C. M., Li, N., & Gardner, R. G. (2011). The five-factor model of personality traits and organizational citizenship behavior: A meta-analysis. *The Journal of Applied Psychology*, *96*(6), 1140–1166. doi:10.1037/a0024004 PMID:21688883

Chibnall, J. T., & Detrick, P. (2003). The NEO PI-R, Inwald Personality Inventory, and MMPI-2 in the prediction of police academy performance: A case for incremental validity. *American Journal of Criminal Justice*, *27*(2), 233–248. doi:10.1007/BF02885696

Cochrane, R. E., Tett, R. P., & Vandecreek, L. (2003). Psychological testing and the selection of police officers. *Criminal Justice and Behavior*, *30*(5), 511–537. doi:10.1177/0093854803257241

Costa, P. T. Jr, & McCrae, R. R. (1985). *The NEO Personality Inventory manual*. Odessa, FL: PAR.

Costa, P. T. Jr, & McCrae, R. R. (1992). *NEO PI-R professional manual*. Odessa, FL: PAR.

Costa, P. T. Jr, & McCrae, R. R. (1995). Domains and facets: Hierarchical personality assessment using the revised NEO Personality Inventory. *Journal of Personality Assessment*, *64*(1), 21–50. doi:10.1207/s15327752jpa6401_2 PMID:16367732

Costa, P. T. Jr, Terracciano, A., & McCrae, R. R. (2001). Gender differences in personality traits across cultures: Robust and surprising findings. *Journal of Personality and Social Psychology*, *81*(2), 322–331. doi:10.1037/0022-3514.81.2.322 PMID:11519935

Costa, P. T. Jr, & Widiger, T. A. (2002). *Personality disorders and the five-factor model of personality* (2nd ed.). Washington, DC: American Psychological Association. doi:10.1037/10423-000

De Fruyt, F., McCrae, R. R., Szirmak, Z., & Nagy, J. (2004). The Five-factor Personality Inventory as a measure of the Five-Factor Model: Belgian, American, and Hungarian comparisons with the NEO PI-R. *Assessment*, *3*(3), 207–215. doi:10.1177/1073191104265800 PMID:15358876

Detrick, P. (2014). *NEO Personality Inventory-Revised*. Retrieved from: http://lib.post.ca.gov/Publications/PsycScreeningManual/NEO_PI-R.pdf

Detrick, P., & Chibnall, J. T. (2006). NEO PI-R personality characteristics of high performing entry-level police officers. *Psychological Services*, *3*(4), 274–285. doi:10.1037/1541-1559.3.4.274

Detrick, P., & Chibnall, J. T. (2013). Revised NEO Personality Inventory normative data for police officer selection. *Psychological Services*, *10*(4), 372–277. doi:10.1037/a0031800 PMID:23398091

Detrick, P., Chibnall, J. T., & Call, C. (2010). Demand effects on positive response distortion by police officer applicants on the Revised NEO Personality Inventory. *Journal of Personality Assessment*, *92*(5), 410–415. doi:10.1080/00223891.2010.497401 PMID:20706927

Detrick, P., Chibnall, J. T., & Luebbert, M. C. (2004). The Revised NEO Personality Inventory as predictor of police academy performance. *Criminal Justice and Behavior*, *31*(6), 676–694. doi:10.1177/0093854804268751

Dilchert, S., Ones, D. S., Viswesvaran, C., & Deller, J. (2006). Response distortion in personality measurement: Born to deceive, yet capable of providing valid self-assessment? *Psychological Science*, *48*, 209–225.

Edens, P. S., & Arthur, W. (2000, April). *A meta-analysis investigating the susceptibility of self-report inventories to distortion.* Paper presented at the 15th annual conference of the Society for Industrial and Organizational Psychology, New Orleans, LA.

Forbey, J. D., Lee, T. C., Ben-Porath, Y. S., Arbisi, P. A., & Gartland, D. (2013). Associations between MMPI-2-RF validity scale scores and extra-test measures of personality and psychopathology. *Assessment*, *20*(4), 448–461. doi:10.1177/1073191113478154 PMID:23443819

Griffith, R. L., Chmielowski, T., & Yoshita, Y. (2007). Do applicants fake? An examination of the frequency of applicant faking. *Personnel Review*, *36*(3), 341–355. doi:10.1108/00483480710731310

Hogan, R. (2005). In defense of personality measurement: New wine for old whiners. *Human Performance*, *18*(4), 331–341. doi:10.1207/s15327043hup1804_1

Hogan, R. T. (1991). Personality and personality measurement. In M. D. Dunnette & L. M. Hough (Eds.), *Handbook of industrial and organizational psychology* (2nd ed.; pp. 873–919). Palo Alto, CA: Consulting Psychologists Press.

Hough, L. M., & Ones, D. S. (2002). The structure, measurement, validity, and use of personality variables in industrial, work, and organizational psychology. In N. Anderson, D. S. Ones, H. K. Sinangil, & C. Viswesvaran (Eds.), *Handbook of industrial, work & organizational psychology* (2nd ed.; Vol. 1, pp. 233–277). London, United Kingdom: Sage.

Hough, L. M., & Oswald, F. L. (2005). They're right, well. . . mostly right: Research evidence and an agenda to rescue personality testing from1960s insights. *Human Performance*, *18*(4), 373–387. doi:10.1207/s15327043hup1804_4

Hurtz, G. M., & Donovan, J. J. (2000). Personality and job performance: The big five revisited. *The Journal of Applied Psychology*, *85*(6), 869–879. doi:10.1037/0021-9010.85.6.869 PMID:11125652

International Association of Chiefs of Police, Police Psychological Services Section. (2014). *Preemployment psychological evaluation guidelines.* Retrieved from: http://www.theiacp.org/portals/0/documents/pdfs/Psych-PreemploymentPsychEval.pdf

McCrae, R. R., & Costa, P. T. Jr. (2010). *NEO Inventories professional manual for the NEO Personality Inventory-3, NEO Five-Factor Inventory-3, and NEO Personality Inventory-Revised.* Lutz, FL: PAR.

Metchik, E. (1999). An analysis of the "screening out" model of police officer selection. *Police Quarterly*, *2*(1), 79–95. doi:10.1177/109861119900200104

Morasco, B. J., Gfeller, J. D., & Elder, K. A. (2007). The utility of the NEO PI-R validity scales to detect response distortion: A comparison with the MMPI-2. *Journal of Personality Assessment*, *88*(3), 276–283. doi:10.1080/00223890701293924 PMID:17518549

Morey, L. C., Quigley, B. D., Sanislow, C. A., Skodol, A. E., McGlashan, T. H., Shea, M. T., & Gunderson, J. G. et al. (2002). Substance or style? An investigation of the NEO PI-R validity scales. *Journal of Personality Assessment*, *79*(3), 583–599. doi:10.1207/S15327752JPA7903_11 PMID:12511022

Mount, M. K., & Barrick, M. R. (1995). The Big Five personality dimensions: Implications for research and practice in human resource management. *Research in Personnel and Human Resource Management*, *13*, 153–200.

Mount, M. K., Barrick, M. R., & Stewart, G. L. (1998). Five-factor model of personality and performance in jobs involving interpersonal interactions. *Human Performance*, *11*(2-3), 145–165. doi:10.1080/08959285.1998.9668029

Mount, M. K., Barrick, M. R., & Stewart, G. L. (1998). Five-factor model of personality and performance in jobs involving interpersonal interactions. *Human Performance*, *11*(2-3), 145–165. doi:10.1080/08959285.1998.9668029

Mount, M. K., Barrick, M. R., & Strauss, J. P. (1994). Validity of observer ratings of the big five personality factors. *The Journal of Applied Psychology*, *79*(2), 272–280. doi:10.1037/0021-9010.79.2.272

National Advisory Commission on Criminal Justice Standards and Goals. (1973). *Task force on police*. Washington, DC: Author.

Ones, D. S., Viswesvaran, C., & Dilchert, S. (2004, November). *Personality and police officer work performance: A construct-based, comprehensive meta-analysis and implications for pre-offer screening and psychological evaluations*. Paper presented at the annual meeting of the International Association of Chiefs of Police, Los Angeles, CA.

Ones, D. S., Viswesvaran, C., & Reiss, A. D. (1996). Role of social desirability in personality testing for personnel selection: The red herring. *The Journal of Applied Psychology*, *81*(6), 660–679. doi:10.1037/0021-9010.81.6.660

Piedmont, R. L. (1998). *The Revised NEO Personality Inventory: Clinical and research applications*. New York, NY: Plenum. doi:10.1007/978-1-4899-3588-5

Reid-Seiser, H. L., & Fritzsche, B. A. (2001). The usefulness of the NEO PI R positive presentation management scale for detecting response distortion in employment contexts. *Personality and Individual Differences*, *31*(4), 639–650. doi:10.1016/S0191-8869(00)00168-9

Rosse, J. G., Stecher, M. D., Miller, J. L., & Levin, R. A. (1998). The impact of response distortion on preemployment personality testing and hiring decisions. *The Journal of Applied Psychology*, *83*(4), 634–644. doi:10.1037/0021-9010.83.4.634

Salgado, J. F. (1997). The five-factor model of personality and job performance in the European community. *The Journal of Applied Psychology*, *82*(1), 30–43. doi:10.1037/0021-9010.82.1.30 PMID:9119797

Schinka, J. A., Kinder, B. N., & Kremer, T. (1997). Research validity scales for the NEO PI-R: Development and initial validation. *Journal of Personality Assessment*, *68*(1), 127–138. doi:10.1207/s15327752jpa6801_10 PMID:16370773

Schmit, M. J., & Ryan, A. M. (1993). The Big Five in personnel selection: Factor structure in applicant and nonapplicant populations. *The Journal of Applied Psychology*, *78*(6), 966–974. doi:10.1037/0021-9010.78.6.966

Scrivner, E. M. (1995). Community policing: New roles for police psychology. In M. I. Kurke & E. M. Scrivner (Eds.), *Police psychology into the 21st century* (pp. 419–433). Hillsdale, NJ: Erlbaum.

Sellbom, M., & Bagby, R. M. (2008). The validity and utility of the positive presentation and negative presentation management scales for the Revised NEO Personality Inventory. *Assessment*, *15*(2), 165–176. doi:10.1177/1073191107310301 PMID:18463407

Spilberg, S. W., & Corey, D. (2014). *Peace officer psychological screening manual.* Sacramento, CA: California Commission on Peace Officer Standards and Training.

Tett, R. P., Jackson, D. N., & Rothstein, M. (1991). Personality measures as predictors of job performance: A meta-analytic review. *Personnel Psychology*, *44*(4), 703–740. doi:10.1111/j.1744-6570.1991.tb00696.x

Viswesvaran, C., & Ones, D. S. (1999). Meta-analyses of fakability estimates. Implications for personality measurement. *Educational and Psychological Measurement*, *59*(2), 197–210. doi:10.1177/00131649921969802

Woods v. Town of Danville, WV, 712 F. Supp. 2d 502 - Dist. Court, SD West Virginia (2010).

Young, M. S., & Schinka, J. A. (2001). Research validity scales for the NEO PI-R: Additional evidence for reliability and validity. *Journal of Personality Assessment*, *76*(3), 412–420. doi:10.1207/S15327752JPA7603_04 PMID:11499455

Chapter 5
Current Issues in Psychological Fitness-for-Duty Evaluations of Law Enforcement Officers:
Legal and Practice Implications

Martin J. Mayer
Jones & Mayer, USA

David M. Corey
Corey & Stewart, USA

ABSTRACT

Courts throughout the United States have ruled that that the "awesome powers" entrusted to law enforcement officers, and the safety-sensitive nature of their positions, impose on their public employers a responsibility to ensure that they are fit to perform their duties. But, as with an officer's powers, the authority of a police employer to mandate a psychological fitness-for-duty evaluation (FFDE) is not without boundaries. This chapter addresses the legal authority of a police employer to require an FFDE, the limits to that authority, and the implications of these constraints both for police employers and the psychologists who conduct these evaluations on their behalf. Written by two prominent experts in police employment law and police psychology, this chapter concerns itself with both the law and professional standards of practice. Key topics include the legal threshold for requiring an FFDE, limitations to the content of an FFDE report, and evaluator qualifications.

INTRODUCTION

A long series of statutory and case law authority dating back more than 50 years establishes both the right and the obligation of police employers to ensure that their officers are physically and mentally fit to perform their job duties and exercise the powers of a law enforcement officer (*Bonsignore v. City of New York,* 1982; *Conte v. Horcher,* 1977; *People ex rel. Ballinger v. O'Connor,* 1982). Although quite broad, the authority of a police employer to order an officer to submit to a psychological fitness-for-

DOI: 10.4018/978-1-5225-0813-7.ch005

duty evaluation (FFDE) is not without restrictions. The law—comprised of statutes and regulations, and court decisions that interpret the meaning and application of both—also places constraints on the scope of the evaluation, the acquisition and communication of private information, the role of a mental health expert in making employment decisions, and, in some jurisdictions, who is qualified to perform these evaluations. Standards of practice and ethics also serve to guide a police psychologist's decisions concerning the antecedent conditions, informed consent, assessment methods, reporting constraints, and other considerations associated with FFDEs (American Psychological Association [APA], 2015; International Association of Chiefs of Police [IACP], 2013).

Indeed, it is where the law and standards of psychological practice intersect that the parameters of a proper FFDE can be found. In this chapter, we focus on this intersection and discuss emerging trends in the law and their practice implications for both the police employer and psychologist. This chapter is not intended to provide legal advice, which necessarily requires an attorney's consideration of the facts of a particular case in combination with state and federal law, provisions of any collective bargaining agreement, institutional policies and procedures, and local risk management decisions. Furthermore, this chapter is intended to supplement, not supplant, existing treatises on the topic (e.g., APA, 2015; Corey, 2011; Corey & Borum, 2013; Fischler, McElroy, Miller, Saxe-Clifford, Stewart, & Zelig, 2011; Gold & Shuman, 2009; Piechowski & Drukteinis, 2011; Rostow & Davis, 2004; Stone, 2000) by focusing on contemporary issues and controversies.

The Legal Threshold

Once an employee is on the job, actual performance is generally the best measure of the employee's ability to do the job (Equal Employment Opportunity Commission [EEOC], 1995). Courts have long held that capricious, retaliatory, or punitive demands for psychological evaluations of incumbent employees "*based solely on the will and not the reason of the public employer*, would constitute an arbitrary and unlawful imposition of terms and conditions of public employment" (*Hill v. City of Winona,* 1990, at 661, footnote 1, emphasis added; see also *McGreal v. Ostrov,* 2004; *Merillat v. Michigan State University,* 1994; *Watts v. Alfred,* 1992). On the other hand, courts also have given broad authority to employers to mandate medical evaluations of their employees, particularly those engaged in safety-sensitive work, when doing so serves the goal of reducing the risk of injury to the employee or others. The standard for justifying an FFDE is often referred to as the "threshold" (cf. APA, 2015; IACP, 2013). We next discuss three elements of the legal threshold question: when FFDEs *may be* conducted (including when they do not violate an employee's legal rights), when they *should be* conducted, and when they *should not be* conducted.

When Fitness-for-Duty Evaluations May Be Conducted

The Americans with Disabilities Act of 1990 (ADA, 1990) is the federal statute with the greatest controlling authority over an employer's ability to require a medical evaluation of an employee. However, it must also be noted that state laws may provide greater protections than do the ADA. In California, for example, the Fair Employment and Housing Act (FEHA, 2011) is just such a law.

According to the ADA, when an employer has a reasonable belief, based on objective evidence, that a police officer may have a psychological condition that impairs his or her ability to perform essential job functions or poses a direct threat, an FFDE is "job-related and consistent with business necessity"

(42 U.S.C. §12112[d][4][A]; 29 C.F.R. §1630.14[c]). Case law has established that an employer need not wait for objective evidence of impaired performance before justifying an FFDE when the employee is engaged in dangerous work.

In *Brownfield v. City of Yakima* (2010), a federal circuit court upheld the validity of a police chief's order for an FFDE even before there was any evidence of impaired work performance, noting, "Police officers are likely to encounter extremely stressful and dangerous situations during the course of their work. When a police department has *good reason* to doubt an officer's ability to respond to these situations in an appropriate manner, an FFDE is consistent with the business necessity" (at 1147, citations omitted, italics added). Setting new legal ground, the Court held that the business necessity standard can be met *even before* an employee's work performance declines when the employer is engaged in dangerous work and "is faced with significant evidence that could cause a reasonable person to inquire as to whether an employee is still capable of performing his job" (at 1146, citations omitted).

In the federal law enforcement context where the legal standard for justifying a psychological FFDE is not the ADA, but rather 5 C.F.R. § 339.206 (cf. *Slater v. Department of Homeland Security,* 2008), the legal threshold is lower for positions in which a reasonable probability of substantial harm can be anticipated from the nature of the position (*Lassiter v. Department of Justice,* 1993). In *Butler v. Thornburgh* (1990), a federal circuit court held that "where the employee's position implicates the safety of others, and the potential harm is severe, even a low probability that the harm will occur may be sufficient to establish a direct threat" (at 876). Other courts have reached similar decisions (e.g., *Hogarth v. Thornburgh,* 1993; *Myers v. Hose,* 1995).

Indeed, in *Brownfield v. City of Yakima* (2010), the Court acknowledged that its "consideration of the FFDEs' legitimacy is heavily colored by the nature of Brownfield's employment" (at 1146) as a police officer. The Court pointed out that officers are engaged in "extremely stressful and dangerous situations" and are placed "in positions where they can do tremendous harm if they act irrationally" (at 1147, citing *Watson v. City of Miami Beach,* 1999).

In *City of Greenwood v. Dowler* (1986), an Indiana appellate court held that the attempted suicide of a police officer was sufficient grounds to terminate a police officer, whereas it might be inadequate to warrant termination of other public employees. The appeals court panel wrote,

A policeman frequently works alone, wields authority, carries lethal weapons which he is empowered to use in proper circumstances, and exercises wide discretion continuously while on and off duty. He must, at a moment's notice, be prepared to pursue dangerous criminals and shoot them if necessary, or be shot. He may expect high speed chases. He is confronted with extricating hurt, dead, and dying people from vehicular accidents. In short, it is not an occupation for the fainthearted, a person with weak nerves, or a person with questionable emotional maturity. Such unfortunate afflictions go to the very heart of the qualifications of a police officer. Lack of control and bad judgment can result in grave consequences .... From all the evidence, reasonable people may conclude (though reasonable people could disagree) that [the officer] had become sufficiently emotionally unstable as to be unreliable as a policeman in stress situations. (at 1085-1086)

The "business necessity standard" articulated in the ADA has generally been understood to require some level of *objective evidence* giving rise to reasonable concerns about a *particular* individual's medical fitness to justify an employer-mandated FFDE. This interpretation derives from the EEOC's enforcement guidance:

An employer's reasonable belief that an employee's ability to perform essential job functions will be impaired by a medical condition or that s/he will pose a direct threat due to a medical condition must be based on objective evidence obtained, or reasonably available to the employer, prior to making a disability-related inquiry or requiring a medical examination. Such a belief requires an assessment of the employee and his/her position and cannot be based on general assumptions. (EEOC, 2000, Question 5)

The EEOC's long-held position has been that the ADA's business necessity standard does not permit medical testing of an incumbent employee unless and until the employer has an individualized, reasonable suspicion of impairment or direct threat due to a medical condition. As a result, the practice of routinely referring police officers involved in shootings and other traumatic events for fitness evaluations has been argued to violate the ADA's prohibition against medical examinations that are not job-related and consistent with business necessity (cf. Corey, 2011; Trompetter, Corey, Schmidt, & Tracy, 2011). Recent federal case law challenges this position.

For example, in *EEOC v. U.S. Steel Corporation* (2013), the Court examined U.S. Steel's union-approved practice of conducting random drug and alcohol testing on its probationary employees, which the EEOC insisted was in violation of the business necessity standard. However, the Court held that the alcohol testing policy—which had no individualized assessment component based on suspicion, reasonable or otherwise, but rather was an "across-the-board" policy devoid of any individual consideration—served the business necessity of eliminating hazards in the workplace.

In finding for U.S. Steel, the Court held that the medical examination or inquiry at issue must genuinely serve the asserted business necessity and be "no broader or more intrusive than necessary" (at 61, quoting *Conroy v. New York State Dep't of Correctional Servs.*, 2003). The Court concluded, "Where employers advancing safety as the business necessity demonstrate that the medical test or inquiry 'makes even a small contribution to reducing the risks posed by unfit [employees], it is amply justified'" (at 66, quoting *Transport Workers Union of Am., Local 100, AFL-CIO v. N.Y. City Transit Auth.*, 2004), particularly when "employees are charged with performing dangerous and safety-sensitive duties" (at 70).

Notably, the EEOC conceded that the business necessity exception articulated in 42 U.S.C. § 12112(d)(4)(A) encompasses periodic across-the-board drug and alcohol testing of police officers, firefighters, private security officers, and other positions affecting "public safety." In *EEOC v. U.S. Steel,* the Court rejected this exemption as being too narrow:

Even if police officers and firefighters can be distinguished as being public servants whose jobs are to protect the public, the agency ignores that private security officers, bus drivers, flight attendants, and nuclear plant operators have no such overriding duty to protect the public. These are jobs that, if performed badly, could result in harm to others in the general public. Yet, there is no reason to deem the lives of those in the general public less worthy of protecting than the lives of one's co-workers. Where the guiding principle of the business necessity exception is to permit employers to take preemptive steps to protect people from injury, the Court sees no reason to make a distinction in the kinds of people that such employers are allowed to protect. The life of a person is no less valuable simply because he or she decided to work in a factory rather than take a walk through the park. (at 83)

Under the reasoning of *EEOC vs. U.S. Steel* (2013), police employers may be able to adopt a policy to routinely evaluate police officers who have been exposed to a significant trauma (e.g., officer-involved shooting) or stressful assignment (e.g., prolonged undercover or child sex crime unit assignment) with high potential to impair job functioning ***when*** the purpose of the policy is to protect the officer, fellow officers, or the public; the scope of the evaluation is no broader or intrusive than necessary; and the medical examination is reasonably expected to reduce the risk of harm. Again, it must be noted that individual state laws and/or labor agreements might require the employer to meet with and secure support from the relevant labor organizations, as did U.S. Steel in this case.

Practice guidelines that cast such employer policies as violating the ADA's prohibition against unwarranted medical examinations and inquiries on the basis that they are contrary to the EEOC's enforcement guidance should be revisited. However, the fact that such medical evaluations may be legally permissible does not necessarily render those evaluations equivalent to FFDEs, inasmuch as these latter evaluations, by definition, tend to be evaluations in which the referral is justified by objective and individualized evidence. In addition, local employer/employee labor agreements might limit the employer's ability to compel such tests.

Each of the federal cases just discussed (*Brownfield v. City of Yakima,* 2010; *EEOC vs. U.S. Steel,* 2013; *Lassiter v. Department of Justice,* 1993; *Slater v. Department of Homeland Security,* 2008; *Transport Workers Union of Am., Local 100, AFL-CIO v. N.Y. City Transit Auth.,* 2004) joins a legacy of similar cases establishing that neither the ADA, nor the Code of Federal Regulations, bars an employer from requiring a medical evaluation as a condition of an employee's continued employment when (1) the employer is engaged in safety-sensitive work; (2) the consequences of impaired work performance may have catastrophic consequences for the employee being referred for evaluation or for others; and (3) the mandated evaluation is reasonably expected to serve the employer's safety goals.

Until recently, the courts have held the position that employees released from medical leave under the Family & Medical Leave Act (FMLA) of 1993 are to be afforded special consideration, and this position has also been reflected in professional practice (Corey, 2011). More recently, this position has come under challenge.

The FMLA stipulates that when an employee returns from medical leave the employee is entitled to be reinstated to his or her position or an equivalent position (29 U.S.C. § 2614[a][1]). If the employer has a uniformly applied practice or policy requiring it, the employer also may require each employee taking FMLA leave to provide certification from the employee's health care provider that the employee is able to resume work (29 U.S.C. § 2614[a][4]). Most courts have interpreted the FMLA as prohibiting an employer from compelling an employee returning from FMLA leave to submit to an independent evaluation of his or her fitness for duty once certified by the treating health care provider as ready to return to work, although pre-leave or post-return behavior may justify an FFDE (*Albert v. Runyon,* 1998; see also *Brumbalough v. Camelot Care Centers*, 2005). When an employer is able to establish that it would have ordered an FFDE *had the employee not taken leave*, courts have generally held such an examination to be permissible once the employee has been reinstated (*Carrillo v. National Council of Churches of Christ in the USA*, 1997).

In *White v. County of Los Angeles* (2014), the Court held that an employer is permitted to seek its own evaluation of an employee's fitness for duty—after returning the employee to work but before returning him or her to duty—when it is not satisfied with the employee's health care provider's certification and there was a "pre-leave" basis to justify an FFDE. Susan White was employed as a Senior District Attorney Investigator with the Los Angeles County District Attorney's Office, a position requiring peace officer status under California Government Code § 1031. In 2009, White began experiencing emotional difficulties and was observed acting erratically at work "with very high emotional highs and very low lows." In early 2010, White made a poor tactical decision while serving a search warrant, which jeopardized her own and others' safety and led to her coworkers being concerned that she was psychologically unstable.

White disclosed to coworkers and her supervisors that she was on medication, and she was seen crying, anxious, and exhibiting mood swings. Although White's behavior improved briefly after her supervisors discussed their observations with her, concerns about her fitness for duty culminated in early 2011 when she gave court testimony containing significant factual errors. Shortly after, White tearfully told her supervisors that she needed to take off a month for inpatient and outpatient treatment, which was later extended to three months. At the end of that treatment period, White's health care provider wrote a letter to her employer stating that she would be able to return to work and perform the essential functions of her position, effective September 7, 2011.

On September 6, 2011, the employer notified White that she would be placed on paid administrative leave and reassigned to her home effective September 7, 2011. She was subsequently ordered to submit to an FFDE. White sought a court injunction against the FFDE, arguing that requiring her to perform the medical reevaluation violated her right under the FMLA to be restored to employment on her doctor's certification alone. The lower court issued a permanent injunction preventing the District Attorney (DA) from requiring White to submit to the FFDE based on her pre-leave conduct, stating, "Nobody is disputing based on the facts of 2010, 2011 that Ms. White should be reevaluated. The whole point of the [FMLA] is that she was[,] by her own psychologist."

The DA appealed and the Court of Appeal addressed the question of whether, after an employee has been returned to work as required by the FMLA, the employer is prohibited by the FMLA from requiring a medical reevaluation related to the serious health condition for which the employee was granted leave. The Court concluded that "it is not [prohibited from ordering an FFDE], even where such reevaluation involves matters existing prior to the FMLA leave."

The Court's rationale in *White* rested on a 2008 addition in the language of the U.S. Department of Labor's FMLA regulations: "Requirements under the Americans with Disabilities Act (ADA), as amended, apply. After an employee returns from FMLA leave, the ADA requires any medical examination at an employer's expense by the employer's health care provider be job-related and consistent with business necessity" (29 C.F.R. § 825.312[h]).

The Court made note of the Department of Labor's explanation for this change, including, in part, that the added language "intends to make clear that, once an employee returns to work and is no longer on FMLA leave, an employer may require a medical exam under the guidelines and restrictions imposed by the ADA. At that point, the FMLA's fitness-for-duty regulation no longer applies" (73 Fed. Reg. 67934-01, 68036). The Court wrote,

Thus, it is clear that the Department [of Labor] intended to clarify that a bright line exists at the employee's return to work. Before the return to work, the employer must accept the employee's physician's certification and return the employee to employment; after the return to employment, the FMLA protections no longer apply, and the employer may require a FFDE consistent with the ADA. (at 704)

A Justified FFDE Does Not Violate an Employee's Rights

In *Dengel v. Waukesha County* (2014), after several disturbing workplace incidents, Dengel was referred to the Employee Assistance Program (EAP). Due to a dispute regarding disclosure of information, he refused to return. Dengel's attorney requested that the County provide reasons for its concern with Dengel's mental state. In response, the County stated that it did not believe Dengel had a medical issue—merely a behavioral one. It also clarified that it was no longer seeking a fitness-for-duty evaluation, but that it still needed a return-to-work release. Dengel disagreed, and when his leave expired without him taking any action, Human Resources sent him a letter informing him that it viewed him to have voluntarily terminated his employment.

Dengel subsequently filed suit alleging, among other things, ADA violations. The Court held, "Inquiries into an employee's psychiatric health are often permissible when they reflect concern for the safety of employees and the 'public at large,' especially in jobs affecting public safety.... Moreover, where there is evidence of instability or potential danger, employers are generally justified in seeking mental evaluations" (at 993). Reviewing all of the County's concerns, the Court said, "Dengel's behavior and his sensitive position show that the County's requirement that Mr. Dengel visit EAP and obtain a return to work authorization were clearly job-related and consistent with a business necessity."

In *Franklin v. City of Slidell* (2013), Franklin, a minority senior corrections officer, brought action against the city alleging that he was required to take a fitness-for-duty evaluation and was relieved of his duties in retaliation for filing a discrimination complaint and civil lawsuit in violation of Title VII of the Civil Rights Act of 1964. Additionally, he alleged that he was required to take a medical and psychological fitness-for-duty evaluation before returning to work from medical leave in violation of the Americans with Disabilities Act (ADA).

The Court found that "[p]laintiff engaged in erratic behavior before and during his period of medical leave, ... and it was necessary and appropriate to require Plaintiff to pass a fitness for duty examination before resuming his duties as a senior corrections officer in light of the nature of that position and City policies. In light the City's proffered nondiscriminatory reasons for its actions, the burden shifts to Plaintiff to produce evidence that these proffered reasons are merely pretext for retaliation." In *Franklin,* the plaintiff failed to provide such evidence.

When Fitness-for-Duty Evaluations Should Be Conducted

The previous discussion highlights the foundational standard that FFDEs, like all medical evaluations of incumbent employees, must be legally justified. But beyond the right of an employer to require an FFDE is its *obligation* to do so under circumstances that put the officer, fellow officers, or the public in peril. Many jurisdictions throughout the country impose upon law enforcement management the duty to ensure that law enforcement officers are both physically and psychologically fit for duty. This is due, in part, to the authority exercised by law enforcement officers, as well as statutory law and court decisions.

In *Thomas v. Johnson* (1968), the federal court held that "[t]he municipal employer will generally be held liable where it has retained an agent whose past history did in fact, *or should have*, put the municipality on notice of the *agent's* propensity for violence or *instability*" (at 1031; emphasis added). The *Johnson* court stated further, "[I]f negligence in the selection of unfit persons or *retention of known incompetents* can be shown on the part of members of the appointing authority, recovery of damages against the municipality will follow subject to the proximate cause limitation" (at 1031; emphasis in original).

In *Moon v. Winfield* (1973), the federal court stated that where the head of a law enforcement agency "is under some affirmative duty to act and he fails to act accordingly, he may be held negligently responsible for his omission" (at 845). The Court noted that there are several situations which could impose a duty on the agency head to act. For example, knowledge of situations involving a history of misconduct, or complaints regarding "physical abuse or malicious or threatening conduct towards civilians," or instances of "questionable mental stability," raise issues of fact as to the possible negligence on the part of the head of an agency if nothing is done to determine fitness for duty (at 845, emphasis added). Under those circumstances, the Court states, the officer should be assigned "to some other duty where he is under close supervision and has limited contact with the public" (at 845).

Under federal civil rights statute 18 U.S.C. § 1983, a plaintiff may sue public employers and supervisors who negligently hire, supervise, and retain an employee. To establish such negligence, a plaintiff must prove that (1) the employer and/or supervisor had actual or constructive knowledge that his or her subordinate was engaged in conduct that posed a pervasive and unreasonable risk of constitutional injury to citizens; (2) the employer's or supervisor's response to that knowledge was so inadequate as to show "deliberate indifference" to, or tacit authorization of, the alleged offensive practices; and (3) there was an affirmative causal link between the employer's or supervisor's inaction and the alleged constitutional injury.

Courts have frequently referred to the fact that law enforcement agents are entrusted with an "awesome power" (e.g., *In re Muhammed C.,* 2002; *People v. Quiroga,* 1993). In *Duran v. City of Douglas* (1990), the Court stated when discussing derogatory language used toward law enforcement officers that, "while police, no less than anyone else, may resent having obscene words and gestures directed at them, they may not *exercise the awesome power at their disposal* to punish individuals for conduct that is not merely lawful, but protected by the First Amendment" (at 1378, emphasis added). Because of the awesome power granted to peace officers, numerous restrictions and obligations are imposed on those officers and/or their employer.

For instance, in California, the Government Code mandates that one must be free from certain emotional or mental conditions in order to possess the powers of a peace officer. Government Code § 1031 states, in part, "Each class of public officers or employees declared by law to be peace officers shall meet all of the following minimum standards: (f) Be found to be free from any physical, emotional, or mental condition that might adversely affect the exercise of the powers of a peace officer." Similar laws containing exclusionary criteria exist in Arizona (Arizona Regulation 13-4-107), Georgia (Georgia Administrative Rules and Regulations 464-3-.02), Idaho (Idaho POST Council Administrative Rules 11.11.058), and no fewer than 11 other states (cf. Corey & Borum, 2013).

It is an erroneous assumption, however, that state statutes pertaining to a law enforcement officer's eligibility for employment pertain only to preemployment requirements. In *Sager v. County of Yuba* (2007), the California Court of Appeal held that this statute, and the associated regulations of the California Peace Officer Standards and Training (POST) Commission, apply equally to incumbent law enforcement officers. The Court wrote that "the section 1031 standards must also be maintained throughout a peace officer's career. Section 1031 reflects a minimum set of standards for allowing a new recruit to become a peace officer and it would be illogical to conclude the Legislature believed those standards disappeared once an officer began working" (at 8).

In *Brown v. Sandy City Appeal Board* (2014), the Utah Court of Appeals reached a similar decision and, like the *Sager* court, approved the use of the California POST Commission's psychological screening dimensions in a psychological FFDE. In *Brown,* the Court permitted the application of these California screening criteria to the FFDE of a Utah police officer to "flesh out" the more general Utah requirement of mental competence, stating:

We view [the psychologist's] consideration of the California POST standards as analogous to the way that a court might use case law from sister jurisdictions—not as binding authority but as a reference to consider how other courts have analyzed and resolved a particular issue. Here, California and Utah apparently share a common requirement that peace officers be mentally fit for duty. However, unlike Utah, California has provided additional guidance for evaluating officers' mental competence. (at 771)

Laws defining the psychological standards for both initial and *ongoing* eligibility as a law enforcement officer—in combination with state and federal statutes that make it possible to sue public employers and supervisors for negligent hiring, training and retention—establish a professional duty to mandate FFDEs when public safety is in peril. In *Conte v. Horcher* (1977), the Illinois Appeals Court held that a police chief's order for a police lieutenant to submit to an FFDE was "not only valid and proper, but *also necessary to assure the effective performance of the department*" (at 569). In *Bonsignore v. City of New York* (1982), the federal court held that "[t]he City could reasonably have anticipated that its *negligence* in failing to identify officers who were unfit to carry guns would result in an unfit officer injuring someone using the gun he was required to carry" (at 638, emphasis added). These landmark decisions have been followed by a long line of similar court decisions granting police employers the authority to mandate FFDEs when justified by safety considerations (cf. *Kraft v. Police Commissioner of Boston* [1994], holding that a police chief could require a reinstated detective to pass a psychological evaluation before recertifying him to carry a firearm; *Krocka v. City of Chicago* [2000], finding that it was "entirely reasonable, and even responsible" for the Chicago Police Department to evaluate the officer's fitness for duty "once it learned that he was experiencing difficulties with his mental health" [at 515]; *Watson v. City of Miami Beach* [1999], deciding that "[i]n any case where a police department reasonably perceives an officer to be even mildly paranoid, hostile, or oppositional, a fitness-for-duty examination is job-related and consistent with business necessity" [at 935]).

The case of *Keslosky v. Borough of Old Forge* (2014) illustrates an employer's authority to mandate an FFDE when ongoing eligibility is reasonably in doubt. Keslosky began working as a police officer on September 1, 1979. On March 13, 1998 he stopped working, claiming to be suffering from a stress-related work injury due to harassment at work. He received treatment from a family physician, a psychologist, and a psychiatrist. The psychiatrist, Dr. David Liskov, opined that he would "be very reluctant to psychiatrically clear this individual to continue in the capacity of a Police Officer if paranoid symptoms are indeed pathological (which they appear [to be] at this time)" (at 5).

The situation continued for several years but eventually Keslosky was ordered to return to work. However, the Municipal Police Officers Education and Training Commission noted that his certification had expired in 1999 and outlined the steps he needed to take to become eligible for certification as a police officer, including medical examinations. Keslosky was notified of the requirements and his attorney responded, stating that Keslosky would not submit to either the physical or psychological examination. As a result, he was suspended without pay.

Keslosky filed suit and the trial court upheld the suspension due to his refusal to submit to the medical evaluations. The trial court concluded that Keslosky's suspension was proper because he lacked a valid police officer certification. The trial court also concluded Keslosky was ineligible to receive compensation after his certification expired and denied him back pay. The appeals court affirmed.

The obligation of a police employer to require an otherwise justifiable FFDE is also established by the Occupational Safety and Health Act (1970). In passing this law, Congress acknowledged a broad employer obligation to protect the safety and health of all employees (Morgan & Duvall, 1983).

But even when an FFDE is squarely within the employer's rights, and even when it is clear that the employer must take action to fulfill its obligations to maintain safety in the workplace and the community, an FFDE is not always the *best* choice. The IACP FFDE Guidelines (IACP, 2013) acknowledge this:

When deciding whether or not to conduct an FFDE, both the agency and examiner should take into account its potential usefulness and appropriateness given the specific circumstances, and the agency should consider whether other remedies (e.g., education, training, discipline, physical FFDE) might be more appropriate or useful instead of, or in addition to, a psychological FFDE. (Guideline 4.2)

In *Conroy v. N.Y. State Dep't of Corr. Serv.* (2003), the Second Circuit Court of Appeals endorsed the opinion of the Ninth Circuit decision in *Cripe v. City of San Jose* (2001), which held that "[t]he business necessity standard is quite high, and is not [to be] confused with mere expediency" (at 890). The *Conroy* court went on to write,

An employer cannot simply demonstrate that an inquiry is convenient or beneficial to its business. Instead, the employer must first show that the asserted "business necessity" is vital to the business. For example, business necessities may include ensuring that the workplace is safe and secure or cutting down on egregious absenteeism. The employer must also show that the examination or inquiry genuinely serves the asserted business necessity and that the request is ***no broader or more intrusive than necessary.*** *The employer need not show that the examination or inquiry is the only way of achieving a business necessity, but the examination or inquiry must be a reasonably effective method of achieving the employer's goal. (at 97-98, emphasis added)*

Certainly there are instances in which an impaired officer, once confronted with the concerns of the employer, agrees that he or she is unfit for duty, in need of mental health care, and voluntarily agrees to obtain that care while on medical leave. However, this situation does not obviate the need for an independent FFDE upon certification by the employee's treating provider of the employee's eventual readiness to return to work.

When Fitness-for-Duty Evaluations Should Not Be Conducted

The preceding discussion underscores the broad legal authority and responsibility granted to law enforcement employers when a police officer's fitness for duty is reasonably placed at issue. However, the reasonableness of an employer's fitness concerns is a critically important factor in determining the legitimacy of any requirement that an incumbent employee submit to a medical examination, even when engaged in safety-sensitive work.

When an employer determines that an employee's conduct warrants termination based upon his or her behavior, an FFDE would be inappropriate and unnecessarily complicate the record in the event of appeal or adjudication. Should the conduct-based termination be later overturned by an arbitrator or other trier of fact, an FFDE may then be required if otherwise justified, but the timing of that evaluation would be placed where it is most meaningful: namely, in proximity to the employee's return to duty.

In *Palmer v. Circuit Court of Cook County* (1997), the Seventh Circuit Court of Appeals affirmed an employer's right to terminate a mentally ill worker who repeatedly threatened to kill her superior and sought reasonable accommodation. The Court held,

[I]f an employer fires an employee because of the employee's unacceptable behavior, the fact that that behavior was precipitated by a mental illness does not present an issue under the Americans with Disabilities Act. The Act does not require an employer to retain a potentially violent employee. Such a requirement would place the employer on a razor's edge—in jeopardy of violating the Act if it fired such an employee, yet in jeopardy of being deemed negligent if it retained him and he hurt someone. The Act protects only "qualified" employees, that is, employees qualified to do the job for which they were hired; and threatening other employees disqualifies one. It is true that an employer has a statutory duty to make a "reasonable accommodation" to an employee's disability, that is, an adjustment in working conditions to enable the employee to overcome his disability, if the employer can do this without "undue hardship." But we cannot believe that this duty runs in favor of employees who commit or threaten to commit violent acts. The retention of such an employee would cause justifiable anxiety to co-workers and supervisors. It would be unreasonable to demand of the employer either that it force its employees to put up with this or that it station guards to prevent the mentally disturbed employee from getting out of hand. (352-353)

Other courts have held that an employee's simple misconduct, without a reasonable basis for inferring a mental health impairment, does not meet the legal requirement for a medical evaluation (*Maplewood and Law Enf. Labor Services,* 1996; *McGreal v. Ostrov,* 2004; *Merillat v. Mich. St. Univ.,* 1994; *Watts v. Alfred,* 1992). Avoiding unwarranted FFDEs is particularly important given the broad recognition that a mandatory psychological examination may constitute "a stigma, an official branding" of the employee (*Stewart v. Pearce,* 1973).

Even in instances in which an FFDE *should be* mandated, it may be preferable to postpone the evaluation until other less privacy-intrusive measures have been carried out. For example, when an employee requests permissible leave (e.g., sick leave, FMLA) to obtain treatment, it may be preferable to allow the employee the opportunity to obtain the needed intervention before requiring an independent evaluation of his or her fitness. Doing otherwise is more likely to require two evaluations—the first to document what the employee already concedes, and the second to assess the employee's fitness after some period of treatment—when only the latter evaluation may be needed.

It is important to keep in mind that even when an FFDE may be justified under one statute (e.g., the ADA), it may be prohibited under another. A particularly relevant exception involves returning U.S. military reservists. The Uniformed Services Employment and Reemployment Rights Act of 1994 (USERRA, 1994; USERRA Final Rule, 2006) entitles veterans to reemployment after military service in either the position they would have held absent their departure for military service "or a position of like seniority, status and pay" (38 U.S.C. § 4313[a][2][A]; see *Petty v. Metropolitan Government of Nashville-Davidson County*, 2008). However, similar to an employer's right to require an FFDE of an employee returning to service from FMLA leave (*White v. County of Los Angeles,* 2014), an employer may require an *otherwise justified* FFDE after properly reemploying the veteran.

Procedural Issues in Conducting Fitness-for-Duty Evaluations

As we have discussed, police employers are granted wide but not unlimited authority to require FFDEs of law enforcement officers reasonably suspected of a mental health condition that substantially limits their ability to safely and effectively perform the duties of their position. We turn next to a discussion of three important procedural issues in conducting FFDEs that, if inadequately considered, may pose liability to both the employer and examiner and may diminish the probative value of the examination in determining the ultimate question of the officer's psychological fitness for duty. These issues are (1) the scope of the FFDE, (2) the content of the FFDE report, and (3) the qualifications of the fitness examiner.

The Scope of the Fitness-for-Duty Evaluation

Once justified, an FFDE must be restricted either to the condition discovered by the employer or to the condition(s) reasonably linked to the behavioral issues giving rise to the employer's concerns. Under the ADA, "[t]he inquiries or examinations must not exceed the scope of the specific medical condition and its effect on the employee's ability, with or without reasonable accommodation, to perform essential job functions or to work without posing a direct threat" (EEOC, 1997, p. 10). Although, as discussed previously in this chapter, an employer may require a medical examination when an employee who has been on medical leave seeks to return to work, "[t]he employer may not use the employee's leave as a justification for making far-ranging disability-related inquiries or requiring an unrelated medical examination" (EEOC, 2000 at Question 17). Instead, medical inquiries and requests for medical documentation must be limited to what is needed to assess the employee's ability to work and, as noted by the court in *Conroy v. N.Y. State Dep't of Corr. Serv.* (2003), must be "no broader or more intrusive than necessary" (at 98).

Corey (2011) has suggested that when it is not yet confirmed that the subject of an FFDE actually has a medical or mental health condition, as when the referral results from a sudden, adverse change in behavior or work performance,

[T]he scope of the examination should be narrowed to those conditions reasonably linked to the problem behavior or other objective evidence giving rise to the referral. On the other hand, when an employee with a previously diagnosed condition is referred for evaluation to determine his or her readiness to return to work, the scope of the evaluation must be limited to that condition. In any case, an examination for either inability to perform essential functions of the job or possible direct threat must be narrowly tailored to seek only that information necessary to address those referral questions. (p. 278, citations omitted)

The IACP FFDE Guidelines (IACP, 2013, Guidelines 7 and 9) also provide guidance on the sources and types of information that would likely be included in the scope of a properly conducted FFDE, noting that "all collected information be clearly related to job performance issues and/or the suspected job-impairing mental condition" (Guideline 7.4). These include:

1. A written description of the objective evidence giving rise to concerns about the employee's fitness for duty and any particular questions that the employer wishes the examiner to address.
2. Background and collateral information regarding the employee's past and recent performance, conduct, and functioning, including:
    a. Job class specifications and/or job description.
    b. Performance evaluations.
    c. Previous remediation efforts.
    d. Commendations and testimonials.
    e. Internal affairs investigations.
    f. Formal citizen/public complaints.
    g. Use-of-force incidents.

h. Reports related to officer-involved shootings.
i. Civil claims.
j. Disciplinary actions.
k. Incident reports related to any triggering events.
l. Medical records.
m. Prior psychological evaluations.
n. Other supporting or relevant documentation related to the employee's psychological fitness for duty.

The guidelines also stipulate that, "[i]n some cases, an examiner may ask the examinee to provide relevant medical or mental health treatment records and other data for the examiner to consider" (Guideline 7.4). The EEOC provides the following guidance on this topic:

[I]n most situations, an employer cannot request an employee's complete medical records because they are likely to contain information unrelated to whether the employee can perform his/her essential functions or work without posing a direct threat. (EEOC, 2000, Question 13)

Thus, when requesting any of the records set forth above, examiners should consider whether the request is, as the ADA requires, "no broader or intrusive than necessary," and whether they may be disclosed under state law.

Employers occasionally withhold from the examiner important medical and personnel records that they have in their possession, often due to the mistaken belief that the Health Insurance Portability and Accountability Act (HIPAA; 2000a, 2000b) requires the employee's authorization to release them. Two facts oppose this practice.

First, HIPAA's Privacy Rule (2000b) does not apply to the employer in its role as custodian of employment-related records, including those held in the employee's separate medical file. Second, when conducting employer-mandated medical evaluations, the examiner is an agent of the employer (*Jimenez v. Dyncorp International,* 2009); consequently, information held by the employer may be disclosed to the examiner as long as it is reasonably expected to further the purpose of an otherwise justified evaluation. Instances in which the employer fails to do so can pose significant liability when the withheld records are later determined to be "a moving force" behind harm caused by an employee erroneously found to be fit for duty as a partial consequence of the examiner's blocked access to the withheld information (cf. *Colon v. City of Newark,* 2006).

One aspect of the scope of the fitness evaluation that is often overlooked by an examiner is the question of fitness *sustainability.* Under the terms of the ADA Amendments Act (2009) and the final regulations, an impairment that is episodic or in remission meets the definition of disability if it would substantially limit a major life activity when active. According to the EEOC (2015),

This means that chronic impairments with symptoms or effects that are episodic rather than present all the time can be a disability even if the symptoms or effects would only substantially limit a major life activity when the impairment is active. The Appendix [Section 1630.2(j)(1)(vii) and corresponding Appendix section] provides examples of impairments that may be episodic, including epilepsy, hypertension, asthma, diabetes, major depressive disorder, bipolar disorder, and schizophrenia. (Question 11)

Thus, an evaluative focus on the employee's current functioning without also considering the positive and negative effects from an individual's use of one or more mitigating measures (that is, measures intended to eliminate or reduce the symptoms or impact of an impairment, including medication and counseling) is incomplete. An individual could erroneously be regarded as having no disability (and therefore not eligible for reasonable accommodation, even if requested) simply because mitigating measures rendered the employee non-symptomatic at the time of the FFDE, even when the impairment is episodic or recurring.

At the same time, an individualized assessment may show that such an employee, as a result of the past pattern of his or her impairment, the normal course of the impairment, the employee's history of treatment non-compliance, and the limitations and/or negative effects of the mitigating measures, may pose an elevated risk of near-term relapse. In such a case, even if the employee is for all intents and purposes fit for duty at the time of the evaluation, the *sustainability* of that fitness may be unreliable and, as a consequence, pose a direct threat. For this reason, it is important that the scope of the evaluation consider the episodic or recurring nature of an impairment, in addition to the positive and negative effects of mitigating measures when assessing fitness for duty.

Content of the FFDE Report

Within the broad subject of FFDEs, there is probably no topic more controversial, or more fraught with potential liability, than what information the employer is entitled to receive from the examiner after the FFDE is completed. The ADA itself is silent on the topic; it is the EEOC's enforcement language that is instructive: "An employer is entitled only to the information necessary to determine whether the employee can do the essential functions of the job or work without posing a direct threat" (EEOC, 2000, Question 13).

But what information from an FFDE is needed for the employer to reach this determination? And what impact, if any, do state confidentiality statutes have on the answer? As we illustrate below, the answer to this second question varies greatly along state laws.

In *Sangirardi v. Village of Stickney* (2003), the Illinois Court of Appeals held that the state's "Confidentiality Act" (740 ILCS 110/1 et seq.) did not preclude a police employer from receiving the results of a mandated FFDE:

The authority to order fitness exams is justified by the unique, almost paramilitary nature of police departments and the critical importance of police officers to public health and safety. By necessary implication, the police department must have access to the ***ultimate fitness determination*** *of such exams in order to determine whether officers are capable of performing their duties. (at 798, emphasis added)*

Further, the Court found that Sangirardi had no reasonable expectation that the results of the FFDE would be kept confidential from the police chief because "fitness exams are part and parcel of the process officers must undergo in order to be hired and retained" (at 799). However, a year later, in *McGreal v. Ostrov* (2004), the Seventh Circuit Court of Appeals held that the *Sangirardi* decision did not entitle the police employer to "anything other than the fitness for duty determination. They were not entitled under any Illinois law to force the disclosure of the intimate and irrelevant details of [the employee's] home life" (at 690).

California confidentiality law, on the other hand, differs in important ways from Illinois law, and evaluating psychologists should be cautioned to learn what their respective jurisdictions require for a legally enforceable consent form and what information can be disclosed to a police employer in the absence of such consent. In the case of *Pettus v. Cole* (1996), the California Court of Appeal ruled, among other questions, on whether and to what extent medical information obtained during the psychiatric examination of an employee may be disclosed to the employer by a psychiatrist without the employee's authorization or consent, where the employee has requested leave from work because of a stress-related disability, the examination is required under the employer's short-term disability policy, and the examination is arranged and paid for by the employer.

Noting that the psychiatrists failed to obtain a specific written authorization to disclose their findings to the employer, the Court held that the psychiatrists violated Pettus's privacy rights under the state's "Confidentiality of Medical Information Act" (CMIA). As with Illinois's Confidentiality Act, the CMIA strictly prohibits the disclosure of medical information except when specifically authorized by the individual using a compliant form. The *Pettus* court concluded:

The Legislature recognized ... that the ability of employers to obtain some medical information without employee authorization may serve a legitimate purpose under some circumstances. At the same time it sought to preserve the employee's interest in maintaining the confidentiality of sensitive medical information in the employment context. To balance these interests, the Legislature restricted the information that may be disclosed without authorization to only that which is necessary to achieve the legitimate purpose. (at 66)

Absent a written authorization from the employee, the CMIA stipulates that an employer is entitled only to a description of the functional limitations of the employee that may entitle him or her to leave from work for medical reasons or limit the employee's fitness to perform his or her employment, provided that no statement of medical cause is included in the information disclosed. Notably, the CMIA includes an exception when the examination is conducted at the specific prior written request and expense of the employer and the disclosure is limited to that part of the information that is relevant to a lawsuit, arbitration, grievance, or other claim or challenge to which the employer and the employee are parties and in which the employee has placed in issue his or her medical history, mental or physical condition, or treatment, provided that the information is used or disclosed only in connection with that proceeding (Civil Code § 56.10[c][8]). Indeed, it is this latter exception that permits an evaluating psychologist in California to release to the employer a comprehensive written report once the employee challenges the psychologist's fitness determination.

It is important to note that both the *Pettus* and *McGreal* courts found that the examiners failed to obtain consent and authorization from their examinees using the forms required by the respective confidentiality statutes. In *McGreal,* the Court wrote that use of the form in that case would have "served the competing public policy interests in maintaining mental health confidentiality and ensuring a mentally fit police force" (footnote 4). The Court went on to write,

For example, if the officer disobeyed a reasonable order to submit to a mental health exam and refused to sign a valid consent to the disclosure necessary to determine fitness for duty, then the police department would be justified in discharging the officer. An officer could choose not to consent to disclosure but could not, in that instance, retain his position as a police officer. (footnote 4)

In *Pettus,* the Court limited its holding to instances in which CMIA-compliant consent and authorization is *not* obtained.[1] In *Anthony v. Village of South Holland* (2013), the federal district court enjoined Anthony's police employer from requiring him to irrevocably release his mental health records and ordered that the employer use a consent form that conforms to the Illinois Confidentiality Act, which includes "the right to revoke the consent at any time," among other provisions. However, when the employee does not give the necessary authorization, the examining psychologist is limited by statute to disclosing to the employer only that information permitted in the absence of consent (e.g., a description of the functional limitations of the employee that may entitle him or her to leave from work for medical reasons or limit the employee's fitness to perform his or her employment, provided that no statement of medical cause is included in the information disclosed).

In tension with any solution that deprives the employer of information pertaining to medical causation is the employer's need for sufficient medical information to determine whether the employee's functional limitations derive from a disability (EEOC, 2000) and, ultimately, whether the employee is psychologically fit for duty. In *Sager v. County of Yuba* (2007), a California appeal court held that the determination of a law enforcement officer's fitness for duty is a matter for the employer to decide, with consideration of, but not blind deference to, the opinion of its medical expert. In *Slater v. Department of Homeland Security* (2008), the Merit System Personnel Board concluded that FFDE reports that were "entirely conclusory, devoid of any medical documentation or explanation in support of their conclusions" carried less "credibility and reliability" than one that was "a thorough, detailed, and relevant medical opinion addressing the medical issues of the agency's removal action" (at 16).

The utility of a non-cursory report is also seen in the case of *Michael v. City of Troy Police Department* (2014). Michael was hired as a police officer by Troy in 1987. In March, 2000, he was diagnosed with a brain tumor and underwent a craniotomy that same month to remove the tumor. He subsequently underwent two more such operations in 2002 and 2009. "Because of certain incidents of what defendants regarded as odd behavior in the several months before plaintiff's third craniotomy, defendants required Michael to undergo a neuropsychological evaluation to determine his fitness to return to work after the surgery" (at 2-3).

Dr. Firoza Van Horn, a neuropsychologist, evaluated Michael on December 7, 2009 and reported that Michael's test results revealed several significant cognitive deficits. Dr. Van Horn concluded that "there is convincing evidence that Officer Michael is not competent to handle his duties as a police officer" (at 4).

Subsequently, five different doctors rendered opinions regarding Michael's fitness for duty with some finding that he was fit for duty and others finding that he was not. In March of 2012, Michael requested a "civilian desk position" and permission to work outside the department in security or asset protection. Both requests were denied. Michael filed his complaint in this matter on July 30, 2012, bringing two counts in his complaint: disability discrimination and retaliation, both in violation of the ADA.

Michael alleged he is not disabled but is perceived as disabled by the defendants. The defendants argued that Michael could not establish the second element of his prima facie case of discrimination—namely, that he is "otherwise qualified" to work as a police officer—and they moved for summary judgment which, ultimately, was granted.

The federal district court ruled that "[a]n employer may, in certain circumstances, rely on the results of a medical examination to determine that a person cannot perform the essential functions of a position for purposes of the ADA. Specifically, the ADA 'mandates an individualized inquiry in determining whether an employee's disability or other condition disqualifies him from a particular position'" (at

23; internal citation removed). The Court held that Dr. Van Horn's evaluation was a "thorough medical assessment" and "qualifies as an individualized inquiry for purposes of the ADA" (at 24), ruling that Michael "has not presented sufficient evidence that he is 'otherwise qualified' under the ADA to work as a Troy police officer" (at 33). Importantly, Michael disagreed with the conclusions from Dr. Van Horn's evaluation thereby putting it "at issue" and justifying disclosure of the full report.

Citing *Wurzel v. Whirlpool Corp.* (2012) and *Jennings v. Dow Corning Corp.* (2013), the Court noted that an individualized inquiry focuses on the individual's actual medical condition, and its impact, if any, on that individual's ability to perform the job in question. In addition, the inquiry must be conducted by an examining doctor who (1) is familiar with the relevant job duties; (2) obtains "much individualized information" about the employee's medical condition; (3) has current knowledge of the employee's medication condition; (4) examines the employee in person; and (5) reviews the records of the employee's other treating physicians. As such, employers may only rely on evaluations that meet this standard.

Both the law and professional standards of practice are in harmony on the question of whether the FFDE report should address reasonable accommodation unless specifically requested by the referring source. Said succinctly, the answer is no. The EEOC admonishes the following:

A doctor who conducts medical examinations for an employer should not be responsible for making employment decisions or deciding whether or not it is possible to make a reasonable accommodation for a person with a disability. That responsibility lies with the employer. The doctor's role should be limited to advising the employer about an individual's functional abilities and limitations in relation to job functions, and about whether the individual meets the employer's health and safety requirements. (EEOC, 2002, at 6.4)

Beyond the question of responsibility for making employment decisions, professional standards of practice make clear that psychologists who conduct evaluations for third parties should be guided in their decisions about report content by the employer's referral questions; applicable policies, procedures and provisions of any collective bargaining agreement; relevant law; and informed consent (APA, 2015, Guideline 11; IACP, 2013, Guideline 10.1.1). Examiners who opine on topics not solicited by the referral source, whether or not it is within the examiner's clinical expertise (e.g., reasonable accommodation, treatment recommendations, prognosis for recovery) are acting outside of their contractual role and do a disservice to the referring party (Corey, 2011). As Gold and Shuman (2009) assert, "When specific questions are asked, evaluators should limit themselves to providing opinions and supporting data responsive only to these questions unless otherwise specified" (p. 153).

Qualifications of the Fitness Examiner

When mandating an FFDE that is job-related and consistent with business necessity, the ADA entitles an employer to require that the employee be evaluated by a doctor of its own choosing, so long as the employer foots the bill. In its enforcement guidance, the EEOC states,

The determination that an employee poses a direct threat must be based on an individualized assessment of the employee's present ability to safely perform the essential functions of the job. This assessment must be based on a reasonable medical judgment that relies on the most current medical knowledge and/or best objective evidence. To meet this burden, an employer may want to have the employee examined by a health care professional of its choice who has expertise in the employee's specific condition and can provide medical information that allows the employer to determine the effects of the condition on the employee's ability to perform his/her job. (EEOC, 2000, Question 12)

But the fact that the employer is entitled to select a particular doctor does not mean that the chosen doctor is necessarily well-suited for the task. It is an established ethical standard that psychologists decline to conduct evaluations that fall outside of their competence (APA, 2010). This is especially critical when conducting occupationally-mandated psychological evaluations where the stakes are as high as they are in FFDEs of police officers and other safety-sensitive positions (APA, 2015, Introduction).

The IACP FFDE Guidelines (IACP, 2013) list the following minimum qualifications for examiners conducting these evaluations:

1. Be licensed psychologists or psychiatrists with education, training, and experience in the diagnostic evaluation of mental and emotional disorders;
2. Be competent in the evaluation of law enforcement personnel;
3. Be familiar with the essential job functions of the employee being evaluated and the literature pertinent to FFDEs, especially that which is related to police psychology;
4. Be familiar with, and act in accordance with, relevant state and federal statutes and case law, as well as other legal requirements related to employment and personnel practices (e.g., disability, privacy, third-party liability);
5. Be familiar with, and be guided by, other applicable professional guidelines, including, but not limited to, the *Specialty Guidelines for Forensic Psychology*;
6. Satisfy any other minimum requirements imposed by local jurisdiction or law;
7. Recognize and make ongoing efforts to maintain and develop their areas of competence based on their education, training, supervised experience, consultation, study, and professional experience; and
8. Seek appropriate consultation, supervision, and/or specialized knowledge to address pertinent issues outside their areas of competence that may arise during the course of an FFDE. (Guidelines 5.1.1 through 5.1.8)

In addition, the guidelines stipulate that "[w]hen an FFDE is known to be in the context of litigation, arbitration, or another adjudicative process, the examiner should be prepared by training and experience to qualify as an expert in any related adjudicative proceeding" (IACP, 2013, Guideline 5.2).

An illustration of how local law may impose other minimum requirements is seen in *White v. County of Los Angeles* (2014). Here the California Appeal Court held that a police employer's freedom to require an employee returning from FMLA leave to submit to a fitness evaluation after being returned to paid status is in part justified by the fact that California law permits only licensed psychologists meeting certain requirements of experience, training and competence to assess a police applicant's or officer's psychological fitness and the doctor who cleared her to return, following the FMLA leave, did not have that background.

Psychological FFDEs are often contentious examinations in which the employee being evaluated has much to lose, public and officer safety is at risk, and the likelihood of an administrative grievance, arbitration or litigation is high, particularly when the officer is deemed to be unfit for duty and the results are contested. The Montana Supreme Court case of *City of Livingston, Montana v. Montana Pub. Empl. Assoc.* (2014) illustrates what can go wrong.

Matthew Tubaugh was hired as a police officer with the City of Livingston in 2004.[2] Tubaugh initially met or exceeded expectations as an officer. Prior to 2011, he had received only a few minor reprimands. A series of incidents that occurred in 2011 and 2012, however, led Police Chief Darren Raney to issue a letter of reprimand to Tubaugh on June 28, 2012 as a result of several troubling incidents. The first of these occurred during a City Court trial in December 2011 when he told the judge that he disagreed with a ruling of the court and later became aggressive and argumentative toward the defendant. The second took place in January 2012 when Tubaugh disagreed with his supervising officer and attempted to confront the County Attorney. After being told that the County Attorney was unavailable, he made a profane outburst. Then, in April 2012, Tubaugh lost his composure following an arrest, called the arrestee a "small child" and a "baby," and slammed down his clipboard. He then inserted himself into the booking process and charged the arrestee with obstruction of justice after the arrestee was reluctant to provide an address.

Finally, on June 8, 2012, Tubaugh criticized a co-worker, Jessica Kynett, for using the internet at work and for missing work for physical therapy. The interaction became confrontational and Tubaugh ignored an order from a supervisor to "knock it off." On June 23, 2012, Tubaugh and another officer made another arrest, this time for disorderly conduct. At the detention center, Tubaugh's conduct escalated the situation and ultimately provoked a physical altercation, after which Tubaugh charged the arrestee with assault for the altercation in addition to the initial charges.

Chief Raney's letter of reprimand was primarily for the confrontation with Kynett, but the letter also referenced other incidents of inappropriate conduct, including a letter of complaint that was filed concerning Tubaugh's behavior during one of the arrests. On July 25, 2012, Tubaugh was placed on paid administrative leave. Subsequent investigations conducted by Chief Raney found that Tubaugh had engaged in unprofessional conduct and that his use of force against one of the prisoners was not objectively reasonable. Chief Raney also became concerned that Tubaugh had displayed "an increasing tendency to respond to disrespectful or insufficiently deferential behavior with charges such as disorderly conduct, resisting arrest, obstruction, or assaulting an officer" (at para. 7).

Chief Raney determined that a fitness-for-duty examination was needed, and he ordered Tubaugh to complete an examination with a psychologist "with a focus on law enforcement fitness for duty" (at para. 7). The psychologist concluded that,

Tubaugh suffered from a personality disorder, and that he exhibited symptoms of paranoia, narcissism, and histrionic personality disorder. [The psychologist] concluded that he was unable to recommend that Tubaugh continue as an officer. After reviewing [the psychologist's] report and providing Tubaugh the opportunity to respond, Raney recommended Tubaugh's discharge. The recommendation was accepted and Tubaugh was discharged on October 29, 2012. (at para. 7)

Tubaugh protested his discharge pursuant to his rights under the collective bargaining agreement (CBA) in effect at the time between the City of Livingston and the Montana Public Employees Association (MPEA). Pursuant to the CBA's binding arbitration provision, an arbitration hearing was held. On May 20, 2013, Arbitrator Anne MacIntyre determined that while there was just cause to discipline Tubaugh, the proper disciplinary action was a three-month suspension without pay. She ordered that the City of Livingston reinstate Tubaugh to his previous position or to one of comparable pay, and pay Tubaugh back pay and benefits until his reinstatement. She also ordered that the City of Livingston expunge the fitness for duty examination from Tubaugh's personnel file.

Arbitrator MacIntyre's principal concerns about the examining psychologist's "troubling" examination were that his sole interview with Tubaugh took place in a public venue, that he relied on statements from people who were not identified in the report, and that Tubaugh never had the opportunity to rebut or challenge the bases for the psychologist's conclusions. "The Arbitrator did not hold that the City could not require its officers to complete a fitness for duty examination; instead, she held that the fitness for duty examination here was not credible or reliable because of the manner in which it was conducted" (at para. 30).

The City of Livingston petitioned to vacate the arbitrator's award and, following briefing and oral argument on the petition, the district court issued an order vacating it, noting in part that Chief Raney had given Tubaugh an opportunity to provide additional information after the examination. The MPEA appealed the ruling before the Montana Supreme Court. The Court reversed the district court's ruling, stating,

The Arbitrator did not order that the examination be destroyed. She merely ordered it removed from Tubaugh's personnel file to prevent it from being used for disciplinary purposes in the future. ... Removal from the personnel file of an examination report that the Arbitrator determined should not have been the basis for discharge was a form of relief within the Arbitrator's broad powers under the CBA. The District Court erred when it held that the Arbitrator exceeded her authority by directing removal of the examination from Tubaugh's personnel file. (at para. 37)

The arbitrator raised concerns about a "troubling" FFDE evaluation that was conducted in a public venue, that relied on statements from people who were not identified in the report, and that denied the examinee the opportunity to rebut or challenge the bases for the psychologist's conclusions. It is instructive that the *McGreal* (2004) court expressed similar doubts about an FFDE evaluation that, "[f]or reasons not explained in the report … apparently credited only the versions of those stories presented by the defendants and their lawyer" (at 13).

Corey (2011) pointed out that "third-party information, primarily consisting of documents and interviews with collateral informants, is especially important given the elevated potential in FFD evaluations for either party to provide an incomplete picture of the relevant facts" (p. 278). To help balance the potential for bias, Corey advised that an examinee "be provided with a full opportunity to tell his or her side of the story as it pertains to the issues underlying the referral, including alternative explanations and perspectives" (p. 279).

Professional practice guidelines also acknowledge that occupationally-mandated psychological evaluations "frequently occur in contexts in which the referral source, the examinee, and collateral information sources (e.g., supervisors, coworkers, human resource personnel) have preexisting and complex relationships, often with competing interests and motives" (APA, 2015, pp. 18-19). Consequently, it is important that evaluating psychologists strive to be "dispassionate advocates for their evidence-based findings and the job-relevant inferences to be drawn from them rather than for particular outcomes" (p. 19).

Summary

A substantial body of law affirms a public safety employer's authority to order a psychological fitness-for-duty evaluation of an employee when it is job-related and consistent with business necessity. As we have shown, this standard is met when facts give rise to reasonable questions about the employee's ability to perform in a safety-sensitive position.

Nevertheless, the law also places constraints on when fitness evaluations can be required, the scope of the evaluation, the acquisition and communication of private information, the role of a mental health expert in making employment decisions, and, in some jurisdictions, who is qualified to perform these evaluations. These restrictions are clarified further by professional practice guidelines and ethical standards. Together, these laws and professional standards have significant implications for the police employer and the evaluating psychologist.

When the employer has met the legal threshold for mandating an FFDE, the evaluation itself must nevertheless be carried out in a manner that is no broader or more intrusive than necessary. This includes the requirement to receive and review employment and health care records which, when relevant and properly limited, cannot be unreasonably withheld by either party.

Furthermore, when evaluating psychological fitness for duty in a safety-sensitive position, examiners are cautioned to attend both to current fitness and the sustainability of fitness. The latter is especially important when a condition's symptoms or treatment effects are episodic rather than persistent.

A particularly controversial and high liability topic involves the information to which an employer is entitled to receive from the examiner after the FFDE is completed. The statutory and case law we reviewed in this chapter highlights the importance of knowing and conforming to state laws pertaining to the disclosure of confidential medical information, as well as the importance of obtaining consent or authorization from the employee using state-compliant authorization forms before disclosing any information to the employer other than a description of any functional limitations of the employee and the ultimate fitness determination.

However, this is not to say that an evaluator should not prepare a thorough written report. Indeed, a comprehensive report should always be written, citing all relevant findings and describing their relationship to the evaluator's opinions about the employee's fitness for duty. But in the absence of written authorization that conforms to statutory requirements, the comprehensive report should be prepared and retained by the psychologist pending the employee's challenge to the psychologist's determination.

Whether or not the employee authorizes the evaluating psychologist to disclose the personal health information supporting the fitness determination, both the law and professional standards of practice agree that the psychologist should not address reasonable accommodation, including treatment recommendations, unless specifically requested by the referring party. Instead, psychologists who conduct these evaluations should constrain their opinions to those that respond to the referral questions.

Although employers are entitled to select a professional of their own choosing to conduct an FFDE, psychologists are required by state law and ethical standards to decline to conduct evaluations that fall outside of their competence. This is especially critical when an FFDE is known to take place in the context of litigation, arbitration, or another adjudicative process. Local laws may impose additional minimum requirements on the qualifications of psychologists who conduct these evaluations.

REFERENCES

ADA Amendments Act of 2008. *Pub., L,* 110–325, (2009).

Albert v. Runyon, 6 F.Supp.2d 57, 1998 U.S. Dist. Lexis 7505 (D.Mass., 1998)

American Psychological Association. (2010). *Ethical principles of psychologists and code of conduct.* Washington, DC: Author. Retrieved February 12, 2016, from https://www.apa.org/ethics/code/principles.pdf

American Psychological Association. (2015). *Proposed professional practice guidelines for occupationally-mandated psychological evaluations.* Washington, DC: Author. Retrieved December 13, 2015, from http://apacustomout.apa.org/commentcentral/commentcentralPDF/Site44_OMPE%20Practice%20Guidelines%20Final%20Draft%2011-13-2015.pdf

Americans with Disabilities Act of 1990, Pub. L. No. 101-336, §2, 104 Stat. 328 (1991).

Anthony v. Village of South Holland, #13 C 3068, 2013 WL 5967505, 2013 U.S. Dist. Lexis 159990 (N.D. Ill. Unpublished, Nov. 8, 2013)

Bonsignore v. City of New York, 683 F.2d 635 (1982)

Brown v. Sandy City Appeal Board, 2014 UT App 158

Brownfield v. City of Yakima, 612 F.3d 1140 (9th Cir. 2010)

Brumbalough v. Camelot Care Centers, Inc., No. 04-5543, 427 F.3d 996 (6th Cir. 2005)

Butler v. Thornburgh, 900 F.2d 871 (5th Cir. 1990), cert. denied, 498 U.S. 998 (1990)

California Confidentiality of Medical Information Act, California Civil Code § 56.11 (2012).

California Fair Employment and Housing Act. Cal. Code Regs. tit. 2, § 7285-7297.11 (2011).

Carrillo v. National Council of Churches of Christ in the USA, 976 F.Supp. 254 (SDNY 1997)

City of Greenwood v. Dowler, 492 N.E.2d 1081 (Ind.App. 1986)

City of Livingston, Montana v. Montana Pub. Empl. Assoc., 2014 MT 314, DA 14-0083

Colon v. City of Newark, #A-3260-03T23260-03T2, 2006 WL 1194230 (N.J.A.D. 2006)

Conroy v. N.Y. State Dep't of Corr. Serv., 333 F.3d 88 (2d Cir. 2003)

Conte v. Horcher, 365 N.E.2d 567 (Ill. App. Ct. 1977)

Corey, D. M. (2011). Principles of fitness-for-duty evaluations for police psychologists. In J. Kitaeff (Ed.), *Handbook of police psychology* (pp. 263–293). New York, NY: Routledge Psychology Press.

Corey, D. M., & Borum, R. (2013). Forensic assessment for high-risk occupations. In R. K. Otto & I. B. Weiner (Eds.), *Forensic psychology* (2nd ed.; vol. 11, pp. 246-270). Hoboken, NJ: John Wiley & Sons, Inc.

Cripe v. City of San Jose, 261 F.3d 877 (9th Cir. 2001)

Dengel v. Waukesha County, 16 F.Supp.3d 983 (E.D. Wis. 2014)

Duran v. City of Douglas, 904 F.2d 1372 (9th. Cir. 1990)

EEOC v. U.S. Steel Corp., No. 10-1248 (W.D. Pa. Feb. 20, 2013)

Equal Employment Opportunity Commission. (1995). ADA enforcement guidance: Preemployment disability-related questions and medical examinations: Compliance manual (Vol. 2, Sect. 902, No. 915.002). Washington, DC: Author.

Equal Employment Opportunity Commission. (1997). EEOC enforcement guidance on the Americans with Disabilities Act and psychiatric disabilities: Compliance manual (Vol. 2, Sect. 902, No. 915.002). Washington, DC: Author.

Equal Employment Opportunity Commission. (2000). *Enforcement guidance on disability-related inquiries and medical examinations of employees under the Americans with Disabilities Act: Compliance manual* (Vol. 2, Sect. 902, No. 915.002). Washington, DC: Author.

Equal Employment Opportunity Commission. (2002, October 29). *ADA technical assistance manual: January 1992.* (Publication EEOC-M-1A, Addendum).

Family & Medical Leave Act, 29 U.S.C. §2601 (1993).

Fischler, G. L., McElroy, H. K., Miller, L., Saxe-Clifford, S., Stewart, C. O., & Zelig, M. (2011). The role of psychological fitness-for-duty evaluations in law enforcement. *The Police Chief*, *78*, 72–78.

Franklin v. City of Slidell, 969 F.Supp.2d 644 (August 27, 2013)

Gold, L. H., & Shuman, D. W. (2009). *Evaluating mental health disability in the workplace*. New York, NY: Springer Science & Business Media. doi:10.1007/978-1-4419-0152-1

Health Insurance Portability and Accountability Act (HIPAA). (2000a). *Title 45, Subtitle A, Subchapter C, Part 160*. General Administrative Requirements.

Health Insurance Portability and Accountability Act (HIPAA) Privacy Rule. (2000b). *Title 45, Subtitle A, Subchapter C, Part 164*. Subpart E, Privacy of Individually Identifiable Health Information.

Hill v. City of Winona, 454 N.W.2d 659 (1990)

Hogarth v. Thornburgh, 833 F.Supp. 1077 (SDNY 1993)

Illinois Confidentiality Act, 740 ILCS 110/1 et seq. (1998).

In Muhammed C., 116 Cal. Rptr. 2d 21 (2002)

International Association of Chiefs of Police, Police Psychological Services Section. (2013). *Guidelines for psychological fitness-for-duty evaluations*. Arlington, VA: Author.

Jennings v. Dow Corning Corp., No. 12-12227, 2013 WL 1962333, 10 (E.D. Mich. 2013)

Jimenez v. Dyncorp International, 635 F.Supp.2d 592 (W.D. Tex. 2009)

Keslosky v. Borough of Old Forge et al., No. 3:2008cv01240 Doc. 171 (M.D. Pa. 2014)

Kraft v. Police Commissioner of Boston, 417 Mass. 235 (1994)

Krocka v. City of Chicago, 203 F.3d 507 (7th Cir. 2000)

Lassiter v. Department of Justice, 60 M.S.P.R. 138 (1993)

Maplewood and Law Enf. Labor Serv., *108 LA (BNA) 572*. (Daly 1996).

McGreal v. Ostrov, #98-CV-3958, Docket entry No. 177 (N.D. Ill. Oct. 1, 2004); interim ruling on a Motion at 2004 U.S. Dist. Lexis 18420, on remand from 368 F.3d 657, #02-3405, 2004 U.S. App. Lexis 9059 (7th Cir. 2004)

Merillat v Michigan State University, 207 Mich. App. 241 (1994)

Michael v. City of Troy Police Department, 2014 U.S. District Lexis 149367 (E.D. Mich. 2014)

Moon v. Winfield, 368 F. Supp. 843 (N.D. Ill. 1973)

Morgan, D. L., & Duvall, M. N. (1983). OSHA's general duty clause: An analysis of its use and abuse. *Berkeley Journal of Employment & Labor Law, 5,* 283-321. Retrieved November 21, 2015, from http://scholarship.law.berkeley.edu/bjell/vol5/iss2/3

Myers v. Hose, 50 F.3d 278 (4th Cir. 1995)

Occupational Safety and Health Act of 1970, 29 U.S.C. § 654, Pub. L. 91-596, 84 Stat. 1590, 91st Congress, S.2193 (1970).

Palmer v. Cir. Ct. of Cook County, Illinois, 117 F.3d 351 (7th Cir. 1997)

People ex rel. Ballinger v. O'Connor, 13 Ill. App.2d 317 (1957)

People v. Quiroga, 16 Cal. App. 4th 964 (1993)

Pettus v. Cole, 57 Cal.Rptr.2d 46 (Cal. App. 1 Dist. 1996)

Petty v. Metropolitan Government of Nashville-Davidson County, 538 F.3d 431 (6th Cir. 2008)

Piechowski, L. D., & Drukteinis, A. M. (2011). Fitness for duty. In E. Y. Drogin, F. M. Dattilio, R. L. Sadoff, & T. G. Gutheil (Eds.), *Handbook of forensic assessment: Psychological and psychiatric perspectives* (pp. 571–591). New York, NY: John Wiley & Sons, Inc. doi:10.1002/9781118093399.ch25

Rostow, C. D., & Davis, R. D. (2004). *A handbook for psychological fitness-for-duty evaluations in law enforcement*. Binghamton, NY: The Haworth Clinical Practice Press and The Haworth Reference Press.

Sager v. County of Yuba, 68 Cal.Rptr.3d 1 (Cal. App. 2007)

Sangirardi v. Village of Stickney, 342 Ill.App.3d 1, 276 Ill.Dec. 28, 793 N.E.2d 787 (2003)

Slater v. Dept. of Homeland Security, 2008 M.S.P.B. 73, Docket No. SF-0752-06-0805-I-2

Stewart v. Pearce, 484 F.2d 1031 (9th Cir. 1973)

Stone, A. V. (2000). *Fitness for duty: Principles, methods and legal issues*. Boca Raton, FL: CRC Press.

Thomas v. Johnson, 295 F. Supp. 1025 (D.C. Cir. 1968)

Transport Workers Union of Am., Local 100, AFL-CIO v. N.Y. City Transit Auth., 341 F. Supp. 2d 432 (S.D.N.Y. 2004)

Trompetter, P. S., Corey, D. M., Schmidt, W. W., & Tracy, D. (2011). Psychological factors after officer-involved shootings: Addressing officer needs and agency responsibilities. *The Police Chief*, *78*(1), 28–33.

Uniformed Services Employment and Reemployment Rights Act of 1994 (USERRA), Pub. L. 103-353, 38 U.S.C. §§4301-4335 (1994).

USERRA Final Rule, 20 C.F.R. Part 1002 (2006).

Watson v. City of Miami Beach, 177 F.3d 932 (11th Cir. 1999)

Watts v. Alfred, 794 F.Supp. 431 (D.D.C. 1992)

White v. County of Los Angeles, No. B243471 (Cal. Ct. App. Apr. 15, 2014)

Wurzel v. Whirlpool Corp., 482 F. App'x 1 (6th Cir. 2012)

ENDNOTES

1 The California CMIA (Civil Code § 56.11) requires the following elements: (1) the name or functions of the provider disclosing the medical information; (2) the name or functions of the persons or entities to receive it; (3) the specific uses and limitations on the use of the information; (4) a specific date after which the provider is no longer authorized to disclose the information; and (5) notice that the person signing the authorization may receive a copy of the authorization. Similarly, the Illinois Confidentiality Act expressly requires that a consent form must include "the right to revoke the consent at any time" (740 Ill. Comp. Stat. 110/5[b]). It also must specify (1) the person or agency to whom disclosure is to be made; (2) the purpose for which disclosure is to be made; (3) the nature of the information to be disclosed; (4) the right to inspect and copy the information to be disclosed; (5) the consequences of a refusal to consent, if any; and (6) the calendar date on which the consent expires.

2 The factual summary of this case derives from the narrative of the Court's decision and, while not quoted verbatim in its entirety, it borrows heavily from the language of the Court.

Section 3

Clinical Intervention and Prevention

Chapter 6
Critical Incident Interventions:
Crisis Response and Debriefing

Emily Brucia
Palo Alto University, USA

Matthew J. Cordova
Palo Alto University, USA

Josef I. Ruzek
National Center for PTSD, VA Palo Alto Health Care System, USA & Palo Alto University, USA & Stanford University, USA

ABSTRACT

Police officers are exposed to many critical incidents throughout their careers. This chapter discusses critical incident exposure and psychological sequelae in police officers, police culture, obstacles to mental health care, currently utilized early interventions, existing research for these approaches, alternative evidence-based early interventions, emerging models, and directions for future research. Given the frequency and potential impact of critical incidents, early intervention for exposed police officers is of central importance. One of the most commonly utilized group early interventions, Critical Incident Stress Debriefing (CISD), has limited empirical support, such that some departments are being advised against its use. That said, there are important challenges in identifying better, evidence-based alternatives.

INTRODUCTION

Police officers are exposed to many critical incidents throughout their careers (Carlier et al., 2000; Malcolm et al., 2005). A critical incident may be defined as, "A potentially traumatic event which may cause a given individual's emotional resources to become over-taxed, resulting in a spectrum of reactions from exhaustion to increased and unrelenting mental health symptomology" (Maguen et al., 2009, p. 754). Critical incident exposure is one of the reasons some have considered policing to be the world's most psychologically dangerous job (Marin, 2012).

DOI: 10.4018/978-1-5225-0813-7.ch006

Given the frequency and potential impact of critical incidents, early intervention for exposed officers is of central importance. In practice, one of the most common formal interventions following a critical incident is an individual meeting with a mental health professional that has an in-depth understanding of the law enforcement culture (typically an in-house or contracted police psychologist). The goal of such meetings is to provide support and education, rather than to treat or prevent traumatic stress reactions (E. Dorian, personal communication, March 16, 2016). However, there is not yet a universally adopted approach or methodology for such contacts and there is no research evidence regarding their effects.

One of the most commonly utilized group early interventions, Critical Incident Stress Debriefing (CISD), has limited empirical support; evidence suggests it may not be helpful and may even be harmful to participants (Mitchell, 1983; Tuckey, 2007). Some organizations are being advised against its general use (Tuckey, 2007) and researchers have recommended that mandated group psychological debriefings should cease (Bisson, McFarlane, Rose, Ruzek, & Watson, 2009). However, there are important challenges to identifying a better, evidence-based alternative.

This chapter will discuss critical incident exposure and psychological sequelae in police officers, police culture and obstacles to mental health care, early interventions in current use, existing research on these approaches, alternative evidence-based early interventions, emerging models, and directions for future research.

Critical Incident Exposure / Sequelae

Police officers are faced with an array of critical incidents during their careers. These may include officer involved shootings, deaths involving children or gruesome scenes, traffic collisions, and line of duty deaths or injuries (Marin, 2012). Although the way critical incidents are defined and documented is not always clear, it has been estimated that a first-year police officer is exposed to an average of 12 critical incidents, and that the average 30-year police officer at the time of retirement has been exposed to an average of 250 critical incidents (Marin, 2012).

Psychological distress in police officers is common in the early weeks following a critical incident; risk factors and vulnerabilities, discussed below, appear to make chronic adjustment problems more likely. In a sample of 89 police officers recently exposed to a potentially traumatic stressor, the most commonly reported emotional reactions at the time of the incident, regardless of whether or not the officer went on to develop posttraumatic stress disorder (PTSD), included helplessness (80%), intense fear (59%), and horror (21%) (Marchand, Boyer, Nadeau, Beaulieu-Prevost, & Martin, 2015). In most cases, these emotions are transient and naturally resolve (Litz et al., 2002). Those whose reactions do not subside within approximately 3 months after an incident are more likely to experience chronic distress (Kessler et al., 1995). Approximately 6.8% of the general American population meets criteria for PTSD (Kearns et al., 2012). Prevalence rates of PTSD in police officers range from 7-19%, suggesting that approximately 135,000 police officers in the United States experience symptoms of PTSD (Komarovskaya et al., 2011; Marin, 2012; O'Hara, 2012).

Risk factors for the development of PTSD have been identified. In the general population, risk factors include prior trauma exposure, psychiatric history, poor social support, perceived life threat during the trauma, and distress during and immediately after the trauma (Kearns et al., 2012). Additionally, younger age and female gender are associated with greater likelihood of developing PTSD following a trauma (Litz et al., 2002).

Risk factors for PTSD in police officers can be grouped by pre-incident, peri-incident, and post-incident factors. Pre-incident factors include family psychiatric history, cumulative exposure to critical incidents within the past year, occupational stressors, and the impact of past personal traumas (Marchand et al., 2015). Pre-existing difficulties with emotional expression, greater anxiety sensitivity, neuroticism, the tendency to dissociate, hypersensitivity to threat, and a slowed un-learning and fear reconditioning (i.e., habituation) process may also increase risk of PTSD among officers (Marchand et al., 2015).

Peri-incident factors, including characteristics of the critical incident itself, confer psychological risk. Duty-related critical incidents most strongly associated with PTSD are killing someone in the line of duty, the death of a fellow officer, and physical assaults (Maguen et al., 2009; Violanti & Drylie, 2008). In a sample of 100 suburban police officers, exposure to death and perceived life threat were the best predictors of subsequent PTSD (Robinson, Sigman, & Wilson, 1997). Perceived threat to one's partner's life or physical integrity and greater distress and dissociation during and immediately after the incident have also been associated with greater risk for PTSD (Marmar et al., 2007).

Post-incident risk factors for PTSD in police officers have also been identified. Dissatisfaction with organizational support and poor social support outside of police work are associated with poorer adjustment. Physical injuries, depression, other negative and stressful life events, and avoidant coping are also associated with greater risk for PTSD (Marchand et al., 2015).

Environmental stress may be an important factor in officers' adjustment to duty-related critical incidents. Police officers are exposed to work environment stress due to conflict with peers and administration, outdated equipment, shift work contributing to irregular sleep hours, abrupt shift rotations, and constant scrutiny by and discord with the public and the media (Brondolo, Wellington, Libby, & Brondolo, 2008; Haugen, Eves, & Weiss, 2012; Marin, 2012). These secondary stressors may contribute to psychological distress following critical incident exposure (Maguen et al., 2009).

Social support is one of the most significant protective factors for police officers. Strong support from colleagues during and immediately following a critical incident, ease of discussing the incident at work, a positive attitude from colleagues and superiors about expressions of emotion, higher perceived availability of and satisfaction with support, and longstanding support all appear to be protective factors (Kleim & Westphal, 2011; Marchand et al., 2015). Less previous trauma and less critical incident exposure have been correlated with lower PTSD symptoms (Kleim & Wesphal, 2011). In female police officers, hardiness (i.e., a sense of commitment, control, and challenge) appears to be a protective factor (Marchand et al., 2015). Greater sense of self-worth and the belief that the world is benevolent also appear to protect officers from developing PTSD (Kleim & Westphal, 2011).

Police Culture

Unique factors in law enforcement culture may pose obstacles to mental health care. While many of these are resilience factors that may be functionally adaptive for police officers, they can also impede recognition of post-incident adjustment issues and willingness to seek treatment. Police culture promotes police officers as invulnerable, heroic protectors, and the police identity is built on principles of self-reliance, toughness, control, strength, vigilance, quick and effective problem-solving, discipline, and resilience (Gilmartin, 2002; Kirschman, 2007; Royle, Keenan, & Farrell, 2009; Violanti & Drylie, 2008; Wester, Arndt, Sedivy, & Arndt, 2010). This identity development begins in the police academy, where, in paramilitary fashion, superior officers and academy instructors reinforce subordinate officers for acting in accordance with this behavioral code (Wester et al., 2010). This socialization may instill unrealistic expectations regarding emotional and physical strength and invulnerability to trauma (Violanti & Drylie, 2008).

The socialization process also promotes "the thin blue line," separating police officers from civilians (Gilmartin, 2002). Though the intention of the thin blue line is to promote fraternalism, it can result in decreased social support from non-law enforcement friends and detachment from psychologically distressed colleagues (Gilmartin, 2002; Violanti & Drylie, 2008). Distressed officers may be rejected and avoided by their colleagues and superiors (Wester et al., 2010). A Senior Investigation Officer in a study on stigma in police culture was quoted as saying, "We're getting the welfare department in tomorrow for any officers who want to talk about this murder. They'll be using the room past my open office door. If I see you walk down that corridor, don't bother coming back" (Royle et al., 2009, p. 83).

Police culture's expectation of psychological invincibility can create difficulties for officers that experience psychological distress. Self-stigma, defined as the negative internalized beliefs about oneself, impedes help-seeking behavior (Wester et al., 2010). Distressed officers may feel inferior and unacceptable. Royle et al. (2009) found that male police officers believed they would be perceived by others as weak or inferior if they sought counseling. Self-stigmatizing beliefs may then be compounded by external stigma, the perception that psychological distress is an egregious violation of police cultural norms (Wester et al., 2010). Officers with PTSD have reported feeling devalued, isolated, and ostracized by their peers and unsupported by their superiors (Marin, 2012). Thus, officers may go to great lengths to suppress and deny their symptoms.

These aspects of police culture and identity complicate delivery of post-critical incident mental health care. The hyper-masculine principles that make up police culture may render officers unwelcoming of psychological "weakness," unpredictability, uncontrolled emotions, and the perceived inability to cope (Violanti & Drylie, 2008). In stark contrast, counseling may encourage officers to confront and express painful emotions and to develop more flexible coping mechanisms (Kirschman, Kamena, & Fay, 2014). Moreover, officers often learn through their police work to be skeptical or distrustful of others, which may contribute to difficulties in establishing a working therapeutic alliance and concerns about confidentiality (Kirschman, Kamena, & Fay, 2014). Officers may also be dissuaded from seeking therapy due to real or perceived concerns about being deemed unfit for duty and professional repercussions (e.g., being placed in the "rubber gun squad") (Wester et al., 2010). Some distressed officers may face negative job changes (e.g., being labeled unfit for duty, assigned to recuperative duties, reduced pay) and difficulty with the workman's compensation process (e.g., having to take unpaid leave if a claim is rejected and sick- or vacation-leave has been depleted) (Haugen et al., 2012; Wester et al., 2010). These officers report being further isolated, punished, and degraded through their assignments to recuperative duties (Royle et al., 2009). These factors may keep police officers from admitting to post-critical incident distress and from seeking needed psychological treatment.

Current Interventions

Psychological debriefing originated during World War I and World War II. Developed by battlefield psychiatrists, debriefing was based on the premise that if soldiers shared combat stories after significant battles, in close proximity to the battlefield, immediately following combat, and with the expectation that they return to duty, they would be better prepared for future battles (Litz et al., 2002). Psychological debriefings remain a frequently employed intervention for emergency responders following critical incidents, across cultures and countries, including in the U.S. (Tuckey, 2007).

There remains much confusion in the research literature and in clinical practice about the definition of "debriefing." The term "debriefing" is frequently utilized to describe a variety of interventions including, but not limited to, emotional debriefing, psychological debriefing, Critical Incident Stress Debriefing, pastoral counseling, and psychological first aid (Bisson et al., 2009; Litz et al., 2002). The lack of specificity with which the term debriefing is used makes it challenging to 1) determine what specific interventions are actually being practiced in various agencies and departments, and 2) definitively apply conclusions from the research literature on debriefing (reviewed in the next section) to current practices in the field. Proper and accurate use of terminology will enhance the reliability and validity of research outcomes and will reduce confusion for researchers, clinicians, and police leadership and organizations.

The most frequently implemented group intervention for emergency responders is Critical Incident Stress Debriefing (CISD) (Malcolm et al., 2005). CISD was designed by a former Baltimore County firefighter in the 1970s due to concern about emergency responders following critical incidents (Litz et al., 2002; Mitchell, 1983). CISD is based on the principle of early intervention and the belief that talking aids in recovery from psychological trauma. CISD was intended to be administered in a group format, to emergency responders who were deployed to the same critical incident, and by culturally competent mental health professionals (ideally who work in the same field) and trained peer support staff (who enhance credibility of the intervention). The goals of CISD include education about stress reactions and coping skills, normalization of stress reactions, promotion of sharing and emotional processing of the event, and provision of information regarding referrals (Litz et al., 2002).

CISD is comprised of seven phases (Mitchell, 1983). In the Introduction Phase, leaders describe the process of CISD, informed consent, confidentiality, and expectations. In the Fact Phase, participants are asked to state their identity and their role in the critical incident. In the Thought Phase, participants are asked to share their thoughts during and/or immediately after the critical incident. In the Reaction Phase, participants are asked to explore their personal reactions to the event. In the Symptom Phase, leaders provide psychoeducation about critical incident stress and normalize and validate participants' experiences. In the Teaching Phase, leaders describe coping skills for critical incident stress. In the Re-entry Phase, participants are encouraged to ask questions and/or address other concerns (Mitchell, 1983).

In the 1990s, Mitchell and Everly collaboratively developed the multi-component stress management model known as Critical Incident Stress Management (CISM), of which CISD is one component (Everly et al., 2000; Everly et al., 2000; Mitchell & Everly, 2001). CISM is a strategic stress management model designed to meet the needs of emergency responders, their families, and their organizations (Everly & Mitchell, 1999). Several integrated components of CISM are intentionally designed to intervene at various time points (Everly, Flannery, & Mitchell, 2000). Prior to involvement in a critical incident, emergency responders receive education about stress reactions, stress management, and coping skills. During or after the critical incident, CISM assesses and supports the needs of first responders through crisis intervention and stress management. Within 12 hours post-critical incident, a defusing intervention may be administered in small groups to assess mental health symptoms. In the days or weeks that follow, CISD may be administered in a small group format to address symptoms and facilitate processing of the critical incident. CISM also provides peer support and chaplaincy services to the involved emergency responders and their families (Sheehan, Everly, & Langlieb, 2004). CISM includes consultation with community and organization leaders to coordinate and adapt services to their specific settings. In addition, CISM facilitates referrals for ongoing symptoms of distress, and provides debrief-the-debriefer sessions (Sheehan et al., 2004).

Commonly cited intended effects of CISD are 1) mitigation of acute psychological distress, 2) prevention of posttraumatic stress symptoms, and 3) promotion of an accelerated and normal recovery (Everly, Flannery, & Mitchell, 2000; Tuckey, 2007). However, the multi-faceted, comprehensive CISM was not designed to interfere with the natural recovery process or to replace more intensive mental health counseling or therapy (Malcolm et al., 2005). CISD was included as one component of CISM, and was not intended to be the sole way of addressing critical incident stress (Everly et al., 2000; Wessely & Deahl, 2003). Published CISD manuals explicitly state that CISD is a necessary, but insufficient, intervention for traumatized individuals with ongoing distress and impairment in functioning following a critical incident (Mitchell & Everly, 1996).

CISD/Psychological Debriefing Research

Various forms of psychological debriefing have been evaluated. In published studies, there is considerable methodological diversity with respect to the type of debriefings, format, timing, sample size, and population. This section will first review meta-analytic studies of CISD and CISM that included investigations involving a mix of participants, including police officers. It will then review individual studies that have specifically evaluated the effects of debriefing interventions on first responders in general. Finally, it will review individual studies that have assessed the effects of debriefing interventions on police officers.

Meta-analytic studies have concluded that single-session individual or group psychological debriefings do not prevent PTSD and do not reduce psychological distress; regardless of which intervention is used (i.e., CISD vs. non-CISD), people tend to improve over time (Bisson et al., 2009; NIMH, 2002; National Collaborating Center for Mental Health, 2005; Rose, Bisson, & Wessely, 2009; Van Emmerik et al., 2002). Rose et al.'s (2002) Cochrane report conducted a meta-analysis of 15 randomized controlled trials (RCT) that evaluated whether single-session psychological debriefing delivered within 1 month of a traumatic event was effective in preventing PTSD and mitigating psychological distress. In these studies, "psychological debriefing" encompassed multiple interventions, including CISD, crisis intervention, psychiatric stress debriefing, multiple stressor debriefing, and trauma debriefing. Debriefings were administered in individual or group format. All of the RCTs included a single-session debriefing that employed normalization of stress reactions and emotional processing and/or ventilation through recollection and/or reworking of the event. Results suggested that compared to control groups, single-session debriefing did not prevent PTSD or reduce psychological distress. Further, in two long-term RCTs, one of which conducted a three-year follow-up, debriefed individuals were at a higher risk of developing PTSD. Rose et al. (2002) concluded that there is no evidence supporting the use of single-session debriefing, and that compulsory debriefing of trauma survivors should cease.

Van Emmerik et al. (2002) conducted a meta-analysis of seven studies: five included CISD interventions, six used no-intervention control groups, and three used non-CISD interventions (30 minutes of counseling, education, historical group debriefing). Included studies were a mix of individual and group psychological debriefing. All of the studies administered a single-session debriefing within 1 month of the critical incident and conducted assessments pre- and post-intervention with psychometrically sound measures. CISD showed no better outcomes than alternative interventions and wait-list control groups receiving no care (Van Emmerik et al., 2002).

Bisson et al. (2009) conducted a systematic review of 12 RCTs of psychological debriefing. Psychological debriefing was defined by the researchers as a, "Brief preventative technique that occurs within 1 month of a traumatic event" (Bisson et al., 2009, pp. 91). All of the studies administered a single psychological debriefing or similar interventions within 1 month of a trauma. All but one study implemented individual psychological debriefing. Of the ten studies comparing individual PD with no intervention, two were positive, five were neutral, and three were negative. Bisson et al. (2009) concluded that there is no evidence to suggest that debriefing is effective in preventing PTSD and that future research efforts should focus on developing and evaluating multilevel, tailored interventions for high-risk populations, including emergency workers.

Other meta-analyses have reviewed the effectiveness of multi-component CISM interventions. Everly et al. (2002) conducted a meta-analysis assessing the effectiveness of eight CISM interventions in reducing PTSD symptoms, frequency of assault, and other adverse outcomes. All of the studies assessed individual or group interventions consistent with CISM. Large mean effect sizes supported CISM's utility in mitigating the negative psychological sequelae of trauma. Everly et al. (2002) acknowledged that most of the CISM studies were naturalistic and called for RCTs.

Roberts and Everly (2006) conducted a meta-analysis of 36 studies assessing the effectiveness of crisis intervention (CISM or another form of crisis intervention) in family preservation and reduction of psychological co-morbidity. All of the studies had a clearly stated research design and conducted baseline and follow-up assessment with specific outcome measures. CISM interventions consisted of a minimum of three sessions (range: 4 to 12), including pre-crisis training, individual or group crisis intervention immediately post-critical incident, and post-critical incident crisis counseling at 1-month. A large mean effect size of multicomponent CISM was reported, but the effects of CISM on psychiatric morbidity were unclear (Roberts & Everly, 2006).

In studies of single-session group CISD applied to non-police emergency responders (e.g., firefighters, soldiers) results are mixed (Deahl et al., 2001; Eid et al., 2001). As discussed later in this chapter, these studies have several methodological and conceptual limitations.

In a RCT involving British servicemen ($N = 106$) returning from a Bosnia peacekeeping operation, soldiers were randomized to receive a single session group psychological debriefing or no intervention (Deahl et al., 2001). At 12-month follow-up, the debriefed group showed a greater reduction in possible alcohol abuse than the no intervention group. Deahl et al. (2001) proposed that research on the effectiveness of debriefing should include a wider range of outcome variables, including substance misuse.

Eid et al. (2001) evaluated the effect of group psychological debriefing on acute stress reactions in military personnel ($n = 9$) and firefighters ($n = 9$; 6 were volunteer civilians) involved in rescue work following a fatal traffic accident. Both groups participated in an operational debriefing (e.g., discussion of the planning, organization, execution, and outcome of a given operation). Military personnel also participated in a voluntary two and a half hour group psychological debriefing carried out by two experienced military psychologists (one with extensive CISD training). Two weeks later, the firefighters (without psychological debriefing) endorsed more sleep disturbance, mood swings, and jumpiness than their psychologically debriefed military counterparts. Eid et al. (2001) concluded that group psychological debriefing reduced acute stress reactions for the military personnel. Perrin et al. (2007) demonstrated greater prevalence of PTSD in World Trade Center recovery workers that had less training. This may explain, at least in part, the greater symptoms in Eid et al.'s (2001) sub-sample of mostly volunteer firefighters and suggests the importance of including appropriate control groups in outcome studies.

Wee et al. (1999) surveyed 66 emergency medical services personnel involved in the 1992 Los Angeles Civil Disturbance. Those that attended a group CISD intervention ($n = 42$) approximately 2 months prior were compared to those who declined CISD ($n = 23$). The researchers did not specify whether CISD involved single or multi-session debriefings. Debriefed emergency services personnel showed reduced arousal, intrusion, and stress-related symptoms (Wee et al., 1999).

The few published studies that have evaluated a single-session, group CISD intervention with police officers have concluded that a stand-alone CISD does not prevent the onset of PTSD symptoms, and may contribute to greater symptoms in this population (Carlier et al., 1998; Carlier et al., 2000). Carlier et al. (1998) were commissioned to conduct a field study of police officers involved in rescue work after a cargo plane crashed in Amsterdam in 1992. Approximately 200 police officers were involved in the rescue work. Due to operational demands, less than half of those involved were able to participate in voluntary group CISD. The study compared debriefed ($n = 46$) and non-debriefed ($n = 59$) officers. For practical reasons (e.g., funding, recruitment), data collection began several months post-critical incident. At 8 months post-incident, participants were asked to recall their pre-event and early symptoms. At 8 and 18 months post-incident, they were asked to rate their current symptoms. The debriefed and non-debriefed groups did not differ with regard to retrospectively recalled early or post-event symptoms. At 8 months, the groups did not differ in the rate of PTSD diagnosis. However, at 18 months post-critical incident, debriefed officers reported more hyper-arousal symptoms than non-debriefed officers, suggesting that debriefing contributed to the exacerbation or maintenance of hyper-arousal symptoms (Carlier et al., 1998).

Carlier et al. (2000) utilized a non-randomized pre-test/post-test design to compare police officers ($n = 86$), who were voluntarily individually debriefed with CISD at 24 hours, 1 month, and 3 months following a variety of critical incidents, to non-debriefed internal ($n = 82$; officers exposed to trauma but declined debriefing) and external ($n = 75$; drawn from a previous study of traumatized police officers before debriefing was available) control groups. The groups did not differ in psychological morbidity at pre-test (conducted post-incident and shortly before the beginning of debriefing), 24 hours, or 6 months; however, at 1 week post-critical incident, debriefed police officers endorsed greater PTSD symptomatology than non-debriefed officers. Reported satisfaction with CISD was high but was unrelated to symptom improvement.

Bohl (1995) assessed the effectiveness of group CISD for male police officers in Southern California. The officers included in the study had been exposed to only one critical incident in the past 3 months. Debriefed participants ($n = 40$) showed decreased symptoms of depression, anger, nightmares, flashbacks, and appetite changes compared to non-debriefed participants ($n = 30$). This study did not utilize randomization, participants came from various departments and had been exposed to different types of critical incidents, and data were only collected 3 months post-intervention.

In sum, meta-analyses have concluded that single-session psychological debriefing does not prevent PTSD or reduce psychological distress. Only three published studies (Bohl, 1995; Carlier et al., 1998; Carlier et al., 2000) have researched CISD applied to police officers; they used relatively weak methodologies and yielded inconclusive results. Many types of debriefings are described in the literature, contributing to confusion and some contention among researchers and clinicians regarding the ongoing use of CISD. Based on findings of well-conducted RCTs, there is little evidence to support the effectiveness of psychological debriefing of police officers.

Conceptual and Methodological Challenges

The outcome literature on CISD must be considered in the context of several conceptual and methodological challenges. "Debriefing" has been used to refer to a range of interventions and the methodological heterogeneity of existing studies makes it difficult to draw conclusions about debriefing's utility (Malcolm et al., 2005; NIMH, 2002).

The research methodology on group psychological debriefing has been critiqued (Tuckey, 2007). Meta-analytic reviews have included studies involving participants from different "cultures" (e.g., motor vehicle accident survivors, non-police first responders, police officers). Given the unique nature of police culture, these findings may not be generalizable to the police officer population. Additionally, many studies included in the previously reviewed meta-analyses involved individual, single-session debriefing. CISD was intended to be a one-time, small group intervention existing within the context of the multi-component CISM program, not a one-off, individual intervention (Mitchell, 1983; Tuckey, 2007).

The timing of the debriefing is another key methodological issue (Tukey, 2007). CISD was intended to be administered in the immediate aftermath of a critical incident (1 to 10 days, or 3 to 4 weeks for mass disasters), not months later (Everly & Mitchell, 2000). Across studies, the timing of debriefings ranged from 24 hours to 6 to 9 months post-critical incident (Bohl, 1995; Chemtob et al., 1997; Jenkins, 1996; Stallard & Law, 1993; Wee, 1995). Further, some critical incidents themselves are prolonged for days or months (e.g., Boeing plane crash; Carlier et al., 1998). Meta-analyses were based on studies in which the intervention was delivered at various times following critical incidents of variable duration (Tukey, 2007).

Additionally, there are concerns regarding the training of debriefing facilitators (Tukey, 2007). CISD was designed to be delivered by facilitators experienced and competent in debriefing, such as those trained by the International Critical Incident Stress Foundation (ICISF). Inclusion of facilitators without standardized training may threaten the fidelity and replicability of the intervention (Tuckey, 2007). Further, without cultural competence in working with a given population, such as police officers, debriefing facilitators may contribute to negative outcomes (Tuckey, 2007).

For reasons articulated above, many have identified the need for reliable, valid, controlled research on group CISD (Tuckey, 2007). However, debriefing research in general, and with police officers specifically, poses many methodological challenges. First, critical incidents are sudden and unpredictable, particularly in police work. This creates obstacles to organizing and planning CISD outcome research (Litz, 2008).

Second, obtaining baseline and pre-intervention data is difficult (Litz et al., 2002; Robinson & Mitchell, 1993). Individuals and organizations in the midst of crisis are unlikely to prioritize research assessments (Everly et al., 2000). For example, for administrative reasons, Carlier et al. (1998) were delayed for several months post-incident/CISD in beginning data collection; 8 months later, officers were asked to report their recollections of their early symptoms. Similarly, Jenkins (1996) asked emergency medical workers that had responded to a mass shooting to retrospectively rate their symptoms the week before the event. Data from these studies were vulnerable to distortions in recall and mood-dependent memory.

Third, the lack of validated self-report measures for police officers calls into question the quality of assessments utilized in CISD outcome studies with this population (Best, Artwohl, & Kirschman, 2011). The most commonly used critical incident exposure measure is the Police Stress Survey (Spielberger, Westberry, & Greenfield, 1981), published in 1981. Despite the increased interest in the police culture and well-being, the Critical Incident History Questionnaire, aimed at assessing the range of critical incident exposure in police officers, was not published until 2010 (Chopko, Palmieri, & Adams, 2015).

Fourth, randomization and inclusion of appropriate control groups, vital if strong conclusions about effectiveness are to be reached, are challenging in debriefing research. Many debriefing and CISM studies lack random assignment for ethical and functional reasons, so most participants are self-selected (Litz et al., 2002). Those choosing to participate in debriefing may differ in many ways from individuals who do not. Between group differences in distress, motivation, prior trauma exposure, social support, and co-morbidity may threaten internal validity and make findings impossible to interpret (Malcolm et al., 2005; Tuckey, 2007).

There are no RCTs of individual or group debriefings of police officers in the research literature. This may be due to the methodological challenges highlighted above. Skills for conducting this research are not likely to be present in the staffs of most police departments, so that collaborations with academic researchers are needed.

Intervention for Acute Stress Disorder and PTSD

In the last decade, international evidence-based guidelines for the treatment of stress and trauma-related disorders, including Acute Stress Disorder and PTSD have emerged (Forbes et al., 2011). These standards also provide early intervention recommendations in the immediate aftermath of trauma exposure (APA, 2004; Department of Veterans Affairs/Department of Defense, 2004). These interventions include Psychological First Aid, Skills for Psychological Recovery, Cognitive Behavior Therapy for Acute Stress Disorder, Prolonged Exposure, Cognitive Processing Therapy, and Eye Movement Desensitization and Reprocessing.

Psychological First Aid is an evidence-informed early intervention for trauma survivors that was created, in part, to address concerns about the effectiveness of psychological debriefing (National Child Traumatic Stress Network and National Center for PTSD, [NCTSN-NCPSD] 2006). Psychological First Aid was designed to be utilized in disaster response and to be administered in the immediate aftermath following an emergency, disaster, or act of terrorism, with goals of supporting individual and community resiliency, reducing acute distress, and fostering short and long term adaptive coping and functioning. Psychological First Aid includes 8 components: 1) contact and engagement, 2) safety and comfort, 3) stabilization, 4) information gathering regarding current needs and concerns, 5) practical assistance, 6) connection with social support, 7) information on coping, and 8) connection with appropriate services (NCTSN-NCPSD, 2006; Ruzek et al., 2007; Uhernik & Husson, 2009). Psychological First Aid is intended to be consistent with the literature on risk and resilience, pragmatic for field settings, appropriate across lifespan development, and adaptable across cultures, including first responders. Although Phillips and Kane (2006) consider Psychological First Aid to be the "best practice" intervention for first responders in the immediate aftermath of a disaster, it has not been subjected to rigorous empirical evaluation (Forbes et al., 2011).

Skills for Psychological Recovery is another evidence-informed, early intervention for trauma (Berkowitz et al., 2010). Skills for Psychological Recovery was designed to follow Psychological First Aid in the weeks and months following mass trauma exposure, with an emphasis on building coping skills to manage post-disaster stress, distress, and hardship (Berkowitz et al., 2010; Forbes et al., 2010). Skills for Psychological Recovery uses several counseling sessions to teach skills for problem solving, positive activity scheduling, managing emotional and physical reactions, promoting helpful thinking, and enhancing social connection (Berkowitz et al., 2010). The goal of Skills for Psychological Recovery is to facilitate recovery and adaptive functioning and to prevent unhelpful behaviors (Berkowitz et al.,

2010). As with Psychological First Aid, the effectiveness of Skills for Psychological Recovery has not yet been evaluated in research.

Bryant (2007) developed Cognitive Behavioral Therapy for Acute Stress Disorder with the goal of preventing the development of PTSD. Post-trauma distress naturally resolves for most survivors; however, approximately 75% of those who meet criteria for Acute Stress Disorder (diagnosed between 2 to 4 weeks post-trauma) go on to develop PTSD (Bryant, 2007; Creamer, O'Donnell, & Pattison, 2004). Thus, Cognitive Behavioral Therapy for Acute Stress Disorder is introduced following the early weeks of adaptation, when some of those at greatest risk for long-term distress can be identified (Bryant, 2007). Cognitive Behavioral Therapy for Acute Stress Disorder consists of five sessions focused on education (common symptoms, treatment rationale), breathing retraining, imaginal and in-vivo exposure to trauma memories or stimuli, and cognitive restructuring to challenge negative thoughts about the trauma, self, others, and the world (Bryant, 2007). Ehlers and Clark (2003) reviewed seven trials (mostly RCTs) of Cognitive Behavioral Therapy for those with early symptoms of PTSD or Acute Stress Disorder. CBT was more effective than supportive counseling in reducing PTSD, anxiety, and depression, both at post-treatment and for as long as 4 years post-treatment (Bryant et al., 1999; Bryant, Moulds, & Nixon, 2003; Ehlers & Clark, 2003). Cognitive Behavioral Therapy for Acute Stress Disorder is the best-supported preventive early post-trauma intervention at the current time. To date, Cognitive Behavioral Therapy for Acute Stress Disorder has not been evaluated in police officers.

For individuals whose symptoms progress beyond 1 month, evidence-based interventions for PTSD, such as Cognitive Processing Therapy, Prolonged Exposure, and Eye Movement Desensitization and Reprocessing, may be delivered. Cognitive Processing Therapy is a manualized, 12-session treatment for PTSD that can be delivered in individual or group format (Powers et al., 2006; Resick & Schnicke, 1996). Cognitive Processing Therapy is based on information processing theory, focuses on modifying cognitions around the themes of safety, trust, power and control, esteem and intimacy, and addresses a range of emotions (Powers et al., 2006; Resick & Schnicke, 1996; Resick et al., 2008). Treatment sessions include 1) introduction and education, 2) discussion of the patient's written account about the meaning of the event, 3) identification of thoughts and feelings, 4) remembering the trauma, 5) identification of stuck points (e.g., conflicting or negative beliefs that create negative emotions and unhealthy behavior), 6) challenging questions, 7) faulty thinking patterns, 8) safety issues, 9) trust issues, 10) power and control issues, 11) esteem issues, and 12) intimacy issues and meaning of the event (Resick & Schnicke, 1996). RCTs have demonstrated that Cognitive Processing Therapy is an effective treatment for PTSD among survivors of an array of traumatic events, including military trauma and childhood sexual abuse (Forbes et al., 2012).

Although Cognitive Processing Therapy has not been evaluated in first responders, multiple studies have evaluated its effectiveness in treating military-related trauma (Alvarez et al., 2011; Chard et al., 2010; Forbes et al., 2012; Monson et al., 2006). For example, Monson et al. (2006) conducted an RCT of Cognitive Processing Therapy vs. a wait-list control in veterans ($N = 60$) with military-related PTSD. Post-treatment, 40% of those in the Cognitive Processing Therapy condition no longer met criteria for PTSD; 50% experienced a significant change in PTSD symptoms post-treatment and at 1-month follow-up. Improvements were also found in depression, anxiety, affect functioning, guilt, and social adjustment. Alvarez et al. (2011) used a cohort design to compare group Cognitive Processing Therapy ($n = 104$) to treatment as usual ($n = 93$) in male veterans in a Veterans Affairs PTSD Residential Rehabilitation Program. Cognitive Processing Therapy resulted in greater improvement in PTSD and a variety of other outcomes.

Prolonged Exposure is a manualized PTSD treatment consisting of 9 to 12 weekly, 90-minute sessions (Foa et al., 2007; Tuerk et al., 2011). Prolonged Exposure is based on emotional processing theory and focuses on reducing trauma-related conditioned responses that occur in the absence of realistic threat. Prolonged Exposure includes education about normal trauma reactions and the rationale for treatment, breathing retraining, in-vivo exposure to avoided trauma-related situations or objects, and imaginal exposure to trauma-related memories. Imaginal and in-vivo components are conducted in a repeated, prolonged fashion and take place both in and out of session.

While RCTs of Prolonged Exposure have not been conducted in police officers, it has been shown to be an effective treatment for PTSD in veterans and military personnel (Eftekhari et al., 2013; Forbes et al., 2012; Jeffreys et al., 2013; Powers et al., 2010; Rauch et al., 2009; Tolin & Foa, 1999; Schnurr et al., 2007; Tuerk et al., 2011; Yoder et al., 2012). For example, Tuerk et al. (2011) conducted a post-hoc analysis of the effectiveness of Prolonged Exposure for PTSD in combat veterans (N = 65) that had served in Iraq and Afghanistan. Three-quarters of treatment completers scored below the clinical cutoff for PTSD. Tolin and Foa (1999) reported a time-series case study of a police officer with PTSD due to a work-related critical incident, demonstrating a reduction in PTSD symptoms that was maintained at 6-month follow-up.

Eye Movement Desensitization and Reprocessing has also received empirical support as a treatment for PTSD (Shapiro, 1989a, 1989b). Eye Movement Desensitization and Reprocessing consists of 8 phases: client history and treatment planning, preparation, assessment, desensitization, installation, body scan, closure, and reevaluation (for further details of the phases of EMDR, see Shapiro [1989a, 2001]). A distinguishing characteristic of this intervention is holding trauma-related memories in awareness while conducting bilateral eye movements. Eye Movement Desensitization and Reprocessing has been evaluated in police officers. Wilson and colleagues (2001) compared Eye Movement Desensitization and Reprocessing with a traditional stress management program in police officers (N = 62) with PTSD. Officers that received Eye Movement Desensitization and Reprocessing endorsed lower PTSD symptoms, subjective distress, job stress, and trait anger, and higher marital satisfaction than officers that did not (Wilson, Tinker, Becker & Logan, 2001). Lansing, Amen, Hanks, and Rudy (2005) conducted a non-controlled study of Eye Movement Desensitization and Reprocessing in a sample of (N = 6) police officers with duty-related PTSD. From pre- to post-intervention, participants showed an almost complete elimination of PTSD symptoms.

Given barriers to mental health care in police culture, identifying evidence-based PTSD treatments that are acceptable to law enforcement personnel may increase treatment engagement. Becker et al. (2009) investigated PTSD treatment preferences in a sample (N = 379) of active law enforcement personnel (n = 156), cadets (n = 108), and criminal justice students planning on entering a law enforcement career (n = 99), with varying trauma histories. Treatment options included Cognitive Processing Therapy, Exposure Therapy, Pharmacotherapy (sertraline), Eye Movement Desensitization and Reprocessing, Psychodynamic Therapy, and Brief Eclectic Therapy (a combination of Cognitive Behavioral Therapy and dynamic therapy). CISD was included but not compared with the other interventions. Participants were instructed to read a police traumatic event and imagine they developed PTSD. Participants were then instructed to rate the credibility of the treatment options and to choose their most and least preferred treatment options.

Cognitive Processing Therapy (36.9%) and Exposure (25.9%) were the two most preferred treatment options. In a sub-sample of participants who endorsed actual prior exposure to a traumatic event (n = 218), which included participants with likely PTSD, Cognitive Processing Therapy (39%) and Exposure

(20.6%) were the top two preferred treatment options. In another sub-sample of participants meeting criteria for PTSD (n = 36), Cognitive Processing Therapy remained the top choice (39%) followed by Psychodynamic Therapy (25%). Only 11% of the sub-sample of participants with PTSD endorsed exposure as their top choice; however, 52% endorsed exposure as their second choice. Across all participants, Eye Movement Desensitization and Reprocessing was the least preferred modality for PTSD treatment. Such findings may inform police department decision-making regarding offering evidence-based treatments (Becker et al., 2009).

Emerging Models

Given the apparent limitations of single-session interventions, such as CISD, alternative intervention models for police officers have been developed. Cumulative stress debriefings, peer support, and residential treatment programs reflect efforts to provide more intensive and/or ongoing intervention. While initial research suggests that these approaches have promise, they are yet to be rigorously evaluated.

Multi-session supportive interventions have been studied. Doctor, Curtis, and Isaacs (1994) randomly assigned police officers (N = 61) to 12 weeks of hour-long group therapy, designed to promote ventilation of feelings and reduce denial, or to a control condition. No significant differences were found. Young (2012) assigned officers to periodic group stress debriefings (n = 20) or a or control condition (n = 17); no differences were found in effects on PTSD, depression, coping skills, perceived organizational support, or quality of life. Results of these studies suggest that multi-session supportive group interventions are ineffective.

Peer support programs have been forwarded as another way that law enforcement agencies can augment psychological services (Kamena, Gentz, Hays, Bohl-Penrod, & Greene, 2014). Peer support programs are intended to provide social, emotional, and practical support to police officers in distress for personal or professional reasons, help officers navigate the psychological challenges of their work, and provide day-to-day support (International Association of Chiefs of Police, 2011).

Peer support members are specially trained co-workers, who may therefore be more acceptable, non-threatening, and better positioned than family members and mental health professionals to normalize both tactical and emotional decisions officers face (Kirschman et al., 2014). Peer support officers may be well positioned to detect officers with elevated levels of distress and impaired functioning and to help guide these officers to formal mental health services. Police officers on administrative leave as a result of legal and/or department policy are at risk of isolation from their co-workers. In such situations, ongoing contact with a peer support officer may reduce feelings of shame, embarrassment, abandonment, and rejection (Kirschman et al., 2014; Rowland, 2011).

Berg, Hem, Lau, Haseth, and Ekeberg (2005) found that in a nationwide sample of Norwegian police (N = 3272), those who worked in districts lacking peer support programs and whose populations were greater than 50,000 endorsed more work injuries and job pressures. However, there are no published trials of the effectiveness of police peer support at reducing psychiatric morbidity.

Residential treatment programs provide an alternative form of treatment for first responders. The Veterans Health Administration (VHA; U.S. Department of Veterans Affairs, 2010) provided guidelines to match patient needs with appropriate level care. The VHA articulates that residential treatment programs are intended to provide veterans with a semi-structured environment to address PTSD, substance abuse, medical problems, other psychological issues, and reintegration into the community. Similarly, police officers most appropriate for residential treatment may be those exhibiting severe symptoms and functional impairment.

Two residential treatment programs specialize in the treatment of first responders. Founded in the 1990s, the On-Site Academy in Westminister, MA, offers residential and non-residential short- and long-term programs for rescue workers experiencing work-related acute, cumulative, or delayed critical incident stress reactions (On-Site Academy, n.d.). Staff are licensed clinicians, advanced CISM peers, national trauma consultants, and other support staff from the police, fire, and emergency medical services. Interventions delivered at On-Site Academy include CISM debriefings, Thought Field Therapy, Alpha-Stim, Eye Movement Desensitization and Reprocessing, and substance use treatment.

The West Coast Post-Trauma Retreat and Significant Others and Spouses programs were modeled after the On-Site Academy (Fay, Kamena, Benner, & Buscho, 2006). West Coast Post-Trauma Retreat and Significant Others and Spouses fall under the umbrella of the First Responder Support Network, a non-profit organization whose mission is to provide educational and therapeutic treatment programs for first responders and their families with the goal of promoting recovery from critical incidents and stress (First Responder Support Network, 2015; Heglund, 2009). West Coast Post-Trauma Retreat is a 6-day residential treatment program for first responders who present with symptoms of depression, PTSD, anxiety, sleep disorders, and substance use. Treatment is highly structured, consisting of psychoeducation, group therapy, individual therapy, Eye Movement Desensitization and Reprocessing, and milieu therapy with peer support and clinicians. Staff are licensed clinical psychologists, therapists, police chaplains, and peer support (including many former clients. Approximately 60% of the clients are law enforcement, 21% are fire or emergency medical service, and 19% are from corrections, military, probation, or other civil services (Fay et al., 2006). First Responder Support Network also offers Significant Others and Spouses retreats to support the spouses and partners of first responders with their own depression, anxiety, and vicarious traumatization (Fay et al., 2006; First Responder Support Network, 2015). There are no published studies of the effectiveness of such residential treatment programs.

Organizational Issues

Organizational issues may complicate decision-making regarding early intervention for police officers following exposure to a critical incident. First, determining which events warrant early intervention is a conceptual challenge that may be compounded by organizational cultural differences. For example, organizations may offer or mandate CISD following critical incidents such as an officer involved shooting or line of duty death. However, other critical incidents with potentially substantial emotional impact (e.g., infant deaths, motor vehicle accidents, bearing witness to tragedy) may occur without acknowledgement of impact by the organization, and involved officers may feel uncomfortable asking for a formal intervention from the department (N. Schlitz, personal communication, March 18, 2016). Second, critical incidents may tax organizational resources. In incidents involving officers and other staff across multiple shifts, the time and person-power needed to schedule and implement assessment and intervention may be prohibitive. Third, ethical and legal issues emerge around the monitoring of post-incident reactions. In peer support programs, confidentiality may be difficult to ensure given discrepancies between laws and departmental policies (International Association of Chiefs of Police, 2011); thus officers may have concerns regarding trust, disclosure, and the referral process.

Police organizations also need to be aware of and address other sources of employee stress. Organizational stress results from perceptions of politics, poor leadership, and lack of administrative support, conflict with administration, outdated equipment, inadequate training, poor communication from superiors about roles and expectations, and criticism from the media and public (Brondolo et al., 2012; Kirschman, 2007; Maguen et al., 2009; Marin 2012; Regehr & Bober, 2005). Evidence suggests organizational stress may be as important as critical incident exposure in determining officers' emotional well-being (Collins & Gibbs, 2003; Liberman et al., 2002; Patterson, 1999).

Recommendations

Clearly, deriving evidence-based recommendations for early intervention for police officers exposed to critical incidents is challenging. Based on research findings, it is easier to offer evidence-based cautions. Specifically, organizations are cautioned against holding mandatory group psychological debriefings that involve recounting details of the event. Given that officers may differ in level of exposure, emotional reactions, and coping responses to the same event, and given the lack of evidence that CISD-type interventions are effective in preventing PTSD or other negative sequelae of critical incidents, alternative care models are suggested.

Several evidence-informed recommendations can be made. First, education regarding mental health issues, adaptive coping, self-care, and peer support should be introduced in the police academy and integrated through police officers' careers via continued training. Such training may reduce stigma, facilitate recognition of emotional states and behaviors that pose risk for longer-term adjustment difficulties, and increase acceptance of mental health intervention. Second, as a simple first intervention, mental health professionals and law enforcement personnel should consider being trained in the administration of Psychological First Aid (NCTSN/NCPTSD, 2006). Psychological First Aid is widely endorsed and has been designed to pose little threat to adverse reactions; however it has yet to be studied in randomized trials. Third, police departments should provide a framework for monitoring staff reactions and referral to more intensive evidence-based treatments when needed. This may mean locating practitioners or having in-house police psychologists trained in evidence-based psychological treatments for PTSD (i.e., Cognitive Processing Therapy, Prolonged Exposure, Eye Movement Desensitization and Reprocessing) to promote effective referral and treatment. Fourth, departments should implement confidential, ongoing peer support programs. Training respected peers in provision of support, detection of distress, risk assessment (e.g., suicidal ideation), and referral can decrease isolation and stigma and enhance transition to more formal individual, family, and group therapy, substance use programs, and residential treatment.

Future Research

In light of the conceptual and methodological challenges in designing and researching early interventions for police officers, several directions for future research are indicated. Aside from anecdotal reports, research has not assessed the nature of the interventions police departments are currently administering, whether the terminology being used (e.g., debriefing) accurately describes the content of the interventions, or the perceived outcomes (e.g., participant and departmental satisfaction). Research should clarify what interventions are being administered, whether they map onto evidence-based treatments, whether police officers and departmental leadership perceive them to be helpful, and whether they are associated with positive objective outcomes (e.g., reduced distress, improved functioning, fewer missed work days or workman's compensation claims).

Given the limited evidence for the impact of single-session individual or group debriefing methods, and the promise of brief multiple-session counseling approaches like Cognitive Behavioral Therapy and Skills for Psychological Recovery, it is important to increase research on these brief interventions. Psychological First Aid and Skills for Psychological Recovery are yet to be evaluated in RCTs with civilians or in any study with police officers. There is also a need for studies evaluating multi-component incident and stress management programs, given that police departments will be implementing a set of services that need to be evaluated, not isolated interventions.

Further, assessment of a broader range of outcomes of early intervention for police, beyond PTSD and depression, is needed. For example, the impact of early interventions on perceived stigma, alcohol/substance use, marital/family and occupational functioning, and acceptance of referral to more intensive forms of treatment must be evaluated. Lastly, it remains to be determined whether pre-emptive primary prevention interventions (before exposure to incidents), designed to enhance resiliency factors and adaptive coping skills, could buffer officers from the challenges inherent in policing (Whealin et al., 2008).

Determining clinician competency and qualification to administer interventions to law enforcement is also an important topic. There is great variability across clinicians practicing in the field, including degree (e.g., masters vs. doctoral level), discipline (e.g., psychology, social work), law enforcement background (e.g., military vs. police vs. civilian), and areas of training and expertise (e.g., training and board certification status in Police Psychology). Whether these clinician variables are differentially associated with intervention outcomes must also be studied. Guidelines regarding competency and specialization in Police Psychology might guide such investigations (see American Board of Police and Public Safety Psychology at www.abpp.org).

Perhaps most critical, police departments should explore collaborative relationships with local academic partners to evaluate the ways in which they are supporting their personnel, and test the effectiveness of newer, potentially more effective models of critical incident assistance, to move toward effective prevention of problems for police officers whose vital societal role may place them at risk for experiencing significant personal and family difficulties.

REFERENCES

Alvarez, J., McClean, C., Harris, A. H. S., Rosen, C. S., Ruzek, J. I., & Kimerling, R. (2011). The comparative effectiveness of cognitive processing therapy for male veterans treated in a VHA posttraumatic stress disorder residential rehabilitation program. *Journal of Consulting and Clinical Psychology*, *79*(5), 590–599. doi:10.1037/a0024466 PMID:21744946

American Psychiatric Association (APA). (2004). *Practice guidelines for the treatment of patients with acute stress disorder and posttraumatic stress disorder*. Arlington, VA: American Psychiatric Association.

Becker, C. B., Meyer, G., Price, J. S., Graham, M. M., Arsena, A., Armstrong, D. A., & Ramon, E. (2009). Law enforcement preferences for PTSD treatment and crisis management alternatives. *Behaviour Research and Therapy*, *47*(3), 245–253. doi:10.1016/j.brat.2009.01.001 PMID:19200945

Berg, A. M., Hem, E., Lau, B., Haseth, J., & Ekeberg, O. (2005). Stress in the Norwegian police service. *Occupational Medicine*, *55*(2), 113–120. doi:10.1093/occmed/kqi023 PMID:15757985

Berkowitz, S., Bryant, R., Brymer, M., Hamblen, J., Jacobs, A., Layne, C., … Watson, P. (2010). *Skills for Psychological Recovery: Field Operations Guide.* The National Center for PTSD & the National Child Traumatic Stress Network.

Best, S., Artwohl, A., & Kirschman, E. (2011). Critical incidents. In J. Kitaeff (Ed.), *Handbook of police psychology (pp. 491 – 507).* New York, NY: Routledge, Taylor and Francis Group.

Bisson, J. I., McFarlane, A. C., Rose, S., Ruzek, J. I., & Watson, P. J. (2009). Psychological debriefing for adults. In E. B. Foa, T. M. Keane, M. J. Friedman, & J. A. Cohen (Eds.), *Effective treatments for PTSD (pp. 83 - 104).* New York, NY: The Guilford Press.

Bohl, N. (1995). The effectiveness of brief psychological interventions in police officers after critical incidents. In J. Reese, J. Horn, & C. Dunning (Eds.), *Critical incidents and police, revised.* Washington, DC: Dept Justice.

Brondolo, E., Wellington, R., Brady, N., Libby, D., & Brondolo, T. (2008). Mechanism and strategies for preventing post-traumatic stress disorder in forensic workers responding to mass fatality incidents. *Journal of Forensic and Legal Medicine*, *15*(2), 78–88. doi:10.1016/j.jflm.2007.04.007 PMID:18206823

Bryant, R. A. (2007). Early intervention for post-traumatic stress disorder. *Early Intervention in Psychiatry*, *1*(1), 19–26. doi:10.1111/j.1751-7893.2007.00006.x PMID:21352105

Bryant, R. A., Moulds, M. L., & Nixon, R. V. D. (2003). Cognitive behaviour therapy for acute stress disorder: A four-year follow-up. *Behaviour Research and Therapy*, *41*(4), 489–494. doi:10.1016/S0005-7967(02)00179-1 PMID:12643970

Bryant, R. A., Sackville, T., Dang, S. T., Moulds, M., & Guthrie, R. (1999). Treating acute stress disorder: An evaluation of cognitive behavior therapy and supportive counseling techniques. *The American Journal of Psychiatry*, *156*, 1780–1786. PMID:10553743

Brymer, M., Jacobs, A., Pynoos, R., Ruzek, J., Steinberg, A., Vernberg, E., & Watson, P. (2006). *Psychological First Aid: Field Operations Guide* (2nd ed.). Available on www.ncptsd.va.gov

Carlier, I. V. E., Lamberts, R. D., Van Uchelen, A. J., & Gersons, B. P. (1998). Disaster-related post-traumatic stress in police officers: A field study of the impact of debriefing. *Stress Medicine*, *14*(3), 143–148. doi:10.1002/(SICI)1099-1700(199807)14:3<143::AID-SMI770>3.0.CO;2-S

Carlier, I. V. E., Voerman, A. E., & Gersons, B. P. R. (2000). The influence of occupational debriefing on post-traumatic stress symptomatology in traumatized police officers. *The British Journal of Medical Psychology*, *73*(1), 87–98. doi:10.1348/000711200160327 PMID:10759053

Chard, K. M., Schumm, J. A., Owens, G. P., & Cottingham, S. M. (2010). A comparison of OEF and OIF veterans and Vietnam veterans receiving cognitive processing therapy. *Journal of Traumatic Stress*, *23*(1), 25–32. PMID:20146255

Chemtob, C., Tomas, S., Law, W., & Cremniter, D. (1997). Postdisaster psychosocial intervention: A field study of debriefing on psychological distress. *The American Journal of Psychiatry*, *154*(3), 415–417. doi:10.1176/ajp.154.3.415 PMID:9054792

Chopko, B. A., Palmieri, P. A., & Adams, R. E. (2015). Critical incident history questionnaire replication: Frequency and severity of trauma exposure among officers from small and midsize police agencies. *Journal of Traumatic Stress*, *28*(2), 157–161. doi:10.1002/jts.21996 PMID:25808672

Collins, P. A., & Gibbs, A. C. (2003). Stress in police officers: A study of the origins, prevalence and severity of stress-related symptoms within a county police force. *Occupational Medicine*, *53*(4), 256–264. doi:10.1093/occmed/kqg061 PMID:12815123

Creamer, M. C., O'Donnell, M. L., & Pattison, P. (2004). The relationship between acute stress disorder and posttraumatic stress disorder in severely injured trauma survivors. *Behaviour Research and Therapy*, *42*(3), 315–328. doi:10.1016/S0005-7967(03)00141-4 PMID:14975772

Deahl, M. P., Srinivasan, M., Jones, N., Neblett, C., & Jolly, A. (2001). Evaluating psychological debriefing: Are we measuring the right outcomes? *Journal of Traumatic Stress*, *14*(3), 527–529. doi:10.1023/A:1011160606866 PMID:11534883

Department of Veterans Affairs/Department of Defense (VA/DoD). (2004). *VA/DoD Clinical practice guideline fro the management of post-traumatic stress, version 1.0*. Washington, DC: Veterans Health Administration, Department of Defense.

Devilly, G. J., Gist, R., & Cotton, P. (2006). Ready! Fire! Aim! The status of psychological debriefing and therapeutic interventions: In the workplace and after disasters. *Review of General Psychology*, *19*(4), 318–345. doi:10.1037/1089-2680.10.4.318

Doctor, R. S., Curtis, R., & Isaacs, G. (1994). Psychiatric morbidity in policemen and the effect of brief psychotherapeutic intervention – a pilot study. *Stress Medicine*, *10*(3), 151–157. doi:10.1002/smi.2460100304

Eftekhari, A., Ruzek, J. I., Crowley, J. J., Rosen, C. S., Greenbaum, M. A., & Karlin, B. E. (2013). Effectiveness of national implementation of prolonged exposure therapy in veterans affairs care. *JAMA Psychiatry*, *70*(9), 949–955. doi:10.1001/jamapsychiatry.2013.36 PMID:23863892

Ehlers, A., & Clark, D. M. (2003). Early psychological interventions for adult survivors of trauma: A review. *Biological Psychiatry*, *53*(9), 817–826. doi:10.1016/S0006-3223(02)01812-7 PMID:12725974

Eid, J., Johnsen, B. H., & Weisaeth, L. (2001). The effects of group psychological debriefing on acute stress reactions following a traffic accident: A quasi-experimental approach. *International Journal of Emergency Mental Health*, *3*(3), 145–154. PMID:11642192

Everly, G. S., Boyle, S. H., & Lating, J. M. (1999). The effectiveness of psychological debriefing with vicarious trauma: A meta-analysis. *Stress Medicine*, *15*(4), 229–233. doi:10.1002/(SICI)1099-1700(199910)15:4<229::AID-SMI818>3.0.CO;2-M

Everly, G. S. Jr, Flannery, R. B. Jr, & Mitchell, J. T. (2000). Critical incident stress management (CISM): A review of the literature. *Aggression and Violent Behavior*, *5*(1), 23–40. doi:10.1016/S1359-1789(98)00026-3

Everly, G. S., Lating, J. M., & Mitchell, J. T. (2000). Innovations in group crisis intervention: Critical incident stress debriefing (CISD) and critical incident stress management (CISM). In A. Roberts (Ed.), *Crisis intervention handbook: Assessment, treatment, and research* (pp. 77–97). New York, NY: Oxford University Press.

Everly, G. S., & Mitchell, J. T. (2000). The debriefing "controversy" and crisis intervention: A review of lexical and substantive issues. *Journal of Emergency Mental Health, 2*(4), 211–225. PMID:11217152

Fay, J., Kamena, M. D., Benner, A., & Buscho, A. (2006). A residential milieu treatment approach for first-responder trauma. *Traumatology, 12*(3), 225–262. doi:10.1177/1534765606294991

First Responder Support Network. (2015). *First responder support network.* Retrieved from http://www.frsn.org

Foa, E. B., Hembree, E. A., & Rothbaum, B. O. (2007). *Prolonged exposure therapy for ptsd: Emotional processing of traumatic experiences.* New York, NY: Oxford University Press.

Forbes, D., Fletcher, S., Wolfgang, B., Varker, T., Creamer, M., Brymer, M. J., & Bryant, R. A. et al. (2010). Practitioner perceptions of skills for psychological recovery: A training programme for health practitioners in the aftermath of the Victorian bushfires. *The Australian and New Zealand Journal of Psychiatry, 44*(12), 1105–1111. doi:10.3109/00048674.2010.513674 PMID:21070106

Forbes, D., Lewis, V., Varker, T., Phelps, A., O'Donnell, A. P., Wade, D. J., & Creamer, M. et al. (2011). Psychological first aid following trauma: Implementation and evaluation framework for high-risk organizations. *Psychiatry, 74*(3), 224–239. doi:10.1521/psyc.2011.74.3.224 PMID:21916629

Forbes, D., Lloyd, D., Nixon, R. D. V., Elliott, P., Varker, T., Perry, D., & Creamer, M. et al. (2012). A multisite randomized controlled effectiveness trial of cognitive processing therapy for military-related posttraumatic stress disorder. *Journal of Anxiety Disorders, 26*(3), 442–452. doi:10.1016/j.janxdis.2012.01.006 PMID:22366446

Forbes, D., Lloyd, D., Nixon, R. D. V., Elliott, P., Varker, T., Perry, D., & Creamer, M. et al. (2012). A multisite randomized controlled effectiveness trial of cognitive processing therapy for military-related posttraumatic stress disorder. *Journal of Anxiety Disorders, 26*(3), 442–452. doi:10.1016/j.janxdis.2012.01.006 PMID:22366446

Gilmartin, K. (2002). *Emotional survival for law enforcement: A guide for officers and their families.* Tuscon, AZ: E-S Press.

Haugen, P. T., Evcs, M., & Weiss, D. S. (2012). Treating posttraumatic stress disorder in first responders: A systematic review. *Clinical Psychology Review, 32*(5), 370–280. doi:10.1016/j.cpr.2012.04.001 PMID:22561967

Heglund, J. (September 2009). Helping first responders withstand traumatic experiences. *FBI Law Enforcement Bulletin,* 1 – 4.

International Association of Chiefs of Police. (2011). *Peer support guidelines.* Retrieved from http://www.theiacp.org/portals/0/documents/pdfs/Psych-PeerSupportGuidelines.pdf

Jeffreys, M. D., Reinfeld, C., Nair, P. V., Garcia, H. A., Mata-Galan, E., & Rentz, T. O. (2013). Evaluating treatment of posttraumatic stress disorder with cognitive processing therapy and prolonged exposure therapy in a VHA speciality clinic. *Journal of Anxiety Disorders*, *28*(1), 108–114. doi:10.1016/j.janxdis.2013.04.010 PMID:23764125

Jenkins, S. R. (1996). Social support and debriefing efficacy among emergency medical workers after a mass shooting incident. *Journal of Social Behavior and Personality*, *11*(3), 477–492.

Kamena, M. D., Gentz, D., Hays, V., Bohl-Penrod, N., & Green, L. W. (2011). Peer support teams fill an emotional void in law enforcement agencies. *The Police Chief*, *78*(8), 80–84.

Kearns, M. C., Ressler, K. J., Zatzick, D., & Rothbaum, B. O. (2012). Early intervention for ptsd: A review. *Depression and Anxiety*, *29*(10), 833–842. doi:10.1002/da.21997 PMID:22941845

Kessler, R. C., Sonnega, A., Bromet, E., Hughes, M., & Nelson, C. B. (1995). Posttraumatic stress disorder in the national comorbidity survey. *Archives of General Psychiatry*, *52*(12), 1048–1060. doi:10.1001/archpsyc.1995.03950240066012 PMID:7492257

Kirschman, E. (2007). *I love a cop: What police families need to know* (Rev. ed.). New York, NY: The Guilford Press.

Kirschman, E., Kamena, M. D., & Fay, J. (2014). *Counseling cops: What clinicians need to know*. New York, NY: The Guilford Press.

Kleim, B., & Westphal, M. (2011). Mental health in first responders: A review and recommendation for prevention and intervention strategies. *Traumatology*, *17*(4), 17–24. doi:10.1177/1534765611429079

Komarovskaya, I., Maguen, S., McCaslin, S. E., Metzler, T. J., Madan, A., Brown, A. D., & Marmar, C. R. et al. (2011). The impact of killing and injuring others on mental health symptoms among police officers. *Journal of Psychiatric Research*, *45*(10), 1132–1336. doi:10.1016/j.jpsychires.2011.05.004 PMID:21658717

Lansing, K., Amen, D. G., Hanks, C., & Rudy, L. (2005). High-resolution brain SPECT imaging and eye movement desensitization and reprocessing in police officers with ptsd. *The Journal of Neuropsychiatry and Clinical Neurosciences*, *17*(4), 526–532. doi:10.1176/jnp.17.4.526 PMID:16387993

Liberman, A., Best, S., Metzler, T., Fagan, J., Weiss, D., & Marmar, C. (2002). Routine occupational stress and psychological distress in police. *Policing: An International Journal of Police Strategies & Management*, *25*(2), 421–439. doi:10.1108/13639510210429446

Litz, B. T. (2008). Early intervention for trauma: Where are we and where do we need to go? A commentary. *Journal of Traumatic Stress*, *21*(6), 503–506. doi:10.1002/jts.20373 PMID:19107726

Litz, B. T., Gray, M. J., Bryant, R. A., & Adler, A. B. (2002). Early intervention for trauma: Current status and future directions. *Clinical Psychology: Science and Practice*, *9*(2), 112–134. doi:10.1093/clipsy.9.2.112

Maguen, S., Metzler, T. J., McCaslin, S. E., Inslicht, S. S., Henn-Haase, C., Neylan, T. C., & Marmar, C. R. (2009). Routine work environment stress and PTSD symptoms in police officers. *The Journal of Nervous and Mental Disease*, *197*(10), 754–760. doi:10.1097/NMD.0b013e3181b975f8 PMID:19829204

Malcolm, A. G., Seaton, J., Perera, A., Sheehan, D. C., & Van Hasselt, V. B. (2005). Critical incident stress debriefing and law enforcement: An evaluative review. *Brief Treatment and Crisis Intervention, 5*(3), 261–278. doi:10.1093/brief-treatment/mhi019

Marchand, A., Boyer, R., Nadeau, C., Beaulieu-Prevost, D., & Martin, M. (2015). Predictors of post-traumatic stress disorder among police officers: A prospective study. *Psychological Trauma: Theory, Research, Practice, and Policy, 7*(3), 212–221. doi:10.1037/a0038780 PMID:25793514

Marin, A. (2012). *Line of duty: Investigation into how the Ontario Provincial Police and the Ministry of Community Safety and Correctional Services have addressed operational stress injuries affecting police officers, (Ombudsman Report, October 2012)*. Onatrio, Canada: Andre Marin.

Marmar, C. R., McCaslin, S. E., Metzler, T. J., Best, S., Weiss, D. S., Fagan, J., & Neylan, T. et al. (2006). Predictors of posttraumatic stress in police and other first responders. *Annals of the New York Academy of Sciences, 1071*(1), 1–18. doi:10.1196/annals.1364.001 PMID:16891557

Mitchell, J. T. (1983). When disaster strikes… The critical incident stress debriefing process. *Journal of Emergency Services, 8*, 36–39. PMID:10258348

Monson, C. M., Schnurr, P. P., Resick, P. A., Friedman, M. J., Young-Xu, Y., & Stevens, S. P. (2006). Cognitive processing therapy for veterans with military-related posttraumatic stress disorder. *Journal of Consulting and Clinical Psychology, 74*(5), 898–907. doi:10.1037/0022-006X.74.5.898 PMID:17032094

National Collaborating Centre for Mental Health. (2005). *Post-traumatic stress disorder. The management of PTSD in adults and children in primary and secondary care*. Leicester, UK: British Psychological Society & Gaskell.

National Institute of Mental Health. (2002). *Mental health and mass violence: Evidence-based early psychological intervention for victims/survivors of mass violence. A workshop to reach consensus on best practices. NIH Publication No. 02- 5138*. Washington, DC: U.S. Government Printing Office.

O'Hara, A. (2012, August). Badge of life: Police mental health. *Badge of Life Newsletter,* 1 – 3.

On-Site Academy. (n.d.). *On-Site academy: Serving those who serve*. Retrieved from http://www.on-siteacademy.org

Patterson, G. (1999). Coping effectiveness and occupational stress in police officers. In J. Violanti & D. Paton (Eds.), *Police trauma: The psychological aftermath of civilian combat* (pp. 214–226). Springfield, IL: Charles Thomas.

Perrin, M. A., Digrande, L., Wheeler, K., Thorpe, L., Farfel, M., & Brackbill, R. (2007). Differences in PTSD prevalence and associated risk factors among world trade centre disaster rescue and recovery workers. *The American Journal of Psychiatry, 164*(9), 1385–1394. doi:10.1176/appi.ajp.2007.06101645 PMID:17728424

Phillips, S. B., & Kane, D. (2006). *Guidelines for working with first responders (firefighters, police, emergency medical service and military) in the aftermath of disaster.* New York, NY: American Group Psychotherapy Association. Retrieved from http://www.agpa.org/home/practice-resources/group-interventions-for-trauma/general-information-on-trauma-for-clinicians-and-the-public-at-large/guidelines-for-working-with-first-responders-(firefighters-police-emergency-medical-service-and-military)-in-the-aftermath-of-disaster

Police & Public Safety Psychology. (n.d.). Retrieved March 2, 2016, from http://www.abpp.org/i4a/pages/index.cfm?pageid=3606

Powers, M. B., Halpern, J. M., Ferenschak, M. P., Gillihan, S. J., & Foa, E. B. (2010). A meta-analytic review of prolonged exposure for posttraumatic stress disorder. *Clinical Psychology Review*, *30*(6), 635–641. doi:10.1016/j.cpr.2010.04.007 PMID:20546985

Rauch, S. A. M., Defever, E., Favorite, T., Duroe, A., Garrity, C., Martis, B., & Liberzon, I. (2009). Prolonged exposure for PTSD in a Veterans Health Administration PTSD clinic. *Journal of Traumatic Stress*, *22*(1), 60–64. doi:10.1002/jts.20380 PMID:19145643

Regehr, C., & Bober, T. (2005). *In the line of fire: Trauma in the emergency services*. New York, NY: Oxford University Press, Inc. doi:10.1093/acprof:oso/9780195165029.001.0001

Resick, P. A., Galovski, T. E., Uhlmansiek, M. O., Scher, C. D., Clum, G. A., & Young-Xu, Y. (2008). A randomized clinical trial to dismantle components of cognitive process therapy for posttraumatic stress disorder in female victims of interpersonal violence. *Journal of Consulting and Clinical Psychology*, *76*(2), 243–258. doi:10.1037/0022-006X.76.2.243 PMID:18377121

Resick, P. A., & Schnicke, M. K. (1996). *Cognitive processing therapy for rape victims*. Newbury Park, CA: Sage Publications, Inc.

Roberts, A. R., & Everly, G. S. Jr. (2006). A meta-analysis of 36 crisis intervention studies. *Brief Treatment and Crisis Intervention*, *6*(1), 10–21. doi:10.1093/brief-treatment/mhj006

Robinson, H. M., Sigman, M. R., & Wilson, J. P. (1997). Duty related stressors and PTSD symptoms in suburban police officers. *Psychological Reports*, *81*(3), 835–845. doi:10.2466/pr0.1997.81.3.835 PMID:9400075

Robinson, R. C., & Mitchell, J. T. (1993). Evaluation of psychological debriefings. *Journal of Traumatic Stress*, *6*(3), 367–382. doi:10.1002/jts.2490060307

Rose, S. C., Bisson, J., Churchill, R., & Wessely, S. (2002). Psychological debriefing for preventing post traumatic stress disorder (PTSD). *Cochrane Database of Systematic Reviews*, (2): CD00560. doi:10.1002/14651858.CD000560 PMID:12076399

Royle, L., Keenan, P., & Farrell, D. (2009). Issues of stigma for first responders accessing support for posttraumatic stress. *International Journal of Emergency Mental Health*, *11*(2), 79–86. PMID:19927494

Ruzek, J. I., Brymer, M. J., Jacobs, A. K., Layne, C. M., Vernberg, E. M., & Watson, P. J. (2007). Psychological first aid. *Journal of Mental Health Counseling*, (29): 1, 17–49.

Schnurr, P. P., Friendman, M. J., Engel, C. C., Foa, E. B., Shea, M. T., Chow, B. K., & Bernardy, N. et al. (2007). Cognitive behavioral therapy for posttraumatic stress disorder in women: A ramdonized controlled trial. *JAMA Psychiatry*, *297*(8), 820–830. PMID:17327524

Shapiro, F. (1989a). Eye movement desensitization: A new treatment for post-traumatic stress disorder. *Journal of Behavior Therapy and Experimental Psychiatry*, *20*(3), 211–217. doi:10.1016/0005-7916(89)90025-6 PMID:2576656

Shapiro, F. (1989b). Efficacy of the eye movement desensitization procedure in the treatment of traumatic memories. *Journal of Traumatic Stress*, *2*(2), 199–223. doi:10.1002/jts.2490020207

Shapiro, F. (2001). *Eye movement desensitization and reprocessing (EMDR): Basic principles, protocols, and procedures* (2nd ed.). New York, NY: The Guilford Press.

Sheehan, D. C., Everly, G. S., & Langlieb, A. (2004). Current best practices coping with major critical incidents. *FBI Bulletin*, *73*(9), 1–13.

Spielberger, C. D., Westberry, L. G., Grier, K. S., & Greenfield, G. (1981). *The police stress survey: sources of stress in law enforcement*. Tampa, FL: Human Resources Institute.

Stallard, P., & Law, F. (1993). Screening and psychological debriefing of adolescent survivors of life-threatening events. *The British Journal of Psychiatry*, *163*(5), 660–665. doi:10.1192/bjp.163.5.660 PMID:8298836

Tolin, D. F., & Foa, E. B. (1999). Treatment of a police officer with PTSD using prolonged exposure. *Behavior Therapy*, *30*(3), 527–538. doi:10.1016/S0005-7894(99)80023-9

Tuckey, M. R. (2007). Issues in the debriefing debate for the emergency services: Moving research outcomes forward. *Clinical Psychology: Science and Practice*, *14*(2), 106–116. doi:10.1111/j.1468-2850.2007.00069.x

Tuerk, P. W., Yoder, M., Grubaugh, A., Myrick, H., Hamner, M., & Acierno, R. (2011). Prolonged exposure therapy for combat-related posttraumatic stress disorder: An examination of treatment effectiveness for veterans of the wars in Afghanistan and Iraq. *Journal of Anxiety Disorders*, *25*(3), 397–403. doi:10.1016/j.janxdis.2010.11.002 PMID:21131170

U.S. Department of Veterans Affairs & Department of Defense. (2010). *VA/DoD clinical practice guideline for management of post-traumatic stress* (2nd ed.). Washington, DC: Author.

Van Emmerik, A., Kamphuis, J. H., Hulsbosch, A. M., & Emmelkamp, P. M. G. (2002). Single session debriefing after psychological trauma: A meta-analysis. *Lancet*, *360*(9335), 766–771. doi:10.1016/S0140-6736(02)09897-5 PMID:12241834

Violanti, J. M., & Drylie, J. J. (2008). *Copicide: Concepts, cases, and controversies of suicide by cop*. Springfield, IL: Charles C. Thomas Publisher, LTD.

Wee, D. F., Mills, D. M., & Koehler, G. (1999). The effects of critical incident stress debriefing (CISD) on emergency medical services personnel following the Los Angeles civil disturbance. *International Journal of Emergency Mental Health*, *1*, 33–37. PMID:11227752

Weiss, D. S., Brunet, A., Best, S. R., Metzler, T. J., Liberman, A., Pole, N., & Marmar, C. R. et al. (2010). Frequency and severity approaches to indexing exposure to trauma: The critical incident history questionnaire for police officers. *Journal of Traumatic Stress*, *23*(6), 734–743. doi:10.1002/jts.20576 PMID:21171134

Wessely, S., & Deahl, M. (2003). Psychological debriefing is a waste of time. *The British Journal of Psychiatry*, *183*(1), 12–14. doi:10.1192/bjp.183.1.12 PMID:12835237

Wester, S. R., Arndt, D., Sedivy, S. K., & Arndt, L. (2010). Male police officers and stigma associated with counseling: The role of anticipated risks, anticipated benefits and gender role conflict. *Psychology of Men & Masculinity*, *11*(4), 286–302. doi:10.1037/a0019108

Whealin, J. M., Ruzek, J., & Southwick, S. (2008). Cognitive behavioral theory and preparation for professionals at risk for trauma exposure. *Trauma, Violence & Abuse*, *9*(2), 100–113. doi:10.1177/1524838008315869 PMID:18367753

Wilson, S. A., Tinker, R. H., Lecker, L. A., & Logan, C. R. (2001). Stress management with law enforcement personnel: A controlled outcome study of EMDR versus a traditional stress management program. *International Journal of Stress Management*, *8*(3), 179–200. doi:10.1023/A:1011366408693

Yoder, M., Tuerk, P. W., Price, M., Grubaugh, A. L., Strachan, M., Myrick, H., & Acierno, R. (2011). Prolonged exposure therapy for combat-related posttraumatic stress disorder: Comparing different outcomes for veterans of different wars. *Psychological Services*, *9*(1), 16–25. doi:10.1037/a0026279 PMID:22449084

Young, A., & Parr, G. (2004). An examination of the effectiveness of period stress debriefings with law enforcement personnel. In G. R. Walz & R. K. Yep (Eds.), *VISTAS: Perspectives on counseling, 2004* (pp. 145 - 152). Alexandria, VA: American Counseling Association.

Young, A. T. (2012). The effectiveness of cumulative stress debriefings with law enforcement personnel. *International Journal of Emergency Mental Health*, *14*(1), 29–35. PMID:23156960

Chapter 7
First Responder Psychological Recovery Following a Mass Casualty Event

Sara Garrido
Nicoletti-Flater Associates, USA

John Nicoletti
Nicoletti-Flater Associates, USA

ABSTRACT

Mass Casualty Events (MCE) have an extraordinary impact on an entire community. The impact on victims' families, survivors, and community members is often the subject of significant attention; however, rarely does the impact on first responders (law enforcement officers, firefighters, dispatchers, crime scene investigators/photographers, etc.) garner the same coverage. Additionally, agencies can quickly become overwhelmed by the magnitude of the response causing them to overlook the psychological impact of these incidents on their personnel. Serving as specialists in police and public safety psychology, crisis intervention, and trauma recovery, the authors reflect on lessons learned from their response to multiple MCEs, including the 1999 Columbine High School shooting and the 2012 Aurora Century 16 Theater shooting, and offer recommendations to agencies regarding crisis response and trauma recovery.

INTRODUCTION

At approximately 12:40am on July 20, 2012 members of the Aurora Police Department responded to the Century 16 Theater following the largest mass shooting in Colorado's history. Twelve were killed, including a six-year-old girl, and an additional 70 were wounded in the shooting. After 1,132 days, the shooter was sentenced to 12 life sentences without the possibility of parole for 1st Degree Murder and 3, 318 years for 64 counts of Attempted 1st Degree Murder, Attempted 2nd Degree Murder, and one count of Possession of Deadly Explosives. The investigation and prosecution involved nearly the entire Aurora Police Department, both sworn and civilian, as well as personnel from more than 40 additional local, state, and federal agencies. From emergency responders who carried victims from the theater rushing

DOI: 10.4018/978-1-5225-0813-7.ch007

them to local hospitals in the back of police vehicles, to crime lab personnel who sifted through blood and debris while processing the crime scene, to homicide detectives working tirelessly on the case for more than three years, the horrific nature of this incident and the prolonged exposure to it in preparing for trial left a tremendous psychological footprint. On August 26, 2015 during the last day of the sentencing hearing, Judge Samour spoke to the defendant saying, "You will never set foot in free society again… the defendant does not deserve any sympathy…Sheriff, get the defendant out of my courtroom please. (O'Neill, 2015, Paragraph 3)." Although there was a community wide sigh of relief at the conclusion of the trial and a great deal of discussion regarding closure being provided at long last, the psychological footprint remains and for many of the first responders, the wounds are still visible.

On December 2, 2015 at approximately 11am, Sayed Rizwan Farook and his wife, Tashfeen Malik, opened fire at a San Bernardino County, CA Department of Public Health training event and holiday party, of about 80 employees. The Public Health event began as semi-annual meeting and training, and was transitioning to the luncheon/holiday party when the shooting began (Lin & Winton, 2015). Farook and Malik entered the room armed with semi-automatic pistols and rifles, in black ski masks and tactical gear. They fired between 65 and 75 rounds (Aisch et al., 2015). In addition, the assailants left three explosive devices, which failed to explode, and likely were set to target first responders (Aisch, et al., 2015). The first police units were on scene within four minutes of the initial 911 emergency call (Lin & Winton, 2015). Two police officers arrived on the scene first, and another officer arrived several minutes later. Overall, approximately 300 officers and agents from the area responded to the active shooter event (Lin & Winton, 2015). The first responders entered a chaotic and unpredictable situation, knowing that initially they would not have cover (Jacobo, 2015). One officer, who entered the banquet room where the shooting took place, described it as "surreal" and "unspeakable carnage," adding that survivors had "pure panic" on their faces (Jacobo, 2015, Paragraph 7). Another officer reported, "My body went numb…It was overwhelming and surreal" (Jacobo, 2015, Paragraph 13). The suspects fled in a black SUV before police arrived. A witness was able to provide Farook's name to the police, who were then able to track Farook's vehicle (Lin & Winton, 2015). After the SUV was stopped, the couple exchanged fire with police and both were killed in the shootout (Aisch, et al., 2015). A total of seven police agencies were involved in the shootout (Lin & Winton, 2015). Overall, 14 civilians were killed in the mass shooting and 24 people, including two police officers, were injured. After an investigation by the FBI, the shooting was deemed an act of terrorism (Jacobo, 2015). The long-term psychological impact of this mass casualty event on the community and on first responders' remains to be seen.

This chapter is intended to emphasize for readers the impact MCEs have on first responders and the authors hope to educate readers on:

1. The impact of trauma contamination on first responders following a MCE, and common symptoms of distress in first responders. Research is clear that because of an increased exposure to life threatening situations, first responders are also at an increased risk of experiencing trauma-related symptoms (Weiss et. al., 2010). Exposure is either direct when the responder is the victim (officer involved shooting) or vicarious when he or she is the responder (MCE). Whether the exposure is direct or vicarious, the distress involved in these types of incidents can be significant. Training first responders on the detection, prevention, and mitigation of vicarious trauma symptoms can mitigate symptom severity and duration following an incident. This section will include recommendations based on the training the authors provide to agencies around the state of Colorado and across the country on trauma response and recovery.

2. Developing Health & Wellness programming to assist in the psychological recovery of first responders. Agencies must understand the need to provide support services not only for the impacted responders but also for their families. This begins proactively with events such as Family Nights in which new first responders meet with members of an agency's Peer Support Team as well as the contracted police and public safety psychologists to learn about the impact of the job on their loved ones and how best to support each other following a critical incident. Following an incident, outreach should be provided to families of first responders whenever possible to assist in the recovery process (Kirschman, 2007).
3. The role of police psychologists in providing Psychological First Aid (PFA). This chapter will detail services offered to first responders following several high profile mass casualty incidents including the Columbine High School Shooting and the Aurora Century 16 theater shooting. The authors offer unique insights only afforded to those that work with first responders and have responded to multiple large-scale mass casualties. Both the Columbine and Century 16 shootings were very unique incidents given the number of victims and the experience for first responders given the scale and target of the attacks. More specifically, Columbine High School was considered the worst school shooting of its time and the Aurora Century 16 shooting was the first mass casualty theater shooting in the United States. The exceptionality of these events had a unique impact on first responders, which was noticeable in the defusing and debriefings that took place in the hours, days, and weeks following these events.
4. Providing ongoing support to first responders during drawn out legal proceedings. Readers of this book likely have base knowledge regarding the importance of processing through traumatic events. It is also important to understand that first responders are often under a gag order by the courts following a mass casualty incident, which severely limits their ability to process through their own trauma. Police psychologists must work with agencies to manage this impact as well as the impact of ongoing media coverage.
5. Addressing the impact of media on law enforcement agencies and personnel following a MCE. Media coverage can be both beneficial and detrimental to the recovery of first responders. The coverage itself can unfortunately trigger trauma symptoms for many first responders. Media coverage does, at times, praise the efforts of first responders and community support is of course very appreciated. However, the media and community response to media reports can also at times be very critical of first responders, often without full knowledge or understanding of actual events. This can be exceedingly frustrating and hurtful yet first responders are rarely able to address this with their community. Lack of acknowledgement for their efforts or, even worse, critical critiques of their efforts can prolong the recovery process.

BACKGROUND

Sundnes and Birnbaum (2003) report that between 1951 and 2000, there were 7,312 documented disasters, resulting in more than nine million deaths and costing the United States more than $960,000,000. Historically, providing emergency psychological care has consistently been shown to reduce chronic mental illness in trauma survivors and it is widely accepted that officers involved in shootings or other significant critical incidents, such as a MCE, require immediate support (Best, Artwohl, & Kirschman, 2011). Raphael (1986) provided the first descriptions of interventions to be delivered to survivors in the aftermath of a disaster. A total of 11 intervention components were identified including: comforting and consoling; immediate care for basic physical necessities; identifying and providing referrals to those needing traditional mental health services; and ensuring the individual was linked to an ongoing system of support (Lewis, Phelps, Gavel, & Forbes, 2013). In 1989, the International Critical Incident Stress Foundation (ICISF) formalized an international network of more than 350 crisis response teams specially trained in a standardized and comprehensive crisis intervention model. The goals of this new model included: 1) stabilization and mitigation of acute stress symptoms, 2) reduction of functional impairment, and 3) restoration to an individual's previous level of functioning. This model was utilized following the 1995 bombing of the Federal Building in Oklahoma City and again after the TWA 800 mass air disaster (Levy, Stewart, & Buirski, 2003). The terrorist attacks of September 11, 2001 again demonstrated the extent to which first responders are impacted both physically and psychologically by a large-scale tragedy. Since 9/11, the potential negative psychological consequences of mass casualty work resulting from personal exposure to traumatic events, as well as responding to and working with traumatized communities, has increasingly been the subject of considerable investigation. First developed in the early 1980s, Critical Incident Stress Debriefing (CISD) has been relied on heavily over the years. In 2001, the U.S. government and American Red Cross clarified the definition of a critical incident debrief explaining this typically represents a single-session intervention promoting disclosure of traumatic experiences while also providing both education and reassurance related to the range of normal trauma and stress reactions. Debrief participants are encouraged to utilize healthy coping strategies or seek more intensive services as needed to assist (Ruzek & Watson, 2001). Debriefing sessions are typically offered within 72 hours of the trauma and are intended to offer participants an opportunity to vent, receive psychoeducation, and emotional processing. However, a review of evidence-based literature states that this CISD can have either no effect, or may even be psychologically injurious for responders who have not yet had an opportunity to sleep, let alone process their own experiences before being asked to speak about their experience, often in a group setting (Raphael & Wooding, 2004). Over the last decade, there has been the emergence internationally of evidence-based recommendations for an intervention that is more likely to positively assist first responders, known as Psychological First Aid (PFA). This was developed by the Department of Veterans Affairs National Center for Posttraumatic Stress Disorder and the National Child Traumatic Stress Network and has since been adopted for use after a MCE by a number of disaster response organizations and agencies, including the Red Cross. PFA is designed to reduce the initial distress caused by traumatic events; address essential physical needs first such as safety, food, and communication with loved ones; help to facilitate adaptive individual and group methods or coping; and normalize emotional responses. First responders, such as police and fire personnel, typically establish individual command centers within a larger disaster response environment and a Psychological Incident Commander should be appointed to assist with ensuring responders are being provided PFA as they process through the command center. By providing a framework for active listening, a focus on safety and immediate needs, and a way to bring up essential coping strategies (such as: spend time with loved ones, eat, sleep), PFA helps traumatized individuals to collect themselves. The use of PFA was demonstrated at the Pentagon following the 9/11 attacks. Here, multidisciplinary teams provided initial triage, psychosocial support, and referral for further assessment and treatment, as well as leadership consultation to public health workers (Benedek, Fullerton, & Ursano, 2007). This same technique was utilized at Columbine High School where teams entering the school were provided psychological inoculation to assist with mitigating the trauma reaction and later provided PFA as their on-scene duties were completed. The Psychological Incident Commander can organize meetings with first responder units, assess individuals, and review organizational support and resources to provide a plan for psychological help, support, and ensure special attention is provided to any high-risk individuals or groups. However, a lesson learned from the psychological response of Columbine was that proactive follow-up outreach should also be provided to first responders during the weeks and months following the event and while the investigation and media attention remains ongoing. This was offered to first responders involved in the Century 16 Theater shooting with positive results.

Research consistently shows that while significant psychopathology post-incident is not commonly experienced, there is a regular pattern of observed emotional distress related symptoms present in first responders following an MCE (Honig & Sultan, 2004). Commonly observed symptoms include anxiety, hyperarousal, hypervigilance, intrusive thoughts, anger, and grief (Stewart, Mitchell, & Wright, 2004). Additionally, there is evidence suggesting that disaster work often shatters the basic assumptions first responders have with regard to their own vulnerability and sense of natural justice in the world (Palm, Polusny, & Follette, 2004). Following the 2001 terrorist attacks in New York, 12% of the 28,000 police first responders involved reported symptoms of acute stress and anxiety (Dowling, Moynihan, & Genet, 2006). In a study comparing 709 police first responders with 317 civilians exposed to a variety of critical incidents, Fikretoglu (2006) found that panic symptoms mediated the relationships among fear, helplessness or horror responses, and dissociation in civilians, while only partially mediating such relationships in police first responders. The study supports the theory that extreme fear may mediate the development of PTSD and proper stress inoculation training provided to first responders may protect against the development of PTSD.

A number of additional protective factors are associated with an individual's psychological response to a traumatic event. These factors can be categorized as: 1) pre-event threshold factors (what is done before an event is even on an agency's radar), 2) event horizon factors (what is done during an MCE), and 3) post-event horizon factors (what is done to support psychological recovery after an MCE).

Pre-Event Threshold Factors

First responder personalities often include trait resiliency, which has emerged from multiple research studies as a predictive factor associated with how well first responders cope after completing duties associated with an MCE. Dr. Al Siebert (2010), an internationally recognized expert on the nature of highly resilient individuals, describes resiliency as the ability: to sustain mental and physical health during high levels of ongoing disruption and pressure; to overcome adversities and bounce back from setbacks; to actively pursue a new way of functioning when an old way is no longer possible; and to do all of this without acting in dysfunctional or harmful ways. Resiliency also generally refers to an ability to view events as largely under an individual's own control, as a challenge as opposed to a threat, and as meaningful rather than merely as both unpredictable and pointless (Alexander, Psychol, & Klein, 2009). Resiliency is the result of individual characteristics, personality traits, and past experiences and these qualities can come naturally or can be learned through interactions with peers.

Resiliency training, as well as trauma inoculation training, also both appear to serve as protective factors. Agencies around the country currently utilize a number of programs aimed at highlighting the importance of resiliency and general officer wellness. For example:

1. **Peer Support Teams:** According to the International Association of Chiefs of Police, the goal of peer support is to provide all public safety employees within an agency the opportunity to receive support through times of high personal or professional stress (IACP, 2011). Peer Support Team (PST) members are trusted, trained and experienced colleagues, generally considered by their supervisors and peers to be resilient, who offer confidential assistance and guidance to employees and their family members who are dealing with emotional distress, acute stress symptoms of PTSD, job-related stress and problems, and/or any marital or family issues that could potentially cause problems at work or a personal or professional crisis. The overall goal of a peer support program is to establish a support network for members of an agency who can assist in helping first responders and their families understand, adjust to, and recover from incidents that can be overwhelming. Most first responders perceive talking to a fellow officer as a less formal method of garnering psychological support than talking to a professional; therefore, it makes sense for those peers to be trained to help fellow first responders access professional mental health supports if needed.
2. **Family Night Events:** Family Nights, which are generally facilitated by an agency's mental health providers and peer support team members, offer an opportunity for first responders and their spouse or partner to receive training on critical incident stress, coping strategies, resiliency, high-risk relationships, and substance abuse. Many agencies offer Family Night programming to each new graduating academy class while others offer annual Family Night events that are open to the entire agency. Having a member of the command staff provide an introduction to the curriculum and, even participate with their own spouse or partner, lends credibility to involvement in these events and the agency's overall investment in officer wellness.
3. **Kids Academy Programming:** Kids Academy is a unique type of programming that Nicoletti-Flater Associates produced in collaboration with the Denver Police Department in response to an intense increase in national outrage against law enforcement. This program is an opportunity for the children of law enforcement officers to have a positive experience with law enforcement and learn about police activities and safety measures. Participants are offered a variety of interactive activities to learn about law enforcement work including an obstacle course, arrest control demonstration, scavenger hunt in the scenario house, fingerprinting lifts, police vehicle rides, and equipment try-on. Law enforcement officers staff each activity station so that kids have a chance to ask questions and get to know officers on a personal level. Departmental police psychologists are also in attendance at this event to answer questions for children and their parents regarding law enforcement stress, coping strategies, general parenting, etc. More than 150 kids attended the first Denver Police Department Kids Academy and the response was so positive that it was quickly determined it should be an annual event. Any opportunity for an agency to positively engage officers and their families will likely have a positive impact on morale and offers an opportunity for law enforcement families to build strong relationships which will serve the agency well should it become impacted by an MCE.

Additionally, agencies should offer Trauma Contamination Training, aimed at educating officers and all those involved in investigating a MCE on the science of human performance factors that influence behavior during high stress, time pressured, deadly force confrontations (Honig & Lewinski, 2008). This training should address what first responders might expect to experience not just during but also after responding to a critical incident. Most mass casualty responders may experience mild, transient distress such as sleep and concentration disturbances or increased emotionality following an incident.

However, healthy adjustment and resiliency should be expected in most and responders experiencing transient symptoms will likely return to normal levels of functioning without significant psychological treatment. The primary interventions helpful for this category of responders are community support and educational interventions. A smaller group of responders may experience moderate symptoms such as persistent insomnia, higher levels of anxiety, or impaired interpersonal functioning. Impairments in functioning do not necessarily meet threshold criteria for a formal mental health diagnosis; however, these symptoms will likely benefit from psychological intervention. A small subgroup may meet criteria for Posttraumatic Stress Disorder (PTSD) or Major Depressive Disorder requiring ongoing specialized treatment to return them to a previous level of functioning. The most significant predictors of outcome severity include proximity, duration, and intensity of exposure (Carlier, Lamberts, & Gersons, 1997). Man-made deliberate attacks are also generally associated with greater pathology than natural disasters (Benedek, Fullerton, & Ursano, 2007).

Emotional restraint on the job is encouraged, and for very good reason given that there are typically severe consequences for any officer that expresses a great deal of emotion while on the job. To maintain emotional restraint, an individual often learns to desensitize to violence. When faced with an incident that is either too similar (i.e., an officer personalizes a child death because the child is the same age as her or his own) or too different (i.e., responding to a mass casualty for the first time), it is more difficult to remain emotionally restrained. It can be disconcerting for an officer who is accustomed to being emotionally restrained who now finds it difficult to regulate his or her emotional expression. Such an officer may engage in what is known as "seepage and leakage," meaning the emotions seem to ooze out, often in inappropriate ways and at unacceptable environments (e.g., yelling at a civilian during a traffic stop). Not surprisingly, many first responders feel something is wrong when they experience strong emotions after a traumatic incident. Yet those reactions are quite normal. Remember, resilience is not the absence of emotional reactions but rather the process of overcoming considerable emotional distress.

After a stressful event or critical incident, a person may find himself or herself experiencing physical symptoms, such as shaking of the hands. The shaking is not usually associated with a fear response; it is actually associated with the body being flooded with adrenaline. There is a lack of oxygen and blood flow going to the small muscles in the body (i.e., the hands), thus impairing the individual's ability to function normally. Other normal experiences associated with an adrenaline dump include:

1. **Tunnel Vision:** Tunnel vision refers to the narrowing of the visual field and the visual cues being attended to (Lewinski, 2008). It is actually biologically adaptive to lose peripheral vision during a fight or flight experience. If an individual chooses to fight, he or she will generally only need to focus on the thing that poses the biggest risk (gun, knife, etc.). If flight is chosen, only the escape route needs attention. First responders, who are accustomed to being extremely vigilant of their surroundings, often express concern that they did not see certain aspects of a scene (i.e., a pedestrian walking by, a car driving by, etc.) during a critical incident, but there is an adaptive reason for this.
2. **Auditory Exclusion:** This refers to the experience of tunnel hearing. That is, the brain only focuses on the sounds that it perceives as essential for survival while filtering out any other extraneous sounds (Shomstein & Yantis, 2004). Like with tunnel vision, there is a physiological explanation for auditory exclusion. First responders may report not hearing gunfire or, conversely, hearing it but reporting that the gunfire sounded muffled. There is nothing wrong with the officer; it simply means the brain prioritized what it attended to and the gunfire did not "make the cut."

3. **Dissociation:** Dissociation, or a cognitive disconnect from certain events or memories, is another common occurrence after a highly stressful event that involved adrenaline (Artwohl, 2003). In general, research suggests that high levels of stress can negatively impact memory, particularly short-term memory for simple facts. Again, the brain, when faced with "fight or flight" decisions, is concerned with survival not detail. Following an officer-involved shooting, investigators might ask an officer how many rounds were fired from her or his weapon. In some cases, officers may not know how many times they fired because the brain is not concerned with bullet count; the brain is concerned with stopping the threat.
4. **Stomach "Butterflies":** Once again, the primary function of the fight or flight response is to successfully survive a threatening situation. To that end, all non-essential systems in the body shut down so that energy can be directed to systems needed in fight or flight. This includes the digestive system. Normally, throughout the day, the digestive tract is constantly moving and contracting as part of the digestive process. When this stops, it creates a sensation of butterflies or knots.

Expecting not to feel anything after witnessing and responding to a MCE is like expecting not to bleed from a deep cut. There is a biological reaction to a traumatic event that the body experiences, just as there is with a physical injury (Klinger, 2001). However, just as physical injuries can be tended to, so can psychological reactions, and it is important for individuals to recognize that appropriate care prevents future complications. Talking to friends and family, being part of a community, and peer support are among the more reliable sources of resiliency in first responders. Further, talking to a mental health professional allows first responders to recognize and understand what is happening, and find out what measures could help them process these very common reactions. Professional support also helps identify when an immediate coping-mechanism – such as burying oneself in work or increased substance use to get to sleep – turns into an unhealthy strategy that could result in long-term problems. Again, a deep cut likely requires stiches, preferably with the help of a trained professional. Most do not question the need for a doctor to assess and treat a severe physical injury yet many automatically evaluate weakness following a psychological injury. It stands to reason that a psychological injury would also benefit from professional assistance to avoid ongoing issues.

A trauma response may be acute, delayed, or cumulative. An acute response means that symptomatology will be experienced right away; however, not everyone experiences this. Some people will not experience any symptoms for days or even weeks after a trauma. They might think they are "fine" and then all of a sudden they have nightmares, become moody, etc. There is nothing wrong if one experiences a delayed response to an incident; however, it is important to educate responders on this possibility and encourage them to seek assistance and/or activate healthy coping strategies whenever they do become aware of symptoms. A cumulative response to trauma is one that all first responders need to be mindful of. Think of the slowly boiled frog that does not even know that it is being cooked until it is too late. When an individual is constantly exposed to trauma, it can start to feel "normal," limiting awareness regarding the impact the trauma is having on psychological wellbeing. Friends and family members of a first responder may notice small changes in functioning first; however, they may hesitate to point this out for fear of the responder's reaction. Training should highlight the importance of accepting constructive feedback from friends and loved ones given that their alertness to symptoms may serve as an early warning sign.

Event Horizon Factors

In the immediate aftermath of a MCE, responders are generally so focused on their assigned duties they have little time to process their emotional reaction. Although they may not be aware of it, their senses are likely being contaminated by everything going on around them. For example, handling the bodies of children (i.e., sense of touch and sight) almost universally has disturbing effects on first responders. First responders tasked with clearing the movie theater after the Century 16 Theater shooting also reported that hearing the ringing of cellphones (i.e., sense of hearing) lying next to the deceased was very upsetting. Teams entering Columbine High School had to contend with the sight of multiple dead and wounded children. In addition to sensory contamination, other disaster-related factors that appear to increase the likelihood of developing distressing psychological symptoms include 1) a human-caused disaster rather than a naturally occurring event, 2) feeling unsafe in the disaster zone, 3) the development of an empathic attitude to survivors, 4) experiencing helplessness in the disaster zone, and 5) the intensity of exposure to traumatic scenes (Norris, Friedman, & Watson, 2002). Event horizon factors that appear to be consistently protective against the adverse impact of MCEs include organizational support of officer wellness, clear definition of duties, attention to personal physical needs, teamwork, and a sense of being appreciated.

First responder reports indicate that events felt most threatening not when their own personal safety was threatened but rather events felt threatening with regard to their inability to manage the physical or emotional trauma being suffered by victims (Honig & Sultan, 2004). Lack of control for the suffering of others was a critical factor in the amount and degree of distress experienced by responders (Frye & Stockton, 1982). One of the officers transporting victims after the Century 16 theater shooting testified that he could hear blood from the victims "sloshing around" in his patrol car and that he recalled begging one victim not to die on him as he rushed him to the hospital (Bryan, 2013). It has also been noted that the trauma of dealing with human remains can be countered by mentally distancing oneself from the deceased by not looking at their faces, not learning the name or personal details of the deceased, or by reframing the work through translating it into something positive and meaningful rather than experiencing it as purely awful. First responders are often known for their dark sense of humor, and there is evidence that this serves this particular population as a healthy coping strategy, particularly in the face of death; however, it is rarely viewed as an option for managing the distress of working with dead children. The lack of ability to utilize a key coping strategy with these severely disturbing cases may also speak to the acutely difficult psychological recovery from these events.

Given the necessity for an agency to manage an overwhelming number of critical tasks, having a Psychological Incident Commander can be invaluable to an agency. This person could be a police psychologist, trusted employee assistance provider, or a senior member of the Peer Support Team.

The Psychological Incident Commander's Responsibilities during the Event Horizon Phase

1. Monitoring the first responders on scene for signs of acute distress requiring immediate assistance.
2. Ensuring that a mental health provider or supervisor has a brief personal contact with each first responder (sworn and civilian) before the end of his or her shift.
3. Being available to consult with command staff.
4. Sharing information about available mental health services with first responders.

5. Connecting with and answering questions for first responders' family members if needed.
6. Coordinating with the employee assistance provider and other agency mental health service providers to organize follow-up.

Post-Event Horizon Factors

First responders experience a wide variety of reactions related to their assignments on the day of the event. Many first responders would prefer to work the crime scene than be responsible for assisting victims' families, especially during the awful task of delivering death notifications. Working the crime scene naturally feels like a more valuable contribution during a MCE. First responders assigned to crowd control, or tasked with responding to routine calls for service, may feel inept or as if their contributions are not important. First responders who were on off-duty, on vacation, or otherwise unavailable to respond may feel excluded because they did not share in the experience and did not contribute. The importance of all contributions should be noted and actively respected by an agency.

First responders are also commonly exposed to numerous ongoing consequences of a MCE including ongoing media interest and lengthy legal proceedings. Additionally, upon completion of their mass casualty related duties, first responders are typically expected to return to routine operation duties where they may be exposed to other disturbing and potentially overwhelming events. There is a complex interaction between the cumulative impact of trauma exposure and coping. Exposure to stressful life events in one's personal life may compromise the emotional welfare and functioning of first responders. The cumulative nature of vicarious trauma underscores the need for long term monitoring of the welfare of first responders after they have completed their mass casualty related duties.

For many first responders, the emotional rollercoaster that started immediately after the event will continue for weeks, months, and even years depending on the length of the investigation and their involvement with legal proceedings. Individual reactions to traumatic events and acute stress vary greatly, and can change quickly. As the brain and body begin processing the experience there is a wide range of usual responses including: numbness, grief, guilt, anger and sadness. Some first responders may worry that something is wrong with them if they feel fine and are able to go about their work and life as normal; however, this too is on the continuum of normal response. Some first responders may start asking "why" questions. "Why did the perpetrator kill innocent people?" "Why did I live when others did not?" "Why did God allow this to happen?" These questions generally do not have fully satisfactory answers and responders may frustrate themselves trying to make sense of an event that is ultimately senseless. First responders often feel a strong sense of obligation to push themselves during the event recovery phase, to contribute and support their colleagues, victims' families, and their community, which can greatly affect a responder's personal and professional functioning. For example, some first responders will want to work around the clock. Others will not leave an injured victim's hospital bed. Some will take a day off and then find it hard to return. Those who were off duty when the event happened may experience guilt, and some may overwork themselves trying to make up for not being there that day. Civilian employees, who are holding down the fort, fielding hundreds of calls, may become overwhelmed. Dealing with the logistical challenges can also be incredibly frustrating. Rather than moving the community forward, it can feel like an occupying force has overrun the community and their job is just to stem the tide. First responders may resent assignments that feel trivial, like escorting a visiting VIP or doing crowd control.

The constant media presence rehashing every detail of the event, giving attention to the perpetrator, questioning the police response--all can have the unintended consequence of re-traumatizing first responders who cannot escape the barrage of attention and questions. Misreporting and inappropriate behavior by media representatives can also contribute to mounting resentment and cynicism. After the Columbine High School shooting, members of the press posed as mental health professionals in an attempt to gain more access to the scene and to the victims' families. Again, an experienced Psychological Incident Commander can assist with managing these logistics and help prevent some of the unintended psychological consequences that come with an aggressive media presence or intensely concentrated community response.

In the days and weeks that follow a MCE, there may be conflicts around overtime, time off and Workers' Compensation within an agency. First responders may be upset if someone takes time off and perceive that as not pulling one's weight or instead taking advantage of the situation to get maximum time off or to set the stage for a disability claim down the line. While there may be an occasional abuse of the system, for first responders who truly need time off or psychological support, there may be unnecessary pressure to show up as usual or even work extra. Simply asking people how they are doing or if they need time off will not necessarily solicit an honest response so it is important to work with the Psychological Incident Commander to develop a standardized method for evaluating recovery needs. In addition, resentment can arise in connection with awards and honors. First responders in one agency may feel that other first responders are inflating how important their role was in responding to the incident, or that particular responders are being singled out for heroic actions when others are not. Additionally, those that receive special recognition for heroic actions may feel the honor is not deserved and may actually feel worse for receiving special attention. Conflicts can also arise around gifts and donations that come to the agency. Appreciative community members or businesses may donate tickets to a sporting event or trays of food, and first responders can get upset if someone takes (or is given) more than one's fair share. Some of these issues may seem petty, but when people are upset about something they cannot change--like the fact that someone killed people in their community--they may redirect their anger and frustration onto something seemingly within their control. It is a lot easier to get angry with a living person, or with a frustrating situation, than it is with a deceased perpetrator. This is known as displaced anger and although it does need to be dealt with and managed appropriately, it represents a very understandable impulse to a situation that feels chaotic or out of control (Kirschman, 2007).

Since there are such a variety of reactions to traumatic experiences, anyone in an agency, whether they were on-scene during the incident or not, may be affected. Some staff may react more strongly than expected due to difficulties outside of work or previous experience with traumatic events, therefore frequent casual check-ins with all staff members in the first weeks are essential. If time and resources are limited, the Psychological Incident Commander will likely organize check-ins in the following order:

1. First responders to the scene including command staff;
2. First responders who were on-scene and arrived after the shooting was over, including those assigned to work with victims, their families or the media;
3. Detectives assigned to process the scene; and
4. Dispatchers, other civilian staff and anyone who was off-duty.

Incidents of extremely emotional distress will unfortunately not necessarily occur only during normal business hours; therefore, responders should be able to reach a supportive listening ear--a trained professional or a peer—at any time of day or night. This means that peer support team members offer a phone number to call and that mental health staff are integrated into the day-to-day operations of any agency so that first responders have many opportunities to develop trusting relationships with them long before a MCE. At the same time, support service providers need to take a proactive approach to offering outreach to all staff members. It should be made clear during these check-ins that they do not represent an official fitness-for-duty assessment but are rather intended as an informal opportunity to touch base. Officers should have at least one such opportunity available to them in the first few days following the event. Some agencies decide to make check-ins mandatory so that there is less associated stigmatization. The people who really need support do not necessarily take advantage of it for fear of appearing weak. Following the Century 16 shooting, Nicoletti-Flater Associates was provided a list of every person who responded in the theater by the Aurora Police Department Chief of Police. This list was divided up among the staff and every responder was mandated to speak with a staff member at least once. In addition to mental health professionals, supervisors should also personally check in with front-line staff, and have an increased awareness should any significant deviation from baseline functioning become apparent in their personnel.

After a critical incident, first responders are often concerned about how they reacted physiologically and emotionally, and whether these reactions are "normal." Therefore, post-incident interventions should remain focused on education as this reassurance reduces worry, anxiety, and negative self-assessment (Honig & Sultan, 2004). Much of the time, normalization and education on the impact of acute stress on the body, ways to stay resilient, and where to seek support affords sufficient support (Artwohl, 2002). Intense discussions regarding details of the response and the psychological impact should not be done in a group format early on. It is also best to delay tactical debriefings to give first responders time to prepare themselves for discussing and learning from the event. Because of the emotional impact, first responders may need some time before engaging in a conversation on what could have been done better.

Spouses and children often need education and support when an officer has experienced a trauma as well (Kirschman, 2007). They are also a good source of information. Some agencies have conducted a brief anonymous online survey of family members, asking for their observations. The Peer Support Team and the Psychological Incident Commander can utilize the results of this type of survey to specially tailor support services. Offering Family Night activities with a brief educational component can also be beneficial and allow both a forum for processing the impact of the MCE on the family while also gaining insight on how to best support the responder and recover as a family. Allowing first responders to connect with survivors has also proven to be a powerful way to help responders process and find support. Organizing a breakfast and inviting survivors, first responders, and even hospital personnel offers a chance to spend time with others that went through the same traumatic event and builds community and resilience. Allowing first responders private time with families at the memorial site preferably away from the public can also be a useful way for first responders to process their experience.

CONCLUSION

It is clear that providing mental health services to first responders following a mass casualty event is an essential part of the recovery process and agencies should take steps to ensure they have access to mental health providers that have a working knowledge of both first responder culture and crisis intervention. There is currently limited research on what specific techniques are most beneficial when working with responders impacted by a MCE. Moving forward, the field would benefit from research addressing the efficacy of individual models as it pertains to the recovery of responders following these types of events. It should be noted that due to the chaotic nature of these situations, it may remain difficult to structure studies around the recovery process, especially given the response and recovery transitions are so fluid. In the absence of formalized studies, it is hoped that agencies and mental health professionals will continue to ensure that the lessons learned from each of these tragedies are made widely available to ensure that what assistance can be offered to others is shared.

REFERENCES

Aisch, G., Fessenden, F., Keller, J., Park, H., Parlapiano, A., Shaver, J., . . . Yourish, K. (2015, December 10). What investigators know about the San Bernardino shooting. *The New York Times*. Retrieved February 20, 2016, from http://www.nytimes.com/interactive/2015/12/02/us/california-mass-shooting-san- bernardino.html?_r=0

Alexander, D., Psychol, C., & Klein, S. (2009). First responders after disasters: A review of stress reactions, at-risk, vulnerability, and resilience factors. *Prehospital and Disaster Medicine*, *24*(2), 87–94. doi:10.1017/S1049023X00006610 PMID:19591301

Artwohl, A. (2002). Perceptual and memory distortions in officer-involved shootings. *FBI Law Enforcement Bulletin*, *71*(10), 18–24.

Artwohl, A. (2003). No recall of weapons discharge. *Law Enforcement Executive Forum, 3*(2), 41-49

Benedek, D., Fullerton, C., & Ursano, R. (2007). First responders: Mental health consequences of natural and human-made disasters for public health and public safety workers. *Annual Review of Public Health*, *28*(1), 55–68. doi:10.1146/annurev.publhealth.28.021406.144037 PMID:17367284

Best, S., Artwohl, A., & Kirschman, E. (2011). Critical incidents. In J. Kitaeff (Ed.), *Handbook of police psychology* (pp. 491-507). New York, NY: Routledge, Taylor and Francis Group.

Bryan, A. (2013, January 7). Aurora theater shooting officer: So much blood I heard it 'sloshing around'. *WTVR*. Retrieved April 3, 2016, from http://wtvr.com/2013/01/07/aurora- theater-shooting-officer-so-much-blood-i-heard-it-sloshing-around/

Carlier, I., Lamberts, R. D., & Gersons, B. P. (1997). Risk factors for posttraumatic stress symptomatology in police officers: A prospective analysis. *The Journal of Nervous and Mental Disease*, *185*(8), 498–506. doi:10.1097/00005053-199708000-00004 PMID:9284863

Dowling, F., Moynihan, G., Genet, B., & Lewis, J. (2006). A peer-based assistance program for officers with the New York City Police Department: Report of the effects of Sept. 11, 2001. *The American Journal of Psychiatry*, *163*(1), 151–153. doi:10.1176/appi.ajp.163.1.151 PMID:16390904

Fikretoglu, D., Brunet, A., Best, S., Metzler, T., & Deluchi, K. (2007). Peritraumatic fear, helplessness and horror and peritraumatic dissociation: Do physical and cognitive symptoms of panic mediate the relationship between the two? *Behaviour Research and Therapy*, *45*(1), 39–47. doi:10.1016/j.brat.2006.01.008 PMID:16516845

Frye, S., & Stockton, R. (1982). Discriminant analysis of posttraumatic stress disorder among a group of Vietnam veterans. *The American Journal of Psychiatry*, *145*, 1289–1291. PMID:7055277

Honig, A., & Lewinski, W. J. (2008). A survey of the research on human factors related to lethal force encounters: Implications for law enforcement training, tactics and testimony. *Law Enforcement Executive Research Forum, 8*(4), 129-152.

Honig, A., & Sultan, S. (2004). Reactions and resilience under fire: What an officer can expect. *The Police Chief, 71*(12), 54–60.

IACP Psychological Services Section. (2011). *"Peer Support Guidelines," ratified at the 118th Annual Conference of the International Association of Chiefs of Police.* Retrieved from http://www.theiacp.org/portals/0/documents/pdfs/Psych-PeerSupportGuidelines.pdf

Jacobo, J. (2015, December 8). San Bernardino shooting first responders describe the chaos, 'unspeakable carnage' they saw. *ABC News*. Retrieved February 20, 2016, from http://abcnews.go.com/US/san-bernardino-shooting-responders- describe-chaos-unspeakable-carnage/story?id=35653728

Kirschman, E. (2007). *I love a cop* (Rev. ed.). New York, NY: Guilford.

Klinger, D. (2001). *Police responses to officer involved shootings*. Washington, DC: US Government Printing Office.

Levy, M., Stewart, M., & Buirski, C. (2003). Denver analysts respond to the Columbine tragedy. *The American Psychoanalyst, 37*(1), 6–7.

Lewinski, W. (2008). The attention study: A study on the presence of selective attention in firearms officers. *Law Enforcement Executive Forum, 8*(6), 107-138.

Lewis, V., Varker, T., Phelps, A., Gavel, E., & Forbes, D. (2014). Organizational implementation of psychological first aid (PFA): Training for managers and peers. *Psychological Trauma: Theory, Research, Practice, and Policy, 6*(6), 619–623. doi:10.1037/a0032556

Norris, F., Friedman, M., Watson, P., Byrne, C. M., Diaz, E., & Kaniasty, K. (2002). Disaster victims speak: Part I. An empirical review of the empirical literature, 1981-2001. *Psychiatry, 65*(3), 207–260. doi:10.1521/psyc.65.3.207.20173 PMID:12405079

O'Neill, A. (2015). Theater shooter Holmes gets 12 life sentences, plus 3,318 years. *CNN.* Retrieved from http://www.cnn.com/2015/08/26/us/james-holmes-aurora-massacre-sentencing/

Palm, K., Polusny, M., & Follette, V. (2004). Vicarious traumatization: Potential hazards and interventions for disaster and trauma workers. *Prehospital and Disaster Medicine, 19*(01), 73–78. doi:10.1017/S1049023X00001503 PMID:15453162

Raphael, B., & Wooding, S. (2004). Debriefing: Its evolution and current status. *The Psychiatric Clinics of North America, 27*(3), 407–423. doi:10.1016/j.psc.2004.03.003 PMID:15325485

Ruzek, J., & Watson, P. (2001). Early intervention to prevent PTSD and other trauma-related problems. *PTSD Research Quarterly, 12*(4), 1–7.

Shomstein, S., & Yantis, S. (2004). Control of attention shifts between vision and audition in human cortex. *The Journal of Neuroscience, 24*(47), 10702–10706. doi:10.1523/JNEUROSCI.2939-04.2004 PMID:15564587

Siebert, A. (2010). *Survivor personality: Why some people are stronger, smarter, and more skillful at handling life's difficulties and how you can be too*. New York, NY: The Berkley Publishing Group.

Stewart, S., Mitchel, T., & Wright, K. (2004). The relations of PTSD symptoms to alcohol use and coping drinking in volunteers who responded to the Swissair Flight 111 airline disaster. *Journal of Anxiety Disorders*, *18*(1), 51–68. doi:10.1016/j.janxdis.2003.07.006 PMID:14725868

Sundnes, K., & Birnbaum, M. (2003). Health and disaster management guidelines for evaluation and research in the Upstein style. *Prehospital and Disaster Medicine*, *17*(3), 1–17. PMID:12938951

Weiss, D. S., Brunet, A., Best, S. R., Metzler, T. J., Liberman, A., Pole, N., & Marmar, C. R. et al. (2010). Frequency and severity approaches to indexing exposure to trauma: The critical incident history questionnaire for police officers. *Journal of Traumatic Stress*, *23*(6), 734–743. doi:10.1002/jts.20576 PMID:21171134

Chapter 8
Transition and Reintegration of Military Personnel to Law Enforcement Careers

Stephen F. Curran
Atlantic OccuPsych, USA

Elizabeth O. Holt
Holt Psychological Services, USA

Joseph H. Afanador
U.S. Army, USA

ABSTRACT

Over two million United States military service members have served in the theaters of Iraq and Afghanistan since 2001. Many of these military service members are seeking employment in law enforcement upon discharge from active duty. The skills acquired from military service are complementary to many of the essential job functions of a law enforcement officer, thus a natural fit. In addition, military reserve police officers have seen activations for deployment to combat regions. These National Guard and Reserve service members make a rapid transition from military fatigues to a police uniform upon their return from deployment. After outlining the scope of the military deployment cycle, reintegration programs and preemployment assessment challenges are described in this chapter. The comprehensive description will provide psychologists working with law enforcement and related public safety agencies the necessary tools for both assessing and supporting the success of those reintegrating to their law enforcement careers.

INTRODUCTION

Wars winding down and military sequestrations have resulted in an increase of military service members seeking employment in law enforcement. Since 2012, the United States Army reduced its force by 80,000 soldiers and in July 2015, they announced plans to reduce their force by another 40,000 members by the end of fiscal year 2018 (Tan, 2015). "Under current reduction plans, the 'Total Army,' which includes

DOI: 10.4018/978-1-5225-0813-7.ch008

active force, the Army National Guard and the Army Reserve, will drop to 980,000 soldiers. That includes 450,000 active soldiers, 335,000 Army National Guard soldiers, and 195,000 Army Reserve soldiers" (Lopez, 2015, para. 30). If "sequestration continues, the active Army is expected to shrink further to about 420,000 soldiers – a loss of an additional 30,000 soldiers" beginning sometime in 2019 (Lopez, 2015, para. 25).

The Washington, DC Metropolitan Police Department (MPD) estimated that 21% of their new hires have prior military experience (www.mpdc.dc.gov). This is relatively consistent with the United States Department of Justice's finding that 23% of the approximately 18,000 law enforcement departments in the country have Guard and Reserve members in their ranks who were activated into military service (International Association of Chiefs of Police, 2010). Therefore, roughly one out of five police applicants have prior military experience. Consequently, the evaluating police psychologist in a preemployment screening must possess a basic understanding of military service, as well as the prevalence of mental health issues in soldiers who have served in combat-related overseas assignments. Asking appropriate questions is critical to understanding each service member's psychological reaction to his/her deployment, and to assess if there are any ongoing mental health concerns that might impair suitability for a position as a law enforcement officer. Additionally, police psychologists play an integral role in easing a police officer's return to work after being activated into military duty, while being mindful of federal laws and regulations that prevent discrimination against service members returning home from military assignments.

Police officers and military service members are kindred spirits (Clark, 2014). The military service member may consider a career in policing due to the similarities between military structure and law enforcement agencies. In turn, law enforcement agencies are interested in recruiting veterans due to their increased patriotism, maturity, leadership skills, tactical knowledge, physical ability, and team orientation (International Association of Chiefs of Police, 2010).

However, police agencies are encouraged to exercise caution before entering into this seemingly beneficial relationship, as the military and civilian police forces have inherently different job descriptions. Moreover, multiple and rapid deployments of military personnel can result in difficulty transitioning and readjusting to the role of a civilian law enforcement officer. This can result in impaired judgment and impulsive behavior, particularly when it comes to the application of use-of-force techniques (International Association of Chiefs of Police, 2010).

Over two million United States Army, Air Force, Coast Guard, Marine Corps, and Navy personnel have served since 2001 in theaters of Afghanistan as part of Operation Enduring Freedom (OEF); since 2003 in Iraq for Operation Iraqi Freedom (OIF); and since 2010 in Iraq and Afghanistan for Operation New Dawn (OND) (Curran, Allen, Clark, Craig, & Gardner, 2014). Of those deployed, approximately 27% were deployed more than once (Sayer et al., 2010). Moreover, "The United States military has fought two major wars in the last 10 years, relying heavily on the ranks of the National Guard and Reserves to bolster the strength of regular troops" (Clark, 2014, para. 23). As of August 11, 2015, there were 10,364 National Guard members deployed, 8,400 of whom were stationed in the Middle East region (National Guard Bureau Public Affairs Office, personal communication, 2015). A significant sub-group of deployed soldiers are National Guard and Reserve members, some of whom are civilian law enforcement officers. These officers must put their law enforcement careers on hold, and face similar challenges as full-time military personnel when they return home from active duty.

The reintegration experience of each service member varies due to numerous factors, such as the location and length of deployment, as well as the specific assignment while deployed. In addition, resiliency factors and community support play a critical role in one's readjustment to society. While some service members describe their deployment experience(s) in a positive manner, others may begin to manifest behavioral and/or psychiatric symptoms as a result of their involvement in military assignments overseas. "Studies estimate that 19-44% of soldiers returning from Afghanistan or Iraq (OEF/OIF) meet the criteria for a mental health diagnosis" (Zinzow, Britt, McFadden, Burnette, & Gillespie, 2012, p. 742). Research by Thomas et al. has suggested that "prevalence rates for PTSD or depression with serious functional impairment ranged between 8.5% and 14.0%, with some impairment between 23.2% and 31.1%" (2010, p. 614). While adjustment, mood, and anxiety disorders are cited as being the most common mental health diagnoses in service members returning home from war, traumatic brain injury, substance abuse issues, and dual diagnoses are also prevalent (Seal, Bertenthal, Miner, Sen, & Marmar, 2007, p.478-9) (Tanielian et al, 2008, p. 12-14). Approximately 25% of military personnel who were deployed to a combat zone within the last 12 months reported frequent binge drinking (Adams, Larson, Corrigan, Horgan, & Williams, 2012).

DEPLOYMENT CYCLE

In the early years after the Cold War era, the United States enjoyed a period of relative calm following the first Gulf War (1990-2001). While the United States was involved in one major conflict (i.e., Operations Desert Shield/Desert Storm) and numerous peacekeeping missions (e.g., Somalia and Bosnia), the majority of service members never saw combat. In fact, the majority of coalition casualties during Operation Desert Storm, also known as the 100-hour war, were caused by coalition friendly fire. As a consequence of the Cold War's end, the U.S. military underwent significant troop reduction and reorganization. During this time, the U.S. Army established a tiered-readiness system which only allowed the Army to fund, resource, and train certain units identified to support an overseas mission or go to war, if the need presented itself (Hemmerly-Brown, 2009). As a result, U.S. Army Reserve (USAR) and Army National Guard (ARNG) units were limited to their one weekend a month and annual 2-week training. Some of these soldiers were tasked with supporting peacekeeping missions in the Sinai and Balkans (United States National Guard, 2015). Still, the majority of individuals serving in the military in the 1990s had never deployed to a combat zone and of those that did, most of them never saw combat. However, since the attacks of September 11, 2001 and the inception of the War on Terror, the U.S. military, especially the active and reserve components (USAR/ARNG) of the Army, have been forced to sustain deployments and combat operations.

In order to meet the deployment demand, the Army created a *cyclic readiness* system establishing "a force generation model," referred to as "ARFORGEN" (United States Army CGSC, 2014). This allowed the Army to maintain a "balanced force capability to provide a sustained flow of forces for current commitments and to hedge against unexpected contingencies" (United States Army CGSC, 2014, F105RA-9). For simplicity, the ARFORGEN cycle can be divided into two parts; *Boots on Ground* or BOG (when a soldier is deployed/supporting an overseas mission), and *Dwell* time (when a soldier is at his/her home station). "To maintain a high number of soldiers in theater, the [active] Army has deployed them at BOG:Dwell ratios between 1:1 and 1:2" (Bonds et al., 2010, p. xi). The Army preferred to deploy the active component at a 1:2 to1:3 ratio and mobilize the reserve component at a 1:3 to1:4 ratio, but in reality, the ratios were closer to 1:1 and 1:2 to 1:3, respectively (Bonds et al., 2010; United States Department of the Army, 2011). In fact, during the 2007-2008 Iraq War surge, the Army had a BOG of

15-months. However, due to the decrease in military combat operations, the Army decreased its BOG time to nine months while increasing Dwell time. According to Army Regulation 525-29, BOG:Dwell ratios are planned for 1:3 for the active component and 1:5 for the reserve component (United States Department of the Army, 2011).

Battle Rhythm

While every deployment experience is unique to the individual, there were a number of trends observed in both Iraq and Afghanistan. Generally, an Army or Marine unit could expect to experience an increase in enemy activity (i.e., combat) during the first and last few months of a deployment. In Afghanistan, the heaviest months of combat and hostile fatalities usually occurred during the late spring/summer months (March-October), with the winter months seeing the least amount due to the harsh weather. However, between 2009 and 2012, service members deployed to Afghanistan were subjected to constant combat. Figure 1 provides an indication of these patterns with yearly totals of U.S. troop casualties in Afghanistan (http://icasualties.org/OEF/ByMonth.aspx).

Whereas service members experienced a cyclical battle rhythm in Afghanistan, those deployed to Iraq were subjected to constant combat. Soldiers and marines experienced a high number of fatalities from 2003 to 2007, with fatalities beginning to decrease in 2008. This coincided with the Iraq troop surge that occurred from March 2007 to July 2008. Figure 2 shows U.S. troop casualties in Iraq by year (http://icasualties.org/Iraq/ByMonth.aspx). Note its contrast with the pattern of casualties in Afghanistan.

Psychological Assessments/Services During Deployment Cycle

Pre-Deployment

Before a soldier ever deploys, he or she is given the opportunity to seek mental health services. Virtually every active duty Army unit has at least one licensed psychologist or social worker assigned to their unit at the brigade level. For those units that do not have mental health providers assigned to them, they can

Figure 1. Afghanistan U.S. fatalities by year (2001-January 2016)

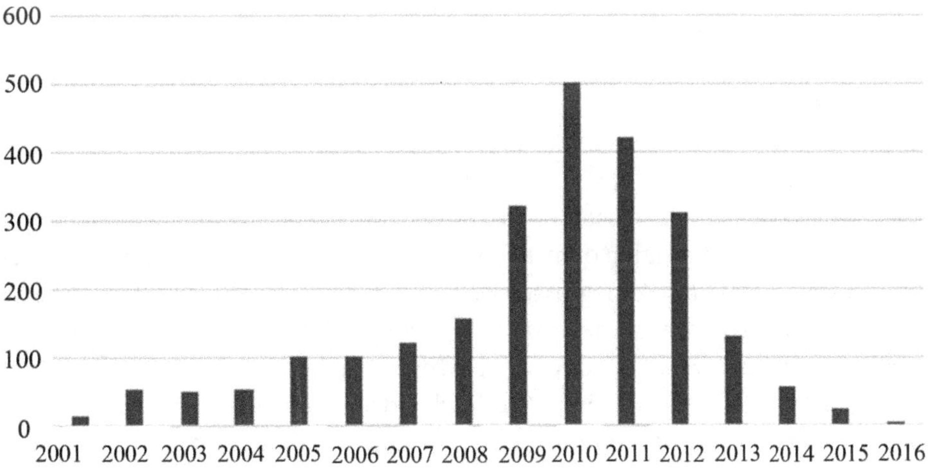

Figure 2. Iraq U.S. fatalities by year (2003-2015)

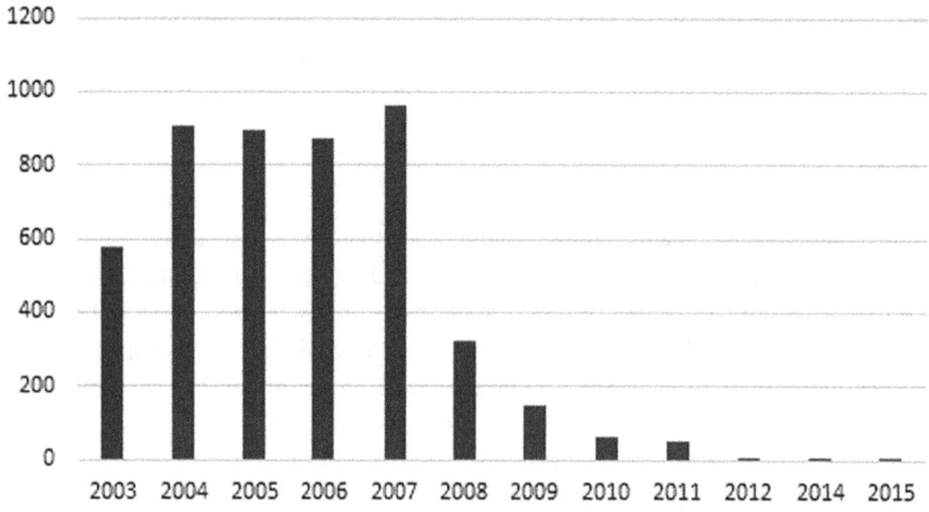

receive support from the local military treatment facility (MTF). However, USAR/ARNG soldiers have to rely on local civilian clinicians to provide that support.

When an Army unit (active or reserve component) has been tasked with a deployment, they are required to go through a Soldier Readiness Processing (SRP) center to update their administrative and medical information. During the medical screening process, they will complete a Pre-Deployment Health Assessment questionnaire followed by a face-to-face interview with a healthcare provider. If the solider has a mental health condition, is taking psychotropic medications, or has a history of violent or suicidal behavior, he or she will be referred to a licensed mental health provider for a more in-depth interview. According to an Assistant Secretary of Defense for Health Affairs memorandum (Woodson, 2013, p. 2), a waiver can be granted if the soldier is stable (no worsening symptoms or changes to medications within three months of deployment), does not have a condition that is likely to worsen during the deployment, and is expected to have access to health care. These waivers are given on a case-by-case basis. In addition to a mental health screening and medication review, every soldier is required to take either the Automated Neuropsychological Assessment Metrics (ANAM) or the Immediate Post-concussion Assessment and Cognitive Testing (ImPACT), a computerized concussion tool, in order to establish a cognitive baseline (Under Secretary of Defense, 2015).

During Deployment

While deployed, soldiers have access to mental health services (i.e., therapy and psychotropic medication). However, the frequency of contact with these services is dependent on the phase of the war (i.e., initial vs. established war) and location of mental health assets. If a service member experiences a mild traumatic brain injury (mTBI), also known as a concussion, for any reason, he or she will be administered the Military Acute Concussion Evaluation (MACE), a concussion screener, and will be removed from duty for observation and recovery. (A copy of the MACE can be downloaded for free at the Defense and Veterans Brain Injury Center website (https://dvbic.dcoe.mil/material/military-acute-concussion-evaluation-mace-pocket-cards.) At a minimum, the impacted soldier will be given 24 hours recovery for his or her first incident and 7 days for a second incident within a 12-month period. If the soldier has three or more mTBI events within a 12-month period, he or she cannot return to duty without a full concussion evaluation. Additionally, a soldier can be referred for a full concussion evaluation at any time (Department of Defense Instruction 6490.07). Such an evaluation will consist of neuroimaging, neuropsychological testing (to include reviewing baseline ANAM/ImPACT scores), and a functional assessment, which may include rehabilitation providers. Within 30 days of demobilization from combat theater, soldiers will complete the Post-Deployment Health Assessment (PDHA), which is a self-report questionnaire that includes demographic, general health and mental health items that might be deployment-related. It also assesses "traumatic stress, depression, interpersonal conflict, suicidal ideation, and interpersonal aggressive ideation, as well as physical symptoms and environmental exposures" (Bliese, Wright, Adler, Thomas, & Hoge, 2007, p. 142). Service members also have the opportunity to have a face-to-face interview with a healthcare provider to discuss any medical or mental health issues that occurred while deployed.

Post-Deployment

Upon returning to their home station, Army units will have an uninterrupted 7-day reintegration period (i.e., reverse Soldier Readiness Processing), which focuses on a range of administrative and medical issues, to include mental health. For the active duty Army, this will occur the day after returning home. Many Army installations have procedures for soldiers identified as high-risk to be immediately screened by a mental health provider upon returning home. A similar process has been established for the USAR and ARNG but may occur at varying degrees. During this time, the military completes post-deployment evaluations on those returning home from war to help identify soldiers in need of mental health treatment. They are also afforded the opportunity to have a face-to-face interview with a healthcare provider. Soldiers that endorse a critical item will be referred to a mental health provider. In addition, every soldier will retake the ANAM/ImPACT. Any soldier who had changes to his or her baseline score or experienced a concussive event while deployed (either reported or documented) will be referred for a neurological evaluation. In addition, soldiers will be reevaluated with the Post-Deployment Health Re-Assessment (PDHRA) 90 to 180 days post-deployment. These forms then become part of the soldier's permanent medical record.

In a longitudinal study conducted by Milliken, Auchterlonie, and Hoge (2007), 88,235 United States soldiers returning from Iraq reported more mental health concerns on the PDHRA than the PDHA. This finding suggests that mental health concerns might be overlooked due to the early timing of the administration of the PDHA. While both active military and reserve soldiers reported similar rates of exposure to potentially traumatic combat experience on the PDHA, researchers found that the USAR and ARNG members endorsed substantially higher rates of interpersonal conflict, depression, PTSD, and overall mental health risk factors. Based on the combined screening, clinicians identified 20.3% of active and 42.4% of reserve component soldiers as requiring mental health treatment (Milliken et al., 2007). Milliken et al. (2007) also noted that guard and reserve members were referred for mental health concerns at higher rates than their active duty military counterparts. While approximately 40% of ARNG soldiers were identified as having a mental health concern three months after returning from deployment, only half of these soldiers accessed mental health services (Milliken et al., 2007; Pfeiffer et al., 2012). Milliken et al. (2007) postulated that the difference in rates between active and reserve component soldiers might be attributed to reservists having difficulty accessing mental health services for deployment-related issues. In addition, reservists quickly disband and make a rapid transition to civilian life. As a result, they might have limited interaction with fellow soldiers and feel isolated from the military community (Gorman, Blow, Ames, & Reed, 2011).

The conclusions of the Milliken et al. (2007) study are likely an underestimate of the prevalence of mental health and behavioral issues after deployment. As previously mentioned, the PDHA and the PHDRA are self-report questionnaires, and soldiers might be reluctant to answer the items in a forthright manner for many reasons, including the stigma surrounding mental health and concerns about what item endorsement could mean to their military career. In a study conducted by Warner et al. (2011), 1,712 out of 3,502 Army soldiers from one infantry brigade completed the PDHA anonymously. Researchers found, "Soldiers reported significantly higher rates for all mental health concerns on the anonymous survey, 12.1% ($n = 207$) met the criteria for either PTSD or depression compared with only 4.2% of all soldiers who completed the routine PDHA" (Warner et al., 2011, p. 1067). Consequently, many soldiers may not be identified as having a mental health issue upon initial completion of the PDHA. As Hoge, Auchterlonie, and Milliken (2006) concluded in their study, less than 10% of service members that received mental health treatment were referred through the PDHA.

Even if soldiers endorse psychiatric and/or behavioral symptoms on the PDHA and are referred for further mental health treatment, they do not always follow through or continue with the recommended psychiatric and/or therapeutic services. According to a study conducted by Hoge et al. (2014), out of the over 45,000 soldiers that completed the PHDA upon return from Afghanistan, 10.3% were referred for further evaluation for any mental health problem. While 75% of those referred followed up with their referral within 90 days, only 33.2% had one or more encounters with mental health providers within the next 90 days, and 5% received a diagnosis of PTSD. Out of the 2,230 soldiers who received a PTSD diagnosis within 90 days of returning home from Afghanistan, 22% had one mental health care visit and 41% had eight or more encounters with mental health personnel over the next 12 months (Hoge et al., 2014). In summary, soldiers that exhibit mental health concerns may *fall through the cracks*, and continue to demonstrate problematic/worsening mental health symptoms and behavioral concerns long after their deployment is over.

Reintegration Programs

Reintegration has been formally defined as the process of transitioning back into personal and organizational roles after deployment (Currie, Day, & Kelloway, 2011). All military branches require their troops to complete reintegration programs prior to discharge (Sayer et al., 2011). While some soldiers seamlessly return to their lives prior to deployment, others face serious obstacles adjusting back to civilian life. The Department of Defense (DoD) is cognizant of the complex issue of reintegration, and each service branch has designed programs to address the psychological wellbeing of active duty service members. However, there is a lack of uniformity between these reintegration endeavors across branches. In addition, "To date, there is no consensus on how to define or evaluate reintegration resources, particularly those that offer support across populations and across the services" (Defense Centers of Excellence, 2012, p. 1). This is further complicated by the fact that some law enforcement agencies are not prepared to address issues faced by their returning veteran and have no strategy in place to promote reintegration into their domestic law enforcement duties (International Association of Chiefs of Police, 2010).

As previously mentioned, research has shown that National Guard and Reserve personnel face more mental health and reintegration issues as compared to their active-duty counterparts. "In addition to demographic differences and geographical dispersion, National Guard and Reserve service members may risk receiving less training and preparation before active duty and are not embedded with their military unit after deployment" (Scherrer et al., 2014, p. 1391). In 2008, the DoD introduced the Yellow Ribbon Reintegration Program (YRRP). This federally mandated program is an effort to help National Guard and reservists and families at all stages of the deployment cycle by providing a wide range of local resources. "Service members and their families attend Yellow Ribbon events, where they access information on healthcare, education and training opportunities, financial services, and legal benefits" (Military OneSource, 2015, para. 1). Service members and their families attend a one or two-day YRRP workshop 30 to 60 days prior to the deployment. While the service member is deployed, family members continue to receive information about various topics such as PTSD and identifying family members who might be at risk. When service members return home, they and their families attend a 1- or 2-day event about available resources and reconnecting with their loved ones 30 to 180 days after deployment. However, in most states, this program officially concludes after 90 days (Jackson, 2009).

In fiscal year 2012, the YRRP hosted 2,028 events and the total number of attendees was 248,352. In total, more than 1.3 million National Guard and reserve services members and their families participated in YRRP events from 2008 to 2013, making it the largest systematic public health campaign in U.S. history (Scherrer et al., 2014). However, there is a lack of research evaluating this program's effectiveness. While Scherrer et al. (2014) found that 83% of respondents found YRRP to be informative and helpful, there have been no follow-up studies to assess if service members and their families accessed these agencies for further assistance, and the outcome results of such interventions have likewise not been assessed.

LAW ENFORCEMENT OFFICERS RETURNING HOME FROM A COMBAT ZONE AFTER DE-ACTIVATION

Police agencies logically want to know if the officer returning from a combat zone is mentally and physically fit for duty (Clark, 2014). Mood alterations such as increased irritability and depression, as well as behavior such as a propensity for anger, low frustration tolerance, substance abuse issues, impulsivity, sensitivity to loud noises, and risk-taking behavior can make it difficult for veterans to function consistently on the job. As a result, police departments are strongly encouraged to have a reintegration plan in place prior to the police officer's military mobilization that is consistent with employment laws and legal precedent.

Veterans have certain rights and protections during both military service and upon return home from active duty (International Association of Chiefs of Police, 2010). Police agencies must be cognizant of and adhere to federal statutes that prevent the discrimination of employment based on genetic information, as well as mental and physical disabilities (Genetic Information Nondiscrimination Act, 2008; the Americans with Disabilities Act, 2000; the Americans with Disabilities Act Amendments Act, 2008). Furthermore, police agencies must comply with the Uniformed Services Employment and Reemployment Rights Act (USERRA, 1994), which ensures that individuals who have served in the Armed Forces, National Guard, Reserves, or other uniformed service, are not disadvantaged in their civilian careers as a result of their military duty. USERRA mandates that returning service members return to the position they would have attained had it not been for their military service, including their rank and benefits. In addition, it requires that police agencies make reasonable efforts to enable veteran officers to update or refresh their skills. The police psychologist will want to be respectful about the implications of USERRA and work with a police agency wanting to formally evaluate a military returnee back to police duties. The case of *Petty v. Metropolitan Government of Nashville-Davidson County* (2008) is representative of the issue. The police agency subjected the returning police officer to a fitness for duty type assessment. The court ruled in favor of the officer, citing USERRA and finding that the re-employment rights of the officer were violated. Thus, a police agency must restore the military reserve police officer to full duty in the position that he/she would have attained had his/her career not been interrupted by being activated into military service. A police agency may not mandate a fitness for duty type evaluation simply because an officer is returning from military service, regardless of whether combat was involved. To reiterate, a police agency must restore the returning military reserve police officer to duty and may only consider a psychological fitness examination when there is evidence of functional impairment related to officer safety or job performance.

In the mid 2000s, the Institute of Law and Justice (ILJ) conducted a study to explore how law enforcement agencies assisted and supported their officers' return to community policing after being activated into military service (Webster, 2012). While some police departments simply have the officer return back to work, other agencies have implemented and designed a structured program to address this issue. Some agencies return the military reserve officer back to duty followed by classroom in-service training, firearms qualification, and a modified phase of Field Training Officer (FTO) supervision. These steps provide ample time for observation of the returned officer. Any documented observations that psychological or medical fitness may be a concern can *then* trigger an assessment of the officer. The assessment of work ability (fitness for duty) then reverts to conducting a comprehensive evaluation.

Police command and human resources play a critical role in the transition of the military returnee. Some agencies have a Military Liaison Officer (MLO) who maintains contact with the service member and his or her family before, during and after deployment. The International Association of Chiefs of Police (IACP; 2010) also recommended that police departments develop a relationship with the military Transition Assistance Officer (TAA) in their state. The TAA serves as a point of contact and can provide information about available resources and military benefits that can be accessed by the employee. In addition, other no-cost implementation strategies, such as a welcome home event, can show appreciation, support, and recognition of the police officer's military service. Military returnees may also be encouraged to reach out to their peer support/assistance team, and it is further recommended that the peer support team include officers with prior military experience and/or specialized training in the challenges of readjusting from military deployment

Police psychologists play an integral role in easing a police officer's return to work after being activated for military duty, as well as providing a comprehensive psychological assessment on veterans applying for a position in law enforcement. Employee Assistance Programs (EAPs) can provide therapeutic support to the law enforcement officer that is activated into military service. Not only can they assist officers in preparation for deployment, they can also ease their return to civilian life. Such reintegration strategies could include a one-time, mandated, psychoeducational consultation with a mental health clinician. The police departments in Dallas, Louisville, Houston, Los Angeles, Kansas City (Missouri), New York City, and Chicago are among those with this requirement (Webster, 2012). However, this does not necessarily mean that new policies need to be developed for the officer returning home from military assignment. For example, for the New York City Police Department, officers who leave and return to the agency for any reason undergo a psychoeducational consultation with a staff psychologist (Webster, 2012). There are training resources available for psychologists and other mental health professionals seeking to acquire these intervention skills. For example, The Center for Deployment Psychology (CDP) provides training for military and civilian behavioral health professionals to provide evidence-based behavioral services to military personnel, veterans, and their families (http://deploymentpsych.org/about). Other resources include two guidebooks published by the IACP. One guidebook is directed at police officers returning from deployment and another is a "Leaders" guidebook for administrators of public safety agencies (IACP, 2009, 2010).

In late 2007, the IACP received funding and guidance from the Bureau of Justice Assistance (BJA) to design a project to better understand the experiences of combat veterans as they transitioned into a law enforcement role. An overview of the IACP's time-phased recommendations is listed below. Some of these recommendations can be easily and immediately implemented, whereas others require long-term discussion and development. For example, within 30 to 60 days after an officer returns home from deployment:

- Publically acknowledge veteran officers for their service on their return to their agency/community;
- Create within-agency focus groups to learn more about veteran officers' needs;
- Develop communication methods with veteran officers and their families throughout the deployment cycle;
- Offer veteran officers a flexible timetable to meet a range of transitional needs;
- Create a specialized Field Training Officer (FTO) type program structured to assist veteran officers;
- Allow the veteran officer to ride-along or job-shadow with a peer;
- Address the confidentiality policies of the services offered and clarify misconceptions;
- Update veteran officers on new policies, procedures, law, and changes in equipment and technology.

ASSESSMENT

Soldiers who screened positive for a mental health concern on the PDHA were significantly more likely to leave military service for any reason during the year following deployment than those who screened negative for all deployment locations (Hoge et al., 2006). Wars winding down have also been correlated with a substantial increase in applicants with prior military service (Dralle & Curran, 2014). This increase has resulted in unanticipated consequences that pose unique challenges to police and public safety psychologists. Thus far this chapter has detailed the foundation of reintegration assessment and intervention related services for active Army components, generalizable to other branches, as well as public safety employer sponsored reintegration of those police officers activated for military deployments. The remainder of this section of the chapter will address the veteran seeking his or her first police officer position and those military reserve police officers already employed with an agency and applying to a new law enforcement employer.

Helping soldiers make a successful transition to civilian life is a shared, societal responsibility. President Barack Obama signed the bipartisan Veterans Opportunity to Work Act (VOW to Hire Heroes Act), which provides additional support to assist unemployed veterans to secure employment in the civilian sector (White House Business Council, 2012). In addition, it provides tax incentives to businesses that hire unemployed former service members. In fiscal year 2012, the Community Oriented Policing Services (COPS), an office in the Department of Justice (DOJ), awarded more than 200 law enforcement agencies over $111 million in grants to fill 800 full-time positions to preserve or re-hire law enforcement officers, and any agency requesting new positions were required to hire a military veteran who served at least 180 days since September 11, 2001 (United States Department of Justice, 2012). This endeavor is also supported at the state and local level with programs such as the Military Police Basic Training Program (MPBTP), which was developed by the Michigan Commission of Law Enforcement Standards (MCOLES). MCOLES has developed a basic military police training program specific to veterans who are interested in civilian policing, provided that the candidate meets all of the pre-requisites, as well as MCOLES pre-employment standards, which includes a physical fitness test and a reading/writing examination (MCOLES, 2015). In addition, the Western Arizona Law Enforcement Academy implemented a Military Police Training Transition Program, which is an eight-week course that gives military police the opportunity to transition directly into a law enforcement position in Arizona upon completion of their active military service (Scarpulla, 2014).

The Prince George's County Police Department in Maryland attends 30 veteran hiring events on an annual basis (Miceli & Rollo, 2015). "On average, each recruit class that enters the academy consists of 45 to 50 recruits, and, typically, 10 to 15 veterans are in each class" (Miceli & Rollo, 2015, p. 36). Commitment to hire individuals with prior military service is apparent in numerous police agencies throughout the United States. Some agencies, such as the Chicago Police Department, have mandated that a minimum of 20% of referred academy applicants be military veterans (Peterson, 2012).

An evaluating psychologist will want to have a solid foundation in a wide variety of subjects prior to assessing those with military service. This may be unfamiliar territory to many psychologists. Knowing the legal precedents under USERRA and Veteran's Administration (VA) Compensation procedures is essential. Further, the evaluating psychologist will need a skill-set for psychometric assessment of Traumatic Brain Injury (TBI), exposure consequences due to Improvised Explosive Devices (IEDs) and assessment of combat exposure such as the Combat Exposure Scale (Keane et al., 1989). Acquiring a foundation in these areas is in addition to being proficient in the police and public safety specialty.

The benefits of hiring police officers with prior military service are numerous and already described above. The majority of these applicants are well-suited and typically display no signs of psychological problems. The challenge is identifying the sub-group of candidates having psychological problems. There is no longitudinal occupational monitoring program in existence that might provide risk rates of prior military members having psychological problems and seeking law enforcement positions. Curran reported:

The evaluating psychologist cannot dismiss the potential negative effects causally related to combat experiences. Exposure to Improvised Explosive Devices (IEDs), for example, may result in blast effects from direct projectile injury or air pressure changes that cause brain concussions and injury. These same IED incidents may be associated with injury and death to unit members. The pre-employment interview is recommended to ask about exposure to IEDs, mortar attacks, and firefights (2014, p. 32).

Data from a retrospective examination of current law enforcement officers with prior combat deployment who were evaluated for a new police agency compared to a group of police officer applicants with prior deployment but no prior police experience reveal possible differences. The currently employed police officers with prior combat experiences had significantly greater scores than the non-police officer applicants across several measures on the Inwald Personality Inventory (IPI) such as Antisocial Attitudes, Phobic Personality, and Rigid Personality Traits (Curran, 2014).

A preemployment psychological assessment protocol typically must be consistently applied to all applicants at the post-conditional offer of employment stage. This does not preclude expansion of inquiries based upon a candidate's history as part of a semi-structured interview. These probes will be important for eliciting signs of possible psychological factors that may impact performing essential job functions of a police officer. Screening questions from the Combat Exposure Scale (Keane et al., 1989) can provide an assessment of exposure at the high, moderate or low range in addition to no exposure. Among the seven questions posed are:

- How often did you fire rounds at the enemy?
- How often did you see someone hit by incoming or outgoing rounds?

An evaluating psychologist is recommended to not assume that a direct correlation between exposure level and psychological symptoms exists. Curran (2014) reported in a study of 133 veterans that those with no combat exposure, but in combat zones, had greater scores on Inwald Psychological Inventory (IPI) scales of Job Difficulty and Family Conflict compared to those with greater combat exposure. Another finding was those with low combat exposure had higher scores on the measure of Alcohol Problems from the IPI scale and Emotional stability from the 16PF compared to veterans with no combat exposure as well as moderate to high ratings on the Combat Exposure Scale. Furthermore, combat experiences have no relationship to suicide post-deployment. The most recent data about suicide finds that veterans with deployment, including multiple deployments, do not have a higher rate compared to veterans who never deployed (Reger et al., 2015). Moreover, these same researchers from the National Center for Telehealth & Technology (T2) found that veterans with an early separation from military service and a less than honorable discharge had greater risk for suicide. Another background factor an evaluating psychologist will find useful is knowledge about locations in Iraq and Afghanistan and timeframe when served "in-country." Obtaining information from a Marine reporting having served in the Anbar Province of Iraq during the 2004 - 2005 timeframe should not be glossed over as a walk in the park. This was one of the most violent and bloody periods for the U.S. military during the Iraq War (see Table 2).

The information gleaned from interview questions will provide data about experiences that may contribute to subsequent problems. Chief among these is the signature wound source from combat operations in Iraq and Afghanistan - the Improvised Explosive Device (IED). Candidates suffering injury from an IED projectile to the head and body are rarely seen for preemployment evaluations due to the severity of these type injuries. In contrast, the blast effects from an IED where no serious observable injury occurs is an altogether different matter. Interview inquiries about each exposure to an IED blast should be conducted. Was the applicant on foot or in a vehicle and, if the latter, what type of vehicle? Was the blast during 2003 to 2005 or later when vehicles had improved armor? Was the applicant within 50 yards of the IED? Was the applicant knocked off his or her feet? Was there loss of consciousness, and if yes, for how long? What about subsequent medical intervention and stand down recovery period? In addition to the blast effects, were bystanders injured or killed? These questions elicit important information to understanding aspects of current psychological functioning. Further interview inquiries based on the above data in areas of attention and concentration will be important. An assessment of recovery from a concussion is relevant on many levels including the candidate's ability to complete an entry-level recruit training program. These inquiries are in addition to any questions about the subsequent development of posttraumatic stress, anxiety disorders, depression, or other concerns.

A dilemma emerges when a candidate presents for the preemployment psychological evaluation while concurrently receiving Veterans Administration (VA) disability compensation for one or more psychiatric conditions. How is the evaluating psychologist to consider the existence of a pre-existing condition? The common thread among each state's standards for police officer suitability is that the candidate must not have a mental or emotional condition that would impair job performance (Commission on Accreditation for Law Enforcement Agencies, 2006). Box 1 defines the VA's rating standards for mental disorders. When a candidate being evaluated reports a 30% VA disability for a mental disorder, does that automatically disqualify the applicant? The same candidate may often state having never been symptomatic, sometimes will report having never required treatment, or if treatment was received, the applicant may report no longer being treated because the symptoms remitted.

The evaluating police psychologist will want to implement the following when presented with a military veteran seeking a police officer (or other public safety related) position. A key element that must be considered throughout the evaluation is the requirement that each candidate be individually assessed (ADA, 2008). A certain percentage of disability rating, such as 30%, cannot be used as an automatic disqualifier. Another key component to the evaluation is not rendering an opinion about psychological suitability and/or stability until treatment records are obtained, including the complete VA Compensation and Pension (C&P) report. The request for records may delay a candidate's entry to a recruit training program therefore the hiring agency will need to understand the potential exposure to liability if a determination is rendered without all relevant records. Additional recommended practices have been described by Curran (2014, 2012, 2010) and Roberts et al. (2015). Another essential element to consider is the candidate's *current* psychological status knowing that an essential job function for police officers is effectively performing under high stress conditions. "Current" for many specialists in police and public safety is within a three-year timeframe. For comparison, if a candidate engaged in theft from an employer resulting in job termination within the past three years, this behavior would reflect negatively upon domains of judgment, integrity, and impulse control. Similarly, a candidate within a three-year time frame of having driving citations related to speeding and/or not using a seatbelt would be assessed negatively on dimensions such as those related to judgment and maturity. Candidates having filed for VA compensation and awarded disability within a three-year timeframe would reasonably be assessed

Box 1. General rating formula for mental disorders

Total occupational and social impairment, due to such symptoms as: gross impairment in thought process or communication; persistent delusions or hallucinations; grossly inappropriate behavior; persistent danger of hurting self or others; intermittent inability to perform activities of daily living (including maintenance of minimal personal hygiene); disorientation to time or place; memory loss for names of close relatives, own occupation, or own name 100%
Occupational and social impairment, with deficiencies in most areas, such as work, school, family relations, judgment, thinking, or mood, due to such symptoms as: suicidal ideation; obsessional rituals which interfere with routine activities; speech intermittently illogical, obscure, or irrelevant; near-continuous panic or depression affecting the ability to function independently, appropriately and effectively; impaired impulse control (such as unprovoked irritability with periods of violence); spatial disorientation; neglect of personal appearance and hygiene; difficulty in adapting to stressful circumstances (including work or a worklike setting); inability to establish and maintain effective relationships 70%
Occupational and social impairment with reduced reliability and productivity due to such symptoms as: flattened affect; circumstantial, circumlocutory, or stereotyped speech; panic attacks more than once a week; difficulty in understanding complex commands; impairment of short- and long-term memory (e.g., retention of only highly learned material, forgetting to complete tasks); impaired judgment; impaired abstract thinking; disturbances of motivation and mood; difficulty in establishing and maintaining Effective work and social relationships 50%
Occupational and social impairment with occasional decrease in work efficiency and intermittent periods of inability to perform occupational tasks (although generally functioning satisfactorily, with routine behavior, self-care, and conversation normal), due to such symptoms as: depressed mood, anxiety, suspiciousness, panic attacks (weekly or less often), chronic sleep impairment, mild memory loss (such as forgetting names, directions, recent events) 30%
Occupational and social impairment due to mild or transient symptoms which decrease work efficiency and ability to perform occupational tasks only during periods of significant stress, or; symptoms controlled by continuous medication 10%
A mental condition has been formally diagnosed, but symptoms are not severe enough either to interfere with occupational and social functioning or to require continuous medication 0%

as having current indicators of problems in adapting to stressful conditions. Psychological conditions such as posttraumatic stress disorder may have a course where symptoms remit then re-emerge when posed with certain triggers. The types of potential triggers presented when in police training and then on patrol are more likely to be of concern than the stressors encountered in occupations such as accounting, carpentry, and a broad range of other non-public safety positions. These are complex issues to resolve prior to rendering a final determination of psychological stability and suitability.

FUTURE IMPLICATIONS/SUMMARY

Wars winding down and military sequestrations have resulted in an increase of military service members seeking employment in law enforcement. Estimates suggest that 20% of police officer applicants have prior military experience. Consequently, the evaluating police psychologist in a preemployment screening must possess a basic understanding of military service, as well as knowledge of prevalence rates of mental health issues in soldiers who have served in combat-related overseas assignments. In addition, police psychologists are encouraged to be familiar with transition and reintegration efforts that are sponsored by the military, as well as public safety agencies. The police psychologist must also be cognizant of laws and legal precedents that prevent discrimination against police officer candidates with prior military experience. Asking appropriate questions is critical in understanding each service member's psychological reaction to deployment(s). Are there are any ongoing mental health concerns that might impair his/her suitability for a position/reinstatement as a law enforcement officer? Additionally, police psychologists play an integral role in easing a police officer's return to work by helping the law enforcement agency implement a reintegration plan based on best practices. An effective reintegration plan includes services to families at each stage of the deployment cycle in addition to clinical services that support the military returnee's transition back to duty.

REFERENCES

Adams, R. S., Larson, M. J., Corrigan, J. D., Horgan, C. M., & Williams, T. V. (2012). Frequent binge drinking after combat-acquired traumatic brain injury among active duty military personnel with a past year combat deployment. *The Journal of Head Trauma Rehabilitation*, *27*(5), 349–360. doi:10.1097/HTR.0b013e318268db94 PMID:22955100

Americans with Disabilities Act Amendments Act, 42 U.S.C. § 12101 (2008).

Bliese, P. D., Wright, K. M., Adler, A. B., Thomas, J. L., & Hoge, C. W. (2007). Timing of Postcombat Mental Health Assessments. *Psychological Services*, *4*(3), 141–148. doi:10.1037/1541-1559.4.3.141

Bonds, T. M., Baiocchi, D., & McDonald, L. L. (2010). *Army Deployments to OIF and OEF*. Retrieved from http://www.rand.org/content/dam/rand/pubs/documented_briefings/2010/RAND_DB587.pdf

Clark, M. (2014). Military vets joining law enforcement. *Police Magazine*. Retrieved March 17, 2016, from http://www.policemag.com/channel/careers-training/articles/2014/01/military-vets-joining-law-enforcement.aspx

Commission on Accreditation for Law Enforcement Agencies. (2006). *Standards for Law Enforcement Agencies, 32.2.8 Emotional Stability/Psychological Fitness Examination.* Gainesville, VA: Author.

Curran, S. F. (2012, September 29). *Progress report: Effects from combat stress upon reintegration for citizen soldiers and on psychological profiles of police recruits with prior military experiences.* Presentation at the International Association of Chiefs of Police, Police Psychological Services Section, Annual Meeting, San Diego, CA.

Curran, S. F. (2014). Assessment and evaluation: Collecting the requisite building blocks for treatment planning. In S. M. F. Clevenger, L. Miller, B. A. Moore, & A. Freeman (Eds.), *Behind the badge: A psychological treatment handbook for law enforcement officers* (pp. 23–43). New York, NY: Houghton Mifflin Harcourt.

Curran, S. F., Allen, S. W., Clark, D. W., Craig, D., & Gardner, L. H. (2014). Managing encounters with returning veterans. *The Police Chief*, *81*, 52–55.

Curran, S. F., & Ritchie, E. C. (2006, October 14). *Warrior transition by Army Reserve and National Guard personnel from combat operations in Iraq to policing in the United States.* Workshop presentation at the International Association of Chiefs of Police 113th Annual Convention, Police Psychological Services Section, Boston, MA.

Currie, S. L., Day, A., & Kelloway, K. (2011). Bringing the troops back home: Modeling the postdeployment reintegration experience. *Journal of Occupational Health Psychology*, *16*(1), 38–47. doi:10.1037/a0021724 PMID:21280943

Defense Centers of Excellence. (2012, February). *A Review of post-deployment reintegration: Evidence, challenges and strategies for program development.* Retrieved from http://www.dcoe.mil/content/Navigation/Documents/Review_of_Post-Deployment_Reintegration.pdf

Department of Defense Instruction (DoDI) 6490.11. (2012). *DoD policy guidance for management of mild traumatic brain injury/concussion in the deployed setting.* DoDI.

Dralle, P. W., & Curran, S. F. (May 16, 2014). *Wars winding down...Now what?* Presentation at the Annual Meeting of the Consortium of Police Psychological Services (COPPS), Amelia Island, FL.

Gorman, L. A., Blow, A. J., Ames, B. D., & Reed, P. L. (2011). National Guard families after combat: Mental health, use of mental health services, and perceived treatment barriers. *Psychiatric Services (Washington, D.C.)*, *62*(1), 28–34. doi:10.1176/ps.62.1.pss6201_0028 PMID:21209296

Hemmerly-Brown, A. (2009, November 19). *AFROGEN: Army's deployment cycle aims for predictability.* Retrieved from: http://www.army.mil/article/30668/

Hoge, C. W., Achterlonie, J. L., & Milliken, C. S. (2006). Mental health problems, use of mental health services, and attrition from military service after returning from deployment to Iraq or Afghanistan. *Journal of the American Medical Association*, *295*(9), 1023–1032. doi:10.1001/jama.295.9.1023 PMID:16507803

Hoge, C. W., Grossman, S., Auchterlonie, J. L., Riviere, L. A., Milliken, C. S., & Wilk, J. E. (2014). PTSD treatment for soldiers after combat deployment: Low utilization of mental health care and reasons to dropout. *Psychiatric Services (Washington, D.C.)*, *65*(8), 997–1004. doi:10.1176/appi.ps.201300307 PMID:24788253

International Association of Chiefs of Police & Bureau of Justice Assistance. (2009). *Employing returning combat veterans as law enforcement officers*. Retrieved from http://www.iacp.org/Employing-Returning-Combat-Veterans-as-Law-Enforcement-Officers

International Association of Chiefs of Police & Bureau of Justice Assistance. (2010). *Law enforcement leader's guide on combat veterans: A transition guide for veterans beginning or continuing careers in law enforcement*. Retrieved from www.iacp.org/portals/0/pdfs/LeadersGuide_300dpi.pdf

Jackson, K. A. (2009). *Strengthening the yellow ribbon reintegration program: Common challenges and policy options to assist returning reservists*. (Master's Thesis). Goldman School of Public Policy, University of California, Berkeley, CA.

Keane, T. M., Fairbank, J. A., Caddell, J. M., Zimering, R. T., Taylor, K. L., & Mora, C. A. (1989). *CES (combat exposure scale)*. Retrieved from http://www.ptsd.va.gov/professional/pages/assessments/assessment-pdf/CES.pdf

Lopez, C. T. (2014, July 9). Army to realign brigades, cut 40,000 soldiers, 17,000 civilians. *Army News Service*. Retrieved from www.army.mil/article/151992/Army_to_realign_brigades_cut_40_000_Soldiers_17_000_civilians

Metropolitan Police Department. (2008). *Employer partnership: The Washington, DC Metropolitan Police Department and the US Army Reserve*. Retrieved from http://mpdc.dc.gov/page/employer-partnership-mpd-and-us-army-reserve

Miceli, T., & Rollo, J. (2015, August). Military veterans and the contemporary challenges in law enforcement. *The Police Chief*, *82*, 36–39.

Michigan Commission on Law Enforcement Standards. (2015, August 13). *Military police basic training program*. Retrieved from http://www.michigan.gov/mcoles

Military OneSource, Department of Defense. (2015). *The yellow ribbon reintegration program*. Retrieved from http://www.militaryonesource.mil/deployment?content_id=266643

Milliken, C. S., Auchterlonie, J. L., & Hoge, C. W. (2007). Longitudinal assessment of mental health problems among active and reserve component soldiers returning from the Iraq War. *Journal of the American Medical Association*, *298*(18), 2141–2148. doi:10.1001/jama.298.18.2141 PMID:18000197

Peterson, N. (2012, April 17). Trading camouflage for badges: Vets going back to work in law-enforcement. *Medill Reports Chicago*. Retrieved from http://newsarchive.medill.northwestern.edu/chicago/news-204277.html

Pfeiffer, P. N., Blow, A. J., Miller, E., Forman, J., Dalack, G. W., & Valenstein, M. (2012). Peers and peer-based interventions in supporting reintegration and mental health among National Guard soldiers: A qualitative study. *Military Medicine*, *177*(12), 1471–1476. doi:10.7205/MILMED-D-12-00115 PMID:23397691

Reger, M. A., Smolenski, D. J., Skopp, N. A., Metzger-Abamukang, M. J., Kang, H. K., Bullman, T. A., & Gahm, G. A. et al. (2015). Risk of suicide among US military service members following Operation Enduring Freedom or Operation Iraqi Freedom deployment and separation from the US military. *JAMA Psychiatry*, *72*(6), 561–569. doi:10.1001/jamapsychiatry.2014.3195 PMID:25830941

Roberts, M., Corey, D., Fischler, G., & Spilberg, S. (July, 2015). *Pre-employment screening of applicants currently receiving compensation for a psychological disability from the Veteran's Administration: Suggested guidelines*. Unpublished. Retrieved from IACP Police Psychological Services list serve.

Sayer, N. A., Frazier, P., Orazem, R. J., Gravely, A., Carlson, K. F., Hintz, S., & Noorbaloochi, S. (2011). Military to civilian questionnaire: A measure of postdeployment community reintegration difficulty among veterans using Department of Veterans Affairs medical care. *Journal of Traumatic Stress*, *24*(6), 660–670. doi:10.1002/jts.20706 PMID:22162082

Sayer, N. A., Noorbaloochi, S., Frazier, P., Carlson, K., Gravely, A., & Murdoch, M. (2010). Reintegration problems and treatment interests among Iraq and Afghanistan combat veterans receiving VA medical care. *Psychiatric Services (Washington, D.C.)*, *61*(6), 589–597. doi:10.1176/ps.2010.61.6.589 PMID:20513682

Scarpulla, C. (2014, August 29). *Military police training transition program*. Marine Corps Air Station Yuma. Retrieved from www.mcasyuma.marines.mil

Scherrer, J. F., Widner, G., Schroff, M., Matthieu, M., Balan, S., van den Berk-Clark, C., & Price, R. (2014). Assessment of a postdeployment Yellow Ribbon Reintegration Program for National Guard members and supporters. *Military Medicine*, *179*(11), 1391–1397. doi:10.7205/MILMED-D-14-00094 PMID:25373071

Seal, K. H., Bertenthal, D., Miner, C. R., Sen, S., & Marmar, C. (2007). Bringing the war back home: Mental health disorders among 103788 US veterans returning from Iraq and Afghanistan seen at Department of Veterans Affairs facilities. *Archives of Internal Medicine*, *167*(5), 476–482. doi:10.1001/archinte.167.5.476 PMID:17353495

Tan, M. (2015). Army lays out plan to cut 40,000 soldiers. *Army Times*. Retrieved March 17, 2016, from http://www.armytimes.com/story/military/pentagon/2015/07/09/army-outlines-40000-cuts/29923339/

Tanielian, T., Jaycox, L. H., Schell, T. L., Marshall, G. N., Burnam, M. A., & Eibner, C. The Invisible Wounds Study Team. (2008). *Invisible wounds of war: Summary and recommendations for addressing psychological and cognitive injuries*. Santa Monica, CA: Rand.

Thomas, J. L., Wilk, J. E., Riviere, L. A., McGurk, D., Castro, C. A., & Hoge, C. W. (2010). Prevalence of mental health problems and functional impairment among active component and National Guard soldiers 3 and 12 months following combat in Iraq. *Archives of General Psychiatry*, *67*(6), 614–623. doi:10.1001/archgenpsychiatry.2010.54 PMID:20530011

Under Secretary of Defense, Department of Defense. (2015). Report to Congress: National Defense Authorization Act (NDAA) for Fiscal Year (FY) 2008, Section 1673; House Report (H.R.) 111-491, Accompanying H.R. 5136 the NDAA for FY 2011, Page 314, Improvement of Medical Tracking System for Members of the Armed Forces Deployed Overseas. Washington, DC: Author.

United States Department of Justice, Office of Community Oriented Police Services. (2012, June). *COPS fact sheet*. Retrieved from http://www.cops.usdoj.gov/pdf/2012AwardDocs/CHP/2012

United States Department of the Army. (2011). *Army force generation. (Army Regulation 525-29).* Washington, DC: Author.

United States Department of Veteran Affairs. (2015). *Schedule for rating disabilities, 38 C.F.R. § 4.130, DC 9411, general rating formula for mental disorders*. Washington, DC: Author.

United States National Guard. (2015). *About the National Guard*. Retrieved from http://www.nationalguard.mil/AbouttheGuard.aspx

Warner, C. H., Appenzeller, G. N., Grieger, T., & Belenkiy, S. (2011). Importance of anonymity to encourage honest reporting in mental health screening after combat deployment. *Archives of General Psychiatry*, *68*(10), 1065–1071. doi:10.1001/archgenpsychiatry.2011.112 PMID:21969463

Webster, B. (June 2012). *Combat deployment and the returning police officer*. Retrieved from http://ric-zai-inc.com/Publications/cops-p150-pub.pdf

White House Business Council. (2012). *Guide to hiring veterans*. Retrieved from www.whitehouse.gov/sites/default/files/docs/white_house_business_council_-_guide_to_hiring_veterans.pdf

Wilcox, S. L., Oh, H., Redmond, S. A., Chicas, J., Hassan, A. M., Lee, P. J., & Ell, K. (2015). A scope of the problem: Post-deployment reintegration challenges in National Guard unit. *Work (Reading, Mass.)*, *50*, 73–83. PMID:25167910

Woodson, J. (2013). *Memorandum, subject: clinical practice guidance for deployment-limiting disorders and psychotropic medications*. Washington, DC: Assistant Secretary of Defense for Health Affairs, Department of Defense.

Yellow Ribbon Reintegration Program. (n.d.). *Yellow Ribbon Reintegration Program overview brief.* Retrieved from http://rwtf.defense.gov/Portals/22/Documents/Meetings/m14/152yrrp.pdf

Zinzow, H. M., Britt, T. W., McFadden, A. C., Burnette, C. M., & Gillespie, S. (2012). Connective active duty and returning veterans to mental health treatment: Interventions and treatment adaptations that may reduce barriers to care. *Clinical Psychology Review*, *32*(8), 741–753. doi:10.1016/j.cpr.2012.09.002 PMID:23063627

Chapter 9
Law Enforcement Officer Suicide

Daniel W. Clark
Washington State Patrol, USA

Elizabeth K. White
Riverside County, USA

ABSTRACT

Suicide is a serious public health problem that impacts individuals, families, communities, and law enforcement personnel. More than 42,000 completed suicides were counted in the United States in 2014. Suicide has long been a concern within law enforcement. In this chapter, the authors explore the current status of Law Enforcement Officer (LEO) suicide research and dispel the myth that officer suicides are dramatically higher than in the general population. We then review general information on suicide prevention, and supplement this general information with law enforcement-specific risk factors, warning signs, variables, tips, and recommendations for intervention and postvention. Additionally, we suggest a range of available resources for further consideration.

LAW ENFORCEMENT SUICIDE

Is a chapter on suicide necessary? We believe it is, because individuals contemplating suicide are generally referred to mental health professionals. Yet, the literature clearly demonstrates that even mental health professionals do not receive adequate training in suicide assessment and management during their graduate programs. Only 55% of psychologists, 25% of social workers, 6% of marriage and family therapists, and 2% of accredited counselors' education programs contain specific training on assessment and management of suicide (Schmitz et al., 2012).

Is a chapter on *law enforcement officer* (LEO) suicide necessary? Again, we believe the answer is yes. For a variety of reasons, research, prevention, intervention and postvention are all slightly more complex in the world of law enforcement. As we proceed through the discussion of each topic, specific differences related to police culture will be highlighted at each step. In this chapter, the authors will explore LEO suicide research, review general information on suicide prevention, and supplement this general information with law enforcement-specific information, recommendations, and available resources.

DOI: 10.4018/978-1-5225-0813-7.ch009

REVIEW OF RESEARCH

The Centers for Disease Control and Prevention (CDC) collects data and tracks trends and patterns in the U.S. on mortality, including deaths by suicide. Suicide rates are expressed as X number of individuals per 100,000 in the population (or X/100,000). This allows one to meaningfully compare rates across different groups. According to the American Association of Suicidology's report for 2014, the suicide rate among U.S. adults ages 18 and older is 13.4/100,000 (Drapeau & McIntosh, 2015).

At this point, it appears deceptively simple to either prove or disprove whether LEOs complete suicide at a rate higher than, equal to, or less than the general population. We need simply compare the suicide rate of the general population with that of LEOs. However, such comparisons are easier said than done. Research related to suicide rates among LEOs has been fraught with problems due to a number of factors. In fact, the greatest challenge in law enforcement suicide research has been the lack of empirical, reliable data on the subject. Previous methodological problems included lack of adequate sample size, inappropriate comparison across different periods of time, no specification of type of police work performed, and/or lack of generalizability (Hem, Berg, & Ekeberg, 2001). Violanti (2010) found support for claims of underreported LEO suicides, and Hem et al. (2001) cited a failure to use appropriate comparison groups, as well as misinterpretations of the research. Studies investigating suicidal ideation and attempts are often difficult due to union negotiated agreements that prohibit surveys and freedom of information demands that are intrusive to law enforcement. There is considerable mistrust on the part of officers that results will truly be anonymous and/or appropriately protected (International Association of Chiefs of Police, 2014; Violanti, 2007).

The police population also differs from the general population in terms of age and ethnicity, which have repeatedly been identified as factors in suicide risk (Aamodt, Stalknaker, & Smith, 2015; Centers for Disease Control & Prevention, 2016). In addition, LEOs are, by definition, employed, which is often considered a mitigating factor (Milner, Page, & LaMontague, 2014). Other complications include agency culture and environment, which can result in inadequate records or mislabeling the cause of death in an effort to protect law enforcement personnel and their families. The impact of preemployment psychological screening, which further differentiates the law enforcement population from the general population, is largely ignored as a possible contaminant. There is not even an agreed upon definition on who qualifies as an LEO in the literature reviewed (Clark, White, & Violanti, 2012).

Despite the issues identified above, a number of studies related to LEO suicide have been completed over time. These studies are the appropriate starting point in identifying a suicide rate to compare to the existing one in the general population. Many have claimed that the LEO suicide rate is two to three times higher than the general U.S. adult population. The media have reported LEO rates of 22/100,000 as compared to the 12/100,000 in the general population, which appears to be based on the 1995 Fraternal Order of Police (FOP) study of insurance claims submitted by 92 local chapters in 24 states (Langston, 1995). The media have also commonly reported 300 or more officer suicides per year and that the police rate is at least double the general population (D'Aurizio, 1997; Loh, 1994).

Research on LEO suicide has produced widely varying rates from 5.8/100,000 per year in London (Heiman, 1975) to 203.7/100,000 per year in Wyoming (Nelson & Smith, 1970). In an effort to shed some light on the matter, *USA Today* published data on five of the nation's largest law enforcement agencies in terms of their LEO suicide rates (per 100,000 individuals per year): New York Police Department- 15.5, Los Angeles Police Department- 20.7; Federal Bureau of Investigation (FBI)- 26.1; Chicago Police Department- 18.1; and San Diego Police Department- 35.7 (Fields & Jones, 1999). The annual combined rate for these LEOs is 16.34/100,000, which is notably less than the 22.0/100,000 asserted by the FOP study (Aamodt & Stalnaker, 2001).

LEO suicide research in the last 15 years strengthens the position that LEO prevalence rates, while not optimal, are definitely not double the rate of the general population. Consider Benner's (2001) study of the San Francisco Police Department from 1965-2000; he reported a prevalence rate of 17.1. Campion (2001) examined 89 law enforcement agencies in Illinois, Indiana, and Minnesota, and reported a prevalence rate of 18.1. Aamodt and Stalnaker (2001) conducted a meta-analysis on the suicide rate of law enforcement personnel reported in research and identified a prevalence rate of 18.1. Loo (2003) conducted a meta-analysis of 101 studies and reported a mean prevalence rate of 22.99. Greater weight should be given to rigorous research, especially where meta-analyses are conducted, as these efforts combine data from numerous research studies, which are carefully screened prior to inclusion, allowing greater confidence in the resulting conclusions.

As previously mentioned, it is essential to use appropriate comparison groups when evaluating the suicide rate of LEOs. When using demographics similar to the LEO population, the matched sample suicide rate was found to be 21.89 according to Aamodt and Stalnaker (2001). In their article, the two researchers were further able to refine their matched sample rate to 18.3 by accounting for the expected deaths by suicide from people with schizophrenia or bipolar disorder, which would likely have been screened out in LEO applicants. And, if the LEO suicide rate is 18.1 when considering more methodologically sound research (Aamodt & Stalnaker, 2001), then the difference between LEOs and the matched sample is actually negligible.

O'Hara and Violanti (2009) and O'Hara, Violanti, Levenson, and Clark (2013) have taken the LEO suicide research one step further into the modern technological age by using Internet surveillance techniques. These authors reasoned that use of the Internet to track reports of police suicide using consistent surveillance terms throughout multiple media sites such as news sites, police websites, blogs, and forums, would yield consistent and more complete data. Their research tracked 119,000 suicide-specific news articles in 2008, which yielded a count of 141 completed LEO suicides for a rate of 16.4/100,000, which is less than the demographically adjusted general population rate of 18.3/100,000 identified by O'Hara and Violanti (2009).

Aamodt, Stalnaker, and Smith (2015) collected information from 12 large agencies between 2010 and 2014, representing 9% of the total law enforcement population (N = 91,025.) This represents the largest profile study of LEO suicides to date. The study evaluated 836 suicides of active, sworn personnel and revealed a rate of 12.62 per 100,000, which is even lower than the LEO rate reported in 2009. The demographic data of the 836 suicides indicated the law enforcement group consisted of 92% males and 80.4% Whites. The national suicide rate for white males between the ages of 20-64 varied between 35.30 and 36.51 per 100,000 from 2010-2013 (Heron 2013, 2015a, 2015b, 2016). In summary, the recent, more rigorous studies provide strong support for the conclusion that the law enforcement suicide rate is well below the rate of a demographically matched general population comparison group.

Despite the data presented above, the belief that LEOs complete suicide at an unusually high rate does persist to some extent for a number of potential reasons. One possible reason is that sensational information is interesting. The news proclaims, "Officers are three times as likely to die by their own hand as the hand of a suspect." Is it true? Yes, although it varies from state to state. Is it significant? The unfortunate reality is that a comparison group matched by age, gender, and ethnicity would result in equally upsetting numbers or worse. Between 2010 and 2014 in the U.S., data retrieved from the Web-based Injury Statistics Query and Reporting System (WISQARS) database of the Centers for Disease

Control and Prevention (CDC) showed that white males between the ages of 20-59 completed suicide 88,278 times and were the victim of homicide 11,957 times. The comparison group was therefore 7.4 times as likely to die by their own hand as by the hand of someone else (CDC, 2016.)

A second potential reason may be the higher visibility in the news of all matters pertaining to law enforcement. If a dentist or a plumber is caught with a prostitute, it may warrant a small mention in the paper, depending on the size of the town. If a law enforcement officer is caught with a prostitute, it is likely to be front page news. For better or worse, law enforcement personnel are higher profile and held to a different standard; consequently, LEO suicides may be more publicized than suicides from other professions.

As the above studies indicate, recent research has repeatedly shown that the suicide rate for LEOs is not significantly higher than that of appropriately matched comparison groups. We contend that one of the major roles of police psychologists may be to provide and explain accurate, research-based information related to suicide in a manner that is respectful of police culture. Such education must continue to occur with the public at large as well. Police psychologists are encouraged to create and maintain a regular suicide forum within police psychology organizations and listservs, monitor and evaluate suicide trends, utilize more innovative prevention program strategies, share preliminary research results, and refine research protocols.

PREVENTION

Suicide is a serious public health problem that impacts individuals, families, and communities. Suicide prevention strives to reduce risk factors and increase protective factors or resilience. Ideally, prevention is multi-leveled and effective at promoting suicide awareness and encouraging a commitment to social change.

Warning Signs and Risk Factors

Increased awareness of warning signs and risk factors may help reduce the suicide rate by educating law enforcement agencies, officers, family members, peer support teams, and supervisors on what to look for in a potentially suicidal individual. If one does not know what the signs of increased suicide risk are, it is unlikely that one can recognize them and intervene in ways needed to mitigate such risk. “Warning signs” indicate *immediate* risk for suicide and only apply to individuals. “Risk factors” indicate someone is at a *heightened* risk for suicide and may apply to individuals or groups (Rudd et al., 2006; SPRC, 2011).

Rudd et al. (2006) detail many warning signs, including individuals talking about or threatening suicide, as well as seeking access to lethal means. Feeling hopeless or that there is no way out of a difficult situation is an important warning sign to monitor. Other warning signs include anger, anxiety, agitation, sleep changes, dramatic changes in mood, and withdrawal from social and familial contact.

The American Association of Suicide (AAS), one of the leading professional organizations concerned with suicide, published the acronym IS PATH WARM regarding warning signs (AAS, 2005). Generally speaking, the more warning signs that are present, the higher the risk level.

I: Ideation
S: Substance Abuse

P: Purposelessness
A: Anxiety
T: Trapped
H: Hopelessness
W: Withdrawal
A: Anger
R: Recklessness
M: Mood Change

Risk factors indicate an increased overall risk level for either groups or individuals. Common risk factors include prior attempts, mood disorders, substance use or abuse, access to lethal means, and interpersonal loss or disruption in an important relationship (Rudd, Joiner, Jobes, & King, 1999; Shea, 2009; SPRC, 2011). Additional risk factors include social isolation, shame, a sense of burdensomeness, sleep disturbance, legal or occupational problems, financial problems, and impulsivity.

Patterson, Dohn, Bird, and Patterson (1983) published the acronym SAD PERSONS to capture these risk factors:

S: Sex (male)
A: Age (15-34)
D: Depression
P: Previous exposure to suicide
E: Ethanol/alcohol/drug abuse
R: Rational thinking loss
S: Social support system lacking
O: Organized plan
N: No spouse or significant other
S: Sickness

Campbell (2004) suggested adding an "A" to this acronym to make it SAD PERSONAS, with the additional "A" referring to access to lethal means. This scale is not linear, but the more statements that are true, the higher the risk level.

Consider a medical example such as a heart attack. Risk factors for a heart attack, or indicators of *heightened risk*, include obesity, tobacco use, and physical inactivity. Warning signs of a heart attack, indicating *immediate risk*, include shortness of breath, chest pains, nausea, and light headedness (SPRC, 2011). Similarly, risk factors for suicide indicate increased risk and warning signs indicate immediate risk that requires immediate attention.

Law Enforcement Specific Warning Signs and Risk Factors

There are a number of cultural variables that impact existing risk factors and warning signs related to LEO suicide, starting with a strong identification with mental toughness and emotional control. Emotional difficulties are often seen as weakness in law enforcement culture.

Most officers identify themselves as problem solvers and self-sufficiency is viewed as an essential attribute. The general public looks to officers to keep the peace, to assist when they are victims of crime, and to protect them from all manner of harm. LEOs may therefore have unrealistically high expectations of themselves when it comes to handling their own problems. Many law enforcement line officers, as well as command staff, have limited awareness of how to identify and secure appropriate treatment from mental health providers (MHPs) skilled in providing services to law enforcement populations. Negative experiences with MHPs who are not familiar with or supportive of law enforcement can discourage or shut down tentative attempts to seek assistance. Lack of support from command staff, either emotionally or through supportive policy and procedure, can also sabotage use of mental health services. Although younger peace officers appear more comfortable with obtaining psychological assistance, even they may be discouraged from seeking help if the agency involved does not provide the assistance, does not make assistance well publicized or easily accessible, or creates an environment that pairs seeking assistance with weakness, failure, shame, or job consequences (International Association of Chiefs of Police, 2014; Violanti, 2003).

If services are available, there may be a significant fear of consequences for seeking help, including concerns about immediate career impact, such as a loss of reputation or being assigned to desk duty if the officer admits to difficulties (International Association of Chiefs of Police, 2014). Additional concerns include long term consequences, such as failure to promote or even referral for a fitness for duty evaluation and possible termination.

Violanti (2003) discussed the need of officers to put up an emotional barrier to protect themselves from the human misery they witness. This can result in a fairly rigid system in which emotions are generally suppressed; it can also result in a form of depersonalization. Violanti went on to postulate that such a system may carry over into the home environment, creating a world that does not allow for an outlet of emotions. Such a system can also negatively impact interpersonal interactions with friends and family. Aamodt and Stalnaker (2001) also noted in a separate article that relationship problems were the most frequently identified reason for an officer to complete suicide, playing a role in 26.6% of suicides. In more recent research with a larger sample group, Aamodt, Stalnaker, and Smith (2015) confirmed that relationship issues and legal problems were the top two identified reasons for a completed LEO suicide.

Officers are taught early on to suppress, or at a minimum, hide emotion, particularly in the field. While such skills are mandatory for survival, when overdeveloped, they create an individual who is quite skilled at not showing feelings of distress, sadness, etc. When considered with the obstacles noted above, such as fear of being seen as weak or fear of job consequences, an officer is very likely to be quite good at not showing or discussing distress, regardless of inner pain. As such, officers may not display many of the signs normally observed in individuals contemplating suicide or they may display them in unique ways. For example, an officer might become more productive at the worksite if the officer is experiencing impulses towards increased risk taking as a means of indirect suicidal ideation or intent, either consciously or unconsciously. Such an officer might suddenly become the first to respond to every high risk call. Rather than being looked at as a warning sign, such behavior may be praised and even rewarded. While most people are familiar with the term "Suicide by Cop," few consider the alternative, which the authors describe as "Suicide by Suspect." Such a death allows the officer to provide for his or her family, avoids some of the potential shame and trauma related to suicide, and guarantees support and respect from the law enforcement community.

The cohesiveness of law enforcement officers and the tendency to socialize with other officers off duty creates a homogeneous environment that reinforces positive and negative aspects of law enforcement culture, both on and off the job. Due to the emphasis on mental toughness and the ability to hide emotion, an officer experiencing distress may look to other officers and make negative comparisons.

If no one else "appears" to be experiencing problems, the officer may refrain from bringing up his or her issues due to embarrassment for not being an adequate enough problem-solver. Officers may be even less willing to seek support from someone outside of law enforcement, whom they believe will not understand their world or their issues. The enhanced identification with the job that occurs among many officers can have significant impact if an officer is facing potential loss of the job due to allegations of misconduct, injuries on the job, or potential negative findings in a fitness for duty evaluation. The mindset of established LEOs can be an "all or nothing" style: "I am a cop or I am nothing." This thinking can increase risk for suicide and prevent officers from finding healthy compromises or alternatives that individuals in other professions may more comfortably access. In addition, as the majority of an officer's friends are often other officers (Bishop & Boots, 2014), loss of position likely will result in perceived or actual loss of access to social support (Waters & Ussery, 2007).

Police culture historically condoned, or at least ignored, use of alcohol as a coping method (Bishop & Boots, 2014; Violanti, 2004). The acceptance of alcohol as a coping method increases the risk for impulsive or disinhibited behavior. While alcohol abuse is rarely identified as the reason for suicide among law enforcement personnel (just 4% of LEO suicides, according to Aamodt, Stalnaker, & Smith, 2015), in the authors' experience a large number of officers who complete suicide are found to be under the influence at the time of their death. In a recent study of suicidal ideation in law enforcement, alcohol consumption among LEOs was identified on a scale of 1-4 (1=no drinks, 2=1-3 drinks, 3=4-10 drinks and 4=11 or more drinks per week). The authors found that for each unit increase on the scale of 1 to 4, the corresponding incidence of suicidal ideation in their LEOs increased by 25%, which further supports the role of alcohol's interaction with suicide for law enforcement (Bishop & Boots, 2014.)

The presence of firearms has long been known to increase the risk for completed suicides in any household due to ease of access to lethal means. Aamodt and Stalnaker (2001) found that over 90% of LEO suicides involved a firearm. In an updated study by Aamodt, Stalnaker, and Smith (2015) using more recent data, the percentage was found to be 96.4% compared to the national rate of 50.9% (56.4% for males). Data retrieved from the WISQARS database of the CDC showed white males between the ages of 20-59 completed suicide with a firearm 52.5% of the time during the same time period of the study (CDC, 2016).

The various stressors impacting LEOs, while not always unique, do add to the risk factors for suicide. Commonly identified factors involved in LEO suicides include: job related stress, traumatic exposure, the dissolution of one's primary relationship, clinical depression, and substance abuse or dependence. Other factors reported in the research include police corruption, misconduct, bureaucracy, alienation, lack of control over working conditions, illness/injury incurred on or off the job, and impending retirement (D'Angelo, 2001; McMains & Mullins, 2001).

Officers face threats to their own lives on a fairly regular basis. Officers are frequently exposed to human suffering, the inhumanity in the actions of one person against another, assaults against children, and other critical incidents that may cause secondary trauma. Violanti (2010) found that certain traumatic experiences increased the risk of PTSD and suicidal ideation in LEOs. The combined impact of PTSD and alcohol use led to a ten-fold increase in risk of suicidal ideation among officers. Lastly, the current negative climate towards law enforcement is also a stressor. There have been a number of ambush killings of officers reported in recent headlines and in the authors' experiences, many officers are experiencing an increased sense of vulnerability.

Many individuals involved in the field of suicide have recently advocated a zero event goal in suicide prevention. There is even a "Zero Suicide" initiative identified by the U.S. Department of Health and Human Services, National Action Alliance for Suicide Prevention (2012). The concept has been endorsed by a number of other health agencies and there are websites now exclusively devoted to the concept (Suicide Prevention Research Center, 2016). Question, Persuade and Refer (QPR) for Law Enforcement (2016) also supports this concept specifically for law enforcement officers. Such a goal, while a noble aspiration, may not be realistic for law enforcement due to the very aspects of law enforcement culture identified above. This goal also does not take into account the concept of the "impulsive suicide" (Anderson, 2008). A number of individuals who go on to complete suicide do so after a relatively brief amount of consideration, sometimes less than five minutes. The signs and symptoms normally displayed across time are missing and the means are often more lethal. The equation appears to be a combination of ease of effort, speed of access, and certainty of death, which make firearms a ready choice. There is less likely to be a history of depression or mental illness. There is some evidence to suggest that the ease and fast access actually drives the act. As officers almost always have access to firearms and tend to be decisive and action oriented, they may be more vulnerable to such acts and there may be little or no warning signs involved (O'Hara & Violanti, 2009; Violanti, Vena, & Marshal, 1996).

While extensive budget resources are devoted to physical training and firearms accuracy, training devoted to resilience, stress management, and critical incident recovery is often lacking. Direct training related to suicide prevention is unusual. While LEOs frequently come into contact with suicidal individuals in the field, they often receive little or no training on the topic, much less how to react to or prevent suicide among their own ranks. Smaller departments may not have the budget or resources to present trainings in these areas. Command staff, who are often slightly older than line officers, may be even more entrenched in police cultural values emphasizing emotional control and toughness. Specialized mental health services and/or training may not be high priority when it comes to budget allocation and/or union negotiations. Finding psychologists to effectively teach LEOs may also be a challenge as there has traditionally been some standoffishness between the two professions.

In summary, any prevention plan involving law enforcement personnel must take into consideration the additional risk factors and warning signs that are unique to law enforcement. It is important to recognize that the absence of warning signs should never be used as a reason for not "asking the question." It should be remembered that LEOs may have many of the risk factors even if they display none of the warning signs delineated above and the potential for impulsive suicide may mean high risk even if no signs are present.

Protective Factors

Protective factors are skills, strengths, or resources that help people deal more effectively with stressful events. Protective factors for suicide risk include coping skills, problem solving skills, family and community support, a sense of connectedness, and perhaps cultural or religious beliefs that affirm the importance of life (Joiner, Walker, Rudd, & Jobes, 1999; SPRC, 2011).

Protective factors can counterbalance risk factors and warning signs. Picture a teeter-totter on a playground. On one side of the teeter-totter are the risk factors and warning signs weighing that side of the teeter-totter down. On the other side are protective factors that may serve as protective mechanisms. Unfortunately, some of the risk factors and warning signs, such as age, race, gender, and prior exposure to suicide are virtually unchangeable. With the teeter-totter analogy, however, we can view the protective factors as counterbalancing those factors that are not amenable to change.

Resources

General resources for prevention include the American Association of Suicidology (AAS), which serves as a national clearinghouse for information on suicide, www.suicidology.org. The Suicide Prevention Resource Center (SPRC) has a Best Practice Registry (BPR) comprised of evidence-based programs, expert/consensus statements, and relevant standards, www.sprc.org/bpr.

The National Strategy for Suicide Prevention (NSSP) calls for clearly identifying populations that will benefit from each intervention and the program as a whole; specifying the outcomes to be achieved; using interventions known to affect a particular outcome; coordinating and organizing the community to focus on the issue; and basing a suicide prevention effort on a clear plan with goals, objectives, and implementation steps (US HHS, 2001). Recently, several reviews examined the application of the NSSP and suggested updates to the recommendations (SPRC, 2010; US HHS, 2012).

The CDC approach to preventing suicide is similar. It includes goals such as describing and tracking the problem of suicide behavior, increasing understanding of suicide trends and patterns, studying the causes and consequences of suicide behavior, evaluating and demonstrating ways to prevent suicide behavior, and communicating scientific information about suicide behavior (CDC, 2015).

Another resource to review is the suicide prevention plan for each state in the United States. The Suicide Prevention Resource Center (SPRC) lists all the state plans; for more information, see www.sprc.org/states/materials/plans. Each plan may address currently available resources.

Law Enforcement Specific Resources

The International Association of Chiefs of Police (IACP) and the Office of Community Oriented Policing Services (COPS Office) united to identify initiatives regarding LEO suicide prevention (IACP, 2014.) These initiatives focused on refining the law enforcement leadership role; empowering leaders to create culture change; encouraging collaboration between police and mental health professionals to ensure new approaches and create best practices; and identifying state-of-the-art mental wellness programs and suicide prevention strategies available for replication. In 2015, IACP and others released a 12-minute video, *Breaking the Silence: Suicide Prevention in Law Enforcement*, available at youtu.be/fBJbo7mnnBs.

In September of 1999, the FBI hosted the Suicide and Law Enforcement Conference, which generated a compilation of articles targeting LEO suicide. There are 61 articles across six sections which address suicide from different perspectives such as organizational, psychological, behavioral, and quantitative approaches. The file is available for download from www.ncjrs.gov/pdffiles1/193528-193589.pdf.

In 2007, the California Peace Officer Standards and Training (POST) Training Network produced a video directly addressing law enforcement suicide, *Preventing Law Enforcement Officer Suicide* (Commission on POST, 2007). The video provides vignettes and a training curriculum for discussing suicide signs, symptoms, and responses. The video is available through CA POST at post.outpostnetworks.com/postcatalog/catalogue/c12/p225.

In 2008, the IACP, the Bureau of Justice Assistance, the U.S. Department of Justice and EEI Communications partnered to produce a compilation of suicide prevention resources from leading agencies across the country. This resource CD includes steps to developing a law enforcement-specific suicide prevention program and provides sample training materials and presentations as well as sample funeral protocols for completed suicide for use with law enforcement families and agencies. The CD is available through the National Criminal Justice Reference Service at www.ncjrs.gov/App/Publications/abstract.aspx?ID=246399.

ACT to Prevent a Suicide is a 45-minute interactive training DVD filmed using Los Angeles Police Department (LAPD) personnel, equipment, and locations in order to help a law enforcement audience relate to the subject matter. The training not only identifies the signs and symptoms of someone who might be contemplating suicide, but also asks viewers to consider what steps they would take to help a friend or colleague showing such signs. Realistic scenarios are presented and viewers are challenged to Ask, Care, and Transport (ACT): *Ask* the difficult question about suicide, show that someone *cares*, and *transport* the employee to help. *ACT to Prevent a Suicide* can be obtained from Behavioral Science Services of the LAPD (www.lapdonline.org).

QPR stands for Question, Persuade, and Refer — three simple steps anyone can learn to help save a life from suicide. People trained in QPR learn how to recognize the warning signs of a suicide crisis and how to question, persuade, and refer someone to help. QPR for Law Enforcement is a registered best practice training program listed in the National Registry of Evidence-based Programs and Practices. The QPR Institute offers a 6-hour training course focusing on protecting law enforcement co-workers, friends, family, and community from suicide (courses.qprinstitute.com).

INTERVENTION

After identifying that someone is potentially suicidal, the question becomes: "What do I do next?" Whether the identified individual is an officer, a non-officer employee, or a family member, the next step is to evaluate the individual, preferably by a mental health professional such as a psychologist or psychiatrist with experience working with law enforcement.

Assessment is key to effective intervention. In the previous section, the authors addressed risk factors, warning signs, and protective factors. As part of intervention, clinicians need to complete the assessment by determining the level of suicidal ideation, the amount of planning the individual has completed, and the access to lethal means.

How does one determine if an individual is suicidal? Ask about suicidal ideation in a straightforward, non-biased manner such as, "Have you thought about hurting or killing yourself?" or "Have you thought about suicide?" (AAS, 2015). These two questions pull for a "yes" or "no" answer without biasing the individual's response. Alternatively, if one asked, "You aren't thinking of doing something stupid like killing yourself, are you?," the questioner has now likely influenced the individual's answer toward a socially desirable reply such as, "No, I'm not going to do anything stupid."

Most people, even LEOs, are likely to give an honest answer to the question of having suicidal ideation. In the author's experience, some will not give an honest response but these are the minority. Remember that it is important to work on building rapport and trust with an LEO before asking questions about suicidal ideation. A good rapport is likely to result in an even greater likelihood of an honest response.

Useful questions as follow-up to a "yes" answer to the question, "Are you thinking of hurting or killing yourself?" include: "Have you thought about how you might end your life?," "Do you have the means available?," "Any family history of suicidal behavior?," and "Have you ever made a suicide attempt yourself?"

Two additional questions that may help the clinician formulate the risk assessment are, "What has been keeping you alive so far?" and "What do you think the future holds in store for you?" The first question assesses an individual's ambivalence, or the ongoing struggle with, "Should I live or should I die?" The second assesses feelings of hopelessness. Most people struggle with defining or identifying hopelessness, so rather than asking about hopelessness directly, the authors recommend exploring an individual's thoughts about his or her future. If the individual responds, "Future? What future? Nothing is ever going to change. I'll always feel this way, so why should I keep living?," then the presence of hopelessness has been demonstrated.

Now that the "data collection" portion of the assessment is complete, the next step is the formulation of risk. As clinicians, we are not expected to predict the future and determine who will end their life. Our responsibility is to detect increased risk. Simon (2002, 2011), as well as Berman and Silverman (2013) and Silverman and Berman (2013), agree that clinicians cannot predict with certainty which individuals will complete the act of suicide and that the formulation or estimation of risk is a judgment call based on the clinician's training, background, and experience.

Simon (2002, 2011) describes a systematic assessment of risk, but adds that systematic does not mean perfect or exhaustive. Simon also recommends that risk assessment be considered a *process*, not an event. Silverman and Berman add, "Denial of suicidal ideation is insufficient to constitute a complete SRA (suicide risk assessment)" (2013, p. 8). These authors recommend that clinicians go beyond the initial question of, "Are you thinking of hurting or killing yourself?" and probe further, if the patient/client's history or presentation warrants.

Granello (2010) articulates 12 core process principles that guide suicide risk assessment. These principles serve as a complement to the current focus on content in suicide assessment, and include principles such as considering suicide assessment as "treatment" and "collaborative." A collaborative approach enlists the patient/client's input in the process, and emphasizes "we" language and statements such as, "Let's put our heads together and we'll try to figure this out."

Suicide risk exists on a continuum, from no risk to high risk, and intervention options are keyed to the level of risk. One method of rating risk severity is Joiner et al.'s (1999) model of nonexistent, mild, moderate, severe, and extreme. This method communicates the clinician's assessment clearly and effectively. Lower risk individuals are thinking, or ideating, about suicide. They may wonder if life is worth living or if they want to continue fighting whatever is troubling them.

Talking with someone is important, and many options are available including a faith based individual, a mental health professional, the person's primary care physician, a trained peer supporter, or someone from the individual's Employee Assistance Program (EAP). Another option is a helpline or hotline such as the National Suicide Prevention Lifeline. Family members and friends may provide important ancillary support.

As risk level increases, the intervention emphasis should shift to the professional end of the spectrum. On the low risk end of the continuum, peer supporters may be especially helpful in noticing changes in the individual and asking about suicidal thoughts. On the high risk end of the continuum, the mental health professional providing the intervention should question whether inpatient treatment is needed, and discuss this with the employee at risk.

As part of the assessment and formulation of suicide risk, mental health professionals should ask if the individual has a plan for suicide. One of the reasons to learn about the suicide plan is to reduce access to those lethal means, where possible. An informal guide in suicidology is that once individuals have begun to develop a plan, they tend to stick to that particular method, and do not easily switch to another method (Draper, 2008).

Law Enforcement Specific Intervention Factors

A common, and effective, suicide intervention with the general population is to reduce access to lethal means. This can, of course, be problematic with LEOs. Officers have access to lethal means every shift they work, and they should be evaluated with this in mind. The authors have two comments. First, seriously consider if removal of firearms is a necessary step. A gun and badge are part of an officer's identity, and to remove either can be a significant blow to his or her identity at a time when he or she is already likely experiencing hopelessness, anxiety, anger, and/or depression. If, in the interest of the officer's safety, removal of firearms is deemed a necessary step, then removal of *all* firearms is important. Many officers carry at least one backup weapon, plus many become firearms collectors and may have additional firearms at home.

Second, who assumes temporary custody of these firearms? Mental health professionals strive to protect privileged information as much as possible, even when someone is suicidal. Temporary disposition of the individual's firearms should be treated similarly to other privileged information. Options for temporary, safe storage of firearms to discuss with the suicidal individual include a family member, a trusted coworker or friend, or perhaps the officer's department or agency itself.

The authors have discussed limiting access to firearms and the potential impact on LEOs. In addition to firearms, it is important to acknowledged that there are other lethal means that may be available, such as knives, medications (legal and illegal), household chemicals and other poisons, materials used for hanging or suffocation, and jump sites. Temporarily reducing an individual's access to lethal means may help lower the probability of the individual's completed suicide (Barber & Miller, 2014; Means Matter, 2008).

A common intervention for many individuals experiencing distress and/or considering suicide is for the mental health provider to secure time off for the individual in question. A physician's letter securing time off for a LEO, however, may carry additional ramifications. Anything that raises concerns about the officer's ability to safely and effectively perform his or her duties can result in a fitness for duty evaluation (FFDE) being requested by the employing agency. One alternative strategy is for the officer to request the time off on his or her own behalf, if possible. If the officer has no time off on the books or the agency is too short staffed to allow it, it becomes essential that the mental health professional discuss with the officer the possible ramifications of a request for time off coming from a mental health provider.

A temporary hold or inpatient hospitalization is often used with individuals who are imminently suicidal. An additional factor to consider with law enforcement is what impact such a hold or hospitalization may have on the officer's employment. For example, in California if someone is involuntarily hospitalized for posing a serious threat of harm to self, that individual is not typically permitted to purchase or carry a firearm for five years (Clark & White, 2003). For a sworn officer, this may mean termination from his or her current employment. Should involuntary hospitalization be necessary, the mental health care provider may wish to coordinate with the hospital clinician prior to the officer's discharge to discuss any prohibition on firearms. The psychologist may also want to consider whether a voluntary hospitalization would accomplish the same goals without the added long term constraint of not being able to be armed. One of the complications of a voluntary hospitalization, however, is that the person can voluntarily leave the hospital just as he or she voluntarily entered the hospital. Although most psychologists do not have admitting privileges, and rely on the hospital to reevaluate the suicidal individual, the risks and benefits of hospitalization should be discussed with the person, whenever possible.

Resources

Resources for intervention include the long-standing practice for many mental health professionals of having a suicidal or potentially suicidal person agree to a "no-harm/no-suicide contract" (Simon, 1999). Forty years ago, the intent of such a "contract" was to assist in suicide risk evaluation and treatment planning, sharing the responsibility with the patient (Simon, 1999). However, over time the practice has devolved into a substitute for a thorough risk assessment by the clinician (Garvey, Penn, Campbell, Esposito-Smythers, & Spirito, 2009).

The utility of no-harm/no-suicide contracts has been debated for years, and has resulted in mixed reactions. According to several authors (Bongar & Sullivan, 2013; Simon, 2011), such contracts are not legally protective and may actually harm practitioners if they have a completed suicide in their caseload and the family sues for malpractice. In addition, a mere note of "no SI/HI/CFS" (no suicidal ideation/ homicidal ideation/contracted for safety) is considered by the courts to be an insufficient evaluation, and will likely be held against the mental health professional (Simon, 2011).

The Safety Plan Intervention (SPI) is an update and improvement to the no-harm/no-suicide contract (Stanley & Brown, 2012). Composed of 6 steps, it represents an escalating response to suicidal ideation. The process begins with sharing the warning signs of suicide with the suicidal individual. Second, when the individual recognizes he or she is feeling suicidal, the next step is to employ internal coping or distracting strategies, such as going for a walk, listening to music, exercising, or watching a movie. These activities do not require another person, which may enhance a patient's own sense of self-efficacy and create a sense that suicidal urges can be mastered.

Third, if more intervention is needed, the individual may socialize with people who may offer support and/or distraction from the suicidal ideation. This social interaction may occur in the individual's natural social environment, helping distract the person from his or her suicidal thoughts and urges. It may also take place through visiting healthy social settings such as self-help groups, coffee shops, or places of worship.

If the suicidal individual continues to escalate, the fourth step is to involve family members or friends who help in resolving the crisis. This step differs from step three in that the individual reveals that he or she is feeling suicidal, which may be difficult. The fifth step is to contact a mental health professional or an agency to request professional help. The sixth step is to reduce access to lethal means.

As part of the fifth step, contacting mental health professionals or agencies, it may be helpful for the individual to contact the National Suicide Prevention Lifeline (800-273-TALK or www.suicidepreventionlifeline.org). The person in question may find it useful to add the Lifeline phone number to his or her cell phone for easy access. This lifeline was established in 2005 and links more than 150 crisis clinics across the country. If the caller is a military veteran and presses "1" during the welcome message, the caller will be directed to a veterans' suicide prevention hotline specialist located in the VA call center in New York.

Additionally, if the individual is a member of the lesbian, gay, bisexual, transgender, and questioning (LGBTQ) community, that person may benefit from knowing the contact information for the Trevor Project (866-488-7386 or www.thetrevorproject.org), a national organization providing crisis intervention and suicide prevention services to LGBTQ young people ages 13-24.

The Safety Plan Initiative has been adapted for use as an app on a smartphone or tablet. Two available apps are *My3* and *Safety Plan*, both available from either the Apple App Store or Google Play for free. Both apps allow the user to follow a script of the above outlined six steps using plans the user has already input. For example, on My3, the user inputs internal coping strategy suggestions, such as exercise or watching a favorite movie for step two and contact information for three family members or friends he or she could contact when having suicidal thoughts for step four.

A third app which clinicians might find useful is from Substance Abuse and Mental Health Services Administration (SAMHSA) and is called *Suicide Safe* (store.samhsa.gov). Published in 2015, this free app is a resource for clinicians, and includes conversation starters, case studies, and a list of training and other resources. In addition, the app can assist in locating local behavioral health resources.

Law Enforcement Specific Resources

Safe Call Now (206-459-3020 or www.safecallnow.org) is a resource for public safety employees to speak confidentially with officers, former officers, public safety professionals, and/or mental health professionals who are familiar with emergency responders. Safe Call Now was designed as a safe place for law enforcement personnel to obtain assistance from individuals who understand the demands of a law enforcement career. These trained peer supporters provide assistance and referrals for any public safety personnel and their families who are experiencing an emotional crisis or want someone with whom to talk. LEOs experiencing suicidal thoughts or concerns may want to incorporate Safe Call Now as a resource for step 5 of their SPIs.

Additional such resources include the National Law Enforcement Hotline (800-COPLINE), which offers general crisis support and is staffed exclusively by retired law enforcement officers. There are also state specific programs such as Cop 2 Cop, a New Jersey based 24-hour hotline (866-COP-2COP or ubhc.rutgers.edu/cop2cop/) offering services to law enforcement officers and their families in the state of New Jersey. Numerous groups provide information related to law enforcement suicide: e.g., BadgeofLife.com, Tears of a Cop.com, and Copline.net.

LAW ENFORCEMENT-SPECIFIC POSTVENTION

As described earlier in this chapter, although the rate of suicide within law enforcement is much lower than has often been reported, approximately 140 suicide deaths do occur every year among LEOs in the U.S. (O'Hara & Violanti, 2009). Each death is tragic and has a devastating impact on all those involved. Postvention refers to an organized response following a suicide to facilitate the healing of individuals from the grief and distress of suicide loss, to mitigate other negative effects of exposure to suicide, and/or to prevent suicide among people who are at high risk after exposure to suicide (National Action Alliance for Suicide Prevention, 2015).

But is postvention any different for law enforcement personnel than it is for the general population? The same cultural and systemic issues in law enforcement discussed earlier may play a role in postvention as well.

Connections between academy mates, radio car partners, and LEOs in general are quite strong. Following the death of an officer, that officer's family often stretches to include colleagues, both sworn and civilian, as well as supervisors in the grieving process. The degree of identification among police officers is high. For example, law enforcement funerals are attended by local officers, as well as officers from all over the state and sometimes neighboring states as well. Many of the attending officers do not even know the fallen officer. This same web of connections will carry the impact of a suicide across shifts, units of assignment, and even agencies.

Law enforcement bereavement has a number of traditions that provide comfort and meaning to LEOs after the painful loss of a fellow officer. Almost every law enforcement agency has a Line of Duty Death (LODD) policy with explicit and detailed steps. However, not many agencies have a similar policy for employees who die by suicide.

When an agency loses an employee to suicide, one of the most important steps it can take is to respond in a compassionate and respectful manner. Unfortunately, a common response is to attempt to disassociate that employee as much as possible from his or her agency (Force Science Institute, 2013). The officer may be perceived as having "broken the code" of behavior that is acceptable for law enforcement. Senior leaders may not know what to do following a suicide and may react in a negative manner, such as denying their employees the opportunity to participate in the funeral or remembrance ceremony. Other employees may label the deceased in pejorative terms, such as "coward" or "weak."

A Force Science Institute newsletter (Force Science Institute, 2013) reported that after three officers in his command took their lives, the chief emailed his department that "these suicides were about personal choices, selfishness, and weakness." The widow of one of the suicides stated her husband would not have felt comfortable seeking help. "He would have said, 'If I were ever to go to counseling or seek help, people would think I was crazy, and they wouldn't think I could do my job and they wouldn't respect me'" (p. 3). Attitudes such as that described in the newsletter referenced above are likely to increase the perceived stigma surrounding suicide, and may decrease the probability that other employees will be willing to seek help if they are feeling suicidal.

Rather than developing an explicit policy for responding to an employee suicide similar to an LODD policy (IACP, 2014), we recommend chiefs quickly assemble an *ad hoc* committee to address each death by suicide individually (Clark & White, 2002). For example, an agency would probably treat a completed suicide by an officer who was in intractable pain following an on-duty accident differently than an officer who was accused of sexually assaulting multiple individuals he or she contacted in an official capacity. An *ad hoc* committee composed of individuals such as a senior leader, the department psychologist or a member of the agency's Employee Assistance Program, a chaplain, someone from Human Resources, and a member of the union or association could be tasked with recommending how the agency addresses the complicated issues following each unique employee suicide.

We are not advocating that an LODD and a completed suicide be treated identically. We are advocating that the completed suicide be treated respectfully, perhaps similarly to an employee who dies in a non-duty related motor vehicle accident or heart attack. Funerals or memorial services are to honor the individual's entire life, not the manner in which he or she died (Clark & White, 2002; IACP, 2014).

A second factor to consider is that LEOs may be impacted by suicide in a number of ways. Cerel, McIntosh, Neimeyer, Maple, and Marshall (2014) recommend revising how we refer to "suicide survivors," focusing on a more dimensional picture with four concentric circles: exposed to suicide, affected by suicide, suicide-bereaved short-term, and suicide-bereaved long-term. These four terms are nested, with "suicide-bereaved long-term" in the center of the nested circles and "exposed to suicide" on the outermost circle.

As a function of the job, many LEOs are "exposed" to suicides in the population they serve, but their reactions to this exposure may be minimal or fleeting. Officers may also be "affected" by suicide in terms of experiencing some distress in the short-term, perhaps because they knew the decedent, it was a particularly gruesome scene, or based on more personal factors.

Officers, employees, and/or family members may be "suicide-bereaved short-term" if they had a close attachment or relationship with the decedent and are impacted by the death. This group may benefit from crisis intervention and support services, such as are outlined next. Finally, a small group of officers, employees, and/or family members may be "suicide-bereaved long-term." This group is likely to have had close personal relationships with the decedent and they may struggle longer term with significant responses that impact their daily functioning. This group is the closest to the earlier definitions of "suicide survivors," and may benefit from crisis intervention and support services, as well as therapy.

In addition to the funeral, other postvention options include offering Crisis Management Briefings (CMB) designed to: disseminate accurate, factual information about the death; provide information about suicide in general; and remind attendees of additional sources of support (Clark, Thompson, & Welzant, 2007; Mitchell, 2015). Most people are not usually interested in talking about suicide – until it touches them directly. Then, for a brief period of time, the survivors of the suicide loss may want to understand more about what happened to their spouse/significant other, family member, coworker, or friend, etc. This brief window of time allows mental health professionals and peer supporters the opportunity to talk about suicide in a group, explain additional resources, and then address individual concerns once the CMB has concluded. Jordan, paraphrasing the influential suicidologist Edwin Shneidman, wrote, "Effective postvention for suicidally bereaved families may be one of the most important forms of multigenerational prevention available to mental health professionals" (2001, p. 99).

Individual crisis interventions with peer supporters, mental health professionals, and/or faith-based individuals may be helpful to employees struggling to understand the death of one of their coworkers. Group crisis interventions, such as Critical Incident Stress Debriefings, encourage survivors of suicide loss to talk about the loss and emotions they are experiencing. In the authors' experiences, two issues which often arise are the emotion of anger at the deceased and the "God question"—"Is my coworker/friend in hell forever because of ending his/her own life?"

It is important to identify and consider those individuals who may be considered "collateral damage" – dispatchers, coworkers, former coworkers, support staff, supervisors, academy training cadre, academy classmates, and extended family members. This may be regarded as a kind of triage, where the injured or impacted are prioritized by their need for care or intervention. The highest priority response is for those closest to the deceased and at greatest risk for distress or impairment. The next level of concern is likely to be those impacted on a secondary level, followed by anyone who may benefit from an intervention but who are less in need of urgent attention.

Working with the deceased employee's family and respecting their needs is critical. For example, if the employee's death was by gunshot, the family may respond negatively to a 21-gun salute at the funeral or memorial service. It is important to respect the family's wishes; however, a 21-gun salute is a show of respect and is deeply rooted in law enforcement culture. How might an agency resolve this potential conflict? One option may be to offer the 21-gun salute after the family has left the funeral or memorial service area. This plan respects both the law enforcement culture and the family's sensitivity to gunfire in the aftermath of their loss.

Resources

Resources for postvention include *Responding to Grief, Trauma, and Distress After a Suicide: U.S. National Guidelines* (National Action Alliance for Suicide Prevention, 2015). The *National Guidelines* were written by the Survivors of Suicide Loss Task Force of the National Action Alliance for Suicide

Prevention. The Task Force's vision was for: "A world where communities and organizations provide everyone who is exposed to a suicide access to effective services and support immediately — and for as long as necessary — to decrease their risk of suicide, to strengthen their mental health, and to help them cope with grief" (2015, p. i). The report calls for the creation and sustainment of the resources, infrastructure, services, and systems necessary to effectively respond to any incidence of suicide in the United States. The report is available for download from actionallianceforsuicideprevention.org.

Bolton's *My Son, My Son* is a classic in postvention work with survivors of suicide loss (Bolton, 1983). The Boltons wrote this book following the death of their son by suicide. Many survivors of suicide loss groups hand this book out as an excellent resource to new survivors of suicide loss who visit the group.

Survivors of Law Enforcement Suicide (SOLES) has a page on the Tears of a Cop website specifically for those who have lost a law enforcement family member to suicide (www.tearsofacop.com/police/SOLES.html).

CONCLUSION

Suicide is a serious, *preventable* public health problem that impacts individuals, families, communities, and law enforcement. More research is needed to further refine our understanding of the incidence of suicide in law enforcement and to improve methods of both prevention and intervention; however, even more important is the need to take action. Many resources already exist to assist mental health professionals, law enforcement agencies, and police chiefs in combatting this blight. These include peer support programs, wellness programs, and chaplaincy programs, as well as training and support resources such as were outlined in this chapter. A broad range of recommended programs and established protocols are currently available and relatively inexpensive for agencies to implement. It is essential that law enforcement agencies become proactive in addressing this complex issue.

REFERENCES

Aamodt, M. G., & Stalnaker, N. A. (2001). Police officer suicide: Frequency and officer profiles. In D. Sheehan, & J. Warren (Eds.), *Suicide and Law Enforcement Conference. Suicide and Law Enforcement* (pp. 383-398). Washington, DC: Federal Bureau of Investigation.

Aamodt, M. G., Stalnaker, N. A., & Smith, M. (2015, October). *Law enforcement suicide: Updated profiles and the quest for accurate suicide rates.* Paper presented at the annual meeting of the Society for Police and Criminal Psychology, Atlanta, GA.

American Association of Suicidology. (2005). *IS PATH WARM?* Retrieved from http://www.suicidology.org/resources/warning-signs

American Association of Suicidology. (2015). *Understanding and Helping the Suicidal Individual.* Retrieved from http://www.suicidology.org/Portals/14/docs/Resources/FactSheets/UnderstandingHelpingSuicidalIndividual.pdf

Anderson, S. (2008, July 6). Urge to end it all. *The New York Times.* Retrieved from http://www.nytimes.com/2008/07/06/magazine/06suicide-t.html

Barber, C. W., & Miller, M. J. (2014). Reducing a suicidal person's access to lethal means of suicide: A research agenda. *American Journal of Preventative Medicine, 47*(3S2), S264–S272.

Benner, A. (2001). Suicide in San Francisco: Lessons learned and preventions. In D. Sheehan, & J. Warren (Eds.), *Suicide and Law Enforcement Conference. Suicide and Law Enforcement* (pp. 31-44). Washington, DC: Federal Bureau of Investigation.

Berman, A. L., & Silverman, M. M. (2013). Suicide risk assessment and risk formulation Part II: Suicide risk formulation and the determination of levels of risk. *Suicide & Life-Threatening Behavior*, *44*(4), 432–443. doi:10.1111/sltb.12067 PMID:24286521

Bishop, S., & Boots, P. D. (2014). General strain theory, exposure to violence, and suicide ideation among police officers: A gendered approach. *Journal of Criminal Justice*, *42*(6), 538–548. doi:10.1016/j.jcrimjus.2014.09.007

Bolton, I. (1983). *My son, my son: A guide to healing after death, loss, or suicide.* Atlanta, GA: Bolton PR.

Bongar, B., & Sullivan, G. (2013). *The suicidal patient: Clinical and legal standards of care.* Washington, DC: American Psychological Association. doi:10.1037/14184-000

Campbell, W. H. (2004). Revised 'SAD PERSONS' helps assess suicide risk. *Current Psychiatry*, *3*(3), 102.

Campion, M. A. (2001). Police suicide and small departments: A survey. In D. Sheehan, & J. Warren (Eds.), *Suicide and Law Enforcement Conference. Suicide and Law Enforcement* (pp. 417-430). Washington, DC: Federal Bureau of Investigation.

Centers for Disease Control and Prevention. (2015). *Featured Topic: World Health Organization's (WHO) report on preventing suicide.* Retrieved from http://www.cdc.gov/violenceprevention/suicide/who-report.html

Centers for Disease Control and Prevention. (2016). *WISQRS - Web-based Injury Statistics Query and Reporting System.* Available from http://www.cdc.gov/injury/wisqars/index.html

Cerel, J., McIntosh, J. L., Neimeyer, R. A., Maple, M., & Marshall, D. (2014). The continuum of "survivorship": Definitional issues in the aftermath of suicide. *Suicide & Life-Threatening Behavior*, *44*(6), 591–600. doi:10.1111/sltb.12093 PMID:24702241

Clark, D. W., Thompson, D. J., & Welzant, V. (2007). *Suicide: Prevention, intervention, and postvention* (2nd ed.). Baltimore, MD: International Critical Incident Stress Foundation.

Clark, D. W., & White, E. K. (2002, April). *After a peace officer suicide: Helping your agency recover.* Paper presented at the 35th Annual American Association of Suicidology Conference, Bethesda, MD.

Clark, D. W., & White, E. K. (2003). Clinicians, cops, and suicide. In D. P. Hackett & J. M. Violanti (Eds.), *Police Suicide: Tactics for Prevention* (pp. 16–36). Springfield, IL: Charles C. Thomas.

Clark, D. W., White, E. K., & Violanti, J. (2012). Law enforcement suicide: Current knowledge and future directions. *The Police Chief*, *79*(5), 48–51.

Commission on Peace Officer Standards and Training. (2007). *Preventing law enforcement suicide – Code 3 officer needs assistance*. California POST Training Network.

D'Angelo, J. J. (2001). Spirituality and police suicide: A double-edged sword. In D. Sheehan, & J. Warren (Eds.), *Suicide and Law Enforcement Conference. Suicide and Law Enforcement* (pp. 503-510). Washington, DC: Federal Bureau of Investigation.

D'Aurizio, E. (1997, February 16). Sobering truth: Cops high suicide rate. *Bergen County Record*, p. N1.

Drapeau, C. W., & McIntosh, J. L. (2015, December 22). *U.S.A. suicide 2014: Official final data*. Washington, DC: American Association of Suicidology. Retrieved from http://www.suicidology.org

Draper, J. (2008). *Suicide prevention on bridges: The National Suicide Prevention Lifeline position*. The National Suicide Prevention Lifeline. Retrieved from http://www.suicidepreventionlifeline.org/learn/factsheets.aspx

Fields, G., & Jones, C. (1999, June 1). Code of silence doesn't help. *USA Today*, pp. A1-A2.

Force Science Institute. (2013). FS instructor offers insights into chief's comments on officer suicides. *Force Science News, 225*. Retrieved from http://www.forcescience.org/fsnews

Garvey, K. A., Penn, J. V., Campbell, A. L., Esposito-Smythers, C., & Spirito, A. (2009). Contracting for safety with patients: Clinical practice and forensic implications. *The Journal of the American Academy of Psychiatry and the Law*, *37*(3), 363–370. PMID:19767501

Granello, D. G. (2010). The process of suicide risk assessment: Twelve core principles. *Journal of Counseling and Development*, *68*(3), 363–370. doi:10.1002/j.1556-6678.2010.tb00034.x

Heiman, M. F. (1975). The police suicide. *Journal of Police Science and Administration*, *3*(3), 267–273.

Hem, E., Berg, A. M., & Ekeberg, O. (2001). Suicide in police—A critical review. *Suicide & Life-Threatening Behavior*, *31*(2), 224–233. doi:10.1521/suli.31.2.224.21513 PMID:11459255

Heron, M. (2013). *Deaths: Leading causes for 2010. National Vital Statistics Reports, 62(6)*. Hyattsville, MD: National Center for Health Statistics.

Heron, M. (2015a). *Deaths: Leading causes for 2011. National Vital Statistics Reports, 64(7)*. Hyattsville, MD: National Center for Health Statistics.

Heron, M. (2015b). *Deaths: Leading causes for 2012. National Vital Statistics Reports, 64(10)*. Hyattsville, MD: National Center for Health Statistics.

Heron, M. (2016). *Deaths: Leading causes for 2013. National Vital Statistics Reports, 65(2)*. Hyattsville, MD: National Center for Health Statistics.

International Association of Chiefs of Police (IACP). (2014). Breaking the silence on law enforcement suicides. *IACP National Symposium on Law Enforcement Officer Suicide and Mental Health*. Washington, DC: Office of Community Oriented Policing Services.

Joiner, T. E., Walker, R. L., Rudd, M. D., & Jobes, D. A. (1999). Scientizing and routinizing the assessment of suicidality in outpatient practice. *Professional Psychology, Research and Practice*, *30*(5), 447–453. doi:10.1037/0735-7028.30.5.447

Jordan, J. R. (2001). Is suicide bereavement different? A reassessment of the literature. *Suicide & Life-Threatening Behavior*, *31*(1), 91–102. doi:10.1521/suli.31.1.91.21310 PMID:11326773

Langston, E. (1995). *Police suicide: A nationwide problem*. Washington, DC: Center for Criminal Justice Studies.

Loh, J. (1994, January 23). Keeping the job from becoming a killer: Counselors fight rising police suicide rate. *Fort Worth Star-Telegram*, pp. A4.

Loo, R. (2003). A meta-analysis of police suicide rates: Findings and issues. *Suicide & Life-Threatening Behavior*, *33*(3), 313–325. doi:10.1521/suli.33.3.313.23209 PMID:14582841

McMains, M. J., & Mullins, W. C. (2001). *Crisis negotiations: Managing critical incidents and hostage situations in law enforcement and corrections*. New York, NY: Anderson Publishing.

Means Matter. (2013). *Lethal means counseling for clinicians*. Retrieved from https://www.hsph.harvard.edu/means-matter/recommendations/clinicians/

Milner, A., Page, A., & LaMontagne, A. (2014). Cause and effect in studies on unemployment, mental health and suicide: A meta-analytic and conceptual review. *Psychological Medicine*, *44*(05), 909–917. doi:10.1017/S0033291713001621 PMID:23834819

Mitchell, J. T. (2015). *Group crisis intervention* (5th ed.). Baltimore, MD: International Critical Incident Stress Foundation.

National Action Alliance for Suicide Prevention. (2015). *Responding to Grief, Trauma, & Distress after a Suicide: U.S. National Guidelines*. Washington, DC: National Action Alliance for Suicide Prevention.

Nelson, Z. P., & Smith, W. E. (1970). The law enforcement profession: An incident of high suicide. *Omega*, *1*(4), 293–299. doi:10.2190/WEFX-85W4-01BX-R73F

O'Hara, A. F., & Violanti, J. (2009). Police suicide – A comprehensive study of 2008 national data. *International Journal of Emergency Mental Health*, *11*(1), 17–23. PMID:19637497

O'Hara, A. F., Violanti, J., Levenson, R. L., & Clark, R. G. (2013). National police suicide estimates: Web Surveillance Study III. *International Journal of Emergency Mental Health and Human Resilience*, *15*(1), 31–38. PMID:24187885

Patterson, W., Dohn, H., Bird, J., & Patterson, G. (1983). Evaluation of suicidal patients: The SAD PERSONS scale. *Psychosomatics*, *24*(4), 343–349. doi:10.1016/S0033-3182(83)73213-5 PMID:6867245

Question Persuade Refer (QPR) Institute. (2016). Zero suicide training programs. *QPR for Law Enforcement*. Retrieved from http://courses.qprinstitute.com/

Rudd, M. D., Berman, A. L., Joiner, T. E., Nock, M. K., Silverman, M. M., Mandrusiak, M., & Witte, T. et al. (2006). Warning signs for suicide: Theory, research, and clinical applications. *Suicide & Life-Threatening Behavior*, *36*(3), 255–262. doi:10.1521/suli.2006.36.3.255 PMID:16805653

Rudd, M. D., Joiner, T. E., Jobes, D. A., & King, C. A. (1999). The outpatient treatment of suicidality: An integration of science and recognition of its limitations. *Professional Psychology, Research and Practice*, *30*(5), 437–446. doi:10.1037/0735-7028.30.5.437

Schmitz, W. M. Jr, Allen, M. H., Feldman, B. N., Gutin, N. J., Jahn, D. R., Kleespies, P. M., & Simpson, S. et al. (2012). Preventing suicide through improved training in suicide risk assessment and care: An American Association of Suicidology Task Force unabridged report addressing serious gaps in U.S. mental health training. *Suicide & Life-Threatening Behavior*, *42*(3), 292–304. doi:10.1111/j.1943-278X.2012.00090.x PMID:22494118

Shea, S. C. (2009). Suicide assessment Part 1: Uncovering suicidal intent – A sophisticated art. *Psychiatric Times*. Retrieved from http://www.psychiatrictimes.com/articles/suicide-assessment-part-1-uncovering-suicidal-intent%E2%80%94-sophisticated-art

Silverman, M. M., & Berman, A. L. (2013). Suicide risk assessment and risk formulation Part I: A focus on suicide ideation in assessing suicide risk. *Suicide & Life-Threatening Behavior*, *44*(4), 420–431. doi:10.1111/sltb.12065 PMID:25250407

Simon, R. I. (1999). The Suicide Prevention Contract: Clinical, Legal, and Risk Management Issues. *The Journal of the American Academy of Psychiatry and the Law*, *27*(3), 445–450. PMID:10509943

Simon, R. I. (2002). Suicide risk assessment: What is the standard of care? *The Journal of the American Academy of Psychiatry and the Law*, *30*(3), 340–344. PMID:12380411

Simon, R. I. (2011). Improving suicide risk assessment. *Psychiatric Times*. Retrieved from http://www.psychiatrictimes.com/articles/improving-suicide-risk-assessment

Stanley, B., & Brown, G. K. (2012). A brief intervention to mitigate suicide risk. *Cognitive and Behavioral Practice*, *19*(2), 256–264. doi:10.1016/j.cbpra.2011.01.001

Suicide Prevention Resource Center, & SPAN USA. (2010). *Charting the future of suicide prevention: A 2010 progress review of the national strategy and recommendations for the decade ahead*. Newton, MA: Education Development Center, Inc.

Suicide Prevention Resource Center, & Rodgers, P. (2011). *Understanding risk and protective factors for suicide: A primer for preventing suicide*. Newton, MA: Education Development Center, Inc.

Suicide Prevention Resource Center. (2016). *Zero Suicide Website and Tool Kit*. Retrieved from: http://zerosuicide.sprc.org/

U.S. Department of Health and Human Services (HHS) Office of the Surgeon General and National Action Alliance for Suicide Prevention. (2001). *2001 National strategy for suicide prevention: Goals and objectives for action*. Washington, DC: HHS.

U.S. Department of Health and Human Services (HHS) Office of the Surgeon General and National Action Alliance for Suicide Prevention. (2012). *2012 National strategy for suicide prevention: Goals and objectives for action*. Washington, DC: HHS.

Violanti, J., Vena, J. E., & Marshal, J. R. (1996). Suicides, homicides and accidental deaths: A comparative risk assessment of police officer and municipal workers. *American Journal of Industrial Medicine*, *30*(1), 99–104. doi:10.1002/(SICI)1097-0274(199607)30:1<99::AID-AJIM17>3.0.CO;2-3 PMID:8837691

Violanti, J. M. (2003). Suicide and the police culture. In D. P. Hackett & J. M. Violanti (Eds.), *Police suicide: Tactics for prevention* (pp. 66–74). Springfield, IL: Charles C. Thomas.

Violanti, J. M. (2004). Predictors of police suicide ideation. *Suicide & Life-Threatening Behavior*, *4*(3), 277–283. doi:10.1521/suli.34.3.277.42775 PMID:15385182

Violanti, J. M. (2007). *Police suicide: Epidemic in Blue* (2nd ed.). Springfield, IL: Charles C. Thomas.

Violanti, J. M. (2010). Police suicide: A national comparison with firefighter and military personnel. *An International Journal of Police Strategies and Management*, *33*(2), 270–286. doi:10.1108/13639511011044885

Waters, J. A., & Ussery, W. (2007). Police stress: History, contributing factors, symptoms, and interventions. *Policing: An International Journal of Police Strategies & Management*, *30*(2), 169–188. doi:10.1108/13639510710753199

Section 4
Employee Wellness and Support

Chapter 10
Employee Assistance Programs: Counseling and Psychological Services for Law Enforcement Officers

Evan M. Axelrod
Nicoletti-Flater Associates, USA

ABSTRACT

The purpose of this chapter is to introduce and explore counseling and psychological services for law enforcement officers that extend beyond critical incident interventions. In particular, this chapter focuses on Employee Assistance Programs (EAPs), including discussion of how such programs have become an essential tool in supporting and sustaining law enforcement officers, their families, the agencies they work for, and the communities they serve. This chapter discusses what an EAP is, the benefits of EAPs, and the return on investment that public safety agencies can expect when utilizing an EAP. Relevant topics such as confidentiality, internal vs. external EAPs, and the need for specialized EAPs for public safety agencies are addressed. Finally, the chapter also explores non-traditional services that can be offered through EAPs to assist public safety agencies in supporting and sustaining their personnel in meeting their mission of serving the public.

INTRODUCTION

The purpose of this chapter is to introduce and explore counseling and psychological services for police officers that go beyond critical incident interventions. In particular, this chapter examines employee assistance programs (EAPs), discussing how such programs have become an essential tool in supporting and sustaining law enforcement officers, their families, the agencies they work for, and the communities they serve. To gain a full understanding of EAPs and how they fit into the continuum of psychological services utilized by public safety agencies, there are a number of areas that must be reviewed including what constitutes an EAP, what are the benefits of an EAP, and what is a public safety agency's return on investment when utilizing an EAP. Two more areas that are of the utmost importance to understand when considering EAPs for public safety agencies are confidentiality and the different types of programs that are available to an agency. In addition to selecting the optimal type of program, it is important to

DOI: 10.4018/978-1-5225-0813-7.ch010

understand that law enforcement officers require specialized EAPs with clinicians who have an appropriate knowledge base and have been specifically trained in police and public safety psychology. Finally, a thorough discussion of EAPs also needs to address the possibility of non-traditional services that can be offered through such a program that further the program's benefit to law enforcement officers and their families, as well as the agency. It is the author's perspective that EAPs are an invaluable tool for public safety agencies to utilize in supporting and sustaining their personnel in meeting their mission of serving and protecting the public.

WHAT IS AN EMPLOYEE ASSISTANCE PROGRAM?

EAPs are voluntary, work-based programs that offer an array of psychological services to employees. The services, which are also typically offered to the employee's immediate family members, are free to the employee because they are paid for by the employer, often as part of an overall benefits package. EAPs typically offer confidential assessments, counseling, and referrals to address a broad range of issues that may be affecting an employee's mental health, emotional well-being, and/or psychological stability. Some examples of such issues include stress, anger, grief and loss, family related problems, mental health disorders, and substance abuse. By addressing these issues, an EAP attempts to help the employee develop the capacity to solve problems, thereby enhancing the employee's functioning and quality of life. Often times, EAPs will also provide consultation services to managers and supervisors, engage in the prevention of workplace violence, and assist with trauma responses. Ultimately, EAPs are uniquely designed to benefit both the employer and the employee by providing services to employees, their families, and the organization.

EAPs began in the United States in the 1940s and were originally conceived as occupational alcohol programs (Attridge et al., 2009). These programs, which were part alcohol treatment, part social work, were typically provided in-house, meaning they were internal to the organization, and were designed to reduce the number of industrial accidents that occurred related to alcohol consumption. Such programs came into existence for two reasons. First, there was a shortage of skilled male workers as a result of World War II, meaning more males with alcohol problems were inevitably being hired by businesses. Secondly, corporate physicians believed that spending money on rehabilitating workers with alcohol issues would be more cost effective than terminating them and then having to hire and train new workers that may also end up having problems related to alcohol (Attridge et al., 2009).

Beginning in the 1950s, these occupational alcohol programs began to expand their focus to include mental health related problems (Office of Personnel Management, 2016). Like alcohol related problems, corporations began to see that it was more cost effective to rehabilitate trained workers who developed mental health problems than it was to take a chance on hiring and training a new employee. Throughout the 1950s and 1960s, these expanded occupational alcohol programs became even more widely utilized and accepted, solidifying their part in the workplace culture (Attridge et al., 2009).

Based on the need for and success of occupational alcohol programs, The Hughes Act, also known as the Comprehensive Alcohol Abuse and Alcoholism Prevention, Treatment, and Rehabilitation Act of 1970, was signed into law by President Richard Nixon. The Hughes Act created the National Institute of Alcohol Abuse and Alcoholism (NIAAA) and mandated that all Federal employees have access to comprehensive alcohol prevention and treatment programs (Office of Personnel Management, 2016). The 1970s and 1980s continued to see growth in the utilization and acceptance of occupational alcohol programs. This time period also brought about some important enhancements. First, the NIAAA changed the name of the work-based service from "occupational alcohol program" to "employee assistance program." According to Masi (1984), that change in terminology achieved two objectives. First, it conveyed that the program's focus was on assisting employees, regardless of the type of problem from which they suffered. Secondly, it avoided the stigma that may have been associated with the narrower program name, which specifically identified it as being for alcohol or drug problems. The shift to EAPs from occupational alcohol programs was not just a change in name. It also transformed the way services were provided. Masi (2015) explains that changes in the field as a result of the broadened focus with EAPs included professional staffing of service providers, increased focus on general job performance, and more training of management and supervisors on how to make appropriate referrals to EAPs. Finally, the 1980s saw four other developments in EAPs (Attridge et al., 2009). First, EAP benefits were expanded to include family members, recognizing that healthier families meant healthier and more productive employees. Secondly, EAPs began managing situations associated with workplace violence. An additional development during this time period was a move away from internal EAPs to external EAPs. Lastly, EAPs that had historically been more of a referral and care coordination service shifted to more direct provision of care services. By the end of the 1980s, 60%-70% of all EAPs were providing direct care services (White & Sharer, 2003).

Not surprisingly, based on the trend since the 1940s, EAPs continued to grow during the 1990s and 2000s. In fact, between 1993 and 2002 there was a 194% increase in EAP enrollment and by 2006, 71% of all employers in the United States offered some form of an EAP (Masi, 2011). What began as a resource for occupational alcohol prevention and treatment developed into what a special committee appointed by the National Business Group on Health defined as "the human behavior/psychological experts that provide strategic analysis, guidance, and consultation throughout the organization to apply the principles of human behavior to enhance organizational performance, culture, and business success" (Employee Assistance Trade Association, 2013b, p. 1). Employee assistance programs will likely continue to grow and evolve as new demands emerge in the workplace.

BENEFITS OF AN EMPLOYEE ASSISTANCE PROGRAM

Overall, EAPs have been shown to work (Attridge et al., 2009; BadgeofLife.com, 2008; Gupton et al., 2011). Moreover, they help both the individual and the employer. In part, their success is due to the fact that psychological treatment works, particularly when the treatment is tailored to the client's needs and cultural preferences (Duncan, 2009). Furthermore, as Gupton et al. note, "Attending to the psychological health of an employee's home and family life has progressively been recognized as beneficial to the agency as well as to the employee. Such programs are powerful and valuable ways of serving employees by improving their home environments and, therefore, benefiting the law enforcement agency and the communities they serve" (2011, p. 93). In fact, it has even been suggested that because of the benefit that employee assistance can provide, law enforcement officers should "visit a mental health professional once a year, with the same diligence they get their teeth cleaned or go for an annual physical examination" (BadgeofLife.com, 2008, p. 1).

Employers in general have found that proactive, preventative efforts to help employees identify and resolve personal issues before they have serious medical, family, and/or workplace consequences are financially beneficial (Office of Disability and Employment Policy, 2009).

According to the National Business Group on Health (2008), one study showed that the use of EAP services resulted in an avoidance of work loss in 60% of cases, with an average savings of 17 hours per case. Additionally, 72% of the people involved with these cases exhibited improved work productivity, with an average gain of 43%. Other research also supports that user satisfaction with EAPs is generally high. A national study involving an independent firm used follow-up interviews for over 1,300 cases and found that 95% of the EAP users reported being satisfied with their experience (Attridge et al., 2009).

In addition to decreasing work loss and increasing productivity, there are numerous other ways in which EAPs have been demonstrated to benefit both employees and employers. Rothermel, Slavit, and Finch (2008) have discussed three specific ways that employers, including law enforcement agencies, benefit from EAPs.

1. Employee assistance programs leverage the value of an organization's investment in its workforce by:
    a. Encouraging employee engagement;
    b. Improving the abilities of employees and their dependents to successfully respond to life's challenges;
    c. Offering employees short-term problem-resolution services or referring employees and dependents to mental health treatment services when indicated; and
    d. Developing employee and manager competencies in managing workplace stress and improving work team performance.
2. Employee assistance programs address the costs of doing business by:
    a. Reducing workplace absenteeism and unplanned absences;
    b. Decreasing workplace accidents;
    c. Lowering employee turnover and related replacement costs;
    d. Facilitating safe, timely and effective return-to-work for employees after short-term and extended absences;
    e. Reducing healthcare costs;
    f. Improving the value of organizational investments in wellness and health promotion, self-care management, continuity of care, and work-related efforts; and
    g. Increasing efficient use of health care through early identification, care management, and recovery efforts.
3. Employee assistance programs mitigate business risks by:
    a. Reducing the likelihood of workplace violence or other safety risks;
    b. Managing the effect of such disruptive incidents as workplace violence, injury or other crises and facilitating a swift return-to-work after adverse workplace events;
    c. Supporting disaster and emergency preparedness and minimizing disruption after such events;
    d. Smoothing the adjustment to mergers, acquisitions, site closures or other workforce change events;
    e. Reducing the likelihood of legal action or liability, maintaining business practices that promote a violence-free workplace; and
    f. Promoting and supporting drug- and alcohol-free workplace policies and programs.

Based on Rothermel and coauthors' identification of how EAPs benefit both employers and employees, it is clear they can be of great value. However, there are still numerous additional ways in which an EAP can be of value (IHPS, 2015; National Business Group on Health, 2008; Nicoletti-Flater Associates, 2016). Those ways include:

- Strengthen employee morale and reduce turnover;
- Improve relationships between employees, customers, and managers;
- Address numerous inappropriate or dangerous behaviors;
- Train mangers to manage complex emotional, cultural, and diversity issues;
- Build personal resilience by offering employees a way to cope with personal issues that can have a negative impact on their job performance;
- Minimize the costs of insurance plans by staving off stress-related illnesses and decreasing doctor visits;
- Decrease "presenteeism," which refers to when an employee goes to work sick but cannot work at full capacity. Studies show that mental health problems are highly associated with work limitations in time management, interpersonal/mental functioning, and overall output;
- Decrease or mitigate labor disputes;
- Aid in suicide prevention;
- Meet otherwise unmet mental health needs;
- Attract new employees as part of a comprehensive benefits package; and
- Lower Workers' Compensation costs and expedite recovery and return to work, as well as resolve issues that put an employee out of work or led to injuries, reduce stress and depression related to the injury, and function as part of the continuum of care with medical providers and all other involved entities (Richards, 2015).

Like any employer, public safety agencies are capable of reaping all of the benefits from the utilization of an EAP. Additionally, it is well known that high-stress occupations require that employees are able to consistently function at their peak performance levels (Anderson et al., 2015; Nicoletti-Flater Associates, 2016). Mental health problems, even if mild in nature, can generate costly errors for employers in this area. By utilizing an EAP, it has been demonstrated that public safety agencies are able to:

- Decrease/mitigate complaints and investigations;
- Reduce on-the-job accidents;
- Manage training related problems;
- Enhance stress/coping skills;
- Enhance judgment/decision-making;
- Improve peak performance; and
- Avoid costly law suits related to citizen complaints, negligence of duty, and employee dissatisfaction (Gottschalk, 2007; Nicoletti-Flater Associates, 2016).

COST-EFFECTIVENESS OF EMPLOYEE ASSISTANCE PROGRAMS

One common concern from an employer's perspective regarding EAPs is the cost-effectiveness of offering such a program. Typically speaking, an EAP's overall effectiveness is measured by the return on investment (ROI). According to Hargrave et al. (2008), the typical return on investment for an EAP is

$2.00. That is, for every $1.00 invested by the employer into the program, the employer realizes a $3.00 return. LaCroix (2015) demonstrates an even higher ROI. LaCroix asserts that for every dollar spent on an EAP, the employer will see a return of $5.00 to $15.00. The sources of such an ROI reportedly include decreased lost time, decreased use of medical and accident benefits, and reductions in filed grievances (LaCroix, 2015).

ROI can be seen in other ways as well. Consider the findings reported below by a number of investigators.

- One study showed that 57% of employees that utilized EAPs had improved ability to work productively (Attridge, 2003).
- Another study showed that 50% of employees that utilized EAPs had improved attendance and/or productivity (Harlow, 2006).
- According to Amaral (2008), 64% of individuals that utilized EAPs for work specific issues and 46% of cases that utilized such programs for other issues had improvement.
- Mercer's review of EAPs (2008) showed that employers realized a total health benefit per employee of $7,983.00 per year.

Considered from another perspective, there definitely seems to be a cost associated with not utilizing EAPs. As Kendall points out, "From depression to anxiety, from drug abuse to alcohol addiction, common psychiatric disorders take a remarkable, if little-discussed, toll. In lost productivity and absenteeism alone, the cost to business approaches $312 billion annually" (2000, p. 1). There is good reason to expect that law enforcement agencies are among the organizations for which EAPs are likely to represent a worthwhile employee benefit.

CONFIDENTIALITY

Among the important questions that a law enforcement employee is likely to raise regarding whether to utilize an EAP is, "Is it confidential?" Nothing impacts the utilization and success of an EAP more than confidentiality. If law enforcement officers mistrust the program, it is likely the program will be underutilized, resulting in officers not obtaining help they may need and law enforcement agencies assuming greater liability due to employee performance-related problems.

As Gupton et al. (2011) pointed out, all employees, including law enforcement officers, are entitled to confidential counseling and any possibility that their reported difficulties may be disclosed to the employer significantly undermines the counseling process. Of course, there are certain statutory limits to confidentiality such as being a danger to oneself or others, child abuse, elder abuse, or other exceptions that may vary by jurisdiction. Even with these limits to confidentiality, a skilled provider should be able to work with an employee to find potential solutions to most of the challenges to confidentiality that may come up during the course of treatment.

In addition to needing to ensure confidentiality so as to make the EAP safe for employees to access, professional ethics and state and federal law protect the communication between law enforcement officers and employee assistance counselors (American Psychological Association, 2016). Even in the collection of data used for the justification of utilizing an EAP, a public safety agency can only collect basic rate data and cannot collect any data that contains specific, identifying information about who has utilized the services (American Psychological Association, 2016). Without proper written authorization, disclosing who utilized an EAP and for what reason would not only be unethical but illegal, given that disclosures of this nature would violate laws such as the Health Insurance Portability and Accountability Act of 1996 (HIPAA).

INTERNAL VS. EXTERNAL EMPLOYEE ASSISTANCE PROGRAMS

Once a public safety agency has decided to offer an EAP to employees, one important question becomes what type of program it should select, an internal or external EAP. As was previously discussed, EAPs began as programs that were internal to an organization run by occupational physicians and social workers. As those original programs evolved to treat more comprehensive issues, treat family members, and manage issues associated with workplace violence, the provision of services often moved from internally based programs to professionally staffed, externally based programs (Attridge et al., 2009). In fact, Attridge and coauthors report that by 1994 less than 20% of EAPs were internally based (2009).

Sharar, Pompe, and Attridge (2013) examined the differences between internal and external EAPs and found that while there were differences, the two modalities appeared to be equally effective. The following are the most significant advantages and disadvantages that Sharar and coauthors found when looking at internal vs. external programs:

Advantages of internal EAPs:

The organization owns the program;

- ◦ EAP counselors know the organization and the organization's culture;
- ◦ Easier communication within the organization;
- ◦ More credibility with supervisors;
- ◦ Assessments can be made within the organizational context;
- ◦ Mediation services can be readily offered;
- ◦ Counselors can serve multiple roles;
- ◦ Onsite problem assessment capability;
- ◦ Greater coordination of treatment monitoring and follow-up; and
- ◦ The EAP can be better integrated into Human Resources and other benefit programs.

Disadvantages of internal EAPs:

- Too closely identified with a particular department, group, or individual (e.g., Internal Affairs or the Chief/Sheriff);
- Confidentiality is more difficult to maintain;
- Can be more expensive than an external program due to salary/benefit costs, administrative support costs, and logistical costs;
- Smaller organizations may not be able to justify adequate full-time staffing of counselors;
- Less diversity in counseling staff;

- Higher likelihood of staff burnout due to understaffing of the program;
- Assessments may less objective in nature; and
- Counselor's neutrality is more easily compromised.

Advantages of external EAPs:

- Less costly for small or medium-size organizations;
- Confidentiality is stronger and more easily maintained;
- The program is separate from organizational politics;
- More privacy and less stigma associated with accessing external offices;
- More links to community services and referral sources;
- May have more diverse staff;
- More specially trained staff;
- More flexible scheduling options;
- More employee choice in the selection of a counselor;
- Can provide a broad range of related work/life or wellness services;
- The organization is not responsible for any malpractice of the counselors; and
- The organization saves money by not having to hire and manage additional EAP staff.

Disadvantages of external EAPs:

- Counseling is usually not provided in-person at organization worksites;
- Some external programs are unable to be adapted or tailored to the specific needs of an organization;
- Some employees and supervisors may be reluctant to deal with "outsiders" for help;
- May lack knowledge about the organization and its unique culture;
- Communication between the EAP and the organization can be more difficult;
- Less feeling of ownership of the program;
- An external EAP may be for-profit, which may mean that it does not always have the best interest of the organization in mind; and
- Appointments may be less convenient, as employees have to go offsite.

Although Sharar and his collogues concluded that internal and external EAPs are equally effective, this may not be true for law enforcement agencies due to the needs of the agency and the beliefs of the population being served. As noted earlier, one of the greatest concerns that people have when accessing EAPs is the fear that their use of the program will not be confidential (Albrecht, 2014). In fact, this is the main criticism of internal EAPs, that information does not stay confidential, and internal employee assistance counselors face numerous conflicts of interest (Sonnenstuhl & Trice, 1986). Law enforcement officers are no different than anyone else in their concerns regarding confidentiality, resulting in many law enforcement officers being reluctant to obtain services from providers they see as "connected" to their agency (BadgeofLife.com, 2008). Based on the author's experience, law enforcement officers may be inclined to perceive an internal EAP as a direct line to Internal Affairs or the Chief/Sheriff, and therefore as another form of discipline.

Like the majority of organizations that utilize EAPs, public safety agencies have also gravitated toward utilizing external EAPs (Favorini & Spitzer, 1993). This change generally results in higher utilization rates, particularly by the families of law enforcement officers (Employee Assistance Trade Association, 2009). Many of the advantages associated with an internal EAP, including assessing employees within an organizational context, providing onsite counseling/assessment/mediation services, and coordinating treatment monitoring and follow-up, can all be accomplished through specialized external EAPs. Additionally, many of the potential disadvantages associated with external EAPs are fairly easily mitigated. Some of the disadvantages of external EAPs noted earlier included programs not being tailored to the specific needs of an organization, lack of knowledge about the organization and its unique culture, and the risk that the EAP's profit motive could interfere with pursuit of the best interests of the organization. These potential disadvantages can be mitigated when a public safety agency selects and utilizes an EAP that is specialized for the demands associated with law enforcement and staffed by clinicians who specialize in police and public safety psychology.

THE NEED FOR SPECIALIZED EMPLOYEE ASSISTANCE PROGRAM SERVICES FOR LAW ENFORCEMENT

Despite the type of EAP an agency chooses to utilize, it is clear that public safety personnel require a program that is specialized to the unique demands, stressors, and culture of law enforcement (U.S. Department of Health and Human Services, 2015b). Not only do EAP personnel for public safety agencies need to understand the challenges of working in public safety, they also need to understand how mental health problems in high-stress occupations require specialized techniques and approaches to help maintain an employee's optimal level of performance. In addition to dealing with critical incidents, some of the common workplace issues faced by public safety personnel and their families include shift work, attention from mass media and social media, organizational/administrative stress, and a variety of legal issues (ESI Group, 2016

Generally speaking, for any EAP to be successful, counselors need to have an understanding of the culture and dynamics of an agency. For public safety agencies that means counselors should have an understanding of not only law enforcement officer culture, social values, and customs, but also how stress and the demands of the job can impact different personnel differently. For example, in a given situation, how do sworn personnel differ from civilian personnel, and what are the dynamics between the two? It is also imperative for EAPs that serve public safety agencies to understand how vicarious trauma impacts public safety personnel and how resilient they can be. As Best, Artwohl, and Kirschman (2011) point out, when working with police officers it is important to assume that they are resilient and can recover from trauma because as a population, police officers are particularly resilient to post-traumatic stress disorder.

As identified by the U.S. Department of Health and Human Services (2015b), another reason that public safety agencies need a specialized EAP is that counselors with specialized training may be able to help educate and train managers and supervisors to identify when law enforcement officers are having difficulties that are impacting their work. For example, specially trained counselors can help supervisors and managers connect problematic work behaviors such as increased citizen complaints, minor traffic incidents, increased excessive force complaints, and/or increased absenteeism to the possibility of underlying stress-related or other mental health-related origins. Law enforcement personnel may appreciate knowing that EAP clinicians have specialized training in police and public safety psychology. While more research on the topic is needed, such awareness may remove some of the barriers to seeking care, allowing specialized counselors to select interventions that are most relevant—and likely effective—for public safety employees and their families.

Successful EAPs for public safety agencies require not only specialized counselors, but also specialized services. In her discussion of essential features of an EAP that was servicing the Georgia Bureau of Investigation, Lang (2010) identified that it was critical for an EAP serving a public safety agency to have a toll-free telephone number that was accessible 24 hours a day, seven days a week, so all employees, dependents, and household members could contact the program when needed to schedule appointments. Moreover, appointments had to be offered within 48 hours and scheduled within five to seven days of the initial call to the EAP. If an employee or his or her dependent was seeking assistance for an emergency, that individual had to be seen within 24 hours of the request (Lang, 2010). Additionally, Lang recommended that successful and effective EAPs that are designed for public safety agencies should include the following:

- Providing non-critical incident emergency coverage for all eligible employees and dependents that may be covered by the program;
- Law enforcement officers and eligible dependents should be matched to the clinician best suited for their needs. This includes ensuring there is no lengthy intake process or multiple reassignments;
- Multiple office locations for easy access to services; and
- Guaranteed confidentiality.

QUALIFICATIONS OF EMPLOYEE ASSISTANCE PROGRAM PROVIDERS

In addition to needing a specialized EAP, law enforcement agencies also need service providers with specialized qualifications. Roman and Blum (1988), the Employee Assistance Trade Association (2009), and the International Employee Assistance Professionals Association (2011) are among the researchers and organizations that have identified core technology requirements and developed standards that are important to consider in selecting an EAP provider. In addition to having a solid foundation of basic counseling skills and cultural competency, an employee assistance counselor should also have insider knowledge of psychological and social issues that can impact the culture of the workplace. The Employee Assistance Trade Association (2013a) also recommends that agencies should look for counselors who have five years of direct clinical practice, three years' experience in providing EAP counseling, licensure at the highest level of practice for mental health in the state of residence, licenses in good standing, and adequate liability insurance.

EAP counselors should also provide their services in accordance with the Employee Assistance Program Core Technology. Originally developed by Roman and Blum in 1988 and then updated by the International Employee Assistance Professionals Association in 2011, the Employee Assistance Program Core Technology represents the essential components identified by the broader employee assistance profession. Programs that embrace this model are able to provide unique strategies for addressing work-organization productivity issues and employee concerns affecting job performance. Essential components of this approach are described below (Roman & Blum, 1988; International Employee Assistance Professionals Association, 2011).

The Employee Assistance Program Core Technology:

1. Consultation with, training of, and assistance to work organization leadership (managers, supervisors, and union officials) seeking to manage troubled employees, enhance the work environment, and improve employee job performance;
2. Active promotion of the availability of EAP services to employees, their family members, and the work organization;
3. Confidential and timely problem identification/assessment services for employee clients with personal concerns that may affect job performance;
4. Use of constructive confrontation, motivation, and short-term intervention with employee clients to address problems that affect job performance;
5. Referral of employee clients for diagnosis, treatment, and assistance, as well as case monitoring and follow-up services;
6. Assisting work organizations in establishing and maintaining effective relations with treatment and other service providers, and in managing provider contracts;
7. Consultation to work organizations to encourage availability of and employee access to health benefits covering medical and behavioral problems including, but not limited to, alcoholism, drug abuse, and mental and emotional disorders; and
8. Evaluation of the effects of EAP services on work organizations and individual job performance.

There are a number of different types of trained professionals who can provide services for general EAPs in accordance with the Employee Assistance Core Technology. However, it is important to recognize that Police & Public Safety Psychology is a practice specialty that was recognized by the American Psychological Association (APA) in 2013. The American Board of Professional Psychology (ABPP) recognized Police & Public Safety Psychology as a specialty board in 2011. Clinicians providing EAP services to law enforcement agencies should have specific training in the specialty and be familiar with the culture of law enforcement and the specific demands of police officer positions. Advanced knowledge and skills in this distinctive practice area are required. According to the APA, "Police and public safety psychology is concerned with assisting law enforcement and other public safety personnel and agencies in carrying out their missions and societal functions with effectiveness, safety, health, and conformity to laws and ethics" (2015, p. 1).

The APA has also helped define the specialized knowledge and skills that a police and public safety psychologist should possess. Some of the relevant specialized knowledge and skills are summarized in the sections below (APA, 2015).

Specialized knowledge of police and public safety psychologists:

- Understanding of the essential functions of police and public safety organizations and personnel;
- Understanding of the working conditions unique to law enforcement officers' respective positions;
- Understanding of the common and unusual stressors in public safety work;
- Understanding of the normal and abnormal adaptation to occupational stress and trauma;
- Understanding of the research related to resilience and recovery in public safety personnel; and
- Understanding of the unique aspects of confidentiality and testimonial privilege when providing services to public safety personnel and/or agencies.

Specialized skills of police and public safety psychologists:

- Psychological assessment of public safety personnel;
- Short-term cognitive behavioral treatments and approaches;
- Post-shooting incidents intervention;
- Line-of-duty death intervention;
- Deep undercover stress reaction intervention;
- Peer support team intervention;
- Suicide intervention;
- Wellness and coaching intervention;
- Crisis intervention;
- Hostage negotiation;
- Criminal profiling;
- Psychological autopsy; and
- Understanding of epidemiological factors affecting outcomes of various tactical situations.

Ultimately, for an EAP to be successful, the counselors providing the services need to be specially trained as EAP counselors. More specifically to public safety agencies however, not only should a counselor be trained in the Employee Assistance Program Core Technology, he or she should also be specialized in Police & Public Safety Psychology. This second piece is of critical importance. Not only has the U.S. Department of Health and Human Services pointed out that, "Counselors in the regular EAPs do not necessarily have comparable understanding of the law enforcement profession and culture" (2015a, p. 1), but the use of police psychologists by public safety agencies has proven to be a "cost effective asset" to those agencies (Davis, 1993).

Perhaps the strongest argument for the use of specially trained police and public safety psychologists in the provision of EAPs from law enforcement officers is this:

Law enforcement officers are often reluctant to seek professional support for a variety of reasons. Officers, who have been trained to act independently and maintain constant emotional control, may view the need for support services as a sign of personal weakness. Even if they recognize that they would benefit from it. Therefore, the skills that help officers perform their jobs effectively can sometimes work against them at times of stress or hardship. They may avoid asking for help if they believe that EAP counselors will not be attuned to their particular stressors or will not understand the nature of their work. (U.S. Department of Health and Human Services, 2015b, pp. 1-2)

KNOWLEDGE BASE OF PUBLIC SAFETY EMPLOYEE ASSISTANCE PROGRAM PROVIDERS AND TYPES OF SERVICES PROVIDED

As should be clear, based on the nature of organizations, EAP providers need to be able to provide services on several different levels. EAP providers need to be knowledgeable in areas relating to the organization, the supervisors and managers, and the line employees. The U.S. Department of Labor (2015), offers a reasonable model outlining what knowledge EAP providers should have based on the clients they are serving.

Services being provided to the agency/organization as the client:

- Assistance in developing alcohol and drug policies;
- Consultation regarding legal compliance issues;
- Design and selection of health benefit plans;
- Evaluation of health care providers; and
- Compliance with drug-free workplace policies.

Services being provided to supervisors/managers as the client:

- How to make supervisor referrals based on declining job performance;
- Separating performance issues from behavioral health issues;
- Determining the need to intervene with troubled employees; and
- Following up on an employee's progress.

Services being provided to line employees as the client:

- General information and referral resources;
- Crisis intervention;
- Problem identification;
- Short-term problem resolution;
- Substance abuse assessments;
- Referral for diagnosis and treatment or other kinds of help;
- Follow-up contacts or sessions to provide support; and
- Educational seminars and workshops.

The preceding outline by the U.S. Department of Labor is useful in highlighting the importance of remembering that EAP services are delivered across an organization's hierarchy. This outline however does not fully address the wide range of clinical experience and expertise that is needed by EAP providers servicing public safety agencies. Although many problems about which law enforcement officers seek EAP services are either acute or transitory, some officers may also have more chronic conditions. According to Gupton et al. (2011), some of the most commonly identified reasons that law enforcement officers seek employee assistance include:

- Marital or relationship problems;
- Parent-child difficulties;
- Difficulties managing schedule changes;
- Family responsibilities;
- Substance abuse;
- Anxiety;
- On-the-job trauma;
- Organizational stressors; and
- Perceived lack of administration support.

In addition to seeking EAP providers with expertise in the areas identified above, public safety agencies should also look for EAPs that offer a broad range of services. Based on the author's experience, areas where resources or services are likely to be needed include:

- Family conflict;
- Child and adolescent difficulties;
- Depression and suicide intervention/prevention;
- Personal distress;
- Anger management;
- Domestic violence/stalking;
- Eating disorders;
- Grief and loss;
- Stress management;
- Trauma management /post-traumatic stress disorder;
- Critical incident reactions;
- Phobias;
- Panic attacks;
- Sleep disorders;
- Obsessive compulsive disorder;
- Retirement planning;
- Workplace dissatisfaction/conflict resolution;
- Attention-deficit hyperactivity disorder;
- Financial problems;
- Legal concerns;
- Eldercare issues;
- Animal/pet issues;
- Workplace violence; and
- Multitasking.

Most often these problems need to be addressed in a short-term, time-limited fashion, typically four to six sessions (Taranowski & Mahieu, 2013). Due to this aspect of the service, EAP providers need to be experienced in specific types of therapeutic approaches including:

- Behavioral therapy
- Cognitive therapy
- Cognitive-behavioral therapy
- EMDR
- Stress management training
- Anger management training
- Substance use/abuse counseling

To manage the range of problems that are seen by public safety EAPs, it is clear that an effective program will be one staffed by numerous police and public safety psychologists who have further experience and expertise in a multitude of clinical areas and therapeutic approaches. The multifaceted needs of law enforcement employees can also be met through the use of outside referrals. If a law enforcement officer or one of his family members is struggling and the EAP does not include a clinician with expertise in the area of need, the EAP should be able to make a referral to an appropriate treatment provider, facilitate the next appointment, and provide follow-up regarding the referral.

Finally, in addition to the variety of traditional counseling and psychological services that an EAP should be able to provide, today's public safety agency may also be interested in having their EAPs offer other services as well. Some of these additional services that can be provided by EAPs include:

- Case management
- Critical incident management
- Psychological emergency preparedness
- Managing organizational training
- Managing organizational change
- Mediation/motivational mediation
- Anger management classes
- Verbal communication and de-escalation classes
- Managing the challenges of military deployment and homecoming
- Physical health programs
- Weight loss programs
- Disease management programs
- Preventative health programs
- Psychoeducation classes/Seminars
- Financial planning/budgeting
- Outreach to employees and family members
- Life coaching
- Anti-bullying training
- Work team functioning
- Burn-out prevention

Basically, a truly effective EAP should be able, either directly or through referral, to meet all of the psychological and behavioral health care needs of the public safety agency that it serves.

FUTURE DIRECTIONS/INNOVATIONS

Since their inception, EAPs have constantly been evolving to meet the demands of the ever-changing workplace. A review of the literature indicates there are at least seven areas in which EAPs are either adapting or looking to adapt in the future. One of the greatest priorities is to address utilization rates. Across a variety of industries, utilization rates that range from 5% to 30% have been reported in regard to what percentage of employees annually access EAP services (Attridge et al., 2009). Even being optimistic, that means that 70% of employees who could possibly benefit from services are not accessing them. One of the easiest and most effective steps an agency can take to increase EAP utilization is to make the program more visible. Many employees do not utilize these benefits because they do not know they have an EAP or do not know how to access the services. Both EAP providers and agencies can combat this problem by making information about the EAP readily available. The EAP should be advertised on an agency's Intranet and in its handbooks or employee resource guides. In addition, posters and pamphlets can be placed throughout the agency, and program providers should attend agency briefings at least once a year to present the program and the available services to employees.

Employee assistance programs can also increase utilization by connecting with law enforcement officers through multiple mediums and encouraging phone consultations. For example, it is my experience that some public safety agencies have their EAPs provide articles and videos to the agency, as well as use websites and social media to engage employees. Other non-traditional ways to connect with employees might include creating online polls and hosting interactive events such as health or weight-loss challenges. As for phone consultations, many law enforcement officers may be more willing to contact EAPs if they are able to talk to someone over the phone without feeling as if they will have to see someone in person. Often, my experience is that once a person engages with his or her EAP via telephone, that individual more willing to utilize the services in person.

The final way that public safety agencies can increase utilization is by creating a culture within the agency that is positive about program utilization. Based on my experience working with EAPs, this has to be done from the top down. When an agency's administration and supervisors are supportive of using the program, can speak about the program's benefits, and can talk about the confidentiality associated with the program, line law enforcement officers are more willing to access those services.

The next way that EAPs are evolving is in how the delivery of services is managed. Historically, EAP services have been delivered through face-to-face or telephone contacts. Moving forward, EAPs are likely going to be taking greater advantage of technology including Skype, live Internet chatting, online coaching, webinars, and email consultation. Some EAPs are also using social media and mobile apps to better engage employees (Clark, 2015). The following are specific ways in which EAPs can maximize their use of technology and social media when servicing an agency (Attridge et al, 2009; Nicoletti-Flater Associates, 2016; Office of Disability and Employment Policy, 2009):

- Maintain a website containing referral and benefit information;
- Provide detailed information about program services and the process of accessing and utilizing services;
- Offer an online library of information;
- Use social media to engage employees with program information, relevant articles, and interactive surveys;
- Offer online self-assessment tools;
- Host webinars;
- Provide online training courses;
- Offer an online messaging system;
- Make the program more accessible and personal by providing clinician pictures and biographies;
- Host live chat support groups;
- Produce an online magazine/newsletter;
- Allow for public safety agencies to view their account information;
- Provide information and sample disclosures regarding confidentiality;
- Provide intake paperwork;
- Use Skype and other teleconferencing technology in the provision of services; and
- Provide helpful links to additional information and other potential services of interest.

The next two ways in which EAPs are either adapting or looking to adapt in the future are by changing their focus from being reactive to proactive, and by integrating their services with wellness and work-life programs (Employee Assistance Trade Association, 2013b). Traditionally, EAPs have been reactive in nature- employees sought help after experiencing problems. Currently there is a drive to be more proactive by working toward problem prevention and the enhancement of resiliency (Livingston, 2015). This is being accomplished through a variety of means including clinician outreach and provision of more psychoeducational seminars and/or webinars. It is my observation that more emphasis on resiliency-related skill development for law enforcement officers can now be seen in the training academy, as well as other forms of early intervention and training.

Employee assistance programs are also changing their focus by becoming more integrated with wellness and work-life programs. Wellness programs are programs offered by employers that are designed to improve the overall health, fitness, and well-being of employees through the use of preventative interventions, preventative health screenings, and the promotion of healthy activities/choices. Work-life programs are the business practice of creating a flexible, supportive environment to engage employees and maximize organizational performance (U.S. Office of Personnel Management, 2015). Work-life programs are ultimately meant to help employees balance their personal lives with their work lives through creating flexible workplaces, providing financial planning support, caring for dependents, promoting community involvement, encouraging and supporting health and wellness, and providing recognition for work related achievements (World at Work, 2016). Cleary there is overlap between the missions of EAPs, wellness programs, and work-life programs. Combining these programs may serve to maximize a public safety agency's return on investment, enhance the positive outcomes for employees, and allow for a more proactive program than is found with a traditional EAP.

As was previously discussed, both internal and external EAPs appear to be effective and both come with strengths and weaknesses, although many of the concerns regarding external programs can be effectively mitigated. Furthermore, although a small number of internal programs are still in use, many employers, including public safety agencies, appear to prefer external EAPs (Favorini & Spitzer, 1993). Despite these trends, there are still some employees who would be more likely to utilize services if they were located onsite. To meet this challenge, some employers are beginning to look toward hybrid EAP models (Drury, 2016). A hybrid EAP is an externally based program that has clinicians work on-site on a part-time basis. With this model, employees who are concerned about confidentiality and stigma can utilize off-site services, while employees wanting the convenience of not leaving the workplace can utilize the on-site services when they are available.

The sixth way that EAPs are looking to adapt and change is by attempting to further professionalize and standardized the field. Unfortunately, services provided by EAPs can vary widely. This is particularly true when public safety agencies use services that are not provided by police and public safety psychologists. EAP professional organizations have attempted to professionalize and standardize the field though advocating for adherence to the Employee Assistance Program Core Technology and through offering accreditation for EAPs (Employee Assistance Trade Association, 2013b). To date, there are several organizations that offer accreditation for EAPs. These efforts at accreditation have been hampered by two factors. The first challenge is that there are no universal, agreed-upon standards (National Business Group on Health, 2008). The second problem is that becoming accredited is completely voluntary and only about 16% of EAPs are accredited (Taranowski & Mahieu, 2013). The idea behind accreditation is to ensure that employers are receiving a consistently high standard of EAP service delivery from qualified clinicians. Although it is difficult to imagine ever gaining 100% compliance with voluntary accreditation, it is important for public safety agencies to remember that they can take steps to ensure the quality of their EAP by utilizing specially trained police and public safety psychologists, particularly those that have been board certified by ABPP.

The seventh and final way that EAPs are attempting to adapt and change for the future is by strengthening the research foundation on which the field is based (Employee Assistance Research Foundation, 2013). The research that has been conducted on EAPs has been hampered by challenges similar to those encountered by those seeking to standardize and accredit EAPs. Namely, there is a wide variety of programs and providers that are not standardized, making comparisons across EAPs more difficult. Additionally, my conclusion is that although a great deal of research has been done regarding EAPs, much of the research has been focused on three particular areas: rate of utilization, employee satisfaction, and return on investment. Moving forward, more research needs to be done in specific areas such as how differences between programs impact the program's effectiveness, what aspects of an EAP are most important to the program's effectiveness, the effectiveness of different treatment modalities, the effectiveness of proactive EAP interventions, and the effectiveness of newer, technologically based methods of service delivery. In addition, more research is needed specifically on the effectiveness of EAPs within law enforcement organizations.

CONCLUSION

For more than 70 years, EAPs have been an integral part of the organizational landscape. In an effort to maintain a healthier work force, organizations adopted internal alcohol and substance abuse programs that ultimately transformed into mostly external programs that focused on a multitude of problems ranging from mental/behavioral health issues to the support and care needs of employees' family members. As EAPs move into the future and continue to evolve with the changing needs of organizations, they must embrace an even wider mission of helping employees establish better work-life balance and greater overall health and wellness.

Like other organizations, public safety agencies have seen the benefits of offering EAPs to their personnel. Research clearly shows that EAPs offer positive experiences for users and a positive return on investment for the agency. A major obstacle for many law enforcement personnel is concern about whether employee assistance counselors will understand their culture and the nature of their work. One of the ways that public safety agencies can address this issue is by looking for specialized EAPs that are staffed by psychologists who are specifically trained as police and public safety psychologists. Through the use of such professionals, public safety agencies are providing their personnel with psychological services that can help maintain their overall mental health and wellness, while also enhancing their work performance and productivity. By utilizing EAPs, public safety agencies are taking advantage of an invaluable tool that helps with supporting and sustaining their personnel in meeting their mission of safely and effectively serving the public.

REFERENCES

Albrecht, S. (2014). Why don't employees use EAP services? *Psychology Today*. Retrieved from https://www.psychologytoday.com/blog/the-act-violence/201402/why-dont-employees-use-eap-services

Amaral, T. M. (2008). *Global benchmarking and EAP best practices*. Presented at the annual institute of the Employee Assistance Society of North America, Vancouver, BC, Canada.

American Psychological Association. (2015). *Police and public safety*. Retrieved from http://www.apa.org/ed/graduate/specialize/police.aspx

American Psychological Association. (2016). *Protecting your privacy: Understanding confidentiality*. Retrieved from http://www.apa.org/helpcenter/confidentiality.aspx

Anderson, L. C. J., Bazin, L. A., & Graham, G. (2015). *Peak performance in combat*. Retrieved from http://www.benning.army.mil/infantry/magazine/issues/2015/Jul-Sept/pdfs/Bazin-Peak%20Performance_TEXT.pdf

Attridge, M. (2003, March). *EAP impact on work, stress and health: National data 1999-2002*. Presented at the bi-annual conference of the Work, Stress and Health Conference: American Psychological Association/National Institutes of Occupational Safety and Health, Toronto, ON, Canada.

Attridge, M., Amaral, T., Bjornson, T., Goplerud, E., Herlihy, P., McPherson, T., & Teems, L. (2009). History and growth of the EAP field. *EASNA Research Notes*, *1*(1). Retrieved from http://www.easnsa.org

BadgeofLife.com. (2008). *A new police stress management strategy: The annual mental health check*. Retrieved from http://www.badgeoflife.com/prescription.php

Best, S., Artwohl, A., & Kirschman, E. (2011). Critical incidents. In J. Kitaeff (Ed.), *The handbook of police psychology* (pp. 491–507). New York, NY: Routledge.

Clark, A. D. (2015). Quality EAPs carry their weight. *Benefits Magazine*, 42-47.

Davis, J. A. (1993). The use of behavioral scientists in law enforcement. *The Law Enforcement Quarterly*, 20-28.

Drury, M. A. (2016). *Go hybrid...Get more mileage out of your EAP*. Retrieved from http://www.ccainc.com/thought-leadership/position-papers

Duncan, B. L., Miller, S. D., Wampold, B. E., & Hubble, M. A. (Eds.). (2009). *The heart and soul of change: Delivering what works in therapy* (2nd ed.). Washington, DC: American Psychological Association.

Employee Assistance Research Foundation. (2013). *Funded Research*. Retrieved from http://www.eapfoundation.org/research/

Employee Assistance Trade Association. (2009). *Selecting and strengthening employee assistance programs: A purchaser's guide*. Arlington, VA: Employee Assistance Society of North America.

Employee Assistance Trade Association. (2013a). *High quality network provider*. Retrieved from http://www.easna.org/research-and-best-practices/what-is-eap/

Employee Assistance Trade Association. (2013b). *What is EAP?* Retrieved from http://www.easna.org/research-and-best-practices/what-is-eap/

Favorini, A., & Spitzer, K. (1993). The emergence of external employee assistance programs: Report of a survey and identification of trends. *Journal of Employee Assistance Research*, *2*(1), 23–35.

Gottschalk, P. (2007). *Knowledge management systems: Value shop creation*. Hershey, PA: Idea Group Publishing. doi:10.4018/978-1-59904-060-8

Group, E. S. I. (2016). *Public Safety EAP*. Retrieved from http://www.theeap.com/public-safety-eap/

Gupton, H. M., Axelrod, E. M., Cornell, L., Curran, S. F., Hood, C. J., Kelly, J., & Moss, J. (2011). Support and sustain: Psychological intervention for law enforcement personnel. *The Police Chief*, *78*, 92–97.

Hargrave, G. E., Hiatt, D., Alexander, R., & Shaffer, I. A. (2008). EAP treatment impact on presenteeism and absenteeism: Implications for return on investment. *Journal of Workplace Behavioral Health*, *23*(3), 283–293. doi:10.1080/15555240802242999

Harlow, K. C. (2006). The effectiveness of a problem resolution and brief counseling EAP intervention. *Journal of Workplace Behavioral Health*, *22*(1), 1–12. doi:10.1300/J490v22n01_01

Institute for Health and Productivity Studies. (2015). *From evidence to practice: Workplace wellness that works*. Baltimore, MD: Johns Hopkins University.

International Employee Assistance Professionals Association. (2011). *Definitions of an employee assistance program (EAP) and EAP core technology: Updated October 2011*. Retrieved from http://www.eapassn.org/About/About-Employee-Assistance/EAP-Definitions-and-Core-Technology

Kendall, J. (2000). It's your problem too: Anxiety, depression, and addiction among your staff can cost you plenty. Here's how to cope. *Business Week*, (February), 25.

LaCroix, D. (2015). *Employee assistance program costs*. Retrieved from http://business.lovetoknow.com/wiki/Employee_Assistance_Program_Costs

Lang, S. (2010). The value of an employee assistance program. *CALEA Update Magazine*, 107. Retrieved from http://www.calea.org/calea-update-magazine/issue-107/value-employee-assistance-program

Livingston, S. (2015). Employers turn to resilience-building programs to cut worker stress. *Benefits Magazine*. Retrieved from http://www.businessinsurance.com/article/20150607/NEWS03/306079981/employers-turn-to-resilience-building-programs-to-cut-worker-stress

Masi, D. A. (1984). *Designing employee assistance programs*. New York, NY: American Management Associations.

Masi, D. A. (2011). Cost-effectiveness of EAPs. In D. A. Masi (Ed.), *Correct understanding and application of EAP necessary for all entities that implement measures for mental health.* Retrieved from http://archive.hshsl.umaryland.edu/bitstream/10713/3361/1/Cost%20Effectiveness%20of%20EAP.pdf

Masi, D. A. (2015). *EAP counseling: History, core technology, and uniqueness of EAP counseling*. Retrieved from http://www.eaprefer.org/social-workers/from-dr-dale-masis-desk/history-core-technology and-uniqueness-of-eap-counseling/

Mercer, M. (2008). *Survey of health, productivity, and absence management programs 2007*. New York, NY: Marsh & McLennan Companies.

National Business Group on Health. (2008). *An employer's guide to employee assistance programs*. Retrieved from http://www.businessgrouphealth.org/pdfs/FINAL%20EAP_report_2008highres.pdf

Nicoletti-Flater Associates. (2016). *Employee assistance program*. Retrieved from http://www.nicoletti-flater.com/eap.php

Office of Disability and Employment Policy. (2009). *Employee assistance programs for a new generation of employees: Defining the next generation*. Washington, DC: U.S. Department of Labor.

Office of Personnel Management. (2016). *Work life: Employee assistance programs*. Retrieved from https://www.opm.gov/policy-data-oversight/worklife/employee-assistance-programs/

Richards, F. (2015). *Do employee assistance programs decrease Worker's Compensation costs?* Retrieved from http://smallbusiness.chron.com/employee-assistance-programs-decrease-workers-compensation-costs-14246.html

Roman, P. M., & Blum, T. C. (1988). Reaffirmation of the core technology of employee assistance programs. *The Almacan*, *19*(8), 17–22.

Rothermel, S., Slavit, W., & Finch, R. A. (2008). *An employer's guide to employee assistance programs: Recommendations for strategically defining, integrating and measuring employee assistance programs*. Washington, DC: National Business Group on Health.

Sharar, D. A., Pompe, J. C., & Attridge, M. (2013). Onsite versus offsite EAPs: A comparison of workplace outcomes. *Journal of Employee Assistance*, *43*(2). Retrieved from chestnutglobalpartners.org/.../Onsite%20Versus%20Offsite%20EAPs.pdf

Sonnenstuhl, W. J., & Trice, H. M. (1986). *Strategies for employee assistance programs: The crucial balance. Key Issues Series No. 30*. Ithaca, NY: Cornell University, New York State School of Industrial and Labor Relations.

Taranowski, C. J., & Mahieu, K. M. (2013). Trends in employee assistance program implementation, structure, and utilization, 2009 to 2010. *Journal of Workplace Behavioral Health*, *28*(3), 172–191. doi:10.1080/15555240.2013.808068

U.S. Department of Health and Human Services. (2015a). *Federal occupational health: Law enforcement employee assistance program FAQ's*. Retrieved from https://www.foh.hhs.gov/whatwedo/EAP/Law/FAQ.asp

U.S. Department of Health and Human Services. (2015b). *Federal occupational health: Law enforcement medical programs*. Retrieved from http://foh.hhs.gov/whatwedo/EAP/Law/LawAssist.asp

U.S. Department of Labor. (2015). *elaws: Drug-free workplace advisor*. Retrieved from http://webapps.dol.gov/elaws/asp/drugfree/assistance/screen94.asp

U.S. Office of Personnel Management. (2015). *Work-life*. Retrieved from https://www.opm.gov/policy-data-oversight/worklife/

White, W., & Sharar, D. (2003). The evolution of employee assistance: A brief history and trend analysis. *EAP Digest*, *3*(4), 16–24.

World at Work. (2016). *Work-life*. Retrieved from https://www.worldatwork.org/home/html/worklife_home.jsp

Chapter 11
Health and Wellness Programming:
The Added Contribution of an Ethical Mindset

Jennifer Kelly
New Jersey Area Independent Practice, USA

Jack E. Hoban
Resolution Group International, USA

ABSTRACT

The health and wellbeing of our police community has rightfully become a top priority to ensure the viability of this critically important workforce. This chapter defines officer wellbeing, identifies stressors inherent in policing, and explores the impact of stress upon police officers. The potential contributions of an ethical mindset to officer wellbeing are considered, including the concept of the officer as Ethical Protector. Important elements of health and wellness programs are reviewed, with an emphasis on developing resources that support police officers' physical, mental, emotional, and social wellbeing. Police agencies are encouraged to draw from model programs and national guidelines to develop sustainable, cost-effective health and wellness programs. Such efforts are likely to fit local needs, foster positive community relations, and support police officer resiliency.

INTRODUCTION

During the past several years there have been a number of major symposiums, initiatives, and program development efforts focused on improving the health and wellness of police officers. Notable examples include the International Association of Chiefs of Police's (IACP) 2012 creation of the Center for Officer Safety and Wellness (IACP, 2012) and a 2013 national symposium dedicated to law enforcement officer suicide and mental health issues. In 2014, President Barack Obama signed an executive order that established the President's Task Force on 21st Century Policing (COPS Office, 2015). One of the six focal

DOI: 10.4018/978-1-5225-0813-7.ch011

areas identified by the Task Force was dedicated entirely to officer safety and wellness, and included a comprehensive set of recommendations. It is clear that supporting police officer wellness has emerged as a national priority and police psychologists are ideally positioned to make important contributions to this effort. This chapter first defines wellness and identifies the myriad of factors that lead to stress in police officers. It also highlights the essential importance of an individual's ethical standpoint, which cannot be overlooked when creating a comprehensive program aimed at inoculating police personnel against the on- and off-duty stressors in their lives. Finally, a comprehensive list of programming elements is provided from which agencies can draw when creating their own health and wellness programs.

WELLNESS DEFINED

While relatively recent national consideration has been given to addressing the health and wellness of police officers in the United States, comprehensive occupational health and safety programs have been established in Canada and the United Kingdom within police departments for a number of years (Sanberg, Brito, Luna, & McFadden, 2010). These national programs, such as the United Kingdom's 2004 Strategy for a Healthy Police Service, aim to promote the highest level of physical, mental, and social wellbeing in employees; prevent health departures caused by working conditions; prevent illness and injury in the workplace; and place employees in positions for which they are physically and psychologically suited. Specifically with regard to psychological health, the Mental Health Commission of Canada created a national initiative that governs psychological health and safety in the workplace (Canadian Standards Association, 2013). This Standard posits that every workplace has control, responsibility, and influence over certain factors that psychologically impact their employees. National initiatives such as these have led to specific health and wellbeing programs that employers implement to improve lifestyle choices and physical health as a means of preventing chronic illness. Other countries have likewise developed programs that target organizational and environment practices to improve overall employee health (Australian Government, 2010).

The phrase "workplace wellness" has been defined by Berry, Mirabito, and Baun (2010) as "an organized, employer sponsored program that is designed to support employees as they adopt sustainable behaviors that reduce health risks, improve quality of life, enhance personal effectiveness, and benefit the organization's financial position" (p. 106). According to Mattke (2013), the success of wellness programming is dependent on effective communication, employee participation, leadership engagement, use of existing resources, and continuous evaluation of the program. A comprehensive approach, therefore, requires more than just a focus on improvement to emotional and physical health. Employee engagement, satisfaction, and pride become relevant to good health as well as employee effectiveness (World Economic Forum in Partnership with Right Management, 2010). When considering wellness in policing, the primary goals should include increasing resilience and improving mental and physical health in response to stress and adversity through the development of strong ethical principles, physical health, and emotional strength. Although each officer brings different coping capabilities to the policing position, adaptive coping and resiliency skills can be taught, practiced, and learned for the benefit of all officers. These health improvements will in turn benefit the organizations and communities that officers serve.

IDENTIFYING AND ACKNOWLEDING STRESSORS

To mitigate the impact of stress, it is necessary to identify and acknowledge where an officer's stress originates. Every individual is exposed to a variety of sources of stress. There are stressors originating from one's current work situation, social life, financial standing, health status, and domestic relationships, including significant other, children, and extended family. Factors such as work-family conflict alone have been found to predict poorer psychological health in a large police sample (Mikkelsen & Burke, 2004). Moreover, officers' personal life stressors may combine with occupational stress to exacerbate the challenges associated with police work.

Inherent to policing is ongoing exposure to events commonly referred to as critical incidents (Best, Artwohl, & Kirschman, 2011). Best and coauthors assert that the definition of critical incident must be flexible enough to incorporate a broad range of on-duty events that officers experience. A critical incident can vary based on the perception of the individual officer involved and often includes serious threat of injury or loss (Gentz, 1990). Critical incidents place burdens on officers' emotional and coping resources. Policing involves regular exposure to confrontation, violence, and potential harm (Maquen et al., 2009). The potential for harm may include physical injuries from chasing and apprehending subjects, motor vehicle accidents, or needle sticks (Brandl & Stroshine, 2003; Lorentz, Hill, & Samimi, 2000). At the extreme end of potential responses to on-duty critical incidents is the development of Posttraumatic Stress Disorder (PTSD).

Theoretical models of work environment stress in policing additionally include categories of stress involving co-worker factors (e.g., manpower issues, personality conflicts); supervision (poor, inconsistent, lack of recognition); work content (unclear roles, lack of training); and temporal issues (shift work, mandatory overtime) (Hurrell, Nelson, & Simmons, 1998; Brough, 2004). Researchers have found that these routine work stressors constitute a distinct and greater influence on the manifestation of PTSD symptoms than exposure to critical incidents (Liberman et al., 2002). Likewise, an examination of officer self-report yielded higher subjective levels of stress from workplace stressors involving poor communication, lack of support, and an excessive caseload when compared to exposure to critical incidents (Collins & Gibbs, 2003).

As stated above, in order to fully appreciate the need for health and wellness programming for police officers, understanding the cumulative nature of stress and identifying the vast range of stressors impacting the police community is essential. While national attention has recently been placed on improving relationships between the police and communities, the origins of improved relationships can be seen back with the creation of the Office of Community Oriented Policing (COPS) in 1994. COPS (2012) has defined *community policing* as a philosophy that promotes collaborative relationships between police agencies and the individuals and organizations they serve through proactive problem solving and transformation of existing systems. An element often missing in this discussion is the importance of a suitably stable (both physically and mentally) community of police officers. It is impossible to succeed in America's vision of true community policing without having the guardians of society physically and mentally healthy. The bond between police and community can only be cohesive if there exists a culture that is comfortable in acknowledging and addressing the physical and emotional needs of officers.

To maximize the ability of officers to be physically sound and to perform in emotionally and ethically appropriate ways, their emotional wellness should be considered to the same extent as their tactical soundness. Just as officers are reminded of good tactical practices, proper handling of disturbances, and other routine functions of policing, their emotional wellbeing and self-care practices should be encouraged.

From the very inception of community policing in the U.S. it was stressed that this approach should be more than a program but rather a philosophy that promotes healthy, constructive relationships between communities and police (COPS, 2014). Likewise, the health and wellness of police officers should not be just another solitary program, but rather a holistic philosophy that advocates for and improves the wellbeing of every police officer.

IMPACT OF STRESS

It is widely understood that the physiological responses to stress are largely genetically predetermined, but that psychological and behavioral responses to stress are more a product of learning and choice (Nash, 2007). Lazarus and Folkman (1984) describe coping as the constantly changing mental and behavioral efforts to manage the demands placed on an individual in order to not only solve a problem, but also to maintain a positive outlook. In the extreme, when one is exposed to a trauma, a primary tenet for the explanation of a pathological response is that it undermines firmly held beliefs and assumptions about the world (Janoff-Bulman, 1992). This is particularly true when one has taken the life of another and subsequently experiences a disruption to one's sense of one's own goodness, self-esteem, and self-image (Grossman, 1995). Long-term deleterious effects of exposure to the chronic stressors of policing may likewise damage officers' beliefs and assumptions about the world, how they relate to those in it, and how they feel about themselves. As a result, a focus of any health and wellness program for officers must have a component designed to re-calibrate one's ethics and belief systems.

The costs of failing to offer health and wellness programming can be seen in the nation's recent focus on a variety of health problems in police personnel. The National Alliance on Mental Illness has summarized the literature on police suicides indicating the rate of police officer suicide is 2.3 times that of police homicides, with the rate of police suicides being estimated at approximately 18 suicides per 100,000 (Aamodt & Stalnaker, 2001). In addition, almost one in four police officers have had thoughts of suicide at some point in their lives (Violanti et al., 2009), and in small departments the rate of suicide is four times that of the national average of suicides within the general population (Violanti, Mnatsakanova, Burchfield, Hartley, & Andrew, 2012). Similarly, the Buffalo Cardio-Metabolic Occupational Police Stress (BCOPS) Study by Hartley, Fekedulegn, Burchfield, Andrew, and Violanti (2011) found the percentage of police officers with depression was nearly double that of employed personnel in other occupations (12.0% vs. 6.8%). Possibly because police officers are very adept at masking emotions and duress, they do not typically display many of the common warning signs of suicide (O'Hara & Violanti, 2009). The latter is a particular cause for concern and is all the more reason for agencies to establish preventative and proactive wellness programming.

Overall, between 7 and 19% of police officers involved in shootings are believed to have symptoms of PTSD (Gersons, 1989). Far more common, however, is vicarious traumatization (VT)—a framework for understanding the negative impact of exposure to trauma on first responders (McCann & Pearlman, 1990). VT occurs when individuals who are in a position to care for others begin to identify with and feel responsible for them. This sense of responsibility is believed to lead to changes in identity, values, and self-concept; changes in relationships and intimacy levels; as well as changes in tolerance of the helper (Famili, Kirschner, & Gamez, 2014). The ongoing experiences of VT, as well as the exposure to acts of violence and other stressful events, may erode officers' sense of safety and trust in others and lead to feelings of alienation and suspicion.

With regard to physical functioning, Hartley et al. (2011) also found police officers to have one of the poorest cardiovascular disease health profiles of any occupation. Within the BCOPS study between 2004 and 2009, police officers were found to have a more adverse cardiovascular profile than the generally employed U.S. population. A higher percentage of officers were obese (40.5% vs. 32.1%) and they also had higher mean serum total cholesterol levels than the comparison groups of employed persons. Zimmerman (2012) similarly concluded that police officers have an excess number of risk factors for cardiovascular disease than found in the civilian population when measured by level of hypertension, obesity, smoking, and sedentary lifestyles.

Mitigation of the stressors that impact police officers will certainly foster a higher-functioning public safety employee. Prevention is key, as well as a swift response to existing stress. Along with accomplishing the agency's mission, the agency's goal should be healthy employees with the side benefits of employee retention and recruitment, increased job satisfaction and performance, lower absenteeism, and fewer injuries.

THE RELEVANCE OF ETHICS IN A COMPREHENSIVE WELLNESS PLAN

While common wellness programming frequently includes psychological and physical components to assist in the development of resiliency and health, very little discussion has existed relative to the importance of clarifying an officer's self-concept and ethical mindset as a way of increasing wellbeing. Hoban and Gourlie (2014) have articulated in *The Ethical Protector* a system for addressing police officers' numerous stressors and ethical challenges as a means to improve not only health and wellbeing, but also community relations. A synergistic training regimen that combines physical training, verbal conflict resolution skills, and the clarification and activation of an Ethical Protector mindset is designed to decrease the impact of trauma exposure and the risk for burnout and compassion fatigue.

An Ethical Protector is conceptualized as a guardian of one's own life and the lives of all others—including those suspected of violating the law. This identity differs greatly from that of a "law enforcer," and is hypothesized to lead to more respectful community relations and increased officer resiliency. An Ethical Protector has the ability to separate in his or her mind the relative value of behavior (which can be unethical and/or illegal), from the absolute value of life as an inalienable right worthy of respect at all times and under all circumstances. Ethical Protectors respect the lives of everyone, while dealing tactically and professionally with suspected criminal behavior.

Today's police officers regularly face ethical challenges. Hoban and Gourlie (2014) point out that while legally relevant conundrums are often highlighted so to avoid specific liability concerns and improve risk management, those complex factors that are relevant to an individual officer's psychological health—and how they potentially could be positively impacted by an Ethical Protector self-concept—are often left unaddressed.

Looking back to the experiences of service members in active combat during the Vietnam War, Shay (1994) has chronicled the negative impact of dehumanization of the enemy on returned veterans. Veterans who demonized or dehumanized the enemy suffered moral injury and were more prone to depression and alienation upon return from war. According to Shay, restoring the honor of fallen enemy combatants (i.e., respecting the enemy's life, even if killing the enemy was necessary because of life-threatening behavior) is an essential step in recovery from combat PTSD. In Shay's view, the self-respect of service members can never be fully repaired without compensating for the moral injury that may have resulted from their actions or other complex aspects of the wartime experiences in Vietnam.

It is reasonable to posit that dehumanizing behavior by police officers would be similar in character and form to that of military personnel. In his sequel to *Achilles in Vietnam*, Shay (2002) outlined factors that prevent psychological damage in military personnel. Cohesive units, particularly those with supportive leadership that focus on maintaining the ethical integrity of the group, are most likely to resist post-traumatic stress and moral injury. Likewise, training that addresses the total efficacy of the individual—including his or her mind, body, emotions, character, and spirit—will help to inoculate the individual against the stressors of traumatic incidents. The body and mind need to be trained simultaneously to deal with physical dangers, as well as to respond ethically in the face of moral dangers.

Police officers who view all human life as something to be valued, protected, and defended, regardless of the lawfulness of specific acts, are hypothesized to experience benefits such as reduced stress and increased well being. It also seems reasonable to expect that such a stance or outlook would lead officers to act in ways that would result in improved community relations. The value of ethical clarity and calibrating one's moral compass as it relates to improved interactions with others is highlighted in Hoban and Gourlie's (2014) formula: "ethics drive tactics; tactics drive technique" (p. 99). As such, a healthy ethical foundation is hypothesized to lead to better tactical decisions that protect both the officers and citizens with whom they interact. The resulting interactions would then be expected to lead to the best possible results in a conflict situation, to improved resiliency, and to decreased stressors on and off duty. This viewpoint is supported by Anshel's (2011) application of the Disconnected Values Model (DVM) to law enforcement personnel, which posits behavioral change is most successfully precipitated by value acceptance and by holding oneself accountable to acting in accordance with one's values (e.g., an Ethical Protector self-concept, in this case).

So how does one become an Ethical Protector? Specific, synergistic training in ethical clarity, superior communication skills, and physical self-confidence are hypothesized to contribute to this goal. It begins with calibrating one's moral compass as a protector of all life and using force only when necessary to protect life so that the standards of one's actions can be measured. Rather than approaching "ethics training" as an intellectual classroom exercise, the United States Marine Corps has found that the best way to instill moral values is through emotionally impactful stories "tied to" physical training (Hoban & Gourlie, 2014). These "tie-ins" (Shusko, 2015) allow for a personal understanding and appreciation, beyond a purely academic discussion, of the values that will inspire moral behavior and contribute to wellness. These authors believe that the cornerstone of ethical practice is represented in the Dual Life Value, which espouses that all life is worthwhile, even that of one's supposed enemies (Humphrey, 1992). This directly relates to policing if one understands and integrates the belief that valuing one's own life is only half of the equation. An ethical basis will lead to actions that are much more fitting with a police officer's mission to serve and protect. However, let us be clear: A police officer is expected to respect only the intrinsic value of life and not that of illegal or unlawful behavior.

A police officer's fully integrated set of protector values is hypothesized by Hoban and Gourlie (2014) to increase the likelihood that, under stress, these will be the values that are acted upon (e.g., "ethics are moral values in action", p. 28). If one loses sight of the value of an adversary's inalienable right to life, acting in an immoral manner becomes all too easy. In effect, Ethical Protector skills may serve to inoculate the police officer from the psychological and spiritual harm (i.e., moral injury) done by dehumanizing those whose motives are unclear to them (e.g., the suspect or subject). An officer with a solid ethical foundation who is well trained to respond physically and psychologically is likely to be tactically stronger than one without this underpinning. According to Hoban and Gourlie (2014), the basic art of respectful communication, which includes a consistent approach in all encounters, along with clarifying and empathic listening and skillful verbal persuasion, will significantly increase the likelihood of a non-violent outcome. These proposed conflict resolution skills include those espoused in the Vistelar Institute's training on Verbal Defense and Influence (Mangold, 2014).

The final component of the Ethical Protector mindset is the training of police officers in controlling tactical space. The safest place to be in any interaction is one that optimizes the officer's safety as well as the safety of the suspect/subject. Gaining a tactical advantage by skillfully managing the conflict space enhances the police officer's ability to secure safe apprehension and containment, if required. Because conflicts are dynamic, the "space" is ever changing and must be identified at all times. If this ability becomes automatic, then an officer may be more easily able to avoid unhelpful emotional and physiological responses to stressful encounters. The physical training for an Ethical Protector mindset consists of martial combatives and combat conditioning (Hoban & Gourlie, 2014). In theory, physical confidence and moral strength go hand in hand, which leads the Ethical Protector training to incorporate discussions in moral and ethical principles before, during, and after physical conditioning. Certainly more research is needed on the effectiveness and applicability of this model. However, it shows potential for integrating officer health and wellness objectives with efforts at improved community relations and policing.

ELEMENTS OF HEALTH AND WELLNESS PROGRAMS

A variety of health and wellness programming elements for police officers are identified below and can be conceptualized as adding to a model driven by an ethical self-concept such as that of the Ethical Protector. These programming elements include focal areas of physical health, mental health, healthy leadership and milieu, safety and prevention, and financial education/financial health. Each agency should consider this list within the realm of brainstorming as the need for viable and sustainable programming is essential. Some elements are much more tangible than others, given that objectives such as positive leadership and milieu can be much more difficult to quantify. The Major Cities Chiefs Association and the Department of Justice's Officer Safety and Wellness Group have provided examples of large scale case studies and programs to serve as models for agencies to consider, modify, and adopt as practical or relevant in their own settings (Kuhns, Maguire, & Leach, 2015).

For any program to be viable and sustainable, the elements of each organization's model should come from an analysis of what that agency needs. An identified subgroup of the diverse stakeholders in the process is ideal for the identification of essential programming. For example, the health and wellness program should be created as a collaborative effort between representatives from the administration, union, medical staff, mental health staff, and chaplaincy personnel. Before implementation, it would be ideal to hold a forum for employee contributions to the health and wellness program, along with ongoing employee feedback once the program is underway. Agencies may also find it critical to the program's sustainability to appoint an individual who will create policy, implement procedures, design evaluative measures of change, and support the overall milieu of positive change.

Physical Health

Research abounds illustrating that police officers are at high risk for developing cardiovascular disease, high blood pressure, diabetes, and elevations in stress hormones that over time may lead to a variety of health difficulties, including insomnia (Zimmerman, 2012; Arnetz, Nevedal, Lumley, Backman, & Lublin, 2009). Law enforcement agencies interested in combating the negative impact of policing-related stress on their employees' physical health have a myriad of programming options available to them. Access to low-cost medical screenings that evaluate factors relevant to a police officer's high-risk areas, including EKG and lipid testing, dietary and nutritional education, and smoking cessation programs, can potentially impact occurrence rates of injury, time loss due to illness, and medical retirements.

Wellness programming addressing an officer's physical fitness level will similarly reduce risk of injury and deleterious medical conditions. Access to fitness equipment, fitness education by trained personnel, and annual fitness testing and/or voluntary fitness incentives and competitions are also ways agencies can encourage the prevention and amelioration of health-related problems. As an incentive to maintaining optimal physical health, some agencies have begun to allow officers time during their shifts to exercise (Kuhns, Maquire, & Leach, 2015). Exploration into a broader range of exercise options outside those of traditional police training programs such as Crossfit, functional fitness approaches as utilized by the United States Marine Corps, and martial arts may lead to more physically fit officers, thus reducing stress and improving health (USMC, 2006; Kuhns, Maquire, & Leach, 2015; Hoban & Gourlie, 2014).

Anshel (2011) has described the efficacy of health behavior change programming to be somewhat ambiguous, with poor adherence over time being a common outcome. If making radical changes to fitness routines and eating habits were easy, obesity and poor physical fitness would not be so prevalent today. Thus, changing established health behavioral patterns is quite daunting even in those motivated for improvement. Anshel (2011) summarizes his and others' work and identifies five components believed to be needed to change health behavior: (1) having a specific mission and developing a mission statement; (2) obtaining social support; (3) using some identifiable measure of change; (4) developing routines with proper time management strategies; and (5) acknowledging one's values. Health and wellness programming for police officers will do much to increase its success if these five factors are considered at the development stage.

Mental Health

A positive byproduct of the national attention on policing during the past few years has been to identify the lack of focus and resources within the area of officer safety and wellbeing as it relates to police officers' emotional health. *Breaking the Silence: A National Symposium on Law Enforcement Officer Suicide and Mental Health* (2014) was convened by the IACP in partnership with the Office of Community Oriented Policing Services. This symposium resulted in the development of strategies to be used as the foundation for positively impacting the mental health needs of law enforcement. As a national event it highlighted the need for overall milieu changes that should begin with the selection of leaders who openly support and encourage mental health programming. The symposium also encouraged establishing early warning systems and protocols to identify at-risk officers and providing treatment options to meet the needs of officers having difficulties with anxiety, depression, or substance misuse.

Of primary importance when developing treatment access for officers is securing treatment providers who are competent and well versed in police culture. Particularly when the main avenue for therapy is an Employee Assistance Program (EAP), the need is essential for EAP treatment providers who are aware of what police officers do on the job, why they do what they do, and how their activities impact their emotional wellbeing (Kirschman, Kamena, & Fay, 2014). The American Board of Professional Psychology's (ABPP) recent addition of board certification in the specialty of Police and Public Safety Psychology positively impacts agencies' ability to locate culturally competent and qualified clinicians.

Law enforcement agencies are also becoming increasingly aware of the benefit of a well-trained and active peer support program. Development of a peer support program can be utilized to create, maintain, and improve officer wellbeing. While these programs have been in existence for decades (Roland, 2011), they have evolved from alcohol abuse support groups and "stress units" that may respond following a specific line-of-duty critical incident, to proactive teams that offer early assistance when difficulties first occur (Mullins, 1994). One benefit of a well-trained peer support group is the perception that other officers understand the dynamics involved in police work and are in a unique position to offer empathy. Those in need of support may initially be more open to speaking to a peer than to seeking out the assistance of a mental health provider. Particularly when enhanced coping is achieved through shared experiences, the value of the created attachments with peers in further inoculating one against future stressors cannot be overstated (Cohen, Gottlieb, & Underwood, 2000).

A second benefit to the peer support program is its ability to be the conduit to linking the employee in need with a culturally competent mental health provider. The most successful peer support programs are those created with the backing of the agency's leadership (Roland, 2011). Like any internal programming, a program that functions in line with the organization's mission statement will undoubtedly be more successful. Training and selecting the right people to serve as peer supporters are also critical to its success. In developing their own peer support programs, agencies can rely on guidelines established by the IACP Police Psychological Services Section (IACP, 2006). A strong correlate to a peer support program is a formal chaplaincy program that in addition to spiritual resources and ongoing support, offers psychological first aid and a bridge to mental health professionals.

Similar to the peer support program, there is a need for all agencies to have a formal post-critical incident intervention protocol, most typically implemented following an officer-involved shooting. While there is no universally accepted post-critical incident intervention technique (Best, Artwohl, & Kirschman, 2011), psychoeducation following an incident can be expected to assist officers in the acute phase of symptomatology that may result from trauma exposure. Interventions are most typically offered in the form of near immediate psychological first aid, individual debriefings with a mental health provider, or group debriefings that are typically done by a team of professionals and peer support team members. For a comprehensive roadmap for creating a protocol following an officer-involved shooting, readers are encouraged to review the IACP's Officer Involved Shooting Guidelines (2013). The relevance of whether these support services should be offered on a voluntary or mandatory basis is addressed, as is another related and frequently debated topic—confidential "wellness visits."

Akin to post-incident interventions, the need for "wellness visits" or "safeguard debriefings" (Famili, Kirschner, & Gamez, 2014) has been debated for decades. Essentially these "check ins" with the agency-secured mental health professional (whether an in-house psychologist or outside contractor) are confidential meetings designed to be entirely proactive and occur on the basis of a pre-determined frequency rather than as a response to specific events. For example, a larger agency with specialty units such as Homicide, Crime Scene Investigators, and Special Victims may have officers meet with a mental health professional once every six months to address any concerns the officer may be experiencing. While compulsory, these visits do not require the officers to speak about any specific topics and may be largely psychoeducational and support-driven in nature. No information would be reported to the agency with the exception of risk of harm to self or others. Allen (2014) has identified this type of wellness visit as a form of secondary prevention, aimed at targeting groups with elevated risk for psychological difficulty based on their essential job functions. However, as a proactive model for stress reduction, these wellness visits could be offered to every member of a department on an annual basis. Such visits would also encourage connections with mental health professionals.

Trauma resilience training in the form of inoculating police officers against stress reactions and performance deficits in response to critical incidents has been found to be another successful proactive attempt to increase emotional and physical health while optimizing officer performance. Arnetz, Nevedal, Lumley, Backman, and Lublin (2009) found officers to have significantly reduced negative mood, positive physiological benefits, and better performance compared to controls following ten weeks of imagery and skills training with mental skill rehearsal prior to exposure to a critical incident simulation. Police officers learned cue-controlled relaxation methods, participated in group discussion of thoughts and feelings, practiced effective weapons management, and learned ways to navigate new environments. The fact that proactive training can reduce subjective distress and physiological stress reactions while simultaneously improving job performance suggests officers' wellness can be positively impacted with a priori interventions. Because the development of PTSD can be predicted by increases in subjective levels of distress and in heart rate around the time of a trauma, strategies to assist in the amelioration of these effects will naturally benefit the officer's sense of wellbeing and health (Pole 2007; Shalev et al., 1998). Many of the findings discussed above are consistent with those also espoused by Nash (2007) when he suggested that techniques geared toward reducing physiological arousal, maintaining belief systems, and addressing feelings of shame and guilt improve responses to stress.

Regular staff trainings with respect to stress management, emotional resilience, the development of emotional intelligence, critical incident training, and substance abuse prevention are recommended for the sustainment of health and wellness programming. These trainings are likely to be effective only if done in an optimal learning environment. Annual in-service training in which an officer sits in a warm room for seven hours straight with few breaks and little to no interaction with co-workers is unlikely to be optimally effective. Rather, integrating didactic instruction with physical trainings, short five- to ten-minute "main points" presented at roll calls, and the use of everyday technology already in the hands of officers is more likely to maximize acquisition and retention of material being presented. For example, the BLUE application (app) for smartphones (McWilliams & Hamilton, 2015) is an excellent example of bringing health and wellness concepts in line with 21st century technology. This mobile app offers an assessment of suicidality and provides access to the document *Breaking the Silence: A National Symposium on Law Enforcement Officer Suicide and Mental Health.* Online access to trainings and self-assessments, the agency's own "Health and Wellness Manual," and agency-specific protocols for all health-related policies will ensure officers have 24-hour access to the information they need relative to maintaining their health and wellbeing.

Healthy Leadership

Common sense tells us that if leaders espouse the mission statement of an agency and create programming that reflects the stated mission, the employees will believe that mission to be a goal. With regard to health and wellness programming, the department's milieu must support ethical principles, wellness, health, and group cohesion. Executive staff must show open support to the request for mental health services and make it clear that this is not an impediment to one's career (Clark, White, & Violanti, 2012). Executive staff must be comfortable attending debriefing sessions and wellness checks to model these activities as normative. They must support frontline supervisors repeatedly using roll call to educate and sustain wellness programs. It is only from this type of top-down approach that any wellness program will be successful (Zula, 2014).

Officer Safety as Prevention

A plethora of information has become available regarding an officer's physical safety as a result of the IACP's Officer Safety and Wellness Center. Injury tracking programs, injury reduction efforts, and focus on safety education and training are becoming much more commonplace thanks in part to the leadership of IACP and other national organizations. Safety and education training can include assessment of motor vehicle stop responses, use of tactical safety equipment, and more frequent defensive tactics and use of force trainings. Simple interventions such as zero tolerance policies for not wearing body armor, seatbelts, and reflective vests are relatively simple and straightforward responses by administrations to address known causes of officer injuries and fatalities (Czarnecki & McArdle, 2012). Another testament to the relevance and national concern regarding officer safety has been the efforts of groups such as the Bureau of Justice Assistance (an arm of the U.S. Department of Justice) and the IACP to sponsor initiatives focused on officer safety. For example, the Bureau of Justice Assistance Officer Safety and Wellness Initiative: VALOR Program was established in 2010 by the United States Attorney General to respond to the increase in assaults and violence against police officers and to increase officer safety and wellness through training, technical assistance, and specialized programs.

Police officers face significantly greater risk of serious on-the-job injuries or death compared to other industries, with upwards of five times the number of fatalities compared to deaths occurring in all industries during the same time period, and three times as many non-fatal injuries (U.S. Department of Labor, 2014). Agencies nationwide have begun to implement pilot programs to address these alarming trends. Unique features of such efforts have included a variety of medical supports; trauma kit programs that train officers to render aid (including self-aid); tactical telemedicine programs in which officers have real-time video conferencing with local trauma centers; and excited delirium response protocols (Czarnecki & McArdle, 2012).

Finances and Retirement Planning

An often-overlooked area of support for employees is a solid system of support and guidance with regard to planning for retirement. If these benefits or resources exist in a department, they are often triggered when a retirement date is chosen and a police officer begins to "process out" of active duty. Certainly a more proactive approach would be ongoing access to financial planning services throughout the officer's law enforcement career, including estate planning services and retirement fund design. Educating recruits as early as the academy with regard to the pitfalls of factoring in overtime monies to sustain the officer's general lifestyle can prevent a morass of difficulties caused by living beyond one's means. This lifestyle choice can become very problematic very quickly when overtime money is no longer available or injury precludes working extra shifts. A police agency that offers and compiles financial resources for planning will certainly contribute to the overall health of their officers into retirement.

INCLUDING FAMILIES IN HEALTH AND WELLNESS

Health and wellness programming should not be limited to a discussion of the individual employee's needs, but also include the interaction and impact of policing on the law enforcement family. Kirschman, Kamena, and Fay (2014) have described policing as a family occupation. They highlight the fact that the experiences of the officer at work will spill over to the officer's significant other and children, in much the same way that the stresses experienced at home may be brought to the job. As the police officer's family is one of his or her primary supports, it is essential that the family be considered in any health and wellness programming. Education for recruits and their families as early as the police academy should be routinely offered. One of this chapter's authors was recently invited to begin the first family seminar for basic police recruits at the Camden County College Police Academy in Blackwood, New Jersey. The mission of the academy as described by its Executive Director (S. Addezio, personal communication, October 3, 2014) was to provide insights to the recruits and their families with regard to the potential impact policing may have on them individually as well as collectively. The primary goal of this type of seminar is to encourage the development of concrete strategies to manage the challenges unique to police families as a means of proactively building resiliency for individual officers and their families.

These family or spousal academies should serve as an introduction to remaining healthy and well throughout one's career. The participants can receive practical and positively oriented information to help promote resiliency, better understand the unique stressors involved in law enforcement, and normalize their feelings and concerns about their loved one's profession. Family academies are not a substitute for therapy, but rather an opportunity for families to learn about the many resources that they can access when needed. For many, it may be the first time they learn the many ways in which the job can impact an officer's identity, and subsequently an officer's emotional, family, and social life. For example, it helps family members to understand factors such as the officer's need to be chronically hypervigilant, in control, and able to exercise power. Family members also benefit from learning how these factors can impact the officer outside of his or her awareness. The need for focused attention toward maintaining a self-concept steeped in ethical principles, such as those associated with the Ethical Protector model, can also be reinforced and ultimately supported by the officer's family.

Greene and Kirschman (2001) have previously identified factors that appear to promote resiliency in the non-police family member. These include flexibility within family rules, good communication skills, and personal independence. The conflict between being controlled and in command on the street and being open and warm at home has not gone unnoticed by those who work with, or are themselves, in policing or police families. The innate struggle lies between the family's desire for accessibility and vulnerability, and the officer's discomfort in demonstrating these due to the need to avoid these on the job. Particularly useful in family seminars is the inclusion of current police families to serve as a panel of "real life accounts" of how the police family can manage even the mundane stressors associated with shift work, missing holidays, administrative betrayals, fear of trauma and harm to the officer, and firearms in the home. For many families, this is the first time they will have a firearm in the home, and as such, they may have questions regarding issues such as firearm storage and how to speak to children about weapons.

Many families have significant safety concerns for their officers. A review of current statistics in terms of line-of-duty injuries and deaths, with a focus on officer training and use of force procedures, can be used as an educational tool. Additional practical concerns may include communicating with their loved one while on-duty, extended periods of separation, the impact of having a police parent on children, and unfamiliarity with police culture. Family and spousal academies offer a low-stress opportunity to obtain answers to many practical questions in a forum with others experiencing similar issues (Kirschman, 2007).

A more detailed discussion of critical incidents can also be included in the family seminar with respect to the varied experiences that could be considered "traumatic" over and above the obvious or commonly discussed ones. A discussion of what an officer can expect from a crisis debriefing should include a list of typical emotional, behavioral, and cognitive symptoms that may follow exposure to a critical incident, as well as a brief discussion of how *cumulative stress* can be particularly problematic and how it can be managed. Teaching points could include the fact that not everyone reacts the same way to a traumatic event, officers evolve or change over time in how they respond to traumatic events, that there are biological aspects of a traumatic stress reaction, and that ignoring enduring signs of a traumatic stress reaction can lead to harmful outcomes.

The ultimate goal for the family seminar is for the recruit and family to walk away feeling empowered, to be aware of potential areas of concern, and to have a list of tools to prevent or combat likely concerns. At the very least, the family seminar should provide a list of reputable resources for families to access if future assistance is needed. Ideally, family members also leave feeling very confident that the stresses inherent in the job can be managed by good problem solving, remaining flexible, having good communication, effective planning, spending time together as a family, engaging in healthy activities, and structuring and defining family roles (Greene & Kirschman, 2001).

CONCLUSION

It is not a question of whether the field of policing is in dire need of comprehensive health and wellness programming. It is a question of which elements take priority and how that determination will be made. Ancillary questions include the best way to implement programming, as well as the most cost effective manner in which to offer a comprehensive health and wellness program. While there is an obvious need for supporting the physical and mental health of police officers, we believe having an ethical mindset that values all life as the framework for health and wellness programming will not only improve the officer's functioning, but will also dramatically improve the health of the relationships between police officers and the community. Looking forward, research and data collection on health and wellness programming outcomes is essential to determine the efficacy of implemented changes and to provide a basis for cost effectiveness. Agencies will need to become creative in their search for funding to support programming implementation and sustainability.

REFERENCES

Aamodt, M. G., & Stalnaker, N. A. (2001). Police officer suicide: Frequency and officer profiles. In D. C. Sheehan & J. I. Warren (Eds.), *Suicide and law enforcement* (pp. 383-398). Washington, DC: Federal Bureau of Investigation. Retrieved from maamodt.asp.radford.edu/Police%20Research/police%20suicide.pdf

Allen, S. (2014). Keeping our heroes safe: A comprehensive approach to destigmatizing mental health issues in law enforcement. *The Police Chief*, *81*(5), 34–38.

Anshel, M. H. (2011). The disconnected values model: A brief intervention for improving healthy habits and coping with stress in law enforcement. In J. Kitaeff (Ed.), *Handbook of police psychology* (pp. 525–540). New York, NY: Routledge.

Arnetz, B. B., Nevedal, D. C., Lumley, M. A., Backman, L., & Lublin, A. (2009). Trauma resilience training for police: Psychophysiological and performance effects. *Journal of Police and Criminal Psychology*, *24*(1), 1–9. doi:10.1007/s11896-008-9030-y

Australian Government. (2010). *Effective health and wellbeing programs.* Retrieved from https://www.comcare.gov.au/__data/assets/pdf_file/0011/70220/Effective_Health_and_Wellbeing_Programs_Pub_82_PDF,3.63_MB.pdf

Berry, L. L., Mirabito, A. M., & Baun, W. B. (2010). What's the hard return on employee wellness programs? *Harvard Business Review*, *88*(12), 104–112. PMID:21188899

Best, S., Artwohl, A., & Kirschman, E. (2011). Critical incidents. In J. Kitaeff (Ed.), *Handbook of police psychology* (pp. 491–507). New York, NY: Routledge.

Brough, P. (2004). Comparing the influence of traumatic and organizational stressors on the psychological health of police, fire and ambulance officers. *International Journal of Stress Management*, *11*(3), 224–227. doi:10.1037/1072-5245.11.3.227

Canadian Standards Association. (2013). *Psychological health and safety in the workplace— Prevention, promotion, and guidance to staged implementation. CAN/CSA-Z1003-13/BNQ 9700-803/2013.* National Standard of Canada.

Carlan, P. E., & Nored, L. S. (2008). An examination of officer stress: Should police departments implement mandatory counseling? *Journal of Police and Criminal Psychology*, *23*(1), 8–15. doi:10.1007/s11896-008-9015-x

Charles, L. E., Burchfiel, C. M., Fekedulegn, D., Vila, B., Hartley, T. A., Slavan, J., & Violanti, J. M. et al. (2007). Shiftwork and sleep: The Buffalo Police Health Study. *Policing: An International Journal of Police Strategies & Management*, *30*(2), 215–227. doi:10.1108/13639510710753225

Clark, D., White, E., & Violanti, J. M. (2012). Law enforcement suicide: Current knowledge and future directions. *The Police Chief*, *79*(5), 48–51.

Cohen, S., Gottlieb, B., & Underwood, L. (2000). Social relationships and health. In S. Cohen, L. Gottlieb, & B. Gottlieb (Eds.), *Social support measurement and intervention: A guide for health and social scientists* (pp. 3–28). New York, NY: Oxford University Press. doi:10.1093/med:psych/9780195126709.003.0001

Collins, P. A., & Gibbs, A. (2003). Stress in police officers: A study of the origins, prevalence and severity of stress-related symptoms within a county police force. *Occupational Medicine*, *53*(4), 256–264. doi:10.1093/occmed/kqg061 PMID:12815123

COPS Office. (2012). *Community policing defined.* Washington, DC: Office of Community Oriented Policing Services. Retrieved from http://ric-zai-inc.com/Publications/cops-p157-pub.pdf

COPS Office. (2014). *20 years of community oriented policing*. Washington, DC: Office of Community Oriented Policing Services.

COPS Office. (2015). *President's Task Force on 21st century policing implementation guide: Moving from recommendations to action*. Washington, DC: Office of Community Oriented Policing Services.

Czarnecki, F., & McArdle, D. Q. (2012). A synopsis of some featured departments providing medical support to police field operations. *The Police Chief*, *79*(12), 70–75.

Famili, A., Kirschner, M., & Gamez, A. (2014). Vicarious traumatization: A guide for managing the silent stressor. *The Police Chief*, *81*(9), 26–30.

Gentz, D. (1990). The psychological impact of critical incidents on police officers. In J. T. Reese, J. M. Horne, & C. Dunning (Eds.), *Critical incidents in policing* (pp. 175–181). Washington, DC: Federal Bureau of Investigation.

Gersons, B. P. (1989). Patterns of PTSD among police officers following shooting incidents: A two-dimensional model and treatment implications. *Journal of Traumatic Stress*, *2*(3), 247–257. doi:10.1002/jts.2490020302

Greene, L., & Kirschman, E. (2001). *On-line education, resources, and support for law enforcement families: Final report. (Document No. 186749)*. Washington, DC: U.S. Department of Justice.

Grossman, D. (1995). *On killing: The psychological cost of learning to kill in war and society*. Boston, MA: Little, Brown.

Grossman, D. (2004). *On combat: The psychology and physiology of deadly conflict in war and peace*. St. Louis, MO: PPCT Research Publications.

Hartley, T. A., Fekedulegn, D., Burchfield, C. M., Andrew, M. E., & Violanti, J. M. (2011). Health disparities in police officers: Comparisons to the U.S. general population. *International Journal of Emergency Mental Health*, *13*(4), 211–220. PMID:22900455

Hoban, J. E., & Gourlie, B. J. (2014). *The Ethical protector: Essays on police ethics, tactics, and techniques*. Spring Lake, NJ: RGI Media and Publications.

Humphrey, R. L. (1992). *Values for a new millennium*. Spring Lake, NJ: The Life Values Press.

Hurrell, J. J., Nelson, D. L., & Simmons, B. L. (1998). Measuring job stressors and strains: Where we have been, where we are and where we need to go. *Journal of Occupational Health Psychology*, *3*(4), 368–389. doi:10.1037/1076-8998.3.4.368 PMID:9805282

International Association of Chiefs of Police. (2006). *Peer support guidelines*. Retrieved from http://www.theiacp.org/psych_services_section/

International Association of Chiefs of Police. (2012). *Center for Officer Safety and Wellness*. Retrieved from http://www.theiacp.org/centerforofficersafetyandwellness

International Association of Chiefs of Police. (2013). *Officer involved shooting guidelines*. Retrieved from http://www.theiacp.org/psych_services_section/

International Association of Chiefs of Police. (2014). *IACP National Symposium on Law Enforcement Officer Suicide and Mental Health: Breaking the Silence on Law Enforcement Suicides*. Washington, DC: Office of Community Oriented Policing Services.

Janoff-Bulman, R. (1992). *Shattered assumptions: Towards a new psychology of trauma*. New York, NY: The Free Press.

Kirschman, E. (2007). *I love a cop: What police families need to know* (Rev. ed.). New York, NY: The Guilford Press.

Kirschman, E., Kamena, M., & Fay, J. (2014). *Counseling cops: What clinicians need to know*. New York, NY: The Guilford Press.

Kuhns, J. B., Macquire, E. R., & Leach, N. R. (2015). *Health, safety, and wellness program case studies in law enforcement*. Washington, DC: Office of Community Oriented Policing Services.

Lazarus, R. S., & Folkman, S. (1984). *Stress, appraisal, and coping*. New York, NY: Springer Publishing Company.

Liberman, A. M., Best, S. R., Metzler, T. J., Fagan, J. A., Weiss, D. S., & Marmar, C. R. (2002). Routine occupational stress and psychological distress in police. *Policing: An International Journal of Police Strategies & Management*, *25*(2), 421–439. doi:10.1108/13639510210429446

Lorenz, J., Hill, L., & Samimi, B. (2000). Occupational needlestick injuries in a metropolitan police force. *American Journal of Preventive Medicine*, *18*(2), 146–150. doi:10.1016/S0749-3797(99)00137-3 PMID:10698245

Mangold, K. (2014). *Confidence in conflict for everyday life*. Milwaukee, WI: Truths Publishing.

Maquen, S., Metzler, T. J., McCaslin, S. E., Inslicht, S. S., Henn-Haase, C., Neylan, T. C., & Marmar, C. R. (2009). Routine work environment stress and PTSD symptoms in police officers. *The Journal of Nervous and Mental Disease*, *197*(10), 754–760. doi:10.1097/NMD.0b013e3181b975f8 PMID:19829204

McCann, L., & Pearlman, L. A. (1990). Vicarious traumatization: A framework for understanding the psychological effects of working with victims. *Journal of Traumatic Stress*, *3*(1), 131–149. doi:10.1007/BF00975140

McWilliams, S., & Hamilton, I. (2015). BLUE: Starting the conversation about officer stress and depression. *The Police Chief*, *82*(5), 22–25. PMID:26705371

Mikkelsen, A., & Burke, R. (2004). Work-family concerns of Norwegian police officers: Antecedents and consequences. *International Journal of Stress Management*, *11*(4), 429–444. doi:10.1037/1072-5245.11.4.429

Nash, W. P. (2007). Combat/operational stress adaptations and injuries. In C. R. Figley & W. P. Nash (Eds.), *Combat stress injury* (pp. 33–63). New York, NY: Routledge.

O'Hara, A. F., & Violanti, J. M. (2009). Police suicide: A web surveillance of national data. *International Journal of Emergency Mental Health*, *11*(1), 17–23. PMID:19637497

Pole, N. (2007). The psychophysiology of posttraumatic stress disorder: A meta-analysis. *Psychological Bulletin*, *133*(5), 725–746. doi:10.1037/0033-2909.133.5.725 PMID:17723027

Roland, J. (2011). Developing and maintaining successful peer support programs in law enforcement organizations. In J. Kitaeff (Ed.), *Handbook of police psychology* (pp. 509–524). New York, NY: Routledge.

Sanberg, E. L., Brito, C. S., Luna, A. M., & McFadden, S. M. (2010). *A guide to occupational health and safety for law enforcement executives*. Washington, DC: Police Executive Research Forum.

Shalev, A. Y., Freedman, S., Peri, T., Brandes, D., Sahar, T., Orr, S. P., & Pitman, R. K. (1998). Prospective study of posttraumatic stress disorder and depression following trauma. *The American Journal of Psychiatry*, *155*(5), 630–637. doi:10.1176/ajp.155.5.630 PMID:9585714

Shay, J. (1994). *Achilles in Vietnam: Combat trauma and the undoing of character*. New York, NY: Scribner.

Shay, J. (2002). *Odysseus in America: Combat trauma and the trials of homecoming*. New York, NY: Scribner.

Shushko, J. C. (2015). *Tie-ins for life*. Spring Lake, NJ: RGI Media and Publications.

UK Parliament Select Committee on Work and Pensions. (2004). *Strategy for a healthy police service*. Retrieved from http://www.publications.parliament.uk/pa/cm200304/ cmselect/cmworpen/456/4051908.htm

United States Marine Corps. (2006). *A Concept for Functional Fitness*. Washington, DC: USMC. Retrieved from http://library.crossfit.com/free/pdf/USMCFunctionalFitnessConcept.pdf

U.S. Bureau of Labor Statistics. (2014). *Fatal occupational injuries in 2014*. Retrieved from http://www.bls.gov/iif/oshcfoi1.htm

Violanti, J. M., Fekedulegn, D., Charles, L. E., Andrew, M. E., Hartley, T. A., Mnatsakanova, A., & Burchfield, C. M. (2009). Suicide in police work: Exploring potential contributing influences. *American Journal of Criminal Justice*, *34*(1-2), 41–53. doi:10.1007/s12103-008-9049-8

Violanti, J. M., Mnatsakanova, A., Burchfield, C. M., Hartley, T. A., & Andrew, M. E. (2012). Police suicide in small departments: A comparative analysis. *International Journal of Emergency Mental Health*, *14*(3), 157–162. PMID:23894796

World Economic Forum in Partnership with Right Management. (2010). *The wellness imperative: Creating more effective organisations*. Geneva, Switzerland: World Economic Forum.

Zimmerman, F. H. (2012). Cardiovascular disease and risk factors in law enforcement personnel: A comprehensive review. *Cardiology Review*, *20*, 159–166. PMID:22314143

Zula, K. (2014). Workplace wellness programs: A comparison between best practice guidelines and implementation. *Journal of Applied Business Research*, *30*(3), 783–792. doi:10.19030/jabr.v30i3.8564

Chapter 12
Peer Support in Public Safety Organizations

Nancy K. Bohl-Penrod
The Counseling Team International, USA

Daniel W. Clark
Washington State Patrol, USA

ABSTRACT

Peer supporters are a vital resource for members of the public safety community. Peers are often the first to notice when colleagues are exhibiting symptoms of psychological distress. Due to the cultural norms and the personality traits of those drawn to this career field, many public safety officers prefer to confide in peers rather than to obtain the assistance of mental health professionals. Further, peer supporters can give public safety officers the reassurance and support they need to enlist the services of mental health professionals. This chapter reviews the development and application of peer support teams, addresses issues in selecting peer support team members and developing a program, reviews team organization options and training needs, and addresses common challenges.

INTRODUCTION

Peer support is a vital resource for members of the public safety community that emerged in many major law enforcement agencies in the 1980s (Reese, 1995). Leaders of the Boston (MA) Police Department, Washington State Patrol, Los Angeles (CA) Police Department (LAPD), and San Bernardino County (CA) Sheriff's Department were among those who early on recognized the importance of having a formal peer support program. Today, those four peer support programs, and many others, are thriving and continue to make a difference in the lives of officers who need help. In this chapter, the authors review the development and application of peer support teams, as well as address issues in selecting peer support team members and developing a viable program. Peer supporters are those individuals that work for a law enforcement agency in any capacity and attend peer support training to become members of the peer support team (see section on Training Peer Supporters). In addition, this chapter reviews team organization options and training needs, and addresses common challenges.

DOI: 10.4018/978-1-5225-0813-7.ch012

THE IMPACT OF PEER SUPPORT

In 2015, the Baltimore (MD) Police Department arrested an African American male, Freddie Gray. While transporting him, he suffered massive spinal injuries that lead to his death in the hospital. There were on-going protests after his funeral, which turned into the Baltimore riots. In the wake of the Baltimore disturbances, police officers there faced intense scrutiny and pressure as they watched their actions and motives being questioned by everyone from social media bloggers to television pundits (Laughland & Swaine, 2015). The criticism surrounding the city's police did not abate after the flames were extinguished or the debris cleared from the streets. Citizens also criticized the police officers for intentionally using aggressive driving to rough up African American suspects while in transit in departmental vans.

After indictments were handed down against six Baltimore police officers surrounding the in-custody death of Freddie Gray, some Baltimore police officers felt abandoned by their leaders and feared the possibility of criminal prosecution (Baldwin & Ford, 2015). During this tumultuous time, when trusting someone could have dire consequences if confidences were broken, Baltimore police officers received support from members of the New York (NY) Police Department peer support team, who have often faced their own tremendous public scrutiny and pressure. The peer supporters from New York Police Department (NYPD) watched their fellow officers in Baltimore struggle and it did not take long for them to provide help to their colleagues. Ten members of the NYPD peer support team provided what few others could — understanding from a trusted and respected source (Celona & Fredericks, 2015).

Peer supporters are a vital resource because peers are often the first to notice when colleagues are exhibiting symptoms of psychological distress (Everly, 2015). Due to the cultural norms and the personality traits of those drawn to police work, the authors' experiences as police psychologists for over two decades lead us to conclude that many public safety officers are more likely to confide in peers than to obtain the assistance of mental health professionals. Unlike mental health professionals, peer supporters have the potential for instant credibility and are in a unique position to provide colleagues with a much-needed sense of normalcy after a critical incident. A critical incident refers to an event that is outside the normal range of experiences and, many times, can challenge a first responder's ability to cope (Everly, 2015). Contact with peer supporters may give public safety personnel the reassurance, support, and encouragement they need to enlist the services of mental health professionals. For example, after the San Bernardino terrorist attack of December 2, 2015, the first author received 45 calls from police officers who had previously been supported by peer support team members. Because of this earlier contact, these officers likely felt more comfortable reaching out to their mental health providers.

Several members of the Washington State Patrol's (WSP) peer support team and the second author traveled to New York City following the tragic events of 9/11 to support members of the NYPD and the New York City Fire Department (FDNY). As we walked around the impacted area, the WSP peers would approach NYPD or FDNY personnel with a WSP shoulder patch in their left hand and offer a handshake with their right hand, saying, "Hi! We're troopers with WSP, and we're here for a week to offer our support. Would you like one of our patches?" This simple, but highly straightforward approach seemed to result in expressions of gratitude and statements about how only other officers could understand what they had been through.

Peer supporters may be an invaluable resource when officers are depressed or suicidal. Peer supporters are trained to identify behaviors associated with suicidality and to begin the intervention process that may then result in a referral to the next higher level of care, such as a mental health professional, chaplain, or crisis intervention service (Kamena, Gentz, Hays, Bohl-Penrod, & Greene, 2011). Peer supporters are with officers on the front lines, may be available at all times, and bring empathy and a keen awareness of the importance of maintaining confidentiality. Peer supporters are in a unique position to provide their colleagues with a sense of normalcy, validation, and acceptance.

Given the cultural norms and stigmas that continue to surround the use of mental health services, public safety officers are more likely to confide in peers than to seek out mental health professionals (Kamena et al., 2011). Peer supporters serve as conduits or "bridges," providing peers with information about the benefits of counseling, as well as encouraging them to seek these services (Allen, Jones, Douglas, & Clark, 2014; Grauwiler, Barocas, & Mills, 2008). Access to support, from either peers or mental health providers, can result in a reduction of depressive symptoms such as isolation, shame, and hopelessness, providing much needed psychological relief.

Utilizing peer supporters has proven to be one of the most effective tactics for public safety officers to cope in the aftermath of critical incidents (Clark & Haley, 2007; Force, 2013; IACP, 2011; Lott, 2013; Roland, 2011; Trompetter, Corey, Schmidt, & Tracy, 2011). Several studies have shown the power of peer support, both alone and as part of the "Helping Triad" (e.g., Bohl, 1998).

The "Helping Triad" is composed of Mental Health Professionals, Chaplains, and Peer Supporters. When these three different resources synchronize their efforts to help departments/agencies and offer their assistance as a team, the competiveness which can occur among these three different support services is minimized. Ideally, these three services train together and develop the ability to work side by side when responding to critical incidents. Since law enforcement personnel vary greatly in their willingness to seek help and from whom, the "Helping Triad" provides them the opportunity to turn to whichever of the three support services they are most comfortable reaching out to for assistance. Whether it is for spiritual encouragement, professional help, or co-worker peer support, employees benefit from the advantage of having access to all three services. In fact, there is research evidence that police officers who made greater use of peer support following a line-of-duty shooting experienced less severe trauma symptoms (Solomon & Horn, 1986).

In addition to major critical incidents and traumas, peer supporters may also be helpful in providing support following a variety of personal life events such as relationship problems, death of a loved one, financial setbacks, etc. (Kamena et al., 2011). Other reasons to access peer support might include health concerns, parenting challenges, burnout, and anxiety. Peer support may also be useful for family members (Gupton, Axelrod, Cornell, Curran, Hood, Kelly, & Moss, 2011), for assisting ill and injured officers, and in addiction treatment (Kroll, 2014).

Creamer et al. (2012) assert that peer supporters should be used as a routine part of employee health and wellness, not just for high risk events or critical incidents. For example, employees struggling with a new supervisor, new or revised job responsibilities, job situations triggering past personal struggles, retirement worries, Internal Affairs investigations, or being placed on a job improvement plan may all benefit from peer support.

MECHANISMS OF ACTION FOR PEER SUPPORT

What are the mechanisms of action for peer support? One is the camaraderie of sharing an experience with someone who truly understands. For example, a peer support team member who has used lethal force in the line of duty may be in a position to provide peer support to another officer who had to use lethal force in carrying out his or her duties (Everly, 2015). A "peer" is someone who has similar training, background, and work experiences. The closer to a "true peer" we can provide, the more likely a solid rapport or connection will build between the peer supporter and the person seeking the support (Everly, 2015). For example, provide a peer supporter from dispatch when a dispatcher is looking for someone to talk with, and provide an officer who has been involved in a shooting to talk with another officer who was involved in a recent shooting, etc.

The question of whether a dispatcher can provide peer support for an officer, or if an officer can provide peer support for administrative or clerical staff is likely to be asked. Our perspective is that they can; however, logic and experience suggest the closer one gets to a "true peer," the more likely the individual seeking peer support is to have a positive and helpful interaction from the very beginning. Certainly more research is needed on the relationship of occupational similarity to the effectiveness of peer support efforts in law enforcement settings.

On a recent disaster response, the second author was asked to talk with the flight crew of a helicopter. He asked a peer with flight experience on similar missions to be his team member. When the flight crew began talking about an indicator light that forced them to the ground for a safety check, the peer knew exactly which warning light the crew was complaining about. This indicator light is infamous (according to the peer) for just being a burned out bulb; however, protocol was to return immediately to base to have the situation investigated, much to the frustration of the flight crew because they were involved in ongoing rescues. The tight peer-to-peer connection with a knowledgeable, credible, and experienced peer appeared to greatly assist the helicopter flight crew in addressing their reactions.

Peer support is particularly helpful when working with groups who are specially trained or who have a unique culture, such as law enforcement (Everly, 2015). This is fully consistent with our experience working in law enforcement but also with other groups such as firefighters, school personnel, and nurses. Peers understand the culture, including the specific terms and slang used in specific occupational contexts. For employees receiving peer support, a key benefit may be the greater perceived empathy and respect from talking with a peer who understands the nuances of the situation. This can build initial trust and rapport in the relationship. The second author often talks in training about the "been there, done that badge," which lends peer supporters credibility. This is not a competitive, "I can top your story" mindset but a sense of empathy and, "I understand what you are experiencing because I've been there."

"Tommy," a WSP trooper, was assaulted during a traffic stop that ended in a struggle for his firearm. Fortunately, Tommy regained control of the situation and subdued the suspect. Peer support responded and provided assistance. Tommy was so impacted by this support that he contacted the second author and asked to join the Peer Support Team. Shortly after his peer support training, several young troopers in his district were involved in a pursuit which ended in shots fired. None of the troopers were injured, but this was a critical incident for them. As the second author drove to the district, Tommy contacted him and asked to sit in on the small group support discussion (often referred to as a *defusing*, a more immediate and smaller version of a formal psychological debriefing group with homogeneously exposed participants). During the defusing with the impacted officers, the second author provided psychoeducation about critical incidents, how they can impact people, and the importance of self-care. The young troopers listened and nodded, saying, "Thanks, Doc." Then, Tommy shared his story and how his incident had impacted him, and the young troopers listened *intently*. Although both shared approximately the same ideas, these young troopers truly listened to their peer with the "been there, done that badge," highlighting for the second author the absolute importance of using peers.

LIMITED RESEARCH

Much of the literature regarding peer support is anecdotal or descriptive. Peer support services are consumer driven and voluntary, limiting the opportunity for randomized clinical trials. Further, many peer support programs are built around a philosophy of inclusion, again limiting the use of randomized clinical trials (Grauwiler, Barocas, & Mills, 2008; Resnick & Rosenheck, 2008).

Resnick and Rosenheck (2008) compared the Vet-to-Vet program, a peer education and support program, to standard care without peer support in samples of veterans who were seeking care at the Community Reintegration Program at the Errera Community Care Center, a VA program for veterans with severe mental illnesses. They concluded that veterans enrolled after the implementation of the Vet-to-Vet program showed superior outcomes compared to veterans who received standard care on measures of general empowerment.

Two studies examined guidelines for peer support programs whose employees were at high risk of exposure to potentially traumatic events. First, Sheehan, Everly, and Langlieb (2004) surveyed 11 federal, state, and city law enforcement agencies, looking for best practices in coping with major critical incidents. They reported five key findings: (a) all 11 law enforcement agencies recognized the value of early psychological intervention, (b) all agencies used a phase-sensitive, multi-component crisis intervention system, (c) each agency viewed peer support as a "virtual imperative" for a successful program, (d) all agencies recognized the importance of specialized crisis intervention training prior to introducing the program, and (e) all agencies used a variety of tactical tools to deliver services, including 1:1 crisis intervention or peer support, small and large group interventions, and family support.

Second, Creamer et al. (2012) conducted an international survey of recognized experts in order to develop a consensus on evidence-informed peer support guidelines for high-risk organizations. They asked 92 clinicians, researchers, and peer support practitioners from 17 countries to rate statements generated from the existing literature using a 3-round web-based Delphi process. From this, eight key recommendations were developed regarding the goals of peer support, selection of peer supporters, training and accreditation, mental health professional use, peer support roles, access to peer support, caring for peer supporters, and program evaluation.

DEVELOPING A PEER SUPPORT PROGRAM

Peer support programs require some effort to establish, but with the proper infrastructure in place, they can be run without extensive oversight or significant time-consuming efforts. Experts recommend having a steering committee comprised of a mental health professional, sworn and non-sworn employees, management, and supervisory personnel (Kamena et al., 2011). Essential to this process is support from department administration and leaders of the employee association or union. Without this support, the program may struggle to gain widespread acceptance, which could result in animosity between the rank and file and management, according to Finn and Tomz (1997). In some cases, peer support programs have failed because the program was forced on management teams before they were ready or had a complete understanding of what such a program entailed (Finn & Tomz, 1997). When a program has the support of management, management will likely allow for marketing the program and for the peer supporters to provide support while on duty.

Peer support experts also recommend that teams craft their own unique peer support policy manual that spells out the specific details of the policies and procedures for the program's daily operations. Furthermore, the policy manual should detail the kinds of tools used by peer supporters when helping peers, especially when engaging those in emotionally intense situations (Kamena et al., 2011).

Peer support policies should contain a mission statement, so all in the program and those who will use the program understand the mission of the peer support program. This allows everyone to understand the mission and goals of the peer support team, alleviating misunderstandings regarding the concept. For example, the International Association of Chiefs of Police (IACP) Police Psychological Services Section approved a set of Peer Support guidelines that states, "The goal of peer support is to provide all public safety employees in an agency the opportunity to receive emotional and tangible support through times of personal or professional crisis and to help anticipate and address potential difficulties" (IACP, 2011, p. 1).

In the policy, the duties, responsibilities, and expectations of peer supporters are explained, along with the benefits and limitations to peer support assistance. For instance, a peer supporter cannot provide the professional care a mental health professional can, nor can they provide the same level of confidentiality protection. On the other hand, peer supporters are often more accessible than mental health professionals because they may already be on scene or on their shift at the time a coworker seeks the assistance of a peer supporter.

Most peer support policies address when and if peer supporters are compensated by the department for their off-duty peer support activities. There are departments that will compensate their peer supporters if the department asks them to respond to assist during or after an incident, while others consider peer support activities voluntary and do not offer compensation. It is important that the policies also cover critical issues such as confidentiality, discipline, and the role of peer support personnel in internal investigations.

Many peer support teams assign different levels of oversight, which should be delineated in the policy so everyone understands the different roles. Many assign an employee as the coordinator to run the program, and to work closely with a mental health professional who may also be their agency consultant or in-house police psychologist. The coordinator does not work alone, and since a coordinator does not have the same protection as a mental health professional regarding information disclosed to him or her, it helps protect the agency/department when a mental health consultant is involved. The coordinator can lean on the consultant as someone who can help out in difficult situations. The consultant will help shoulder any problems that may occur inside the department because of the peer support program. In addition, as noted earlier, an advisory board or steering committee should be formed to help with creative ideas and guidance. Establishing the criteria for removing a peer support team member is also important. The criteria for removal from the program often include issues such as breaching confidentiality, being subject to workplace discipline, or failing to attend mandatory trainings (Kamena et al., 2011).

Peer supporters should be provided with the opportunity to request a hiatus from their duties when their personal or professional obligations become overwhelming. Peer supporters should be encouraged to engage in self-care and take needed time off to prevent burn out. A "Memorandum of Understanding" (MOU) between the department and the individual peer support team member should be signed before anyone becomes part of a peer support program. Employees who become peer supporters should be willing to agree to the following: attending the basic 2-5 day training course; attending 1 day of updated training once a year; completing the monthly data summary reports; maintaining confidentiality (unless reporting is necessary); informing the program coordinator if they need to withdraw from the program temporarily due to personal or professional circumstances; and accepting that they serve at the direction and pleasure of their department leader and can be removed from the program at any time without cause.

The IACP peer support guidelines are well developed and can be used as a template. These guidelines spell out the importance of confidentiality, the need for training from a mental health professional, and the recommended steps for selection and non-selection of potential peer supporters (IACP, 2011). This policy is reviewed and updated by the Police Psychological Services Section every 5 years, then reapproved by the IACP senior leadership.

The IACP guidelines cover the purpose of having peer support programs and address the differences regarding privacy, confidentiality, and privileged communication. These three concepts are critical to peer support. Privacy is a personal right which limits the access of others to certain information about one's self, body, mind, etc. Confidentiality is a moral, ethical, professional duty to refrain from speaking about matters disclosed during a peer support contact, with the exception of certain mandated reporting criteria such as child abuse, elder abuse, suicidal or homicidal intent, etc. Privileged communication is a legal protection which provides relief from the duty to speak in court proceedings about certain matters. Privileged communication is most often applied to relationships such as doctor-patient, attorney-client, priest-confessor, and between spouses. Some states have included trained peer supporters on this select list (IACP, 2011).

The IACP guidelines also cover the potential role conflicts a peer supporter may experience and the requirements regarding reporting to a supervisor any information that must be divulged. It contains a section explaining the administrative policies that are set forth by management staff. Selection and de-selection are reviewed, as well as how mental health professionals provide ongoing consultation to the peer support team. The importance of basic and advanced training is discussed along with listing what types of content domains should be covered (see section on Training Peer Supporters).

SELECTING PEER SUPPORTERS

Peer support programs are not without their challenges. Peer supporters must maintain confidentiality and be careful not to use their position to feed the rumor mill or their own personal or professional agendas. Unlike mental health professionals, in some states, peer supporters are not bound by any legal or ethical authority to maintain the confidences of the colleagues they aid. However, in other states, such as Washington, most communications to peer supporters are regarded as privileged and legal protections are in place (see Revised Code of Washington 5.60.060 (6)(a)). Peer Support Team leaders are encouraged to check their local statutes and consult with an attorney. Lapses or misconduct by peer supporters can have devastating effects on those who trust them. Given the power and influence peer supporters may wield, it is imperative to take great care when evaluating candidates for peer support positions.

The screening process begins by sending out a request for volunteers. This "memorandum" explains the purpose of the program, and what the expectations are from the Chief or Sheriff. To ensure that recruitment is seen as fair and impartial, maximum distribution of this memorandum or advertisement is crucial. Those wanting to be peer supporters are asked to fill out an application and write a short paragraph explaining their motivation to be in the program. Their statements should address the strengths they possess which make them qualified to be peer supporters and what experiences they have had that would qualify them to serve with the program (Creamer et al., 2012).

Some agencies or departments add an additional step in the process and publish the list of applicants so the entire department has an opportunity to nominate those they want to be in the program. The "Nominations for Peer Supporters" forms are sent to the offices of the consulting mental health professional, who tallies the votes. This is to ensure privacy and prevent the department from knowing how many votes a person did or did not receive. These nominations are cross-referenced with those that want to be in the program and those that were chosen to be in the program. The department receives a list of the applicants with the most nominations, often the top 10 candidates.

With or without this additional step, the peer supporter applicants are now scheduled to go through an oral interview. It is imperative that these candidates have the respect of their peers and that they have good reputations (Creamer et al., 2012). This increases the trust in the program and gives the program credibility. It may also increase supervisors' willingness to refer to the program, as well as their willingness to allow peer supporters to assist while on duty.

Interviews with potential peer supporters should be conducted by a group including the department's designated mental health professional, as well as other peer supporters. The IACP guidelines recommend peer supporters enter the screening process in good standing with the department and recommended by their supervisors (IACP, 2011). The selection committee should take into account the applicant's exposure to traumatic situations, maturity, credibility, and motivation for volunteering to become a peer supporter. Some suggest providing applicants with possible scenarios to ascertain how they would handle delicate situations and to gain some insight into their empathy and judgment (Kamena et al., 2011).

TRAINING PEER SUPPORTERS

Communication skills and good judgment are critical skills for a peer supporter. As a result, training must focus on communication skills, such as active listening and learning how to assess problem situations. Furthermore, the peer supporters must learn when personal relationships would make it inappropriate for that peer supporter to be involved due to conflicts of interest (Creamer et al., 2012; Kamena et al., 2011).

Initial Training

The first training sessions typically span between 2-5 days, and should address the importance of privacy, confidentiality, ethical issues, and stress management skills. While lecture is an important component to instruction, trainees should also be required to demonstrate the ability to use the skills that are covered in the trainings. Role playing, small group exercises, and "fish bowl" (a fish bowl activity is when a learner role plays in front of the other attendees) are all adult learning activities that are incorporated into the training. Although many trainees are initially reluctant to engage in role plays, our experience is that comments on training course evaluations often refer to role plays as one of the most effective aspects of the training. Training should also include education about alcohol and substance abuse, suicide assessment, and crisis intervention (Kamena et al., 2011).

A mental health professional should be involved in the development of the training program as well as in determining if a trainee has demonstrated the required skill set (Creamer et al., 2012; Kamena et al., 2011; Woods, 2014). Training should continue on a regular basis, ideally provided by the mental health professional who provided the original training, and who may also serve as the consultant or lead for the team. Attendance should be required of all peer supporters throughout the year.

The Police Psychological Services Section of IACP (2011) recommends the following training topics for peer support teams. Many of these topics may be taught in the initial training, and others may be included in subsequent trainings. Peer support training is not "one and done," but should be supplemented with at least annual updates. Recommended topics include:

1. Confidentiality
2. Role conflict
3. Limits and liability
4. Ethical issues
5. Communication facilitation and listening skills
6. Nonverbal communication
7. Problem assessment
8. Problem-solving skills
9. Cross-cultural issues
10. Psychological diagnoses
11. Medical conditions often confused with psychiatric disorders
12. Stress management
13. Burn-out
14. Grief management
15. Domestic violence
16. HIV and AIDS
17. Suicide assessment
18. Crisis management intervention
19. Work-related critical incident stress management
20. Alcohol and substance abuse
21. When to seek licensed mental health consultation and referral information
22. Relationship issues and concerns
23. Military support
24. Local resources (e.g., social services, AA meetings, childcare resources, etc.)

Additional Topics

Other subjects presented may include topics such as grief, helping someone from the LGBTQ community, and how to handle a line-of-duty death. Critical incidents in policing are explained so the peer supporter has a good understanding of the emotional aftermath of a significant traumatic event that can impact the employee and/or department. Some officers have reported feeling that they are "going crazy" because of the emotional intensity of their reactions (to a traumatic event). Such officers need to know that what they are experiencing are normal reactions to abnormal situations. A fellow officer can provide the validation of their emotional responses, given his or her status as one who has "been there."

It is essential that peer supporters understand they are not providing therapy. They are taught not to call themselves "peer counselors" because that term may be misleading. They are providing support and are trained to refer to a mental health professional or chaplain if necessary. Understanding the limits of peer support is just as important as knowing the value of peer support. Peer supporters should be comfortable asking questions and understanding their limits (Finn & Tomz, 1997). There are legal limits to confidentiality such as threats to self, threats to others, and any criminal activity. Every department should set up their guidelines for confidentiality, and peer supporters are expected to adhere to their specific departmental guidelines and state requirements.

In the training, peer supporters are taught when and where to refer someone whom they know needs more help than a peer supporter can offer. Providing a guest speaker from the Police Chaplains Corps during training is essential, both to address how chaplains may be helpful during a crisis and to introduce peer supporters to a referral option. Other referral options may be to a book, mobile apps, journal article, mental health professional, physician, self-help group, hotline, etc.

Crisis intervention is covered in the basic class to help those who need immediate assistance due to a crisis the peer might be experiencing. The "Middleton Model" (US Immigration and Customs Enforcement, 2013) is a three-step model easily remembered by those wanting to become peer supporters. Family and relationship issues are discussed, as well as how a peer supporter can assist someone who is having personal problems outside of work.

Getting the Word Out

After selection and training of the peer supporters, teams need to let their agency/department know who is on the team. This can be accomplished in several ways. One is by word of mouth, but this is likely to provide spotty notification. Although personal recommendations carry a lot of weight with officers, officers who have been helped by a peer supporter may not want to advertise this.

Second, brochures or flyers posted in prominent places may be helpful. The WSP Peer Support Team printed posters and attached flyers and business card holders to the poster, so interested parties could take either a flyer or business card in order to contact someone on the team.

Third, it may be worthwhile to request that the agency's Public Information Office interview team members and publish an article about the team in the daily/weekly/monthly agency newsletter. In such publications, it may help to include a phone number or website address where additional information could be obtained.

Fourth, publish the team roster on the agency website. The WSP Peer Support Team has a webpage listing all team members, their photo, and the contact information each peer supporter chooses to publish. This encourages employees to self-select their peer supporter from the published list of trained peers (Creamer et al., 2012).

Fifth, add the team list to the Computer Aided Dispatch (CAD) system the agency/department uses. When employees contact dispatch seeking a peer supporter, dispatchers can quickly access the list and provide options to the employee.

TEAM ORGANIZATION

The authors are aware of two types of teams and two primary organization styles. The two types of teams are single agency and multi-agency. If an agency or organization has enough personnel, it may choose to staff an internal peer support team. Larger agencies, such as WSP, LAPD, or Los Angeles Sheriff's Department, have such an internal team. These teams may reach out to outside entities, but their primary duty is to their own agency. For example, the WSP team has 40-50 members, all WSP employees, who focus on supporting the agency's 2,100+ employees; however, members of the WSP team may be "loaned" to other organizations who have a need and request support, upon approval of the WSP Chief. WSP's Peer Support Team reached out to support state employees following an earthquake in 2001 whose epicenter was near the state capital, and which impacted many state employees. Peer support team members spoke to several hundred state employees over a two-day period when the employees were allowed to return to their work sites.

The second type of team is multi-agency, and may be based on geography such as a county focused team. These teams may have members from not only other agencies but other disciplines, such as police, fire, emergency medical services (EMS), dispatch, and search and rescue. This second type of team may be arguably more versatile, due to the varied disciplines of their members. In more rural areas, where an incident may involve multiple officers from multiple jurisdictions, multiple dispatchers, an ambulance crew, and a fire engine crew, the multi-agency team has the ability to "match" support team members with the responders.

Both types of teams typically select either a team structure where a mental health professional (MHP) leads the team or the MHP acts as a consultant to the team. Many teams lead via a steering or advisory committee that may be composed of the MHP, an administrator, and several senior peers. This steering committee makes policy decisions regarding the team, selects new team members, and disciplines team members when needed (IACP, 2011).

COMMON CHALLENGES

One of the most significant challenges to a successful peer support program is a perceived lack of confidentiality, whether due to an actual breach of confidentiality by a peer support team member, the perception of a breach by a team member, or by an agency not respecting or protecting the need for confidentiality of a peer support team. One of the reasons employees seek out peer support is the confidential nature of the contact. When confidentiality is perceived to be violated, confidence in the entire team is likely to be jeopardized.

How does the team "fix" a perceived confidentiality problem? First, explore what happened to determine if there actually was a violation and, if so, make what reparations are possible with the aggrieved employee/s. The steering committee needs to decide if the peer supporter responsible needs to be removed from the team. If there was no violation, explain to the aggrieved party the circumstances and the limitations of confidentiality.

The possibility that the agency itself did not respect the confidentiality of the peer support team may be addressed through developing an MOU outlining the importance of confidentiality and the agency's support for the team. An important next step is to have the Chief or Sheriff endorse the MOU. Ideally, this should be done proactively, perhaps as an attachment to the aforementioned team policy.

Lack of support by either management or the relevant association/union is a potential challenge. Ideally, such support is sought during the team development phase so that it is a non-issue. However, sometimes events occur where either management or the association/union is concerned about the team's functioning. Collaborative discussions with the concerned parties will hopefully address their concerns. This is where keeping statistics and having a well thought out policy can be instrumental. Teams can demonstrate their usefulness by citing the number of people or hours peer support members have spoken with employees.

Compensation for peer support team members may be another challenge. Most peer support teams are composed of volunteers; however some agencies offer compensation to team members. What about providing support during non-work hours? If the peer supporter is providing support on his or her own time and needs to travel to do so, the authors recommend the peer supporter call his or her watch commander or equivalent supervisor so this notification can satisfy legal and insurance concerns. The peer supporter can then work with his or her chain of command to arrange for comp time, or some other form of compensation. At times, the chain of command may call for an off-duty peer support person, e.g., in the event of an employee injury, a gruesome accident, or difficult crime scene. These call-out times are generally covered in the peer supporter's general bargaining agreement.

At times, peer supporters themselves experience challenges in their own personal or professional lives that may lead to decreased effectiveness or impairment. Or, they may be assigned to a position that is incompatible with peer support, such as an internal affairs assignment. In either case, a temporary leave of absence from the team may be the most effective resolution to this challenge. This is an issue best addressed in the peer support team policy.

Removal of a team member is a difficult issue. This may be due to a perceived breach of confidentiality or the team member may no longer be considered in good standing within the agency. Team member removal is another issue best addressed in the peer support team policy, and presented during initial training of the team member.

Countertransference, or over-identifying with the person seeking peer support, can be a challenge. Ideally, the peer supporter needs to be able to identify with the person seeking help and empathize with that employee; however, over-identifying with the help-seeker is often counterproductive and may even be harmful (Everly, 2015). The best way to remedy the situation may be to find another peer supporter for the help-seeker to speak with or for the peer supporter to realize what is happening and take a mental and/or emotional step back, plus consult with the team mental health professional.

Finally, team- and self-care may be a challenge. As team members, peer supporters are exposed to other people's trauma, and even strong peer supporters can become overwhelmed, especially in large-scale incidents such as disaster response or the trauma of a line-of-duty death. Team care is not only the responsibility of the team leadership or steering committee, but much like a sports team, the peer support team needs to care for itself and be aware of, and reach out to, team members who are struggling (Creamer et al., 2012).

A common tactic for caring for the team is called "debrief the debriefers" or "post action staff support" (PASS). Not only is this good team self-care but it also demonstrates that the peer support team is practicing what it is teaching. A PASS is similar to a critical incident stress debriefing, but is shortened from seven phases to three phases. A PASS may be provided to peer support team members by other team members, or the team may want to ask an outside team member to lead the PASS (Potter, 2007). When Critical Incident Stress Management (CISM) teams deployed to New York to assist NYPD's peer assistance teams after the terrorist attacks of September 2011, one of the conditions was the deploying teams had to arrange for a PASS upon their return. The second author deployed to New York with members of his WSP Peer Support Team, and arranged for a PASS to be provided by the local Coast Guard Peer Support Team when the WSP team returned.

CONCLUSION

Peer support programs are uniquely positioned to help law enforcement personnel obtain assistance when facing professional or personal challenges. It appears likely that important ingredients of successful peer support programs include the shared backgrounds between peer supporters and support seekers, the sense of camaraderie that often prevails among police and public safety officers, as well as the maturity, interpersonal skills, and training of peer supporters. Through listening, understanding, and providing appropriate referrals, peer support programs serve proactively as an early-warning detection system to help individuals handle their personal problems. Peer support helps decrease the day-to-day stress of the law enforcement profession. It can also counter-balance the emotional strain of critical incidents, as well as prevent the accumulation of frustration, anger, and helplessness that could lead to substance abuse, depression, domestic violence, or suicide. Confidentiality and trust are critical components of a successful peer support program. A careful team member selection process and a well-conceived training program are likewise important. Not every police or public safety officer makes a good peer supporter. Those who are selected for peer support programs need to have their hearts in the right place and must learn how to provide support in effective ways. When a peer support program becomes an integral part of a law enforcement department's culture, the officers and other personnel in that department are likely to reap important, perhaps life-changing benefits. A peer support program also promotes trust and encourages the use of a department's mental health counseling services.

REFERENCES

Allen, S., Jones, C., Douglas, F., & Clark, D. (2014). Keeping our heroes safe: A comprehensive approach to destigmatizing mental health issues in law enforcement. *The Police Chief*, *81*, 34–38.

Baldwin, B., & Ford, D. (2015, June 10). Baltimore police officers break silence on riots, murder spike and Freddie Gray. *CNN*. Retrieved from http://www.cnn.com/2015/06/10/us/baltimore-police-officers-interview/

Bohl, N. (1998). The helping triad. *The Police Chief*, *98*, 135.

Celona, L., & Fredericks, B. (2015, May 26). NYPD visits Baltimore to help cops cope after riots. *New York Post*. Retrieved from http://nypost.com/2015/26/nypd-visits-baltimore-to-help-cops-cope-after-riots

Clark, D. W., & Haley, M. (2007). Crisis response tools for law enforcement. *The Police Chief*, *74*, 92–101.

Creamer, M. C., Varker, T., Bisson, J., Darte, K., Greenberg, N., Lau, W., & Forbes, D. et al. (2012). Guidelines for peer support in high-risk organizations: An international consensus study using the Delphi method. *Journal of Traumatic Stress*, *25*(2), 134–141. doi:10.1002/jts.21685 PMID:22522726

Everly, G. S. Jr. (2015). *Assisting individuals in crisis* (5th ed.). Baltimore, MD: International Critical Incident Stress Foundation.

Finn, P., & Tomz, J. E. (1997). *Developing a law enforcement stress program for officers and their families*. Washington, DC: US Department of Justice, Office of Justice Programs, National Institute of Justice.

Force, M. (2013). Compassion in law enforcement. *The Police Chief, 80*, 10–12.

Grauwiler, P., Barocas, B., & Mills, L. G. (2008). Police peer support programs: Current knowledge and practice. *International Journal of Emergency Mental Health, 10*(1), 27–38. PMID:18546757

Gupton, H. M., Axelrod, E., Cornell, L., Curran, S. F., Hood, C. J., Kelly, J., & Moss, J. (2011). Support and sustain: Psychological intervention for law enforcement personnel. *The Police Chief, 78*, 92–97.

US Immigration and Customs Enforcement. (2013). Crisis intervention in immigration and customs enforcement. In *Immigration and customs enforcement student handbook* (pp. 10-69). Washington, DC: U.S. Government Printing Office.

International Association of Chiefs of Police. (2011). *Peer support guidelines*. Retrieved from http://www.theiacp.org/portals/0/documents/pdfs/Psych-PeerSupportGuidelines.pdf

Kamena, M. D., Gentz, D., Hays, V., Bohl-Penrod, N., & Greene, L. W. (2011). Peer support teams fill an emotional void in law enforcement agencies. *The Police Chief, 78*, 80–84.

Kroll, R. (2014). Managing the dark side: Treating officers with addiction. *The Police Chief, 81*, 48–51.

Laughland, O., & Swaine, J. (2015, July 8). Baltimore police chief fired amid crime spike: 'Families are tired of feeling this pain'. *The Guardian*. Retrieved from http://www.theguardian.com/us-news/2015/jul/08/baltimore-police-chief-fired-freddie-gray-protests-report

Lott, L. (2013). Planning for a critical incident involving an officer. *The Police Chief, 80*, 14–15.

Potter, D. (2007). *Post Action Staff Support (PASS): A method for evaluating team member skills*. Retrieved from http://www.kantu.org/adobe/PASS Article 07.pdf

Reese, J. T. (1995). A history of police psychological services. In M. I. Kurke & E. M. Scrivner (Eds.), *Police psychology into the 21st century* (pp. 31–44). Hillsdale, NJ: Lawrence Erlbaum.

Resnick, S. G., & Rosenheck, R. A. (2008). Integrating peer-provided services: A quasi-experimental study of recovery orientation, confidence and empowerment. *Psychiatric Services (Washington, D.C.), 59*(11), 1307–1314. doi:10.1176/ps.2008.59.11.1307 PMID:18971407

Roland, J. E. (2011). Developing and maintaining successful peer support programs in law enforcement organizations. In J. Kitaeff (Ed.), *Handbook of police psychology* (pp. 509–524). New York, NY: Routledge Taylor & Francis Group.

Sheehan, D. C., Everly, G. S. Jr, & Langlieb, A. (2004). Current best practices: Coping with major critical incidents. *FBI Law Enforcement Bulletin, 73*, 1–13.

Solomon, R. M., & Horn, J. M. (1986). Peer support: A key element of coping with trauma. *Police Stress, 9*, 25–27.

Trompetter, P. S., Corey, D. M., Schmidt, W. W., & Tracy, D. (2011). Psychological factors after officer-involved shootings: Addressing officer needs and agency responsibilities. *The Police Chief, 78*, 28–33.

Woods, J. P. (2014, June). Prioritizing emotional & mental health through peer support. *The Police Chief, 81*, 10–11.

Section 5
Operational Consultation

Chapter 13
The Evolution of Police Interactions with People with Mental Health Problems:
The Third Generation (Strategic) Approach

Dorothy Cotton
PMHL Solutions, Canada

Terry G. Coleman
PMHL Solutions, Canada

ABSTRACT

As early as the 1970s, some police agencies began to develop education and training initiatives as well as specialized response initiatives to assist police in responding to calls for service involving people with mental health problems. Various versions of Memphis's Crisis Intervention Team program as well as various co-response models have become increasingly common. However, the effectiveness of these often stand-alone programs remains unclear. What has become clear is that police agencies require a strategic approach to interactions between police and vulnerable populations including those with mental health problems. This chapter, which provides an overview of the evolution of these specialized police responses, proposes that there is a need for a more comprehensive third generation approach—a strategic approach—rather than solely a "program" approach. Identification is made of specific areas in which the unique skills of psychologists are important in furthering the success of the necessary strategic approach.

INTRODUCTION

Interactions between police and people who appear to be experiencing mental health problems (P/MHP)[1] are both common and problematic. Although reliable data have been scarce, it appears that such interactions might be more frequent in recent years (Boyce, Rotenberg, & Karam, 2015). However, it is less clear whether there has been an actual increase in the number of situations or if the apparent increase

DOI: 10.4018/978-1-5225-0813-7.ch013

in numbers is attributable to improved identification and recording of such events by police. Certainly, there is an increase in the attention that this issue has garnered, both from police and the public.

The nature and causes of these interactions is complex. Although deinstitutionalization during the 1950s and 1960s has been generally viewed as a major causative factor, there are a variety of other forces which also come to play. For instance, on the one hand, improved treatments have increased the likelihood that people who were formerly confined to institutions are now able to live in the community. Furthermore, legislation has changed to reflect a greater focus on human rights and freedoms for P/MHP; this makes it more likely that their desire to live in the community will be honored.

On the other hand, the views of much of society have tended to shift to the right of the political spectrum; the apparent result is less tolerance of P/MHP for what might be perceived by some as deviant behavior. This "law and order" mentality has influenced law and policy and, thus, arguably the nature of police responses. These and other factors such as the relative inaccessibility of community-based services in many jurisdictions and the persistent perception of an association between mental health problems and violence have led to a sometimes uneasy situation in which police are active participants in the everyday life of many P/MHP, sometimes ambivalently (Brink et al., 2011). Of note, a significant proportion of people with mental health problems have their first encounter with the mental health system as the result of a police interaction (Brink et al., 2011).

The nature of police interactions with P/MHP is highly variable. While some such interactions are crisis situations that might result in an apprehension under a mental health act or an arrest for criminal behavior, many interactions—perhaps even most interactions—are not crises. These might include:

- Minor and non-criminal disturbances in which a person appears to be mentally ill, emotionally disturbed or cognitively impaired;
- Situations in which a P/MHP is the victim of or witness to an offence;
- Situations in which family and support persons of P/MHP call police for assistance; and
- Situations involving social support and informal contacts by police.

Consistent with the fundamental principles of contemporary policing (Coleman & Cotton, 2014a, p. 16), many police organizations have worked to improve their ability to respond to situations involving P/MHP. The two predominant initiatives in this area over time have involved (1) education and training of police officers and other police employees about mental health problems and the mental health system, and (2) specialized police responses, generally in the form of add-on focused operational programs oriented toward response to calls-for-service involving P/MHP. However, while much progress has been made through the implementation of these two types of initiatives, the issue does not appear to have abated—and indeed, appears to be more complex than ever. This complexity suggests a broader strategic approach is likely more appropriate; this approach is one that focuses not only on a case-by-case response to specific situations involving a person with a mental illness, but also addresses the much broader issues of similar vulnerable populations, and the wide variety of situations in which police might encounter members of these populations. In essence, a strategic approach elevates these issues within the organization to a position in which the problem itself can be addressed, rather than simply the symptoms.

The objective of this chapter is to track the evolution of police responses to this important social issue by way of providing:

- An overview of the *first generation approach*- education and awareness;
- A discussion of the *second generation approaches*- add-on/stand-alone programs;[2] and
- The rationale and framework to move to a *third generation approach*- a systemic strategic approach.

THE EVOLUTION OF POLICE RESPONSES TO POLICE INTERACTIONS WITH PEOPLE WITH MENTAL HEALTH PROBLEMS

The First Generation: Education and Awareness

Although, arguably, police have interacted with P/MHP since at least the naissance of modern policing in the early-mid 1800s, there is a sense by some that such interactions are now more frequent. Substantial literature indicates this situation is not unique to Canada and the U.S. but is a factor across at least the "western" world. Although some police officers might not agree that interactions with persons with mental health problems are "real" police work, Hoover (2007) pointed out that "serving as first responders during mental health crises is a long-standing [police] responsibility" (p. 7). Furthermore, notwithstanding that those who adhere to the more traditional policing model do not view interacting with P/MHP as "core" policing, Hoover (2007) maintained that "among the 'legitimate' safety functions of the police is dealing with people with mental health problems" (pp. 7-8).

Not surprisingly, the situations that attract the most attention—from police and from the public—are those in which a P/MHP dies in an interaction with police. The single most common recommendation by coroners' inquests and similar inquiries related to deaths of people with mental health problems in interactions with police has been that there is a need for increased education and training related to mental health problems (Coleman & Cotton, 2005; Police Complaints Authority, 2003), to the extent that such education is now commonplace (McAfee & Musso, 1995; Coleman & Cotton, 2010). For instance, in recognition of the frequency and importance of calls involving P/MHP, most police colleges/academies in North America provide at least nominal training and education in this area, and many police agencies provide additional training to some, or all, personnel including call takers and dispatchers.

But what constitutes effective and sufficient education? Arguably, the most comprehensive review and analysis of the essential components of an effective education and training regime are contained in reports commissioned by the Mental Health Commission of Canada (Coleman & Cotton, 2014a; Coleman & Cotton, 2010). For instance, the TEMPO (Training and Education about Mental Illness for Police Organizations) learning framework is a key component for the operationalization of a mental health strategy for Canadian police agencies (Coleman & Cotton, 2014a). Such a mental health strategy will be discussed later in this chapter as the *Third Generation*.

TEMPO articulates learning objectives and key principles in order to ensure the framework is applicable to a wide range of police agencies and individual jurisdictional needs. In addition to providing a firm basis of knowledge for police personnel,[3] the framework embraces a human rights/anti-stigma philosophy, provides for a range of education appropriate to diverse police audiences, emphasizes a systems approach to police/mental health liaison activities and addresses issues related to the design, delivery and implementation of police education and training.

TEMPO proposes to address gaps that may be evident in some education programs and to assist individual police agencies in carrying out gap analyses of their own education programs. Unfortunately, there are few studies and scant data that adequately address the question of outcomes and effectiveness of different approaches to police/mental health education and training. Many studies use indirect measures such as behavioral intentions and attitudes (as opposed to actual behavior) (see for example, Hansson & Markstrõm, 2014; Pinfold et al., 2003; Horace, 2014) or merely assess the personal satisfaction of the participants post training. A notable exception is the recent work by Krameddine, Demarco, Hassel and Silverstone (2013) in which direct observation of police behavior following a less traditional and a more experiential approach to learning about mental health problems reportedly led to behavioral change.

Many other studies which attempt to measure the outcome of learning are embedded in more complex studies of multi-faceted programs such as the Crisis Intervention Team Model (see, for example, Compton et al., 2014a, 2014b), which make it difficult to draw conclusions about what the essential components are, and whether the observed changes in attitudes and behavior are attributable to education or to some other variable. There is also little consistency about what has constituted "training" when considering that education and training in police colleges/academies has varied from one hour to more than 40 hours (Cotton & Coleman, 2008).

Many learning programs also tend to be relatively narrow and specific in terms of the vulnerable populations that they include and the types of responses they envision. At the level of the front line officer, the seemingly arbitrary distinction that mental health professionals might make between psychiatric disorders, intellectual disabilities, neurodevelopmental disorders, substance use problems, and acquired brain injury (to mention a few) might be not only meaningless but also impossible. Yet many police education programs focus only on major psychiatric disorders.

There are however some common and promising practices that merit inclusion in police education and training. These include considerations not only about the content of learning but also related to the manner in which learning is conducted, the people who both deliver and receive learning, and the need for ongoing education and training. While knowledge and skills are essential to the way in which police interact with P/MHP and, thus, form the bulk of any educational endeavor, as Coleman and Cotton (2014a) made clear it is also essential to integrate:

- Anti-stigma education to challenge the attitudinal barriers that lead to discriminatory action;
- The de-escalation/defusing of interactions with P/MHP by means of effective verbal and non-verbal communications; and
- Ethical decision-making, human rights protection and social responsibility (Coleman & Cotton, 2014a).

With these central principles in mind, the recommended learning spectrum of TEMPO is founded on seven essential areas:

1. Knowledge and skills related to the broad systems and context within which interactions with people with mental health problems occur. Employees of police organizations will acquire an understanding of:
    a. The importance of adherence to the fundamental principles of contemporary policing, such as:
        i. a client focus;
        ii. ethical conduct;
        iii. procedural justice;

    iv. relationship building;
    v. an outcome focus; and
    vi. a multi-agency approach
  b. The role of police personnel in encounters with P/MHP; and
  c. The role of mental health professionals, family and community supports in police encounters with P/MHP, consistent with a systems approach; and
  d. The importance of addressing stigma and bias; the role of the United Nations Convention on Rights of Person with Disabilities, Human Rights Codes, the Americans with Disabilities Act and similar legislation in interactions with P/MHP.
2. Knowledge and skills related to understanding the nature and effects of mental health problems and mental disability including:
  a. The symptoms such as hallucinations, delusions, paranoia, thought disorder, mood disturbances, intellectual impairments, memory problems, disinhibition, behavioral disturbances and other signs and symptoms that might accompany major mental health problems and related problems;
  b. The ability to recognize the above signs and symptoms sufficient to make an assessment about the influence that mental health problems might be having on a person's behavior and ability to comprehend and respond to a police officer's requests or instructions; and
  c. An appreciation of the interplay between culture, race, gender and other person- specific characteristics that affect the experience of mental health problems.
3. Knowledge and skills about the specific local environment within which police-P/MHP interactions occur including:
  a. The importance of fostering police/mental health agency relationships;
  b. The importance of information sharing protocols between police and mental health agencies;
  c. Local mental health legislation sufficient to take appropriate action when necessary;
  d. Other relevant legislation including that which defines privacy rights and human rights;
  e. The function of local mental health agencies and options and where/how to call for consultation and/or assistance and/or to make referral(s); and
  f. Organizational policies and procedures relevant to police-P/MHP encounters.
4. Knowledge and skills in relation to intervention strategies including:
  a. How to use communication skills and de-escalation techniques for defusing and calming situations involving P/MHP;
  b. How to determine whether it is likely that the P/MHP is capable of understanding and responding to the directions given by police; and
  c. How to integrate knowledge about a person's mental health status into implementation of the use-of-force model.
5. Knowledge and skills in relation to risk assessment including:
  a. An understanding of the relationship between mental health problems and dangerousness; and
  b. The ability to assess suicide risk, differentiate between suicidal intent and self-harm and how to contain the situation and/or when to intervene accordingly.
6. Knowledge and skills in relation to use of discretion and ethical decision-making processes with members of these populations (Coleman & Cotton, 2014a).

The TEMPO recommendations are embedded in a context which also suggests that (1) learning should be adapted to the nature of the employee receiving the learning (e.g. new officers versus specialized teams or dispatchers or coach officers or supervisory personnel), (2) issues in regard to this population be integrated into education for crisis resolution and judgment/use of force training,[4] (3) trainers/facilitators of learning are committed to the strategic direction of the police agency and are seen as credible role models within the organization, and (4) it is also critical that consumers—those people affected by mental health and related problems—are involved in both the design and delivery of education.

The literature is clear that whenever possible responding police officers should try to use verbal and nonverbal communication to de-escalate a situation. The TEMPO framework identifies this as essential in the interest of safe outcomes for all parties to the interaction, including the P/MHP (Coleman & Cotton, 2014a). While response models and police activities should, and in most case do,[5] focus on positive outcomes for all police interactions with P/MHP, unfortunately, despite efforts to successfully conclude an interaction, on some occasions it is necessary to use some level of police force. In some cases, this has resulted in serious injury or death of a person in crisis. Police must therefore know not only how to take time and patience to de-escalate but to know when and how to use any level of force.

A note about use of force training is particularly relevant here. "Use of force" skill training has usually appeared as a stand-alone topic in police training, and is typically taught by instructors who are indeed adept at using force. When stand-alone education and training about mental illness including the communication necessary to de-escalate situations, is not well integrated with stand-alone use of force training, it is unlikely to have the desired effect of reducing the potential for the use of force against P/MHP. Similarly, as long as officers harbor beliefs that P/MHP are inherently dangerous, that calls for service which involve P/MHP are more likely to result in use of force and that to some extent use of force is unavoidable in these instances, then the use of force will not decrease. There is also some evidence (Watson & Angell, 2013) that as long as P/MHP expect that police will utilize force, then P/MHP are more likely to respond to police aggressively. Thus, the engagement of P/MHP in education and training of police is essential at a variety of levels in order to avoid this circular escalation of use of force. Furthermore, police officers should requalify at least every three years in their crisis communications skills in a similar manner in which they periodically requalify with their firearm(s) (Coleman & Cotton, 2014a).

The fact that it appears most police academies and agencies now include education about mental health problems speaks to the recognition by police leaders of a need for this as a pre-requisite for positive outcomes to police interactions. Nevertheless, in the absence of contrary evidence, there is also little doubt that taken alone, education is insufficient. Notwithstanding this, effective and relevant education and training is deemed a critical component necessary for successful implementation of not only the *second generation* but also the strategic—*third generation*—approach.

Second Generation: Specialized Police Based Programs

While the intent of providing education and training to police officers so that they would be more prepared to manage interactions with P/MHP was, and is, laudable, it has been readily apparent that education and training alone is not sufficient and, furthermore, there needs to be a context within which the knowledge can be applied. Hence, by the 1970s (in Canada) and the 1980s (in the U.S.), specialized police based responses to P/MHP were beginning to emerge. By far the most well-known model (program) in the U.S. of police-based response to P/MHP is the Crisis Intervention Team (CIT) model, which originated in Memphis, Tennessee in 1988. However, it is important to note that this is not the only model and not necessarily the most appropriate program for every jurisdiction. It is also worth noting that substantial success enjoyed by the CIT, particularly in the U.S., has led to a tendency to use the term CIT to refer to any of a variety of different types of police/mental health response programs. However, as Reuland (2012) pointed out, the appropriate question to ask is not so much which program is best but rather which model, or program, is most appropriate and meets the requirements of the respective jurisdiction. Reuland, as well as Cordner (2006), noted that selection of an appropriate model for police encounters with people with mental health problems will, to some extent, be determined by the nature of the challenges confronting the local jurisdiction.

Reuland identified a variety of possible issues, which in large part are dependent on the varying types of interactions between people and mental health problems. For instance, is the issue one of unsafe outcomes of encounters between police and people with mental health problems? Is it a matter of the frequency of interactions and demands on police resources? Is the issue primarily overutilization of emergency services? Or….? In addition to determining the nature of the issue, however, there is also need to determine the nature of the community. Reuland (2012) advocated for types of responses that are tailored to community characteristics such as:

- The nature and style of leadership in the police agency;
- Required procedures for medical clearance and admission to mental health facilities in the region;
- The nature and availability of mental health resources in general;
- The specific legislation at both local and national or federal level that might determine the options available to police; and
- The demography and geography of the specific jurisdiction.

Similarly, Cordner (2006) addressed the need to involve stakeholders and analyze local resources in order to formulate local needs and, therefore, local responses. The take-home message from both Reuland and Cordner's work is that there is not a single preferred model or response program; each community should have solutions tailored to their individual local characteristics including available resources. Having said that, preparations – the necessary learning – for police personnel for interactions with P/MHP have numerous common elements as documented in TEMPO recommendations (Coleman & Cotton, 2014a).

What are the options? While there are a number of different types of response programs that have been developed in North America and elsewhere, there are two predominant response models: CIT and co-response.

1. Crisis Intervention Team (CIT) Model

The roots of CIT (frequently referred to as the Memphis Model) lie in a crisis; in this case, a situation in which Memphis police shot and killed a young man with a history of mental health problems. CIT, at its 1988 inception, was a police initiated program designed to reduce, and ideally eliminate, tragedies involving police officers and P/MHP. The concept was to better prepare a select group of police officers to handle contact with P/MHP. This was achieved by educating and training sufficient police officers as CIT officers such that on any shift and in any part of the city skilled CIT officers would be available as either first responders or back-up responders to situations that appeared to involve P/MHP.

The education and training to qualify as a CIT officer has typically been a 40-hour course. In addition to the education component, CIT emphasizes the need to develop working relationships with the local mental health establishment in order to facilitate speedy and appropriate resolution of non-criminal interactions with P/MHP. Since Memphis's initial success, CIT, as a brand, has expanded considerably across much of the U.S. as well as into several other countries with the result that CIT is no longer a homogenous product. This, of course, complicates the evaluation and comparisons of CIT across different jurisdictions. Moreover, notably, many agencies that describe themselves as adhering to a CIT approach in reality simply provide CIT or similar training for their police officers—thus, essentially maintaining a *First Generation* approach to the issue at hand. According to Dupont, Cochran and Pillsbury (2007), a comprehensive CIT approach requires several components:

Partnerships: Police/Law Enforcement, Advocacy, Mental Health

1. Police/Law Enforcement Community;
2. Advocacy Community; and
3. Mental Health Community.

Community Ownership: Planning, Implementation and Networking

1. Planning Groups;
2. Implementation; and
3. Networking.

Policies and Procedures

1. CIT (or similar) Education and Training;
2. Police/Law Enforcement Policies and Procedures that are congruent with that of mental health partners; and
3. Access to Mental Health Emergency Policies and Procedures for mental health organizations within the jurisdiction.

Although Watson, Angell, Morabito, and Robinson (2008) pointed out that the literature is not specific about which components of CIT are most important to which outcomes, or under what conditions CIT is likely to be most effective, Steadman, Deane, Borum, and Morrisey (2000) concluded that the deployment of CIT in Memphis was successful in that it reduced the arrest rate resulting from police and P/MHP contact as well as increasing referrals to appropriate mental health resources.

Recent studies by Compton et al. (2014a; 2014b) concluded that CIT training also appears to increase the likelihood of referral and transport to mental health services and decrease the likelihood of arrest. Although CIT training did not have a prominent effect on the use of force, Compton et al. (2014b) suggested CIT appears to be effective concerning pre-booking diversion from the criminal justice system. Heilbrun and Bingham (2013) noted in their review that there is some evidence that in individual interactions, CIT trained officers might be less likely to arrest; however, in the longer term it does not appear to reduce the future involvement of the same individuals in the criminal justice system.

Canada, Angell, and Watson (2010) found that CIT trained officers tended to utilize a wider range of response options in their daily interactions compared to officers who had not received CIT training. Despite questions about evaluations to date, Watson et al. (2008) agreed that "the current research supports CIT as a promising approach to improving police response to persons with mental health problems" (p. 366).

2. Co-Response Models

There are a number of response models in which police and mental health practitioners work together to meet the needs of P/MHP. These types of co-response teams are known by a variety of names; for instance, they might be variously called a Police and Crisis Team (PACT), a mobile crisis team, a joint response team, a police/mental health liaison program, mobile crisis services, or ride-along services. For the purpose of consistency, in this chapter the term "co-response model" will be used and is intended to include all the various types above. In each case, the essential component of such programs is that a police officer and a mental health worker of some sort respond jointly, usually arriving in the same vehicle, to situations in which there has been, or is about to be, a contact between a P/MHP and a police officer.

Notably, while the CIT model appears to be predominant in the U.S., this has not been the case in Canada. The first documented Canadian police response program was a co-response police/mental health model that originated in Vancouver, British Columbia in the late 1970s. According to Levine (1979), Vancouver's Car 87 program was established in the context of a justice reform movement the aim of which was "to explore new avenues to solve old problems" (p. II-2), and to identify ways to use police and community resources to develop diversionary and preventative programs including methods of informal dispute resolution. The resulting program was a joint police/mental health co-response program, in which a police officer and a mental health worker would respond jointly to those calls, which involved a person who appeared to have a mental illness.

There are two reasons why this short historical overview is salient. First, it speaks to Reuland's observation above that rather than trying to identify a "best" model, it is essential to identify the model appropriate for a particular jurisdiction. While the impetus for a specialized police response in the U.S. arose out of concerns for safety and the desire to reduce loss of life and injury, this was not the case in Canada, where such occurrences have been relatively rare. Second, it foreshadows the *Third Generation* approach described later in this chapter, which emphasizes the need for a coherent and strategic approach to the issue rather than often simply the creation of many programs operating in relative isolation of each other.

Since establishment of Car 87 in the 1970s, co-response models have proliferated in Canada and elsewhere but there is little consistency between, or across, these programs. Aside from the essential component that a police officer and a mental health worker respond jointly, programs are highly variable. They might be based in either the police agency or a mental health service; they might be first responders or follow up services; they might provide only crisis intervention or ongoing contacts; they might serve only specific vulnerable populations or a wide variety; they might employ nurses, social workers, psychologists or other mental health personnel; teams might respond in marked or unmarked vehicles; police sometimes wearing uniforms and sometimes not...and so forth.

Given the nature of the variability of the programs and services, it is not surprising that data about outcomes are somewhat equivocal. Shapiro et al. (2014) reviewed both the peer review literature and much of the gray literature about co-responding police mental health programs. Not surprisingly, they found that evidence of the benefit of these programs was inconsistent. Although little data have been collected about the extent to which co-response teams decrease injury in either police officers or P/MHPs, there is some evidence which suggested that compared to "usual service," (e.g. a response by first responders with no particular expertise or specialized services) there tended to be a reduced use of force when using a co-response model (Allen Consulting Group, 2012), although the difference was small.

Regrettably, most studies describing co-response initiatives do not address the issue of the use of force. This might be because, as noted above, decreasing the use of force and reducing injuries has not been the primary focus of these types of programs, or it might be simply because the use of force has been such a small percentage of total interactions that statistical analysis becomes difficult. Other outcome variables discussed by Shapiro et al. (2014) and their general conclusions included:

- **Linking P/MHP with Community Services:** there is some evidence that co-response models are more likely to result in referral of individuals to other mental health agencies (Kisely et al., 2010; Finn & Sullivan, 1989).
- **Reducing Pressure on the Justice System:** there is some evidence that P/MHP have lower arrest rates when they are involved with a co-response model, at least in the short term. There is also some evidence that co-response teams decrease the amount of time police first responders are involved in these situations, thus reducing the burden on police.
- **Improving Officers' Perception of Individuals who have Mental Health Problems**: Some studies have suggested that police exposure to a co-response team might result in improved understanding on the part of police of mental health problems in regard to the issues facing a person with a mental health problem.
- **Reducing the Number of Hospital Admissions:** the evidence here is mixed. In one study, 55% of emergencies handled by a co-response team were managed without psychiatric hospitalization compared to 28% of a control group (Scott, 2000). However, other studies did not find that the co-response model itself contributed to a reduction of hospital admissions. The difference might also depend on the nature of a Memorandum of Understanding (MOU) that police have with their local hospital.
- **Cost Effectiveness:** much of the evidence for cost effectiveness is subjective. As Kisely et al. (2010) pointed out, "those holding the purse strings feel the arrangements are sufficiently beneficial to have funded them without serious hesitation for many years" (p. 13). Scott (2000) found that on the average, each person served by a co-response model cost 23% less when measured through psychiatric hospitalization savings.
- **Program Perception:** on the whole, most staff and community stakeholders regarded the programs as well received and providing a good level of service and reasonable outcomes. However, there was less overall satisfaction with the outcome of the interactions, primarily because of the difficulty that even these co-response teams sometimes have identifying and connecting with limited community resources. Participants who were in receipt of services from a co-response team provide some evidence that this is a preferred model as opposed to a police-based CIT type model; primarily because of the inclusion of mental health practitioners and, thus, usually a presence which looks less police-like (Boscarato et al., 2014).

3. Other Models

While CIT styled responses and co-response programs/tactics are the most common types of police-based response, there are other approaches. Three worthy of mention are:

1. Comprehensive Advanced Response Model

Probably the most basic type of response "program," this model simply stipulates that all police first responders should possess a level of knowledge and skills essentially akin to what specialized officers might have in models such as CIT or a co-response model. In the past, some jurisdictions have developed practices whereby all police first responders receive advanced mental health problems education and training. All police officers are then expected to handle most situations involving P/MHP. While this model might have practicality and utility in smaller police agencies as well as rural areas, the logistical and financial challenges of educating and training all police personnel in a large police agency to the level required is difficult to achieve.

The key point in regard to this "model" is that whereas in the past education and training for police officers was viewed as an adequate solution to interactions with P/MHP (*First Generation*), the contemporary viewpoint would be more that education and training is an essential but insufficient ingredient in a comprehensive police/mental health strategy; that is, it is an important means to an end rather than an end in itself.

2. Sequential Response Models (SRM)

Given that one of the most frustrating aspects of interactions with P/MHP for police has been prolonged wait times at hospitals (and the associated likelihood that the person in question will be quickly released), a number of jurisdictions have established agreements with local mental agencies whereby P/MHP who appear to need assistance might be taken to a non-hospital agency, which will then take over responsibility for the person, leaving the police to return to other duties (see Cotton & Coleman, 2010, for examples of this type of model). In the U.S., this type of response is sometimes referred to as the Reception Center Model, and is often used in conjunction with a CIT response. In most instances (that we are aware of) the mental health agency has a policy of accepting such clients in all cases; there is no screening or refusal. In some instances, the mental health agency also has a working relationship with a hospital emergency department so that P/MHP who are screened and assessed at the agency and deemed to require a hospital admission are processed more quickly or as a priority at the hospital if they are eventually taken there.

The SRMs are essentially a transfer of care for the P/MHP with no questions asked. This service tends to be used when:

- Police feel the person is in need of services or assistance but do not feel the person meets the legal requirement for involuntary hospital admission or treatment;
- Police would like a second opinion—and, in particular, an opinion from a mental health practitioner—as to whether the person in question should be taken to a hospital;
- Police feel that the P/MHP would be best served by removing him/her from the present situation but have no grounds to either arrest or apprehend; and
- There is no local hospital and the time and expense involved in taking a P/MHP to a distant hospital might not be justified.

3. Telephone Consultation Models

A continuing challenge for police is in rural and remote areas where there is no local mental health service, no hospital, and an insufficient number of calls for service to justify any formal type of response such as a CIT or co-response team. There are no obvious solutions to this, but some areas have developed either formal or informal understandings whereby a police officer might obtain advice and guidance from a mental health professional by telephone. The types of inquiries that might be made can include:

- General advice about how to interact with and best serve a P/MHP based on a description of the current situation;
- Specific advice about a P/MHP who might be known to the mental health agency; and
- Advice about the most appropriate disposition of a situation—e.g. to take them to hospital or make some other choice.

In some ways, hospitals are best suited to provide this service to the police as they are also open and available 24/7. Furthermore, there would usually be some kind of medical or psychiatric professional on duty (not limited to physicians but including nurses, psychologists, social workers, crisis counsellors). However, such consultations are often problematic unless they take place in the context of a formal Memorandum of Agreement (MOU) and legal structures.

4. Jurisdiction-Specific Approaches

There is of course no finite list of models and frameworks that are specific to an individual jurisdiction. In most cases, there is not literature available for these idiosyncratic models—yet they do illustrate the point that Reuland (2012) has repeatedly made that any model should reflect the local needs and resources of the individual community. For example, in Honolulu, Hawaii, psychologists employed by the police service act as consultants and respond to calls from all front line officers who seek guidance in the handling situations involving P/MHP. In Ottawa, Canada, a pilot program ran for several years in which psychiatric residents (e.g. psychiatrists in training) responded to specific calls with police. There are several smaller jurisdictions who have worked out informal mechanism by which officers may call a receiving hospital to inform them that they might be arriving with an apprehended P/MHP, and in other settings paramedics or ambulance personnel may respond rather than police to some calls for service. In all cases, the main importance of these kinds of models is that they reflect the existing level of knowledge of officers and other first responders, and the availability of mental health services and mental health professionals.

Third Generation: A Strategic Approach

While increased knowledge and education in combination with add-on and focused programs have arguably improved police response to P/MPH over time, there is no doubt that significant unaddressed problems remain. Most notably, these include:

- The tendency for educational initiatives to address only a subgroup of diagnostic groups or problem types: interestingly, there is no common language or term that is used to describe the large number of vulnerable people, whose difficulties involve not only mental illness but also cognitive impairment and developmental disabilities, including brain injury, autism, dementia and so forth. While this might not be salient to mental health professionals working within the mental health system, for police officers and other first responders, their response and approach is most likely to be determined by the type of symptoms they observe rather than by an individual's specific diagnosis—which of course is often unknown during a street encounter. Arbitrarily separating out these clinical groups at the frontline level is extremely difficult, and providing separate education and training for every different diagnostic group is impractical. A comprehensive education and training program needs to reflect the needs of all these groups;

- Educational initiatives are also often isolated from other police learning; in particular there is rarely integration with use of force training;
- Both education and response programs often do not reflect interactions with P/MHP in a wide variety of contexts; furthermore, such interactions sometimes co-occur in areas in which there may be other focused police programs or initiatives—such as homelessness, situations involving use of force (e.g. SWAT or ERT responses), domestic violence, elder abuse, victim services, initiatives aimed at special populations such as youth, GLBTQ+ populations, specific community groups defined by either location or ethnic composition...and so forth;
- Education and training initiatives might not reflect the current state of knowledge about adult learning styles or issues and thus might not include sufficient or appropriate learning techniques;
- Education often is overly focused on knowledge acquisition as opposed to skill acquisition;
- Much of the focus on police based programs has been on "crisis intervention," yet the majority of police interactions with P/MHP do not involve a crisis (Brink et al., 2011; Belleville Police Service, 2007). Most stand-alone programs are not designed to provide response to all police interactions with P/MHP; moreover, most interactions continue to be handled by first responders rather than specialized teams. In particular, there has been little in the way of developed responses to frequent users of police services; that is, the minority of P/MHP who make numerous demands on police services;
- Stand-alone programs also often fail to recognize that interactions with P/MHP might occur in almost any police context—whether it is a mental health act apprehension, a traffic stop, a well-being check, a situation in which a P/MHP is a victim or a witness; and
- Measurement of outcomes is problematic. Many programs have lacked a clear statement, or even an understanding, of goals; this, consequently, makes rigorous evaluation and the determination of a successful outcome difficult. Is the goal to reduce injury? Reduce hospital wait times? Decrease the number of arrests? Improve relations with the mental health community? Increase referrals to other community agencies? Decrease the likelihood of re-involvement with police? Or all of the aforementioned?

These limitations point to the long overdue need for a broader strategic approach to interactions with P/MHP; that is, an approach based on a police agency's mental health strategy which, in turn, is congruent with the police agency's organizational (corporate) strategy. To advance, enhance and embed this important area of policing in the way a police agency conducts business, it is necessary for police leaders to take a strategic approach as opposed to only the tactical/program approach of the past; this will help ensure a planned integrated approach that will facilitate resource justification and acquisition as well as identifying the desired outcomes of these interactions in the best interest of the P/MHP and the community in general.

Although some progressive police leaders embrace strategic leadership and management and, thus, operate their police agency strategically, it is apparent that many, in particular mid-sized and smaller police agencies, do not. At the core of a strategic approach is the necessity and establishment of a clear organizational (corporate) strategy that is well communicated both internally and externally. Such a corporate strategy is usually composed of several components not least important of which are the agency's mission, vision and corporate values (Thompson, 2003; Jones, 2004). This is what guides strategic leadership and management and also enables the community to hold their police agency accountable for results.

Congruent with the respective organizational (corporate) strategy, functional strategies are necessary to shape and guide the police agency's decisions and actions (tactics) (Beamish & Woodcock, 1999). In the context of this chapter, one such functional strategy a police agency should establish is a mental health strategy[6] for the police organization.[7] In much the same way as progressive police organizations, for example, establish functional strategies such as an *Organized Crime Strategy* or a *Domestic Violence Strategy*, a *Mental Health Strategy* would make a clear declaration about the organization's position and intent, including the commitment of related resources, concerning all aspects of interactions with P/MHP ranging from proactive as well as reactive.

A well-crafted mental health strategy, established in consultation and collaboration with the community and mental health stakeholders, makes the position and goal(s) of a police organization and its activities regarding interactions with P/MHP clear both externally (to the public) as well as internally (to fellow employees). That is, such a strategy is an important means of communication as well as a means of establishing and achieving objectives as well as maintaining direction and commitment to achieve an integrated comprehensive approach and fulfill the agency's mission. Furthermore, the establishment of strategic outcome goals reflected in related programs enable the critical rigorous evaluations that in large part have been missing from a solely program (tactical) approach.

The goals and objectives, including desired outcomes, of the mental health (functional) strategy are achieved by means of the programs/tactics derived from, and linked to, the strategy. That is, programs are no longer a random mix of orphan programs. They are designed to satisfy goals of the mental health strategy and, thus, the strategic goals of the police agency. Examples, of such programs/tactics are those discussed above such as the various co-response teams, CIT programs or other programs that fit the strategy. Arguably, if a program/tactic is not congruent with the mental health strategy it is not the right program. Similarly, if the activities of a program/tactic are not meeting strategic goals, then it is likely the program is improperly implemented, requires a redesign or requires replacement.

This begs the question: what should be included in a mental health strategy for a police organization? Although examples even internationally are few, one example from Australia is worthy of note. Their strategic document, *Policing People who appear to be Mentally Ill,* is comprehensive and clear (Policing People, 2012). Another recent well-constructed and articulated police mental health strategy is that of the Ontario Provincial Police, Ontario, Canada (Ontario Provincial Police, 2015).

The foundation of a mental health and policing strategy should likely include a *Guiding Principle* similar to the following (Cotton & Coleman, 2006):

That each police organization should foster an organizational culture in which people with mental health problems are treated with respect, with the same attention paid to their rights as are other members of society and, furthermore, that procedural justice principles are adhered to and criminalization is minimized.

Without being prescriptive or limiting the scope of a police organization's mental health strategy regarding interactions with P/MHP, arguably, such a strategy will:

1. Focus on root causes of a problem rather than continually addressing the symptoms of a problem;
2. Maximize the likelihood of positive outcomes of police interactions with people with mental health problems;

3. Ensure that the intended nature of police interactions with P/MHP reflects sensitivity to local issues including demographics and cultural factors;
4. Ensure that police agencies work effectively with the mental health system as well as other government and non-government agencies that are involved with P/MHP;
5. Focus on the outcomes of proactive as well as reactive police activities related to interactions with P/MHP; and
6. Facilitate a change of police organizational attitudes and culture with regard to mental health problems.

The last point, of course, relates to the necessity to educate police personnel so that stigma and stereotypes about mental health problems are no longer a negative factor in police organizations.

Of importance to note is that in a strategic approach related to police interactions with P/MHP (*Third Generation*), education and training (*First Generation*) is critical to the preparation of personnel to operationalize the programs and tactics (*Second Generation*) developed pursuant to the mental health strategy and, thus, satisfy the goals of the mental health strategy and in turn meet the agency's organizational goals subject of the strategic approach—the *Third Generation* approach.

While few police agencies at present have formal mental health strategies to address this complex issue, there are a few police agencies in North America that appear to embrace the concept of a system-wide multi-faceted response strategy. For example:

Vancouver Police

Current mental health initiatives of Vancouver Police are:

- A Mental Health Unit, led by a sergeant who coordinates all activities related to P/MHP;
- Police inclusion in Mental Health Care Teams, which provides for exchange of information between the medical system and the police when appropriate;
- The Car 87 program (co-response program);
- Downtown Community Court;
- An Assertive Community Treatment (ACT) team which includes a police officer;
- A homeless outreach co-ordinator—a position that also provides a focus on the role of mental health problems in homelessness;
- A Sex Trade Liaison Officer—again, providing recognition of the role of mental health problems and substance use in this population; and
- Project Link: a joint activity of the police and Vancouver Coastal Health Board, whose goals include both improved outcomes for clients as well as improved and more efficient use of both police and mental health resources (Vancouver's Mental Health Crisis, 2013).

Hamilton (Ontario) Police and the COAST Model

Hamilton Police in conjunction with St. Joseph's Healthcare Center in Hamilton, Ontario have been leaders for many decades in their work related to police interactions with people with mental health problems. While they are probably best known for their co-response team COAST,[8] they now also have several different co-response teams; a mobile response that does not include police, and a rapid-response team for crisis situations which require immediate response and greater overall police involvement—all for improving outcomes for P/MHP. Specific initiatives include:

- A high visibility foot/bike patrol team in the downtown core where about 80% of their mental health encounters occur. This team is supported by a social navigator who proactively helps to prevent crises by linking individuals to services and providing supports to community partners;
- Several co-response teams which include a mental health worker and a police officer; these include teams focused on providing services to adults, children and family, and seniors;
- The COAST program which also operates a suicide prevention helpline;
- Almost half of frontline police officers have completed the 40 hour crisis intervention team training and currently the Hamilton Police are training all personnel with a program specific to suicide presentation;
- A Mobile Crisis Rapid Response Team (MCRRT) in which a mental health worker and a police officer in the same police vehicle provide a first response to situations involving P/MHP; and
- The development and utilization of the patient transfer document (MOU) developed in partnership with St. Joseph's Hospital which has succeeded in reducing wait times in the emergency room from an average of 2.5 hours to 70 minutes in general and to under an hour for the MCRRT.

One of the striking features about the comprehensive approach that Hamilton Police and the COAST programs have developed is the extent to which they are driven by local community needs, informed data collection, outcome measures and evaluation. The Hamilton models are a good example of the value of close partnerships and the evolution of a coordinated, comprehensive and integrated police/mental health response that has developed over time in response to their local situation.

Los Angeles Police Department

Like many—or even most—large urban police agencies, the Los Angeles Police Department (LAPD) has traditionally delivered a number of response initiatives related to their interactions with P/MHP. These include:

- The SMART program—or Systemwide Mental Health Assessment Team, which is a co-response model; and
- A CIT program, which not only provides training for officers assigned to the CIT team but also is open to other officers who might encounter P/MHP in their work.[9]

In addition, in 2005, the LAPD Mental Health Evaluation Unit (MEU) developed a Case Assessment and Management Program (CAMP), the purpose of which is to identify and track frequent users and construct customized responses to their problems; that is, a problem solving approach. The CAMP program co-locates a police officer with various mental health professionals, and is geared toward long-term solutions rather than call-by-call interventions. All of these programs operate under the umbrella of the MEU which has existed for over four decades (Specialized Policing, n.d.; Mental Health Evaluation, n.d.[10]; LAPD Mental Health, 2014).

These programs are not completely unique in and of themselves (although case management programs are somewhat rare). What is unique is the integration of a variety of services under one umbrella—in this case the MEU—which reflects the acknowledgement that there is no "one size fits all" model for solving the situations when P/MHP interact with the police. More striking is that all of these MEU programs are embedded within a functional activity called the Mental Health Crisis Response Program (MHCRP), which not only oversees all specific programs but carries out a wide variety of other functions and activities including:

- Acting as an advisory board;
- Conducting analyses of legislation that affects P/MHP;
- Auditing the use of force that involve P/MHP;
- Ensuring maintenance and analysis of relevant data; and
- Reviewing departmental policies, strategies and procedures related to the handling of persons with mental health problems.

The Role of the Psychologist in Developing and Operationalizing a Mental Health Strategy for a Police Organization

Finally, an important ingredient of a successful strategic approach related to this matter is the inclusion of all stakeholders, including the community, in the establishment of the necessary strategies and the design of programs/tactics as well as the design and delivery of the important education and training. One of those stakeholders often overlooked even at the *First and Second Generation* levels is that of the psychologist. Arguably, the expertise of psychologists has been, with rare exception, one of the missing links in the evolution we describe in this chapter. Curiously, psychologists have played only a limited role to date in the development of police-based responses to P/MHP. While much of the actual "work" of first response can indeed be carried out by any one of many different kinds of mental health professionals, there are a number of unique skills that psychologists bring to the table, including several which have been alluded to above:

- In regard to *first generation* approaches, many education/training programs do not utilize existing knowledge about adult learning styles, educational technology, and generalization of knowledge in areas in which educational psychologists might have specialized knowledge;
- Much of the research to date has concentrated on changing attitudes and knowledge rather than behavior; social psychologists are well equipped to address the complex relationship between attitudes and behavior in such a way as to maximize the likelihood of behavior change;
- Pre-employment selection procedures might be adapted so that consideration is given in the psychological assessment to identifying police candidates who might have stigmatizing and intolerant attitudes;
- As noted, one of the most significant gaps in the literature is the failure to adequately define and measure outcomes—of both education programs as well as of interventions. Psychologists typically possess the ability to develop tools and measures to conduct the necessary evaluation/research;
- While there are some studies that have assessed single aspects of police response at a program level in a before/after manner, there is a dearth of research which allows for comprehensive evaluation across time; there is a need for more sophisticated research incorporating more complex statistical analysis (as opposed to simple pre/post designs);

- Inherent in the adaptation of a strategic approach to any problem is reliance on evidence-based and evidence-informed practice. While, as noted, there is a dearth of research available, psychologists are, arguably, most likely to have ready access to relevant research or to initiate same; and
- Industrial/organizational psychologists might be in an ideal position to contribute to the development of a specific functional strategy which aids in the integration of issues related to P/MHP into the broader organizational structure.

CONCLUSION

Whether or not the number of interactions of P/MHP with police personnel has increased in recent time, it is a social issue deserving of continued attention by all relevant agencies, not least of which are police agencies that are usually available 24/7. In recent years, there have been significant developments in terms of education and training as well as development of a variety of focused and specific intervention strategies. Police personnel are now much better informed and police agencies, through a variety of response models, are better positioned from the perspective of both being effective as well as efficient. Although this evolution is encouraging, further improvement for the benefit of P/MHP and police agencies can be made by taking a strategic approach to addressing the issue. Such an approach will embed this important social matter into police business and develop an approach that instead of repeatedly trying to address symptoms will, in concert with other social agencies, address the problem(s).

Although problem solving is a tenet of contemporary policing, unless a strategic approach is taken, problem solving is unlikely to be effective due to the often overwhelming caseload when only taking a tactical (program) approach. The strategic approach, proposed in this chapter, will elevate the matter to the executive level of a police agency and will facilitate the justification of necessary resources and implementation of the strategy by means of the development of the various necessary programs (tactics). It also allows for a clearer definition of goals and thus the measurement of outcomes—as opposed to outputs. In the case of police agencies, it can provide the opportunity to address, in conjunction with other social and human service agencies, root causes instead of repeatedly responding to symptoms of greater issues.

REFERENCES

Allen Consulting Group. (2012). *Police, Ambulance and Clinical Early Response (PACER) evaluation: Final report.* Melbourne, Australia: Department of Health, State of Victoria.

Beamish, P. W., & Woodcock, C. P. (1999). *Strategic management: Text readings and cases* (5th ed.). Toronto, Canada: McGraw-Hill Ryerson.

Belleville Police Service. (2007). Police interactions with emotionally disturbed/mentally ill people: A comprehensive analysis and review. Belleville, Canada: Author.

Boscarato, K., Lee, S., Kroschel, J., Hollander, Y., Brennan, A., & Warran, N. (2014). Consumer experience of formal crisis response services and preferred methods of crisis intervention. *International Journal of Mental Health Nursing, 23*(4), 287–295. doi:10.1111/inm.12059 PMID:24575860

Boyce, J., Rotenberg, C., & Karam, M. (2015). *Mental health and contact with police in Canada, 2012*. Ottawa, Canada: Juristat, Canadian Center for Justice Statistics, Statistics Canada. Retrieved September 17, 2015, from http://www.statcan.gc.ca/pub/85-002-x/2015001/article/14176-eng.htm?WT.mc_id=twt

Brink, J., Livingston, J. D., Desmarais, S., Greaves, C., Maxwell, V., & Michalak, E. (2011). *A Study of How People with Mental Illness Perceive and Interact with the Police*. Retrieved September 5, 2015, from http://www.mentalhealthcommission.ca/English/document/437/study-how-people-mental-illness-perceive-and-interact-police

Canada, K. E., Angell, B., & Watson, A. C. (2010). Crisis intervention teams in Chicago: Successes on the ground. *Journal of Police Crisis Negotiations*, *10*(1/2), 86–100. doi:10.1080/15332581003792070 PMID:21113318

Coleman, T., & Cotton, D. (2005, July). *A Study of Fatal Interactions between Canadian Police and Mentally Ill*. Paper presented at the 2005 International Association of Law and Mental Health Annual Conference, Paris, France.

Coleman, T., & Cotton, D. (2014b). TEMPO: A contemporary model for police education and training about mental health problems. *International Journal of Law and Psychiatry*, *37*(4), 325–333. doi:10.1016/j.ijlp.2014.02.002 PMID:24720915

Coleman, T. G., & Cotton, D. H. (2010a). *Police interactions with persons with a mental health problem: Police learning in the environment of contemporary policing*. Mental Health and the Law Advisory Committee, Mental Health Commission of Canada. Retrieved on September 4, 2015, from http://www.mentalhealthcommission.ca/English/Pages/ThePoliceProject.aspx

Coleman, T. G., & Cotton, D. H. (2014a). *TEMPO: Police interactions: A report towards improving interactions between police and people living with mental health problems*. Ottawa, Canada: Mental Health Commission of Canada. Retrieved September 5, 2015, from http://www.mentalhealthcommission.ca/English/document/36596/tempo-police- interactions-report- towards-improving-interactions-between-police-and- pe#sthash.QzZpLDsB.dpuf

Compton, M. T., Bakeman, R., Broussard, B., Hankerson-Dyson, D., Husbands, L., Krishan, S., & Watson, A. C. et al. (2014a). The police-based crisis intervention team (CIT) model: II. Effects on level of force and resolution, referral, and arrest. *Psychiatric Services (Washington, D.C.)*, *65*(4), 523–529. doi:10.1176/appi.ps.201300108 PMID:24382643

Compton, M. T., Bakeman, R., Broussard, B., Hankerson-Dyson, D., Husbands, L., Krishan, S., & Watson, A. C. et al. (2014b). The police-based crisis intervention team (CIT) model: I. Effects on officers' knowledge, attitudes, and skills. *Psychiatric Services (Washington, D.C.)*, *65*(4), 517–522. doi:10.1176/appi.ps.201300107 PMID:24382628

Cordner, G. (2006). *People with Mental Health problems. Problem oriented Guides for Police. Problem-specific guides series no. 40.* US Department of Justice, Office of Community Oriented Policing Services. Retrieved September 1, 2015, from http://www.popcenter.org/problems/mental_health problems/

Cotton, D., & Coleman, T. (2006). *Contemporary policing guidelines for working with the mental health system*. Ottawa, Canada: Canadian Association of Chiefs of Police.

Cotton, D., & Coleman, T. (2008). *A study of police academy training and education for new police officers related to working with people with mental illness.* Ottawa, Canada: Mental Health Commission of Canada. Retrieved September 14, 2015, from http://www.mentalhealthcommission.ca/English/document/438/study-police-academy-training-and-education-new-police-officers-related-working-people- #sthash.7RbR3o8X.dpuf

Cotton, D., & Coleman, T. (2010). Canadian police agencies and their interactions with persons with a mental illness: A systems approach. *Police Practice and Research, 11*(4), 301–314. doi:10.1080/15614261003701665

Dupont, R., Cochran, S., & Pillsbury, S. (2007). *Crisis Intervention Team Core Elements.* Memphis, TN: The University of Memphis School of Urban Affairs and Public Policy Department of Criminology and Criminal Justice, CIT Center 1. Retrieved September 17, 2015 from http://www.citinternational.org/images/stories/CIT/SectionImplementation/CoreElements. pdf

Ellis, H. A. (2014). Effects of a Crisis Intervention Team (CIT) training program upon police officers before and after Crisis Intervention Team training. *Archives of Psychiatric Nursing, 28*(1), 10–16. doi:10.1016/j.apnu.2013.10.003 PMID:24506981

Hansson, L., & Markström, U. (2014). The effectiveness of an anti-stigma intervention in a basic police officer training programme: A controlled study. *BMC Psychiatry, 14*(55). PMID:24568685

Heilbrun, K., & Bingham, A. (2013). Community mental health: Innovations in diversion from prosecution of people with mental health problems. In J. Rosenberg & S. J. Rosenberg (Eds.), *Community mental health: Challenges for the 21st century* (2nd ed.; pp. 63–74). New York, NY: Routledge/Taylor & Francis Group.

Hoover, L. (2007). Atypical Situations-Atypical Responses. In T. J. Jurkanin, L. T. Hoover, & V. A. Sergevnin (Eds.), *Improving police response to persons with mental health problems* (pp. 5–23). Springfield, IL: Charles C. Thomas.

Jones, G. R. (2004). *Organizational theory, design and change: Text and cases* (4th ed.). Upper Saddle River, NJ: Pearson Education, Inc.

Kisely, S., Campbell, L. A., Peddle, S., Hare, S., Psyche, M., Spicer, D., & Moore, B. (2010). A controlled before-and-after evaluation of a mobile crisis partnership between mental health and *police* services in Nova Scotia. *Canadian Journal of Psychiatry, 55*(10), 662–668. PMID:20964945

Krameddine, Y. I., Demarco, D., Hassel, R., & Silverstone, P. H. (2013). A novel training program for police officers that improves interactions with mentally Ill individuals and is cost-effective. *Front Psychiatry, 4*(9), 1–10. PMID:23515226

LAPD Mental Health Unit Handout. (2014). Los Angeles, CA: Los Angeles Police Department.

Levine, P. (1979, April). *Cars 86 and 87: A review.* A report prepared for the City of Vancouver Emergency Services Implementation Committee. Vancouver, BC. Retrieved January 15, 2015, from http://searcharchives.vancouver.ca/cars-86-and-87-review

McAfee, J. K., & Musso, S. L. (1995). Training police officers about persons with disabilities: A 50-state analysis. *Remedial and Special Education*, *16*(1), 53–63. doi:10.1177/074193259501600107

Mental Health Evaluation Unit. (n.d.). Los Angeles, CA: Los Angeles Police Department. Retrieved September 17, 2015, from https://csgjusticecenter.org/documents/0000/0913/Los_Angeles_PD_MEU_Overview.pdf

Ontario provincial police mental health strategy: Our people, our communities. (2015). Ontario Provincial Police, Ontario, Canada. Retrieved 15 January 2016, from http://www.opp.ca/ecms/files/289727191.pdf

Pinfold, V., Huxley, P., Thornicroft, G., Farmer, P., Toulmin, H., & Graham, T. (2003). Reducing psychiatric stigma and discrimination: Evaluating an educational intervention with the police force in England. *Social Psychiatry and Psychiatric Epidemiology*, *38*(6), 337–344. PMID:12799785

Police Complaints Authority. (2003). *Review of shootings by police in England and Wales from 1998 to 2001*. London, UK: Police Complaints Authority.

Policing people who appear to be mentally ill. (2012, November). Victoria, AU: Victorian Government Printer. Retrieved September 17, 2015 from http://www.parliament.vic.gov.au/file_uploads/Policing_people_who_appear_to_be_ment ally_pyt8YbmN.pdf

Reuland, M. (2012). Tailoring the police response to people with mental health problems to community characteristics in the USA. In D. Chappell (Ed.), *Police responses to people with mental health problems: Global challenges* (pp. 27–41). London, UK: Routledge.

Scott, R. L. (2000). Evaluation of a mobile crisis program: Effectiveness, efficiency, and consumer satisfaction. *Psychiatric Services (Washington, D.C.)*, *51*(9), 1153–1156. doi:10.1176/appi.ps.51.9.1153 PMID:10970919

Shapiro, G. K., Cusi, A., Kirst, M., O'Campo, P., Nakhost, A., & Sterngiopolous, V. (2014). Co-responding police-mental health programs: A review. *Administration and Policy in Mental Health.* DOI: 10:1007/s10488-014-0594-9.

Specialized policing responses: Law enforcement/mental health learning sites. (n.d.). Washington, DC: Bureau of Justice Assistance, U.S. Department of Justice. Retrieved September 17, 2015, from http://csgjusticecenter.org/documents/0000/0895/Los_Angeles_PD_One_Pager.pdf

Steadman, H. J., Deane, M., Borum, R., & Morrissey, J. (2000). Comparing outcomes of major models of police responses to mental health emergencies. *Psychiatric Services (Washington, D.C.)*, *51*(5), 645–649. doi:10.1176/appi.ps.51.5.645 PMID:10783184

Thompson, J. L. (2003). *Strategic management* (3rd ed.). London, UK: Thomson Learning.

Vancouver's mental health crisis: An update report. (2013, September). Retrieved September 15, 2015, from http://vancouver.ca/police/assets/pdf/reports- policies/mental-health-crisis.pdf

Watson, A., & Angell, B. (2013). The role of stigma and uncertainty in moderating the effect of procedural justice on cooperation and resistance in police encounters with persons with mental illnesses. *Psychology, Public Policy, and Law*, *19*(1), 30–39. doi:10.1037/a0027931 PMID:24920876

Watson, A. C., Angell, B., Morabito, M. S., & Robinson, N. (2008). Defying negative expectations: Dimensions of fair and respectful treatment by police officers as perceived by people with mental health problems. *Administration and Policy in Mental Health*, *35*(6), 449–457. doi:10.1007/s10488-008-0188-5 PMID:18661226

ENDNOTES

1 Given the lack of a common term or label for individuals whose needs are reflected in this chapter, for convenience and clarity this chapter uses *people who appear to be experiencing mental health problems* (P/MHP), since this is the identification that police would make based on behavioral observations. The phrase is intended to include people such as those known to have mental health problems, people experiencing an emotional crisis and people with other related cognitive or behavioral problems such as an intellectual disability, dementia, autism, and fetal alcohol spectrum disorders.

2 In many cases, these could be called *orphan programs* as they originated in response to calls for police "to do something" but were not anchored in a strategic approach that looked for solutions to a problem rather than repeatedly responding to symptoms.

3 TEMPO stresses that learning should be targeted at all police personnel who have direct or indirect contact with the public, i.e., the focus should be on more than only police officers.

4 Traditionally this has been referred to as use of force training. This presupposes that the use of force will be an inevitable outcome. Increasingly this "training" is now being called *judgment training*.

5 Boyce et al. (2015) determined that nearly one million interactions occur each year between police in Canada and persons with mental health and substance abuse problems. Although each one is tragic, only a very few each year result in death or serious injury due to the use of force by police.

6 This strategy could also be a *Vulnerable Persons Strategy*. If that were the case then the scope would be wider, while still including mental health, and the number of related programs would be more.

7 Such a mental health strategy should be focused on the interactions of police personnel with P/MHP they encounter while working with the public. Although outside the scope of this chapter, a police mental health strategy could also include a second part–the important issue of mental wellness in the police workplace.

8 COAST is the acronym for Crisis Outreach and Support Team.

9 This also compares to some extent with the previously described comprehensive *advanced response* approach.

Chapter 14
Police Interactions with Persons-in-Crisis:
Emergency Psychological Services and Jail Diversion

Michael E. Christopher
Honolulu Police Department, USA

Vincent G. Tsushima
Hawaii Pacific University, USA

ABSTRACT

This chapter addresses the interaction of law enforcement officers and people who are psychologically impaired as a result of mental illness, emotional disturbance, or severe intoxication. The chapter consists of three major sections. Part One provides an overview of the larger legal and social factors that increasingly require law enforcement to develop specialized programmatic responses for responding to a Person-in-Crisis (PIC). Part Two provides an overview of different types of programmatic attempts to address the problems associated with these at-risk populations. Part Three offers recommendations to police psychologists on how to develop programmatic solutions to the challenges faced by law enforcement when dealing with PICs.

INTRODUCTION

Law enforcement agencies are increasingly developing programs for responding to a *Person-in-Crisis* (PIC), i.e., an individual who is significantly psychologically impaired as a result of mental illness, emotional disturbance, or substance intoxication. PICs may or may not be a danger to self or others, but they are experiencing psychological impairment and difficulty coping with the stressors of life that is sufficient to generate a state of crisis characterized by short-term, reactive, or defensive thought and behavior.

The new law enforcement-based programs for responding to PICs are designed to accomplish two goals: (1) de-escalate and provide emergency psychological services for PICs, and (2) divert as many

DOI: 10.4018/978-1-5225-0813-7.ch014

people as appropriate from the criminal justice system into the mental health system (CMHS, National Gains Center, 2007; Hails & Borum, 2003). Emergency psychological services, sometimes referred to as crisis services, are in some sense the logical extension of Emergency Medical Services (EMS). Emergency psychological services and EMS focus on providing immediate interventions to prevent death, harm, and suffering, and also to connect the PIC to appropriate follow-up treatment.

In this chapter we address: (1) social and legal changes necessitating the development of these programs, (2) different types of programmatic responses, and (3) recommendations for creating, improving, and maintaining such a program. Our geographic focus is the United States as a whole, but we will highlight data derived from one such program, with which we are associated, the *Honolulu Emergency Psychological Services and Jail Diversion Program* (HEPSJDP).

PART ONE: SOCIAL FACTORS AND LAW ENFORCEMENT RESPONSES TO PICs

In 2014, there were approximately 12 million people in the United States with a serious mental illness (Centers for Disease Control and Prevention, 2013; Kids Count Data Center, 2015). A significant portion of this population will have one or more mental health crises during their lifetimes that will result in encounters with law enforcement. A study of 174 police departments across the United States found that 7 to 10% of all police interactions involved individuals experiencing symptoms of serious mental illness (SMI; Deane, Steadman, Borum, Veysey, & Morrissey, 1999). While we do not have historical data for comparison, it appears likely that these encounters have dramatically increased in recent decades (Hails & Borum, 2003). The reasons for the likely increases in these interactions cannot be accounted for by increases in rates of mental illness or drug abuse (NIH, 2015) and, therefore, have to be understood in terms of changes in public policy (Torrey, 2014).

Deinstitutionalization

Prior to the 1970s, police had far fewer encounters with people suffering from SMI because a much higher percentage of people with SMI were institutionalized, often for life (Torrey, 2014). Beginning in the 1950s, a variety of scientific, medical, moral, and legal changes lead to a new and radically different public mental health care policy that has come to be known as *deinstitutionalization* (Torrey, 2014). Deinstitutionalization is a general term for a set of policies intended to reduce the number of people in mental health hospitals. In the 1950s, mental health hospitals began shutting down in response to lawsuits, government investigative findings of inhumane conditions, and the hopes generated by the development of new psychotropic medications (Torrey, 2014). Over the last half century, the primary effect of deinstitutionalization has been, as intended, to release hundreds of thousands of people with SMI from mental heath hospitals, and prevent others from being institutionalized.

Unfortunately, many people who were released from hospitals have not received adequate outpatient care, and have instead simply been re-institutionalized in jails and prisons, or left to live on the streets as chronically ill and homeless persons (Torrey, 2014). While the failure to fully fund community health care centers that were intended to provide outpatient mental health care for the people released from hospitals is probably the most important factor in the increase in interactions between PICs and law enforcement officers (LEOs), it is also true that community-based treatments often fail (Torrey, 2014).

The data are also clear that while most people with SMI can live safely in the community with adequate health care and sufficient social support, some people with serious and persistent mental illness cannot live in the community continuously (Torrey, 2014).

Re-Institutionalization

While deinstitutionalization is the primary reason for the increase of people with SMI living outside of hospitals, it is important to remember that in no period in the past was everyone, or even most people, with SMI institutionalized for life. Prior to the 1950s, most people with SMI were cared for by their families (Roleff & Egendorf, 2002; Torrey, 2014). In 2002, Roleff and Egendorf concluded that as a result of deinstitutionalization, approximately 763,000 people who would have been housed in mental institutions 40 years earlier were living outside of mental hospitals. Fourteen years later this number is approximately equal to the number of people with SMI who are currently either homeless or being housed in jails and prisons (U.S. Department of Housing and Urban Development, 2014; Torrey et al., 2003; Torrey, Zdanowicz, Kennard, Eslinger, Biasotti, & Fuller, 2014). In 2010, a person with SMI was 3.2 times as likely to be housed in prison or jail as he or she was in a mental hospital (Torrey, Kennard, Eslinger, Lamb, & Pavle, 2010). Arrests of persons with SMI are usually for minor crimes that are primarily a function of their mental illness. Currently, the United States maintains a population of about 365,000 seriously mentally ill persons in jails and prisons (Torrey et al., 2014). Forty years ago, almost this entire population would likely have been institutionalized in mental health hospitals, often for life. Today approximately 500,000 people with SMI cycle in and out of jail and prison, serving sentences of a few months or years, unless they are diverted into an appropriate mental health treatment program (Torrey et al., 2014). Of the approximately 763,000 people who would have been hospitalized 40 years ago, somewhere between 263,000 and 443,000 are now living in the community and functioning at various levels, while 320,000 to 670,000 people with SMI are in prison or jail on any given day (Torrey et al., 2014). This means that people with SMI are 300-700% more likely to be housed in prison/jail than in a hospital. The result is that 15-25% of the incarcerated population in the United States suffers from SMI (Torrey et al., 2014).

Homelessness

Part of the increase in encounters between LEOs and people with SMI is a function of deinstitutionalization. However, another problem adding to the increase is the declining stock of affordable housing (National Low Income Housing Coalition, 2015). People with SMI are especially vulnerable to becoming homeless because as a population, they have lower incomes and their illness often makes it difficult or impossible for them to take advantage of the limited resources available to low-income people. According to the Treatment Advocacy Center (2009), in 2014 there were 150,000 to 200,000 people with SMI living on the streets on any given day. Research indicates that people with SMI become more ill as a consequence of being homeless (Scott, 1993; Kushel, Vittinghoff, & Haas, 2001; Salit, Kuhn, Hurtz, Vu, & Mosso, 1998), which likely increases the frequency at which they become involved in interactions with LEOs. While the numbers fluctuate, more people with SMI are living on the streets than receiving care in hospitals. In fact, only 0.7% of all people with SMI are in a hospital at any given time. Research shows that people with SMI are 150% to 200% more likely to sleep on the street than in a hospital (Torrey et al., 2005). Persons with serious and persistent mental illness who are not receiving adequate services tend to cycle in and out of the criminal justice system. However, it is important to keep in mind that there are approximately 12,000,000 persons in the United States who suffer from SMI, most of whom have never been imprisoned and are functioning independently in the community.

Other Factors Increasing Interactions Between Law Enforcement and PICs

While the single largest factor accounting for the increase in interactions between law enforcement officers and PICs is deinstitutionalization, followed by the affordable housing shortage, it is important to keep in mind that there are at least two other key factors driving the reports of increasing rates of interactions between LEOs and PICs. First is a chronic lack of effective community mental health treatment programs and services (Torrey, 2014). The treatment programs that are highly effective for people with serious and persistent mental illness, such as Assertive Community Treatment (ACT), tend to be the most expensive mental health treatments (Lehman et al., 1999). Therefore, they are the most likely to be cut from public services and the least likely to be paid for by insurance companies. The fact that even the most expensive mental health treatment involving long-term hospitalization is less expensive than the costs of re-institutionalizing the person in the criminal justice system or abandoning him or her on the street, where the costs of emergency psychological services and EMS are frequently higher than the more effective services of long-term hospitalization, does not change the fact that individual institutions can cut their budgets by pushing these costs onto other institutions (Poulin, Maguire, Metraux, & Culhane, 2010). When every other institution fails to address the needs of persons with SMI, the institution of last resort is always law enforcement.

The second factor beyond deinstitutionalization and the housing shortage that is likely contributing to increased interactions between PICs and LEOs is that as training of LEOs improves, they become better at recognizing PICs. For instance, data from the HEPSJDP show a 300% increase in calls involving PICs between 2007 and 2013, and we attribute the majority of the change to increased recognition of PICs by officers due to improved training.

New Legal Standards for Law Enforcement Responses to PICs

Along with the increase in encounters between PICs and LEOs, there has also been greater legal scrutiny of how people with SMI are treated by law enforcement (*San Francisco v. Sheehan*, 2015; Portland State University Criminology and Criminal Justice Senior Capstone, 2012). One area of potential liability involves situations in which the actions of LEOs endanger PICs. A second area of potential liability involves situations in which the actions of officers violate a PIC's civil rights by failing to adhere to section 1983 of the Civil Rights Acts and other legislation, such as the Americans with Disability Act (ADA), that clarify these obligations. Departments need to create policy that not only adheres to state and federal statutes, but also takes into account the multiple, changing, and often conflicting court decisions regarding these interactions. One of the most important of these decisions was *City of Canton v. Harris* (1989). In this decision the court declared that all LEOs are expected to: (1) recognize that persons are engaged in unusual, bizarre, and abnormal behavior, (2) use alternative field tactics when responding to PICs, and (3) ensure these alternative tactics have been designed to take into account the mental status of the person. In *Walker v. City of New York* (2nd Circuit, 1992), the court went further, making it clear that law enforcement agencies must also provide training for dealing with these situations.

Another area in which the courts have given additional guidance is on the issue of what constitutes appropriate use of force for LEOs when they are interacting with PICs. In *Deorle v. Rutherford* (9th Circuit, 2001) the court ruled that when an officer is deciding how much force to use in controlling an agitated person, he or she must take into account the person's mental state and the risk that individual poses to self and others, separate from the degree to which that individual is cooperating with law enforcement. Officers are required to attempt to de-escalate, rather than simply overpower, uncooperative PICs. And, once a PIC is detained or taken into custody, the officer is responsible for the safety, care, and well-being of the PIC. In general, the courts have identified three kinds of scenarios in which LEOs must take into account a person's mental status: (1) the individual is manifestly in need of emergency medical or psychiatric treatment, (2) the individual is mentally incapacitated and thus unable to survive safely in the community without care, and (3) the individual poses an "imminent" danger to self or others. Law enforcement may, and in some circumstances must, arrange transport to a hospital for a PIC. Arresting the PIC does not eliminate this duty.

If the PIC is not under arrest and refuses treatment, the duty to protect the PIC and the community becomes more complex. It is a violation of a person's 4th Amendment rights to unlawfully detain a person who is not under arrest, and a person has the right to refuse to undergo any medical procedure, including a psychiatric evaluation, against his or her will unless very specific conditions are met (*Young v. Romero*, 1982). Therefore, an agency needs a policy that provides a procedure by which officers can, if needed, temporarily suspend a person's civil rights for the protection of the PIC or others. How law enforcement reconciles the duty to arrest with policies designed to prevent arrests while also detaining individuals for the purpose of requiring them to obtain help is unique to each department. The U.S. Supreme Court has ruled that law enforcement agencies can be found guilty of "deliberate indifference" under Section 1983 of the Civil Rights Act if they 1) fail to develop policy for any situation a reasonable person could anticipate, 2) fail to train personnel in the policy, or 3) fail to enforce the policy (*Estelle v. Gamble*, 1976; *City of Canton, Ohio v. Harris*, 1989).

Understanding the legal issues affecting interactions between LEOs and PICs starts with recognizing the way in which the law that structures these interactions is derived primarily from the 8th and 14th Amendments to the Constitution. The 8th Amendment prohibits cruel and unusual punishment, as well as excessive bail or fines (U.S. Const. amend. VIII). In *Estelle v. Gamble* (1976) the court decided that the 8th Amendment requires that prisoners deserve a minimum level of treatment, and that this minimum level of treatment includes mental health care. The definition of what constitutes a prisoner has changed over time, but is now generally understood to be someone whose activity is being restricted by law enforcement. In other words, when a person has been arrested the responsibility is clear: the duty to provide care starts as soon as an officer stops or detains a person for any reason. Law enforcement-based crisis services and jail diversion programs must also be careful not to violate the 14th Amendment's (1868) Due Process Clause, which states that individuals shall not be deprived of life, liberty, or property, without due process of law (U.S. Const. amend. XIV). This ultimately means that law enforcement and other agencies or institutions acting on the behalf of the government must use the least restrictive means available to accomplish the government sanctioned action (*Jackson v. Youngblood*, 1972). LEOs must also be cognizant of the implications of the Americans with Disabilities Act (ADA, 1990), which extend specific civil rights protections to all people who have physical and/or mental disabilities.

Interactions between LEOs and PICs are further complicated because the law makes it clear that a "competent" person has the right to refuse help, including medical treatment, even if that refusal will hasten his or her death (*Matter of Conroy*, 1985). However, the courts have not been as clear on how the issue of competency is to be decided outside of a court. The result is the law requires that a person be treated as competent, except in some emergency situations such as crisis interactions with police, until found incompetent by a court (*Union Pacific Railway Co. v. Botsford*, 1990; *Cruzan v. Director, Missouri Depart. of Health*, 1990). Even in emergency situations, officers must follow specific procedural processes designed to spell out the precise situations under which a PIC's civil rights can be temporarily suspended.

The courts have acknowledged exceptions to the general right to refuse treatment. There are basically two types of exemptions: (1) the person is not competent to make rational decisions (*Canterbury v. Spence*, 1972), and (2) the State has sufficient interests to override the rights of the individual <u>and</u> also has a specific procedure that addresses the individual's "due process" rights (*Cruzan by Cruzan v. Harmon*, 1988). The first exception comes into play when the individual is unconscious or otherwise incapable of consenting, and the harm of not treating is imminent and outweighs any harm threatened by the proposed treatment (*Canterbury v. Spence*, 1972). A PIC obviously cannot consent to emergency psychological services if he or she is unconscious, however, the issue of "otherwise incapable of consenting" comes down to being "competent" to make rational decisions. In *Cobbs v. Grant* (1972) the court stated, "A patient should be denied the opportunity to weigh the risks only where it is evident he cannot evaluate the data, as for example, where there is an emergency, or the patient is a child or incompetent" (p. 243). Although this decision is referring to patients in hospitals, it opens up two issues that are relevant to law enforcement. First, interactions between LEOs and PICs often do constitute an "emergency." And second, the PIC may be in a psychological state that the law would recognize as temporarily "incompetent," but making this judgment often requires more psychological training than any LEO could be reasonably expected to possess. A licensed mental health professional working with law enforcement may be able to assess a PIC's capacity for rational decision-making, but once the "emergency" has passed only a court can declare a person incompetent (*Matter of Conroy*, 1985).

In addition to the issue of competency, the court recognizes that the State may have interests that can in limited circumstances override the interests of the individual. Over the years the State has carved out categories of "compelling interests" on which it has, at times, successfully justified the right to compel a PIC to undergo involuntary treatment/evaluation, some of which apply even if the person is legally competent (*Canterbury v. Spence*, 1972). The State has argued it has an interest in (1) preserving life, (2) protecting the interests of innocent third parties, (3) preventing irrational suicide, and (4) maintaining the ethical integrity of the medical profession (Standley, 2012). However, the only situation under which all courts have consistently recognized the State's right to override a person's civil right to refuse treatment is when the PIC is not competent (*Cruzan v. Harmon*, 1988). The issue then comes down to how to determine if the person is not competent to refuse medical treatment, and there has never been a consensus on this issue. The Supreme Court has left it up to each state to devise a procedure for allowing LEOs and/or health care professionals to override an individual's refusal to accept medical care (Stettin, Geller, Ragosta, Chen, & Ghowrwal, 2014). The result is every state does it a little differently, and case law often raises issues that only get addressed many years later, if ever.

PART TWO: PROGRAM OPTIONS FOR RESPONDING TO PICs

In addition to helping PICs recover, jail diversion and emergency psychological services programs help reduce jail overcrowding, mitigate burgeoning court dockets, lower the cost of providing expensive medication and treatment services within jails, and free up space for more serious felons (Massaro, 2004). These programs can also be advantageous for mental health providers by fostering coordination of treatment without interruption. Continuous treatment can provide opportunities for greater stability and fewer crises, while mandated treatment can provide an additional mechanism for treatment adherence.

Emergency Psychological Services and Jail Diversion

Emergency psychological services are part of but distinct from jail diversion services, though each is more effective when they are combined. Emergency psychological services direct PICs into treatment and support services with no regard to whether they have committed a crime. They focus on, first, providing immediate interventions to prevent death, harm, and suffering and, second, connecting the person to appropriate follow up treatment. In contrast to emergency psychological services, jail diversion programs identify PICs who could be arrested, or have already been arrested, in order to redirect them from the criminal justice system into the mental health and social support systems. Often the practical lines between these two types of services are blurred.

Emergency psychological service programs are for the most part pre-booking programs, while jail diversion programs can take place: prior to arrest, after arrest but prior to booking, after booking but prior to court, or during court. Most jail diversion programs are court-based, rather than law enforcement-based. In 1992 there were 52 such programs in the United States and by 2010 the number had grown to 560 programs across 47 states (CMHS National GAINS Center, 2010).

There are other types of programs that involve the criminal justice system and mental health treatment, which are distinct from but, nonetheless, essential to successful law enforcement-based jail diversion programs. For instance, jails and prisons increasingly provide a range of mental health, transition, or discharge planning services in order to reduce recidivism (Aufderheide, 2014). These programs are distinct from law enforcement-based programs, but they share the goals of reducing criminal recidivism and improving the mental health of people who come into contact with the criminal justice system.

All of these programs share the goal of reducing the number of mentally ill people in jail by diverting them into the mental health system, but they operate at different points in what the GAINS Center for Behavioral Health and Justice Transformation (a program of the Substance Abuse and Mental Health Services Administration [SAMHSA]) calls the *Sequential Intercept Model* (CMHS National GAINS Center, 2007). The five intercept points are: (1) law enforcement and emergency services; (2) initial detention and initial hearings; (3) jails, courts, forensic evaluations, and forensic commitments; (4) reentry from jails, state prisons, and forensic hospitalization; and (5) community corrections and community support services. Law enforcement programs primarily involve intercept one, but they can also extend into intercept two. One of the biggest stumbling blocks to long-term effectiveness of these programs is failure to integrate the different intercepts, which is primarily about failure to share information (Torrey et al., 2014; CMHS National GAINS Center, 2007; CMHS National GAINS Center, 2010).

In this chapter we focus on two types of law enforcement based programs, which are defined by the point in the criminal justice process where diversion occurs: pre-booking and post-booking law enforcement programs. Post-booking jail diversion programs are further divided into different types of jail-based programs and court-based programs. Jail-based programs are further differentiated according to the agency running the jail. Many law enforcement agencies have their own jails or detention facilities where individuals are taken to be booked, prior to being transferred to jails that are associated with either the court system or the post-conviction penal system. Court-based programs are further separated into specialty courts (e.g., mental health and drug courts) and regular dispositional courts (CMHS National GAINS Center, 2007).

Both pre- and post-booking approaches have been shown to be highly effective in reducing crime and preventing harm to the mentally ill and the public, while also saving money for taxpayers. Steadman and Naples (2005) reported (as cited in CMHS National GAINS Center, 2007) that jail diversion reduces time spent in jail for people with mental illness and co-occurring substance use disorders, links these individuals to community-based services, results in lower criminal justice costs, and does not increase public safety risks.

Pre-Booking Programs

Pre-booking jail diversion primarily involves emergency psychological services. The goal is to immediately divert the person from the criminal justice system into the mental health system. A fundamental principle upon which all jail diversion programs should be based is the idea of providing the least restrictive treatment intervention. In general, there are three basic types of pre-booking programs, all of which rely on developing effective interactions between the police and community mental health services (CMHS National GAINS Center, 2007). The different types are (1) police-based specialized police response programs, (2) police-based specialized mental health response programs, and (3) mental health-based specialized mental health response programs. The first two types of program are law enforcement-based, the third is mental health services-based. The success of each model depends upon the mental health resources in the community that police can access for a PIC on a 24-hour basis (Reuland, 2005). Programs are more effective if in addition to emergency room services, they have access to services for people who are in crisis but who do not need the services of an emergency room. These crisis services include: crisis stabilization units, mobile crisis teams, homeless shelters, and detoxification facilities (Reuland, 2005).

Most pre-booking programs are *police-based specialized police response programs* (Hails & Borum, 2003). The best known and most common program of this type is the Crisis Intervention Team (CIT). This approach is sometimes referred to as the "Memphis Model" because it was developed in Memphis, Tennessee. The *Police Executive Research Forum* (PERF) asked law enforcement agencies that have adopted the CIT model why they selected this approach (Reuland, 2005). Many agencies reported that the CIT model is realistic and efficient. Law enforcement agencies often choose the CIT model over a mental health-based model (e.g., mobile crisis team) because they prefer for the police to remain in control of determining how to assist PICs.

Lattimore et al. (2003) explain (as cited in CMHS National Gains Center, 2007) that the CIT approach involves the use of specially trained officers who determine whether an arrest or mental health intervention is appropriate. This model of emergency psychological services and jail diversion is the only one that has an organization, CIT International, dedicated to its advancement and propagation. According to the National Alliance on Mental Illness (NAMI), over 2,700 law enforcement agencies now have CIT programs (NAMI, n.d.). While there have been efforts to ensure that when a specific program is referred to as an example of a CIT program it meets some unified standards (McLean, 2011), at present what constitutes a CIT program varies enormously. The following are the 10 "core elements" of CIT, organized into four categories (Dupont, Cochran, & Pillsbury, 2007).

Ongoing elements:

1. Partnerships: Law enforcement, advocacy, and mental health
2. Community ownership: Planning, implementation, and networking
3. Policies and procedures

Operational elements:

4. CIT: Officer, dispatcher, and coordinator
5. Curriculum: CIT training
6. Mental health receiving facility: Emergency services

Sustaining elements:

7. Evaluation and research
8. In-service training
9. Recognition and honors
10. Outreach: Developing CIT in other communities

The list of core elements is a good general guide for the many components that potentially determine the success or failure of law enforcement-based emergency psychological services and jail diversion programs. As the name implies, CIT is organized around creating a team of officers with special skills and duties. To facilitate a sense of unit cohesion, the Memphis Model stresses using special pins, ceremonies, awards, and rewards for the members. The team or unit must be large enough that a member can respond to every call involving a PIC. In practice this means that in order to have a CIT member on duty for every shift in every sector 365 days per year, the CIT unit usually needs to consist of about 25% of the total number of officers in a department (Dupont, Cochran & Pillsbury, 2007). In small to medium sized departments, this kind of scheduling is often feasible, but in large departments the difficulty of scheduling can become an obstacle in itself. All programs entail training for law enforcement officers, but many departments do not adopt the full 40 hour CIT training program.

In the HEPSJDP we have developed an alternative training program that is only 24 hours long. The HEPSJDP is an example of the second type of police-based program, the *police-based specialized mental health response program.* We refer to it as the *Honolulu Model* to distinguish it from the Memphis Model. Police-based specialized mental health response programs are less common than police-based specialized police response programs because they require police departments to hire mental health consultants to provide on-site and/or telephone consultation to officers (CMHS National GAINS Center, 2007). Like police-based specialized police response programs (e.g., CIT), these programs are run by police departments, but unlike the police-based specialized police response programs they have in-house mental health professionals who consult in real time with LEOs sharing some of the responsibility for determining when and what mental health intervention is appropriate. In these programs LEOs are also specially trained to recognize and respond to people with mental illness, but the amount of training may be less because they have access to professional mental health consultants.

Police-based special mental health response programs come in a variety of forms depending on the type of mental health professionals that are involved and the particular role they play. The Honolulu Model includes specially trained psychologists who are on-call for phone consultation 24/7 to police officers, but there is no special police unit. At this time all officers are trained to the same level. Training emphasizes when and how to consult with the police psychologist. Unlike the Memphis Model, which was created by a police officer and a mental health professional from outside the department in collaboration with community advocacy groups, the Honolulu Model was created by police psychologists who work inside the Honolulu Police Department and provide a full range of psychological services to officers and the department. So far as we know, this is the only program developed under the direction of a police psychologist with an emphasis on the ways in which stress responses of LEOs and PICs impact each other. This approach to training came out of an extensive review of published curriculum and program training guidelines, as well as police psychology literature.

While the development of the Honolulu Model was quite different than the Memphis Model, it also has not been evaluated in any comparative research. The only evaluations of the HEPSJDP to date are internal training surveys that consistently report that 90-95% of participating LEOs are satisfied or very satisfied with the training. The Honolulu Model is also different from the Memphis Model in that it places a much larger emphasis on training officers to recognize the universal biological, psychological, and sociocultural dynamics of being a PIC. The hypothesis behind this approach is that by enabling officers to better understand the universal factors of human crisis situations they are less likely to view PICs as "the other," i.e., as people with whom they share nothing in common. In the Honolulu Model, rather than just focusing on recognizing and responding to PICs as in the Memphis Model, the training focuses on how officers can avoid being overcome by the situational psychological forces that are intrinsic to human beings coping with perceived threats. The goal of the Honolulu Model is to develop an all-inclusive mental health training program that addresses the psychological needs of both LEOs and PICs, within a universal understanding of human nature. It is our position that such a foundation may make it possible for departments to consolidate other kinds of officer-focused mental health training, such as parenting skills, stress management, and officer-involved domestic violence, into the formal training on responding to PICs.

Another version of police-based specialized mental health response program is the Houston Model, which combines a special CIT unit with mental health professionals (Kissinger, 2014). Unlike the Honolulu Model, mental health workers in Houston Model programs tend to be entry-level mental health workers or case managers, who were trained as mental health counselors or social workers. The degree of training and whether they are licensed is often determined by the details of their actual roles. Mental health workers may simply assist officers in obtaining mental health and social services for the PIC and, therefore, do not need to be licensed or have doctoral level training. On the other hand, there may be occasions where mental health professionals are needed to make legal determinations about a person's mental status and whether or not an individual can be transported to a mental health facility for an involuntary evaluation, as the psychologists often do in the Honolulu Model. In such cases the mental health professional must be specially trained and licensed. In the Memphis Model, officers conduct an initial mental health assessment at the scene and make all decisions regarding mental health interventions, whereas in the Honolulu Model officers are trained to recognize PICs and then to call the on-call psychologist for a consultation. In the latter example, the officer decides if there is to be an arrest and the psychologist decides if there is to be a mental health intervention and what that intervention should be. In the Houston Model, officers and licensed counselors work together at the scene to come up with the best mental health intervention.

The third type of program is the *mental health-based specialized mental health response program*. These programs usually provide emergency psychological services, but are not jail diversion programs and are not run by law enforcement agencies. They involve some kind of mobile crisis team that, like with EMS, responds when requested by police. These teams vary greatly in their level of training. This approach sometimes involves a special ambulance service for PICs that provides on-scene medication, but sometime they only provide on scene assistance without the capacity to transport the PICs to services (Deane, Steadman, Deane, Borum, Versey, & Morrissey, 1999).

Post-Booking Programs

Post-booking jail diversion programs are the most prevalent type of diversion program in the United States (CMHS National GAINS Center, 2007). As of mid-2007, there were approximately 500 jail diversion programs in the U.S., and 65% were post-booking programs. The term "booking" refers to being processed after being arrested. The term "jail" refers to different types of facilities in which people are detained after booking, ranging from a holding cell in a police station, to a pre-trial holding facility at court, to a detention facility for certain types of crimes after sentencing. Some jail facilities hold only people who have been convicted of crimes, while others hold people awaiting trial, and some hold both populations. Post-booking programs can be police-based or court-based. Our focus is police-based programs, but it is important to understand how court-based programs can be integrated with police-based programs. Police-based post-booking systems are generally pre-court and operate in police detention centers. A court-based post-booking program operates at either the jail or court arraignment that: 1) screens people potentially eligible for diversion for the presence of mental illness; 2) evaluates their eligibility for diversion; 3) negotiates with prosecutors, defense attorneys, mental health providers, and the courts to produce a disposition outside the jail in place of prosecution or a reduction in charges; and 4) connects people to an individualized array of community-based services (CMHS National GAINS Center, 2007). These programs are beyond the scope of this chapter, but for all jail diversion to work effectively the various agencies and programs need to be able to share data.

In a post-booking program, an individual may be diverted: (1) at or immediately after booking into jail, before the filing of charges with the court; (2) upon release from pre-trial detention with the condition of participation in treatment; (3) prior to disposition (e.g., upon the prosecutor's offer of deferred prosecution); (4) at disposition or sentencing; and (5) when at risk of, or following, a violation of probation (SAMHSA, 2014). Specialty courts, such as drug courts or mental health courts, are a specific type of post-booking jail diversion program founded on the concept of "therapeutic jurisprudence" (CMHS National GAINS Center, 2007).

Court-based programs typically dismiss charges after completion of a mental health program as an incentive to participate in treatment. By contrast, jail-based programs are operated by pre-trial service personnel or by specialized jail personnel, often for individuals who have more severe charges and/or mental health problems, or who simply have not been identified earlier in the process.

The *Pre-trial Services Resource Center* (PSRC) conducted a survey of pre-trial release and deferred prosecution programs throughout the U.S., examining information from 14 jurisdictions. Twelve of the programs met the model criteria for pre-trial release decision- making and two used mental health screening and assessment procedures for the deferred prosecution decision (Clark, 2004). The results showed that jurisdictions used a range of community treatment options tailored to the individual's needs, including both inpatient and outpatient treatment. Further, in all the jurisdictions those defendants needing related services (e.g., housing, medical assistance, financial assistance) could receive assistance ' part of the supervision of pre-trial release or deferred prosecution. As of 2004, the results showe in most jurisdictions persons with mental illness did not have the same opportunities for pre-tr' and deferred prosecution as other defendants (Clark, 2004). In many jurisdictions there is no court- or jail-based agency that gathers information and develops options for the decision-maker shortly after arrest for defendants. Only 257 jurisdictions were identified by this survey as having a formal pre-trial release or deferred prosecution program (Clark, 2004). Moreover, only 12 out of 203 responding jurisdictions met the model criteria for programs that target people with mental illness.

The post-booking component of the HEPSJDP uses specially trained Advanced Practice Registered Nurses who work in the Honolulu Police Department Central Receiving cellblock to screen detainees. Screening includes face-to-face evaluations and checking a database kept by the Department of Health. When the HEPSJDP began in 2008, about 25% of detainees were identified as suffering from SMI or severe substance intoxication. In 2014, the percentage was up to 50%, double the national average. It is unlikely this rate was due entirely to higher rates of SMI and substance abuse in the communities served by the Honolulu Police Department. Instead, our experience is that as mental health screening improves, the percentage of individuals identified as experiencing SMI or substance abuse increases significantly.

PART THREE: CONSIDERATIONS IN DEVELOPING PROGRAMS FOR PICs

Despite the fact that interactions between PICs and LEOs are some of the most psychologically demanding and dangerous interactions faced by LEOs, police psychologists have until recently not seen this as a central focus of police psychology. This chapter was written with the hope of focusing police psychologists' attention on the complexity of these interactions and the importance of developing coherent programmatic responses that integrate the specialized knowledge of police psychology with a "big picture" understanding of how the criminal justice and mental health systems respond to PICs.

Police Culture

The relative neglect of attention on interactions between PICs and LEOs within police psychology may be a function of the fact that police psychologists tend to focus on what law enforcement command focuses on. When we began the HEPSJDP it was common for officers to characterize responding to PICs as "not real police work," despite the fact these encounters constitute 7-10% of all police officer interactions (Deane et al., 1999; Watson & Fulambarker, 2012). Part of this attitude comes from the historically erroneous idea that professional police work was originally only about arresting people for breaking the law. LEOs have been involved in identifying and transporting the mentally ill to mental health hospitals in the U.S. since Americans first started building hospitals for the mentally ill in the early 19th century (Torrey, 2014). What is different in contemporary programs is the attempt to provide basic training for LEOs on how to recognize and effectively respond to psychologically impaired people.

Building officer confidence in the program is critical to overcoming resistance to program implementation (Reuland, 2005). In our experience with the HEPSJDP, two factors were most responsible for overcoming this resistance. First, the HEPSJDP involves having police psychologists on-call 24 hours a day, 365 days a year. Over time the officers have come to see the psychologists as an asset, and will call them for a consult even before they encounter a PIC to get advice on a possible scenario or how to deal with a particularly difficult person with whom they have had frequent contact. The other factor most responsible for overcoming resistance is the training itself. In our experience, many officers are hungry for a better understanding of mental illness and human behavior, particularly if they can apply such insight to situations in their personal as well as professional lives. We have found that the key to using training to overcome resistance to emergency psychological services and jail diversion programs is to start from the officers' perspective, rather than the perspective of the PIC, and then engage LEOs in trying to reconcile their perspectives with those of the PIC. In our experience the fact that the program is designed and run by police psychologists who demonstrate an understanding of the difficulties and stresses of law enforcement work and the personal lives of LEOs goes a long way toward overcoming resistance to these programs and securing buy-in.

Strategic Planning

Most first generation emergency psychological services and jail diversion programs began with the attempt to solve a local problem. For example, the 1988 shooting by Memphis, TN police officers of Joseph D. Robinson, who suffered from schizophrenia, gave rise to CIT (Watson & Fulambarker, 2012). However, there are now enough functioning programs to make it possible for those wishing to develop a program to create a strategic plan based on the experience of established programs. According to the CMHS National GAINS Center (2007), effective strategic planning involves the following key steps:

1. Create a shared vision among stakeholders;
2. Identify a target population as the primary focus of the program;
3. Determine the services that the target group requires;
4. Examine current programs serving the population and identify service area gaps or failures; and
5. Examine this local assessment in terms of different model programmatic approaches, and consider how existing models can be adapted to fit local contexts and constraints.

Developing a strategic plan will involve "mapping the system," i.e., identifying gaps and needs in the system and prioritizing action planning by making choices on where to initially invest resources (CMHS National GAINS Center, 2007). To avoid "reinventing the wheel" and duplicating services, one needs to have a good understanding of the full range of treatment, housing, and services for individuals with mental illness in contact with the justice system. This also means learning what services are deemed by the research literature and professional experts to be most effective. System mapping also entails using what SAMHSA refers to as the sequential intercept model to determine the key points at which individuals with mental illness receive services once they become engaged in the criminal justice system. Good strategic planning includes having an action plan that articulates specific steps and objectives for each set of stakeholders (CMHS National GAINS Center, 2007). A program's stakeholder groups should include the following:

1. Hospitals
2. Community mental health service providers
3. Mental health advocacy groups such as National Alliance on Mental Illness and Mental Health America
4. Consumers
5. Law enforcement

Budgeting is also a key aspect of strategic planning. Most programs begin with a budget that combines federal and local funding. Most federal funding for starting these programs requires at least one law enforcement agency and one mental health agency committed to working together (CMHS National GAINS Center, 2007). Planners need to determine a mix of funding sources that respond to the specific needs of the consumers and reflect the ways in which services are funded and delivered in the local community. Finally, devising a marketing strategy is also critical (CMHS National GAINS Center, 2007) in order to: (1) educate the general public about the importance of mental health and the effectiveness of treatment; (2) get the word out about the people a program serves, its goals, and how potential consumers can be referred to the program; and (3) be prepared, in advance, to respond to incidents that may attract negative attention to the program.

Training

By their basic nature, all successful pre- and post-booking law enforcement-based programs involve training LEOs to: (1) recognize mental illness, (2) de-escalate emotionally disturbed persons, and (3) connect PICs to mental health and social services. While LEOs are always trained, others who need training, such as radio dispatchers, are often overlooked. Though everyone who is trained needs training in the three basic domains listed above, training should also be customized for each group to address the unique issues associated with different roles.

Deciding how many officers to train and to what level is critical. A viable program requires at least one adequately trained officer in every sector 24 hours a day, 365 days a year. If the department is in a medium or large sized city, it is going to need multiple adequately trained officers in every sector to ensure they can respond in a timely manner to all incidents. In addition to the fact that costs of training increase with the size of the department, the larger the department the more complex the scheduling of trained officers becomes. One approach is to train everyone to the highest standard, but since the size of classes is limited, this strategy can take a very long time. If the department has 10,000 officers and each class includes 25 of them, it would take 16,000 hours to provide 40 hours of training to every officer. Even if a department has the funding to pay for the training, the time involved in providing this much training for all personnel could be years. As a result, many medium to large departments develop two levels of training: one for a special unit of officers and a shorter version for the remaining officers (Pauly, 2013). To meet all the scheduling requirements of having at least one highly trained officer in every sector for every shift, a special unit usually has to be about 25% of patrol officers.

One way to reduce the amount of needed training is to incorporate a mental health professional into a program as we have done with the HEPSJDP. If the professional is available 24 hours a day in real time to consult with officers, less training for officers is required. However, it is important to remember that mental health professionals need training as well. Although all licensed mental health professionals are trained to recognize and treat mentally ill and emotionally disturbed persons, most are not trained to assist PICs in the context of interactions with law enforcement. It is our opinion most mental health professionals are not adequately trained for this role and can actually make situations worse and more dangerous in their attempts to help. Misguided attempts to help may also undermine support for these programs. In the HEPSJDP we have on-the-job training for all psychologists responding to calls from police officers. In our experience if the psychologists are not police psychologists, they will need to be trained in some of the basic duties and challenges that LEOs face on the job, particularly when responding to PICs.

Training in a law enforcement agency involves an instructor teaching recruits or officers the knowledge, skills, and attitudes the department wants them to acquire. Mental health training should always involve didactic instruction but it should also include some kind of scenario training. Scenario training often involves live re-enactments of different types of interactions. This kind of live scenario training is excellent for teaching de-escalating skills (Krameddine, DeMarco, Hassel, & Silverstone, 2013). However, these scenarios are not actual encounters with PICs. The HEPSJDP makes extensive use of videos of actual encounters, usually acquired from YouTube. The HEPSJDP is also experimenting with online training.

Training may also include "experience exchange." For example, police departments can offer ride-along programs that expose mental health professionals to the day-to-day experiences of police officers. Or police officers can observe mentally ill persons in contexts other than interactions with police. Another mode of training is cross-training of agencies. This can save money and ensure that agencies interact with each other. Cross-training can also help ensure everyone involved in the program has a common core skill set. Cross-training of staff is also an excellent way to promote cooperation, build a common knowledge base, and create understanding and respect among professionals from diverse training backgrounds.

Collaboration and Integration of Services

Law enforcement programs can only be successful at helping PICs to the extent that they are integrated with other services. Steadman, Morris, and Dennis (1995) recommended (as cited in CMHS National GAONS Center, 2007) that the services that should be integrated and coordinated in diversion programs include: social services, housing, health care services, mental health treatment, substance abuse treatment, local law enforcement and corrections, courts, workforce development, and Medicaid. This integration has to occur at the level of service providers if it is to be effective. Our experience is that when integration is imposed from the top, it often results in mandates that simply cannot be fulfilled due to the complexity of cooperation across multiple bureaucracies, each with its own rules. This is not to say that agency leaders and politicians should not be involved. They often have a broad scope of understanding that is lacking on the "front line," but they also cannot possibly have the detail of knowledge that is needed to ensure smooth and efficient integration of services on a day-to-day basis. Front line workers are the professionals most likely to have viable solutions, but they can only implement them with the active support and engagement of agency leaders and other authorities.

The Council of State Governments (2002) asserted (as cited in CMHS National GAINS Center, 2007) that the single, most significant coordination factor in successful diversion programs is a close working relationship between at least two key stakeholders -- one from the criminal justice system and the other from the mental health care system. Reuland and Cheney (2005) found that, among surveyed agencies participating in law enforcement-based diversion programs for the mentally ill, all of the agencies participated in multidisciplinary committees at some point. These committees, which typically met monthly or quarterly, involve a variety of functions and enhance success by providing a forum for discussion about progress and an opportunity to develop solutions to problems. Part of the coordination process involves developing memoranda of understanding (MOU) or interagency agreements (Massaro, 2004). MOUs are formal agreements between parties regarding cooperative efforts. One of the most common reasons for an MOU is to agree on who is responsible for providing specific resources. For instance, the HEPSJDP is staffed entirely by Honolulu Police Department personnel, but has been funded at different times with city, state, and federal funds. MOUs may also include agreements about sharing information. Such agreements must meet state and federal confidentiality requirements. MOUs can also address many other functions, such as defining referral processes. Ultimately, the key to creating law enforcement-based programs that can respond to the needs of PICs is to integrate pre- and post-booking law enforcement-based services with each other and with the follow up services provided by the courts, health care organizations, and other stakeholders.

In order to provide emergency psychological services and/or jail diversion services, the evaluation of a PIC's mental status should begin at the first contact with an LEO. If all officers are not equally trained in how to respond to PICs, they all should at least be trained regarding when to call for an officer with more training. If the program involves on-call mental health professionals, the officers need to know when and how to contact them. A program must also have clear guidelines on how to acquire different types of voluntary or involuntary services, and who is allowed to make the determination as to what an appropriate intervention is for a PIC. The process for gaining access to whatever services are determined to be appropriate must also be clear. The most psychologically and legally complex of these determinations involves the decision to transport a PIC involuntarily to a hospital or other designated facility for a professional psychological or psychiatric screening, followed by appropriate treatment.

In law enforcement-based post-booking programs, the PIC is already detained in a cellblock and the timeframe for an evaluation has more to do with how long he or she will be held before being transferred to court or another holding facility. This means that the department must have mental health staff available 24 hours a day who are trained in doing emergency mental health evaluations (Clark, 2004). It is important to keep in mind that most mental health professionals are not trained to conduct these kinds of evaluations. This means recruiting for these positions must be done with the assistance of one or more mental health professionals with the relevant training to help ensure that only qualified persons are hired. Police psychologists can play a key role in such recruitment efforts, regardless of whether they are participating in conducting the actual evaluations.

Steadman, Morris, and Dennis (1995) reported (as cited in CMHS National GAINS Center, 2007) that a successful emergency psychological services or jail diversion program requires a strong leader to network and coordinate activities. A full-time position dedicated to coordinating the program provides officers and mental health providers with someone to answer questions and address concerns (Reuland & Cheney, 2005). Part of that leadership requires the individual to be a "boundary spanner," someone skilled at helping the professionals and staff involved to bridge the mental health and criminal justice systems so that problems and challenges are effectively managed (CMHS National GAINS Center, 2007). According to Reuland and Cheney (2005), to be successful, programs need commitment and support from leadership within law enforcement, mental health services, and the community. Clark (2004) reports that similar conditions and resources are needed for the success of post-booking programs. Another often-overlooked ingredient of successful programs is to provide officer recognition for exceptional performance related to the programs (Reuland & Cheney, 2005).

Data Collection, Sharing, and Analysis

To plan effective services for persons with complex needs, it is necessary to be able to share information about the treatment and services they require (CMHS National GAINS Center, 2007). First, it is important to learn as much as possible about local, state, and federal laws that govern the exchange of information between mental health providers and law enforcement. Next, one should establish a committee of stakeholder groups to review or develop policies that facilitate information sharing, including the development of a standardized release of information form that meets legal requirements. The federal

Health Insurance Portability and Accountability Act (HIPAA) does not apply to most of what transpires in these programs, and it includes exceptions for some "emergency" situations that might involve "covered entities." However, other state or local regulations may be stricter than HIPAA requirements and therefore must be thoroughly researched and understood (National Institute of Health, n.d.). A guiding principle is that every effort should always be made to protect the privacy rights and the dignity of PICs.

Data collection and analysis are essential for program evaluation and for building support for diverting people with mental health problems from the criminal justice system into the mental health system. Politicians and legislators need comprehensive and compelling data to do their part in promoting and justifying such efforts. Once a program is up and running, continued data collection and analysis are essential for sustaining and expanding a program's efforts beyond the preliminary stage (CMHS National GAINS Center, 2007). Lastly, data collection and analysis are critical to assisting other agencies in developing adequate mental health treatment plans and programs. A law enforcement-based program designed to assist PICs can only be successful to the extent that the officers are able to connect PICs to needed mental health services. If appropriate services are not available, the data collected in a new program are often essential for helping ensure that elected officials and administrators reprioritize resources in order to develop adequate services.

Agencies should measure both quantitative changes (e.g., changes in the number of certain occurrences such as calls for service or injuries) and qualitative changes (e.g., such as changes in the nature or character of the interactions between officers and PICs) (Reuland & Cheney, 2005). It is also essential to collect information about the PICs who are participating in emergency psychological services or jail diversion programs (CMHS National GAINS Center, 2007). Variables of interest include gender, race/ethnicity, age, psychiatric diagnosis, presence of co-occurring substance use, other relevant health issues, criminal charge(s), prior convictions, number of prior arrests, and jail days. Outcome measures should be designed to address public safety, criminal recidivism, and mental health symptoms. Although difficult to measure, a jail diversion program should also ideally track variables related to consumer functioning and satisfaction with services. Other important variables to consider include housing status (e.g., number of days homeless vs. housed, type of housing, etc.), employment, income, eligibility for veterans' benefits or services, family relationships, social support, satisfaction with services, and quality of life. Reuland and Cheney (2005) reported that the goals of agencies participating in police-based diversion programs for PICs often included safety of officers and civilians; increased officer understanding of mental illness; reduced numbers of individuals with mental illness going to jail; and improved relationships with the community, particularly with mental health professionals, but also with individuals with mental illness and their families. Reuland and Cheney (2005) reported that in several agencies, the numbers of police shootings, assaults and batteries, and use of force incidents decreased as a result of specialized police approaches to addressing the needs of those with mental illness. Some of the desired outcomes such as change in officers' attitudes about, and empathy for, individuals with mental illness, and officers' translation of skills learned for dealing with PICs into other areas of policing and life, can have big payoffs to law enforcement agencies and communities, despite being difficult to measure.

At the very least, a program should track the number of calls for service for PICs, the number of calls for special teams, the types of situations LEOs encounter in responding to PICs (e.g., suicide threats or attempts), disposition outcomes (e.g., arrest or transport to a mental health facility), incidents involving use of force, and officer or citizen injuries (Reuland & Cheney, 2005). However, it is important to keep in mind that increases or decreases in some of these events or factors, such as number of calls, are often hard to interpret. In the beginning of a diversion program, more responses mean that more problems are being addressed. However, if there is an increase in calls involving the same PICs, consideration should be given to whether different mental health interventions or LEO responses are needed. Some agencies collect qualitative data on the satisfaction of law enforcement officers, mental health professionals, consumers, and family members. This can be very helpful in monitoring program effectiveness and impact. Such data may also shed light on the level of burnout and cynicism versus optimism and engagement among the personnel doing the work, factors that likely impact the long-term viability of the program. Agencies can also use program data to calculate savings and efficiencies that may accrue to the agency and its funding sources.

CONCLUSION

Like any system, the planning, organization, and development of a sustainable emergency psychological services or jail diversion program is a complex process. It involves the close cooperation and communication of multiple parties with vested interests in a shared vision, and it requires strong leadership. Based on our experience with the HEPSJDP, we believe that police psychologists are ideally positioned to provide leadership and direction in developing these programs.

REFERENCES

Americans with Disabilities Act (ADA) 42 U.S. Code Chapter 126 (1990).

Aufderheide, D. (2014). Mental illness in America's jails and prisons: Toward a public safety/public health model. *Health Affairs Blog*. Retrieved from http://healthaffairs.org/blog/2014/04/01/mental-illness-in-americas-jails-and-prisons-toward-a-public-safetypublic-health-model/

Canterbury v. Spence, 464 F.2d 772, 788 (D.C. Cir., 1972).

Centers for Disease Control and Prevention. (2013). *Burden of mental illness*. Retrieved from http://www.cdc.gov/mentalhealth/basics/burden.htm

Christopher, M., Kracher, S., & Balcom, S. (2013). *Honolulu Emergency Psychological Services and Jail Diversion Program: 2013 summary report*. Unpublished manuscript.

City and County of San Francisco, California et al. v. Sheehan, 575 U.S. ___ (2015).

City of Canton v. Harris, 489 U.S. 378 (1989).

Clark, J. (2004). *Non-specialty first appearance court models for diverting persons with mental illness: Alternatives to mental health courts*. Delmar, NY: Technical Assistance and Policy Analysis Center for Jail Diversion.

CMHS National GAINS Center. (2007). *Practical advice on jail diversion: Ten years of learning on jail diversion from the CMHS National GAINS Center*. Delmar, NY: Author.

CMHS National GAINS Center. (2010). Getting inside the black box: Understanding how jail diversion works. Delmar, NY: Policy Research Associates, Inc., CMHS National GAINS Center.

Cobbs v. Grant, 8 Cal.3d 229, 502 P.2d 1 (1972).

U.S. Const. amend. VIII U.S. Const. amend. XIV

Cruzan by Cruzan v. Harmon, 760 S.W. 2d 408, 419 (Mo. 1988).

Cruzan v. Director, Missouri Depart. of Health, 497 U.S. 261, 270 (1990).

Deane, M., Steadman, H., Deane, M., Borum, R., Veysey, B., & Morrissey, J. (1999). Emerging partnerships between mental health and law enforcement. *Psychiatric Services*, *50*(1), 99–101. doi:10.1176/ps.50.1.99 PMID:9890588

Deorle v. Rutherford, 272 F.3d 1272 (9th Cir. 2001).

Dupont, R., Cochran, S., & Pillsbury, S. (2007). *Crisis Intervention Team core elements*. Retrieved from http://cit.memphis.edu/pdf/CoreElements.pdf

Estelle v. Gamble, 429 U.S. 97 (1976).

Fixsen, D. L., Naoom, S. F., Blase, K. A., Friedman, R. M., & Wallace, F. (2005). *Implementation research: A synthesis of the literature*. Tampa, FL: University of South Florida, Louis de la Parte Florida Mental Health Institute, The National Implementation Research Network (FMHI Publication #231).

Foley, G., & Ruppel, E. (2008). *The EXIT program: Engaging diverted individuals through voluntary services*. Delmar, NY: CMHS National GAINS Center.

Hails, J., & Borum, R. (2003). Police training a specialized approach to people with mental illness. *Crime and Delinquency*, *49*(1), 52–61. doi:10.1177/0011128702239235

Jackson v. Indiana, 406 U.S. 715 (1972).

Kids Count Data Center. (2015). *Total population by child and adult populations*. Retrieved from http://datacenter.kidscount.org/data/tables/99-total-population-by-child-and-adult#detailed/1/any/false/869,36,868,867,133/39,40,41/416,417

Kissinger, M. (2014, September 27). Milwaukee police promise on mental health training unmet. *Journal Sentinel*. Retrieved from http://www.jsonline.com/watchdog/watchdogreports/milwaukee-police-promise-on-mental-health-training-unmet-b99347957z1-277344381.html

Krameddine, Y. I., DeMarco, D., Hassel, R., & Silverstone, P. H. (2013). A novel training program for police officers that improves interactions with mentally ill individuals and is cost-effective. *Frontiers in Psychiatry*, *4*, 9. doi:10.3389/fpsyt.2013.00009 PMID:23515226

Kushel, M. B., Vittinghoff, E., & Haas, J. S. (2001). Factors associated with the health care utilization of homeless persons. *Journal of the American Medical Association*, *285*(2), 200–206. doi:10.1001/jama.285.2.200 PMID:11176814

Lehman, A. F., Dixon, L., Hoch, J. S., Deforge, B., Kernan, E., & Frank, R. (1999). Cost-effectiveness of assertive community treatment for homeless persons with severe mental illness. *The British Journal of Psychiatry*, *174*(4), 346–352. doi:10.1192/bjp.174.4.346 PMID:10533554

Massaro, J. (2004). *Working with people with mental illness involved in the criminal justice system: What mental health service providers need to know* (2nd ed.). Delmar, NY: Technical Assistance and Policy Analysis Center for Jail Diversion.

Matter of Conroy. 486 A.2nd, 1209, 1225 (N.J., 1985).

Mayer, M. (2013). *Law enforcement responses to mentally ill persons: California peace officers*. Retrieved from http://californiapeaceofficer.org/2013/01/Law-Enforcements-Response-to-Mentally-Ill-Persons/

McLean, B. (2011). *National collaboration aims to ensure unity in CIT*. Retrieved from http://www.citinternational.org/standards/242-national-collaboration-aims-to-ensure-unity-in-cit.html

National Alliance on Mental Illness. (n.d.). *Law enforcement and mental health*. Retrieved from http://www.nami.org/Get-Involved/Law-Enforcement-and-Mental-Health

National GAINS Center for People with Co-Occurring Disorders in the Justice System. (2002). *The Nathaniel Project: An alternative to incarceration program for people with serious mental illness who have committed felony offenses. Program Brief Series*. Delmar, NY: Author.

National Institute of Health. (2015). *Drug facts: National trends*. Retrieved from https://www.drugabuse.gov/publications/drugfacts/nationwide-trends

National Institute of Health. (n.d.). *To whom does the privacy rule apply and whom will it affect?* Retrieved from https://privacyruleandresearch.nih.gov/pr_06.asp

National Institute of Justice. (2015). *Program profile: Mental health courts (multisite)*. Retrieved from https://www.crimesolutions.gov/ProgramDetails.aspx?ID=398

National Low Income Housing Coalition. (2015). Affordable housing is nowhere to be found for millions. *Housing Spotlight, 5*(1). Retrieved from http://nlihc.org/article/housing-spotlight-volume-5-issue-1

Pauly, M. (2013, October 11). How police officers are (or aren't) trained in mental health. *The Atlantic*. Retrieved from http://www.theatlantic.com/health/archive/2013/10/how-police-officers-are-or-aren-t-trained-in-mental-health/280485/

Portland State University Criminology and Criminal Justice Senior Capstone. (2012). *Police use of force: A review of the literature*. Retrieved from http://pdxscholar.library.pdx.edu/ccj_capstone/6/

Poulin, S. R., Maguire, M., Metraux, S., & Culhane, D. P. (2010). Service use and costs for persons experiencing chronic homelessness in Philadelphia: A population-based study. *Psychiatric Services (Washington, D.C.), 61*(11), 1093–1098. doi:10.1176/ps.2010.61.11.1093 PMID:21041347

Reuland, M. (2005). *A guide to implementing police-based diversion programs for people with mental illness* (Rev. ed.). Delmar, NY: National GAINS Technical Assistance and Policy Analysis Center for Jail Diversion.

Reuland, M., & Cheney, J. (2005). *Enhancing success of police-based diversion programs for people with mental illness*. Delmar, NY: GAINS Technical Assistance and Policy Analysis Center for Jail Diversion.

Roleff, T. L., & Egendorf, L. K. (2002). *Mental illness: Opposing viewpoints*. San Diego, CA: Greenhaver Press, Inc.

Salit, S. A., Kuhn, E. M., Hartz, A. J., Vu, J. M., & Mosso, A. L. (1998). Hospitalization costs associated with homelessness in New York City. *The New England Journal of Medicine*, *338*(24), 1734–1740. doi:10.1056/NEJM199806113382406 PMID:9624194

Scott, J. (1993). Homelessness and mental illness. *The British Journal of Psychiatry*, *162*(3), 314–324. doi:10.1192/bjp.162.3.314 PMID:8453425

Standley, R. B. (2012). *Legal right to refuse medical treatment in the USA*. Retrieved from www.rbs2.com/rrmt.pdf

Stettin, B., Geller, J., Ragosta, K., Cohen, K., & Ghowrwal, J. (2014). *Mental health commitment law: A survey of the states*. Retrieved from http://tacreports.org/storage/documents/2014-state-survey-abridged.pdf

Substance Abuse and Mental Health Services Association. (2014). *What is jail diversion?* Retrieved from http://gainscenter.samhsa.gov/topical_resources/jail.asp

Torrey, E. F. (2014). *American psychosis: How the federal government destroyed the mental illness treatment system*. New York, NY: Oxford University Press.

Torrey, E. F., Kennard, S. A. D., Eslinger, S. D., Lamb, R., & Pavle, J. (2010). *More mentally ill persons are in jail and prisons than hospitals: A survey of the states*. Arlington, VA: Treatment Advocacy Center.

Torrey, E. F., Zdanowicz, M. T., Kennard, A. D., Lamb, H. R., Eslinger, D. F., Biasotti, M. C., & Fuller, D. A. (2014). *The treatment of persons with mental illness in prisons and jails: A state survey*. Arlington, VA: Treatment Advocacy Center.

Treatment Advocacy Center. (2009). *Homelessness: One of the consequence of failing to treat individuals with severe psychiatric disorders*. Treatment Advocacy Center Briefing Paper. Retrieved from http://www.treatmentadvocacycenter.org/storage/documents/homelessness--apr_09.pdf

Treatment Advocacy Center. (2011). *Emergency hospitalization for evaluation: Assisted psychiatric treatment standards by state*. Retrieved from http://treatmentadvocacycenter.org/storage/documents/Emergency_Hospitalization_for_Evaluation.pdf

Union Pacific Railway Co. v. Botsford, 141 U.S. 250, 251 (1990).

U.S. Department of Housing and Urban Development, Office of Community Planning and Development. (2014). *The 2013 annual homeless assessment report to congress*. Retrieved from https://www.hudexchange.info/onecpd/assets/File/2013-AHAR-Part-2-About-This-Report.pdf

Walker v. City of New York, 974 F.2d 293 (2nd Circuit, 1992).

Watson, A. C., & Fulambarker, A. J. (2012). The crisis intervention team model of police response to mental health crises: A primer for mental health practitioners. *Best Practices in Mental Health*, *8*, 71. PMID:24039557

Young v. Romero, 457 U.S. 307 (1982).

Section 6

Current Trends and Developments

Chapter 15
Social Climate Change and the Modern Police Department:
Millennials, Marijuana, and Mass Media

Adrienne C. Bradford
City of Atlanta Psychological Services/Employee Assistance Program, USA

Heather K. McElroy
Stone, McElroy & Associates, USA

Rachel Rosenblatt
Stone, McElroy & Associates, USA

ABSTRACT

The advent of social media, blogs, smartphones, and the 24-hour all access news channels make information available to us constantly on the television, the internet, and even while mobile. This chapter highlights contemporary social and generational trends including the arrival of the Millennial generation into the workforce, legalization of marijuana, the mainstream acceptance of body art as a form of self-expression, and the influence of mass media on the lives of police officers, particularly in officer-involved shootings. These emerging factors challenge law enforcement managers to consider complex issues in the workplace while maintaining the core values, camaraderie, and professional standards inherent in policing. The public safety psychologist's role is also evolving with new technology, social developments, and organizational challenges. This chapter aims to encourage dialogue between mental health professionals, law enforcement managers, and policy-makers.

INTRODUCTION

Over the last 10 years, Americans have experienced significant changes in how we communicate. The advent of social media, blogs, smartphones, and the 24-hour all access news channels make information available to us constantly on the television, the internet, and even while mobile. The Millennials born into this age of technology differ significantly from the preceding generations, and these differences impact

DOI: 10.4018/978-1-5225-0813-7.ch015

the available applicant pool for law enforcement agencies (Wilson, Dalton, Scheer, & Grammich, 2010). As the Millennials move into the workforce, and societal trends and practices change, the acceptance of tattoos and body art and the legalization of marijuana alter the landscape of hiring, policy, and operations of police agencies across the country. This chapter highlights contemporary social and generational trends including the arrival of the Millennials into the workforce, legalization of marijuana, the mainstream acceptance of body art as a form of self-expression, and the influence of mass media on the lives of police officers, particularly in officer-involved shootings. These emerging concerns challenge law enforcement managers to consider complex issues in the workplace while maintaining the core values, camaraderie, and professional standards inherent in policing. The public safety psychologist's role is also evolving with new technology, social developments, and organizational challenges. The content of this chapter ideally brings contemporary issues in policing to the forefront, which will hopefully encourage dialogue among mental health professionals, law enforcement managers, and policy-makers as they wrestle with the benefits and risks that often accompany change. Our goal is to enhance the personal and professional lives of the men and women who choose daily to work in the field of law enforcement.

THE NEXT GENERATION

As we progress into the new millennium, it is clear that society is changing rapidly. The invention of social networking and the development of technology for smartphones have drastically changed the volume of information available and the way in which we communicate. The technology boom provides the user with immediate access to worldwide data, 24-hour access to news sources, and encourages the sharing of personal videos, photos, thoughts, and ideas instantaneously with vast numbers of people worldwide.

Facebook, a social networking site launched in a college dormitory room by Mark Zuckerburg in 2004, changed the way we share information and made it possible for people from all over the world to have instant access to others' personal information, perspectives, photographs, and video (Carlson, 2010). In October 2012, a short 8 years after its creation, Facebook had passed the monthly active users mark of one billion members who visit the site at least once a month. The company has an estimated 600 million mobile users and 140 billion friend connections since its inception. In each of the first 3 months of 2014, over one billion users logged into their Facebook account on a mobile device, doubling the amount from only 2 years prior, suggesting massive increases in the mobility, ease, and speed of information sharing (McDuling, 2014). The recent dramatic advances in technology and the use of social media accounts creates new challenges for public safety psychologists and law enforcement commanders, especially those tasked with maintaining legally defensible hiring practices and those providing oversight and intervention after a deadly force encounters.

The number of viewers using mobile devices to access video content increases daily. These devices capture digital images, video, and audio files that can easily be transferred to the internet and viewed immediately by up to millions of viewers worldwide. In fact, almost 30% of smartphone consumers access the local news primarily with their mobile devices, and almost the same number use these devices to view news videos (Smith, 2015).

The Millennials are the generational members born into this age of technological advances. The constant ease and influx of information sharing and the entry of Millennials into the workforce is creating cultural change, necessitating a shift in law enforcement recruitment, technology, and procedures. These technological advances shape the new generation of officers and change law enforcement operations and procedures, particularly concerning the dissemination of information, hiring practices, and departmental responses to critical incidents. The technology of today means that many life experiences can be instantly recorded, independently edited, and immediately disseminated.

As of 2015, Baby Boomers born between 1943 and 1960 comprise the majority of leadership roles in police agencies, and many astute police executives are planning for major social and generational shifts in employee demographics. As the Baby Boomers continue to age, many are preparing for retirement, potentially creating a vacuum in leadership. As of 2015, Generation X, successors to the Baby Boomers, are in their 30s and 40s. Though many will ascend to positions of authority and management in police departments, current projections indicate that it is the Generation Y workers, or the Millennials born between 1985 and 2000, who will eclipse the Generation X employees. In fact, by 2020, it is estimated that the majority of police officers will be members of the Millennials, creating a generational and technological shift in law enforcement hiring practices and operations (Henchey, 2005).

Parenting of the Millennial generation is very different from that of Generation X. "Helicopter parenting" is a term used to describe parents who tend to be overly involved in their children's lives and insulate them from common failures or disappointments. Many members of the Millennial generation grew up with helicopter parents who continue to shelter and manage many aspects of their lives well into adulthood (Rochman, 2013). Helicopter parenting may produce adults who lack the life skills necessary to succeed in a typically competitive and complex workplace and economic environment (Rochman, 2013). Millennials who had helicopter parents may have difficulty managing their own personal time and engaging in accurate self-assessment. Growing up in an environment of "trophy kids" where everyone who participates is deemed worthy of an award may lead to a generation of adults entering the workforce with increasingly unrealistic expectations for promotion, a belief that everyone is exceptional, and a general inability to cope with criticism or disappointment (Graham, 2013).

Due to the recent changes in societal trends and the economic downturn, most college graduates are returning home to live with their parents rather than getting jobs and moving out on their own to begin adulthood (Hartogs, 2013). In fact, a record 21.6 million young adults in America were living with their parents in 2012, resulting in an increasing number of applicants to police departments who have not lived independently, who anticipate gaining stable employment despite possessing minimal work experience, and who harbor unrealistic expectations for rapid promotion (Hartogs, 2013). Those unrealistic expectations are likely to lead to Millennial employees changing jobs more frequently than their predecessors. Research suggests that up to 91% of Millennials expect to stay in a job for less than 3 years (Meister, 2012). Therefore, law enforcement agencies may battle high rates of turnover, difficulty recruiting, and increased early departure—either to another agency or out of the field of law enforcement altogether—, after investing thousands of dollars into training.

Furthermore, the Millennial generation's tendency to remain in their positions for shorter periods of time may impact the eligible applicant pool. More applicants have criminal records, have used drugs, are not in optimal physical health, and have a history of financial instability, particularly as society becomes more accepting of marijuana use, body art, foreclosures, and bankruptcy (Wilson et al., 2010).

According to one study, about half of all 12th-graders reported having smoked marijuana and one in four had used some illicit drug other than marijuana by the end of the 12th grade year (Wilson et al., 2010). Wilson and coauthors reported that these prevalence rates were well above those reported in the early 1990s, signaling important changes. Younger generations, from which police departments would normally draw recruits, also have higher amounts of debt than youths of previous decades (Wilson et al., 2010). After the housing crisis in 2007, more people have filed for bankruptcy, experienced foreclosure on their homes, and had significant credit problems, factors that have typically raised concerns about suitability for a position in law enforcement. All of these circumstances reduce the available recruitment pool and require departments to either relax their standards or place increasingly more work on an already physically and emotionally taxed police force.

Changes in generational values regarding off-duty life also may be impacting law enforcement hiring and retention. The younger generation appears to place much more emphasis on flexibility and emotional control/independence in the workplace, which is inconsistent with the typical way in which law enforcement departments operate (Wilson et al., 2010). As of 2003, less than half of American youths considered a police department or agency a "desirable" or "acceptable" place to work, thereby further tightening the belt on the applicant pool and encouraging existing younger generational officers to seek employment elsewhere (Wilson et al., 2010). That sentiment seems to have only increased, especially with the recent scrutiny of law enforcement, creating officer safety concerns. According to Hladkey, "A series of ambush-style attacks on cops around the nation, and a barrage of anti-police commentary on social media have left officers stressed and hyper-vigilant" (2015, p. 1). These factors have likely contributed to a smaller applicant pool and higher turnover rates. Individual police agencies must do a better job of providing structured career development programs for future leaders. Police executives concerned with sustaining the viability of their agencies will have to become more intentional and adopt a more progressive mindset to recruit and retain their next generation of employees. This may be especially challenging to more traditional members of the law enforcement community. Such individuals may initially express reservations, but will likely realize that organizational change is necessary for effective policing in the 21st century.

Law enforcement managers can identify and prioritize the desirable characteristics of the work environment and then restructure recruitment/retention plans to provide hiring packages and incentives attractive to this new generation of employees (e.g., take-home vehicles, non-traditional work shifts, retention pay, etc.). Furthermore, training and development policies and practices should more closely align with and address the unique characteristics of these younger adults interested in entering law enforcement. A focus on adopting newer technologies, software, and equipment (e.g., providing internet accessibility in the patrol vehicles and the integration of body worn cameras) may be useful in strengthening recruitment and retention efforts.

The new generation of officers, the turnover created by the retirement of the preceding generation, the overwhelming rate at which technology is advancing, and the immediacy of information-sharing are creating a rapid shift in the climate of law enforcement. Therefore, it is imperative for law enforcement administrators and managers, as well as those involved in the hiring process (i.e., background investigators, police psychologists, training instructors, recruiters, etc.), to critically examine the landscape of this next generation of officers. It is crucial to the future of policing for department personnel to assess carefully how their respective agencies can recruit and retain employees and attend to the unique challenges that these employees may face as a result of cultural and technological advances that set them apart from preceding generations.

SOCIETAL SHIFTS IN THE ACCEPTANCE OF BODY ART

Many departments have elected to adjust their hiring standards regarding body art in order to accommodate recent societal changes. Today's law enforcement departments struggle with maintaining a standard of professionalism while also accepting that many of those in the applicant pool have body art, including tattoos and piercings. A Harris Poll conducted in 2012 found that one in five U.S. adults now has at least one tattoo, a 16% increase over the rate indicated in a 2003 poll (Braverman, 2012). As departments struggle to fill vacancies, they have become increasingly lenient with their hiring standards and more accepting of officers having visible body art while in uniform. For example, in 2013 the Tarpon Springs, FL Police Department revised its previous policy against hiring officers with visible body art while in uniform and now allow tattoos that do not cover more than a quarter of an exposed body part (Thompson, 2013).

While some departments have shown a greater degree of flexibility in their hiring standards, some larger city agencies, including the Chicago, IL and Oklahoma City, OK Police Departments, have retained policies that ban visible tattoos in uniform. In fact, the Chicago Police Department adjusted its policy as recently as 2015 after discovering an increasing number of officers who presented with multiple visible and elaborate tattoos, an image that the department claimed was inconsistent with its professional image. In response, three Chicago police officers filed a lawsuit against the department claiming that the policy violated their First Amendment rights of freedom of expression and speech (Gorner, 2015). Officers also complained that the new policy's requirement of wearing additional clothing or cover-up tape to mask tattoos created undue discomfort and skin irritations, particularly when working in the heat. The lawsuit was ultimately thrown out in federal court because the judge ruled that the city's goal to have a professional-looking department outweighed the officers' interests in expressing themselves (Gorner, 2015). Nevertheless, the complaints and lawsuits that emerged after this policy change further highlight the challenge departments face as they try to navigate emerging social trends while maintaining a professional image. The Phoenix, AZ Police Department is yet another large department that revised the tattoo policy to preserve a professional image for the officers. Enacted in August 2011, the revised policy forbids any visible tattoos on officers' arms larger than a 3x5 index card. Further, the policy prohibits any visible tattoos or body art on the neck, hands, or face, along with any offensive imagery or language (Lacey, 2011).

A major challenge in dealing with increasing amounts of body art is the determination of the acceptability of the artwork. Content and location of the tattoo may be particularly relevant if the body art is perceived by the public as offensive or if it creates a negative public impression of the officer (e.g., pornographic, culturally or racially insensitive, or profane body art content). The content of the body art may be quite relevant at the pre-employment stage because tattoos are also typically seen as self-expression. For example, if an applicant has visible tattoos that indicate gang affiliation or racially/culturally offensive material, the department may be concerned about possible involvement in illegal gang activity, or racial or cultural intolerance. Rather than expend the additional resources investigating potentially offensive visible tattoo content or determining acceptable tattoo size and location, some agencies such as the Chicago Police Department opted for a simpler blanket policy banning all visible tattoos. Even if tattoos are not visible, their content can often provide the department with information about the applicant's background and thought processes.

Police departments also have to manage the issue of incumbent officers acquiring tattoos after hire. In these situations, the department should consider a few issues. First, it is important to determine if the tattoo location or content violate the department's documented tattoo policy. If the location of the tattoo violates the policy then the officer may be required to take steps to cover the tattoo, either with additional clothing or skin-tone colored tape. If the content of an officer's tattoo is at issue, it may require a more involved department response as it could be suggestive of certain characteristics or affiliations that are inconsistent with a law enforcement position and the standards of the agency. Specific examples could include tattoos displaying certain gang affiliations or offensive symbols such as swastikas.

While tattoos are certainly one of the most prolific forms of body art, piercings have also become more popular in both men and women and may be a potential consideration in the hiring process. Though women have pierced their ears for some time, it has become more common for both men and women to pierce other body parts and to purposefully alter or mutilate body parts as a form of art (e.g., earlobe stretching, implants under the skin, etc.) (Laumann & Derick, 2010). Some departments have policies prohibiting men from wearing any piercings on duty and limit the piercings of female officers to one or two "tasteful" earrings in the ear lobe (AELE, 2007).

Though some degree of body art can be covered to conform to a department's desire to present a professional image, there may be psychological correlates of body mutilation that impact suitability for hire. Multiple studies have demonstrated that individuals with tattoos and body piercings are more likely to have engaged in high-risk behavior including risky alcohol and drug use (e.g., Burger & Finkel, 2002; Drews, Allison, & Probst, 2000). However, the link between body art and psychopathology and deviant behavior appears to be complex, since tattoos and body art have become more mainstream in recent years. Thus, researchers have cautioned against making over-generalizations about this group. In one study, researchers found there were three primary motivations underlying participants' decision to acquire body art, including sub-threshold psychopathology, an experimenting/creative personality style, and low self-esteem (Nathanson, Paulhus, & Williams, 2006). Thus, for some, acquiring body art may simply be a way to express their uniqueness and creativity. Further, a study by Koch et al. (2010) found that there was a distinction between individuals with only one or two tattoos or body piercings and those who were heavily tattooed and/or pierced. Specifically, the study found that relative to participants with no piercings, participants who reported having seven or more piercings were approximately twice as likely to have also reported monthly marijuana use, other drug use, and an arrest history beyond traffic violations. There was no distinction found between those with no piercings and just a few (i.e., less than seven). However, the presence of four or more tattoos was significantly correlated with monthly marijuana use, a history of other drug use, binge drinking, and an arrest history beyond traffic citations.

Overall, researchers suggest that the presence of tattoos and body piercings, particularly multiple types of body art, can be a valid area to query for the psychological examiner in a preemployment screening. However, appropriate caution should be exercised against making presumptions that body art is suggestive of psychopathology or a deviant history. The content of tattoos and the motivation behind a decision to have body art is an area that may be worthy of exploration and could offer insight into a law enforcement applicant's personality, affiliations, and level of tolerance of other groups.

SOCIETAL CHANGES IN THE ACCEPTANCE OF LEGALIZED MARIJUANA

Another emerging social trend affecting law enforcement agencies is the increasing social and legal acceptance of marijuana use. The decriminalization of marijuana has opened the door for laws allowing the recreational and medicinal use of marijuana, reflecting a shift in societal beliefs about the drug. As law enforcement agencies continue to experience overwhelming vacancies and an increased number of applicants in the potential hiring pool that have used marijuana, agencies are also relaxing their policies related to previous drug use. This easing of pre-employment drug use policies has been seen most prominently in states that have legalized marijuana for adult recreational use and in larger departments that have more vacancies to fill. For example, a month after Washington became the first state to legalize marijuana use in 2012, the Seattle, WA Police Department relaxed its rule against hiring candidates with previous marijuana use from 3 years to 1 year prior to application. However, this has not held true for every department in states with less stringent marijuana laws. For example, although the state of Colorado legalized marijuana in 2012, the Denver, CO Police Department still regards marijuana as an illegal drug because it is considered an illegal, controlled substance under the Federal Controlled Substances Act. For that particular agency, any marijuana use within the past 3 years is still a disqualifier, despite its legalization at the state level (City and County of Denver Civil Service Commission, 2014). More recently, Alaska and Oregon legalized marijuana use in November 2014. It will be interesting to see how law enforcement departments in those states grapple with this issue over the next few years.

Beyond relaxing attitudes about marijuana and the easing of legal penalties, there are some correlates between marijuana use in public safety applicants and other negative behaviors. One study by Roberts and Roberts (2014) showed that among the 66,479 public safety applicants in their sample (including police, fire, corrections, probation, and dispatch applicants), less than 5% reported having used marijuana over 20 times. Among that 5%, applicants were more likely to report other negative pre-hire behaviors including harder drug use, heavier regular drinking habits, blackouts due to heavy drinking, two or more arrests, driving while under the influence of illegal drugs, two or more fights as an adult, and domestic violence. The study further examined the relationship between recency of marijuana use and other negative behaviors. Similar to their findings related to the frequency of use, applicants who reported having used marijuana within 1-2 years of their application were more likely to report other problematic behaviors in their histories than were applicants who had either never used marijuana or had used more than 3 years ago. Specifically, applicants with use within 1-2 years of their application were more likely to report having experienced blackouts due to drinking, heavier regular use of alcohol, use of harder drugs, two or more arrests, and driving under the influence of illegal drugs.

A recent study conducted by Pardini et al. (2015) found that males in their mid-30s were more likely to exhibit antisocial personality features and have more drug-related legal problems if they had engaged in chronic marijuana use between their adolescence and 20s, relative to those who reported infrequent or no use. Further, in a slightly earlier longitudinal study (Brook et al., 2011), participants who were identified as non-users or experimental users of marijuana demonstrated fewer externalizing behaviors (specified as delinquency, rebelliousness, tolerance of deviance, and aggressive behaviors) and higher levels of the personal protective factors (e.g., self-control) than chronic users. The study also found that chronic marijuana users showed a higher degree of internalizing symptoms (e.g., depression, anxiety, and interpersonal problems) than non-users, but there were no significant distinctions among other levels of marijuana use (experimental, occasional, etc.).

While the existing body of research demonstrates a clear pattern that more frequent and more recent marijuana use is related to other negative behaviors, the challenge with the majority of the existing research is that it was conducted on individuals who used marijuana illegally. Thus, it could be argued that those individuals were more inclined to violate rules and laws in other respects as well. Now that marijuana has been legalized in some states, it will be important to do follow-up research in those states to determine if these same findings are consistent over the long term. In the meantime, however, background investigators and public safety psychologists performing pre-hire psychological screenings of public safety applicants should be mindful of negative behavioral indicators associated with past marijuana use and carefully consider the potential implications of suitability for public safety positions. Clearly, the changing social climate and the incoming generation of Millennials alters the current recruiting strategies utilized by law enforcement agencies and also significantly impacts the size of the available applicant pool.

THE IMPACT OF SOCIAL MEDIA ON HIRING POLICE PERSONNEL

In light of the public nature of the internet, employers, especially those in law enforcement, have started reviewing the social media profiles of job applicants and incumbent employees. The inappropriate content contained on an employee's or police applicant's social media accounts could bring an employer's reputation into disrepute and provide grounds for a negligent hiring lawsuit. In the case of public safety agencies, inappropriate content could also create mistrust and a loss of faith among the public that officers are sworn to protect and serve. Cybervetting, as it has become known, is now a fairly common hiring practice in law enforcement agencies. For example, a survey conducted by the International Association of Chiefs of Police (IACP) in 2010 found that one-third of the 728 agencies surveyed acknowledged reviewing applicants' social media presence as part of the background screening process (Johnson, 2010), and that number has likely increased exponentially. Reviewing an applicant's social media presence may shed light on an applicant's social attitudes, beliefs, activities, and the quality of his or her associates that can guide decisions about potential suitability for hire. However, departments also must be cautious to avoid making hiring decisions based on either erroneous information found on a social media page or protected information such as ethnicity, disability, religion, or family medical history.

Imagine a scenario where an uninformed background investigator learns from a review of an applicant's Facebook page that the applicant has multiple family members with psychiatric problems. Fearing that this family history may be suggestive of mental health problems in the applicant, the investigator chooses to dismiss the applicant from the hiring process, unwittingly making the department vulnerable to a discrimination lawsuit. Given the potentially sensitive nature of information gleaned from social media sites and the possible legal ramifications if this information were misused, departments are encouraged to adopt policies and procedures for the appropriate use of social media materials for pre-employment screening and ensure that those employees accessing such materials for hiring purposes are carefully trained. In formulating these policies, departments should consider reviewing the materials provided by IACP (Rose et al., 2010).

Departments must also carefully consider how to use the information they uncover about an applicant on social media sites and also be aware of the legalities in their states for accessing this information. Many departments require that public safety job applicants provide departments with their passwords or ask the applicant to log into their social media accounts in the presence of the background investigator, allowing the investigator unfettered access to their pages. States' legislators are increasingly passing laws to restrict such access. Information that is not covered by privacy constraints is still considered suitable for consideration; however, many states have determined that requiring job applicants to share password-protected information is an invasion of privacy. These laws have been met with frustration by law enforcement agencies that assert that such restrictions make it difficult to thoroughly vet a potential employee. A listing of the most recent state-by-state legislation on social media privacy in the hiring process is detailed on the National Conference of State Legislatures website at http://www.ncsl.org/.

Law enforcement managers also must weigh the legality and importance of ensuring that incumbent officers' social media postings do not contain material that could tarnish the reputation of the officer or the organization. Though the information posted may initially seem innocuous, the officer's reputation could be irreparably damaged when the information is made available and open to the subjective interpretation of innumerable potential viewers. Consider the following real world scenario. In 2011, local media sources in Albuquerque, NM retrieved Officer Trey Economidy's Facebook page content after his involvement in a deadly on-duty shooting. The officer listed his occupation as "human waste disposal" on his Facebook profile (Goode, 2011). In light of the posting, citizens and officials raised concerns, questioning if the officer sincerely believed that his role as a law enforcement officer was to rid the city of unwelcome individuals and if his characterization of the role was endorsed by other departmental employees and managers. Though the officer was disciplined, the image of the department was tarnished by his personal use of social media. Clearly, this example illustrates the damaging impact on the reputation of the organization that can be caused by departmental employees' use of personal social media. Over the past few years, astute agency managers have developed policies to guide the private use of social media by police officers, which is especially critical in light of the greater use of the internet by Millennial officers. It is noteworthy that shortly after the Officer Trey Economidy incident, the Albuquerque Police Department revealed new guidelines to oversee the personal use of social media sites for departmental personnel. Many organizations have followed suit including the New York, NY Police Department (NYPD), the nation's largest police department. The NYPD disseminated stringent guidelines in 2013, instructing police personnel to examine personal social media accounts, including Twitter and Facebook. Employees were urged to be cautious of personal information posted online, including any references, postings, or pictures referring to their work as law enforcement officers (Goodman & Ruderman, 2013).

THE RISE OF THE CITIZEN JOURNALIST AND MEDIA COVERAGE OF LAW ENFORCEMENT OPERATIONS

The rise of social media, increased access to technology, and ubiquity of smartphones have contributed significantly to the proliferation of citizen journalism. These citizen reporters use digital photos or videos to publicly and immediately share their first-person accounts or perspectives of law enforcement encounters. These witnesses capture and disseminate information, often without any training in law enforcement policy or procedure. These accounts are circulated without the fact-checking standards or source verification typically embraced by mainstream media outlets.

Increasingly, the public is using modern technology to capture and disseminate information on deadly force encounters, especially between police officers and ethnic minority members. In Ferguson, MO, citizens transformed into journalists and documented the unrest that gripped the town after the officer-involved shooting death of Michael Brown in the late summer of 2014. These citizen journalists used their mobile devices to share video and digital images of the demonstrations and ongoing police actions, illuminating a strong divide between the Ferguson Police Department and members of the African American community. These images, in concert with the work of the traditional media reporters, brought global awareness to the death of Michael Brown and a public perception of "law enforcement's disproportionate response to the ensuing protests" (Gilmor, 2014, p. 1).

Though the legality of the public documenting these police interactions may be debated, federal and state judges support the public's right to capture digital photos and videos of police in public spaces as long as they are not directly interfering (Wagtendonk, 2015). Increased distribution of personal citizen videos of deadly police encounters often fails to accurately portray all aspects of the incident, creating a skewed view of the interaction and fostering increased mistrust of law enforcement. Police department leaders also criticize the media for sensationalized reporting and providing intense and unbalanced coverage of misconduct in the absence of positive portrayals of law enforcement activities. In response, the law enforcement community is focused on providing alternate perspectives, emphasizing that officer misconduct and mistrust of officers portrayed by the media are the exceptions rather than the norm (Tooley, Linkenbach, Lande, & Lande, 2009).

Over the past few years, instant access to the internet and 24/7 news coverage, linked with enduring societal factors, including racial tensions and long-standing perceived police injustices, particularly those committed against African Americans, have collectively reached a boiling point. The result is an increased public scrutiny of law enforcement personnel, especially in deadly force encounters. These critical incidents are highly publicized and contribute to heightened emotions, increased conflict, and mistrust between the public and the respective law enforcement organizations.

The unending media coverage of officer-involved shootings in the U.S. in 2014 and 2015 has created a public outcry from citizen groups and civil rights organizations and led to a passionate national debate. These issues and the technological improvements over the past 10 years require leadership within public safety organizations to thoughtfully weigh the advantages and disadvantages of incorporating high-tech advances into contemporary law enforcement practices. In the report authored by the President's Task Force on 21st Century Policing, the task force members delineated six "pillars" or main topic areas. In Pillar Three, *Technology and Social Media*, the task force urged police departments to embrace the new technology and "to fully engage and educate communities in a dialogue about their expectations for transparency, accountability, and privacy" (Office of Community Oriented Policing Services, 2015, p. 31). However, the task force members also cautioned that the inclusion of these new technologies must be evaluated appropriately, to ensure that the individual rights of citizens are not violated.

Recently, advocates and citizen reform groups have demanded that police departments incorporate body worn cameras (BWC) to record interactions between officers and the public and to identify potential officer misconduct. Law enforcement organizations are being encouraged to integrate BWCs to enhance officer training and performance, provide a more precise record of encounters, and build agency accountability and transparency (Miller, Tolivar & Police Executive Research Forum, 2014). As support for the use of BWCs mobilizes, police administrators are justifiably cautious and recommend that their respective agencies proceed methodically with the adoption of this technology. In a related example, following the fatal shooting of Michael Brown in Ferguson, MO, the Atlanta, GA Civil Service Review Board (ACRB) conducted a study in 2014 to examine the adoption of BWCs for the City of Atlanta's Police Department. The authors of the study suggested that the use of BWCs could provide an unbiased tool to document the interactions between the departmental officers and members of the public. However, they cautioned, "As with every new technological tool, a thorough analysis of the benefits and concerns must be conducted to ensure that the technology yields the anticipated results." (The Atlanta Citizen Review Board, 2014, p. 8). Many police departments across the country are developing pilot programs and establishing policies that will guide officers integrating this promising technology.

SOCIAL MEDIA, TECHNOLOGY, AND CONSIDERATIONS FOR OFFICER INVOLVED SHOOTINGS

In light of the increased scrutiny on law enforcement, it is important to address how social media and technological advances also impact the law enforcement department's response to officer-involved shootings (OIS), especially deadly force encounters. In the aftermath of an OIS, law enforcement officials must rapidly address and manage complex on-site demands. The homicide investigator ensures the preservation of the integrity of the crime scene to prevent degradation of the forensic evidence. Reporters often dash to the location and demand instant access and information about the suspect/shooting victim and the specifics of the encounter. The family members of the suspect/shooting victim may also be present to gather information on the status of their loved one. Other police personnel may be nearby due to peripheral involvement in the incident or to check on the involved officer. The agency managers and supervisors may also arrive with the goals of minimizing any potential liability and preserving the reputation of the department.

Historically, the laws governing disclosure vary across states, but open records acts determine the information disclosed, withheld, or redacted (Georgia Bureau of Investigation, 2005). In spite of these laws, many public safety organizations have historically withheld the identity of officers involved in shootings, and in certain states, police departments were not obliged to disclose the name of an officer involved in a shooting if there were viable public safety threats. The California Supreme Court recently ruled that police organizations must disclose the names of officers implicated in on-duty shootings, with a few specific exceptions being made in cases of verifiable safety concerns (Dolan, 2014). In this age of instant access and heightened scrutiny, the story of a deadly force encounter appears immediately on the television and internet news, often interrupting normal programming as a "breaking story," and the police agency is inundated with requests for information on the identities of the officer and the deceased. Following the death of Michael Brown, the Ferguson, MO Chief of Police, Thomas Jackson, delayed releasing the name of the involved officer because of concerns for the officer's safety (Dahl, 2014). Chief Jackson also indicated that death threats were made against members of the department on social media. The American Civil Liberties Union (ACLU) of Missouri and the National Association for the Advancement of Colored People (NAACP), along with other prominent organizations, asked the department to release a copy of the police investigation that identified the involved officer (Bendery, 2014). Chief Jackson subsequently withdrew his objections and released the name of the officer, highlighting the pressures law enforcement leadership often face to release personal identifying information once a story gains strong media attention.

Police commanders understand and wrestle with demands from the general public to receive instant information, including the identity of the involved officer and the deceased, especially after a deadly force encounter. In 2012, then Police Commissioner Charles Ramsey of the Philadelphia, PA Police Department requested that the United States Department of Justice conduct an investigation of the agency after 58 people were shot by the police during that year. The agency had been criticized for a lack of transparency, especially in investigations of departmental shootings. The findings were summarized in a report that was released in March 2015 (Faziollah & Purcell, 2015). Based on the results of the investigation, Commissioner Ramsey decided that the agency would now disclose the name of any officer involved in a shooting within 72 hours unless there were viable threats or public safety concerns. Since the policy change, tensions have escalated and the police union officials have angrily opposed this decision due to officer safety concerns. In response, Pennsylvania State Representative Martina White sponsored a bill that would guarantee the anonymity of the involved officer and ensure that the officer is safe and protected from any potential retaliation. The bill dictates that the officer's name would be disclosed at a later date, either once the investigation was closed or if the officer were charged with a crime. This proposed legislation has garnered support from the Fraternal Order of Police (FOP), which cites the safety and recent attacks on police officers as a primary reason to withhold the name of the police officers involved in shootings (Denardo, 2015).

Clearly this issue creates passionate debate on both sides, and it remains to be seen how law enforcement agencies will balance safety for the officer with the public's need to know in the aftermath of an OIS. Though the safety of the officer remains a salient concern for all departmental personnel impacted by an OIS, the police psychologist has the additional responsibility of facilitating care for the officer's psychological well-being. The mental health professional working with the involved officer must consider how the additional stressor of increased media scrutiny as well as how the release of the officer's identity will impact the officer's emotional health and subsequent recovery process.

Agency commanders are concerned about physical and psychological injury to officers involved in shootings and deadly force situations, but the police psychologist has a unique responsibility to attend to the emotional well-being of any personnel involved following a firearm discharge. In 2013, members of the Police Psychological Services Section (PPSS) of the IACP ratified the Officer-Involved Shooting Guidelines to provide direction to departments and mental health providers on how to manage post-shooting situations (IACP, 2013).

After a deadly OIS, the primary goal for the mental health provider is to ensure that the psychological well-being of the involved officer is optimized. In light of the recent scrutiny on deadly police encounters, it is imperative that police psychologists and agency administrators consider the emotional impact on the officer, especially when the community uses social media to disseminate private and possibly inaccurate information about the shooting. The ability to immediately share this information, without vetting procedures to ensure information accuracy, dramatically changes the way OIS data are disseminated and perceived by the public.

Historically, since many police agencies did not immediately release the name of the officer involved in a shooting, there was some available time for the officer to share his or her involvement with significant others before specific identifying information was released to the public. This standard operational practice is shifting as the public demands information about the officer and details of the investigation immediately after a shooting. The officer's opportunity to privately inform significant others of involvement in a shooting, while maintaining anonymity, has been significantly altered. Many officers have discussed the time-sensitive pressure of ensuring that loved ones do not first learn specifics about the shooting from news or social media sources. In the aftermath of an OIS, most departments provide the officer with the opportunity to contact the immediate family to assure them that their loved one is safe, or in the case of injury, that he or she is receiving medical attention. However, with the advent of instant media attention, and in scenarios in which the officer may be injured or unable to make the initial contact with his or her family, police organizations may need to develop and implement policies to identify and train trusted, designated members of the department. These individuals could then be tasked to provide basic, permissible communication to the officer's family if the officer is unable to make the notification.

The intense media scrutiny in the aftermath of an OIS also hinders the officer's ability to have adequate "down time" to process the event in a private manner. In many instances, the officer now has to contend with the demands from the public to release identifying information, as well as the endless news coverage of the incident. Additionally, the intensity of video images of deadly police encounters captured by eyewitnesses and the constant replaying of the incident on both the internet and the 24/7 news channels may also impact the officer's ability to decompress fully in the aftermath of a shooting. Police psychologists assigned to provide emotional assistance to officers involved in shootings should also weigh these concerns and consider that the officer's recovery process may be negatively impacted. Future researchers should investigate how instant media access and dissemination impact the psychological healing of officers involved in shootings, now that officers are tasked with processing the emotional impact of shootings under the scrutiny of an often critical public.

In the aftermath of a deadly encounter, the involved officer may also experience professional stressors including job preservation concerns, isolation from colleagues during the investigation, and intense scrutiny of personnel records and disciplinary history (Artwohl & Christenson, 1997). Policy dictates that officers remain on administrative leave during an investigation, also limiting their ability to work extra jobs for additional income, often creating financial strain. To combat isolation from colleagues, many officers involved in critical incidents use online social support networks to overcome the loneliness and loss of camaraderie that can occur following a shooting.

There are numerous websites and online communities developed by and targeted to law enforcement personnel to provide training opportunities, to share coverage of noteworthy news events, to enhance connections, to promote safety, and to offer emotional support. Some of these online communities may allow officers to log on anonymously, whereas others such as PoliceOne.com require that officers register and be vetted before accessing forums. User data on the PoliceOne.com site indicate that it has over 3 million visitors monthly, and over 500,000 registered users (PoliceOne.com, n.d.).

Many officers positively embrace online social support networks, especially Millennials because of their general comfort with and connection to the internet and social media. However, officers involved in publicized shootings may find passionate scrutiny of their actions by members of the law enforcement community. The social media feedback or criticism may be harsh and judgmental, particularly since posts on some sites may be made anonymously. An officer's actions may be critiqued, and personal information can be publicly disclosed by the law enforcement community at large or specifically by members of the officer's agency, who may be intimately familiar with facts of the investigation. It is possible that the officer who turned to social media for online support to mitigate his or her feelings of social isolation may now experience additional stress from being rejected by law enforcement peers. Officers using social networking sites as an outlet and source of support should do so with an appreciation for the inherent risks associated with such sites.

If information about a critical incident, including private officer information (name, address, etc.), is disseminated to the public, the involved employee and his or her family may also be targeted by the media. Mundane activities like going to the local grocery store may now involve maneuvering news trucks, onlookers, and reporters. Releasing personal information could also increase the likelihood of threats of harm to the officer and his or her loved ones from the general public, anti-police individuals, and/or protest groups.

These concerns are magnified by current events, including officers killed in ambushes in patrol cars in New York City, or at a gas station outside Houston, TX. Vitriolic comments made anonymously online by anti-police advocates, activist movements protesting police brutality, and the personal attacks generated by media reporters primarily interested in presenting sensationalized or one-sided reports to garner higher ratings also raise genuine concerns about officer safety when personal information is provided to the public.

The instantaneous access to information garnered through the proliferation of social media platforms has created additional stress and strain upon the lives and well-being of current officers. Police psychologists and department decision makers should consider these technological advances and their impact on the emotional recovery process for both the involved officer and his or her significant others, especially after a deadly force encounter. The well-informed police psychologist must consider the myriad of sources of potential stress on an officer in the aftermath of a critical incident and help the officer to develop appropriate coping strategies.

To that end, the IACP Officer-Involved Shooting Guidelines highlight that "officers are encouraged to be mindful that accessing online media sites, especially those that contain negative commentary can complicate post-incident thoughts and emotions" (IACP, 2013, p. 5). Department supervisors should encourage all officers to be conscious of any postings on social media at all times, particularly after involvement in a critical incident. Department policy may also include requiring officers involved in deadly force situations and critical incidents to limit public access. The department administrators and police psychologists should also assist the officer in dealing with the emotional correlates of his or her private life being publicized and analyzed. These stressors are often compounded with complex legal proceedings that can linger for long periods of time and may lead to feelings of anger, frustration, sadness, and anxiety.

SUMMARY

The authors have written this chapter as a resource for graduate students, law enforcement commanders, agency executives, and police psychologists to initiate future research and foster continuing dialogue. Hopefully, these efforts lead to more informed policy development and improved organizational procedures. The world is is becoming more technologically sophisticated, especially as Millennials enter law enforcement in greater numbers. Additionally, as we move into the 21st century, the existing practices of law enforcement must adapt to incorporate the ideals of transparency and accountability demanded by an informed public.

REFERENCES

Artwohl, A., & Christensen, L. W. (1997). *Deadly force encounters*. Boulder, CO: Paladin Press.

Bendery, J. (2014, August 13). ACLU files Sunshine Law requests to ID officer who shot Michael Brown. *Huffington Post*. Retrieved October 23, 2015 from www.huffingtonpost.com/2014/08/13/michael-brown-shooting_n_5675660.html

Bosman, J., & Eckholm, E. (2014, August 13). Anonymity in police shooting fuels anger in Missouri. *The New York Times*. Retrieved November 2, 2015 from http://www.nytimes.com/2014/06/14/us/missouri-teenager-and-officer-scuffled before-shooting-chief-says.html?_r=0

Bravermen, S. (2012, February 23). One in 5 U.S. adults have a tattoo. *Harris Interactive*. Retrieved October 4, 2015, from http://www.harrisinteractive.com/NewsRoom/Harris Polls/tabid/447/ mid/1508/articleId/970/ctl/ReadCustom%20Default/Default.aspx

Brook, J. S., Zhang, C., & Brook, D. W. (2011). Developmental trajectories of marijuana use from adolescence to adulthood: Personal predictors. *Archives of Pediatrics & Adolescent Medicine*, *165*(1), 55–60. doi:10.1001/archpediatrics.2010.248 PMID:21199981

Burger, T. D., & Finkel, D. (2002). Relationships between body modifications and very high-risk behaviors in a college population. *College Student Journal*, *36*, 203–213.

Carlson, N. (2010, March 5). At last: The full story of how Facebook was founded. *Business Insider*. Retrieved November 20, 2015 from http://www.businessinsider.com/how-facebook-was-founded-2010-3

City and County of Denver Civil Service Commission. (2014). *Police officer examination informational booklet*. Retrieved October 17, 2015 from https://www.denvergov.org/ Portals/590/documents/Police%20 Candidate%20Informational%20Booklet.pdf

Dahl, J. (2014, August 13). Ferguson chief: Race relations a top priority post-shooting. *CBS News*. Retrieved November 10, 2015 from http://www.cbsnews.com/news/ferguson-missouri-police-chief-race-relations-a-top-priority-post-shooting

Denardo, M. (2015, September 2). FOP backs bill preventing release of names of officers in shootings. *CBS Philly*. Retrieved November 20, 2015 from http://philadelphia.cbs.local.com/2015/09/02/fop-backs-bill-preventing-release-of-officers-names-invovled -in-shootings-during-ongoing-investigations

Dolan, M. (2014, May 29). Court backs disclosure of officers' names in shooting cases. *The Los Angeles Times*. Retrieved November 23, 2015 from http://latimes.com/local/la-me-in-officer-names--20140529-story.html

Drews, D. R., Allison, C. K., & Probst, J. R. (2000). Behavioral and self-concept differences in tattooed and non-tattooed college students. *Psychological Reports*, *86*(2), 475–481. doi:10.2466/pr0.2000.86.2.475 PMID:10840898

Faziolah, M., & Purcell, D. (2015, October 15). New rules for when Philadelphia police shoot. *The Philadelphia Inquirer*. Retrieved November 5, 2015 from http://articles.philly.com/2015-10-19/news/67591744_1_naming-police-officers-police-advisory-commission-police-misconduct

Georgia Bureau of Investigation. (2014). *Open records handbook*. Retrieved March 20, 2016 from http://gbi.georgia.gov/publications

Gillmor, D. (2014, August 16). Ferguson's citizen journalists revealed the value of an undeniable video. *The Guardian*. Retrieved November 1, 2015 from http://www.theguardian.com/commentisfree/2014/aug/16/fergusons-citizen-journalists video

Goode, E. (2011, April 6). Police lesson: Social network tools have two edges. *The New York Times*. Retrieved October 30, 2015 from http://www.nytimes.com/2011/04/07/us/07police.html

Goodman, J. D., & Ruderman, W. (2013, March 28). Police department sets rules for officers' use of social media. *The New York Times*. Retrieved November 10, 2015 from http://www.nytimes.com/2013/03/29/nyregion/new-york--police-dept-issues-guidelines-for-social-media.html?r=0

Gorner, J. (2015a, July 3). Chicago police officers sue over tattoo cover-up rule. *The Chicago Tribune*. Retrieved October 4, 2015, from http://www.chicagotribune.com/news/local/breaking/ct-chicago-police-tattoo-lawsuit-met-20150702-story.html#

Gorner, J. (2015b, October 29). Judge tosses lawsuit challenging CPD policy on tattoos. *The Chicago Tribune*. Retrieved March 28, 2016, from http://www.chicagotribune.com/news/local/breaking/ct-judge-tosses-lawsuit-challenging-cpd-policy-on-tattoos-20151028-story.html

Graham, J. (2013, November 4). A generation of idle trophy kids. *The Boston Globe*. Retrieved November 20, 2015 from https://www.bostonglobe.com/opinion/2013/11/04/idle-millennials-are-victims-their-parents-success/2rWDFWXQHo290FqUpz0HOO/story.html

Grooming and appearance rules for public safety workers. (2007). *AELE Monthly Law Journal*. Retrieved October 17, 2015 from http://www.aele.org/law /2007FPFEB/2007-02MLJ201.pdf

Hartogs, J. (2013, August 1). Study: Record number of young adults living with their parents. *CBS News*. Retrieved November 20, 2015 from http://www.cbsnews.com/news/study-record-number-of-young-adults-living-with-their-parents

Henchey, J. P. (2005). Ready or not, here they come: The Millennial generation enters the workforce. *The Police Chief*, *72*(9), 108–118.

Hladkey, G. B. (2015, November 2). Conn. police worried by ambush assaults, social media hostility. *PoliceOne.com*. Retrieved November 10, 2015 from http://www.policeone.com/pc_print.asp?vid=35092006

International Association of Chiefs of Police. (2013). *Officer-involved shooting guidelines*. Retrieved November 1, 2015 from www.theiacp.org/portals/0/documents/pdfs/Psych-OfficerInvolvedShooting,pdf

Johnson, K. (2010, November 11). Police recruits screened for digital dirt on Facebook, etc. *USA Today*. Retrieved October 17, 2015 from http://usatoday30.usatoday.com/tech/news/2010-11-12-1Afacebook-cops12_ST_N.htm

Koch, J. R., Roberts, A. E., Armstrong, M. L., & Owen, D. C. (2010). Body art, deviance, and American college students. *The Social Science Journal*, *47*(1), 151–161. doi:10.1016/j.soscij.2009.10.001

Lacey, M. (2011, August 11). Booking criminals and comparing ink. *The New York Times*. Retrieved February 16, 2016 from http://www.nytimes.com/2011/08/11/us/11phoenix.html?_r=2

Laumann, A., & Derick, A. (2010). *Tattoos and body piercings in the United States: A national data set*. Retrieved on October 4, 2015 from http://www.bxscience.edu/ourpages/ auto/2010/5/13/44313724/TATTOOS.pdf

McDuling, J. (2014). Facebook's mobile user base has crossed the 1 billion threshold. Retrieved November 20, 2015 from http://qz.com/202349/facebook-mobile-user-base-has-crossed-the-1-billion-threshhold

Meister, J. (2012, August 14). Job hopping is the 'new normal' for Millennials: Three ways to prevent a human resource nightmare. *Forbes*. Retrieved on November 20, 2015 from http://www.forbes.com/sites/jeannemeister/2012/08/14/job-hopping-is-the-new-normal-for-millennials-three-ways-to-prevent-a-human-resource-nightmare

Miller, L., Tolivar, J., & Police Executive Research Forum. (2014). *Implementing a body-worn camera program: Recommendations and lessons learned.* Washington, DC: Office of Community Oriented Policing Services.

Nathanson, C., Paulhus, D. L., & Williams, K. M. (2006). Personality and misconduct correlates of body modification and other cultural deviance markers. *Journal of Research in Personality*, *40*(5), 779–802. doi:10.1016/j.jrp.2005.09.002

Office of Community Oriented Policing Services. The President's Task Force on 21st Century Policing. (2015). *Final report of the President's Task Force on 21st Century Policing. Recommendations and lessons learned.* Washington, DC: Office of Community Oriented Policing Services.

Pardini, D., Bechtold, J., Loeber, R., & White, H. (2015). Developmental trajectories of marijuana use among men examining linkages with criminal behavior and psychopathic features into the mid-30s. *Journal of Research in Crime and Delinquency*, *29*(June). doi:10.1177/0022427815589816 PMID:26568641

PoliceOne.com. (n.d.). About us. *PoliceOne.com*. Retrieved November 22, 2015 from http://policeone.com/about

Roberts, M., & Roberts, R. (2014, October). *Marijuana use by police and public safety applicants: Negative background correlates of frequency and recency of use.* Presented at the International Association of Chiefs of Police Convention, Orlando, FL.

Rochman, B. (2013, February 22). Hover no more: Helicopter parents may breed depression and incompetence in their children. *Time*. Retrieved on February 16, 2016 from http://healthland.time.com/2013/02/22/hover-no-more-helicopter-parents-may-breed-depression-and-incompetence-in-their-children/

Rose, A., Timm, H., Pogson, C., Gonzalez, J., Appel, E., & Kolb, N. (2010, December). *Developing a cybervetting strategy for law enforcement-special report.* Retrieved on March 38, 2016 from http://www.iacpsocialmedia.org/Portals/1/documents/CybervettingReport.pdf

Smith, A. (2015). *U.S. smartphone use in 2015.* Retrieved on November 20, 2015 from http://www.pewinternet.org/2015/04/01/us-smartphone-use-in-2015

The Atlanta Citizen Review Board. (2014). *The Atlanta Citizen Review Board study on body-worn cameras (BWCs) & discussion of concerns and recommendations on BWCs for Atlanta police officers.* Atlanta, GA: The City of Atlanta ACRB.

Thompson, S. (2013, August 11). Law enforcement agencies ease rules for inked officers. *The Tampa Tribune*. Retrieved October 4, 2015 from http://www.tbo.com/pinellas-county/law-enforcement-agencies-ease-rules-for-inked-officers-20130811

Tooley, M., Linkenbach, J., Lande, B. J., & Lande, G. M. (2009). The media, the public and the law enforcement community: Correcting misperceptions. *The Police Chief*, *76*(6), 62–67.

Wagtendonk, A. V. (2015, April 10). How and why you should record the police. *PBS Newshour*. Retrieved November 17, 2015 from http://pbs.org/newshour/update/6-rules-follow-citizen-journalist

Wilson, J., Dalton, E., Scheer, C., & Grammich, C. A. (2010). *Police recruitment and retention for the new millennium: The state of knowledge*. Retrieved November 20, 2015 from http://www.rand.org/content/dam/rand/pubs/monographs/2010/RAND_MG959.pdf

Chapter 16
Emerging Ethical Issues in Police and Public Safety Psychology:
Reflections on Mandatory vs. Aspirational Ethics

Jeni L. McCutcheon
Phoenix Area Independent Police & Public Safety Psychology Practice, USA

ABSTRACT

This chapter presents commonly experienced ethical dilemmas among police and public safety psychologists. Real-world, relevant examples are offered with an emphasis on emerging ethical issues. Related American Psychological Association (APA) ethical principles and standards for psychologists and codes of conduct are highlighted. The possibility that ethical dilemmas go unrecognized due to a focus on mandatory rather than aspirational ethics is considered. Solutions for resolving ethical dilemmas are presented.

INTRODUCTION

Ethical issues abound in the specialty of police and public safety psychology. Psychologists working in this specialty encounter ethical dilemmas that are thought-provoking and challenging. These dilemmas are likely among the toughest aspects of police and public safety psychology practice. A paucity of research exists about commonly experienced ethical dilemmas among police and public safety psychologists. Zelig (1988) surveyed police psychologists and found that the three most encountered ethical dilemmas involved multiple relationships, confidentiality concerns, and resolution of conflicts between professional standards and an organization's needs. Multiple studies of psychologists nationally and internationally have resulted in similar findings, with concerns related to confidentiality and multiple relationships cited as the most frequently experienced ethical challenges in psychology practice (Colnerud, 1997; Pettifor & Sawchuk, 2006; Pope & Vetter, 1992; Slack & Wassenaar, 1999). Zelig (1988) also found that many

DOI: 10.4018/978-1-5225-0813-7.ch016

police psychologists reported they did not experience any ethical dilemmas. This too was consistent with the results of Pope and Vetter (1992), who reported that 134 of their 679 psychologist respondents did not encounter a single ethically troubling incident in the last year or two prior to the survey.

Several reasons likely exist for a lack of identified ethical dilemmas. Psychologists may fail to recognize ethical challenges. They have busy practices or copious work to complete within an agency and may overlook such issues. Conversely they may think too concretely and miss the complexity of situations. Over time, they may have encountered similar dilemmas and have become immune to them. Alternately, perhaps with experience, they become better at managing dilemmas, such that situations are no longer viewed as anything out of the ordinary. Perhaps some police and public safety psychologists fail to consider potential differences between mandatory and aspirational ethics. Ethical dilemmas may go unrecognized due to a focus on mandatory ethics.

Practicing mandatory ethics involves only acting in compliance with enforceable standards. This approach involves following the letter of the law or the specifics of a code. The focus is on conforming to requirements. Close considerations include risk management, avoidance of harm, adherence to requirements and recognition of "right" action. Mandatory ethics are the "floor" of expectations in resolving any given ethical challenge.

Aspirational ethics involve striving for the best possible ethical outcome. In contrast to the floor example of mandatory ethics, aspirational ethics are the "ceiling" in any given ethical dilemma. Goals include pursuing the best outcome for the involved parties and seeking to "do good." This involves embracing principles, a philosophical stance, or an overarching thinking style to resolve ethical dilemmas. The APA's ethical principles for psychologists—in contrast to the enforceable (mandatory) principles—are aspirational in nature. They call upon psychologists to adopt core beliefs rather than simply following a set of rules, laws, or codes.

In considering aspirational ethics, there are multiple relevant areas of the APA Ethics Code. The General Principles relate to and address the need for psychologists to do good, avoid doing harm, be aware of their influence, have integrity, be conscientious and attuned to their responsibilities, be fair, exercise good decision-making, and recognize their biases and the limits of their competence (APA, 2002).

ETHICAL DILEMMAS OF POLICE AND PUBLIC SAFETY PSYCHOLOGISTS

Police and public safety psychologists experience a multitude of ethical dilemmas in different areas. Concerns about confidentiality, multiple relationships, managing conflicts between ethics and organizational demands, and professional competence are particularly relevant for police psychologists. Each of these key areas is addressed in the next section of this chapter and may be associated with a variety of ethical challenges. Psychologists encounter dilemmas when working in any of the four core functional domains of police and public safety psychology: assessment, intervention, consultation, and operations (Aumiller et al., 2007).

Confidentiality

Codes regarding confidentiality address the need for police and public safety psychologists to maintain confidences, identify the client or patient and other involved parties, clarify and make explicit these relationships, and acquire informed consent. The APA Ethical Principles of Psychologists and Code of Conduct (2002) Standard 4, Privacy and Confidentiality, that apply are:

Maintaining Confidentiality

Psychologists have a primary obligation and take reasonable precautions to protect confidential information obtained through or stored in any medium, recognizing that the extent and limits of confidentiality may be regulated by law or established by institutional rules or professional or scientific relationship.

Discussing the Limits of Confidentiality

(a) Psychologists discuss with persons (including, to the extent feasible, persons who are legally incapable of giving informed consent and their legal representatives) and organizations with whom they establish a scientific or professional relationship (1) the relevant limits of confidentiality and (2) the foreseeable uses of the information generated through their psychological activities. (b) Unless it is not feasible or is contraindicated, the discussion of confidentiality occurs at the outset of the relationship and thereafter as new circumstances may warrant. (c) Psychologists who offer services, products, or information via electronic transmission inform clients/patients of the risks to privacy and limits of confidentiality.

Minimizing Intrusions on Privacy

(a) Psychologists include in written and oral reports and consultations, only information germane to the purpose for which the communication is made. (b) Psychologists discuss confidential information obtained in their work only for appropriate scientific or professional purposes and only with persons clearly concerned with such matters.

Disclosures

(a) Psychologists may disclose confidential information with the appropriate consent of the organizational client, the individual client/patient, or another legally authorized person on behalf of the client/patient unless prohibited by law. (b) Psychologists disclose confidential information without the consent of the individual only as mandated by law, or where permitted by law for a valid purpose such as to (1) provide needed professional services; (2) obtain appropriate professional consultations; (3) protect the client/patient, psychologist, or others from harm; or (4) obtain payment for services from a client/patient, in which instance disclosure is limited to the minimum that is necessary to achieve the purpose.

Difficulties with confidentiality can be many. Complications may present when the relationship is hazy and fails to be properly identified, defined, or made clear to the involved parties. Consider the example of a psychologist having breakfast with a Chief of Police who asks about an officer the chief regards as reactive and knows is seeing the psychologist. The ethical police psychologist does not nod and stay quiet, or expound on the identified officer's virtues or troubles. Instead, the ethical psychologist clarifies the relationships, with a polite reminder of the importance of confidentiality. An ethical psychologist would also realize that multiple relationships exist and would therefore clarify the relationship with the chief. Reminding the chief that the current conversation is confidential, the psychologist might then suggest that the chief speak directly with the officer about the stated concerns.

Other ethical dilemmas about confidentiality may arise in regard to practical and business details of police and public safety psychology practice. Sometimes these concerns are about records. Consider, for example, a firefighter sent to see a psychologist following a child drowning incident. The psychologist provides a confidential therapy session or sessions to this patient and may provide a letter verifying attendance to the agency. Importantly, the details of the session, the disclosures, and certainly the subsequent records remain private and confidential. However, the records may no longer be confidential if this same firefighter decides that, after a third child drowning, he/she is distressed and no longer able to perform the job. If that individual seeks a medical retirement or files a Workers' Compensation claim, the psychological treatment records may be required to be disclosed to the employer's Workers' Compensation company in accordance with a state statute. The ethical psychologist will have covered such potentialities in the first meeting with the patient and will have obtained the patient's expressed written consent to these exceptions to confidentiality.

Other related examples include assessment and evaluation subjects who have misimpressions about their rights and roles in the evaluation processes. This often occurs despite repeated verbal and written informed consent procedures prior to and during the course of the evaluation. These procedures clarify the role of the agency as the client and the role of the subject as participant who is not privy to any of the findings, results, recommendations, or the final report. Consider the pre-employment evaluation subject who demands to know psychological test results, "Especially that Wonderlic score, because I want to know how I compare to the guys in the NFL who get that test, too." Or, the peace officer applicant not recommended for hire who does not understand that the agency is the hiring authority after being told by the department's background investigator, "We can't hire you because you failed your psych." This applicant then repeatedly calls the psychologist's office demanding a sit-down discussion to plea for a change in rating. An ethical police and public safety psychologist politely reiterates the relationship, directs the subject back to the hiring agency, and informs the agency commander of the situation. The psychologist may also discuss with the commander the agency's candor, clarifying the psychologist's role as a consultant in the pre-employment process.

Additional concerns about confidentiality arise in the context of providing assessment services as a police psychologist. Though all of the traditional doctor-patient expectations regarding confidentiality may not apply in such evaluations, only relevant details should end up in the assessment reports. In the case of a fitness-for-duty evaluation, detailed information about the individual may not be included in the report sent to an agency, and the psychologist may arrange with the agency to provide a simple fit or unfit recommendation. In the case of a pre-employment psychological screening evaluation, sensitive and private disclosures may be withheld from the report. As an example, consider the applicant with suicidal ideation with a plan in the past year. Instead of detailing this information in the report, the psychologist might identify "recent and significant concerns about emotional instability" in the relevant psychological and mental health history section of the report. Similarly, instead of reporting that the subject of the pre-employment evaluation had numerous previous mental health contacts consisting of medication to decrease symptoms of depression and therapy to cope with the sudden death of a parent, the now-stable applicant's report may read, "Past treatment, no recent or current concerns, currently emotionally stable." In addition, personal information that is not directly job relevant should often be omitted from psychological reports. Examples include an evaluation subject who is cohabitating with a partner and who is not fully out as a lesbian. The report may list the person as "single," and if reference is made to the partner, for example, and a loud verbal argument that led to a welfare check by a local police agency, the report may describe this situation as "a loud verbal altercation with a romantic partner."

In many cases, inquiries about family are limited, if conducted at all, due to consideration of federal laws such as the Genetic Information and Nondisclosure Act (GINA). GINA mandates that genetic information about a job applicant's family members is not queried about or even addressed in a pre-employment psychological evaluation, let alone included in employment-related evaluation reports. This becomes a careful task for the interviewing psychologist, as far as ferreting out appropriate, germane, and job-related details in a pre-employment screening decision and report.

Irrelevant details should not be disclosed in pre-employment psychological screening reports of law enforcement applicants. As an example, consider the psychologist who asks a young applicant about a history of fighting in school, school suspensions, and later mental health treatment. The applicant discloses "having a fairly messed up childhood and dealing with problems with my family." The applicant's father and several uncles were in and out of prison for drug-related charges, and this may be relevant to the screening decisions, since the applicant may have been routinely exposed to illegal behavior. The psychologist may question the applicant's handling of family functions, fraternization with inmates and felons, as well as possible ongoing exposure to illegal drugs due to family members' involvement. What should not be considered or explored, and what may call for a GINA admonishment, would be the content disclosed in a statement such as, "My father was depressed and had a drug problem. I think that is why he used to be so mean, and why I was such an angry kid." An admonishment in this type of scenario might be phrased as follows: "I hear what you are saying, and due to the Genetic Information and Nondisclosure Act, we cannot pursue this area of conversation about your father's health problems. Instead, please tell me about what you do now at the family barbecues, where as you reported, your uncles smoke marijuana in the backyard."

A firm stance on confidentiality in police and public safety psychology practice is needed. This author's recommendation is to become adept at defining all relationships from the first contact, stating these explicitly, identifying other involved parties, and also defining rights and duties inherent with these professional relationships.

Unless otherwise explicitly arranged or as mandated by law, informal contacts and services should be treated entirely as confidential. Examples include a phone call to the psychologist's office inquiring about services, an officer's disclosures made to a psychologist during a ridealong with the officer, a question a dispatcher asks of a psychologist during a sit-in at a call center, a firehouse conversation with a firefighter, or a detention officer's comment in a jail facility's control room about her difficulty coping with her husband's illness. When contacts between a psychologist and public safety personnel occur physically in the field and out of the office, they are confidential, and this often needs to be stated and affirmed.

Confidentiality prevails in formal services as well. When contacts are formal sessions, meetings, or in-office services, these services are defined by written documentation, and expressed written consent is obtained. When services are not confidential, such as pre-employment evaluations, the limits of confidentiality are provided in written form and verbally reviewed, with the expressed written consent of the subject obtained. Finally, in situations where there may be a lack of guaranteed confidentiality and/or privilege, such as with a peer support team's services, these limits are openly discussed with the involved parties.

Multiple Relationships

Much has been written about multiple relationships in psychology, and for good reason. Multiple relationships are common and may pose challenges or dilemmas that are difficult for police and public safety psychologists to manage. Multiple relationships occur in several ways. First, they happen when the psychologist has more than one role or relationship with a client or patient. They happen when the psychologist has one original role or relationship with a client or patient and the psychologist intentionally or inadvertently enters into a new or different relationship with that client or patient. Multiple relationships may also exist when the psychologist enters a relationship with another person associated with the original client or patient. The relevant APA Ethical Principles of Psychologists and Code of Conduct (2002) Standard 3: Human Relations, that apply are:

Avoiding Harm

Psychologists take reasonable steps to avoid harming their clients/patients, students, supervisees, research participants, organizational clients, and others with whom they work, and to minimize harm where it is foreseeable and unavoidable.

Multiple Relationships

(a) A multiple relationship occurs when a psychologist is in a professional role with a person and (1) at the same time is in another role with the same person, (2) at the same time is in a relationship with a person closely associated with or related to the person with whom the psychologist has the professional relationship, or (3) promises to enter into another relationship in the future with the person or a person closely associated with or related to the person. A psychologist refrains from entering into a multiple relationship if the multiple relationship could reasonably be expected to impair the psychologist's objectivity, competence, or effectiveness in performing his or her functions as a psychologist, or otherwise risks exploitation or harm to the person with whom the professional relationship exists. Multiple relationships that would not reasonably be expected to cause impairment or risk exploitation or harm are not unethical. (b) If a psychologist finds that, due to unforeseen factors, a potentially harmful multiple relationship has arisen, the psychologist takes reasonable steps to resolve it with due regard for the best interests of the affected person and maximal compliance with the Ethics Code. (c) When psychologists are required by law, institutional policy, or extraordinary circumstances to serve in more than one role in judicial or administrative proceedings, at the outset they clarify role expectations and the extent of confidentiality and thereafter as changes occur.

Conflict of Interest

Psychologists refrain from taking on a professional role when personal, scientific, professional, legal, financial, or other interests or relationships could reasonably be expected to (1) impair their objectivity, competence, or effectiveness in performing their functions as psychologists or (2) expose the person or organization with whom the professional relationship exists to harm or exploitation.

Exploitative Relationships

Psychologists do not exploit persons over whom they have supervisory, evaluative, or other authority such as clients/patients, students, supervisees, research participants, and employees.

Informed Consent

(a) When psychologists conduct research or provide assessment, therapy, counseling, or consulting services in person or via electronic transmission or other forms of communication, they obtain the informed consent of the individual or individuals using language that is reasonably understandable to that person or persons except when conducting such activities without consent is mandated by law or governmental regulation or as otherwise provided in this Ethics Code. (b) For persons who are legally incapable of giving informed consent, psychologists nevertheless (1) provide an appropriate explanation, (2) seek the individual's assent, (3) consider such persons' preferences and best interests, and (4) obtain appropriate permission from a legally authorized person, if such substitute consent is permitted or required by law. When consent by a legally authorized person is not permitted or required by law, psychologists take reasonable steps to protect the individual's rights and welfare. (c) When psychological services are court ordered or otherwise mandated, psychologists inform the individual of the nature of the anticipated services, including whether the services are court ordered or mandated and any limits of confidentiality, before proceeding. (d) Psychologists appropriately document written or oral consent, permission, and assent.

Not all multiple relationships are problematic. Indeed, they are common, navigable occurrences, and with careful attention they can be managed ethically. The main concern is to avoid harm or exploitation to the client or patient, as well as to avoid entering into or maintaining relationships that will impair the psychologist's objectivity, competence, or effectiveness in performing her or his duties. The burden for meeting these requirements, and showing that the requirements have been met if the need arises, is on the psychologist (McCutcheon, 2011; Younggren & Gottlieb, 2004).

Previously, psychologists received a message, whether explicit or implicit, to simply avoid multiple relationships (Younggren & Gottlieb, 2004). This position was espoused in previous ethical codes for psychologists and routinely taught in graduate training programs. This singular client or patient view of maintaining only one relationship or role still exists.

While maintaining only one role or relationship may be a fine, easy, and straightforward choice in an ideal world, this is not necessarily practical, or even representative of the reality that most police and public safety psychologists face. Unless psychologists practice simply in one functional domain (such as assessment) and in only one functional competency (pre-employment evaluations, for example), it is increasingly likely that one will be regularly, if not constantly, bombarded with the task of managing multiple relationships. Fortunately, in both general psychology practice and police and public safety psychology practice, this reality is being recognized. With due regard and to be clear, some relationships, such as those of a sexual nature or in situations involving a conflict of interest, are clearly inappropriate and must always be avoided. With this acknowledgement, the question at hand for most police and public safety psychologists is not, "How does one avoid multiple relationships?" Rather, the quandary becomes how to ethically manage multiple relationships.

The most obvious multiple relationships are those that happen in an unplanned, circumstantial fashion. Police and public safety psychologists, like all psychologists, experience these. They have patients who live in the same communities and whom they bump into at the grocery store, at the dentist's office, at the gym, or at the local gas station. They inevitably see patients and professional contacts in their own friendship networks, religious organizations, and community events and associations. They also have children attending the same schools as the children of their patients and other public safety personnel with whom they work. They see their clinical patients in different roles, whether they are working off-duty as police officers at a concert or at a street fair. All of these ordinary situations, occurring in both big and small cities, need to be navigated carefully. The psychologist must have a plan of managing such circumstances confidentially and without doing harm, being exploitive or losing objectivity.

Aside from these real-world occurrences, police psychology differs somewhat from other specialty areas of psychology in that multiple relationships may increase naturally over time. Aside from practicing in a rural community or perhaps within military psychology settings, police and public safety psychology is likely unique in the existence of these growing relationships. There is often a flow of contacts that leads to multiple relationships in police and public safety psychology, and this occurs inevitably over time because of the frequent contact the psychologist has with client agencies and their personnel. Such contact may be particularly pronounced if one is an in-house psychologist or if one is a consulting psychologist with a busy practice, providing services to multiple agencies. Over a span of years, a psychologist will likely see the same person in many different contexts and roles.

Consider the following example of a psychologist's many roles and relationships over time. A psychologist sees a deputy sheriff applicant for a pre-employment interview. The applicant is hired, eventually advancing to a class sergeant position for the agency's law enforcement training academy where the psychologist teaches. The sergeant and the psychologist discuss concerns about underperforming academy recruits, and the sergeant refers recruits for counseling to the in-house Employee Assistance Plan, which the psychologist runs.

Years later, the psychologist, now in a private practice setting, employs a contract psychologist who performs a pre-employment evaluation on the same sergeant as he successfully laterals to another agency. Afterward, this individual attends a local continuing education seminar, sits near the psychologist who conducted the initial pre-employment screening years earlier, and suggests a marital retreat that he attended with his spouse as a helpful resource. In the course of this conversation, the sergeant discloses some details about his marital and financial difficulties to the psychologist.

Ultimately, this sergeant advances to a lieutenant position in charge of pre-employment processes at the same agency where the psychologist has provided pre-employment services for a decade. The lieutenant contacts this psychologist to discuss the battery being used in psychological pre-employment evaluations and to enlist the psychologist's help in reviewing policies and procedures for promotional exams. This example illustrates how the psychologist's familiarity and demonstrated competence and helpfulness over time lends to the psychologist's credibility in the field and therefore, leads clients and agencies purposefully to seek out these relationships.

Even when ongoing professional contacts inevitably lead to multiple relationships, police and public safety psychologists should be mindful of the possibility for exploitation and harm, as well as loss of objectivity. Recall that multiple relationships are unethical when they impair objectivity or exploit one or more parties or expose one or more parties to harm. When contemplating which path to take (or whether to take any path at all) that creates or continues a multiple relationship, five questions are suggested:

- What are the options?
- What is in the best interest of the client and the other involved parties?
- Are the proposed roles incompatible?
- Would it be best to simply refer out?
- If I engage in these multiple relationships, how do I navigate these different roles so as not to cause harm or lose objectivity?

Managing Conflicts between Ethics and Organizational Demands

Similar to multiple relationships, negotiating conflicts between ethics and organizational demands can be tricky. Such conflicts may arise when there appear to be differences between the standards of practice for the police and public safety psychologist, the APA Ethical Principles of Psychologists and Code of Conduct, and the demands or expectations of the agency. The relevant codes from the APA Ethical Principles of Psychologists and Code of Conduct (2002) Standard 3: Human Relations, that apply include:

Third-Party Requests for Services

When psychologists agree to provide services to a person or entity at the request of a third party, psychologists attempt to clarify at the outset of the service the nature of the relationship with all individuals or organizations involved. This clarification includes the role of the psychologist (e.g., therapist, consultant, diagnostician, or expert witness), an identification of who is the client, the probable uses of the services provided or the information obtained, and the fact that there may be limits to confidentiality.

Cooperation With Other Professionals

When indicated and professionally appropriate, psychologists cooperate with other professionals in order to serve their clients/patients effectively and appropriately.

3.11 Psychological Services Delivered To or Through Organizations

(a) Psychologists delivering services to or through organizations provide information beforehand to clients and when appropriate those directly affected by the services about (1) the nature and objectives of the services, (2) the intended recipients, (3) which of the individuals are clients, (4) the relationship the psychologist will have with each person and the organization, (5) the probable uses of services provided and information obtained, (6) who will have access to the information, and (7) limits of confidentiality. As soon as feasible, they provide information about the results and conclusions of such services to appropriate persons. (b) If psychologists will be precluded by law or by organizational roles from providing such information to particular individuals or groups, they so inform those individuals or groups at the outset of the service.

Managing the conflicts between one's professional ethics and the organizational demands that one encounters can be a difficult aspect of police and public safety psychology practice. Difficulty arises when an agency requests that the psychologist practice in a manner that is outside the standard of practice and that may even be unethical.

Consider this example. A request for proposals for psychological services resulted in bids and a subsequent contract award. Proposal submission review results were published on a website. Here, bidders were privy to their tallied scores and evaluative comments. A recorded weakness of a submitted proposal regarding provision of confidential counseling services was that "the psychologist declines to report violations of law to the agency." Points were also deducted because the psychologist declined to provide both confidential counseling services and subsequent fitness-for-duty evaluations, citing a conflict of interest. In this case, that which was perceived as a weakness was actually appropriate ethical action. Appropriate ethical action included maintaining confidentiality based on standards of practice as defined by relevant police psychology guidelines, applicable case law establishing psychotherapist-patient privilege (e.g., *Jaffee v. Redmond*), APA Ethical Principles of Psychologists and Code of Conduct regarding confidentiality, applicable state statutes, and the applicable state's Board of Psychologist Examiners Rules of Professional Conduct.

Such situations point to the need for education about what constitutes competent police and public safety psychology practice. Agencies are likely unaware of relevant guidelines, ethical codes, and laws that apply to psychological services and practice. Even when they are aware, a key point to consider is that agencies may choose to ignore these requirements, though psychologists who aspire to be ethical will not.

Also to consider is that psychologists have responsibilities to multiple parties. Fisher (2009) wrote about how psychologists often have duties to multiple parties:

If we stopped asking "Who is the client?," what should we ask instead? Regardless of the type of case or the number of relationships it involves, the question psychologists should ask might be "Exactly what are my ethical responsibilities to each of the parties in this case?" (p. 5).

Another example of conflict between ethics and organizational demands occurs due to pressure to make a quick hiring recommendation. Eager to fill an upcoming law enforcement academy class, an agency requests a psychological pre-employment evaluation "pass" or "fail" rating. The psychological screening decision for a particular applicant is deferred because relevant mental health records were not yet received from a recent mental health provider. The quandary here is meeting organizational demands while ethically performing the pre-employment evaluation. Ethical action involves declining to render a screening decision until needed information is received and the evaluation can be fully completed, per usual practice.

Consider a psychologist asked to provide an inappropriate fitness-for-duty evaluation on an incumbent officer. The officer does not meet threshold criteria for a fitness-for-duty evaluation, and the psychologist discerns that appropriate supervisory actions, such as discipline, have not been taken. It appears the agency is likely dealing with a difficult employee and expecting the psychologist to resolve the officer's employment status. When a psychologist works in-house for an agency, conducting this evaluation may be a directive, thus placing the psychologist in a difficult situation. Psychologists in any practice setting should explain the reasons for declining the referral, and through consultation, explore with the referring party ways to address the problematic employee's behavior. They may also educate about threshold criteria for a fitness-for-duty evaluation needing to be met.

Another example involves a request for a marketing blurb describing the pre-employment psychological procedures that will be used to attract applicants and demystify psychological pre-employment screening procedures. The psychologist provides a general description, omitting specific test names to maintain the validity of the pre-employment procedures. The agency requests more detailed test information "to be thorough," challenging the psychologist's refusal to provide test names and descriptions.

How should the psychologist resolve this conflict? In an ideal world, the psychologist explains the concern and make it clear why she/he is taking a particular stand. If needed, the psychologist presents data to the agency's decision makers and involved persons to educate and explain the conflict. Such data may include the relevant APA Ethical Principles of Psychologists and Code of Conduct, applicable guidelines, laws, and the basis for why something is done the way that it is, and the psychologist's experience in providing appropriate services. In an ideal world, this strategy should suffice. However, such matters are not always easy, and sometimes the psychologist is directed to take unethical action. The appropriate response is to decline, but to do so in a professional and respectful manner. To be successful in this process involves presenting information in such a way that the psychologist is perceived as helpful and educative, rather than insubordinate or subversive. This can sometimes be a difficult feat. Strong relationships with key agency personnel are vital. Being perceived as experienced and competent is essential in order to effect change and guide successful resolution of such conflicts.

Competence

Competency is vital for ethical police and public safety psychological practice. Competence involves being current on skills, abilities, and knowledge and is developed through a psychologist's seeking out and participating in relevant continuing education opportunities, reading and reviewing police and public safety literature, and staying up-to-date with evolving practice guidelines. A critical pathway for the development of competence is performing the intervention or other services with appropriate supervision and/or consultation from already competent psychologists. Competence in police and public safety psychology also involves a continuing expansion of knowledge in science, legal, and other areas related to police and public safety psychology. Several areas of the APA Ethical Principles of Psychologists and Code of Conduct (2002) Standard 2, Competence relate to police and public safety psychologists:

Maintaining Competence

Psychologists undertake ongoing efforts to develop and maintain their competence.

Bases for Scientific and Professional Judgments

Psychologists' work is based upon established scientific and professional knowledge of the discipline.

Delegation of Work to Others

Psychologists who delegate work to employees, supervisees, or research or teaching assistants or who use the services of others, such as interpreters, take reasonable steps to (1) avoid delegating such work to persons who have a multiple relationship with those being served that would likely lead to exploitation or loss of objectivity; (2) authorize only those responsibilities that such persons can be expected to perform competently on the basis of their education, training, or experience, either independently or with the level of supervision being provided; and (3) see that such persons perform these services competently.

Codes about competence also point to the need to have supervisees of police and public safety psychologists practice within their competence, and to have the psychologist assume full responsibility for appropriate supervision. Such supervisees may be practicum students, pre-doctoral interns, post-doctoral residents, and even other personnel, such as administrative staff who may assist police and public safety psychologists with their practice.

A newer measure of competence, available to police and public safety psychologists since 2011, is board certification through the American Board of Police and Public Safety Psychology (ABPPSP). Board certification is achieved when psychologists are judged as successfully able to demonstrate competence in the specialty area, as rigorously evaluated by peers through a formalized process. Experienced psychologists working with police and public safety personnel may be competent but choose not to seek board certification. As Corey noted:

To be sure, psychologists who choose for any number of reasons not to pursue board certification may still be competent in the specialty of police psychology, but only ABPPSP-certified psychologists have demonstrated that competence to the satisfaction of their peers through a demanding series of examinations overseen by a nationally recognized certifying organization (2011, p. 104).

ABPPSP has identified ten foundational competencies that must be successfully demonstrated to obtain board certification in Police & Public Safety Psychology. These competencies are Professionalism; Reflective Practice/Self-Assessment/Self-Care; Scientific Knowledge and Methods; Relationships; Individual and Cultural Diversity; Ethical/Legal Standards; Practice Standards; Interdisciplinary Systems; Knowledge of Client Milieu; and Evidence-Based Practice. Detailed descriptions and corresponding behavioral anchors can be found in the Examination Manual (American Board of Police and Public Safety Psychology, 2014, pp. 35-39).

Examples of ethical dilemmas related to competence are plentiful. The clearest example is practicing in an area in which one is not competent to practice. This can present in multiple ways. Consider the psychologist who has never performed a pre-employment evaluation of a police officer applicant, yet secures a contract to provide such services and then inquires of colleagues how to perform these evaluations. Ponder the psychologist who uses outdated test measures in evaluations, or uses as primary assessment measures psychological tests that have not been validated for police psychology applications. Consider also psychologists who perform assessments unethically, such as when a psychologist's meeting with a candidate in a pre-employment evaluation consists of only a 10-minute face-to-face meeting rather than a more standard 40-minute meeting. A final example is the psychologist who does not keep abreast of developments in the field, never attends any relevant continuing education opportunities, and is either unaware of or does not follow relevant guidelines for police psychology practice.

While it is of concern when one practices incompetently, it is often likely not intentional. Practicing competently is difficult if one does not know, or does not take steps to know, the standard of practice. As with most ethical transgressions, problems with competence can be seen as errors. Such errors are not typically deliberate departures from a standard of practice or may not reflect malicious intent. Such errors may be committed because of a lack of knowledge or a lack of application of existing knowledge (Knapp, Bennett, & VandeCreek, 2012). Regardless of intent, when such errors are made it is insufficient to simply cite a lack of knowledge as justification. Therefore, psychologists should strive to gain knowledge to gain and maintain competence.

NEW AND EMERGING ISSUES

Additional and current topics create ethical dilemmas for police and public safety psychologists. While none of the previously covered ethical challenges are necessarily simple to rectify or manage, they seem to pale in comparison to the tough ethical questions and aspirational challenges raised by new and emerging competencies, practices, and issues in police and public safety psychology.

Telehealth is an example of one such emerging practice area that brings with it a multitude of ethical challenges or dilemmas (Drum, 2014; Ragusea, 2012). Many police and public safety psychologists are uncertain of the right way to proceed. Prohibitive licensure laws currently limit interstate practice. For example, currently psychologists may only practice in states where they are licensed, excepting when other states allow for practice on a limited or other basis. Fortunately, an interstate compact is under development (Nordal, 2015). As the rest of the mental health world grapples with determining how telehealth will work, the specialty of police and public safety psychology will do so as well. For example, there is controversy about whether remote pre-employment psychological evaluations are acceptable. The International Association of Chiefs of Police (IACP) has established pre-employment psychological evaluation guidelines that currently call for face-to-face interviews, and while many psychologists view remote video evaluations as acceptable under the guidelines' specifications, some do not. And what about other services? Should law enforcement-related intervention or consultation services be performed via remote technology? Most police and public safety psychologists would likely report that they have at one time, if not routinely, provided executive consultation to command staff via telephone. While there is likely not much difference in providing such consultation services telephonically or through other remote communication means, it is currently unclear how telehealth modalities can be ethically implemented in regard to other functional competencies within police and public safety psychology.

As psychologists embrace telehealth, ethical issues will surface. A need to maintain confidentiality necessitates utilizing secure, private methods of communication. Competence is also an issue. Consider remotely conducted pre-employment evaluations. How will the psychologist assure adequate proctoring of written testing if the testing measures are administered to applicants in another state? Other services will likely expand telehealth delivery methods in police and public safety psychology practice. Perhaps webinars or remote teaching methods will replace in-person classes on mental illness and stress management at law enforcement training academies. A psychologist conceivably could participate as a consultant in crisis negotiations remotely if the technology allows the psychologist to see, hear, and perceive the call-out in real time. Issues of confidentiality and other ethical issues will arise, and will need to be resolved ethically.

Other emerging practice issues present ethical challenges. Maintaining confidentiality in digital or electronic data exchange can lead to ethical and aspirational challenges. As an example, consider the delivery of a pre-employment evaluation or fitness-for-duty report. Fifteen to 20 years ago, psychologists typically printed out and hand-delivered or securely mailed reports to agencies. For in-house psychologists, reports were completed, printed out, and delivered via an interoffice mail system. As time evolved, reports were sent via courier or any variety of secured mail service, with a signature guarantee and to a designated person. And then the Internet was born, accompanied by the expectation for quicker delivery of reports, often to aid in rapid hiring decisions. Many reports are now sent via email or other digital or electronic methods. Attending to ethical guidelines and building in safeguards to maintain confidentiality and privacy of information are important priorities. Safeguards include sending reports to designated personnel only, formatting issues such as converting documents from Word to PDF format, encryption of documents, password protection of documents, access to secure data in the cloud, and use of data storage systems to be accessed remotely by agencies when reports are available.

Proper data storage and backup are also important areas of consideration for police and public safety psychologists. Any busy police and public safety psychologist is already familiar with maintaining data and records and the related physical space challenges. Electronic storage of data has been a helpful convenience for many police and public safety psychologists. Some state statutes now allow for electronic storage of data. Once records are scanned and backed up appropriately, the physical record may be destroyed. While many legal issues are at play, the ethical issues of confidentiality and competence are significant (Gamble et al., 2015). Records need to be maintained securely and remain accessible if and as needed.

It is easy to imagine all that can go awry in this electronic/digital age of information sharing. Recently, a well-regarded psychologist colleague mistakenly sent a report meant for one designee to an active psychology listserv. The report was not password-protected, and because of the collegial tone of the accompanying email, several listserv members clicked on the link to the cloud within moments of receiving the email and accessed the report. This was a humbling and concerning incident for the psychologist in question.

A subject's access to evaluation reports is another recent challenge to forensic practice. Traditionally, pre-employment psychological evaluation subjects are not provided access to copies of their reports, given that the agency is the client. Except as mandated by state statutes, specific agency policy, or by appeal rights, applicants in pre-employment evaluations do not receive evaluation results. It is standard procedure in pre-employment evaluations, as in any third-party or forensic evaluation, for the subject to be asked to sign a waiver to waive the right to access the report, as well as evaluation findings and recommendations typically included in such reports. It should be delineated in the informed consent document who will be informing the applicant of any final decision regarding his or her suitability. Typically the agency makes the hiring decision, dependent also on other data learned across multiple pre-employment hiring processes. The psychologist should not disclose findings about suitability to the examinee without the agency's explicit informed consent to do so (Bush et al., 2006). With the advent of the Health Insurance Portability and Accountability Act (HIPAA), questions arise regarding whether applicants will be privy to evaluation results, especially because of HIPAA requirements, which would typically allow individuals access to their medical information. There is now a reasonable question being asked: Is it ethical for evaluators to require evaluation subjects to sign a waiver relinquishing their right to access their records? Some psychologists argue for transparency in sharing evaluation findings with applicants (Arcaya, 2011). Some psychologists believe that any practitioner who falls under HIPAA has an entire practice that falls under HIPAA (Borkosky, Pellett, & Thomas, 2014). In other words, the police and public safety psychologist who conducts psychotherapy services and submits invoices electronically to agencies falls under HIPAA and therefore may not be able to separately parcel out pre-employment evaluations as HIPAA exempt. Finally, a number of authoritative sources have concluded that it is consistent with ethical practice to require applicants sign a waiver relinquishing their right to access their records (e.g., Spilberg & Corey, 2014). This is certainly a complex and currently controversial area with diverse perspectives on appropriate courses of action.

Psychologists are often faced with assisting police agencies with community relations. Considering aspirational ethics may be key here: psychologists committed to the best possible outcomes may see opportunities to use their competencies to help facilitate improved community relations. Concerns include the increasing public scrutiny of and discontent with law enforcement. One example of scrutiny is 21st century policing controversies including "Warrior vs. Guardian" mindsets. Recent publications about these mindsets originate from a 2014 White House task force's efforts to examine and make recommendations for 21st century policing (President's Task Force on 21st Century Policing, 2015). This task force was created in the wake of highly visible officer-involved shooting incidents and multiple cities entering into settlements or consent decrees with the Department of Justice for unconstitutional patterns of police practices. Another example of public discontent is the growing influence of social media and technology. As reported in a recent publication, it is currently a tough world in which to be a police officer:

In a Gallup survey in June (2015), just 52% of Americans expressed confidence in the police, down 4 points from a year earlier and tying the lowest level since 1993. The atmosphere then was defined by the beating of Rodney King, recorded by a man on the balcony of his Los Angeles apartment with a Sony Handycam. Cops have always been tribal, keeping to their own in the weary belief that what they do is work only another cop could understand. Now everyone is an expert, and the zeal of bystanders "with their cameras out, 'waiting for something to happen,'" as one Philadelphia officer puts it, has altered the fraught dynamic between the arrested and the arresting (Vick, 2015, p.35).

Another current controversial topic in policing is the interplay between public service agencies and military returnees. Departments are dealing with military returnees, both as new applicants for public safety positions and as returning employees, back from deployment and ready to resume positions in law enforcement. While there is a well-intentioned, often political push and a lay-perception that veterans are seemingly well suited and deserving of public safety positions, according to Aamodt (2004), "There is little empirical support for the notion that officers with military experience are more successful than those without such experience" (p. 72).

Sometimes, military returnees are service-connected through the Department of Veteran's Affairs for medical and mental health disabilities. Such disabilities include cognitive disorders, traumatic brain injuries, depressive disorders, and/or trauma-related disorders such as Posttraumatic Stress Disorder. As of 2013,16% of veterans received disability pay (Congressional Policy Office, 2014). Pre-employment evaluations of applicants with these disabilities are complex. The agency has passed along and would like to hire a veteran or reserve. During the pre-employment evaluation, the subject reports being free of mental health problems and able to perform essential job functions for the high-risk, high-stress public safety position for which he or she has applied. On the other hand, during a Disability and Compensation evaluation, the subject has reported to the Veteran's Affairs evaluator, typically also a psychologist, symptoms and reactions to circumstances that have led to a mental health diagnosis, a disability rating, and subsequent financial compensation. The competent police and public safety psychologist recognizes that in each case, an individualized assessment should be performed. An aspirational emphasis here necessitates consideration of all available information, including information from the current evaluation as well as collateral information, such as the Disability and Compensation evaluation rating form, the interview notes that led to the ratings, and if applicable, other relevant medical and mental health records.

In contrast, the already-hired, incumbent public safety employee returning from deployment and military service is better protected from such scrutiny. The Uniformed Services Employment and Reemployment Rights Act of 1994 (USERRA) defines such an individual's rights. Included in these rights is an allowance to return to a previous job without undue scrutiny. Public service agencies are often unaware of or do not understand the implications of USERRA. Agencies sometimes request evaluations of returning veterans "in order to make sure they are okay to go back to work." The ethical psychologist must decline this request and helpfully educate agencies about appropriate reasons to conduct a fitness-for-duty evaluation.

A final area of recent ethical concern in regard to police and public safety psychology relates to the functional domain of operations. Operational and military psychologists, as well as psychology as a whole, have recently come under fire. In 2014, the APA responded, after years of allegations, that they had supported torture and inappropriate "enhanced" torture techniques against prisoners during the war on terror (Risen, 2015). APA hired an independent investigator, David Hoffman, to investigate whether there was proof that the APA covered up activity that would represent collusion with torture. Several psychologists were previously accused of assisting in torture of prisoners during the war on terror. The claim was that leaders within APA turned away or actively colluded with attempts to cover up this information and attempted to manipulate or wordsmith the APA Ethical Principles of Psychologists and Code of Conduct so that they would not be in opposition to the enhanced torture techniques in which psychologists were involved.

The independent review report, known as the Hoffman report, created great controversy in the field of psychology and asserted that allegations were correct, that the APA had acted inappropriately, and that recommendations for change were needed. These recommendations involved scrutiny of APA leadership who had acted unethically (Risen, 2015). Another recommendation that was proposed in the report was to eliminate operational psychology entirely. Operations is one of the core functional domains of police and public safety psychology. Understandably, police and public safety psychologists watched with concern as the APA Council of Representatives convened, discussed, sought input, and ultimately voted on actions based on report recommendations and fallout.

In August 2015, the APA Council of Representatives voted to ban the participation of psychologists in national security interrogations, even non-coercive interviews. This ban, which applies only to national security interrogations, does not apply to psychologists' participation in domestic law enforcement and corrections interviews where detainees are afforded constitutional protections (Risen, 2015).

At the time of publication in 2016, there is a call to revise the relevant code(s) within the APA Ethical Principles of Psychologists and Code of Conduct. Input is sought. Police and public safety psychologists are in a unique position to provide feedback. The importance is two-fold for police psychologists and those psychologists working in public safety settings such as national security and military settings. One concern is that well-intentioned efforts by the greater psychological community to avoid doing harm may not realistically take into account the complexities of operational psychology. Unfortunately, in certain operations, people are sometimes harmed. Similarly, within operational and forensic psychology roles, often psychologists serve several parties. It is important that a revision in the ethics code not marginalize the legitimate practice of operational police and public safety psychology where psychologists are acting ethically.

As an example, consider the functional competency of crisis and hostage negotiation. Police and public safety psychologists routinely serve on crisis negotiation teams. While a goal of crisis and hostage negotiation is de-escalation and a successful outcome for those involved, such incidents are high-stakes situations in which a person has taken hostages. An ethical dilemma and aspirational challenge arises for the psychologist in weighing what "do no harm" means. For instance, if a successful resolution involves hostages being released, unharmed and alive, and the hostage taker surrendering, all is well. However, sometimes tactical action is taken, and quickly, in order to protect the hostages as well as nearby citizens who are at risk. Though ideally the psychologist steps back in those crucial seconds as a situation escalates, and is certainly not a participant in the tactical action, the action may result in the hostage taker's loss of life. In this loss of life, the threat to the hostages, officers, and the public is eliminated. In this day and age of public scrutiny, operational psychologists need to be clear of their role in such negotiations and actions. However, a concern is that police and public safety psychologists who perform operational functions are vulnerable to the scrutiny of others, including fellow psychologists who are not savvy about this work and may not agree with and openly criticize psychologists' involvement in this key operations functional competency.

SOLUTIONS AND RECOMMENDATIONS

Psychologists must strive to do good, avoid doing harm, be aware of their influence, be trustworthy and mindful of responsibilities, be honest, truthful, fair, exercise good judgment, recognize their own biases and limitations of competence, and avoid participation in activities that may harm others (APA, 2002). In addition to consulting the APA Ethical Principles of Psychologists and Code of Conduct, psychologists have other ways to resolve ethical dilemmas including relevant guidelines, consultation, ethical decision-making models and adopting a critical thinking style involving a prioritization of aspirational ethics (Gottlieb & Younggren, 2011; Nagy, 2011). Each of these can assist with ethical police and public safety psychology practice.

There are multiple guidelines from IACP. These guidelines, revised typically every five years on a revolving schedule, are created in coordination with law enforcement command staff and personnel by psychologists of the Police Psychological Services Section of the IACP. The guidelines assist law enforcement agencies by offering best practice recommendations in police psychology service provision, and in being responsive to certain types of situations and critical incidents within law enforcement agencies. An example of such an incident is an officer-involved shooting. While these guidelines fall specifically under the IACP, police and public safety psychologists may follow recommended practices, such as those laid out in Pre-employment Psychological Evaluation Guidelines, with other public safety populations and settings, such as when working with corrections, detention, and fire personnel and agencies. The current guidelines include: Guidelines for Consulting Police Psychologists (2011); Pre-employment Psychological Evaluation Guidelines (2014); Fitness-for-duty Evaluation Guidelines (2013); Officer-Involved Shooting Guidelines (2013); and Peer Support Guidelines (2011). Additionally, as some competencies in police psychology are forensic, the recently revised APA Specialty Guidelines for Forensic Psychology (2013) may also serve as a useful source of information.

Consultation is important in thinking through ethical dilemmas. Easy access to consultation opportunities is found in becoming a participating member of one of the three major police and public safety psychology organizations: the International Association of Chiefs of Police, Police Psychological Services Section (IACP PPSS); the APA, Division 18, Police & Public Safety Section; and the Society for Police and Criminal Psychology (SPCP). Membership in these organizations offers benefits such as collegiality, opportunities for consultation, listservs, networking, and continuing education to increase competence. One of these organizations, IACP PPSS, offers confidential consultation to their police psychologist section members via the IACP PPSS Ethics Consultation Committee. Another way to seek consultation is to locate a board-certified specialist in police and public safety psychology; a current list of board-certified specialists can be found on the website of the American Board of Police and Public

Safety Psychology. Additionally, attorneys and other professionals (such as physicians) who specialize in work with police and public safety psychology may also be valuable resources in resolving ethical dilemmas.

There are many ethical problem-solving models. These all involve a successive and meticulous series of steps to be utilized in considering and resolving ethical dilemmas. Sequential steps often include pinpointing the inherent ethical dilemma(s); identifying pertinent ethical principles and codes, as well as relevant laws, other practice, and professional issues; recognizing and weighing choices with their subsequent pros and cons; identifying and seeking sources for consultation; choosing a prudent course of action; and a thoughtful review and evaluation of the chosen solution. An in-depth discussion of ethical problem-solving models with examples of application in police psychology practice can be found in McCutcheon (2011).

While adherence to the APA Ethical Principles of Psychologists and Code of Conduct is vital, adherence alone is not enough for competent, thoughtful resolution of ethical dilemmas in police and public safety psychology practice. A mindset of thinking aspirationally is encouraged. Instead of thinking about what they must do and must not do, psychologists should first consider what is the very best they are able to do. As one psychologist remarked to me recently, "Each day driving to work I wonder, what are the best things I will do to help today?" Psychologists should not only discern the minimum requirements for action and then complete them, but also strive to consider and opt for the best actions they are able to achieve for the involved parties. Rather than simply finding an applicable code of conduct and applying it to any given ethical dilemma, a psychologist should adopt a mindset of striving for good. This mindset may function as a source of inspiration for best action when a psychologist is faced with difficult ethical decisions. If not already a mindset for the police and public safety psychologist, aspirational ethics need to be encouraged and adopted as a frame of mind in daily police and public safety psychology practice.

Finally, a mindset of thoughtful and patient humility is often called for. Sometimes, no matter how seasoned psychologists are, they do not know the best way to proceed. When a psychologist is uncertain of the best way to proceed, often not acting immediately is the best option, except in emergent situations. When faced with ambiguity, a psychologist may find it helpful to take time to think through the dilemma before acting. An answer or solution may present itself. If a solution does not naturally come to mind for the psychologist, deliberately practicing an aspirational mindset, along with other practical methods to resolve ethical dilemmas, may be beneficial. Such a stance will assist police and public safety psychologists in successfully resolving more traditional ethical dilemmas and dealing effectively with new emerging practice issues.

FUTURE RESEARCH DIRECTIONS

Rich opportunities for research exist regarding ethical dilemmas in police and public safety psychology. An updated survey of psychologists is needed. Areas for investigation include which ethical dilemmas police psychologists most encounter, whether ethical problem solving models are utilized, and what heuristics are employed, such as the distinction presented in this chapter between mandatory and aspirational ethics. Additional research is also needed regarding the resolution of ethical issues involving new and emerging issues in police and public safety psychology. These include ethical issues inherent in telehealth and digital information storage and exchange, as well as the potentially changing views of who is privy to evaluation results.

CONCLUSION

This chapter covered commonly experienced ethical dilemmas and aspirational challenges among police and public safety psychologists. Examples and commentary on emerging ethical challenges were presented. The possibility that ethical dilemmas go unrecognized due to a focus on mandatory rather than aspirational ethics warrants consideration and future research, especially in regard to new and emerging practice issues.

REFERENCES

Aamodt, M. G. (2004). *Research in law enforcement selection.* Boca Raton, FL: BrownWalker Press.

American Board of Police and Public Safety Psychology. (2014). *Examination manual for specialty board certification in police & public safety psychology, 10*, 1-84.

American Psychological Association. (2002). Ethical principles of psychologists and code of conduct. *The American Psychologist, 57*(12), 1060–1073. doi:10.1037/0003-066X.57.12.1060 PMID:12613157

American Psychological Association. (2013). Specialty guidelines for forensic psychology. *The American Psychologist, 68*(1), 7–19. doi:10.1037/a0029889 PMID:23025747

Arcaya, J. M. (2011). Challenging the police de-selection process during the psychological interview: How gullibility spells hiring doom for the unwary. In J. Kitaeff (Ed.), *Handbook of police psychology* (pp. 227–236). New York, NY: Routledge.

Aumiller, G. S., Corey, D., Allen, S., Brewster, J., Cutler, M., Gupton, H., & Honig, A. (2007). Defining the field of police psychology: Core domains & proficiencies. *Journal of Police and Criminal Psychology, 22*(2), 65–76. doi:10.1007/s11896-007-9013-4

Borkosky, B. G., Pellett, J. M., & Thomas, M. S. (2014). Are forensic evaluations "health care" and are they regulated by HIPAA? *Psychological Injury and Law, 7*(1), 1–8. doi:10.1007/s12207-013-9158-7

Bush, S. S., Connell, M. A., & Denney, R. L. (2006). *Ethical practice in forensic psychology: A systematic model for decision making*. Washington, DC: American Psychological Association. doi:10.1037/11469-004

Colnerud, G. (1997). Ethical dilemmas of psychologists: A Swedish example in an international perspective. *European Psychologist, 2*(2), 164–170. doi:10.1027/1016-9040.2.2.164

Congressional Policy Office. (2014). *Veterans' disability compensation: Trends and policy options.* Retrieved from https://www.cbo.gov/publication/45615

Corey, D. M., Cuttler, M. J., Cox, D. R., & Brower, J. (2011). Board certification in police psychology: What it means to public safety. *The Police Chief, 78*, 100–104.

Drum, K. B., & Littleton, H. L. (2014). Therapeutic boundaries in telepsychology: Unique issues and best practice recommendations. *Professional Psychology, Research and Practice, 45*(5), 309–315. doi:10.1037/a0036127 PMID:25414540

Fisher, M. A. (2009). Replacing "Who is the client?" with a different ethical question. *Professional Psychology, Research and Practice*, *40*(1), 1–7. doi:10.1037/a0014011

Gamble, N., Boyle, C., & Morris, Z. A. (2015). Ethical practice in telepsychology. *Australian Psychologist*, *50*(4), 292–298. doi:10.1111/ap.12133

Gottlieb, M. C., & Younggren, J. N. (2011). Do the right thing: If only it were so easy. *Clinical Psychologist*, *64*(3), 9–10.

International Association of Chiefs of Police. (2011a). *Peer support guidelines.* Retrieved from: http://www.theiacp.org/psych_services_section/

International Association of Chiefs of Police. (2011b). *Guidelines for consulting police psychologists.* Retrieved from: http://www.theiacp.org/psych_services_section/

International Association of Chiefs of Police. (2013a). *Fitness-for-duty evaluation guidelines.* Retrieved from: http://www.theiacp.org/psych_services_section/

International Association of Chiefs of Police. (2013b). *Officer-involved shooting guidelines.* Retrieved from: http://www.theiacp.org/psych_services_section/

International Association of Chiefs of Police. (2014). *Pre-employment psychological evaluation guidelines.* Retrieved from: http://www.theiacp.org/psych_services_section/

Knapp, S. J. Bennett, B. E., & VandeCreek, L. (2012). Risk management for psychologists. In S. J. Knapp, M. C. Gottlieb, M. M. Handelsman, & L. D. VandeCreek (Eds.), *APA handbooks in psychology. APA handbook of ethics in psychology, vol. 1. Moral foundations and common themes* (pp. 483-518). Washington, DC: American Psychological Association.

McCutcheon, J. L. (2011). Ethical issues in police psychology: Challenges and decision-making models to resolve ethical dilemmas. In J. Kitaeff (Ed.), *Handbook of police psychology* (pp. 89–108). New York, NY: Routledge.

Nagy, T. F. (2011). *Essential ethics for psychologists: A primer for understanding and mastering core issues.* Washington, DC: American Psychological Association. doi:10.1037/12345-000

Nordal, K. C. (2015). Embracing telepsychology. *The American Psychologist*, *46*(11), 64.

Pettifor, J. L., & Sawchuk, T. R. (2006). Psychologists' perceptions of ethically troubling incidents across international borders. *International Journal of Psychology*, *41*(3), 216–225. doi:10.1080/00207590500343505

Pope, K. S., & Vetter, V. A. (1992). Ethical dilemmas encountered by members of the American Psychological Association: A national survey. *The American Psychologist*, *47*(3), 387–411. doi:10.1037/0003-066X.47.3.397 PMID:11642988

President's Task Force on 21st Century Policing. (2015). *Final report of the President's Task Force on 21st Century Policing.* Washington, DC: Office of Community Oriented Policing Services.

Ragusea, A. S. (2012). The more things change, the more they stay the same: Ethical issues in the provision of telehealth. In S. Knapp, M. Gottlieb, M. Handelsman, & L. VandeCreek (Eds.), *APA handbooks in psychology. APA handbook of ethics in psychology, vol. 2. Practice, teaching, and research* (pp. 183–198). Washington, DC: American Psychological Association.

Risen, J. (2015, August 7). Psychologists approve ban on role in national security interrogations. *The New York Times*. Retrieved from: http://www.nytimes.com/2015/08/08/us/politics/psychologists-approve-ban-on-role-in-national-security-interrogations.html?_r=1

Slack, C. M., & Wassenaar, D. R. (1999). Ethical dilemmas of South African clinical psychologists: International comparisons. *European Psychologist*, *4*(3), 179–186. doi:10.1027//1016-9040.4.3.179

Spilberg, S. W., & Corey, D. M. (2014). *POST peace officer psychological screening manual*. Sacramento, CA: California Commission on Peace Officer Standards and Training.

Stanley v. McCarver and Osborn, Nelson & Carr Portable X-Ray, Inc. 1 CA-CV 02-0328 (Superior Court in Maricopa County, AZ, 2003).

Vick, K. (2015, August 24). What it's like to be a cop in America. *Time Magazine, 186*(7). Retrieved from: http://time.com/magazine/us/3995775/august-24th-2015-vol-186-no-7-u-s/

Younggren, J. N., & Gottlieb, M. C. (2004). Managing risk when contemplating multiple relationships. *Professional Psychology, Research and Practice*, *35*(3), 255–260. doi:10.1037/0735-7028.35.3.255

Zelig, M. (1988). Ethical dilemmas in police psychology. *Professional Psychology, Research and Practice*, *19*(3), 336–338. doi:10.1037/0735-7028.19.3.336

About the Contributors

Cary L. Mitchell, Ph.D., is a Professor of Psychology at Pepperdine University. A licensed psychologist, he has been conducting preemployment psychological screenings of law enforcement applicants for departments throughout California for over 25 years. Formerly a V.A. psychologist, he has worked in two federal prisons and has been a consultant for the U.S. Department of Justice's COPS program. For three decades he has taught graduate assessment courses, chaired dissertations, and served in administrative roles at Pepperdine that included Director of Clinical Training in the Psy.D. program and Associate Dean in the Graduate School of Education and Psychology. He has authored multiple grants and co-directs a mental health clinic at a homeless shelter.

Edrick H. Dorian, Psy.D., ABPP, is a police psychologist with the Los Angeles Police Department (LAPD) and a clinical psychologist in private practice. He is board certified in both Clinical Psychology and Police & Public Safety Psychology by the American Board of Professional Psychology, and a diplomate of the Academy of Cognitive Therapy. At the LAPD, he provides clinical and training services for sworn and civilian law enforcement personnel, responds to critical incidents, serves as a consultant on the SWAT Crisis Negotiation Team, and provides managerial consultation to commanding officers. He has held academic appointments on the adjunct faculties of California State University Northridge, Moorpark College, and the Graduate School of Education and Psychology at Pepperdine University; and as Assistant Clinical Professor of Psychology in the David Geffen School of Medicine at UCLA.

* * *

Joseph H. Afanador, Psy.D., is a Major in the Medical Service Corps of the U.S. Army. He is fellowship-trained in forensic psychology and has had a variety of assignments in operational and clinical settings while serving on active duty.

Evan M. Axelrod, Psy.D., ABPP, received a doctorate in clinical psychology, with an emphasis in behavioral forensics, from the University of Denver. He is a board certified specialist in Police & Public Safety Psychology, and a board certified expert in traumatic stress. Dr. Axelrod has worked in the areas of emergency response and crime prevention, and has experience in both inpatient and outpatient settings. He specializes in preemployment screening, fitness-for-duty evaluation, and threat/risk assessment, while also providing services in the areas of trauma intervention, stress/anger management, conflict resolution, peak performance, verbal communication/de-escalation, understanding mental health, suicide/suicide-by-cop, peer support, and the detection and disruption of violence. Dr. Axelrod is an adjunct faculty member at the University of Denver, Graduate School of Professional Psychology and has authored and contributed to numerous books and articles in the areas of police and public safety psychology, and the detection and disruption of violence.

Yossef S. Ben-Porath, Ph.D., ABPP, is a Professor of Psychological Sciences at Kent State University and a board certified clinical psychologist. He received his doctoral training at the University of Minnesota and has been involved extensively in MMPI research for the past 30 years. Dr. Ben-Porath is a co-developer of the MMPI-2-RF and MMPI-A-RF and co-author of numerous test manuals, books, book chapters, and articles on the MMPI instruments. He is editor-in-chief of the journal *Psychological Assessment*, and a member of APA's Committee on Psychological Tests and Assessment. Dr. Ben-Porath's clinical practice involves supervision of assessments at Kent State's Psychological Clinic, consultation to agencies that screen candidates for public safety positions, and provision of consultation and expert witness services in forensic cases.

Nancy K. Bohl-Penrod, Ph.D., is the director of The Counseling Team International, which provides counseling, critical incident stress management, peer support training, and consultations to more than 80 public safety agencies throughout the United States. She has trained more than 10,000 peer supporters, and guides agencies on how to develop peer support and wellness programs. She has been a frequent guest speaker on subjects related to peer support and wellness for law enforcement and their families for the California Commission on Peace Officer Standards and Training, California Peace Officers Association, Federal Law Enforcement Training Center, Federal Bureau of Investigation, Federal Air Marshal Service, United Nations, and the International Critical Incident Stress Foundation. She is a past president of the Police Psychological Services Section of the International Association of Chiefs of Police, one of the founders of the Public Safety Peer Support Association, and co-author of the *Public Safety Peer Support/Supervisor Coach* app.

Adrienne C. Bradford, Ph.D., is the director of the City of Atlanta's Psychological Services Unit/Employee Assistance Program. She currently supervises the clinical services that are provided to over 8,000 city employees, including police, fire and corrections. She earned her doctoral degree in clinical psychology from Miami University, Oxford, Ohio. Dr. Bradford has worked as a public safety psychologist for over 25 years and has served as a consultant to correctional settings, police and fire departments, and military organizations. She has extensive crisis response and intervention experience and has worked in the aftermath of natural disasters, major aviation accidents, and terrorist incidents, including 9/11 and the Centennial Olympic Park bombing. Dr. Bradford also maintains a busy training and consulting practice and provides specialized services to clients in the government, sports, and entertainment industries.

Emily Brucia, M.S., is a fourth-year doctoral student in clinical psychology at the Pacific Graduate School of Psychology/Palo Alto University, and she received her B.A. in psychology from Whitman College in 2011. Clinically, Ms. Brucia conducts individual and group psychotherapy with veterans and first responders, and she trained on a mobile crisis team. She is researching predictors of PTSD symptom reduction in a population of treatment-seeking police officers. Ms. Brucia is pursuing a career in police psychology and her areas of professional interest include early intervention and police and public safety psychology. She is a student member of the International Society for Traumatic Stress Studies, American Psychological Association, and the California Psychological Association.

John T. Chibnall, Ph.D., received his doctorate in applied psychology from Saint Louis University in 1994. He is currently Professor of Neurology & Psychiatry at Saint Louis University School of Medicine. His research interests are in health psychology and assessment.

Michael E. Christopher, Ph.D., Psy.D., received his Ph.D. in psychology from the University of California, San Diego in 1997, and his Psy.D. from Argosy University, Hawaii in 2006. He works as a police psychologist for the Honolulu Police Department and is the program coordinator for the Honolulu Emergency Psychological Services and Jail Diversion Program. He is also the director of internships for Hawaii Pacific University's Master of Arts in Clinical Mental Health Counseling program, and he maintains a private practice.

Daniel W. Clark, Ph.D., is a licensed clinical psychologist currently working as the Washington State Patrol (WSP) department psychologist; he is also the founder of Critical Concepts Consulting. As the WSP department psychologist for the past 20 years, Dr. Clark provides treatment services, pre-employment psychological screening for several agencies, critical incident response, and consultation and training services. He has numerous presentations and publications related to law enforcement issues and specializes in trauma and suicide. He is a past chair of the International Association of Chiefs of Police - Police Psychological Services Section, a colonel in the U.S. Army Reserves, and has been involved with Concerns of Police Survivors for more than a decade. He is the author of the *Suicide: Prevention, Intervention, and Postvention* curriculum and co-author of the *Strategic Response to Crisis* curriculum. He is an editor for the *International Journal of Emergency Mental Health & Human Resilience*.

Terry G. Coleman, MOM, Ph.D., MHRM, MA, has almost 40 years of policing experience, including over 10 years as Chief of Police in Moose Jaw, Saskatchewan. In 2003, he was invested with the Order of Merit for Police Forces (MOM) by the Governor General of Canada. From 2007 to 2008, Dr. Coleman was the Deputy Minister of Corrections, Public Safety, and Policing for the Government of Saskatchewan; from 2008 to 2009 he was the Deputy Minister of Municipal Affairs. He teaches at Dalhousie University College of Continuing Education, Athabasca University and is an Adjunct Professor at the University of Regina. Dr. Coleman is a consultant with respect to policing, community engagement, and strategic leadership/management in the public sector. He has extensive experience with the Mental Health Commission of Canada and the Canadian Association of Chiefs of Police related to the intersection of persons with a mental illness and the criminal justice system.

Matthew J. Cordova, Ph.D., is a staff psychologist in behavioral medicine at the VA Northern California Health Care System and an Associate Professor at Palo Alto University. He teaches and supervises graduate students, predoctoral interns, and postdoctoral fellows and has published numerous articles and book chapters on traumatic stress and early intervention. He holds a B.S. from the University of California, Davis and a doctorate from the University of Kentucky. He completed an internship at the VA Palo Alto and a postdoctoral fellowship at Stanford University.

David M. Corey, Ph.D., ABPP, has conducted preemployment psychological evaluations of thousands of police and other public safety candidates and incumbents throughout the western United States for more than 35 years. Dr. Corey is the founding president of the American Board of Police & Public Safety Psychology, and a Fellow of the American Psychological Association. Dr. Corey is board certified in

Forensic Psychology and in Police & Public Safety Psychology by the American Board of Professional Psychology. He writes and teaches extensively on assessment-related topics in police psychology, and he is a faculty fellow at Fielding Graduate University in Santa Barbara, California. With Dr. Yossef S. Ben-Porath, he is the co-author of the *MMPI-2-RF Police Candidate Interpretive Report*, the *User's Guide for the Police Candidate Interpretive Report*, and the upcoming *Practical Guide to the Use of the MMPI-2-RF in Police and Public Safety Evaluations*.

Dorothy Cotton, Ph.D., is a clinical and forensic psychologist who consults with police services across Canada in regard to issues related to police interactions with people with mental illnesses. She has been extensively involved with the Canadian Association of Chiefs of Police (CACP) and the Mental Health Commission of Canada (MHCC). Along with Dr. Terry Coleman, she developed the CACP's *Contemporary Policing Guidelines for Working with the Mental Health System* and the MHCC's *TEMPO* framework for police education and training. Dr. Cotton holds degrees from McGill, Purdue, and Queens Universities and teaches at the latter institution as adjunct faculty. She holds diplomate status in Police Psychology from the Society of Police and Criminal Psychology, and is a fellow of the Canadian Psychological Association. In 2012, Dr. Cotton received the Queen's Diamond Jubilee Medal for her work on police interactions with people with mental illnesses.

Stephen F. Curran, Ph.D., ABPP, received his doctorate from the University of Maryland in 1977 and is a licensed psychologist in Maryland and Virginia. He was among the first psychologists awarded board certification in Police & Public Safety Psychology by the American Board of Professional Psychology. Dr. Curran's expertise is in preemployment evaluation of public safety applicants and stress management intervention and training. He coordinates regional and national psychological services programs for DEA, Amtrak Police, and CSX Transportation, among others. Dr. Curran is active in professional police organizations and a member, as well as past-chair, of the International Association of Chiefs of Police - Police Psychological Services Section. He has promoted reintegration programs for police officer-citizen soldiers returning from deployments in support of OIF/OEF, for which he received the Maryland Army National Guard Commendation Medal (2007).

Paul Detrick, Ph.D., ABPP, is the owner of Florissant Psychological Serves and serves as psychological consultant to numerous law enforcement agencies in St. Louis, MO and surrounding areas. He is board certified in Police & Public Safety Psychology.

Sara Garrido, Psy.D., has worked with Nicoletti-Flater Associates since 2009. She received her doctorate in clinical psychology from the University of Denver's Graduate School of Professional Psychology. Dr. Garrido specializes in crisis intervention and trauma recovery as well as in conducting risk assessments for Nicoletti-Flater Associates. Dr. Garrido also provides debriefings for critical incidents and facilitates trainings on a variety of topics, including workplace and school violence, verbal de-escalation techniques, peer support, vicarious trauma, law enforcement resiliency, and stress management. Additionally, she serves as a peer support consultant for multiple agencies in the Denver, CO area.

Jack E. Hoban, MBA, is a subject matter expert for the U.S. Marine Corps Martial Arts Program (MCMAP) and has led over 500 workshops and seminars around the world. Over the last two decades, he has addressed the FBI, NYPD, Chicago PD, Camden County Police Department, universities, and other government and private organizations on ethics. He is author of *The Ethical Warrior* and *The Ethical Protector - Police Ethics, Tactics and Techniques*. Hoban served as a U.S. Marine Corps officer and is a long time practitioner of martial arts. He assisted in the creation of MCMAP and continues to teach the program at the Marine Corps Base in Quantico, VA and elsewhere. For 17 years, Hoban was an associate of the late Robert L. Humphrey, noted conflict resolution specialist. Hoban earned a B.A. degree in political science from Villanova University and an MBA from National University in San Diego.

Elizabeth O. Holt, Psy.D., is the president of Holt Psychological Services, LLC. She conducts preemployment psychological evaluations for law enforcement agencies at the local, state, and federal levels. Dr. Holt has considerable experience in the assessment of candidates for sensitive and high-risk positions. She also has expertise in correctional settings, acute inpatient psychiatric care, and forensic psychology. Dr. Holt conducts risk assessments on violent and sexually violent offenders. She has been qualified as an expert witness in forensic psychology in various jurisdictions throughout Maryland. Dr. Holt graduated with an M.A. in forensic psychology from the City University of New York (CUNY), John Jay College of Criminal Justice in 1999. She received her doctorate in clinical psychology with an emphasis in forensic psychology from the California School of Professional Psychology, San Diego in 2003. Dr. Holt has been a licensed psychologist in the state of Maryland since 2005.

Jennifer Kelly, Ph.D., ABPP, is a New Jersey licensed psychologist and is board certified in Police & Public Safety Psychology by the American Board of Professional Psychology. Dr. Kelly has served as an evaluating and consulting psychologist to approximately 100 public safety agencies, to workman's compensation carriers, and to private attorneys in the areas of employment assessment (preemployment and fitness for duty) and risk assessment. Dr. Kelly's clinical practice also includes treatment and post-incident debriefing services involving public safety personnel. She is active in professional police organizations and is a member of the International Association of Chiefs of Police, the Society for Police and Criminal Psychology, and the American Psychological Association's Division 18 (Psychologists in Public Service) and 41 (American Psychology-Law Society). She has lectured on topics relevant to police psychology and currently serves as the communication chair for the American Academy of Police and Public Safety Psychology.

Martin J. Mayer, J.D., is a name partner in the firm of Jones & Mayer. Mr. Mayer focuses his practice on providing legal advice, guidance, and representation to approximately 70 law enforcement agencies throughout the state. Additionally, he serves as General Counsel to the California Police Chiefs' Association and the California State Sheriffs' Association and has done so for approximately 35 years. Mr. Mayer presents seminars regarding current legal issues on behalf of numerous statewide and national law enforcement associations. In 2005, Mr. Mayer was honored with the Governor's Lifetime Achievement Award for Excellence in Peace Officer Training, which is awarded on behalf of the Governor of California and the POST Commission. Mr. Mayer was also selected as one of southern California's Super Lawyers for the year 2011, in the areas of government law, employment law, and police litigation.

Jeni L. McCutcheon, Psy.D., M.S.C.P, ABPP, is a licensed psychologist in Arizona and Washington and holds board certification in Police & Public Safety Psychology through the American Board of Professional Psychology, where she also serves as national chair of examinations and president-elect. She holds a doctorate in clinical psychology from Pacific University as well as a post-doctoral master's degree in clinical psychopharmacology from Alliant University. Her psychology practice serves police and public safety populations. She has worked in public and governmental agencies, including Indian Health Services, Veterans Affairs Medical Centers, and the Arizona State Hospital. She has also worked in community mental health centers, public and private psychiatric hospitals, at a neuropsychiatric rehabilitation facility, as part of a mobile crisis team, and as a graduate-level instructor. Dr. McCutcheon has presented and published in the area of ethics. She is a past chair of a state ethics consultation committee.

Heather K. McElroy, Ph.D., ABPP, is the managing partner of Stone, McElroy & Associates and a board certified Police & Public Safety Psychologist through the American Board of Professional Psychology. After obtaining her undergraduate degree at Ohio State University, she attended the University of Alabama for doctoral study in clinical and forensic psychology. She completed her internship at the University of South Carolina Medical School. In 2006, Dr. Stone completed her postdoctoral training requirements with Stone & Associates, where she became managing partner in 2010. Dr. McElroy is a POST-certified peace officer working as a reserve officer and hostage negotiator for the Woodstock (GA) Police Department. She serves as the chair of the International Association of Chiefs of Police - Police Psychological Services Section, has written articles for *Police Chief* magazine, and has presented at professional conferences such as the National Internal Affairs Investigators Association and the Georgia Internal Affairs Investigators Association.

John Nicoletti, Ph.D., ABPP, is a board certified specialist in Police & Public Safety Psychology. Dr. Nicoletti specializes in identifying, assessing, and defusing attack-related behaviors and violence in various workplaces and schools. Dr. Nicoletti has written three books in the areas of violence, entitled *Violence Goes to Work* (1994), *Violence Goes to College* (2001), and *Violence Goes to School* (2002). Dr. Nicoletti was on-scene at the Columbine school shooting and testified in front of the Columbine Commission. He also responded to the Platte Canyon High School shooting, the Aurora Theater shooting, and the Arapahoe High School shooting. Dr. Nicoletti was asked to be part of a team to investigate the Arapahoe High School shooting and provide a summary to a legislative committee. Dr. Nicoletti also served as part of a Harvard Medical School team studying the health and mental health services in the outback of Australia.

Rachel Rosenblatt, Psy.D., ABPP, is a staff psychologist at Stone, McElroy & Associates, and is board certified in Police & Public Safety Psychology by the American Board of Professional Psychology. She provides risk-management psychological screening services for police and public safety officers and participates in fitness for duty evaluations, particularly those requiring neuropsychological assessment. Dr. Rosenblatt completed her doctoral studies in psychology at Florida Institute of Technology and her clinical internship at the Northeastern Ohio Universities College of Medicine. She completed a postdoctoral program in forensic and child psychology prior to joining her current firm in 2009. Since that time, she has been exclusively involved in providing risk-management psychological evaluations. Dr. Rosenblatt has extensive training in public safety psychological assessment, supplemented by training offered through national organizations of police psychologists. She has also participated in ride-alongs with police agencies and has completed a number of law enforcement training programs.

Josef I. Ruzek, Ph.D., is a clinical psychologist specializing in treatment of post-traumatic stress problems. He currently serves as director of the Dissemination and Training Division of the U.S. Department of Veterans Affairs National Center for PTSD. He is co-editor of two editions of *Cognitive-Behavioral Therapies for Trauma*, and co-editor of *Caring for Veterans with Deployment-Related Stress Disorders: Iraq, Afghanistan, and Beyond*. Dr. Ruzek specializes in early intervention for trauma survivors and has been active in development and evaluation of early preventive interventions for disaster and terrorism survivors, returning Iraq War personnel, and patients seen in hospital trauma centers. He is an author of the *Psychological First Aid* field guide and of *Skills for Psychological Recovery*, a manualized approach to crisis counseling. He is co-chair of the Early Intervention special interest group of the International Society for Traumatic Stress Studies.

Anthony M. Tarescavage, Ph.D., is a Postdoctoral Research Scholar and Resident of Psychology at Kent State University, where he received his doctorate in 2015. He is co-author of the upcoming book *Using the MMPI-2-RF in Forensic Assessments*, is the lead author on over one dozen MMPI-2-RF articles in peer-reviewed journals, and has received the APA Division 18 Award for Outstanding Student Research in the Field of Police and Public Safety Psychology. His research focus includes use of the MMPI-2-RF in forensic settings, medical settings, and personnel screenings.

Philip S. Trompetter, Ph.D., ABPP, received his doctorate in clinical psychology from the University of Tennessee in 1970 and became a licensed psychologist in California in 1972. He is a board certified specialist in Police & Public Safety Psychology with the American Board of Professional Psychology. He started providing assessment, intervention, and operational consultation services to law enforcement in 1977, as the department psychologist for several northern California law enforcement agencies. Dr. Trompetter was the chair of the International Association of Chiefs of Police - Police Psychological Services Section (PPSS) in 2009-2010. He chaired or co-chaired PPSS committees to establish practice guidelines for police psychology (i.e., fitness-for-duty evaluations, officer-involved shootings). He was the founding national chair of examinations of the American Board of Police & Public Safety Psychology (ABPPSP) in 2011-2014 and is the 2016-2018 ABPPSP president.

Vincent G. Tsushima, Ph.D., J.D., received his doctorate in clinical psychology from St. John's University in 1995, and his law degree from the Fordham Law School in 1999. He has worked as a forensic psychologist and as an attorney. He is now a full-time faculty member and Associate Professor of Psychology at Hawaii Pacific University, and he is also a police psychologist with the Honolulu Police Department.

Elizabeth K. White, Ph.D., ABPP, has worked in the field of law enforcement for 27 years. She currently provides preemployment psychological assessments for the County of Riverside (CA). Previously, Dr. White provided clinical services for the Los Angeles Sheriff's Department (LASD). Her roles included providing training for the LASD academy, peer support program, and officer involved shooting team. She currently teaches the psychological portion of the County of Riverside's POST-approved background investigators class. Dr. White has authored articles and book chapters and taught on various topics related to law enforcement, including critical incident stress, peer support, and suicide. She authored the *LASD Suicide Prevention Program* and assisted California's Commission on POST as a subject matter expert on its suicide prevention training video. Dr. White is a former chair of the International Association of Chiefs of Police - Police Psychological Services Section and served on its committee on law enforcement suicide.

Index

L

M

N

O

P

R

S

T

U

V

W

www.ingramcontent.com/pod-product-compliance
Lightning Source LLC
LaVergne TN
LVHW060416300926
849162LV00006B/1443